# Flash Games Studio

Sham Bhangal
Igor Choromanski
David Doull
Justin Everett-Church
Thomas Poeser
Glen Rhodes
Kevin Sutherland

DESIGNER TO DESIGNER™

# Flash Games Studio

© 2001 friends of ED

All rights reserved. No part of this book may be reproduced, stored in a retrieval system or transmitted in any form or by any means, without the prior written permission of the publisher, except in the case of brief quotations embodied in critical articles or reviews.

The authors and publisher have made every effort in the preparation of this book to ensure the accuracy of the information. However, the information contained in this book is sold without warranty, either express or implied. Neither the authors, friends of ED nor its dealers or distributors will be held liable for any damages caused or alleged to be caused either directly or indirectly by this book.

First printed in August 2001

**Trademark Acknowledgments**

friends of ED has endeavored to provide trademark information about all the companies and products mentioned in this book by the appropriate use of capitals. However, friends of ED cannot guarantee the accuracy of this information.

Published by friends of ED
30 Lincoln Road, Olton, Birmingham. B27 6PA. UK.

Printed in USA

ISBN: 1-903450-67-5

# Flash Games Studio

## Credits

| | |
|---|---|
| **Authors** | Sham Bhangal, Igor Choromanski, David Doull, Justin Everett-Church, Thomas Poeser, Glen Rhodes, Kevin Sutherland |
| **Content Architect** | Ben Renow-Clarke |
| **Editors** | Jim Hannah, Ben Renow-Clarke, Richard O'Donnell |
| **Technical Reviewers** | Marco Baraldi, Sham Bhangal, Dan Bishop, Jonathan Bloomer, Mike Brittain, Gahlord Dewald, Andrés Yánez Durán, Miles Green, Simon Gurney, Vicki Loader, Glain Martin, Steve Mc Cormick, James Penberthy, Gabrielle Smith, Kevin Sutherland, Peter Walker, Andrew Zack |
| **Graphic Editors** | William Fallon, Katy Freer, Deb Murray, David Spurgeon |
| **Author Agent** | Gaynor Riopedre |
| **Project Administator** | Fionnuala Meacher |
| **Index** | Simon Collins |
| **Cover Design** | Katy Freer |
| **Proof Readers** | Lou Barr, Faye Claridge, Joanna Farmer, Mel Jehs, Laurent Lafon, Fionnuala Meacher, Deb Murray, Mel Orgee, Gaynor Riopedre, Joel Rushton, Paul Samuels, Paul Thewlis, Rob Tidy |
| **Team Leader** | Mel Orgee |

# Flash Games Studio

**Sham Bhangal**
Sham Bhangal originally started out as an engineer, specializing in industrial computer based display and control systems. His spare time was partly taken up by freelance web design, something that slowly took up more and more of his time until the engineering had to go. He is now also writing for friends of ED, something that is taking more and more time away from web design...funny how life repeats itself! Sham lives in Manchester, England, with his partner Karen.

**Igor Choromanski**
Most days, Igor can be found in his studio at the foothills of the Sangre de Cristo mountains in New Mexico with the dark eyed figment of his imagination known as Ikaria right by his side. On the muse's days off, it is his custom to retreat to the local monastery where he pleads for rain at the altar of the goddess of high desert sun or attempts to appease her with a sacrifice of his latest dual cylinder thoroughbred. When all else fails, he succumbs to her will and teaches 3d animation and interactivity at the College of Santa Fe.

**David Doull**
David is a passionate Flash application and Flash game developer based in Adelaide, Australia. He's work can be seen at artifactinteractive.com.au and urbanev.com. He is also the guy behind the amazing smallblueprinter.com, a 3D house-plan visualisation application built entirely in Flash. David would dearly like to thank Miriam for all her kindness and support.

**Justin Everett-Church  www.infinitumdesign.com  www.estudio.com**
Justin is the Interactive Director for eStudio.com, a studio specializing in Flash entertainment. When not making games and other fun stuff there, he can be found at home playing games (purely a research activity of course), or hanging out in #flashhelp on IRC, a great resource for Flash developers (look for Beltran). He lives in Fremont, California along with his partner Ray.

# About the Authors

**Thomas Poeser**
After an MA in Electrical Engineering from Darmstadt in Germany, Thomas went on to do post graduate studies in semiotics, and multimedia design. He worked as a freelance designer in Germany for a while, before moving on to work as an interactive designer for 'digit' in London. He has worked on projects for many prodigious companies, such as: MTV2, Expo2000, Independiente, Sonnetti, Disney liveChannel, Fake-i-d/air, and habitat. He likes doing experimental stuff using mostly Director and Flash. If he were less busy, he would like to spend more time making music.

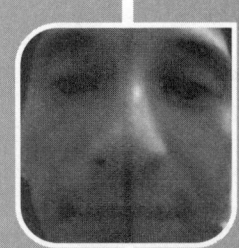

**Glen Rhodes        www.glenrhodes.com**
Glen Rhodes, of Brampton (near Toronto), Canada, splits his passions between computers and music. He currently works at dot com Entertainment Group (dceg.com) as the lead Flash developer, and has been making computer and video games for fifteen years on systems such as DOS, Playstation, Sega, Windows and most recently, Flash. He shares his Flash ideas at www.glenrhodes.com. He is also the co-author of the musical 'Chrystanthia' with Reston Williams, and has been playing piano and writing music all his life. He thanks Lisa Angela, Mom, Dad, Susan, David, Nana, Lol and a little furry friend named Sasha.

**Kevin Sutherland**
A Senior Associate at London & New York based Company-i, specialising in Internet development and technology when the boom of the "Corporate Portal" is keeping him busy with no end of client challenges to work out.
"The simple approach is always the best way to go, the art is in finding a simple approach to a complex challenge, break them down into their smallest components and even the greatest of challenges can be ressolved"

# Flash Games Studio

# Flash Games Studio

**CHAPTER 1   INTRODUCTION TO GAMING**  07
**GLEN RHODES**
　　　Traditional games genres, and how they work in Flash

**CHAPTER 2   OPTIMIZING GRAPHICS FOR GAMES**  35
**GLEN RHODES**
　　　Showing that there's more to making game-friendly graphics than the Optimize Curves Window

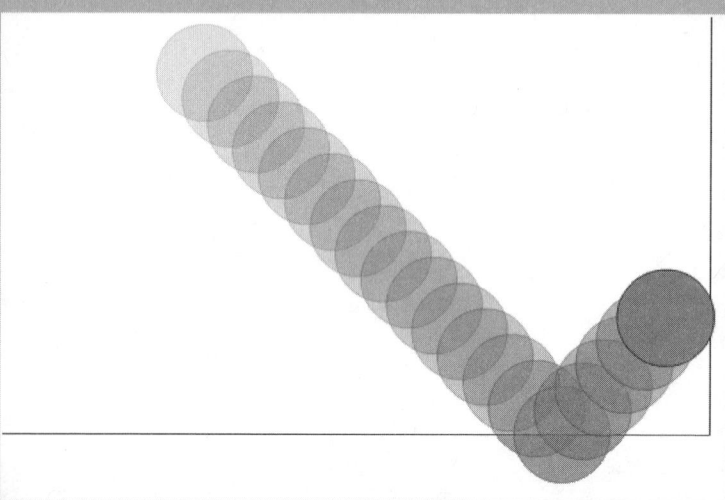

# Palette

**CHAPTER 3    FLASH'S BUILT IN OBJECTS**                                    81
**JUSTIN EVERETT-CHURCH**
   Seeing how your games can benefit from the new Flash objects and methods

**CHAPTER 4    EVENT HANDLING**                                              111
**JUSTIN EVERETT-CHURCH**
   Using the new event structures to ensure smooth yet reactive gameplay

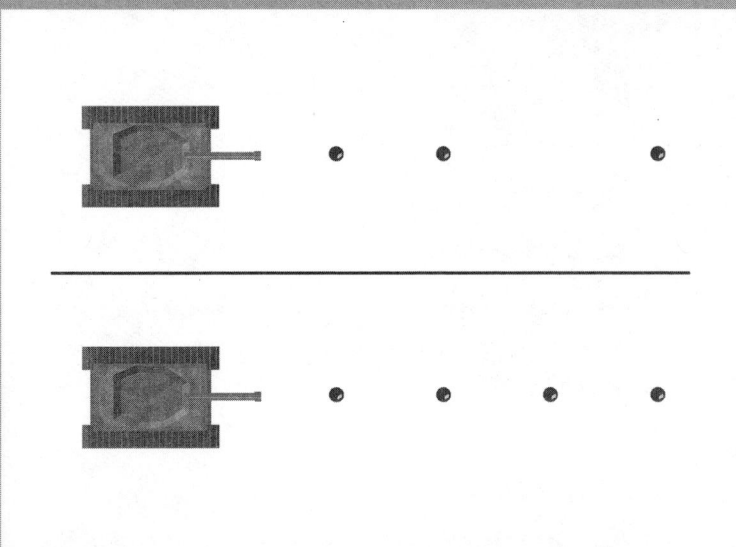

# Flash Games Studio

**CHAPTER 5  TURN BASED GAMES AND ADVANCED LOGIC**  151
**SHAM BHANGAL**
   Take your turn at Tic-Tac-Toe

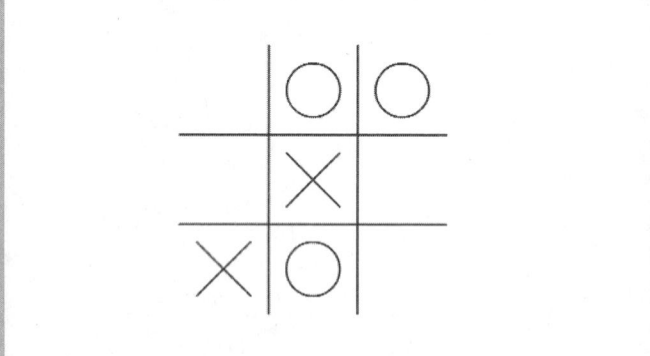

**STRUCTURED REAL-TIME PROGRAMMING**  195
**SHAM BHANGAL**
   gameWorlds, gameSprites and Pong

# Palette

**CASE STUDY  TURN**  263
THOMAS POESER
Complexity from simplicity to create compelling games

**DESIGNING A PLATFORM GAME CONSTRUCTION KIT**  281
DAVID DOULL
Platform games: How to build engines, editors, and enjoyment

# Flash Games Studio

**INTERACTIVE SOUND** 317
SHAM BHANGAL
Making it more than just monaural

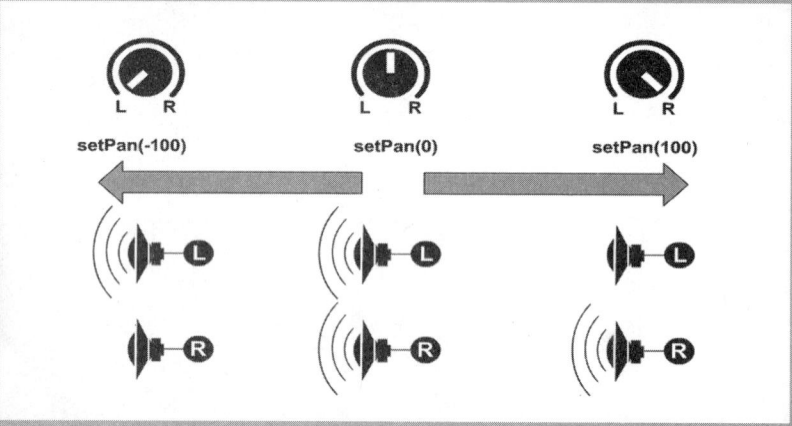

**MUSIC IN GAMES** 353
GLEN RHODES
The fundamental importance of an emotion-enhancing melody

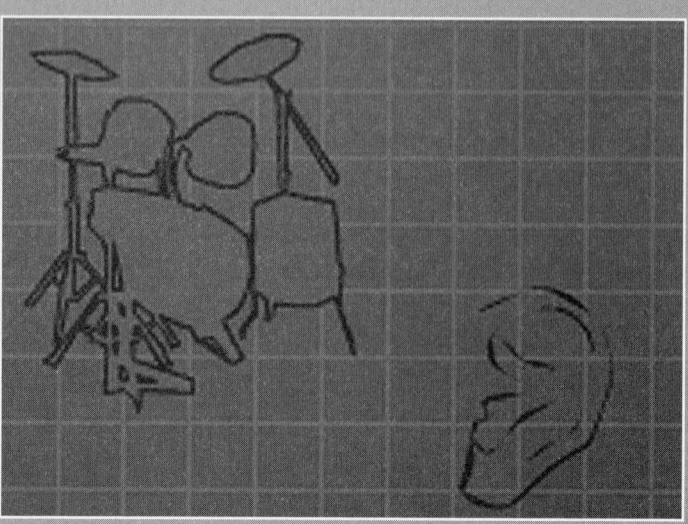

# Palette

**UNDERSTANDING ARTIFICIAL INTELLIGENCE** 379
**IGOR CHOROMANSKI**
    Figuring out fuzzy logic

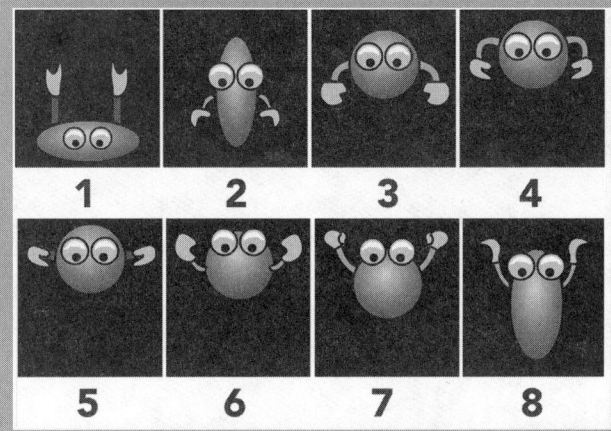

**THE THIRD DIMENSION** 401
**GLEN RHODES**
    Creating faux 3D effects in Flash

# Flash Games Studio

**REAL 3D**     457
GLEN RHODES
    Vectors, z-planes and real 3D

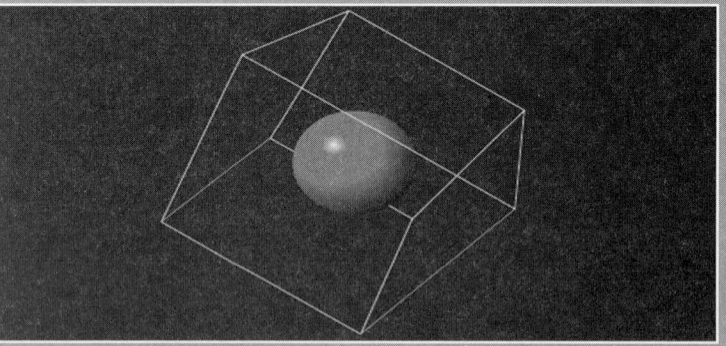

**ULTIMATE 3D**     507
GLEN RHODES
    The hard stuff: Math-based true 3D engines for gaming

# Palette

**MECH ATTACK**  529
**GLEN RHODES**
   Putting all the 3D theory to use

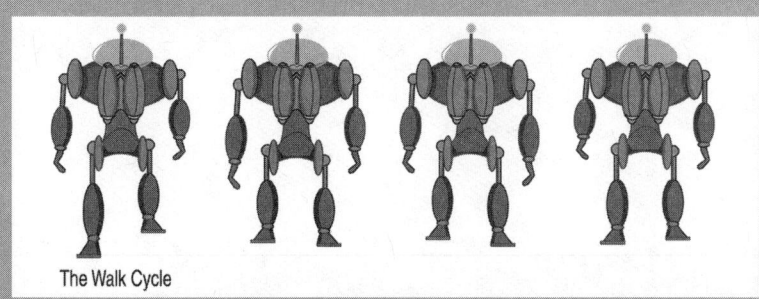

**ONLINE DATA**  595
**KEVIN SUTHERLAND**
   Saving and displaying your high-scores with PHP

# Flash Games Studio

**MULTIPLAYER APPLICATIONS**  623
GLEN RHODES
> Building a web-based multiplayer racing game

**AFTERWORD   DIRECTOR FOR FLASH USER**  681
SHAM BHANGAL
> A path finding approach for those considering the next step

# Palette

# Flash Games Studio

## Palette and Table of Contents
- Layout Conventions ............................................................ 2
- Code Download ................................................................ 4
- Support ........................................................................ 4

## Introduction to Gaming   7
- Enter the Computer .......................................................... 8
- Enter Flash .................................................................... 8
- From the Play Room to the Casino ...................................... 10
- Platform Games .............................................................. 12
- Role-playing Games ......................................................... 13
- First Person Shooters ....................................................... 14
- Sports Games ................................................................ 15
- Fighting Games .............................................................. 16
- Simulations ................................................................... 17
- Writing in Sections .......................................................... 18
- What Makes a Good Game? ................................................ 19
  - Design on Paper .......................................................... 20
  - Keeping your File Size Down ........................................... 21
  - Compression ............................................................... 21
  - Delivery Options .......................................................... 22
    - Online .................................................................... 22
    - Standalone Player ...................................................... 22
  - Performance ............................................................... 22
  - Control ..................................................................... 24
  - Story ....................................................................... 26
  - Challenge .................................................................. 27
  - Reward ..................................................................... 28
  - Demographics ............................................................. 28
  - Testing ..................................................................... 29
  - Standards .................................................................. 29
  - Repeat Playability ........................................................ 29
- Final Thoughts ............................................................... 31

## Optimizing Graphics for Games   35
- A Day in the Life of a Frame .............................................. 37
- The Price of Graphics ....................................................... 37
  - The Pixel ................................................................... 37
  - The Clock .................................................................. 38
  - The Screen Buffer ........................................................ 40
    - A Note About Screen Resolution .................................... 42
- The Price of Vectors ........................................................ 43
  - Scaling and Rotating ..................................................... 48

# Table of Contents

    Line Thickness ........................................................................49
    The Bitmap ............................................................................50
    Alpha ......................................................................................50
    Quality ....................................................................................51
        Anti-aliasing ......................................................................53
    The Killer Text ........................................................................54
    Gradients ................................................................................55
    Performance Statistics ..........................................................63
Simply Simplifying ............................................................................70
    Scrolling ..................................................................................72
File Optimization: Sweetening the Download ................................72
    Breaking It Up To Break It Down ........................................76
Final thought: Think ahead ..............................................................78

## Flash's Built in Objects      81

Defining an Object ............................................................................82
    Types of Objects ....................................................................83
Objects for Games ............................................................................84
    The Object Object ..................................................................84
    The Color Object ....................................................................84
    The Sound Object ..................................................................86
    The Mouse Object ..................................................................87
    The Key Object ......................................................................88
    The Math Object ....................................................................88
    The String Object ..................................................................88
    The Array Object ....................................................................89
    The XML Object ......................................................................89
Getting Intimate with the Movie Clip ..............................................89
    Properties ................................................................................90
        Read Only Properties ........................................................90
        Read/Write Properties ......................................................92
    Animation with Properties ....................................................95
    Hierarchy Revisited ..............................................................103
    Methods ................................................................................104
    Scripting Libraries ................................................................106
    Clip Events Versus Smart Clips ..........................................107
Conclusion ......................................................................................108

## Event Handling      111

Event Handling ..............................................................................112
The onClipEvent Function ............................................................112
    onClipEvent (load) ..............................................................112

# Flash Games Studio

- onClipEvent (enterFrame) ...............................................113
- onClipEvent (unload) ......................................................113
- onClipEvent (data) .........................................................113
- User Interaction ..................................................................113
  - The Keyboard ..............................................................114
  - The Mouse ...................................................................114
- Button Event Handlers .......................................................115
  - onClipEvents for User Input .......................................118
  - Input Properties and Methods ...................................119
- Event Handlers Applied .....................................................120
- Custom Controls ................................................................122
  - Movement ....................................................................123
  - The Tread .....................................................................124
  - Firing ............................................................................125
- Spawning and Initialization ..............................................136
  - Mines ............................................................................136
  - Shots .............................................................................138
  - Speed ............................................................................141
- Collision Detection ............................................................142
  - Collision Detection for Placing Mines .......................142
  - Collision Detection During Play .................................144
  - Shot to Mine Detection ...............................................145
- Timer ...................................................................................146
- Death ...................................................................................147
  - Death by Timeout ........................................................147
  - Death by Collision .......................................................148
- Conclusion ..........................................................................149

## 5  Turn Based Games and Advanced Logic — 152

- Game Definition Fundamentals .......................................153
  - 1. It Has to Create a Game Environment .................153
  - 2. It Has to Create and Enforce Rules ........................153
  - 3. It Has to Include a Method of Controlling
    Non-Player Characters ..................................................154
- Coding a Turn-Based Game ..............................................162
  - Game Creation from Scratch ......................................164
    - A Three Stage Game-Plan .......................................168
    - The Stage ...................................................................168
  - Player Input ..................................................................173
  - Using Event Scripts .....................................................174
  - Final Player Script .......................................................176
  - Emulating Simple Intelligence ...................................180
    - A More Advanced NPC Routine .............................184
  - The Use of Functions in the Game ............................186

## Table of Contents

    Hours of fun! ............................................................................. 190
    Parting shots ........................................................................... 191
  Summary ................................................................................... 192

# Structured Real Time Programming      195

  Structured Real-Time Programming ............................................. 196
  Getting Ready for Real Time ....................................................... 196
    The Flash 5 Plug-in ................................................................ 196
  The Need for Speed .................................................................... 196
    Flash Bottlenecks ................................................................... 197
    Shorthand Coding .................................................................. 197
    Optimizing Code .................................................................... 198
      Optimizing Conditional Logic ............................................. 198
      Event-Driven Interfacing .................................................... 200
      Staggered Update .............................................................. 201
      Look-up Tables .................................................................. 201
      Adaptive Degradation ........................................................ 202
    The Power of Hierarchy ......................................................... 203
  GameWorlds and GameSprites .................................................... 204
  Examples of Our gameWorld ....................................................... 206
  Tennis ........................................................................................ 206
    Defining the Rules ................................................................. 207
    Defining the Game Elements .................................................. 207
    The gameWorld ..................................................................... 208
    Our gameSprites .................................................................... 210
    Our Tennis gameSprites ......................................................... 212
  Our Flash Timelines ..................................................................... 215
    Frame 1: Initialization ............................................................ 216
    Frame 2: Splash Screen .......................................................... 218
    Frame 3: The Game ............................................................... 219
      The Player Bat Script ......................................................... 220
      The NPC Bat ..................................................................... 222
      The Ball Script ................................................................... 223
  Example 2: Building a Scrolling Shoot 'Em Up ............................. 230
    Game Background ................................................................. 232
    Game Graphics ...................................................................... 232
    Gameplay .............................................................................. 234
    Identifying the Components and Workflow ............................ 235
      The Object Definitions ...................................................... 235
    Object Relationships .............................................................. 237
  The Individual Objects ................................................................ 237
    1. The gameWorld ................................................................. 238
      Object Block Diagram ........................................................ 238
      Attached Code .................................................................. 238

# Flash Games Studio

| | |
|---|---|
| Features | 239 |
| 2. The Star | 240 |
|     Object Block Diagram | 241 |
|     Attached Code | 241 |
|     Features | 242 |
| 3. The Terrain | 243 |
|     Object Block Diagram | 243 |
|     Attached Code | 244 |
| 3. The playerShip | 244 |
|     Object Block Diagram | 244 |
|     Attached Code | 244 |
|     Features | 245 |
| 5. The Cursor | 247 |
|     Object Block Diagram | 247 |
|     Attached Code | 247 |
|     Features | 248 |
| 6. The Alien | 248 |
|     Object Block Diagram | 248 |
|     Attached Code | 249 |
|     Features | 249 |
| 7. The Radar | 252 |
|     Object Block Diagram | 252 |
|     Attached Code | 253 |
|     Features | 254 |
| 8. The LaserBeam (plasmaControl) | 254 |
|     Object Block Diagram | 254 |
|     Attached Code | 255 |
|     Features | 255 |
| 9. AlienSpawner | 256 |
|     Object Block Diagram | 256 |
|     Attached Code | 257 |
|     Features | 257 |
| 10. The ScoreKeeper | 258 |
|     Object block Diagram | 258 |
|     Attached Code | 258 |
|     Features | 259 |
| Parting shots | 259 |
| Summary | 260 |

## Turn      263

| | |
|---|---|
| How it works | 264 |
|   Background | 267 |
|   Object-oriented code | 267 |
|   Design | 268 |

# Table of Contents

Turn's FLA structure .................................................................. 269
Creating the game environment ................................................ 270
    Setting specific numbers and paths .................................. 272
The object Movie Clip script – part 1 ........................................ 272
The arms Movie Clip .................................................................. 275
    The object Movie Clip Script – Part 2 ................................ 276
    The Counter ........................................................................ 277
    And that's it! ...................................................................... 279

## Designing a Platform Game Construction Kit    281

The Platform Game ................................................................... 282
How the Game Works ............................................................... 283
    The Level Map .................................................................... 284
    The Game Structure ........................................................... 284
    Scrolling .............................................................................. 285
    Pick-ups and Enemies ......................................................... 286
    Platforms ............................................................................. 288
    The Player ........................................................................... 288
        Increasing the Score ..................................................... 289
        Decreasing the Player's Health ................................... 289
        Losing a Life ................................................................. 289
        Moving to the Left ...................................................... 290
        Jumping Up and Down ............................................... 290
    Player and Platform Collision Detection .......................... 291
        hitTest .......................................................................... 292
    Resetting ............................................................................. 293
    Building Level Maps .......................................................... 294
Building a Level Editor .............................................................. 295
    The Editor Window ............................................................ 296
    Functions ............................................................................ 300
The Data Structure for Levels ................................................... 307
    Loading Levels .................................................................... 308
Displaying Levels ....................................................................... 310
Exending the Level Editor ......................................................... 311
Adapting the Game Engine ...................................................... 312
    New Graphics, New Game Objects .................................. 312
    Super Jumps, Springboards, and Dissolving Platforms ... 313
    A Fixed Player and a Scrolling World .............................. 314
    Conclusion .......................................................................... 314

## Interactive Sound    317

Why Games are Different .......................................................... 318
    Sound File Import Options ................................................. 319
    The Implications of Adding Sound ................................... 319

# Flash Games Studio

- Basic Sound Scripting Actions ..................321
    - Simple Sound Objects ..................322
    - Controlling Linkage Sounds ..................322
        - Stopping Individual Sounds ..................322
        - Offsets and Looping ..................323
        - Using the Root Timeline ..................324
    - Applying Sound to a Game ..................325
        - When to Add Sound ..................325
        - The Sound-building Process ..................326
            - Our ..................327
            - Sample File ..................327
    - Sound Hierarchies – Targeting ..................334
        - Targeted Sound Methods ..................335
        - setVolume ..................335
            - Our Software Model ..................339
            - Combining Linkage Sounds and Targeted Sounds ..................340
        - Adding Stereo Effects with setPan ..................342
        - setTransform ..................346
- Conclusion ..................349

## 9 Music in Games ......... 353

- Let There Be Music ..................354
- Invisible Music ..................354
- Aspects of Music ..................355
    - Tempo ..................355
    - Notes / Melody ..................355
    - Chords ..................356
    - Style ..................356
        - Orchestral ..................357
        - Rock & Electronic ..................357
        - Experimental / Ambient ..................357
        - Ethnic ..................357
    - The Fundamental Truth ..................358
- What Works? ..................358
    - Super Mario Brothers ..................358
    - Warcraft ..................359
    - You Don't Know Jack ..................359
    - Unreal Tournament ..................359
- When and What to Play ..................360
- Software ..................360
- Music in Flash ..................361
- Exporting Music From Flash ..................362
    - Complete Soundtrack ..................365
    - Simple Loop ..................367

# Table of Contents

| | |
|---|---|
| Real-time Mixing/Layering | 369 |
| Finale | 377 |

## Understanding Artificial Intelligence — 379

| | |
|---|---|
| A Being of Your Own | 380 |
| Crisp vs. Fuzzy Logic | 381 |
| Artificial Intelligence | 382 |
| Your First Virtual Pet | 382 |
| Some Gaming Principles | 384 |
| Code | 391 |
| _root, Frame 1 | 391 |
| _root, Frame 2 | 397 |
| mrGreen, Frame 2 | 398 |
| mrGreen, Frame 8 | 398 |
| Conclusion | 398 |

## The Third Dimension — 402

| | |
|---|---|
| Demand for 3D | 402 |
| Minimizing the math | 402 |
| Faking it | 403 |
| Layering and Parallax Scrolling | 404 |
| Pre-rendering | 408 |
| Getting it into Flash | 409 |
| Keeping it Simple | 409 |
| More Complicated Methods | 411 |
| Lighting and shadow | 412 |
| Shine and flaring | 412 |
| Manic Bounce | 417 |
| Star Cruiser | 427 |
| The orb code | 437 |
| The full craft script | 439 |
| Suggested modifications | 446 |
| Isometric 3D | 446 |
| Putting it into practice | 448 |
| Player position and movement | 450 |
| Summary | 454 |

## Real 3D — 457

| | |
|---|---|
| Square One | 458 |
| Defining Shapes | 459 |
| Object Definition | 460 |
| Point | 461 |
| Line | 462 |

# Flash Games Studio

|  |  |
|---|---|
| Quad | 463 |
| Wireframe | 464 |
| Drawing Things | 468 |
| Line engines | 468 |
| Line engine #1 | 468 |
| Line engine #2 | 470 |
| Rendering a Shape | 471 |
| The Concepts | 471 |
| Translation | 472 |
| Scaling | 473 |
| Rotation | 474 |
| Ordering | 475 |
| Projection | 478 |
| Drawing It | 485 |
| Sprites | 492 |
| Cameras | 497 |
| The Objects | 499 |
| The Game Loop | 500 |
| Final Thoughts | 504 |

## 13 Ultimate 3D — 507

|  |  |
|---|---|
| Limitations of Flash | 510 |
| The Flash Polygon Engine | 511 |
| Abracadabra | 513 |
| Making it 3D | 520 |
| Speed Considerations for Games | 526 |
| Limiting the Math | 527 |

## Cs Mech Attack — 529

|  |  |
|---|---|
| The Story So Far... | 530 |
| What's Going on in the Game | 532 |
| The Level Editor | 532 |
| How the Level Editor Works | 533 |
| The Game | 541 |
| The Robot | 542 |
| The Cityscape | 545 |
| The GUI Display | 546 |
| The Crosshair | 549 |
| The Laser | 550 |
| The Streetlamp | 552 |
| Power-ups | 553 |
| Helibombs | 556 |
| The Polygon | 561 |

# Table of Contents

|       |       |
|-------|-------|
| The Loader | 566 |
| The Controller | 571 |
| onClipEvent (load) | 571 |
| Finishing Up | 591 |
| Improvements | 592 |
| Conclusion | 592 |

## Online Data — 595

|       |       |
|-------|-------|
| What is PHP? | 596 |
| What is mySQL? | 597 |
| Reading Minds with Flash and PHP | 597 |
| Think of a number | 599 |
| Player Selection | 601 |
| Am I Right or Am I Wrong? | 602 |
| Looking Back and Looking Ahead... | 604 |
| Displaying messages | 605 |
| Psychic Ability | 606 |
| Game Over | 607 |
| Keeping the score | 608 |
| Our database | 608 |
| Bring on PHP! | 609 |
| Tying it Together | 612 |
| Return to the database | 618 |
| Running out of cache | 619 |
| Systems Architecture | 624 |

## Multi Layer Applications — 624

|       |       |
|-------|-------|
| Peer-to-peer | 625 |
| Client–Server | 626 |
| Internet Protocol Address | 627 |
| Ports | 627 |
| Firewalls | 628 |
| Multiplayer Flash | 629 |
| HTTP | 629 |
| Sockets | 630 |
| Opening and Using a Socket | 631 |
| What to use? | 632 |
| XML | 632 |
| Packets | 634 |
| The Server | 636 |
| Limitations | 636 |
| The Game | 638 |
| Game Screen | 639 |

# Flash Games Studio

| | |
|---|---|
| Control | 640 |
| Converting from angle/speed to square dx and dy | 641 |
| Collision | 644 |
| Colliding with Grass | 644 |
| Obstacles | 645 |
| Shadows | 647 |
| Other Cars | 647 |
| Nodes | 648 |
| Multiple Cars | 650 |
| Packets and Communication in our Game | 652 |
| Client Packets | 653 |
| Server Packets | 654 |
| The Socket Object | 656 |
| Login and Connection | 664 |
| Connect Button Code | 665 |
| Play Local Code | 666 |
| The Car Control Code in Full | 666 |
| Synchronization | 675 |
| The Server | 675 |
| Conclusion | 678 |

## Director Afterword  681

| | |
|---|---|
| Director for Flash Users | 682 |
| Culture Shock | 683 |
| The Interface | 685 |
| The Timeline/Score | 686 |
| The Cast | 689 |
| The Inspectors | 689 |
| The Sprite Editing Windows | 691 |
| Scripting in Director | 691 |
| Conclusion | 693 |

## Index  695

# Table of Contents

# Introduction

# Flash Games Studio

If you've ever wondered how to begin tackling computer game design, this is the place to be. Flash provides a simple but powerful option, with the killer combination of versatility and complexity simmering under its approachable interface. The art of game creation need no longer be a mystery, for here we have the tool to create some genuinely sophisticated and structured, but still ridiculously fun, games.

Flash's vector-based graphics are attractive and easy to create, and, when bundled into movie clips, they're easy to throw around the screen! All of this makes for some good-looking movement – and with a fuel injection of ActionScript they'll soon be tied to some sexy controls as well. It all seems so temptingly easy – and that of course is Flash's strength.

We chart games progression through just about every conceivable genre, looking at the small stuff (how *do* you get the rules right in a game of tic-tac-toe?) and the big stuff (how do you even *begin* to create artificial intelligence?). It outlines the necessity of using ActionScript to control animation, and looks at how Flash's inbuilt objects and methods can help you achieve just what you need. Heck, if the function's not there, it even tells you how to build your own!

There are also all those things we just take for granted when we buy a game from the store. How do you make one object crash into another? And how do you determine the consequences? How do you make one object follow another? How do you make a game play by the rules, or even learn them as it goes along? How do you save a high score over the Internet, and what is the score, anyway? Rest assured it's only our imaginations that keep us in check – everything else can be achieved.

We will also be paying attention to that particular edge that makes a game stand out from the crowd. A game has got to have interest, atmosphere and dynamism. It's got to respond well to its players, and offer a real challenge. But all of this doesn't mean it's got to take an age to download! This is what Flash gaming should be. Why shouldn't your game look the best and feel the best? There is no reason, and this book shows you how to keep those standards at their uppermost.

You will be given a solid ground to keep your feet on, but you will be encouraged to reach for the skies. When the coding gets complex, it's only because you will be experimenting with the upper limits of what Flash can achieve. You will even be toying with some of the things it wasn't ever supposed to do. After all, you are the one who makes the rules; Flash is just there to obey them.

We've tried to keep this book as clear and easy to follow as possible, so we've only used a few layout styles to avoid confusion. Here they are...

- Practical exercises will appear under headings in this style...

## Layout Conventions

**Build this Movie now**

# Introduction

...and where we think it helps the discussion, they'll have numbered steps like this:

1. Do this first

2. Do this second

3. Do this third, etc...

- When we're showing ActionScript code blocks that should be typed into the Actions window, we'll use this style:

    ```
    Mover.startDrag (true);
    Mouse.hide ();
    stop ();
    ```

- Where a line of ActionScript is too wide to fit on the page, we'll indicate that it runs over two lines by using an arrow-like 'continuation' symbol:

    ```
    if (letters[i].x_pos == letters[i]._x &&
    ➥ letters[i].y_pos == letters[i]._y) {
    ```

Lines like this should all be typed as a single continuous statement.

- When we discuss ActionScript in the body of the text, we'll put statements such as `stop` in a code-like style too.

- When we add new code to an existing block, we'll highlight it like this:

    ```
    Mover.startDrag (true);
    variable1 = 35;
    Mouse.hide ();
    stop ();
    ```

- Pseudo-code will appear in this style:

    ```
    If (the sky is blue) the sun is out
        Else (it's cloudy)
    ```

- In the text, symbol names will use this emphasized style: *symbol1*.

- Interesting or important points will be highlighted like this:

> **This is a point that you should read carefully.**

# Flash Games Studio

- `file names` will look like this.
- Web addresses will be in this form: www.friendsofED.com
- New or significant phrases will appear in this **important words** style.

## Code Download

All of the source files for this book can be downloaded direct from the friends of ED website at www.friendsofed.com, from there go to the code section then follow the link to Flash Games Studio to find all the necessary files. If you have any problems with the source files or the downloading, then contact us using one of the methods detailed below and we'll do our best to help.

## Support

If you have any questions about the book, or about friends of ED, check out our web site: there are a range of contact e-mail addresses there, or you can just use the generic e-mail address: feedback@friendsofed.com.

There are also a host of other features up on the site: interviews with renowned designers, samples from our other books, and a message board where you can post your own questions, discussions and answers, or just take a back seat and look at what other designers are talking about. So, if you have any comments or problems, write us, it's what we're here for and we'd love to hear from you.

OK, that's the preliminaries over with. It's time to get busy. Game on!

# Introduction

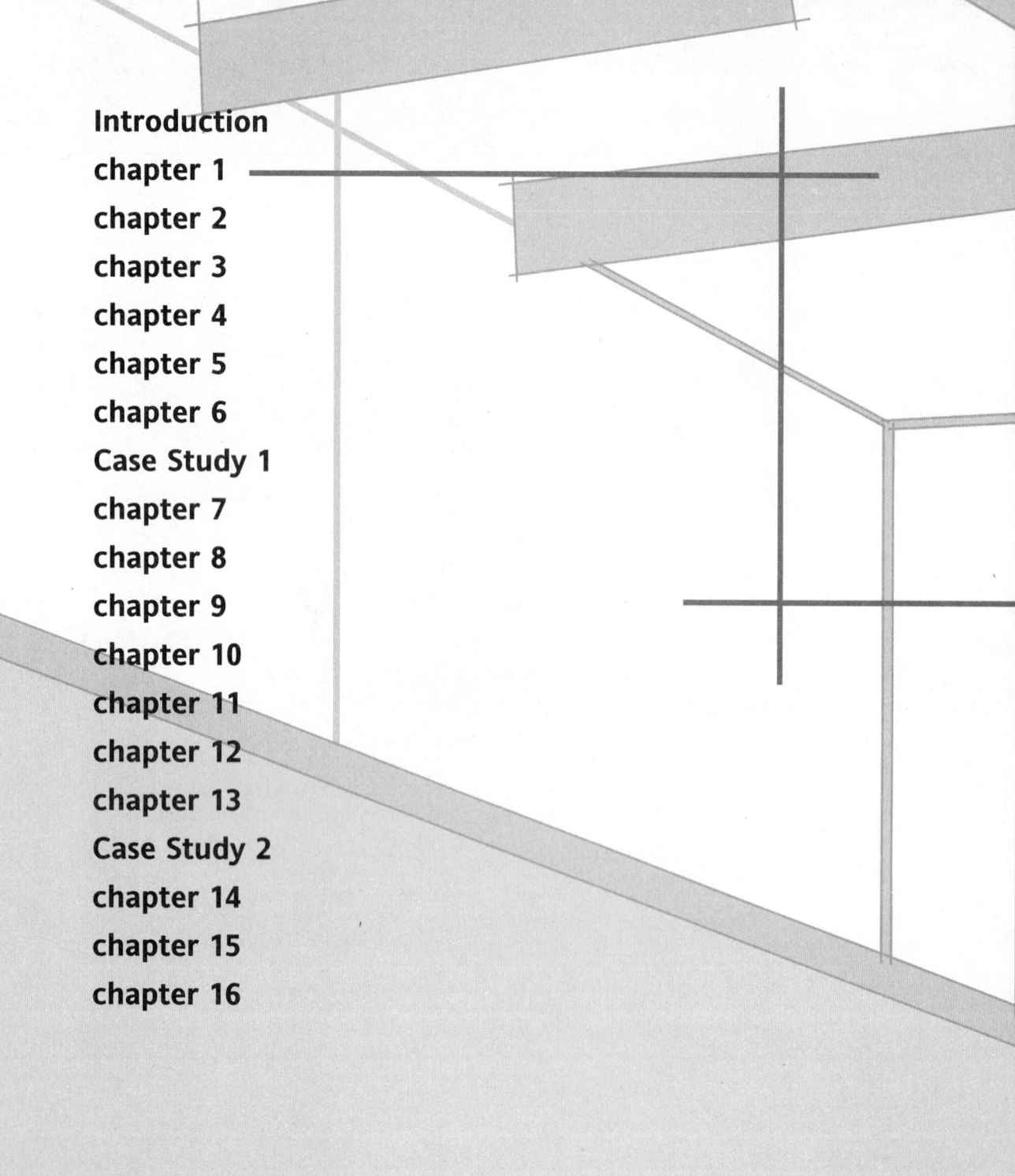

**Introduction**
chapter 1
chapter 2
chapter 3
chapter 4
chapter 5
chapter 6
**Case Study 1**
chapter 7
chapter 8
chapter 9
chapter 10
chapter 11
chapter 12
chapter 13
**Case Study 2**
chapter 14
chapter 15
chapter 16

# Chapter 1
# Introduction to Gaming

# 1 Flash Games Studio

Entertaining the human mind is an ancient preoccupation. Whether it's through the simplicity of skipping stones off the surface of a lake, the excitement of playing hide-and-seek, or the intellectual challenge of chess, games test your skills and provide a break from the workday stress.

In every game of knights and princesses or monsters and magicians, the dreams of the human mind are played out as far as our hearts can carry them, and that is the essence of what it means to be entertained.

In this chapter we're going to have a look at what can be done, what should be done, and how we should go about it. We'll look at:

- What Flash has to offer the game designer – and what it doesn't
- The many types of game on offer, and how we might cope with them in Flash
- What makes a game good, with a look at a few classics
- How to approach game design

## Enter the Computer

In the modern era of bits, bandwidth, pixels and RAM, we have come to accept the computer as part of our daily lives. It works for us, writes for us, calculates and communicates for us. However, there is one thing that the computer doesn't do. It doesn't dream for us. It's up to the modern game designer to take a cold, hard and lifeless collection of electronic hardware and meld it with the human imagination to create strange new worlds.

As the Internet has become more and more widespread, reaching into every aspect of society and culture, so the scope for interactivity has just shot off the scale. A game designer using the Internet might reach more people in one day than Mozart did in his entire life. Millions of people are sitting at their terminals just waiting to be entertained by the next big thing, and this is where you come in.

So, how do you go about making yourself a superstar of game design? Well, the first thing to do is to stop, step back, and understand what the software can and can't do.

## Enter Flash

Here are the facts. If you want to make a game that features a 1024x768 fully texture-mapped 3D world, running at 80 frames per second, with a fully orchestrated CD score, then, unfortunately, Flash is not your best choice. There are a few important things to bear in mind:

- We're working with Flash's resident language, ActionScript. While professional games written in C and Assembly Language are compiled and optimized into sleek streamlined executable files, ActionScript is read and interpreted at run-time by the Flash player or plug-in. This can make it slow.

# Introduction to Gaming

- Flash doesn't have write-access to a player's hard drive. As a result, it is unable by itself to provide the luxury of saved games or player profiles, which make store-bought games so playable. This can be worked around by combining Flash with PHP, and will be discussed later in the book.

- Finally, and crucially, Flash can't access individual pixels. You cannot take an image and change the colors of pixels, or paste a bitmap like a texture onto a polygon.

The bottom line is simply this: Flash is meant for low-bandwidth delivery of vector graphic rich media. It is ultimately best used in presenting simple, smooth, mathematically producible shapes. However, that doesn't mean we have to stop at flying text and pretty patterns. Flash is capable of so much more, as long as the programmer masters ActionScript and makes it work to its full capacity.

So, now we have the conventions out of the way, let's start flouting them. Flash can be enormously powerful. It has that crucial balance of simplicity and great power. It has fantastic sound and represents a major step forward in easy-to-create motion graphics.

Remember the old personal computers? There was no easy way of creating a game with sound, and when you did manage it, it was one channel – so only one event could take place at a time. Arghh! Flash, beautiful Flash, can run anything from event-related sound effects to completely streamed soundtracks, with support for up to 8 channels of audio mixed real-time.

And just look at the graphical possibilities! With the old PC games, making a simple character appear on the screen involved drawing all the pixels of the background, and then going through the sprite (the graphics character) pixel by pixel, to see if each was solid or invisible. This was a tedious process for the computer, but Flash doesn't encounter this problem because it draws actual vector shapes, so it only contends with areas that are part of that sprite, and nothing else. The fact that they define shapes and not just pixels is a distinct advantage of vectors and it means that they can then be drawn directly on to any given background. We'll be going into Flash's graphical capabilities more in the next chapter, and looking at how they can be optimized specifically for games.

Flash also contains complete keyboard handling routines, and with Flash 5, you can now detect the all-important `Key UP` event. It is also resolution independent, meaning that you can have your monitor set at any resolution, and a Flash movie will always look clean and crisp.

So, before getting too bothered about ActionScript's speed issues, there is plenty to get excited about. It has all the major functions of traditional languages like C. All of the math, logic, array and string functions are present. It's possible to create complex programs that can process a variety of things from calculations of space and gravity to graphs and statistics. The main challenge is in knowing how to make Flash do what you want it to do. By the end of this book, you'll have it mastered.

# 1   Flash Games Studio

So, that's a few ground rules out of the way. Let's talk games.

## The Computer Game

There are many different types of computer game, with new types evolving constantly. The first person shooter is currently the hot ticket, but it doesn't mean that it will be in twelve months. However, there are now some clearly defined categories that have become the foundation of the modern gaming world. They include:

- Puzzle Games
- Board Games/Card Games
- Casino Games
- Platform Games
- Role Playing Games (RPG)
- First Person Shooters (FPS)
- Adventure Games
- Sports Games
- Fighting Games
- Simulators
- Strategy games (including Real-Time (RTS)) and many others

## From the Play Room to the Casino

The simplest games, puzzles and brainteasers are very effective in Flash. They are straightforward, but can be made graphically sophisticated. Puzzle games, for example, usually involve a single screen, within which a player works to solve a challenge. Games with blocks and pieces, such as the classic *Tetris* (Nintendo 1989), involve navigating a block around the screen, and fitting it into empty spaces, with the aim of completing and clearing a row.

# Introduction to Gaming

Simple, satisfying and inexplicably addictive:

http://www.shockwave.com/content/tetris/tetris.html

Other puzzle games are based on traditional pre-PC games, such as crossword puzzles, hangman and chess. Occasionally a designer will freak out and insist on animation and interactive eye-candy to liven things up, but these games are essentially stimulating and challenging from their most basic roots.

Aside from making the graphics good and solid, you'll have to think about game logic to create a puzzle in Flash. When you click here, what happens? When this character moves there, what happens? This is perhaps the most involved and intricate part of making a puzzle game, and certainly something to sharpen your ActionScript skills on.

Card games are also relatively easy to develop on computers. All the classic card games have been recreated for the PC generation, from Solitaire to Poker. As with puzzles, the simplicity of these games lends itself well to Flash. There have been some terrific recent examples, including a great adaptation of the ancient Chinese classic, Mahjong:

http://www.flashkit.com/avcode/features/mahjong/mahjong.shtml

For the newcomer to games programming, a board game or card game presents the dual opportunity of creating something that doesn't require a heavy knowledge of sound and graphics,

# Flash Games Studio

while also removing the need to create a new game from scratch. Rather than think up rules and design, the programmer can concentrate on making the game happen, using the established rules.

One more advanced thing that these sorts of games offer is the ability to interact with other users via the Internet. Five years ago, playing a casino computer game was fun, but there was nothing except a pat on your own back for winning the jackpot:

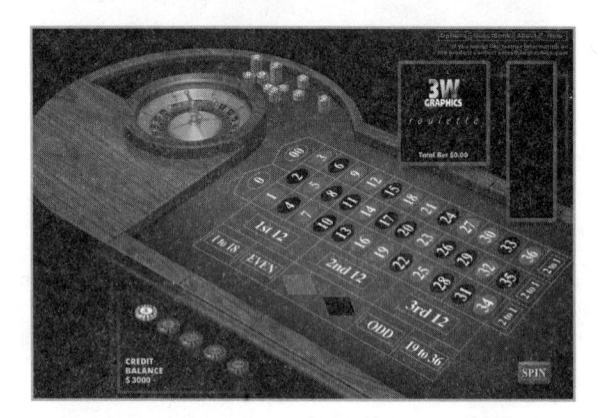

Today, casino games are allowing people to win real money, making them a very big deal indeed. Online casino games offer everything from craps and roulette to card games and slot machines. Community-oriented games such as Bingo are also becoming increasingly popular, and many companies now concentrate on developing sites which provide the full casino experience.

It must be said, however, that to truly build an online casino style game, you must also have a server, or back-end in place; a central computer that your Flash game can communicate with to ensure that player winnings are properly handled, and real-time games like Bingo are synchronized. But of course, that shouldn't deter you from having a little fun with your own programming!

## Platform Games

Early personal computers really began to come into their own with the development of platform games. Take the simple plot device and hazards from an arcade game like Pac-Man (Midway, 1980), add a law of gravity, and you have taken the simple step to platform gaming. This genre presented the first games that simply couldn't exist on paper. Players were required for the first time to control a character, and lead it through a world of life-or-death scenarios.

The formula of dexterity, control and hand-eye coordination generated a blizzard of classic platform games. *Donkey Kong* (Nintendo, 1981), *Manic Miner* (Bug Byte, 1983) and *Chuckie Egg* (A&F, 1983) came along and in turn gave birth to a new concept - the games console – and especially the Nintendo Entertainment System and the Sega Master System. After this, there was no looking back for computer games.

# Introduction to Gaming

In early platform games, players got their first taste of artificial intelligence:

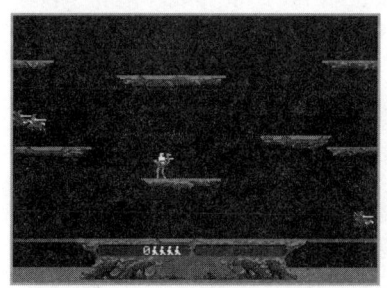

Joust, Williams 1982

In some cases though, it was more artificial than intelligent: enemies who walked into walls or off cliffs didn't display a devastating intellect, but they still worked to add an element of complexity and challenge to the game. At the end of each level a Big Boss monster would provide the most difficult challenge, requiring a bit of problem solving and skill to defeat.

Platform games are easy to design if you have a fertile imagination, but programming them requires a fair degree of technical know-how. When you create a platform game you're implicitly saying that you want full-screen motion. When this is the case with Flash you need to consider frame rate and performance because of Flash's way of rendering graphics. Knowledge of optimization and a fairly strong understanding of physics and movement is indispensable, as these games will see you checking out a few of the boundaries of Flash's capability.

## Role-playing Games

Role-playing games (RPGs) are games in which the player becomes a character and goes on quests and adventures to attain a certain level of experience. The RPG can take many months to play, with much attention paid to detail and the character's evolution. Whereas platform games tend to be linear, with a start and a finish to each level, RPGs tend to be more open, where players can stroll around more or less at will across a large map.

Many great RPGs have been created and have become institutions of the gaming world. Games such as the *Ultima* (Origin), and the *Final Fantasy* (Square Soft) series all created the sense of immersion and depth that define a good RPG.

These games also brought about terrific advances in apparent scale. A really great RPG will seem incalculably huge. This is a very effective tool for immersing a player within a gaming world. Teleportals can provide instant gratification by bandying a player to distant climes, but the sense of what's in between still remains tantalizing.

With RPGs also came a depth of character. Minor details began to matter. Characters were made up of mathematical combinations of strength, stamina, dexterity, magic, stealth, and experience. All of these combined to add to the richness and breadth of the game. And with character came plot, and then story, huge epics that swept away the player to the extent that they couldn't help but suspend their disbelief.

# 1    Flash Games Studio

It is the RPG which has benefited most from the increased popularity of the Internet. Indeed, the marriage of the two has produced many offspring, named Massively Multiplayer Online Role Playing Games. The most famous of these is Ultima Online:

Ultima Online, Electronic Arts 1997

Which, along with games such as *Everquest* (Verant Interactive, 1999) and *Asheron's Call*, (Microsoft, 1999) are literally creating new worlds that bring players together from around the globe. An online game that has 30,000 players at once in various locations all around the game map is an exciting experience that simply didn't (and couldn't) exist five years ago.

On the practical side, when you start writing a role-playing game you'll quickly see that the biggest challenge is handling the scope of data required to keep a whole world running. In a typical RPG, you have thousands of creatures, towns, townsfolk, elements like weather and time of day, and many missions or quests that your character may be carrying out all existing at once. All of this requires some careful ActionScript to get right, but it's worth it when it clicks.

## First Person Shooters

As I said earlier, the first person shooter is today's hot ticket. For years game programmers dreamed of the day when computers could handle real-time 3D material. Now games like *Half-Life*, (Sierra, 1999) *Quake III* (Id Software, 2000), *Tribes II*, (Sierra 2001) and *Duke Nukem Forever* (3D Realms Entertainment) are delivering all that and more. These games are the height of PC realism.

In an FPS, you control your character by moving forward, backward, turning left and right, and looking up and down. Aiming with your gun is accomplished with a crosshair and your projectiles take on a trajectory in 3D space.

The earth-shattering breakthrough in FPS games came with *Doom* (Id Software) in 1993. Never before had people felt so absolutely immersed in a game. Monsters ran around you, bullets flew past you, you could almost feel the fire of a nearby explosion. The FPS insisted on a new skill: the ability to think in three dimensions. New controls and new concepts were created later, when the mouse and the keyboard had to be used together to play the game.

# Introduction to Gaming 1

This was hard and fast gameplay, and to coin the term of the time, "it rocked":

Id Software, 1994

Now, under a decade later, entire generations of console systems have been created just to make 3D technology easier and more powerful.

The FPS also lends itself to the online and multiplayer world with many online FPS games taking shape such as **Quake** (Id Software 1996), **Half-life**, **Counter-Strike** (CSteam 2000) and **Unreal Tournament** (Epic Games 2001). These games provide people with high action multiplayer experiences that add an extra dimension above normal single-player games.

3D in Flash is pretty challenging because it's inherently a 2D platform. Its use of simple vector-based graphics doesn't lend itself well to the types of 3D texture-mapped environments that make other FPSs so successful. However, it's possible to create a completely immersing 3D world in Flash with use of handy tricks such as 3D scaling, pre-rendering and true 3D mathematical motion, and we'll be doing it later in the book.

## Sports Games

Sports games tend to re-create widespread real-life games and are usually very popular with the sport's real-life fans. Practically every existing sport has been turned into a computer game at some point. Indeed, even non-existing games have made it to the console – I'm looking at you, *Speedball* (Imageworks 1988) and *Carmageddon!* (SCI, 1997). Annual releases of hockey, basketball, baseball and football games keep avid fans happy with up-to-date detail and state-of-the-art gameplay. Players have come to expect bone-crunching sound effects and textured, shaded, and motion-captured graphics, and statistics ranging from batting average to eye color.

Less full-on sports games like golf and tennis are also popular, requiring a more careful and precise mastery from the player. There is also sometimes a certain amount of cross-over between sports games and simulations.

# Flash Games Studio

Super-realistic racing games are usually classed as simulations, while their more arcade-like brethren are thrown in with the sports crowd:

Sports games by their very nature are meant for multiple players, whether they're teammates or opponents. This opens up great opportunity for multiplayer play, and so many great two-player, four-player and online sports games have emerged in recent years.

There are numerous challenges in creating a successful Flash sports game. First, you must be able to handle the graphics and the sound requirements to recreate the game. Whether it's a single top-down ping-pong table, or a multi-angled hockey arena, the game must be accurate and clearly displayed. Nothing is more frustrating than not being able to see the ball or the puck.

Mortal Combat, Midway 1992

Secondly, as with puzzles and board games, the rules of a sports game must be handled precisely. Some sports have very simple rules, while others have complex nuances and strange scoring procedures. People also need to be able to develop a level of skill in the game – so it has to have some feel to it. As with real sports, skill makes the difference between good players and great players.

Finally, many secondary skills such as the physics of gravity and projectiles must be brought in to play with certain games. When a baseball is hit, it follows a very precise arc, which determines its height and distance. If these subtleties are handled inaccurately, the game can be gravely affected, and the player's suspension of disbelief will be broken.

## Fighting Games

Fighting legend Bruce Lee popularized a genre of entertainment that involved skilled martial arts and incredible stunts. Modern fighting games capture this on the computer or television screen, with enhancements and brutality that Mr Lee could have only hoped for – or more likely dreaded.

Popular games such as *Mortal Kombat* (Midway, 1992)...

# Introduction to Gaming

...or *Street Fighter* (Caplom, 1987) and *Tekken* (Namco, 1995) are all perfect examples of the fighting challenges that players have come to expect. Over the years they have developed plots and entertaining characters, variously challenging the player's dexterity, control and imagination.

The premise behind a fighting game is simple: one or two players participate, and each controls an on screen character. Combinations of key presses result in your character taking different actions, such as kick, punch, jump or block, and successful attacks cause injury to your opponent. The round progresses until one player is defeated. Certain special combinations of keys, or 'combos' cause your player to perform special, more powerful moves.

The graphics in these games range from simplistic, to ultra-realistic 3D rendered. The amount of blood and carnage in such games has provoked controversy in the past, and they tend to prowl the boundaries of good taste – although not without their own brand of dark humor.

The main task in a fighting game is creating a collision system that allows your fighters to make contact with each other and score damage points. This would involve testing for collision between feet and hands (the offensive) and head and body (the target).

You will also need to create many different animations and graphics to display the various styles of fighting in the game. Different punches, kicks, jumps and other displays must be pre-drawn and then displayed with ActionScript as the game is carried out.

In a fighting game the control system can become quite hectic, with special key combinations producing different moves. Therefore, you will have to write a fairly robust user input handling routine that involves reading keys and keeping track of what has recently been pressed.

## Simulations

A surprisingly early development in computer gameplay was the simulation. The primary goal of course is to accurately mimic a part of real life, whether it be a city, ant colony, hospital, or in the majority of cases a vehicle, such as an airplane or a submarine. In a simulation, the player is presented with a high level of detail and micro-control over the actions and outcomes of whatever it is they're controlling.

# 1 Flash Games Studio

Simulations have matured incredibly over the years. Flight simulators have developed from a single horizontal line across the screen to a fully-realized environment, taking into account the physics and handling of the airplane, so you experience forces such as lift, drag, stall and acceleration:

Often, an element of combat is added to the simulator, creating the dual experience of precision and conflict. Look at the flight simulator again; many popular air combat simulators have been made. Whether you're flying a World War 2 Spitfire or a modern F-16 Eagle, you have the thrill of combat over historical theatres of war, against other aircraft and ground threats.

In a simulator, multiple players can meet up online and take to the skies in an all-out re-creation of Pearl Harbor or take part in bombing raids on London. Fly a night sortie over Baghdad or avoid collision as several friends take turns landing at Los Angeles International Airport – someone else could even be manning the control tower guiding them home.

In Flash, the main difficulty in creating a simulator is the way that 3D graphics are generated. Traditionally, 3D graphics in simulators are fully rendered in true 3D with lines, surfaces and textures. If your simulator has a combat element to it, then you must also create some artificial intelligence – enemies that follow the same physical rules that you do. Aircraft that attempt to intercept and destroy you, ground guns that attempt to shoot you down, and missiles that track you until you evade or destroy them. The thing to remember in simulations is that if it can happen in the real-life situation being simulated, then it should be able to happen in the game. No matter how unlikely it sounds.

There are of course many other types of games, and each type can be combined with another to create new genres. There's still even room for completely new genres to be created, just think of the Japanese Bemani games craze (*Parrapa the Rapper* (SCEI, 1997) for example) that swept the console world not so long ago.

You're probably itching to go already, so let's take a look at a basic game design process.

# Introduction to Gaming

## Writing in Sections

When you start writing a game in Flash (or any language for that matter) you will probably want to break down the writing into manageable sections. Rather than attacking the whole game at once, if you take care of different pieces first, you stand a greater chance of minimizing bugs and other such problems.

As a general guideline, I find it easiest to write in the following flow:

- **Idea** – The first thing is, of course, that spark of inspiration that makes you want to write the game. This can be anything from a simple thought in your head, to a detailed sheaf of scribblings on paper.

- **Engine** – Next, I write the actual brain of the game. The engine is what forms the foundation for the whole game. In a 3D game that would include a polygon engine, sprite engine and a way of sorting it all by depth. Perhaps also a collision engine. The is responsible for driving the major aspects of the game. You can forget about how it works once it's written – you simply need to know that it works.

- **Game play** – This is the stage in which you make your game interactive. Here you add things like gravity, keyboard control and game moves such as jumping and running. Once you have these first two steps written, you'll have something that you can demonstrate to people.

- **Opponents and A.I.** – Eventually it will come time to make your game challenging by providing things that impede the player, and give them a reason to fight back. Elements like spike pits, fire jets and acid pools all fall under this category. This also includes the development of monsters, and their thinking patterns. At this stage you must make monsters that appear to be intelligent, and fight back at you.

- **Specific game elements** – These are the things that add variation and more objectives to the game. Keys, power-ups, health, score-increasing items and mission objects are all objects that add to the overall game as a whole, and give each level a mission and a purpose. You must code different forms of logic to handle things like this, ranging from generic (say, a general 10% health power-up) to specific (say, a secret book on level 4).

- **Plot elements and interstitials** – These are the filler for the games that help forward the plot. When a game is beginning, then you add an introduction, or between levels perhaps you could put an image to imply time passage. These should require little coding except to bring up and play an image (possibly streamed in when needed).

- **Graphical User Interface** (GUI) – This is what allows your player to select different options about the game. Difficulty level, graphics detail, instructions, etc. All the outside-of-game decisions are made through a GUI environment. This should be intuitive and comprehensive.

# Flash Games Studio

- **Sound and Music** – This is a very important step in filling out an entire dimension to your game. Sound and music cues will be vital in enhancing the professionalism and interactivity of any game. We'll go into this in greater detail later in the book.

Of course these guidelines aren't perfect for every game type, for example plot and story might be the first thing developed in an RPG as the rest of the game hinges around them, but they're fine for starters. By following these guidelines, you'll be able to build any game in Flash in a straightforward, timely and rewarding fashion. You will also have built things separately so that you can easily keep different things in their own libraries that can be reused. For example, a polygon engine could be taken and reused again and again in different games, with very little modification.

No matter what type of game you make though, it lives or dies on the strength of that elusive quality: playability. Good games have it, and bad games don't, so let's take a look at some of the steps you can take on your road to finding the playability nirvana.

## What Makes a Good Game?

When it comes down to bare facts, there is no substitute for a good game. All the 3D ray-traced bitmap textured graphics tricks in the world won't save a stinker – and skimming stones off a pond is still more enjoyable than getting to grips with a sloppy game control or a boggy scenario. There are some hard and fast rules to good game design, and you would do well to stick by them. Here's the first brief list of things that we want:

- Performance
- Control
- Story
- Challenge
- Reward
- Repeat Playability

And that's just for the game itself. There are also some other Flash specific issues, the most important of which is: Quick download time.

This is one of the first things you need to be aware of, and pretty much the last thing that will become apparent while you're actually designing. So how can you possibly ever be in control of everything? By practice. The most important thing in a game is the evolving, testing, and tweaking that happens throughout its lifecycle. But before this can happen, you need an idea.

# Introduction to Gaming    1

## Design on Paper

Stop a while, even if you're dying to get programming. There's something that is very appealing about sitting in a quiet spot with no glaring monitors or whirring fans, and just using your hands to draw or write. Get a cup of tea, or some cool water, and just start drawing.

Come on admit it, we've all sat down and created a highly detailed character for no reason and then thrown in a few great bad guys for opposition, before finally trying to incorporate them into a game without a map, and then realizing that the hard drive is already full. First you need to plan, and you need to know what your aims are and how to go about achieving them. Face it: if Flash is going to be unable to meet your requirements, it's far better to realize it early before sweating it out over a hot keyboard. When you design on paper you can:

- Create storyboards that illustrate animated sequences, or general plot sequences

- Design characters and backgrounds

- Map out levels, placing different hazards and bonuses and visualizing how it all works as a whole

- Work out difficult technological problems by sketching out the physics and math and creating a picture that helps you solve it easily

Here's a quick example of a scribbled level map showing all of the major elements of the level:

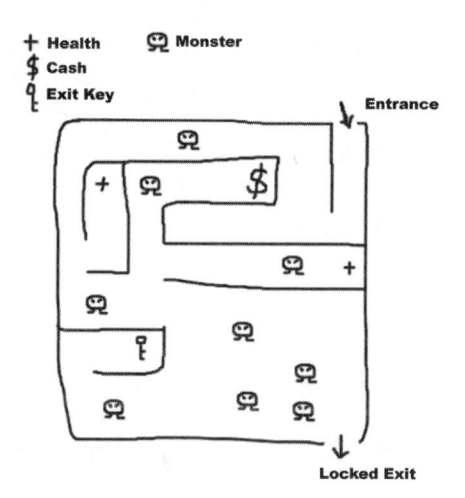

A large commercial game can often have thousands of pages of sketches, designs, layouts and calculations. For our purposes, it helps us to get closer to that ideal balance of the smallest file against the best game.

# Flash Games Studio

## Keeping your File Size Down

It's simple. The larger your file, the longer it's going to take to download, and the more likely your players are to get impatient, give up, and leave. So how long will your movie take to download? Look at the following chart, which indicates a few ideal download times:

| Modem Speed | 50kb file | 100kb file | 500kb file | 1Mb file | 5Mbfile |
|---|---|---|---|---|---|
| 14.4 k (1,800 bytes/sec) | 28 sec | 56 sec | 278 sec | 556 sec | 2,778 sec |
| 28.8 k (3,600 bytes/ sec) | 14 sec | 28 sec | 139 sec | 278 sec | 1,289 sec |
| 56k (7,000 bytes/sec) | 7 sec | 14 sec | 71 sec | 143 sec | 714 sec |
| ISDN (16,000 bytes/sec) | 3 sec | 6 sec | 31 sec | 63 sec | 313 sec |
| DSL (32,000 bytes / sec) | 1 sec | 3 sec | 15 sec | 31 sec | 156 sec |
| Cable (78,000 bytes/sec) | 1 sec | 1.2 sec | 6.4 sec | 13 sec | 64 sec |

Remember that there are still many people out there using 56k and slower modems. Take the time to research your audience, and then make ways of accommodating their needs. If you're appealing to a certain demographic or a certain geographic location, take the time to find out what kind of modem speeds are most prevalent in that market.

> *The reason the chart shows ideal download times is because sometimes things will go slower or faster depending on several factors like traffic, geography and overall speed of the server. If you have connected to a website running on a server that only has an ISDN connection to the internet, then even if you have cable, you can only go as fast as the ISDN – the slower of the two connections. Relative geography plays a big part too. The farther away the player is from the server, the longer the game will take to download.*

## Compression

When you import audio files and bitmaps, make sure you take some time to check the compression on the files. The compression settings can literally make a difference of hundreds of kilobytes to your final file size. Most compression settings can be modified easily by selecting an object in the library, opening its properties, and editing the compression settings within, here are the bitmap compression settings for a sample tree texture:

# Introduction to Gaming

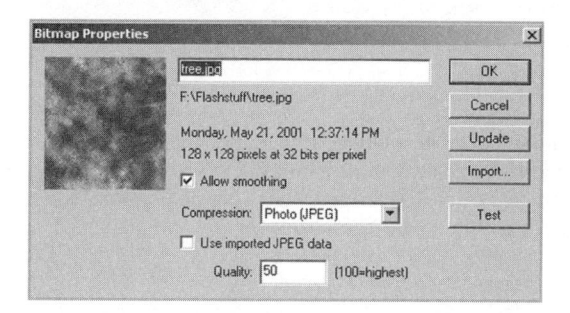

## Delivery Options

Depending on your game, there are a few different ways of deploying it. Each of these ways has different advantages and disadvantages.

### Online

This is the most common method of delivering Flash content. This simply means that it can be found online at a web site, and it runs directly in the browser window. This is the ideal method for delivering an online game that is meant to be part of a web site as a whole. Perhaps it's a game showcase – an online arcade – or a Flash movie that's meant to supplement a major movie. In all these cases, it's best to deliver your Flash content via a web site.

With any online environment, careful consideration has to be given to file sizes, or different methods of content delivery. A definite advantage of delivering your games online is the ease with which the player can get to them. There's very little knowledge required beyond simply clicking on a link or entering the URL.

### Standalone Player

Another option for delivering Flash content (specifically games) is through the standalone player, or projector. When you export a file as a projector, it then becomes an executable file. When you run this, it simply runs your game in a window, with no link to the Internet required.

This gives the player the total experience of immersion in the game by removing all external references like banner ads and navigation bars. The player simply has a self-contained executable file on their computer, and when they run it, the game begins.

This method also overcomes the limitations imposed by downloading a game at runtime. Yes, your player will need to download the game once, but once it's on their hard drive, it will start virtually instantaneously every time they run it, and it should play at a decent speed without the need for streaming.

So, now that we know what we're aiming at in terms of practicality, let's look at some of the other aspects that make a good game standout from a shoddy one.

# 1  Flash Games Studio

## Performance

Performance, performance, performance! This is the single most important aspect of good game design. Without good performance, your gameplay will grind to a halt, and people will run from it like a mailman from a Rottweiler. In fact, fast, playable speed is essentially one of the game programmer's holy grails. When your game runs quickly and plays well, people will line up to play it.

A case in point is the super-successful *Super Mario Brothers* (SMB) for the Nintendo Entertainment System. Before SMB platform games were either simple or slow. But SMB smacked game-players lovingly about the face. It was fast, smooth and beautiful. It was colorful and sparkly and dynamic, and it successfully bridged the gap between games and cartoons:

Nintendo, 1994

Often people design games with only graphics in mind, and then are heartbroken when the game lags along at four frames per second. Games are a fusion of art and technology, and unfortunately the limitations of technology frequently drag the art side down with them.

Some of the best games emerged pre 1995 before good graphics started to become standard. In the early 80s people often made games in their basements with artistry at a minimum, and yet those games became classics simply because those programmers concentrated on making their games playable.

Remember not to be tempted by the beauty of the full motion alpha-faded gradient in Flash. This'll just choke your game and drive away your players. If a game is supposed to mimic a real-life activity like playing tennis, then people expect the game to perform with the same responsiveness and speed of real tennis.

If you've made your game as fast as possible and it still lags, then design the game with a minimum system in mind, and tell your players about it. That way if you say that a Pentium III, 800MHz is required, people running slower systems will understand when the game has performance problems. Let's face it, most of today's games can't run on computers made even just two years ago.

# Introduction to Gaming

A vital aspect of good performance is the download time. If your game takes too long to download, be under no illusions, people will give up. Always create a loader bar, and perhaps some game visuals that will appear right away, while the rest of the game continues loading. If a game is going to take a long time to download, be courteous and inform the player. If they know before hand, they will be more inclined to patience.

Just because a game comes up quickly in the Flash test environment, that doesn't mean it will come up quickly over a modem. While a cable modem and DSL line can load most Flash games in seconds, 56k modem users must still wait patiently for most things to load. The job of entertaining the player starts the moment they arrive at your web site.

## Control

In the context of a game, control can be defined as the ease and success with which a player can make the proper events of the game occur. It doesn't matter whether it's jumping, shooting, or selecting your answer in a trivia question – if the player can't smoothly and confidently perform the actions; frustration and boredom will quickly follow. Game over.

Let's go back to **Super Mario Brothers**. What made this game so great was that not only was it king of performance, it was also beautifully responsive. When you pressed the button, Mario jumped, and if you held the button longer, his arc was a little bit higher. You could make Mario duck and skid to a halt. This exceptional control was the cause of amusing scenes of players lifting and twisting their bodies and thrusting their game controllers from side to side in an attempt to better control Mario.

Realistically and logically, the success of your game depends on the player's ability to play it. Game consoles have ergonomically perfect keypads, whereas you will probably only have a flat keyboard – unwieldy to pick up and brittle when dropped. Choose control keys that are logical, and well placed on the keyboard. The arrow keys are great for controlling movement, they make sense and most computer users are used to moving things like cursors, with those keys.

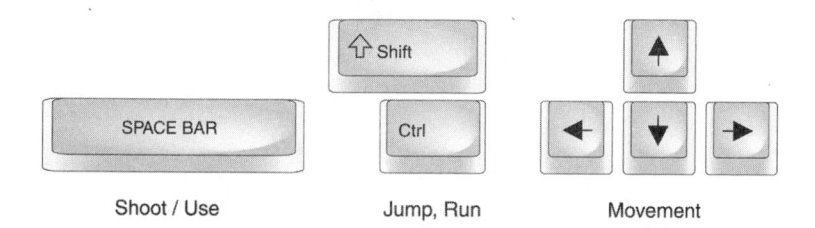

|   |   |   |
|---|---|---|
| SPACE BAR | Shift / Ctrl | ← ↑ ↓ → |
| Shoot / Use | Jump, Run | Movement |

Secondary actions like Jump and Shoot are often controlled with the space bar, the Shift, or control key. Depending on the game, the mouse can also be used to move things around, or open up and navigate through menus.

So what are the indications of good and bad control? Simply stated, the player's actions and key presses should produce the expected result on screen. When this objective is met, then the Control of your game is considered to be intuitive. At this point the game takes on what could be described as an organic feel, and it takes a step along the path of becoming a pleasure to play.

# Flash Games Studio

Much of this is not only achieved through the keyboard, but also by the game physics. When the gravity acting on a player feels accurate and smooth – almost curvaceous – and it combines with intuitive controls, you will then have a game with good control. If your game is rigid and unnatural, then your control will appear to be bad. The key is smoothness. Think of everything happening along curved paths, not rectangles:

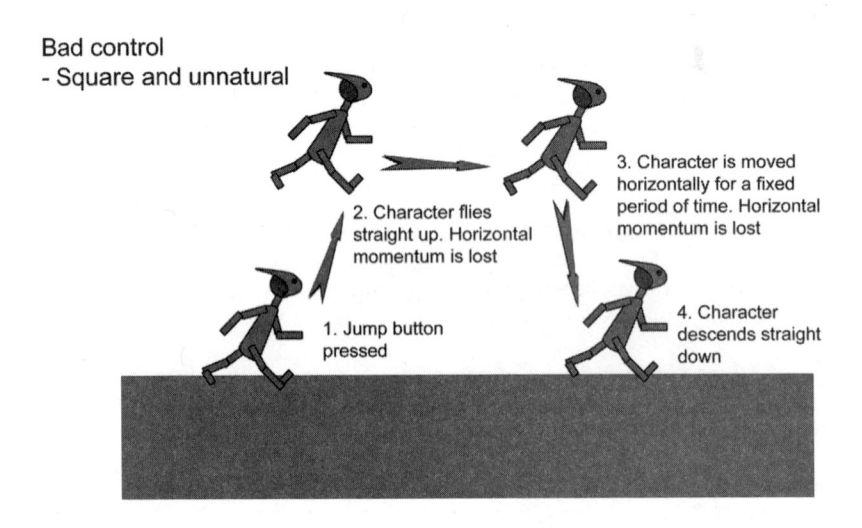

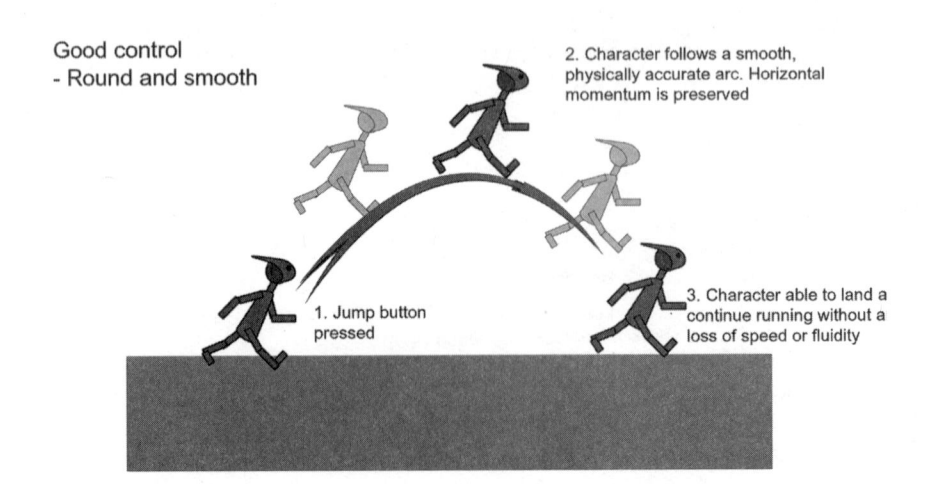

Bad control
- Square and unnatural

1. Jump button pressed
2. Character flies straight up. Horizontal momentum is lost
3. Character is moved horizontally for a fixed period of time. Horizontal momentum is lost
4. Character descends straight down

Good control
- Round and smooth

1. Jump button pressed
2. Character follows a smooth, physically accurate arc. Horizontal momentum is preserved
3. Character able to land a continue running without a loss of speed or fluidity

# Introduction to Gaming

You may have to invest a great deal of time into getting the control to feel natural. Playing around with the different values for friction, gravity or resistance will greatly change the fluidity of your game. Moving with slight acceleration and deceleration will fulfill the requirements of good control.

Game speed, performance and control are all intricately linked, and mastering them all is your first step and your foundation in creating the perfect game.

## Story

Story is an all-encompassing element of good game design. Gone are the days when the story was explained in the liner notes of the program cassette. The story is the reason your player wants to press a number of keys in a particular sequence. There must be motivation and resolution. You must create good guys, bad guys, locations and the often-ignored yet crucial highlight: A plot. The genuinely watertight plots have even made the jump from games to movies – **Tomb Raider** and **Final Fantasy** to name the obvious ones!

Game designers often rush into an idea so quickly that they don't stop to decide what the game is about until they're half done. Could you imagine Stephen Spielberg assembling a cast and crew, and on the first day of shooting stopping to realize he doesn't have any sort of a script?

The story is what forms the all-important emotional attachment to the player. It adds names, feelings and motivation to an otherwise cold and unfeeling medium. It is through the story that we develop people's interest and drive to keep playing the game. When the player feels attached to Jolly Jim the grasshopper trapped in a jar, they will want to endure the challenge of rescuing him to achieve the reward of seeing him hop to freedom:

Maybe they'll even want to get him out of there to see what damage they can do to him. But whatever it is, they want it. Game on!

Research your subject fully. Don't be afraid to go to the library, surf the web, watch documentaries or talk to people who are experts in the topic of your game. For example, war veterans can tell some sobering stories about the realities of war, and then you can take that insight and create a more realistic and emotionally genuine game.

When your story takes on an epic scale then you have achieved the cinematic effect of touching your players deeply and emotionally. Major plot twists and other turns of event will have a profound impact. As the story changes, so too will the player's mood and emotions. You can induce joy, fear, sadness and thrill. These are the goals of a truly great game.

## Challenge

Let's face it; nothing in life is interesting without some sort of effort. Whether you're creating a meal and your challenge is to cook skillfully, or leading a multibillion-dollar corporation where your mission is to become the biggest; challenge is looming. Challenge puts the fun in trying.

Let's look at *Sim City*. When it was first released in 1989, this neat and original game was an instant hit. People could play for hours, creating new communities to lesser or greater success. This is because the blend of challenges in *Sim City* is exactly right. Building a village is a piece of cake, a town, no problem, even reaching city status is well within reach. Maybe, just maybe, you're a natural at this game...?

Electronic Arts, 2000

And then it hits you - the roads are getting a bit busy. Whoah, street shootings are on the rise... Citizens are revolting. Yes, without even trying, you've created a monster. And that's without the natural disasters. The answer? Start again of course.

As you can see, the great games are challenging but not impossible. Players must have the right mix of success and failure so that success is always within reach. Without this, your player will simply get stuck. Game over.

# Introduction to Gaming

In a good game, there are practical elements which mustn't pose too much of a challenge. For example, the control of your game mustn't be so challenging as to become an annoying hindrance. Control should be intuitive, while the scenario itself should be a test. If a character is running towards a wide crevasse, players will want the controls to accurately represent their attempts at making the difficult jump. Eventual success will then be a harmony of player and controls.

On the other hand, don't bore your players by making a game so easy that there's no challenge to completing it. Remember your target audience because different audiences have different types and degrees of skill. Children are generally not as coordinated as adults, while most teenagers will feel patronized by a game that is too childish.

Naturally, as the game progresses, your player's skill levels will increase, and you will have to increase the level of challenge accordingly. This can be accomplished by making enemies more difficult, levels larger and puzzles longer. The process of tweaking the difficulty can be tedious, but it's an integral part of game development.

## Reward

For overcoming challenges and reaching milestones, a good game will offer the player some sort of reward. It could be something that affects their in-game status, like an increase in rank, gaining of experience or eighteen gold pieces, or something for entertainment like an animated sequence.

Be careful – the latter is often known simply as **eye-candy**, or **junkmedia**. This is too often thrown into a game to make it fuller and longer, but it's nothing more than just stuffing. Once again, the cardinal rule stands: if your game is not good on its own, eye-candy will not make it any better. Players will spend no more than five minutes viewing junkmedia, but potentially hours on the game – it is gameplay that matters.

Make sure your game has an ultimate goal because people will grow bored of a game that has no foreseeable ending. It's the pursuit of the goal that keeps players playing. This ultimate goal translates into the ultimate reward: finishing the game.

## Demographics

Remember to consider whom you're writing your game for. Demographics play a large part in how your game is designed and executed. Games for children must be bright and relatively simple, while games for adults can have more subtlety and a greater concentration on plot. If your game is too simple or too convoluted for your demographic, players won't stay.

Also, don't forget gender. Women like different games than men. Generally speaking, men are more interested in violence and physical challenge, while women tend to enjoy more cerebral games like cards or puzzles. Of course this is a generalization, and there are exceptions to everything, but it's something worth bearing in mind.

Some content may also be unsuitable for certain groups. Don't put sex or violence in a game unless you make people aware that it contains some potentially unsuitable subject matter.

## Testing

When your game is finished (or at least at a point where you would consider it to be an accurate representation of the final product) you must start testing. This is the stage at which 90% of your bugs will emerge, and you will probably find yourself fixing things on every level, from the engine to the A.I.

This is a very important stage, so you should find people to test your games who will be professional yet enjoy playing games and will therefore understand what's an error, and what's just work in progress. You need testers to be honest with you, because you don't want to release a game with bugs in it – that is a deadly move and players are often not very forgiving.

## Standards

It's very important that you set your standards high. When you're designing a game from scratch, there's no reason for it to look or feel substandard and amateurish. Always aim for professionalism. This means spending extra time on the graphics, sound, and control, and also ensuring quality at every step of the way with rigorous testing and playing. Accept no less. This is the direction that Flash games will be taking in the near future, and this is what will be required to stay ahead of the pack.

## Repeat Playability

To increase the lifespan of your game, and to keep players happy, it's important to create a reason for your players to want to return to the game and play it again and again.

Making your game non-linear is one effective way to achieve this. If there are multiple paths the player can take when completing the game, they will want to return to explore the other paths to see what they missed. Allowing your game to have multiple variable settings like different weather patterns in a flight simulator, or different arenas in a football game will create many combinations of game, and thus bring players back for more.

Larger games also offer that most precious of gifts: the hidden secret. These games are possible to complete in a relatively linear fashion, but optional secrets are dotted around which require much more lateral thinking from a player. It's almost another game in parallel to the main plot. Finding a secret is very satisfying, and guarantees commitment from a player.

Another trick to ensure repeat business is to introduce random elements to the game. If a level is always different because the computer generates it randomly, then it is certain that every game will be new and unique. However you must be careful not to make your game so random that it has no consistency.

Some games offer a difficulty selection at the start so that the player can choose to play the whole game on easy mode, and then once they've finished, select medium and play again. This goes on until the player has defeated the game at the most difficult setting.

# Introduction to Gaming

Finally – and here's the real gem with an Internet-based baby like Flash – you can't go wrong with multiplayer games. People will always return to play head-to-head many times because of the thrill of the competition and the social aspect of playing with friends.

A terrific example of this is *Half-Life: Counter-Strike*:

CSTeam, 2000

This first person shooter involves strong team play, with each player joining the terrorist or counter-terrorist team. The game is played in rounds, and each player can die only once in a round. Different maps have different objectives. In a bomb map, the terrorists must plant an explosive, and the counter-terrorists must defuse it. In a hostage map, the counter-terrorists must rescue hostages, and the terrorists must stop them. After killing each other, planting the bomb, or rescuing all the hostages, one team will be declared the winner and the other the loser.

The game is great because the opponents are other human players, so there's no predicting how advanced your rivals will be. This provides an unlimited level of challenge and the opportunity to enhance your skills and gain the respect of other players.

*Counter Strike* combines all of the fundamental elements of a good game. It has challenge, reward and definite repeat playability because each game is short, lasting no more than five minutes. Players come back for more because they're constantly trying to improve their skills. Each round offers cash as a reward for skilled playing and to the whole team for winning the round. There are many different variations of game that can be played. You can use a different weapon, join a different team, adopt different strategies and play in different locales. This is the kind of thing you're aiming for, not necessarily an FPS, but an exciting, involving, and rewarding game.

# Flash Games Studio

## Final Thoughts

Game design is a long and involving process, requiring creative, technical, and artistic aptitude. When all the elements come together, you'll find that making a game is a pure pleasure, with satisfaction and benefit every step of the way. Use the short time you have to grab peoples' attention. Tell them stories and make places tomorrow that don't exist today. In the next chapter we'll start with one of the simplest parts of game design, the graphics, but instead of telling you how to draw, we'll tell you what you need to bear in mind when you're drawing to ensure your graphics are tuned to the technology available.

"Feel good about yourself. You are contributing to the cultural wealth of the human race."
- Diana Gruber. **Action arcade adventure set.**

# Introduction to Gaming

Introduction
chapter 1
chapter 2
chapter 3
chapter 4
chapter 5
chapter 6
Case Study 1
chapter 7
chapter 8
chapter 9
chapter 10
chapter 11
chapter 12
chapter 13
Case Study 2
chapter 14
chapter 15
Director Afterword

# Chapter 2
# Optimizing Graphics for Games

# Flash Games Studio

It can't have escaped anyone's notice that the technology of the gaming industry at large has come on in leaps and bounds in recent years. Games can now boast beautifully detailed real-time 3D worlds, with shadows, reflections and subtle lighting. Surfaces are vivid and texturized, grass looks lush and green, and everything is high-resolution in 32-bit color, running at 60 frames per second (fps).

Wouldn't it be nice if we had such graphical luxuries? One of the most important things to remember is that you can have all the complex graphics in the world, but we're making Flash games here, not films. Frame rate is the issue.

When your graphics become too complex and, even worse, hinder the game, then you know you've made a crucial error somewhere along the way. I've seen many artists learn a hard lesson when they created a beautiful main character of 6,000 curves with lush moving background images, only to watch as the game crawled along at 6 fps. For the sake of the game, and your player's enjoyment, cut that character down – sacrifice any grandiose artistic pride – and make the game playable! With a few ninja-like Flash moves, you can knock up some great visuals. All it takes is a couple of ground rules, and amazing graphics will be yours. This chapter will brief you in those rules.

Perhaps the first thing to do is to remember those poor old programmers in the 1980s. They slaved over every single pixel, each one taxing the computer's memory and draining speed. The result of this rationing was a generation of shrewd designers who were constantly coming up with tricks to create visual effects with the barest minimum of resources. Who can forget the genius of using simple flashing black and white blocks at the side of a racetrack to create an illusion of speed? That car was flying along!

These days of course we have a bunch of incredibly powerful PCs, and a temptation to cast off pixel worries and write big fat games. But be warned – pixels still rule the day, and careless designers can still end up in thick performance soup.

In this chapter, we'll be discussing:

- The technical considerations of graphics

- Resolution, Frame rates and Pixels

- Optimizing your images in Flash – things to consider and things to avoid;

- Using ActionScript to help streamline your game

- Optimizing performance and preparing the download

- Pulling in external SWFs to minimize final file size

# Optimizing Graphics for Games    2

## A Day in the Life of a Frame

When we watch television, we are watching a series of still images – frames that zip past at a rate of about 30 per second. So, in one second 30 consecutive images have flashed by and created the illusion of motion.

In Flash, we have the option to choose our desired frame rate:

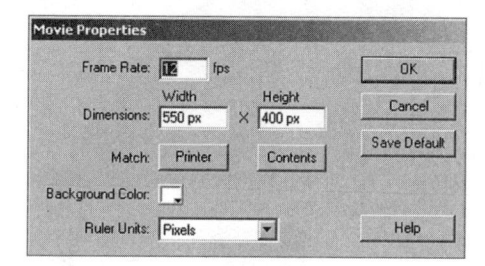

In theory, this all makes sense, and there's nothing more to talk about. However, things aren't quite that simple. Frame rate in Flash can really only be called a desired frame rate, because many things are going to foil your plans for that perfectly smooth 30 fps game.

As each frame passes, Flash must look after a number of things. For a start, it must execute all of the ActionScript in a single frame of your game. So, if you have monsters running around, gravity pulling you down, physics moving you along, and scores to keep, then Flash is already processing a substantial amount of information – and that's before it has even started drawing the images.

## The Price of Graphics

Graphics the single greatest thing that are going to slow down your game. This is simply because there are so many millions of decisions to be made to render the graphics on screen. The task is colossal, and there are a certain number of decisions to be made before you even attempt to bring your image to the screen. If we take it right down to the most basic elements, those decisions should become a lot easier to make.

### The Pixel

A screen is made up of a grid of dots called pixels. The word pixel is derived from 'picture elements'. Take a look at the pixels that make up this image:

# Flash Games Studio

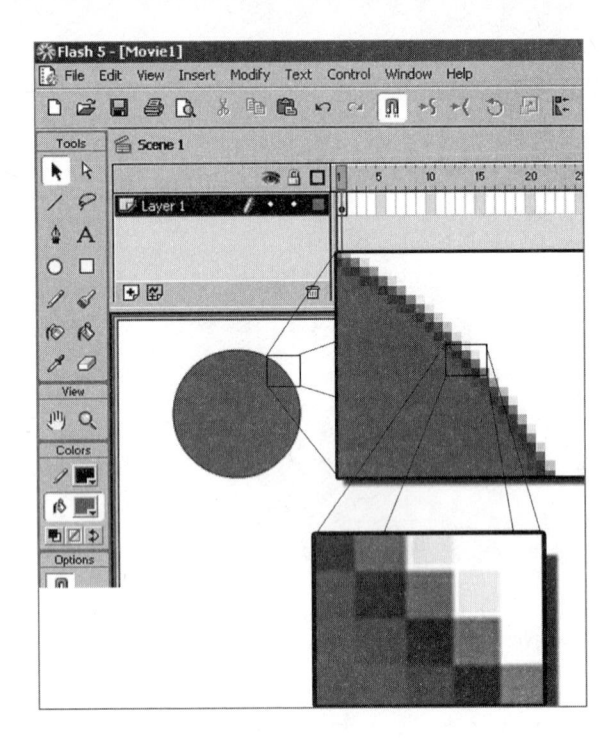

There are a fixed number of pixels from left to right, and from top to bottom. The word to describe the number of pixels on screen is resolution. Modern computers allow you to vary the screen resolution. The higher the resolution, the more pixels you have on screen, and the more detail you can fit on it.

It's important for us to take into account how a computer does what it has to do at the lowest level. At its core, a computer has a clock that ticks at a certain number of times per second. This determines your processor speed.

## The Clock

The master clock is an independent, electrically powered quartz crystal in the CPU of your computer, responsible for keeping every action in your CPU synchronized. Every time this crystal vibrates or 'ticks', it delivers an electrical charge and your computer is able to do one instruction. The number of times that this clock ticks determines the speed of your CPU. 800 MHz is 800 million vibrations/ticks per second. 1.7 GHz is 1.7 billion ticks per second. The faster this clock ticks, the faster your computer can do things. This quartz crystal is your computer's pacemaker; without it your computer wouldn't work.

Every single action your computer performs takes a certain number of clock ticks. For example, let's say that we want the computer to draw one single pixel on the screen, in the upper-left corner - position (0,0) in Flash. Your application goes through several steps to carry out this operation.

# Optimizing Graphics for Games 2

Tick 1: The program tells the computer a graphic instruction is coming up

Tick 2: The program tells the computer a pixel draw is coming up

Tick 3: Your program tells the computer the x coordinate of the pixel

Tick 4: Your program tells the computer the y coordinate of the pixel

Tick 5: Your program tells the computer the color of the pixel

Tick 6: The computer renders the pixel

Ticks 7-12: Overhead calculations the operating system has to perform to actually take the virtual rendered pixel and put it on to the real screen

Say we want to fill the whole screen from top to bottom in one solid color. At an 800 x 600 resolution, that's 480,000 pixels. That's a grand total of 5,760,000 clock ticks to fill the screen. By the time your screen is filled, the computer has done nearly 6 million clock ticks.

Now, let's say we're running on a 600 MHz machine, which means 600 million clock ticks per second. 5,760,000 clock ticks divided into 600 million is about 104. That means that the computer can completely redraw the screen in one solid color 104 times per second, or put another way, at 104 frames per second.

That's a nice frame rate! But keep in mind this is an idealistic example of the computer's efforts. In reality the computer has a lot more to do than just dedicate all of its energies to filling the screen for us. In the world of Windows, Mac OS and multi-tasking, a computer is never doing just one thing at a time. So, realistically speaking, of those 600 million cycles, maybe only 300 are available strictly for our drawing test. Which means our frame rate is:

5,760,000 into 300 million = 53 complete screen redraws per second.

So, our maximum frame rate here is 53 fps. Well, that's still pretty good. The only thing not good about it is that we have achieved a completely blank screen, whatever the color. As soon as we start adding images, things are going to start slowing down, and we only have 23 fps to play with before our 30 fps target is eaten into.

## The Screen Buffer

Rather than rendering directly to your screen, Flash makes use of a screen buffer – which you do not see. If your Flash movie is running in a 550x400 pixel window, the buffer will consider itself 550x400 pixels in size, reserving precisely the amount of RAM required for that number of pixels. When you resize your Flash movie to be larger, then the off-screen buffer will also grow larger – it is entirely related to how big it will appear on screen. In this way your movie is cushioned from the other elements (other programs, the operating system and so on.) that are snaffling your computer's memory.

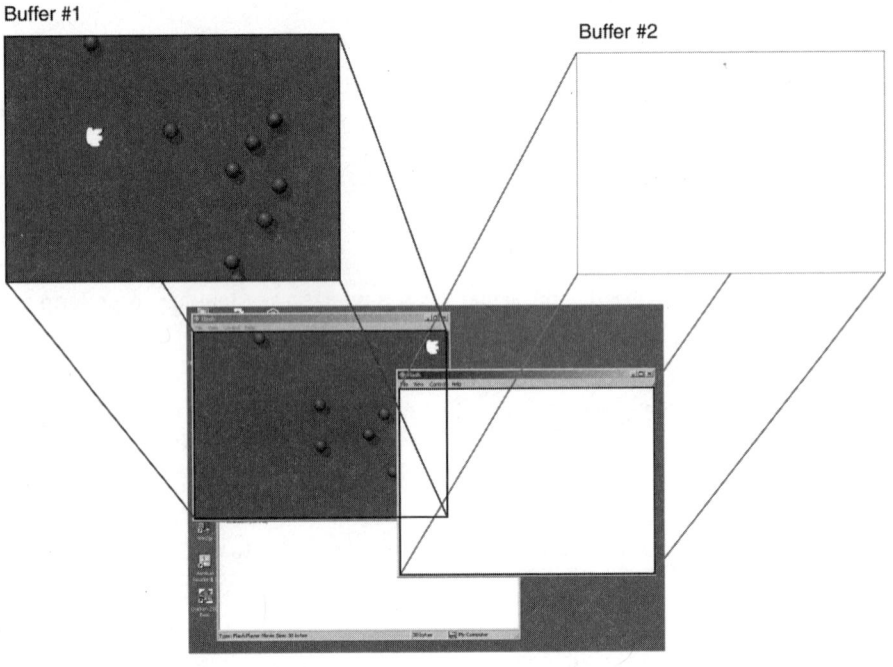

Windows as they appear on-screen

## Optimizing Graphics for Games

Flash treats this buffer as if it actually is the screen, and renders to it. When the final image is complete, the buffer (which is made up of RAM) is pasted into the Video RAM (or VRAM). The VRAM is your screen. Your monitor redraws itself a set number of times per second, by reading the contents of the VRAM.

So you can see there are two rates going on here. There is the rate you set for your Flash movie in frames per second, and then there is the rate at which your monitor refreshes itself via the VRAM.

If you have a modern digital monitor, you've probably got a button on the front that brings up an on-screen menu system with several options including positioning, scaling and refresh rate. This refresh rate is quite important, and indicates how frequently the monitor will update the image it is displaying. Alternatively, in Windows you can change your display settings. Check out the monitor settings in the Control Panel to see the Refresh Frequency in hertz (frames per second).

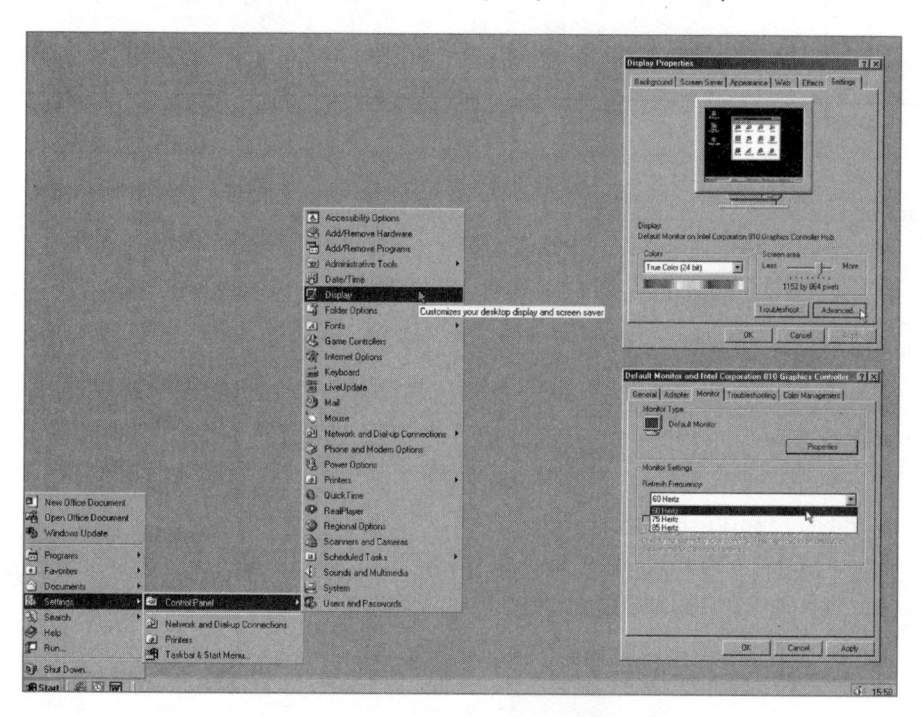

Now, let's say your monitor is refreshing itself at a rate of 60 times per second. Anything that appears on your monitor will run at 60 frames per second. Even if you have a game that boasts a ludicrously quick frame rate (say 120 fps), it will still only appear on the screen at 60 fps.

So a 120 fps game would be wasting its time. It would be rushing to draw all those frames, even though your user would not see half of them.

Right, let's get back to the VRAM. The use of a buffer avoids the messy sight of seeing frames being rendered. If a frame was to be rendered directly to VRAM, and took longer than one monitor refresh to render, then you would see the image in an incomplete state:

How your final frame should look

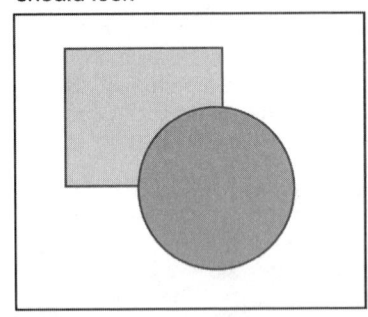

What you might see if a refresh occurs mid-render

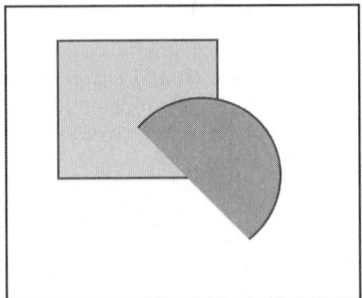

Naturally, at a 60-hertz refresh rate, you would only see that half-rendered image for 1/60th of a second but that is still long enough for your eye to register a distracting flicker.

So if we render the image with all its intricacy and complexity into an off screen buffer, then we can be sure no work-in-progress will be seen by the player, and only when the image is complete will it be switched into VRAM.

Remember that when you don't see something because it is obscured by other images, Flash has still expended effort into rendering it, only to then cover it up and then show you the final product.

### A Note About Screen Resolution

Something Flash has no control over is the resolution of individual users' screens. As a result, you have no control over how big your game will appear:

Crucially for speed, you must make the Flash movie non-scalable and set the scale mode to default, so that the dimensions match the movie you designed. You don't want people to be able to run your game on a 1280x1024 monitor and then scale their browser to full screen – that would make your game crawl. Who are players going to blame? Themselves? No, of course not, they'll blame the designer, so it's up to you to account for all these possibilities.

# Optimizing Graphics for Games    2

A rather hands-on solution to all this is to request that users set their screen resolution to, say, 640x480, thus allowing your 550x400 Flash game to take up a good portion of the screen without losing speed. Bear in mind though, the vast majority of game players will simply not engage in this kind of commitment. Would you?

## The Price of Vectors

Flash is a vector-based program. It's a vector engine. So what is Flash really up to when it's drawing a frame? Why do certain things seem to take longer than others?

First of all, let's make sure we understand what a vector engine is.

Vectors first emerged in the computer world in the 1980s when it was clear that bitmaps were taking up too much precious disk space. Bitmaps are like facsimiles. The computer is not thinking at all – just plotting each pixel one by one and writing it to the screen. As an example, let's look at a simple geometric shape - the rectangle.

In bitmap-speak, if you have a red rectangle that is 100x80 pixels in size, that's a grand total of 8,000 red pixels that must be drawn on screen. Assuming that each pixel takes up 4 bytes (Red, Green, Blue, and Alpha), then that rectangle takes up 32,000 bytes on disk. 32K makes for one fat rectangle.

> *A byte is simply a number from 0 to 255. The standard colorre presentation in Flash is 0 to 255 for Red, 0 to 255 for Green, 0 to 255 for Blue and 0 to 100% for the Alpha channel. This Alpha is still stored as a byte with a value of 0 to 255, but Flash represents this as a percentage within the authoring program itself to make it easier for us humans to visualize. So, any given color is described as R, G, B, and A.*

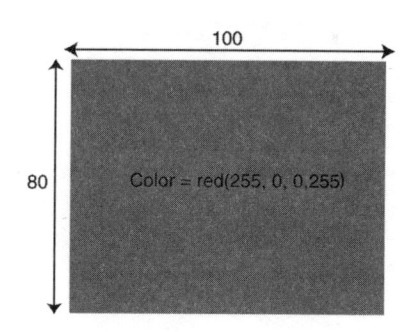

Color = red(255, 0, 0,255)
100
80

But surely there must be a simpler way to create a shape as basic as this? Everyone knows the only important things about a rectangle are its height, width and color. But the bitmap makes each of the 8,000 points just as important as one another. What 80s programmers needed was a way to make the computer work the dimensions out and simply write the pixels from its own calculations, rather having to be told where to plot each individual one. The solution was vectors.

Since the width/height of any rectangle can be fractional (40.32, 12.9, and so on) then we must use 8 bytes each to describe height and width. You see, fractional numbers (also called floating points) require more bytes to remember.

## Flash Games Studio

So, we have:

1. Width (8 bytes – known as a double – 64-bit floating point number);
2. Height (8 bytes – another double);
3. Color (4 bytes – 1 byte each for Red, Green, Blue and Alpha, known as 32-bit color).

Grand total: 20 bytes.

As you can see, there's a substantial difference between 20 bytes to store the vector rectangle, and 32,000 bytes for bitmap rectangle, although both would look identical on screen. Because Flash is delivered on the web, this difference in file size can make or break your download time.

Vectors are a terrific way to optimize graphics, and will certainly help those files sizes plummet. But be warned. This does not give programmers carte blanche to write flabby games. Despite saving time in plotting each pixel, we do now have to allow the computer time to make a few other – often complex – calculations.

Many game vectors are extremely complex. Our friendly red rectangle is quite an easy task for the computer to render. All it must do is start in the upper-left hand corner of the rectangle, and fill in pixels horizontally until the right edge is reached, then it will jump down one pixel and start at the left edge again.

(0, 0) Pixel, upper-left corner of rectangle. Starting point for drawing.

Direction of drawing. One row at a time, left to right.

However, few vector shapes are so simple to draw. Look at this smooth curved vector image:

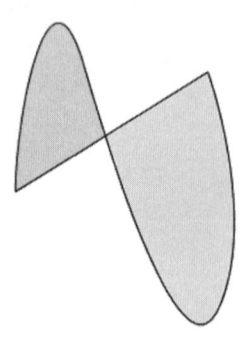

This is a pretty simple image to look at, and it probably doesn't take up many bytes on disk either. It only has two filled regions, two curves and a line. However, we must think from Flash's perspective to understand the issues here.

# Optimizing Graphics for Games 2

One of the unique things about vector graphics is how shapes are defined. Curves in Flash are defined mathematically as objects known as bezier splines. Each spline curve is saved as a series of key values that indicate how the curve behaves. Visually, when you initially draw these curves, you modify the key values by dragging curve points and tangent handles:

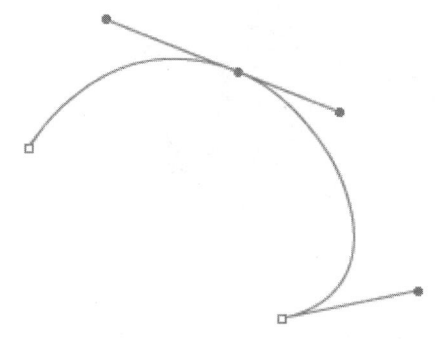

A curve like the one in the diagram is simply saved to the computer as 5 values: 3 Curve points (start, middle and end), and 2 tangents. The formula to draw a bezier curve is a fairly complex one, but luckily Flash seamlessly handles it all for you.

So, what happens when it's time for Flash to draw this object on screen? It must start at the beginning point of the curve and then calculate the next pixel along, based on the influence of the invisible tangents:

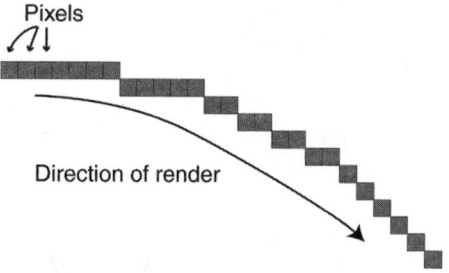

Remember that rendering the rectangle is a simple task of going left to right, top to bottom. However, to the Flash vector engine, curves are logistically more complex. Flash must first perform a calculation to see where the next pixel in the curve is going to be. Only then can it draw the pixel, and proceed with the rest of the curve.

What does this all mean? Clock ticks! The computer doesn't have to do much thinking to render a simple shape like a rectangle, however it must do a substantial amount of processing to calculate and render a curve.

That is why you should always create your images with as few points as possible. Flash has a useful little tool called Optimize, and it's used to remove points that are deemed redundant in the vector image.

Let's look at the complete step-by-step process required to render the following frame, which is frame 1 of our movie:

45

# 2  Flash Games Studio

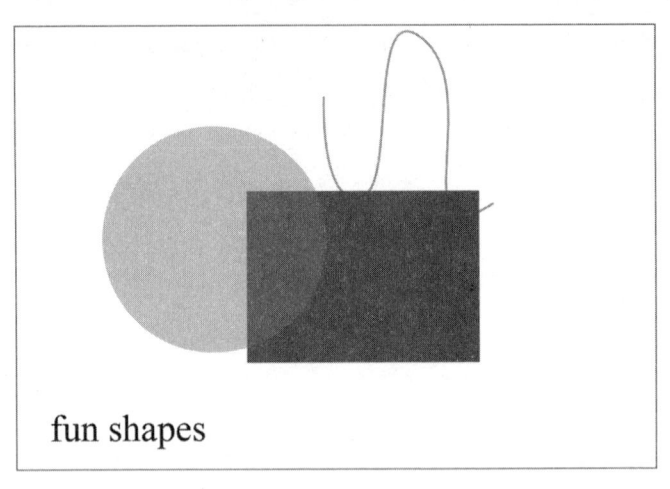

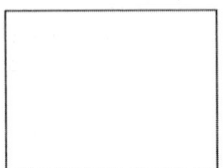

**fun shapes**

1. First the off-screen buffer is cleared white. Or, more technically, it is filled with the color 0xFFFF - Solid white

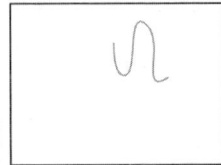

2. An orange bezier curve is drawn. Time is spent calculating the curve, drawing the pixels, and reading the background to apply the antialiasing.

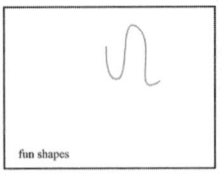

3. Text is printed in the lower left hand corner. This text has many intricate curves and its edges are also antialiased. Drawing this text takes the computer a fair amount of time.

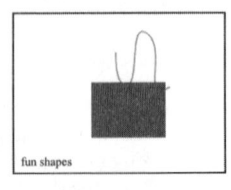

4. A solid blue rectangle is drawn. It is fairly simple to render because of its shape, however at its edges, it must read the background, which will include part of the orange curve, in order to antialias.

5. A 50% alpha green circle is drawn over top of the background and some of the blue square. The vector render engine must perform a read for every pixel of the circle, to ensure proper color mixing.

6. The whole buffer is sent to VRAM, hence becoming visible.

# Optimizing Graphics for Games

## Optimizing Images in Flash

1. First, to use Optimize you must create or import a vector image.

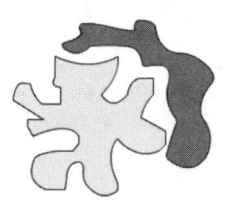

2. Next, highlight and select the image, and choose Modify>Optimize, or press CTRL-ALT-SHIFT-C. You will see the following dialog box:

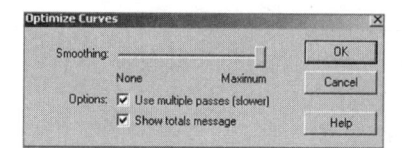

   This will examine the object curve by curve and attempt to remove any curves that are not seen, too small to be seen, or don't follow the overall shape.

3. Move the smoothing slider to specify how much detail to apply and select multiple passes to allow for maximum optimization.

   After this is done, you will see a totals message showing you how much optimization was achieved:

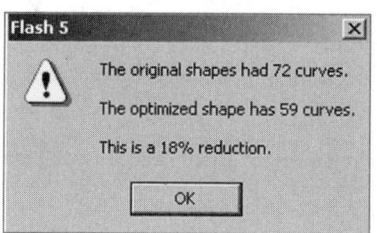

   > The original shapes had 72 curves.
   > The optimized shape has 59 curves.
   > This is a 18% reduction.

4. Once the optimization is complete, you may see some distinct differences. If the change is too much, select undo (CTRL-Z) and try again, with a different optimization setting. This process can take several attempts to achieve the desired results but successful use of the Optimize command will leave you barely noticing the change:

## Scaling and Rotating

One of the distinct advantages of vectors is that mathematical points are convenient to scale and easy to rotate. On the other hand, bitmaps are quite hard to scale and hard to rotate, unless you are using special hardware acceleration.

Imagine a straight line, defined to Flash by the starting point (0,0) and the ending point (9,8). If you want to double the size of that line, all you have to do is multiply all the points by 2.

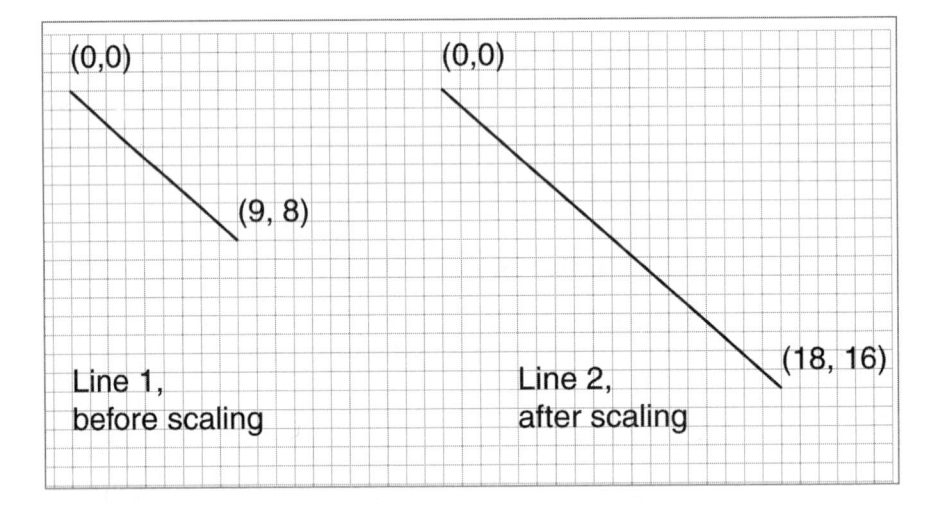

Once the object has been scaled or rotated, Flash then renders the image in exactly the same manner as a non-transformed image. This means that applying transformations to vector objects while your game is running is a safe thing to do, and it does not significantly increase the mathematical workload.

The mathematical workload to plot a small vector shape, and the workload to plot the same shape a million times bigger is identical. However, there is something to keep in mind. Look at the following vector shape:

This is the shape, as it exists in a mathematically perfect world. However, once it is brought on to the screen, as we know, it is converted into pixels. So if the shape was fairly small on screen, it might look something like this when highly magnified:

# Optimizing Graphics for Games

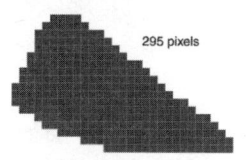

*295 pixels*

Now we tell Flash to double the height and width of our shape on screen. While it is mathematically effortless to plot, something significant changes about what's happening on screen:

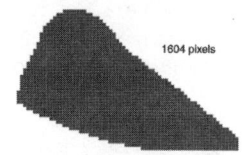

*1604 pixels*

As you can see, we have significantly increased the amount of actual pixel rendering Flash must do and, just as before, each pixel takes up precious clock ticks.

## Line Thickness

Line thickness is handled independently of the actual shapes of the curves and lines. This means that amount of calculation required for thicker lines does not substantially increase. However, on the pixel rendering level, the workload does increase. Take for example our curve from earlier. Let's see that shape rendered with a thicker line:

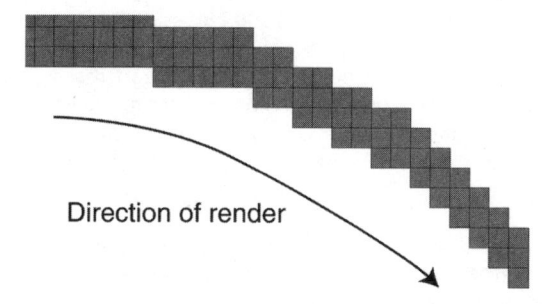

*Direction of render*

As you can see, by increasing our line thickness, we have forced the Flash rendering engine to draw three times as many pixels as in the first curve. This causes an increase in calculations for the visual rendering, meaning an increase in the actual number of pixels that must be drawn, and therefore the number of clock ticks to draw this curve.

It goes without saying then that thick lines are best avoided. Indeed, it is better to use no outlines if at all possible.

## The Bitmap

As you have seen, the bitmap and the vector are rendered differently, with their own complications. Vector curves can require a lot of mathematical overhead to render, while bitmaps are rendered in somewhat the same fashion as the simple rectangle, dot by dot.

The truth of the matter is, there comes a point where the cons of vector plotting begin to outweigh the pros, and it's better to stick with your original bitmap. As a rule of thumb, the number of curves in your vector should be no more than 10% of the number of pixels in the equivalent bitmap.

Take for example the 504x360 pixel title screen pictured; 504 x 360 = 181,440 pixels. At 10%, the vector version ought to be no more than about 18,000 curves.

So, if I was to just use the Trace Bitmap tool in Flash, and convert that into vectors at the most detailed level I would find that, to maintain the quality, the vector equivalent would be obscenely complex. After several minutes of tracing, the image was transformed into a vector containing 46,000 curves - the conclusion from this being that pictures with complex shading and detailed texture should remain as bitmaps.

However, if it is at all possible to create your source image in a vector format, do so. Because, though 46,000 is greater than 18,000, a well-planned vector can be visually stunning, while having only a few hundred curves. In that case, Flash will render the vector image much faster.

## Alpha

One of the most beautiful effects in Flash is a semi-transparent image – an image with an alpha value of less than 100%. However, when you find out what the Flash vector engine is doing to create this subtle blend of colors, you might think twice about using it.

Alpha is also one of the most processor (clock tick) expensive effects to achieve because of what is involved in drawing an object that is semitransparent. When Flash draws any completely solid object, it has to perform one type of pixel operation: **write**. All Flash must do is write pixels to the screen. However, if there is any degree of semitransparency, another pixel operation is introduced: **read**.

# Optimizing Graphics for Games 2

In order to achieve the see-through effect of alpha, Flash must first determine the color of the pixel it intends to draw, then read the color of the pixel beneath, and finally determine what the combined color of the two will be. Only then is it able to draw the pixel.

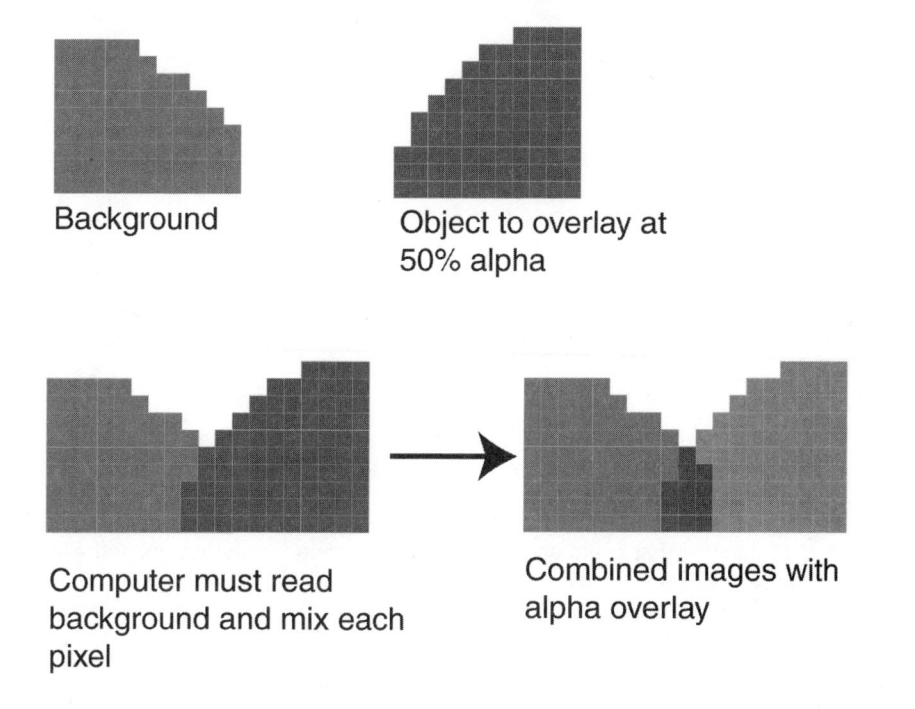

Background

Object to overlay at 50% alpha

Computer must read background and mix each pixel

Combined images with alpha overlay

What this all essentially means is that to draw something semi-transparent requires approximately three times as much work for the computer! This is of course not to say you shouldn't mess with the alpha level, but rather you should be careful exactly how many pixels you commit to semi-transparent images.

## Quality

When you set the quality of a Flash movie, you are telling it to sacrifice some of the image quality for speed. There are several ways to change the quality. First, while running, you can right-click or command-click and set the quality from the menu that appears:

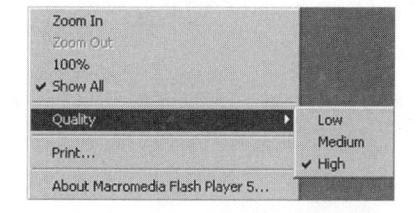

51

# 2  Flash Games Studio

Or you could try your hand at the ActionScript alternative.

## Scripting the Quality

1. Within a new or existing Flash movie on frame 1 create a blank movie clip and call it *quality*.

2. Drag the movie clip named quality from the library on to the stage.

3. Attach the following code to the blank movie:

    ```
    onClipEvent (load)
    {
         _root._quality = "LOW";
    }
    ```

    What this will do is create a movie clip that automatically sets the quality of your entire movie to low.

4. Alternatively, you could attach the following code to any button, and allow users to toggle the movie's quality:

    ```
    on (release)
    {
         _root._quality = "LOW";
    }
    ```

5. Or, if another button is to switch to high quality mode, place the following code inside it.

    ```
    on (release)
    {
         _root._quality = "HIGH";
    }
    ```

    When you set the quality to "LOW", you will see an instant change in the look of your movie.

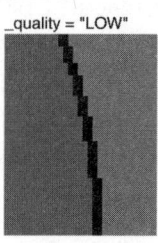

# Optimizing Graphics for Games

Edge of a circle magnified several times

_quality = "HIGH"    _quality = "LOW"

The most noticeable, and unfortunately the most speed-detrimental difference is the presence of antialiasing.

## Anti-aliasing

In the past, when image resolutions used to be quite low, images had a pixelated staircase look (similar to the low quality look in the previous diagram). At that point, the standard resolution for most games was 320x200. This looked fine if an object or sprite was full screen, but the problem was that entire games were supposed to fit in that space, and so a single object or sprite was often very small, like 16 x 16 pixels.

In an effort to make objects look smoother, and hence conceal the low resolution, efforts were taken to insert pixels of an intermediate color. These pixels would act to blend any rough, edge pixels by essentially combining the colors of adjacent pixels.

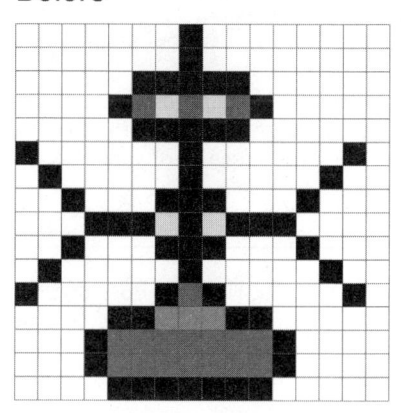

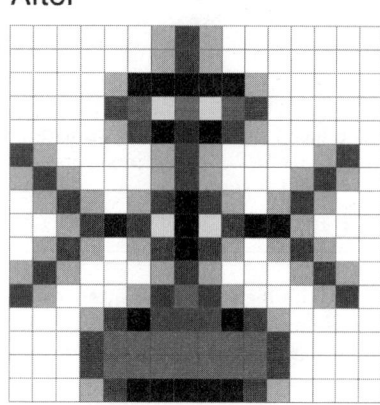

Before    After

Before: Line between pixels of differing colour is harsh

After: Computer takes the average colour between pixels and makes a smoother, "fuzzy" line.

Anti-aliasing is quite similar to alpha or semi-transparent effects, because when the Flash engine is rendering an image, and it encounters an edge, it must read the colors of neighboring pixels and calculate a nice in-between color to place. Again, we have added a read action to our rendering process. However, anti-aliasing an edge does not require as much work as making an entire image semi-transparent, because only edges must be considered. Large areas of solid color in the middle of a shape do not have to be touched by Flash's anti-aliasing brain.

One of the best ways to avoid the need for anti-aliasing is to avoid using sharp, contrasting outlines (black for example). If you avoid using outlines on your shapes in Flash, then you can set the _quality to "LOW" and not severely compromise the visual integrity of your image.

## The Killer Text

Another of the big, processor intensive elements in Flash is text. Not only does text consist of a number of complex curves, but its many edges also tend to need anti-aliasing. This means that text takes a large number of clock ticks to render.

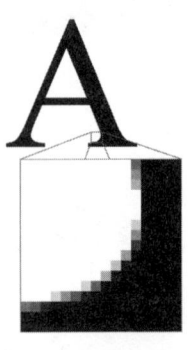

Flash provides one easy way around all this – use dynamic text and don't embed the fonts into the SWF file. If you use one of the three standard fonts (sans, serif, typewriter) then Flash will use a special computer-controlled font-rendering engine.

If you must use non-standard fonts, then try to use fonts that are fairly straight and angular. The more curvaceous your font is, the more computations it requires to render.

If possible, break apart text strings you have created by selecting the text and pressing Ctrl-B. This will allow you to then simplify the curves as much as possible, either by hand, or with Flash's Optimize command (Ctrl-Alt-Shift-C)

# Gradients

Flash has the capacity to draw beautiful gradients. However, that doesn't mean that you should over-use them in games. In fact, you should avoid using gradients as much as possible where speed is a factor.

They are computationally intensive, and they take a lot more clock ticks to render than a solid shape. This is simply because of the amount of calculation that goes into figuring out how to draw the gradient, at any given spot on a shape.

Take for example a linear, left to right, black to white gradient. We know that the left edge will be completely black, and that the right edge will be completely white. This is the simplest gradient, and is the fastest to render. But that's not true for other gradients. A few different things will affect the complexity of a gradient, and hence its hit on performance.

- The size of the gradient. The larger the gradient is, the more real-estate it takes up on screen, the greater the number of pixels that must be rendered, and the slower it will go.

- The number of colors in the gradient, and the more key colors you have in the gradient, the more computation is required to render it.

- The shape of the gradient. Linear gradients are generally faster to render than radial gradients.

If you can do so, try and avoid using gradients that move. These must be redrawn frequently and this will slow down on account of the overhead involved in rendering gradients. If you must use a gradient, place it in the background or somewhere else that is stationary.

Definitely avoid using gradient tweens and other shape tweens. These are very processor intensive, and will affect your game flow. Never use gradients that use alpha-faded colors. This is combining the worst of two slow elements.

# 2 Flash Games Studio

## Optimizing your Graphics Using Movie Clips

Perhaps the best way to create graphics and animation in Flash is through the use of the movie clip, because it is a self-contained object that houses graphics and ActionScript together as one, and it behaves according to the way you tell it.

Movie clips are also vital because they reduce the overall number of graphics in your movie, which in turn reduces file size. Rather than having a stage full of 50 blue squares (each one taking up full vector data) you would create one square, encapsulate it in a movie clip, and then make 50 copies of that movie clip. This would create 50 instances rather than complete copies. Your file size would be tiny.

Let's look at a simple example, a flying ball. For this, I'm going to keep the graphics very simple. In fact, it's just going to be a green circle. I know what you're thinking, "not another bouncing ball", but we'll try and make this one a little different at the end.

To start, you must take the following steps.

1. Open a new movie in Flash.

2. Set its resolution to 550x400 pixels, and frame rate to 30 fps:

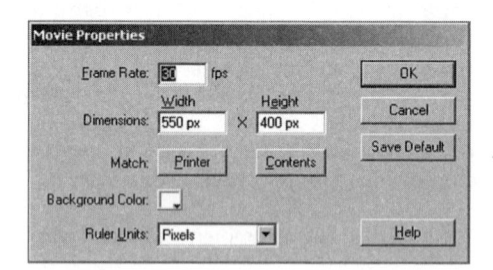

3. Using the circle tool, draw a green circle somewhere near the center of your screen:

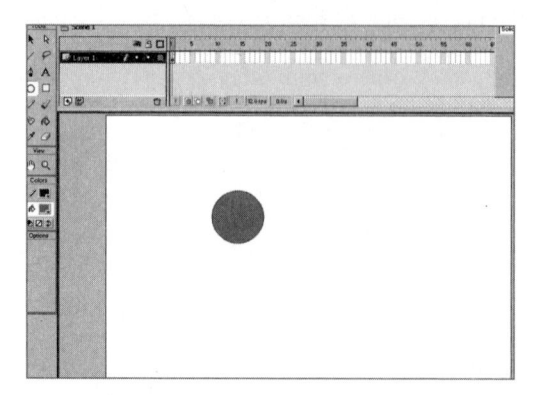

## Optimizing Graphics for Games

Now that we have a graphic of a circle, we must convert it into a movie clip – that vital step that makes our circle into a living, breathing entity.

**4.** Highlight and select the circle, and convert it into a new movie clip symbol (Insert > New Symbol or press CTRL-F8). Give the symbol the name ball.

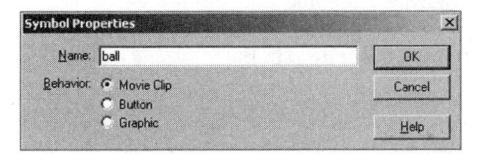

You will now have a movie clip named ball sitting on your stage.

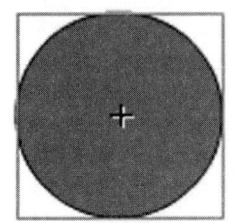

**5.** Now attach the following ActionScript to the ball movie clip:

```
onClipEvent(enterFrame)
{
     _x++;
     _y++;
}
```

This instructs the ball movie clip to increase its _x variable and increase its _y variable by 1 every time it enters a frame. This will have the effect of making the ball move down and to the right.

**6.** Test the movie. You can see the final version as demo2-1.swf in the Chapter 2 source files.

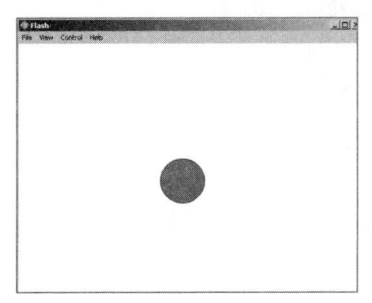

## Flash Games Studio

The ball will now act on its own accord, and we have successfully tied ActionScript to graphics, using the endlessly versatile onClipEvent ().

When you run this sample you'll notice that the ball will eventually reach the edge of the screen and then disappear. Let's give the ball some intelligence here and make it bounce off the walls, keeping it in the screen.

We want to replace the code with the following new ActionScript; I'll explain it step by step:

```
onClipEvent(load)
{
    dx = 4; // set the initial momentum of the ball
    dy = 4;
}

onClipEvent(enterFrame)
{
    _x += dx;        // Move the ball along dx and dy
    _y += dy;

    if (_x < 0)
    {
        _x = 0;      // move it back on screen
        dx *= -1;    // reverse the horizontal momentum
    }
    else if (_x > 550)
    {
        _x = 550;    // move it back on screen
        dx *= -1;    // reverse the horizontal momentum
    }

    if (_y < 0)
    {
        _y = 0;      // move it back on screen
        dy *= -1;    // reverse the vertical momentum
    }
    else if (_y > 400)
    {
        _y = 400;    // move it back on screen
        dy *= -1;    // reverse the vertical momentum
    }
}
```

**7.** In order to make the balls bounce, they must change direction, so introduce two new variables called dx and dy.

```
onClipEvent (load)
{
    dx = 4; // set the initial momentum of the ball
    dy = 4;
}
```

# Optimizing Graphics for Games

8. These next two variables simply represent the amount to increase _x and the amount to increase _y each frame.

    ```
    onClipEvent(enterFrame)
    {
        _x += dx;           // Move the ball along dx and dy
        _y += dy;
    ```

    **Writing** _x++; **is the same as** _x = _x + 1; **and _x += 5; is the same as** _x = _x + 5;

9. Whenever the ball hits the edge, we need to make sure it is still within the screen, and then we change its direction. Add this next section of code:

    ```
    if (_x < 0)
    {
        _x = 0;         // move it back on screen
        dx *= -1;       // reverse the horizontal momentum
    }
    ```

10. Also, when the _x value of the ball is less than 0 (off the left edge of the screen) then we move it back onto the screen, and multiply its dx by –1, thus reversing the direction in which the object is moving:

    ```
    else if (_x > 550)
    {
        _x = 550;       // move it back on screen
        dx *= -1;       // reverse the horizontal momentum
    }
    ```

Since we set the movie's dimensions to be 550x400, when the _x position of the ball is greater than 550 (off the right edge of the screen) then we move it back onto the screen and again reverse the vertical momentum.

## Flash Games Studio

11. Repeat these last two steps for the _y (vertical) movement of the ball:

    ```
    if (_y < 0)
    {
            _y = 0;         // move it back on screen
            dy *= -1;       // reverse the vertical momentum
    }
    else if (_y > 400)
    {
            _y = 400;       // move it back on screen
            dy *= -1;       // reverse the vertical momentum
    }
    }
    ```

    Now, your ball bounces neatly around the Flash window – you can see the effect in demo2-2.swf!

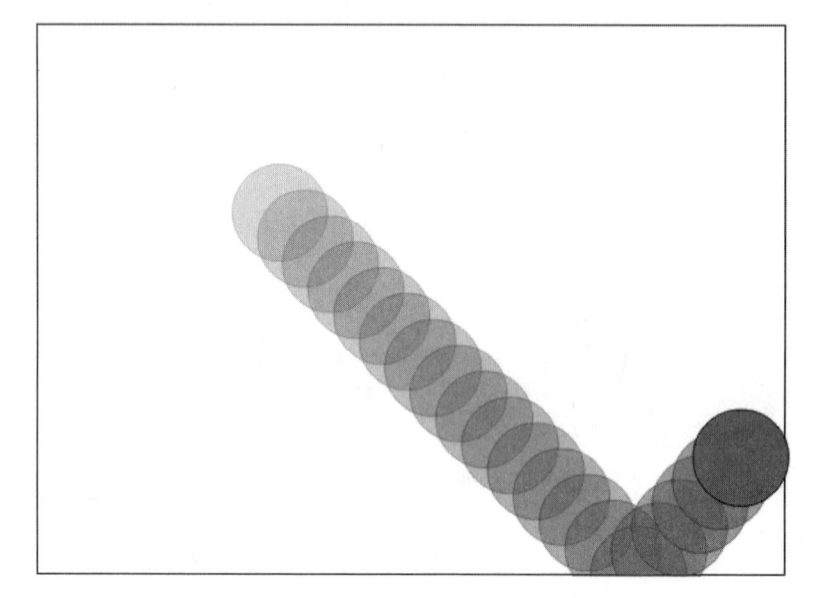

    Finally, let's change two key things about our movie.

12. Let's make the momentum random by updating the movie with the following code:

    ```
    onClipEvent(load)
    {
        dx = Math.random() * 10 - 5;// set the initial momentum of
    ➥the ball
        dy = Math.random() * 10 - 5;
    }
    ```

# Optimizing Graphics for Games

**13.** This will change the ball's initial starting momentum to be completely random. In this case dx and dy will each be a number between −5 and 5. This will allow it to move in any direction.

**14.** Highlight and select the ball movie clip from the stage and copy it.

**15.** Paste it around to create several copies of the ball at different locations all over the stage and test the movie. This version is in the source files as `demo2-3.swf`.

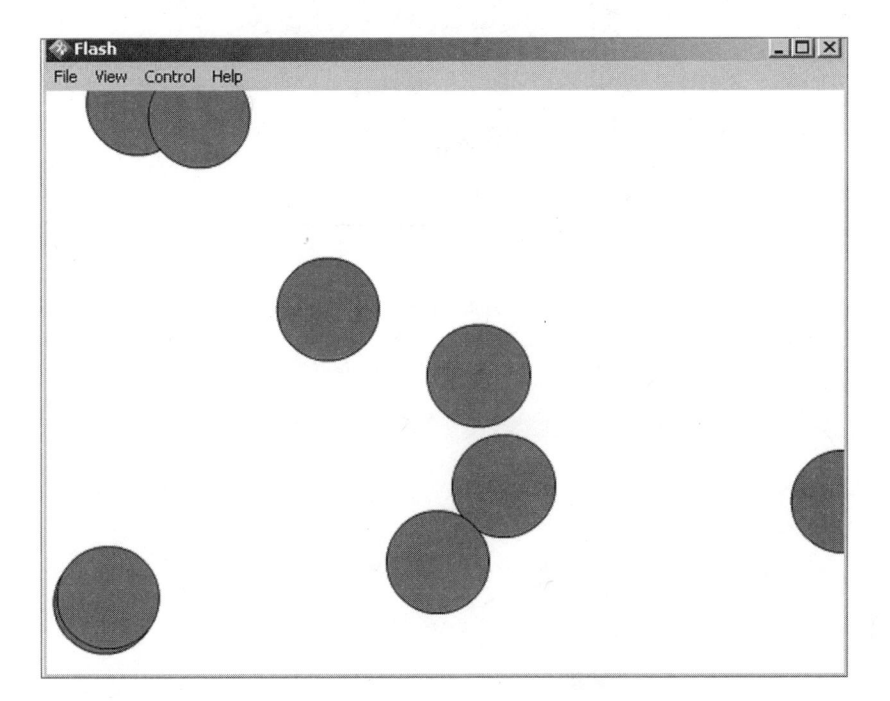

You'll see that each ball is alive. No matter where you place them on the stage they have their own behavior. We have used ActionScript to create animation and breathe life into our circle. Because they are graphical objects with ActionScript attached, they will act independently of one another. This is one of the true benefits of Flash and its movie clip object.

Sometimes, however, it is better to animate traditionally on the timeline instead of using ActionScript. For example, if you wanted each of the balls in the above example to contain a blinking eye, you would edit the timeline of the movie clip itself.

# 2  Flash Games Studio

Within the ball movie clip you would just double-click on any of the balls to edit its timeline, and add frames as you would to any other frame-by-frame animation.

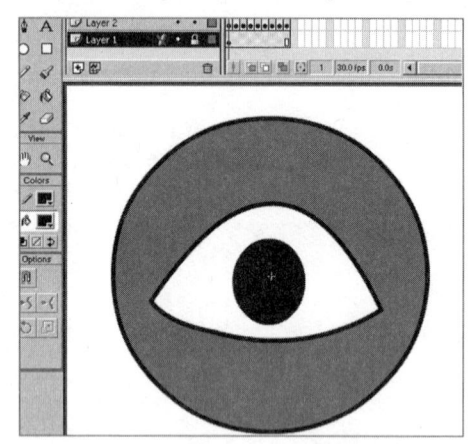

Now, when you test the movie, all the balls will be following their ActionScripted animation, but they will possess timeline animation, and they'll all be blinking at you. So you see you have edited the timeline of the symbol through just one of its instances (see demo2-4.swf).

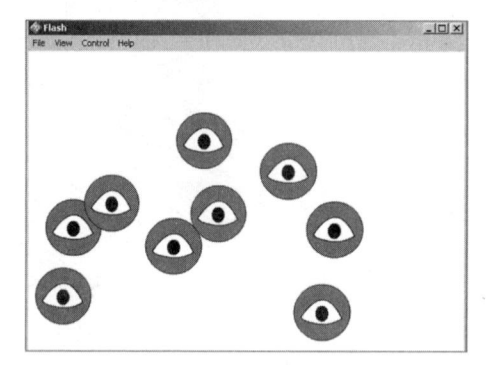

These are simple movie clips, but their applications are far-reaching. You can create monsters, items, rewards and even environmental movie clips that behave according to their own rules, and also according to other global laws such as:

- Gravity, friction and other elements of physics
- 2D and 3D coordinate systems with scaling and transformation
- Artificial Intelligence, offensive and defensive behavior
- Vital statistics and attributes like health and strength

Your creativity is the limit. We'll now move out of the fun realm of flying eyes, and back into the more sobering world of Flash player performance.

# Optimizing Graphics for Games

## Performance Statistics

As a guide, I've put together a table of frame rates for different situations in Flash. These are circumstances that put Flash's render engine to the test. Basically, I put Flash through the wringers to get some hard numbers and see just where it excels or fails at rendering.

The first thing was to create a frame rate counter. This is basically a standalone movie clip that can be dropped into any movie, displaying the frame rate that Flash is achieving.

The frame rate counter is a very simple object to create. You can make your frame rate counter in any style, with any look, but it must have:

- A dynamic text field attached to a variable (this will be the number representing the frame rate);

- A reset button.

Obviously simplicity is the key here. You don't want your frame-rate counter to be a graphics hog slowing down the overall performance. The one pictured is a good example of a simple and functional counter, so let's build it.

## Creating a Frame Rate Counter

1. Within a new blank Flash movie, create a new movie clip and call it frameratecounter:

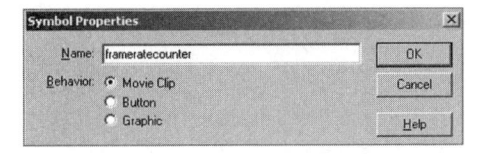

2. To depict the outline of your frame rate counter, draw a yellow box, and place the words "Frame Rate (fps)" within the box:

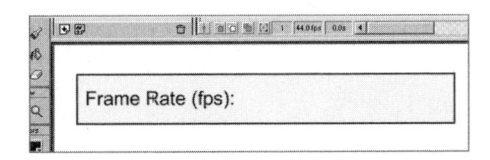

## Flash Games Studio

3. Create a text box to the right of these words.

4. Go to the Text Options tab, and change its type to Dynamic Text. In the Variable field, enter frate.

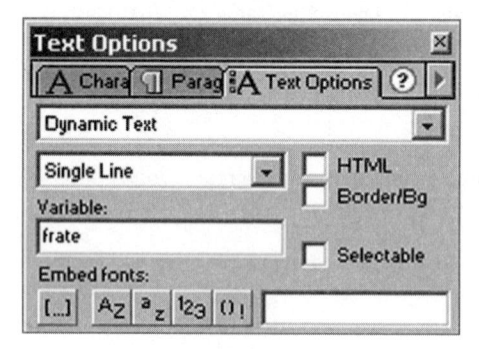

5. On a new layer, draw a red box and place the word RESET over top of it:

   Select it and convert it into a symbol. In the Symbol Properties box, enter resetbutton in the Name field, and set its behavior to Button. Click OK.

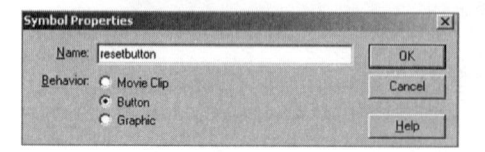

6. Now open the Actions window for the button instance, and enter the following code into the button:

```
on (release)
{
    fcount = 0;
    offset = getTimer();
}
```

# Optimizing Graphics for Games

7. Return to the main timeline and drag the frameratecounter from the Library onto the stage.

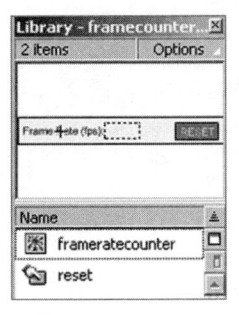

8. Attach the following code to the frameratecounter movie clip.

```
onClipEvent (load)
{
    offset = 0;
    fcount = 1;
}

onClipEvent (enterFrame)
{
    curtime = (getTimer() - offset) / 1000;
    frate = Math.ceil (fcount / curtime);
    fcount++;
}
```

The Math.ceil function here rounds our answer up to the nearest whole number, while getTimer returns the number of milliseconds since the movie started.

That's it! When you test this movie, your frame rate counter will begin to, well, count the frame rate the movie is running at. It should approximately match the frame rate that you have set in the movie properties in Flash.

The fcount is the number of frames that have elapsed since the start of the movie, whilst curtime is the number of seconds since the start of the movie. To get a frame rate we simply divide frames per second or fcount / curtime.

We also include the reset button because the frame rate displayed is an average frame rate reaching back to the beginning of the movie. Sometimes our movie might enter a new section with more detailed graphics, and so we want the new frame rate to be accurately calculated. RESET will essentially set a value called offset to the current value of getTimer(). It will also reset fcount to 0. This will have the effect of restarting the frame rate counter.

The advantage of this frame rate counter is that it can easily be dropped into any movie. All you have to do is select it, and copy it. Then open up any other Flash movie and simply paste it down, preferably on its own layer, and you will have instant frame rate monitoring.

# Flash Games Studio

> *Mac users beware, there are some issues with the frame rate of the Flash player. After testing the frame rate program on a G4-400 running OS 9, we came up with the following results:*

| Frame Rate Requested | Actual Frame Rate |
|---|---|
| 1 | 1 |
| 2 | 2 |
| 3 | 3 |
| 4 | 4 |
| 5 | 5 |
| 6 | 6 |
| 7 | 7 |
| 8 | 8 |
| 9 | 9 |
| 10 | 9 |
| 11 | 10 |
| 12 | 10 |
| 13 | 12 |
| 14 | 12 |
| 15 | 12 |
| 16-20 | 15 |
| 21-30 | 19 |
| 31-58 | 29 |
| 59-120 | 57 |

> *Remember that these are averages so don't be surprised if your Mac gives readings that are a couple of frames higher. Whatever the speed you should still see significant steps in the frame rate that get more and more pronounced towards the higher end of the scale. It's worth bearing these issues in mind if you are planning your game for a Mac or mixed (the web) audience.*

# Optimizing Graphics for Games 2

Now that's clear, let's look at the experiment I carried out.
Several standard objects were created:

1. A solid circle with an outline around it

2. A radial gradient filled circle with an outline around it

3. A linear gradient filled circle with an outline around it

4. A random shape with an outline, consisting of 43 curves

5. A random shape with no outline

6. A solid circle with no outline

7. 25% alpha circle with no outline

8. Bitmap textured circle

9. Complex vector image from a traced bitmap consisting of 240 curves

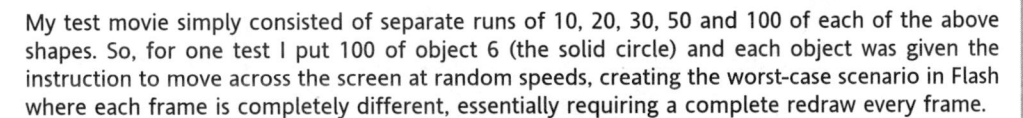

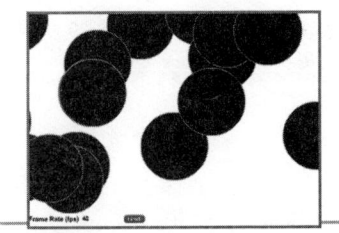

My test movie simply consisted of separate runs of 10, 20, 30, 50 and 100 of each of the above shapes. So, for one test I put 100 of object 6 (the solid circle) and each object was given the instruction to move across the screen at random speeds, creating the worst-case scenario in Flash where each frame is completely different, essentially requiring a complete redraw every frame.

# Flash Games Studio

On top of all that, each test was done three times: Once at high quality, once at medium quality and once at low quality. The following is a list of the resulting measured frame rates in each case.:

**HIGH QUALITY**

| Number of Objects/MC on screen | 10 | 20 | 30 | 50 | 100 |
|---|---|---|---|---|---|
| 1 Solid Circle/outline | 71 | 43 | 34 | 26 | 16 |
| 2 Circle/outline/Radial gradient fill | 57 | 38 | 29 | 22 | 14 |
| 3 Circle/outline/Linear gradient fill | 59 | 40 | 33 | 23 | 14 |
| 4 Random Shapes/outline (43 curves) | 39 | 24 | 16 | 10 | 05 |
| 5 Random Shapes/NO outline | 63 | 43 | 34 | 27 | 17 |
| 6 Solid Circle/NO outline | 85 | 67 | 54 | 46 | 33 |
| 7 25% Alpha Circle/NO outline | 72 | 50 | 32 | 20 | 10 |
| 8 Bitmap Textured Circle | 85 | 57 | 47 | 31 | 17 |
| 9 Complex Vector (traced bitmap) 240 curves | 53 | 33 | 24 | 16 | 09 |

**MEDIUM QUALITY**

| Number of Objects/MC on screen | 10 | 20 | 30 | 50 | 100 |
|---|---|---|---|---|---|
| 1 Solid Circle/outline | 86 | 55 | 47 | 37 | 24 |
| 2 Circle/outline/Radial gradient fill | 69 | 50 | 39 | 31 | 20 |
| 3 Circle/outline/Linear gradient fill | 80 | 51 | 42 | 32 | 21 |
| 4 Random Shapes/outline (43 curves) | 54 | 35 | 25 | 17 | 08 |
| 5 Random Shapes/NO outline | 78 | 55 | 45 | 37 | 24 |
| 6 Solid Circle/NO outline | 95 | 79 | 62 | 56 | 42 |
| 7 25% Alpha Circle/NO outline | 88 | 66 | 44 | 29 | 17 |
| 8 Bitmap Textured Circle | 91 | 60 | 50 | 34 | 19 |
| 9 Complex Vector (traced bitmap) 240 curves | 68 | 45 | 35 | 24 | 14 |

**LOW QUALITY**

| Number of Objects/MC on screen | 10 | 20 | 30 | 50 | 100 |
|---|---|---|---|---|---|
| 1 Solid Circle/outline | 98 | 62 | 54 | 42 | 27 |
| 2 Circle/outline/Radial gradient fill | 75 | 57 | 46 | 36 | 23 |
| 3 Circle/outline/Linear gradient fill | 88 | 57 | 47 | 36 | 23 |
| 4 Random Shapes/outline (43 curves) | 65 | 41 | 30 | 20 | 9 |
| 5 Random Shapes/NO outline | 87 | 63 | 51 | 47 | 27 |
| 6 Solid Circle/NO outline | 103 | 85 | 68 | 61 | 45 |
| 7 25% Alpha Circle/NO outline | 99 | 80 | 48 | 36 | 23 |
| 8 Bitmap Textured Circle | 101 | 69 | 61 | 43 | 27 |
| 9 Complex Vector (traced bitmap) 240 curves | 83 | 57 | 45 | 32 | 18 |

*These experiments were done on a PIII, 800MHz. The movie was running at an on-screen resolution of 550x400.*

# Optimizing Graphics for Games

It's pretty clear to see that the winner was the solid shape (#6), in low quality mode. Even when there were 100 of these solid circles on screen running in high quality mode, the program still effectively maintained a frame rate of 33 frames per second.

At the other end of the scale, the slowest shape was the random shape with outline (#4). When there were 100 shapes at low quality it only attained 9 frames per second.

Also, there is a definite performance difference between shapes with outlines and shapes without. At low quality mode, the solid circle with no outlines (#6) was almost twice as fast as the circle with outline (#1).

As far as alpha goes, the two identical circles with no outlines #6 and #7 only differ in their alpha levels, and yet the frame rates differ substantially especially when there are more objects on screen. This is clearly due to the amount of reading that alpha requires.

For the most part, linear gradients produced faster frame rates than radial gradients.

As we have established, in cases where an image is quite complex, it is often easier to use a bitmap rather than the vector equivalent. In the case between #8 and #9 you can see that the vector data actually ends up being more complex than the pixel data of its bitmap equivalent.

So what conclusions can we draw from this test? Adhere to the following rules, and you'll be an optimization guru:

- Minimize the number of curves in any one object.

- Minimize the use of gradients, and if you must use gradients, try and use simple linear gradients instead of radial gradients.

- Simple solid shapes are by far the fastest. Try and make your game out of those. You can fit 100 or more on screen at once, in full motion and still maintain a good frame rate. That's a lot of objects, and that has a lot of promise for good performance in games. Though they're merely circles, they're representative of any simple shape.

- For very complex images, use a bitmap image of it rather than its vector equivalent.

- Keep your alpha values at 100%, and if you *must* have some semitransparency, keep it stationary and keep its shape simple.

- Remember that *real estate = clock ticks = decrease in performance*. Keep things small because the smaller things are, the fewer pixels must be rendered.

- Try and keep your on-screen resolution low, and increase the perceived real estate by suggesting to your players that they lower the resolution on their monitor.

# 2  Flash Games Studio

One neat trick that you can use is to open two Flash movies in separate browser windows. One of those movies should be very simple and uncomplicated – maybe simply a graphic title. The other should be your game. This takes advantage of a CPU's multi-threaded capability. When you have two Flash threads running simultaneously, the CPU allocates more system resources for the Flash kernel. So, if one of your movies is simple, then effectively the game is handed more of the computer's undivided attention!

## Simply Simplifying

For all the hints and tips about optimizing complex graphics, you might just want to save yourself a headache and design simple.

One of the most naturally low-detail environments is darkness. When we make a game that takes place in outer space, the bottom of the ocean, in a cave, a dark tunnel or from above driving along an asphalt road, we're allowed to leave large portions of the screen real estate black, without too much grumbling from players. Hey, it's atmosphere! The player's mind will fill in the missing information, and Flash will perform better because it doesn't have to contend with any graphics in the darkness (other than the darkness itself, which it will only really need to render once).

Once we have this darkness, we can create the illusion of large-scale movement by moving only reference points in the dark. Take a look at the following example, demo2-8.swf in the source files, where full-screen motion is created with a few visual tricks.

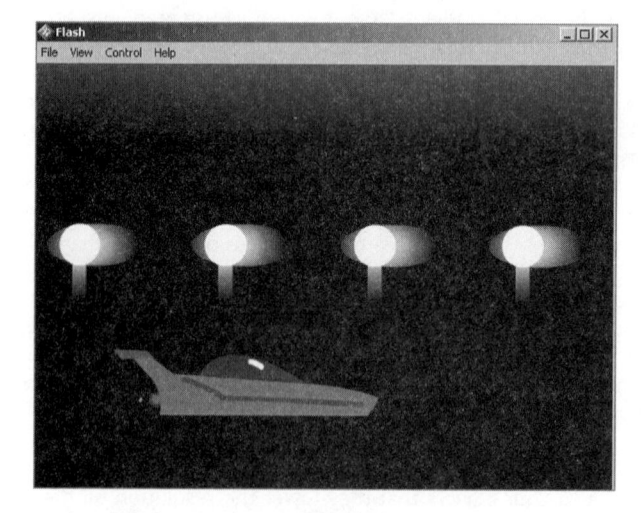

Light from streetlamps zoom by as we move along in our hovercraft. The actual image of the streetlamp is very simple because it is in constant motion and therefore the player's eye does not have a chance to discern it. It has been horizontally stretched to create a motion blurring effect.

# Optimizing Graphics for Games

Then there's the sky; another simple graphical element that serves to create depth while not interfering with the game performance. Because nothing overlaps that sky, it only needs to be rendered once.

Notice the distinct lack of outlines in this example. Because outlines negatively affect performance, I've elected to remove them from all shapes.

Each streetlamp is simply a movie clip with the following code attached to it:

```
onClipEvent(enterFrame)
{
_x -= 20;

    if (_x < -20) _x = 580;

}
```

This simply moves the light to the left until it exits the screen, at which point it is moved to the right hand side of the screen, and the loop continues.

The hovercraft has some code attached to it too:

```
onClipEvent(load)
{
    sy = _y;
    ang = 0;
}

onClipEvent(enterFrame)
{
    _y = sy + 4 * Math.cos(ang+=0.2);
}
```

This is a little bit of ActionScript trickery that uses a cosine wave to make the hovercraft bob slightly up and down smoothly.

A potential modification to this movie would be to make the streetlamp more detailed once the hovercraft comes to a complete stop (the streetlamp stops moving). At this point, the player's eye can recognize more detail, and therefore the stationary streetlamp could have its motion blur turned off, and a few more detailed features are turned on.

The concept of varying the complexity of stationary versus moving graphics is an important one to remember.

## Scrolling

If you are going to create a game that involves a large map (larger than the game screen) then you must consider how you're going to move the screen as your character moves about. When the player reaches the edge of the screen, will the background and foreground begin to scroll along (keeping the player in one position) or will the game simply flip to a new screen, and move the player to the opposite side of the screen?

The obvious advantage to page flipping (or pushing) is the fact that Flash only has to re-render the whole screen once when the player walks off-screen. However, with scrolling Flash is effectively re-rendering the entire scene every time the player moves.

Depending on the player's computer, it might be a good idea to offer them the choice:

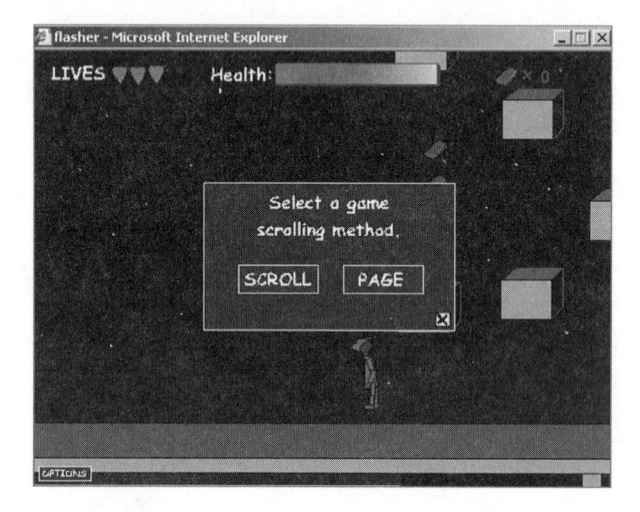

## File Optimization: Sweetening the Download

A lack of optimization will always come back to haunt you, and the first place this can happen is in the download. People don't like to wait. More pertinently, people don't wait. If you have optimized a game down to its underwear and it still takes a year and a day to download, you're going to have to use a different tactic to keep users onboard.

First of all, it is handy to note that objects painted straight on the stage on the main timeline will begin to show up as soon as they're loaded. This means you can place a background image such as a solid color or a title screen on frame 1 of the main timeline, and it will appear almost immediately. Anything else in succeeding frames will be loaded ahead (streamed) while the main timeline begins to play.

If you place a large detailed image within a movie clip on frame 1 of the main timeline, then all playing will halt until that movie clip has been completely loaded. In other words, the movie clip

## Optimizing Graphics for Games 2

and the main timeline will not stream; the movie clip will first need to load, and then the main timeline will continue to stream (at least until another movie clip is encountered).

By placing any such large movie clips on frame 2 of your main timeline, you can place a smaller movie clip on frame 1 to keep your public entertained. This is called a preloader. Before I talk about preloaders however, I would like to mention the handiest of optimization aids.

When you develop Flash applications locally on your computer and then test them, they have a tendency to load instantaneously, no matter how large they are in file size. This is because you're not streaming over a network or Internet connection, rather via the very fast route from your hard drive.

This isn't very useful for testing download times and other file size optimization tricks. Luckily, Flash has a tool called the bandwidth profiler, which allows you to see where your movie is having size and download issues. It also allows you to simulate slow download times right from your hard drive by showing your movie as it would stream over a slow connection.

When you do a test movie (Control Test Movie) your movie will start playing quickly and locally. To enable the bandwidth profiler, while the movie is playing in test mode, go to View>Bandwidth Profiler:

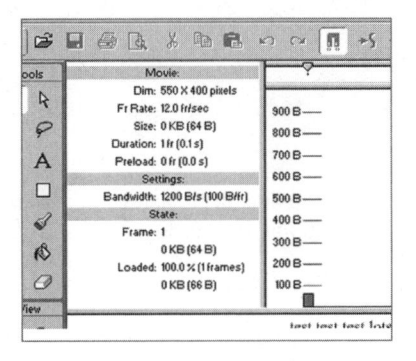

Go to View Show Streaming or hit Ctrl-Enter and the movie will restart but this time it will be simulating a slower connection:

You can set the connection speed you would like to simulate by choosing a value under the Debug menu while your movie is running:

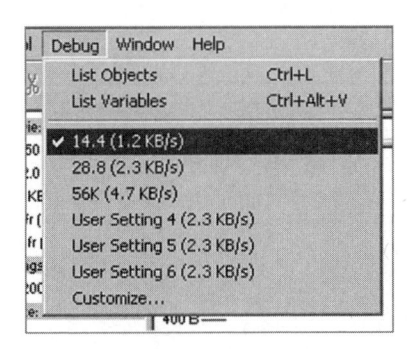

73

## 2  Flash Games Studio

As your movie is streaming, you will see the green streaming bar at the top of the bandwidth profiler that indicates where your movie is while streaming. Now if you find this information about your movie useful, why not let others in on the secret?

If players know exactly how long they are going to have to wait, maybe they'll stick around. Try using a simple meter preloader to gauge the progress.

### A Simple Preloader

1. Create a new blank movie;

2. Create a new movie clip symbol named preloader.

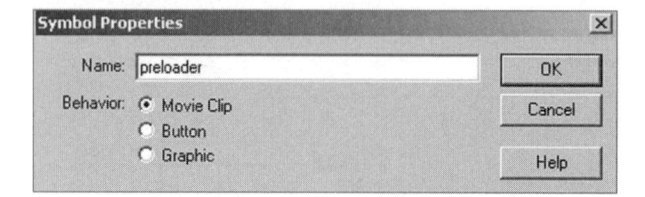

3. Within the new movie clip's timeline, draw a short horizontal line (the needle) starting from the left of the center point (the little cross) and ending at the center point.

4. Return to the main timeline and drag the movie clip preloader on to the stage somewhere.

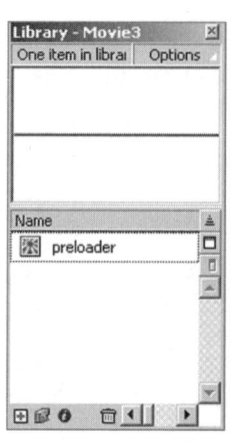

# Optimizing Graphics for Games

**5.** Add the following ActionScript to the preloader movie clip:

```
onClipEvent(load)
{
    _root.stop();
}

onClipEvent(enterFrame)
{
    loaded = _root.getBytesLoaded();
    remaining = _root.getBytesTotal();
    _rotation = (loaded / remaining) * 180;

    if (loaded == remaining)
_root.play ();

}
```

This performs simple math to calculate a fraction of the total size of the movie that is currently loaded, and then scales that by 180 to get an angle. The _rotation of the movie clip is set to be that angle, and there we go – we have a perfectly functional needle.

**6.** Close down the ActionScript window. If you test this movie, you will notice that the arrow is strangely pointing in the wrong direction. Bingo!

It's important that you place this object on its own level and that it only takes up one frame. It should appear before anything else except maybe one frame for graphics painted straight on the timeline. You want your preloader to stop existing once the movie has been loaded in.

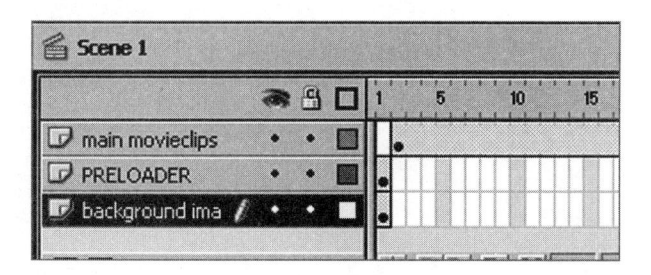

# 2 Flash Games Studio

### Breaking It Up To Break It Down

If your main movie is still going to take too long to download, and even a preloader can't patch up the boredom, you are going to have to do some wholesale restructuring. You might opt to break your movie up. You can get it to pull in external SWF files only when they're needed. This advanced technique ensures that only the necessities of a Flash game are loaded. Elements used later can be loaded in later, perhaps while the user is reading the game instructions, watching the introduction or even playing another mini-game.

Just about anything can be placed in an external SWF file; animations, large graphics – even notoriously memory-quaffing sound tracks.

Let's create an external file that can be pulled into our main game.

## Pulling in an External SWF

1. Create a new, blank movie in Flash. Then, starting with frame 2, create a standard timeline-based animation of about 20 frames. For this example, I created a simple animation of a shape-tweening box that rotates 45 degrees and then stops. This is in the source files as `demo2-6.swf` and `demo2-6.fla`.

    You'll notice I've located this box in the upper-left hand corner of the stage. This is because the upper-left hand corner is of the stage is actually the point that will become the center of our host movie clip in the game. It's the way Flash does it; always design your external movies to be situated around the upper-left corner of the stage.

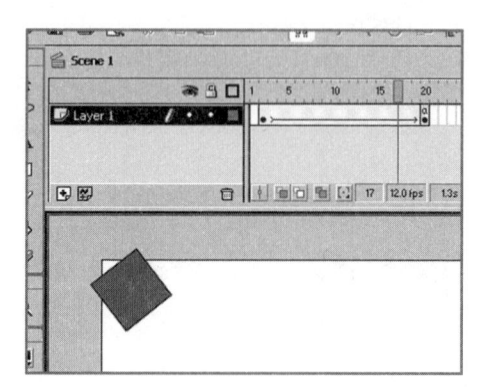

2. Leave the first frame blank and add a `stop()` action to the last frame.

3. Now look in the `demo2-7.fla` and `.fla`, I've created a movie clip that reads "Click here to load", and has a blank button within it. This is the movie clip into which we will load the SWF we created in the previous demo.

# Optimizing Graphics for Games

**4.** Within the button is the following code:

```
on (release)
{
    loadMovie("demo2-6.swf", this);
}
```

This will replace the current contents of the movie clip (the text and the button) with the demo3-6.swf file, which will produce a rotating box on screen. In my sample, I've made several copies of this container movie clip and placed them on the stage.

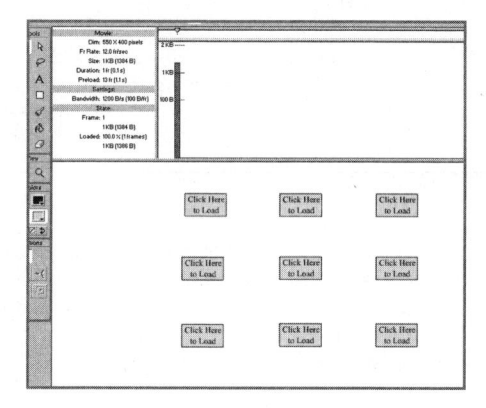

Now, once I've clicked on each button, it will produce the following:

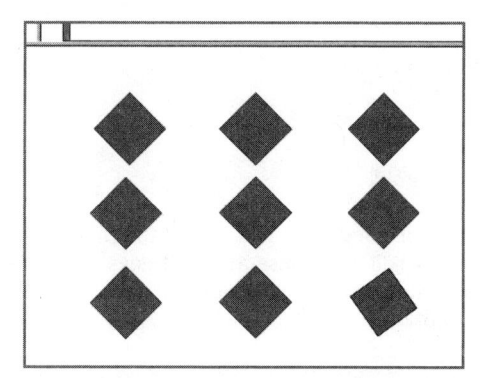

Now, remember that we have a blank frame at the beginning of the loaded-in SWF file. This means that we can effectively remove the SWF file from our game without having to actually unload it and potentially reload it later.

5. Attach the following code to the containing movie clip:

```
onClipEvent(load) {
   gotoAndStop(1)
}
```

Through this you will be telling the movie clip to jump to the blank frame 1. It will then sit there, dormant, or 'parked'. The movie clip will still be in existence, but it will be safely parked on its first frame.

Using this technique you can see how easy it is to load in a user interface quickly and efficiently, and then load the rest of the game as required. Hopefully now your game will be less of a monster, and more popular with those impatient players!

## Final thought: Think ahead

When making your games, you must always be aware of the technical side of the process. At every stage during conception, programming and development, you must always remember to think like the computer and remember what will make or break the game experience.

- Go for solid shapes rather than semi-transparent ones;
- Remove the outlines if you can;
- Simplify your vector images;
- Keep your ActionScript simple.

These are the key points to remember:

- Everything is pixels in the end;
- Clock ticks are gold.

And what's the moral of this long tale? It is simply that making games requires a lot more than just artistic inspiration and skill. Yes, those are the things that make a game fly, however it is the technical considerations that may burden your freedom. Take them, understand them, respect them, and make them work for you.

We'll now turn away from graphics and look into the code that makes up the heart of any game, starting by looking at Flash's objects and how they can be used for gaming.

# Optimizing Graphics for Games

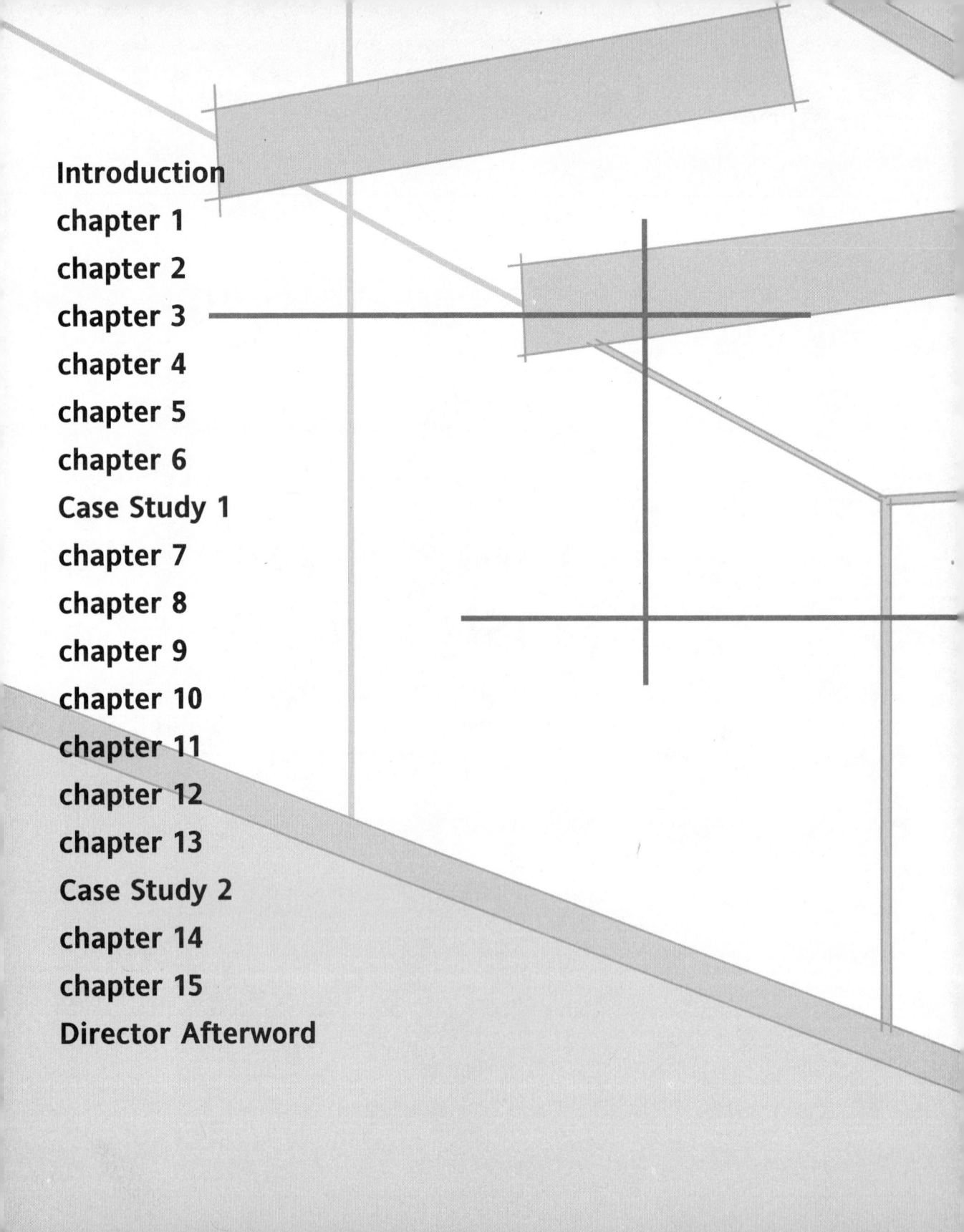

**Introduction**
chapter 1
chapter 2
chapter 3
chapter 4
chapter 5
chapter 6
Case Study 1
chapter 7
chapter 8
chapter 9
chapter 10
chapter 11
chapter 12
chapter 13
Case Study 2
chapter 14
chapter 15
Director Afterword

# Chapter 3
# Flash's Built in Objects

# 3    Flash Games Studio

Objects cover a broad area in Flash but they are particularly relevant to games. By far the most important object type is the **movie clip**. Its various properties and methods have been greatly enhanced in Flash 5, opening up a huge number of possibilities for designers. However, let's not get too biased about our favorites so early on. There's a whole list of other objects that are just as useful, which is exactly what we'll show you in the course of this chapter. The aim is to supply you with a good grounding in Flash objects so that you can take advantage of them as you work through later chapters.

We'll start by outlining some of the elements that all the objects have in common and how to work with them. Then we'll delve right into the objects themselves and look at how we can apply them to games.

Just to get things organized in our minds we can divide all of the specific objects we'll be looking at into three distinct categories, according to how they're used:

1. **Effects**
    Color
    Sound

2. **Inputs**
    Key
    Mouse

3. **Data objects**
    Object
    String
    Array
    Math
    XML

We'll take a detailed look at this complete list, and then wrap up the chapter with a more in depth look at the movie clip object. No one can ever stress enough how important this little item is to us as we program within Flash. Indeed, much of what we discuss over the next few pages will carry over into the next chapter where we talk about event handling and the role that movie clips play in that.

## Defining an Object

Some, objects in Flash, such as Array, Color, and Sound, need to be **defined** before they can be used. Others – for instance, the Math, Mouse or Key objects – are **predefined**, which means they can be called anywhere and will work without any path information.

To define a new object, you use the `new` constructor followed by the object type. These new objects must be given a name, so you set the result of the constructor to its name. For instance, if we wanted an array called `myList`, we'd add the following code:

```
myList = new Array()
```

# Flash's Built in Objects  3

We can create as many new instances of an object type as we like in exactly the same way. Take the **Array** object as an example, you may want to pass several different lists so one instance of the object wouldn't be enough. The same is true for the **Sound** and **Color objects;** you may need to change the color or sound within a particular movie clip in several different ways.

On the other hand, we'd never need to give the Math object multiple instances, since it's there to store methods that return data. You wouldn't need multiple versions of the square root method since it would do the same wherever you put it. In this sense, Math is a bit of a black sheep for our explanation. It serves more as a library, which we can call upon whenever we need to.

Now that we know how to define an object, we still need to know exactly where it's created and how to reference it. Let's shift gears a bit and look at the types of objects available to us in Flash.

## Types of Objects

The objects that come with Flash are organized by functional areas so, as you might guess, the Color object deals with color information, the Key object deals with the keyboard, and so on. What makes these objects unique to their areas are their **methods**.

Methods are operations that an object can perform. For instance, the Mouse object has a method called `hide`. When you call `Mouse.hide`, the cursor disappears until `Mouse.show` is called. If you were to take another object like Sound and try using `hide` on it, nothing is going to happen. That's because there's nothing defined for a Sound object to do that matches `hide`.

Now, at the risk of being a touch confusing, I should mention that some objects have methods with the same name. Both the Color and Sound objects have a `setTransform` method. While they are conceptually similar in what they do (by either transforming a color or transforming a sound), they obviously have to do really different things. This is because the scope of an object applies also to their methods.

Methods can be set just like variables. If there is another method you want your object to be able to perform, you can actually write a function and have it work like a method on a particular object. If you wanted all objects of a particular type to have the same new method, you could easily do it by using `prototype`. Prototype just takes a function and adds it as a method to an object. For example, let's say that we have a function already defined on the _root called `wrap` that wraps the current object to the other side of the screen if it's overstepped a boundary. We're going to have lots of different movies calling this script, so we'd like to save ourselves some hassle and make `wrap` a method of any movie clip. To do that we can add code after the function has been defined telling the `prototype` movie clip to add a method:

```
movieClip.prototype.wrap=_root.wrap
```

Notice that there are no parentheses after either the new method name or the function name. If we had added those parentheses after `_root.wrap`, it would have run the function and set the prototype to any returned value.

# 3  Flash Games Studio

Now we've examined objects in isolation, it's time to see each of them in a gaming context. Not all of the Flash objects will be relevant to you as you build your games so we'll only look in detail at the ones that will be of most use to you to make your game as compelling as possible.

## Objects for Games

If you come from more of a design background, then you may have skipped over many of the built-in objects before. Even if after reading this book you don't, heaven forbid, immediately go off and make your own games, there will still be a lot of information here that will go a long way towards making a website with much more impact. I believe that eventually UI design and game design are going to get a lot closer than they are now, even for Flash which has raised interfaces to such a new high, so with a balance of both skills you'll be one step ahead of the pack.

There's one object that you're no doubt thoroughly familiar with already (or at least you believe you are, we'll see just how much later), it is of course the movie clip. Even though you might not think of it as an object, it most certainly is, and it's one of the most unique and important ones as well. To stop you sitting back on your laurels and getting complacent though, we're going to save that for the end, and instead start with that is potentially the oddest object of them all.

### The Object Object

Yes, there really is something called an Object object. It's the generic object that doesn't come readymade for a particular purpose. When you create a generic object, you can store any type of information you want in it, and fill it with whatever custom methods take your fancy, it's completely up to you.

While a custom object may seem like a nice thing, its application to gaming is actually a little bit limited. Not because it in itself is limiting, but rather because in reality many of the other objects we'll look at require you to make your own custom objects anyway. For instance, the Color object has a method, `setTransform`. For it to work you can pass between 1 and 8 optional parameters to it, since it would be really confusing to try to pass these arguments directly through the method, we create a custom object and set the variables inside it. That way, there is no confusion as to which value goes with which intended argument.

For an example of this, let's jump right into color.

### The Color Object

To define a Color object you must give it the path to the movie clip whose color it will be controlling. Once the Color object has been defined, any methods called on that object will affect the linked movie clip's color properties.

The properties affected by the methods `setRGB` and `setTransform`, are analogous to using the advanced color effects of the Effects palette:

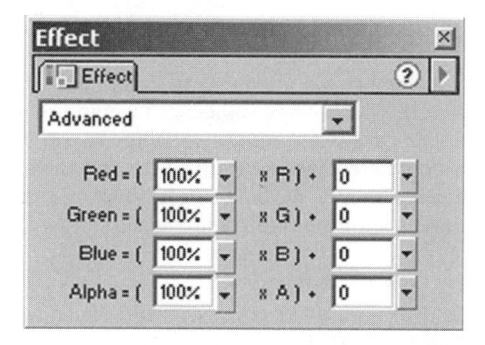

In fact, if you set the color attributes manually in the Flash editing environment, you can access the values by using the `getRGB` and `getTransform` methods in the scripting. The application of the Color object is really just for effects in games. Anywhere you want to programmatically change a movie clip's color you would use a Color object. For instance, if you have an enemy that takes many hits to beat, you could progressively increase the red values of the movie clip until it reaches the fatal amount.

A Color object is linked to a movie by specifying the movie clip's instance name and path as a parameter, so there's no need to have it inside or even near the actual movie. This way, if you want, you could define the Color object near the code that decides what the color settings should be, even if the code is distant from the actual colored movie clip. However, I prefer to keep the Color object close to the movie clip. This way it is all logically together. Let's follow through with our beat'em up enemy example, and say we've got a movie clip on the main stage with the instance name: boss. First of all we need to create our new Color object, we'll be doing this from inside our boss movie clip:

```
myColor = new Color(this);
```

Had we defined the object elsewhere, such as in the _root, we would have had to specify the actual movie clip with any necessary path information.

Setting up the object has really just set up the link. We now need to use the methods to change the color. Due to the complex information that can be used in setting a color, we need to create a generic object to hold the data to pass to the method.

In this object we just need to define variables for whatever aspects of the color we want to change. The variables we can set are based on a percentage of color and an offset. The percentage value changes the relative amount of the color or transparency that are already in the symbol. The offset then adds or subtracts a static amount from each color value. Colors in Flash work on RGB settings with each color ranging from 0 to 255. By using the offset you directly affect that number, thereby affecting the color.

# 3  Flash Games Studio

Let's add our generic object and call it `colorHolder`:

```
myColor = new Color(this);
colorholder = new Object();
```

Now, inside the `colorHolder` object, we just need to define the color properties that we want the movie clip to take on. For the percentage values, you would use variables RA, GA, BA, and AA for red, green, blue, and alpha. The offset uses the variables RB, GB, BB, and AB. So if we wanted to turn the boss movie clip completely red, we'd offset the red value by 255. That way whatever the color value is, it will have red as 255. We'd also need to lower the a values of green and blue to 0, so that they don't combine with the red to make a different color:

```
myColor = new Color(this);
colorholder = new Object();
colorholder.rb = 255;
colorholder.ga = 0;
colorholder.ba = 0;
```

The last thing to do then is to call the `setTransform` method, and supply it with our color object:

```
myColor = new Color(this);
colorholder = new Object();
colorholder.rb = 255;
colorholder.ga = 0;
colorholder.ba = 0;
myColor.setTransform(colorHolder);
```

If you wanted to make it change from its regular appearance progressively towards full red, then you'd use variables instead of static numbers, with the values for red's offset going from 0 up to 255, and the percentage values for green and blue down from 100 to 0.

## The Sound Object

The Sound object works in pretty similar ways to the Color object. Instead of dealing with the color of a movie clip and its contents, the Sound object has methods that will interact with the sounds embedded in the target movie clip, or any sounds that have been programmatically attached to the Sound object.

With the Sound object you can change a sound's volume, pan, or even conduct a very detailed control of the channel output to each of the speakers, allowing you to do all sorts of things such as swapping the right and left channels to the opposite speakers.

These methods, `setVolume`, `setPan`, and `setTransform`, are great for sound effects where you need to place them in a 3D space. You can use the x property of a movie clip to set pan and a hypothetical z coordinate (depth) to adjust volume. The `setVolume` and `setPan` commands operate over a range of numbers, (0 to 100) for volume and (-100 to +100) for pan. Much like the `setTransform` for color, `setTransform` takes an object as its argument, where the object contains variables for the left and right channels for each speaker.

# Flash's Built in Objects

Besides the transformations you can do on a sound object, you can also attach sounds from the Library to the Sound object for code. The process for this will be covered in greater detail in *Interactive Sound* chapter, but it's handy to know that you can use code to play a sound based on a game event.

## The Mouse Object

The Mouse object is pretty simple with only two methods in it, but it's nevertheless a valuable object for gaming. It's one of the objects that you can access globally, without creating an instance, or giving path information.

Using the Mouse object you can hide or show the cursor. Yep. That's it. You just use `Mouse.hide` or `Mouse.show`. The applications are great for gamers. Often a hand or an arrow just isn't right for a game. Now you can get rid of the default cursor and use your own.

When you turn off the cursor, you'd just drag a movie clip that contains your cursor shape. That also means you can script and animate your cursor to do anything you want. For shooting games, or anything else where you need to aim, replacing the cursor with a crosshair would be helpful to your player and also keep more with the game style. As you can see, even with the reticle, having the mouse present can be distracting.

## The Key Object

The Key object is quite a bit more robust than the Mouse object. With the Key object, you can determine what key is pressed, or check the up or down status of any key. As we'll see in the next chapter, it's the Key object that allows us to use multiple keyboard inputs to get around the button event handler limitations.

## The Math Object

If you plan to make games, I'd suggest getting used to dealing with the Math object. Movement in games often requires at least some use of trigonometry, randomization, or one of many other math concepts. This object is another global object that doesn't need an instance or any path information.

This object is filled with all sorts of useful math methods that let you do higher math that simply wasn't possible in earlier version of Flash without building all sorts of lookup tables. You have access to the standard trig methods, such as logarithms, exponents, and square root, and also to some numerical manipulation methods such as round, ceiling, floor, and absolute.

In addition to all of the methods that allow you to compute values, there are also many of the common mathematic constants. For instance, you can look up pi, E (Euler's constant), and some of the common natural logs. I can guarantee that pi is certainly one you'll use a lot in games for anything that requires trigonometry, since trig, in Flash, works in radians, not degrees.

Keep in mind however that speed in a game is crucial and some of the methods here can be somewhat processor intensive. It can sometimes be beneficial to create lookup tables once at the beginning of the game, and those variables when they become necessary. This way the math loses some precision but gains some play speed. We'll see an example of this in the chapter on *Structured Real-Time Programming* later on.

## The String Object

The String object allows you to chop up strings in all sorts of interesting ways. For game application, the String methods are going to be best for parsing information in the background for use by other game elements.

A good example of how the String object can be helpful in a game environment is Simon, the four-color memory game where you have to remember ever-increasing patterns of flashing lights. If you wanted to build this in Flash, you would just make a variable and keep concatenating random variables at each stage. Then, as the player tries to follow the pattern, you can compare their string of entries against the main string.

# Flash's Built in Objects

With the String object, you can do several things. There are numerous substring methods, which will take a large string and, based on the parameters passed to the method, return a small section of it. There are also a variety of index methods, which will search through a large string for a smaller string and return to the position where the string starts. There is even a method that will take a long string and search for a delimiter. Then, at each occurrence of the delimiter, it will break up the string and put it as an element of an array.

Any game that needs to have data parsed is a good candidate for use with the String object.

## The Array Object

Arrays are a very convenient way to make lists. As you add items to an array, you can give them indices so that you can call them later by that number. No matter how much fun parsing may be, for games, I find arrays are usually much more useable than having to do your own parsing using the String object.

For games, I use arrays for a wide variety of tasks, from storing information about all of the enemies on a level, to using it as a container to hold cards when simulating a deck. Any time it would be helpful to store information according to an index is a time for arrays.

Arrays have several methods. You can convert an array to a string, alphabetize it, concatenate two arrays to form one, add or remove an element from the beginning or end of the array, or insert or delete from the middle of the array.

In the card game example, when you need to deal out a card, you can use a `pop` command to return one element from the end of the array and simultaneously remove it. This method is handy because it is such a good analogy for dealing a card from a real deck. As you deal more and more cards, you can then access an array's length to see if it is empty yet. When it is, you simply reshuffle and refill the array and keep going.

## The XML Object

XML is a way of formatting data in a highly organized fashion. Flash 5 now has support for this data type as well as an XML socket that allows for persistent connections to the server to send XML packets to and from the server. This is something that is extremely important for creating multi-user game applications.

Hopefully now that you've seen what Flash's objects can do you're eager to see them put into use throughout the rest of the book, but hang on there's still one very important object left to look at.

## Getting Intimate with the Movie Clip

The movie clip is the only visible object in Flash, and it contains only data. As useful as data is, it's the visuals that make Flash so exciting.

# Flash Games Studio

Each movie clip is a timeline within itself, which runs at the same rate as the movie's frame rate, but is otherwise independent of the stops and starts of other movie clips. Being independent is neat, but it's the fact that it's independent *and* controllable at the same time that makes games possible.

By sending movies to particular parts of their timelines, different code can be executed, different visuals displayed. It can also hold completely different objects, and all of that can be done without disturbing any parent timeline. I say only parent here since while sending a movie clip to another frame doesn't directly affect the child timelines, if the child movie clip isn't on the timeline at the new frame, it'll be destroyed.

Movie clips have methods that allow you to see how much of themselves has loaded, to load new SWF files into a movie, to detect collision with other movies or points, to take you to other web pages by changing the URL, and of course methods that allow you to go to frames, and play or stop the timeline.

In addition to methods, movie clips have properties. Properties are reserved commands that report back a setting of a movie clip. You can get information about a movie's dimensions, position, rotation and scale amongst other things. The best thing about properties is that you can set the majority of them as well as read them. That way if you wanted to move a movie over to the right, you simply adjust its $x$ property. This is so, so invaluable in games. We'll take a detailed look at properties in just a second.

The last of the high points for movie clips are the new clip events. You can now attach code to each individual instance of a movie clip instead of having to have it hard wired into the symbol. There is also some added functionality from using clip events, but we'll spend a lot of time looking at them in the next chapter on *Event Handling*.

## Properties

There are two main types of property: read only, and read/write. As you've probably surmised, the user can only set the values of the latter of the two, but that doesn't make the former any less useful. Let's take a look at them now.

### Read Only Properties

These are the ones that for the most part can't be changed. For instance one of the new properties is the ability to detect the position of the mouse in a given timeline. While you'll find this most useful when it comes to making many types of games, the idea of setting the mouse position via scripting just isn't possible at the moment. Then again, I'm not sure I'd look forward to the ActionScript that would make me move the mouse!

Let's take a look at some of the other read only properties.

The `dropTarget` property will report back the topmost movie clip that is under the cursor. This is truthfully a really strange property on many levels. First it can only be used with a movie clip that's being dragged using the `startDrag` method. Even if a movie clip is being dragged, you still have to use the property of that same movie clip, even though it is impossible to drag more than one movie clip at a time.

# Flash's Built in Objects

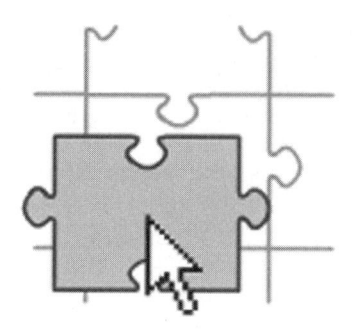

**_dropTarget = /gridSlot3**

Also, notice that it reports back the movie clip touching the mouse, not the dragged movie's origin point. If you are dragging the movie clip right at its center, then there is no difference, but otherwise you aren't really getting any information about what the dragged movie clip itself is doing.

As a nod to backwards compatibility to Flash 4, the data returned by this property is not in the dotted structure we commonly use in Flash 5. Instead, it returns paths using slashes.

The benefits of the `dropTarget` command are patchy, but provided you lock the dragged movie clip to the cursor, it can be used to create drag and drop interfaces for games like jigsaw puzzles. If you'd like more information about how the `startDrag` method works, we'll be looking at it in the methods section shortly.

The `currentFrame` command returns the current frame number of the movie clip. Used in conjunction with a goto command, `currentframe` is very useful for moving a relative number of frames, such as `gotoAndStop(_currentFrame - 5)` will send the timeline five frames back. I should point out that telling movies to go to specific frame numbers is considered a bad idea even in a medium length timeline. If you add frames later, you only have the potential for throwing off your code. Moving relative amounts is much better since it only matters if you've changed the number of frames that you need to travel.

In addition to being able to find what the current frame number is, you can see how many frames there are and how many of them have loaded by using the `totalFrames` and `framesLoaded` properties.

The `totalFrames` property can be used in a variety of ways. You might use it with `currentFrame` to make a ratio of how far the movie has played, or you might use it in a range for a randomization script to send a movie clip to a random frame in its timeline no matter what the length is.

The most common use of `totalFrames` is as a component of a simple preloader. A ratio of frames loaded to total frames for a movie can be easily displayed as a percentage of the load process complete. As we move into the methods section we'll look at another way of doing preloading based on the bytes loaded instead of frames.

The last two I mentioned briefly above, but they deserve a better look since they are used quite frequently in games. xmouse and ymouse report back the coordinates of where the mouse is, but it will do it in the context of whatever movie clip the property is called on. That means that the registration mark for the movie is the (0,0) coordinate, but it also means that if you rotate or scale the movie clip, the coordinates will be affected. Even if you are 10 pixels from the registration mark, but the movie clip that you are using the xmouse and ymouse on is scaled down to 10% it will report back that you are 100 pixels away from the registration mark, since it took that movie's scale into consideration.

**Read/Write Properties**

These properties are going to be the ones that are more likely useful for game applications, especially since they lead so well into our next section on animations using properties. Since there are so many properties, I'd rather not make this section into a repeat of the ActionScript Dictionary, but instead look at the gaming possibilities of each property.

The position of movie clips is controlled by a combination of x and y properties, just like the mouse lookup. The position of the movie clip is in the context of its parent movie, so the same sorts of conditions apply with rotated or scaled movies.

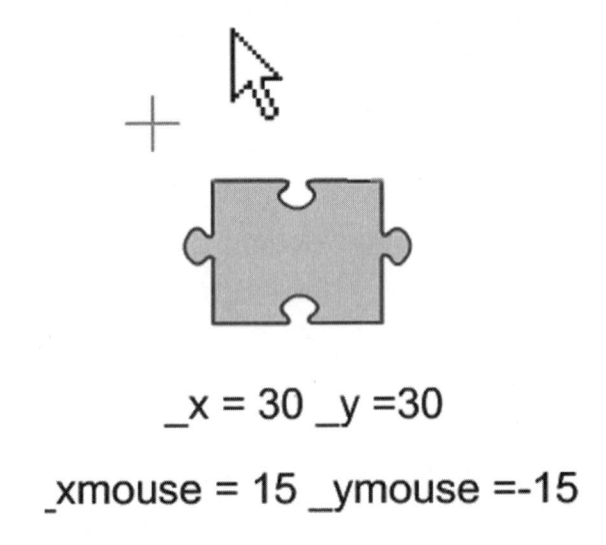

_x = 30 _y =30

_xmouse = 15 _ymouse =-15

Position data can be used to check collision, move the position of the movie clip, or work as part of the arctangent math method to find its angle from it's center. The essential fact here is that this data can be used for a lot of different purposes.

As I mentioned briefly in the last section, you could even take it and use it for purposes other than real positioning. With a sound object you could make the appearance of a sound emitter that adjusts the volume and pan of a sound based on the position of the movie.

# Flash's Built in Objects

In addition to position data we can also get the `rotation` of a movie clip. Whether rotated by setting this property, or rotated in the editing environment, this property will display the rotation the movie in degrees from -180 to 180. When a movie clip is first created, that position is 0 degrees. Any rotation of that object will affect the value that is returned; however if you rotate the contents of the movie clip, you haven't adjusted the orientation of the actual movie clip at all.

If you are interested in top-down games, rotation will prove invaluable to you. There is the obvious use as spinning an avatar to point in a new direction, but also for use in finding headings and determining how to change the position properties of the movie.

Since all of our position data is based on the x and y coordinates we can't just say turn 30 degrees and go forward 10 pixels. The rotation can be taken and used in some of the trigonometric math methods to find out how to break a distance with a heading into its horizontal and vertical components.

By using trigonometry, we can find out what 10 pixels out at 30 degrees would be translated to.

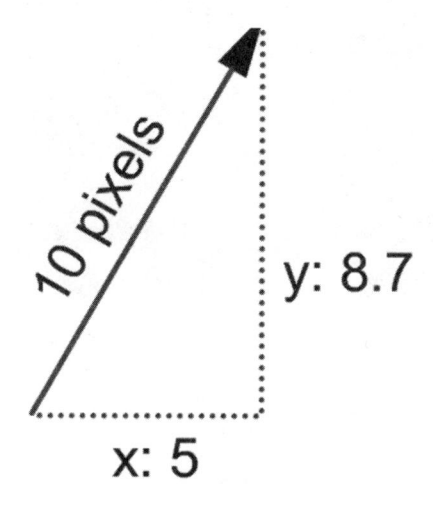

Next we have the dimension properties. You can find the scale of an object, in either horizontal scale (`xscale`) or vertical scale (`yscale`). You can also find the actual `height` and `width` of the movie clip as well. When you create a movie, it starts with scales of 100 and a height and width of whatever the height is (again, in the context of the parent movie). I bring up the absolute dimension and scale at the same time because they are really two sides of the same coin. If you increase the height property, you are also increasing the `yscale` and vice versa.

Which dimension property you choose is really going to depend on your application. In 3D games with perspective, you are going to want to deal with the scales since it will be easier to deal with dimension as a proportion of its normal amount. However if you are making a game that uses one of the line drawing movie clips, it's much easier to affect the height and width since you are trying to make it an absolute size that has little to do with its original size.

# Flash Games Studio

There are two properties that deal with just the appearance of the movie clip. You can adjust the `alpha` (transparency) of a movie clip without using a Color object, or you can completely turn the visibility of the movie clip on or off.

As you can see in the picture below, it is not integral to gameplay, you can use scripted alpha values in games to create more realistic looking effects. The skid marks below are several smaller skid mark movie clips that when they are placed set their alpha based on several settings like speed, and direction the car is traveling in relation to direction the car is rotated.

Changing the `visible` setting makes it so that Flash doesn't have to process the visuals of the movie at all. This is particularly helpful when you need to hide a button that is in a movie clip. When `visible` is set to 0 (off), the hit state of the button is not there and the button does not do anything. If you were to set the same movie clip to an `alpha` of 0 instead of turning off the visibility, buttons would still work and Flash would still be processing the movie, you simply wouldn't be able to see it.

I should mention here that use of alpha should be really limited because of its severe processing requirements. Having too many transparent objects will cause you game to slow down to a crawl.

While on the subject of game speed, let's talk about the `quality` property. This property, when used actually affects the entire movie, not a particular movie clip. What it does is to change the antialiasing method for the movie, making the graphics look smoother the higher the quality setting:

# Flash's Built in Objects

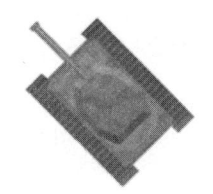

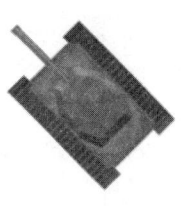

You can set this property to low, medium, high, or best. By default, movies export at high quality. For arcade games, where things are moving fast and there isn't a lot of fine text, medium would work well and provide some additional speed.

Wow, such a palette of actions to choose from! Let's take a look at some of these in action now.

## Animation with Properties

Traditional animation is a great thing in Flash. Some really great movies have even been made without the use of any scripting. That's lovely if you don't want to play a game, but since we obviously do, we need to learn to animate like professional game developers.

The main movements for game characters won't be tweened in games – you have to use scripting to move them. This is because with a tween you have to set up the motion in the editing environment. In a game, movement needs to be determined in real-time, in order to take in reactions to the environment. Traditional animation does still have a strong place in games, although it is now as secondary animation.

Secondary animations are the visual effects that make a game more engrossing and real by adding the details. For games, I tend to think of big animations like walk cycles and other important elements as secondary – though I may refrain from stating this in the presence one of my animator colleagues!

The reason for lumping it all together is that it isn't going to really affect the game if these elements are not there. They're more aesthetic. If your character needs to run to the other side of the screen it will look great if there is a run cycle, but the symbol's sliding across the screen is going to be what is important as far as the scripting of the game. It doesn't matter what position the character's legs are in, the collision detection on the body is going to work just the same. We're currently talking about practical game development over artistry.

# 3  Flash Games Studio

## Beach ball Bouncing

To demonstrate animation through scripting, I'm going to borrow a notorious and evil enemy from my childhood of playing *Keystone Capers* on the Atari. Yes that's right – the beach ball! In this game you ran down long corridors of a shopping mall in pursuit of a crook, dodging a bouncing beach ball along the way:

A bouncing ball will allow us to work on movement using the x and y properties, but will also give us some practice with a couple of the Math object's methods, scale and alpha. We'll start with just rolling the ball, and then add in the bounces. Just to add some effects, we'll also add a shadow that trails along on the ground.

1. To get started, open up a new movie in Flash and go to the movie properties, in the Modify menu. Let's change the frame rate to something faster than 12.

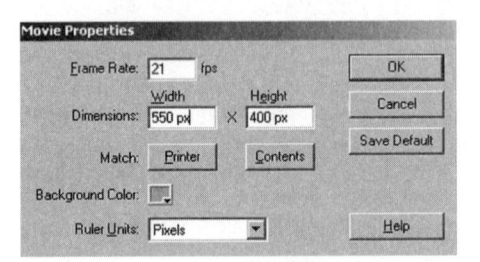

> For games, I like to use to faster frame rates, so that characters move smaller amounts between frames. While it looks much smoother, for scripting it's more beneficial as a way of making sure that a character doesn't move too far at once and miss a collision that should occur.

# Flash's Built in Objects   3

2. To make the artwork for our example, draw a beach ball. When you're done, convert it to a movie clip and give it the instance name `ball`. Select the movie clip and open the Actions panel and add this code:

```
onClipEvent (enterFrame) {
}
```

We're going to talk a lot about clip events later, but for now, just keep in mind that the `(enterFrame)` code will just run anything inside the braces over and over. Since animation is something that has to happen over time, you'll always need to do something to make your scripts run whenever animation is needed.

3. Inside the braces, we want to add code that will move the ball. Since it is a ball that we are going to view from the side we just need it to move horizontally to make it look like it's rolling. To do that, we just take the current x position and add some amount on to it. Eight pixels per frame would be good, but feel free to choose whatever you want.

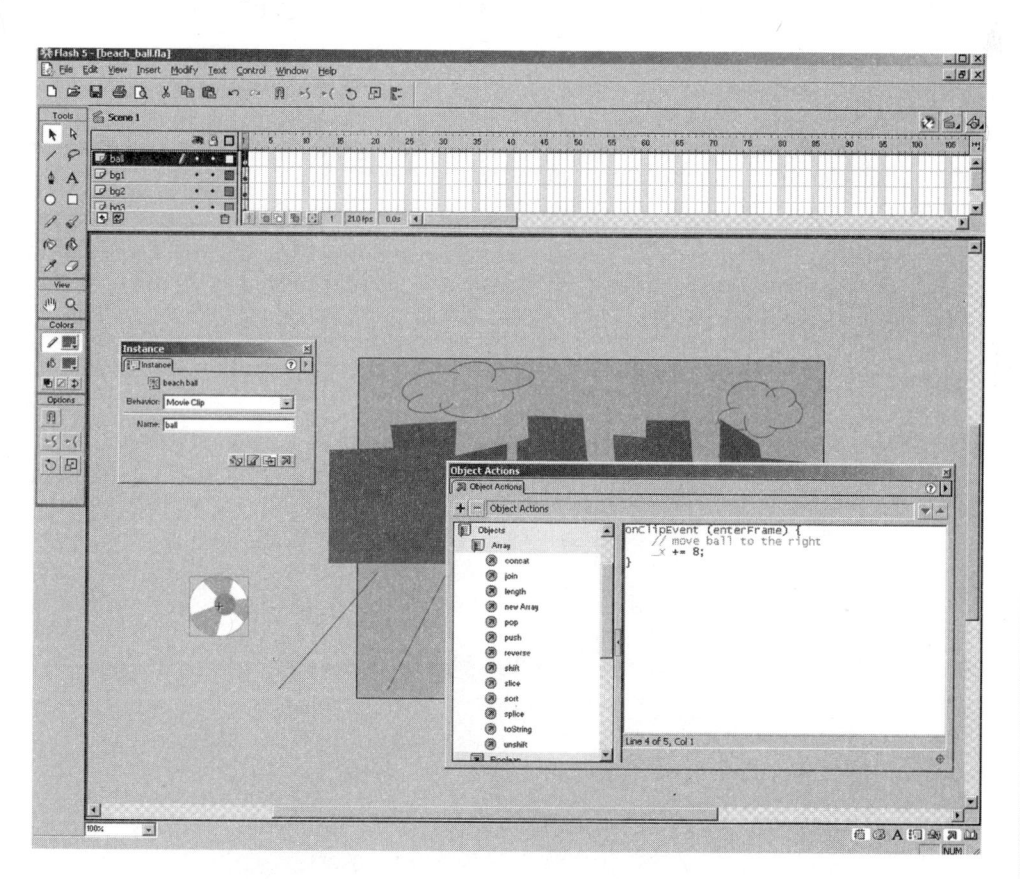

**4.** To add to the current amount we don't have to write something like _x = _x + 8. There is an operator in Flash that will do that for you. To do that, you would use +=. So, to constantly add 8, we'd use the following code:

```
onClipEvent (enterFrame) {
    //move ball to the right
    _x += 8;
}
```

If you test the movie now, you'll see that it slides, but if it were a real ball it would also have to turn. To do the rotation, we could do something very similar to the x animation, but if you give it a try, you'll see that it is hard to get the ball to look like it is rotating at the right rate. To figure out the right rate, we can use some simple math.

As a ball rolls along the ground the distance that it takes for the ball to return to the starting position is the same as the circumference of the ball. If that sounded too technical, think of drawing a circle, breaking it at a point and stretching it out to a line. That line is how far the ball has to roll before it makes a full rotation.

The way to figure out perimeter is that equation you probably learned when you were a little kid, *circumference = 2\*PI\*radius*. We have pi as a member of the math object, and the radius is pretty easy to figure out. It's half the width or height of the ball. So now we have *C=2\*PI\*.5\*width*. Now we are doubling one thing and chopping another value in half. This can all be simplified to *C= PI\*width*.

As we rotate the ball the width is going to change. Normally no matter how you rotate a circle, its width would be the same. Unfortunately with Flash, it adds a bounding box for the movie, which is a rectangle that circumscribes the symbol. As we rotate the ball, we are also rotating that bounding box, and its width would now be the width of the diamond shape made by the corners of the box. Because of this, we want to find out what the width of the ball is once, when it isn't rotated, and then use that value in the script that is repeating all the time:

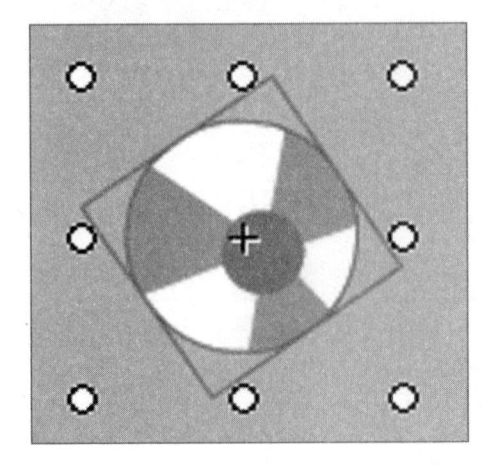

# Flash's Built in Objects  3

5. To do that we are going to use another event clip, this one being a `load` event, which will only happen once.

    ```
    onClipEvent (load) {
    }
    onClipEvent (enterFrame) {
        //move ball to the right
        _x += 8;
    }
    ```

6. Since the circumference isn't going to change for this ball, we can go ahead and figure out that value once and set it to a variable. As we figured out above, the value should be pi* width. To code that, you'd do the following:

    ```
    onClipEvent (load) {
        // find the width for use with rotation
        circumfrence = Math.PI*_width;
    }
    onClipEvent (enterFrame) {
        // move ball to the right
        _x += 8;
    }
    ```

7. Now that we have circumference, we need to do something with it. What we need to know is how many degrees per pixel it takes to for the rotation to occur at the right rate. We can find that out by taking the total degrees in a circle and dividing it by the circumference of the ball. Once we have that, we just multiply it by the current _x position:

    ```
    onClipEvent (load) {
        // find the width for use with rotation
        circumfrence = Math.PI*_width;
    }
    onClipEvent (enterFrame) {
        // move ball to the right
        _x += 8;
        // spin the ball
        _rotation = _x*360/circumfrence;
    }
    ```

    If you test now, you should have a nice rolling beach ball. In the Atari game, the ball bounced so that you could either jump it when it was low, or duck under it when it was high. To make this ball bounce, we need to add a script that just moves the ball up and down since the horizontal motion is already in place.

8. The vertical motion of a ball bouncing along isn't constant. As the ball reaches the top of the arc, the vertical motion needs to slow down, and then as it passes the top, it can begin to speed up again and then repeat the process indefinitely. What we've just described is the top half of a sine wave. Sine waves of course reach a trough, that looks just like an upside down version of the peak.

Plain sine waves oscillate between values of 1 and -1, cycling between peaks and troughs. If we took all of the negative values and made them positive, then we'd have all peaks, with the wave reflecting (bouncing) off of the 0 line. What we've just described is the path we need for the bouncing ball. To convert the negative sine values to positive ones we can use the Math object's abs method to return an absolute value.

9. To get the cyclic values out of the sin method, we need to provide a constant progression of values. For this we can just use the x value since it is getting constantly incremented anyway. The thing is that sin works well with small numbers — one full cycle of the sine wave (two bounces for us) takes places over a range of only 6.283 (2*PI). So, we just need to shrink the amount of x by dividing it by a large number. The larger the divisor is, the broader the bounce will be. I chose 75 as a good amount.

10. We have to take account for is the fact that sin method is going to output very small number (between 1 and -1 before the absolute value). Moving up and down over one pixel will hardly be noticeable, so we just need to multiply what sin returns by a large number, like 100. The number you specify here is the total number of pixels that the ball will rise. Lastly, we need to make the whole amount negative, since Flash's coordinate system has negative values going up and positive values going down:

```
onClipEvent (load) {
    // find the width for use with rotation
    circumfrence = Math.PI*_width;
}
onClipEvent (enterFrame) {
    // move ball to the right
    _x += 8;
    // spin the ball
    _rotation = _x*360/circumfrence;
    // move the ball up and down
    _y = -Math.abs(100*Math.sin(_x/75));
}
```

# Flash's Built in Objects

**11.** Phew! Well that was a drawn out explanation for one little line of code! But if you test now, you'll have a bouncing ball. The only problem is it is now bouncing at the very top of the screen. To correct this, we'll do a non-scripting fix. Out on the main timeline, select the ball movie clip and convert it into a new movie clip. Now it will use the (0,0) coordinates of the movie and you can easily adjust where to put the ball by moving the movie on the main timeline.

**12.** The final thing we are going to do in this example is to create a shadow that follows the ball and sets its size and opacity based on how high the ball is in the air. The effect will be to have a small but opaque shadow when the ball touches the ground and a large diffuse one when it is up in the air:

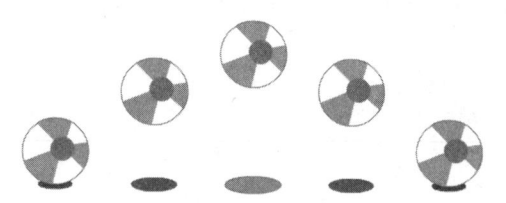

**13.** We should start by creating a shadow. Go into your new movie clip that should right now just hold your ball movie. Draw a shadow in here, and make it into a movie clip, making sure then to reorder the movies so that the shadow is on the bottom. Now go into the actions panel with the shadow selected.

All of the shadow properties we are going to be changing will have values based on some element of the ball movie. Since we are now in a different scope, we'd have to access _parent.ball._property. Instead, let's set the ball object to a variable in the shadow movie. That way, we can save ourselves some typing, and should we ever need to change the relative path of the ball, we just need to change the code in one place.

**14.** Once again, we'll be using a clip event to make sure this code run continuously:

```
onClipEvent (enterFrame) {
    ball = _parent.ball;
}
```

**15.** Now that we have the variable set up to represent the ball movie clip, we can just call properties on it like it was the actual movie. The first thing we need to do is to always keep the shadow directly under ball. This is of course assuming top-down lighting, but since it is a fair bit easier than doing shadows cast from an angle, I think that will be just fine.

```
onClipEvent (enterFrame) {
    ball = _parent.ball;
    _x = ball._x;
}
```

16. Next, we need the scale to fluctuate based on how high up the ball is. The obvious way would be to tie the value to the $y$ position of the ball. The thing is that scale works on a 0-100 range for non-existent to full-size. We need the shadow to always be at least a certain size, so we need to offset the amount. Also, when the ball is at its highest point, $y$ is going to be whatever you stuck as the multiplier in the ball's script. Since that is a pretty big number, let's also cut it in half. Finally, we also need to make scale negative since the $y$ will always be negative.

    ```
    onClipEvent (enterFrame) {
        ball = _parent.ball;
        _x = ball._x;
        _xscale = _yscale=-(.5*ball._y)+50;
    }
    ```

    As you can see there is a nice feature of ActionScript that when you are setting multiple things to the same value, you can set up a chain where all of the variables or properties are set to the value on the far right. By the way, the values that I used as an offset and multiplier on the $y$ value were completely arbitrary; feel free to play with them to achieve a motion that is good for your particular shadow.

17. Last but not least is the opacity change. Alpha works on a 0-100 scale with 100 being opaque. Since we want the movie to be opaque when the ball is low, we need to start off with a large number and subtract from that amount as the ball goes higher. Actually since $y$ is already negative, we just nee to add that amount onto some number like 100. Same as before, we should probably cut the $y$ in half so that it doesn't get too transparent as the ball goes up. Once again, these settings are personal choice and should be set to whatever you want:

    ```
    onClipEvent (enterFrame) {
        ball = _parent.ball;
        _x = ball._x;
        _xscale = _yscale=-(.5*ball._y)+50;
        _alpha = 100+(.5*ball._y);
    }
    ```

    If you test now, you'll see we have a pretty convincing looking ball moving along without even a single tween.

I figure that as long as we are looking at a movie clip whose properties are pretty much slaved to another movie that it would be a good point to revisit hierarchy as well as how to reference between different movies and objects.

# Flash's Built in Objects 3

## Hierarchy Revisited

In our last example we dealt with two sister movies, where one had to access information on the other. There are two ways of getting from one sister object to another. The first is a relative path, which is the way we did it in our example. The other way is by using an absolute path.

With the shadow and the ball in the same movie, it's a very good idea to use a relative path. By going up to the parent object and down to the target movie, all that is required is the target movie is there as the current movie's sister. An absolute path would have been something like `_root.ballAndShadow.ball`. That may not seem so horrible, but if these movie clips were nested further down that path would be much longer. Also if we chose later to encase everything inside another movie clip, the absolute path would be broken. With the relative path, there would be no problem.

If you are just getting started in ActionScript, it may be tempting to use absolute paths for small projects because everything is pretty close to the root anyway. I'd really urge you to start with good habits like using relative paths wherever possible. When you start in on large projects, it's certainly not uncommon to have to change some organization that would throw off absolute paths. What would be a small matter of changing a line or two in a small file could easily become a search for the one broken line of code out of several hundred lines of code in slightly bigger project.

While we're on the topic of nesting and hierarchy, I'd like to give a few examples of how beneficial nesting can be in games. In the next chapter we are going to be building a mini-games based on using a tank. I chose a tank simply for its interesting use of nested movies. As you move the tank around, you'll notice there is a turret for firing. Since the turret movie is nested in the tank, it travels along, without any scripting. When it comes time to aim and fire you can then rotate the turret movie clip, just like any other movie, and it will work as expected. Because of this relationship, you can then move and swing the turret around at the same time, with very simple code:

# Flash Games Studio

If you'd like to take a look at how this game plays, take a look at `introTank.fla`. There may be a lot of code in there that you don't understand. We'll cover it shortly, but for now just take a look at how nested movie clips act dependently and independently from their parent object:

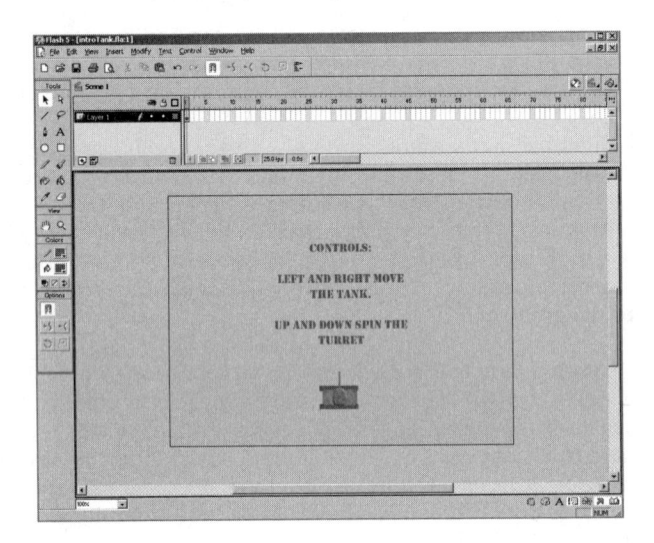

We've taken a good look now at what the properties of movie clips can do for us, but let's also take a look at the methods. The methods of movie clips have some of the most direct gaming applications of any aspect of Flash 5.

## Methods

Looking at the Actions window, not only do you get all of those properties, but you get a whole heck of a lot of methods too. Several of the methods have to do with controlling a timeline. These methods are like the buttons on a DVD player. You can stop or play, go to the next frame or go to the previous one. These methods are all pretty self-explanatory.

There are a couple of things that you should bear in mind when using these methods as to the effect they'll have on your scripts. Any time you use a `gotoAnd...` or `nextFrame`, or `prevFrame`, you immediately jump to that new frame. I know you weren't expecting it to wait to go to the specified frame, but just be aware how immediate "immediately" is! It's so fast that it processes the new frame without ever having rendered the frame that has the `goTo` action in it. Also, if you are already in the frame that you are sending it to, the command is ignored, and the scripts in that frame won't be re-executed.

Other methods deal with the creation or deletion of new movie clips. There is a command to duplicate movies, something that is enormously valuable for games, where you need to spawn a certain number of enemies. When it's time for those movies to go away there is the `removeMovieClip` method to delete them.

# Flash's Built in Objects

If you want to bring in scripts or art assets from external files, you can use the `loadMovieClip` and `LoadMovieClipNum` methods. The difference between them being that the first will replace a specified movie clip that already exists with the contents of the imported SWF. The latter will add the SWF to a new level. The main timeline is level 0, adding a new level will insert the SWF as a sister object to level 1 – though just on top of it. If you want to remove these movies, you can use unload but be aware that it will remove the file from the users cache as well. It's generally better to find some other way of disposing of the movie.

For any of the movies – either those originally present, or those duplicated or loaded, it is possible to change its stacking order dynamically using the `swapDepths` method. Keep in mind that you can only swap depths with sister objects. You can't swap depths with an object nested in a different object.

If instead of loading a movie, you'd rather load data, you can do that with `loadVariables` and `loadVariablesNum`. The distinction between the two is the same as for movies, but this target is where the variables are stored. In this process you can also send data from the movie clip that these methods were called on to the file that you are loading from. If the document targeted is a PHP, ASP page, or CGI script, it can take in the variables and respond accordingly. If you were going to set up a high score list that persisted beyond the instance of the Flash player, you would need to submit the score through this method and wait to hear back with the list of high scores for display purposes.

`getURL` can also send data, but instead of trying to incorporate the data into Flash, it takes the result and pushes it to the browser.

Other methods for movie clips that are of interest to game developers would be those related to **coordinate systems**. In order to compare locations of between two items, it is necessary that they be within the same context. Comparing the coordinates of two movie clips in different timelines is all but useless. The `getBounds` method will take a movie and return an object containing the maximum and minimum x and y values for the specified movie clip. What is even better is that you can specify what movie's coordinate system you'd like the data for.

If you'd rather get information for a particular coordinate translated from one movie clip to the root's context or vice versa, you can use `localToGlobal` or `globalToLocal`. To use these methods, you must create a generic object and to hold your x and y value for the coordinate and then supply it to one of the methods. It will take the specified movie to be the local coordinate system, convert the coordinate values and return them to the same object overwriting your values.

With coordinate data you can also look up to see if that point is inside a movie using the `hitTest` method. You can also compare the bounding boxes of two movies to see if they overlap. This method will return either true or false depending on if the hit was detected. As you might imagine, this is the basis for a lot of the collision detection done in Flash 5. While you still can't check the actual shape of a movie against the shape of another, `hitTest` is still invaluable for making games. We'll take a look at it in greater detail as we build out some of the tank mini-game.

In the properties section we talked about the `dropTarget` property that only works with the `startDrag` method. This method takes a movie clip and moves it around at a one to one ratio with the mouse. There are several options for this method that allow you to lock the movie's center to the cursor point, and others that allow you to constrain the draggable area to a rectangle. When you want to end the drag process you just use `stopDrag`.

If you choose to use both of the features for `StartDrag`, be aware that there is a bug that occurs. The movie clip being dragged is for all intents now your cursor. When its registration point rolls over a button, the button will go into its over state, even if the mouse is outside the constrained rectangle. That also means that if you try to interact with buttons outside the constrained area, they will be buggy since it only partially registers the mouse outside the drag area. On the plus side, when you use both features, the `dropTarget` property will actually return the movie clip that the movie is touching instead of what the cursor is touching.

Lastly, we have the methods that are the second way of building preloaders. Instead of finding out how many frames have loaded, you can get the total number of bytes that have loaded, and the total of number of bytes in a given movie. While building a preloader isn't really a part of the game development process, it is important to know about this technique.

As we saw with the bouncing ball, we are going to rely more on scripting to animate things than tweens over large numbers of frames. Most of my games just don't have content spread out evenly over several frames. Instead I have a few frames that hold the vast majority of the file size. To be able to give any sense of how much has loaded, I have to use a method that returns more useful information than frames.

## Scripting Libraries

As you can see, there are a lot of scripting options available to us to use in making our games. However there are precious few that are specifically geared to a game purpose. There are elements of code that I use in almost any top-down game for instance.

As we talked about before, we can use the prototype command to extend our object to make them more useable to our applications. If you made a blank movie clip that did nothing but store our functions and immediately prototype them to the appropriate objects, you'd have portable code that you would just have to paste into your new movie to have access to all of your game code.

This type of code is pretty generic, but over time you'll start to see code elements that you need over and over. For instance in a top-down game, when a character reaches the edge of the screen, it needs to wrap to the other side. Whether the character is your avatar or a mindless enemy, the code for wrapping will be the same. If you have that set to automatically prototype itself to the `movieClip` object, it will be available to any movie.

As you create more and more of these libraries, you'll notice a significant reduction in the amount of time it takes to develop games, and the organization of your code will increase dramatically.

# Flash's Built in Objects    3

Some of these generic pieces of code will need some information. In the case of a wrap function, you first need to know the dimensions of the stage. Since this is likely to change from game to game, we need to put the custom information somewhere. That leads us into the next section, which compares the benefits of smart clips and the `onClipEvent` event handler.

## Clip Events Versus Smart Clips

One of my favorite features that is new to Flash in version 5 is the fact that you can now have instance-based code. By not having the code in the actual symbol, it is possible to have two instances of the same movie clip doing very different things, without messing up your library with duplicate symbols that only differ in code.

There are two ways of getting instance specific code into a movie. The first is through clip events. As we've seen in the beach ball example, you can add code to the outside of a movie and have it run once at the beginning or all the time. There are actually even more events it handles that we'll see in the next chapter.

With clip events, we can add variables or functions to the movie. Something I like to do is to set up calls inside the symbol to functions I'm going to write on the outside in a clip event. That way I can change the function from instance to instance so that the movie performs differently.

The other way is to use smart clips. Smart clips have been touted as a way to bridge the gap between designer and coder. Without going to the actions panel, you can set variables for an instance of the smart clip. The coder would make the variables settings, and the designer would fill out the form to set the variables appropriately. You can even have a custom interface by creating a SWF to do the form filling with a greater ease and style for the designer.

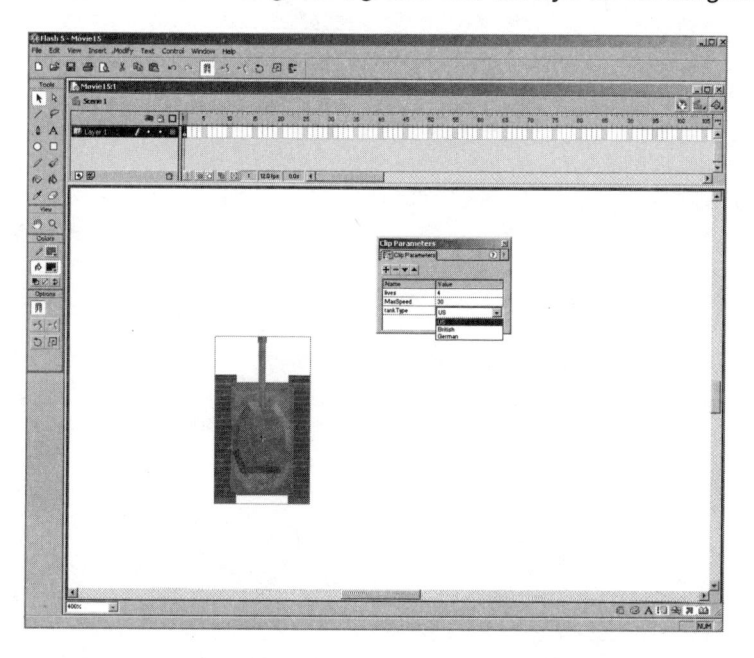

The variables for smart clips are entered into the movie at render before any other variable at load, so that they are immediately available. If you want to have more options for using custom code based on an instance, you would have to write the code in the symbol and have a variable from the smart clip indicating which set of instructions to run.

Both ways have their benefits and pitfalls, but I have to say that I am much more in favor of clip events. There is certainly nothing keeping them from working together, but if you are already in the Actions panel to write a clip event, I'd much rather just add my variables directly on the instance than deal with a custom interface.

In the case of the wrap function, it's a matter of whether you'd prefer to put the screen dimensions in the same area as the code itself, or in an interface for entering specific data. I don't find an extra interface all that necessary. If this would help your code to remain organized, you should definitely consider smart clips.

## Conclusion

Now that you know what all of the objects in Flash have to offer an aspiring game developer, you should start to be getting some ideas about how games will operate in Flash. By knowing what is available to you, it will be easier to look at a game and first know if it is possible to create in Flash, and if it has already been created, you should have some ideas about how the game play is working.

Of course just knowing what tools are available to use won't have you building killer games immediately, but it will make the rest of this book much easier to understand.

# Flash's Built in Objects     3

Introduction
chapter 1
chapter 2
chapter 3
chapter 4
chapter 5
chapter 6
Case Study 1
chapter 7
chapter 8
chapter 9
chapter 10
chapter 11
chapter 12
chapter 13
Case Study 2
chapter 14
chapter 15
Director Afterword

# Chapter 4
# Event Handling

# 4

# Flash Games Studio

In this chapter we're going to explore the exciting new event handling toys on offer in Flash 5, and look at how we can mix and match them to create our own, more complex event handling routines. This is where more advanced gaming really begins to take hold, with the beginning of a sensitive control system.

We will take as a starting point our tank project from the last chapter, and try to evolve it, taking in a few more complex routines along the way. Here's what we'll do:

- Find out how to produce **smooth movement** from the keyboard
- Allow **simultaneous actions**
- Enable the user to **customize keys**
- **Look at spawning** objects and **initializing** them
- Detect **collision** between objects and set the consequences

After all this we should have a pretty responsive and engaging game and, more importantly, a genuine grasp on how to deal with user input in Flash.

## The onClipEvent Function

The main new tool that is going to help us with all this is the onClipEvent function, which lets us detect events that were unusable in Flash 4. Even better is the fact that this code is attached to the outside of the movie clip instance, just like a button's code is on the outside of the button. The result of this is that you can now have any number of instances of a movie clip out on the stage, with each instance having different code.

So then, clip events are pieces of ActionScript attached to the movie instance, which wait to be triggered by an external event. The great thing is, since the code is attached to the movie's Object Actions window, and therefore not actually on its timeline, it doesn't matter what frame your movie clip is on for the code to execute.

This new method allows you to store user controls, collision detection and movement scripts all in one place, making it easier to read through and edit your FLA file at a later date. Anybody who has walked away from a file for a week or so, only to come back and feel like it was written by a stranger, will know that this type of organization is a lifesaver.

Let's start by taking a look at each of the onClipEvent options, and how they are going to help us with game design.

### onClipEvent (load)

With the load event, it's possible to initialize values for a movie clip the moment it appears. This is extremely useful in games, as obstacles or enemies often act within preprogrammed parameters. These parameters can be assigned once here, then other scripts can use the information however they choose. This is also a great place to initialize **functions**, such as the way

# Event Handling

in which an object is to move. Functions only need to be introduced once, so the fact that `load` is only run when the movie clip is loaded makes it the obvious place to put them.

## onClipEvent (enterFrame)

Often going hand in hand with the `load` event is the `enterFrame` event. This event triggers its code at the beginning of each frame. What this means is the code is running constantly, executing at the current frame rate. Because of this, it's a great place to add code that looks after the maintenance of a movie, such as whether or not a bullet has hit anything on its progress across the screen. Later on in this chapter we will be applying an `(enterFrame)` event to our tank's shells in order to check whether they have hit any of the randomly scattered mines.

There is a lot more that can be put in this event handler, such as checks for user controls and timers. Rest assured we'll be looking at those towards the end of this chapter.

## onClipEvent (unload)

The opposite of `load` is the `unload` event. I rarely use this code for games, because the number of events that may prompt an unloading is pretty large. The `unload` event is triggered whenever the movie clip is no longer present, whether that is by simply not being on the timeline anymore, being removed by `removeMovieClip`, or if either happens to any of its parent movie clips. In a lot of games, it's not the simple act of leaving the stage that is significant, but how it leaves.

It's possible for an element to leave the screen for any number of reasons. Maybe it has been destroyed, or maybe it's just the end of the game. In either case, the code for a movie would have been processed. I much prefer to add the code to the event that triggers the object's destruction. Adding this code to the code that causes the `unload` event is going to be easier to read later on.

## onClipEvent (data)

This triggers when either external variables or SWFs are being loaded. Every time Flash receives a section of data for a loaded SWF, or when the last variable of a file loads in, this event is set off. We'll see this in action later in the book when we build a level editor and use the `data` event to check when a new level map has been loaded, and to display it when it has.

Elsewhere in the `onClipEvent` window we have a series of user input related events. These events are `mouseDown`, `mouseUp`, `mouseMove`, `keyDown`, and `keyUp`. In the next section not only will we look at the role of these `onClipEvent` events, but also the events associated with the `on` statements, as part of buttons.

# User Interaction

In Flash we have access to two input devices – the keyboard and the mouse (or whatever you use as the mouse, such as a tablet). Sorry – there is no access to the joystick port, which would be a nice bonus, but you can still create some great interfaces with the standard inputs. Let's start by looking at each of the devices as they apply to making game controls, then we can go through the many different ways of interpreting the input.

# 4  Flash Games Studio

## The Keyboard

Wow, look at all of those keys – so much potential for the world's most complex game! But hold your horses. You need to keep in mind that most of us only have two hands with five fingers to each, and as much as I might like games, it certainly doesn't cover bringing my toes into play.

Certain games call for a lot of different controls, but these are not generally meant to be used at once. For instance, tile-based RPGs will often have a lot of commands, like pickup, drop, inventory, attack, talk, open, and so on, but these are things that you neither have to do quickly nor at once. In an arcade game like a space shooter, you have only a few controls, but you have to do things quickly and often simultaneously.

There is a balance that you as the game designer can decide for yourself, but if your controls are intuitive and comfortable, you should be safe. "Intuitive controls" pretty much means borrowing from what's considered the most common controls. For the keyboard, that often means the arrow keys for the directional controls, or the I, J, K, and L keys which for a long time were considered to be the default direction keys. Whatever you choose, if you design a keyboard interface, make sure your users don't have to play the finger equivalent of a tongue twister before they even get to the actual challenges in the game.

Also bear in mind that there are different keyboard types. Putting a lot of controls in the center of your keyboard may work fine for a standard keyboard but may be awkward on a split keyboard or a laptop keyboard where the player also has to use a track-pad. Also, depending on the type of computer you have, there may be different keys, specific to an operating system, such as the ALT and CTRL keys on the PC, and the COMMAND and OPTION keys on the Mac. While you have access to almost all of the keys on the keyboard, be sure not to choose controls that simply won't work on another keyboard or may be arranged in an unusable way.

## The Mouse

The mouse is a simpler device than a keyboard, but for game play it can have a much more sensitive touch. Like the keyboard, the mouse comes in many different guises. Flash is limited to the two features that are common to every mouse: movement and the main button (commonly the left mouse button for PCs).

Now that we all know about what we have available to us, let's talk about using them to control a game. There are a few different ways of dealing with input from the mouse. Flash has inbuilt event handlers for both keys and mouse, and as we briefly discussed in the `onClipEvent` section, there are also some for movie clips. We can also create scripts that access the status of the mouse or keyboard. We'll touch on these quickly here, but in the large part we'll leave them for the section on building our own checks later.

We'll start off by looking at the button's event handlers, as they will be the most familiar to those of you who have used Flash as a tool for creating user interfaces. After that, we'll look at the `onClipEvent` events that have to do with the keyboard and mouse, and finish off with looking at the properties available to us when we start building our own event handlers.

# Event Handling | 4

## Button Event Handlers

Buttons are a simple way of setting up interactivity; they lay in wait, listening for the correct action from the player, then when the correct action is performed, they merrily respond. Of course, if it's listening for a `keyPress` it really doesn't act like a button; it's a no-frills event handler that doesn't have to be touched in itself. It just holds the code. If on the other hand, a button is listening for a mouse event, it often needs to be physically "pressed" by the cursor. This relies on a hit area – a defined shape where the button exists. As you're no doubt aware, this doesn't have to have anything to do with what the button looks like:

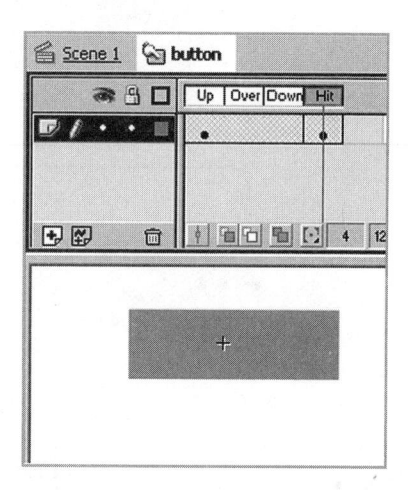

Here the hit area is a bit larger than the actual button graphic, and is just a simple shape. Since you don't ever see it, there is no real reason to decorate it. Also, since the point of a simple button is to be pushed, I often find it a good idea to expand the hit shape of the button to a larger area so that the user has no problem interacting with it. Also keep in mind that hit areas are completely static. No animation can occur. If you place any type of animated symbol in this frame, the hit state will simply be the first frame of that symbol.

Whenever the mouse enters this hit area, the cursor (if visible) will turn into a hand. For a game this can be a good or a bad thing. If you are trying to show your player that this is an area you can interact with, this is an excellent way of doing it since the hand is a symbol users will recognize as an interactive spot. This is helpful in exploratory games where you want to give the user some hints.

On the other hand if you are creating a shooting game, changing the cursor may not be such a great thing. If your targets are marked by a cursor change, that may be giving the user more information than you want since it might be too easy to spot the targets if they are supposed to be hidden.

With the mouse, you can set up handlers that execute code when you enter a button, press it, let go of it, or when you leave the button without letting go, let go outside the button, or enter the button with the mouse button already pressed. With all of that, there are certainly a large number of games where you can use buttons as the main interaction, but these are normally puzzles, or

# Flash Games Studio

other games where you need to choose something, or use a drag and drop style interface. Arcade games made with buttons as the main interaction are generally quite limited to shooting galleries and whack-a-mole style games.

The best way to create a deft control system is by using the keyboard. But we have to be careful; there are limitations that we have to be aware of. The main one of these comes with the `on(keyPress "key")` command, as it works just as if you were typing normally: If you hold down the key, it triggers once, then there is a pause, followed by a repeating trigger:

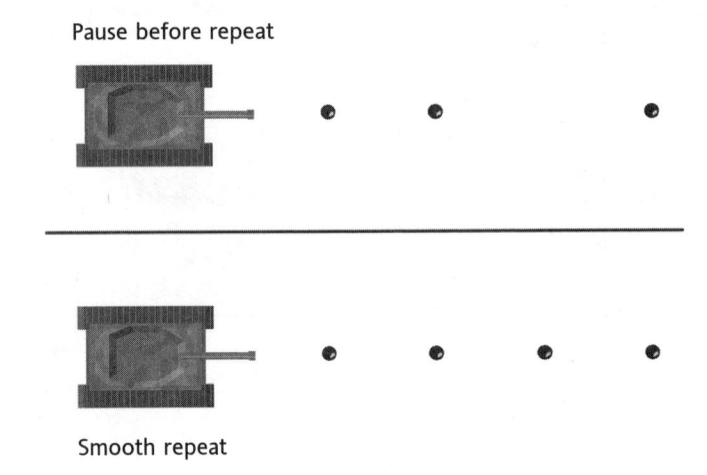

Pause before repeat

Smooth repeat

While that may not seem so bad, a lot can happen in the time it takes for the action to repeat. Also, in most game applications where you need to continuously hold down a key for a persistent effect, it really helps if the action happens smoothly.

Unfortunately, the limitations of the `keyPress` event handler don't finish there. As with typing, you can only have one character being produced at a time. If you hold down two keys, the one that registers second blocks the first, and that command is never received. In the last chapter we looked at the beginning of a tank game where you had to use two controls simultaneously since you had to control the tread independently. This sort of thing would not be possible with the `keyPress` event Handler.

The last major restriction is that unlike the mouse button, using the `on(keyPress)` method you can't detect the release of a key. In games where you need persistent actions, you need to detect when the action stops. For something like a game using a slingshot, if you wanted to have the user hold down a key and let it build up power until the player lets go, you would have to use another solution since there is no easy, accurate way of detecting when the key is released, telling the game to let the slingshot go.

# Event Handling | 4

Let's look at another version of the tank game where it can only move side to side and rotate its turret. In this one, the controls for the tank are the left and right arrow keys to move side to side and the up and down arrows to control the rotation of the turret.

Open up the `tankBlank.fla` file. Inside the tank movie clip there is another movie clip called turret. Also, on a layer beneath the tank and turret, is a very small control button with no hit area. We don't want the mouse to be able to turn into a hand, since all of the controls will be keyboard-based. Within the ActionScript of this button, we'll need to add a total of four `on` statements, one for each of the keys that needs to be listened for. Let's start with the left and right motion of the tank.

Inside the `on` event handler, we need to type `keyPress` as the event and specify the key we want to use. Unlike anywhere else in Flash 5, the `keyPress` event does not use key codes. Instead you put the key you want to use inside quotes. If you are using a special key (any key that is not a number or a symbol), you put the name of the key inside less than, greater than symbols (<>) and also inside the quotes.

When the key is pressed, we are going to want to move the tank, so we just need to add or subtract an amount from its current x position. Like we did in the last chapter you can do that using the addition or subtraction assignment operators (+=, -=_):

```
on (keyPress "<Left>") {
    _x -= 3;
}
on (keyPress "<Right>") {
    _x += 3;
}
```

# Flash Games Studio

If you test here, the tank will move left and right as expected, but you'll see the slight delay after the first hit of the key. In a moment we will look at some very smooth ways of dealing with continuous user input, and removing that annoying delay.

First though, let's add the turret control by inserting two more `on(keyPress)` event handlers. This time they'll be affecting the `_rotation` property of the turret movie clip, so we need to add the appropriate path data:

```
on (keyPress "<Left>") {
    _x -= 3;
}
on (keyPress "<Right>") {
    _x += 3;
}
on (keyPress "<Up>") {
    turret._rotation -= 3;
}
on (keyPress "<Down>") {
    turret._rotation += 3;
}
```

Now when you test it, both the sliding and the turret rotation are functional. The problem is that they won't work at the same time. If you try to spin the turret while also moving the tank, even if you keep holding down the move key, the tank will stop and the turret will rotate.

Even with these limitations though, buttons are still very useful tools. Instead of using them for arcade style controls, they are very good for toggling. If you need to press a key to change a status, such as a selected weapon, a button will be by far the best solution. The same holds true for any not immediately repetitive task, like opening a door, casting a one time spell, or moving in a tile-based game where you can use the pause to allow for precise movement and then the fast repetition for longer movements.

Let's continue on with the movie clip's event handlers to see what else is available.

## onClipEvents for User Input

Movie clips have a certain amount of interactivity to them, but they have other purposes too. As we saw in the last chapter you can adjust a movie clip's position and properties with or without interactivity. Since we've already talked about the `onClipEvent` in general terms, let's now focus on its interactive aspects.

As we touched on before, there are five events that have to do with interactivity: `mouseDown`, `mouseUp`, `mouseMove`, `keyDown`, and `keyUp`. These are fairly similar to some of the events from buttons, but there are some major differences.

As far as the mouse goes, interaction was always in relation to a hit state. This isn't the case with movie clips. `mouseDown` and `mouseUp` are triggered simply by the press and release of the mouse button, regardless of any other condition. This is a good way of tying a major control to the mouse button for when you are using the mouse position for other controls. This way, no matter where you move the mouse, pressing the button will evoke a reaction.

# Event Handling 4

`mouseMove` can be a useful event for mouse-based games. This event runs an action whenever the mouse is moving, independent of frame rate or any other consideration. This means that it could conceivably run several times during a single frame. It can be useful for keeping something aligned with the mouse without using drag operations. Also, if you have an object that moves towards your mouse, you could set a variable with the mouse position so that the mouse position does not have to be accessed every frame as the object moves.

The key-based events, `keyDown` and `keyUp` work much like the `mouseUp` and `mouseDown` events. The code is executed when any key is pressed or released. Unlike the `keyPress`, you aren't able to specify a particular key. By using the key properties though, as we'll discuss next, you can look up which key was last used.

So, we've looked at all the major event handlers for the keyboard and mouse. They are useful, certainly, but yet they're still not delivering in terms of genuinely sensitive game controls. The best way we can keep the controls on our side is to build our own. We won't be completely starting from scratch – far from it – as there are many properties we can check with a bit of help from an `if` statement.

As a prelude to writing our own event handling routines, let's take a quick look at what properties we can get our hands on.

## Input Properties and Methods

At any point in Flash, where you can place code, you're able to access the status of certain elements of both the keyboard and the mouse. Unlike the event handlers, which trigger an action when something occurs, these return a **value**. What you do with these values is up to you.

On the mouse, there are two properties we can access – its horizontal position and its vertical position. These properties, `xmouse` and `ymouse`, return numeric values based on the position of the cursor.

> *It's important to realize that the position of the cursor is relative to particular timelines. If you call _root._xmouse, you'll get the horizontal distance from the upper left hand corner. However, if you were to call it in reference to a movie clip, you would get the position of the mouse in terms of the registration mark of the movie clip.*

What about keys? Well, we can access the state of any key to see whether it's up or down, or even to see what the last key pressed was. Both of these commands can deal with keys as ASCII codes or virtual key codes, rather than as letters or symbols. It's probably easiest to use the key codes rather than the ASCII values as a list of all of the key codes is supplied for you in Appendix B of the **ActionScript Reference Guide** that comes with Flash. If you want to see if the A key is down, you would need to check the value returned by `Key.isDown(65)`. Likewise, `Key.getCode()` will return the code of the last pressed key.

# 4 Flash Games Studio

These sorts of properties will be very useful to us if we want to create our own event handling routines. So, now that we know all of the tools at our disposal for dealing with interaction, let's build our own. The next section will cover making your own customized checks for user input as well as checking for collision (and then dealing with it), and showing you how to turn any available information into a tool for checking the status of a game.

## Event Handlers Applied

In this section we'll build some controls that will function very smoothly for continuous input. Also, we'll look some of the other major events of a game, such as collision detection and the uses of a timer. We'll also take a closer look at using those properties as checks for a game. Since Flash is a tool that wasn't geared especially for games but certainly does allow them, we'll spend a fair amount of our time here building our own checks using simple conditions.

The nice thing about event handlers is that they trigger on their own when the appropriate event occurs. However, this time it's us who needs to do the checking. The way to simulate constant checking is to check the condition extremely frequently. And what did we find was the most frequently run routine? Yes, it's `onClipEvent (enterFrame)`. Inside that, we can place all of the conditions that need to be checked for any of our customized events.

### Controls with enterFrame/if

Let's look again at the tank example where we moved the tank from side to side. You can either continue on with the tankBlank.fla file you just worked on, or use `file tankButton`.fla, which contains the same code.

In order to move smoothly without a typing-style pause, we need to build a script that constantly checks the state of the keys. It will check to see if the right or left arrow keys are pressed and, if so, it will move the tank in the appropriate direction. This eclipses the need to run that troublesome `onKeyPress` command which so hampers us with the keyboard delay. We will also liberate the turret controls with the same technique.

As I mentioned when we started the `onClipEvent` section, one of the organizational benefits of this event handler is the ability to put the code directly on the object, making it easier to find and alter or debug later on. Let's get straight into the code:

1. First, return to the button within the tank movie clip and remove all of the script from its Actions panel. We won't be needing that again!

2. On the main timeline, select the tank. In its Actions panel, add the `enterFrame` event. As we have established, this is the best event to use if we want to constantly run checks.

   ```
   onClipEvent (enterFrame) {
   }
   ```

# Event Handling 4

3. Inside the `if` statement we create a check for the left and right cursor key positions. To find the status we'll be accessing the `key` object and using the `isDown` method. Note that we have to refer to these keys we will use `Key.LEFT` and `Key.RIGHT` within the parentheses, whereas for most keys you would just type their code.

4. If the check finds that the key is indeed being pressed, it will return `true`, causing the script inside the `if` to execute. So, we need to create that script. For the movement commands, to slide the tank to the right and left, we need to adjust the x position by adding or subtracting some amount from the current position. The whole thing so far should look like this:

   ```
   onClipEvent (enterFrame) {
       if (Key.isDown(Key.LEFT)) {
           _x -= 3;
       }
       if (Key.isDown(Key.RIGHT)) {
           _x += 3;
       }
   }
   ```

   If you try the file now, you'll see the tank progress smoothly from right to left without pausing between changing keys. Result! Also – if you press any other key while pressing the arrow keys, you'll notice this does not interfere with the operation of the tank. Our event handler doesn't care about what other keys are doing, because it's not listening to them.

5. Let's now add the last piece of functionality – the turret controls. These will be controlled by using the up and down arrow keys. The turret is a child movie clip of the tank, with the instance name turret. Right under the code for the movement, we can add similar code that alters the rotation of the turret movie clip by adding or subtracting a certain amount:

   ```
   onClipEvent (enterFrame) {
       if (Key.isDown(Key.LEFT)) {
           _x -= 3;
       }
       if (Key.isDown(Key.RIGHT)) {
           _x += 3;
       }
       if (Key.isDown(Key.UP)) {
           turret._rotation -= 3;
       }
       if (Key.isDown(Key.DOWN)) {
           turret._rotation += 3;
       }
   }
   ```

# Flash Games Studio

Just like we added the code to tank, the turret code could have been placed directly on turret. In fact the code could be placed on any movie clip in the Flash file. The main reason for placing it on the tank instead of the turret was to keep all of the code in one place for ease of organization:

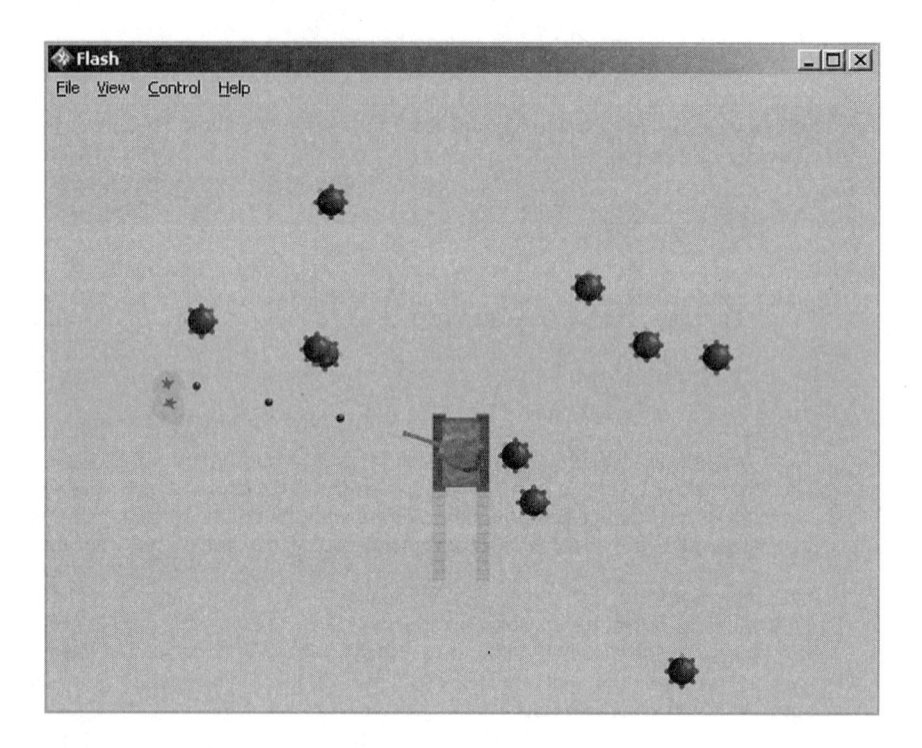

## Custom Controls

Now that we've created a basic set of controls using the key state, let's look at a more robust control mechanism. In the last chapter when we were talking about nested movie clips, we looked at a tank that could turn, and move forwards and backwards while turning and firing the cannon. We're going to start with those controls and then build a menu that'll let the user change the controls to whatever they like. In the end it's a good idea to give the user the final say-so as to what controls are intuitive and comfortable to them, instead of enforcing our own ideas.

The tank example we're going to look at has seven controls, with up to four of them being used at one time. When the controls get that complex it becomes even more important to let users choose their own keys. To get started, open up the `tankFull.fla` file. This is just a copy of the game that we looked at in the previous chapter with hard-wired controls. Our final result will be like `tankCustomKey.fla`.

# Event Handling 4

Though we don't need to know how the controls work in detail to set up custom controls, let's just quickly run through the commands on the tank movie itself to familiarize ourselves with the file. Check out the Actions panel for the tank movie clip:

```
onClipEvent (load) {
    this.swapDepths(100000);
    function move (distance) {
        angle = (_rotation/360)*2*Math.PI;
        _x += distance*Math.sin(angle);
        _y += -distance*Math.cos(angle);
    }
}
```

The first block of code is a `load` statement containing two parts. The first part changes the depth property of the movie up to 100000. This puts it "closer" to the viewer than anything else. When we get to looking at **spawned** objects (those new movie clip instances created by the movie itself) we'll talk about depth in detail but for now it's enough to know that there are going to be a lot of objects placed on the stage and, by moving the tank to a higher depth, it will always appear to be on top of them.

The second part of the `load` statement is a function definition. As we discussed earlier, functions only need to be introduced once to become available. This function takes a distance that needs to be traveled, looks at the direction the tank is pointing in and breaks the distance into its x and y components, and then moves the tank accordingly. This is done using trigonometry through the `Math` object. When they are ready, our controls will call this function and feed it the amount that needs to be traveled.

After initializing these few things, we move on to the more persistent `enterFrame` event of the `onClipEvent`. This is where the checks for the controls actually happen. Let's break this statement into three parts – the movement controls, the tread, and the firing controls.

## Movement

```
onClipEvent (enterFrame) {
if ((Key.isDown(70) || Key.isDown(82)) && (Key.isDown(74) ||
➥ Key.isDown(85))) {
    if (Key.isDown(82) && Key.isDown(85)) {
        move(1);
    } else if (Key.isDown(70) && Key.isDown(74)) {
        move(-1);
    } else if (Key.isDown(70) && Key.isDown(85)) {
        _rotation -= 2;
    } else if (Key.isDown(82) && Key.isDown(74)) {
        _rotation += 2;
    }
    treadcheck++;
}
    if (Key.isDown(69)) {
    turret._rotation -= 3;
    }
```

*continues overleaf*

```
            if (Key.isDown(73)) {
                    turret._rotation += 3;
            }
    }
```

The movement controls are not too different from those we used for the simple tank example. The main difference here is that we need to have something happening with each of the treads to be able to move. Also, we need to make sure that only one of the direction controls is being used for each of the treads.

To do this, I wrote a condition that checks to see if one key from each side is pressed, if not, nothing will happen. This code would allow for more than one key from each side being pressed, but instead of making a longer condition to block that occurrence from doing anything, I've just stacked the conditions to make it favor forward movement. That way if you mash all of the keys you move in a straight line, but it takes using the keys correctly to turn.

Once we know that enough keys are being pressed, (by checking the key status of the control keys), we can then just check for the four possibilities of how the controls are being used. If both treads are moving in the same direction, then depending on which direction that is, the tank will move forwards or backwards. If the treads are going in the opposite direction, then the tank will pivot. The direction of the turn is dependent on which tread is going forwards and which is going backwards.

Inside these conditions, the script for moving or rotating the tank is placed. Movement is achieved by calling the move function we defined in the initial load event, and rotation comes from modifying the _rotation property of the tank movie clip. After all of the movement or rotation has been done, a variable gets incremented confirming that the tank has moved.

The last two movement commands, which control the turret, are just the same as the simple tank example, just with different keys.

### The Tread

Next come the tread marks that get left in the sand. This is a case of something being duplicated and placed on the stage that needs to be beneath the tank. It just wouldn't do to have those tread marks on top! The condition checks to see in the tank has moved at least five times since the last time it put down treads. If it hasn't it just passes by the script and nothing happens. We'll touch on this script again later in the chapter:

```
            onClipEvent (enterFrame) {
                if ((Key.isDown(70) || Key.isDown(82)) && (Key.isDown(74) ||
                ➥ Key.isDown(85))) {
                if (Key.isDown(82) && Key.isDown(85)) {
                        move(1);
                } else if (Key.isDown(70) && Key.isDown(74)) {
                        move(-1);
                } else if (Key.isDown(70) && Key.isDown(85)) {
                        _rotation -= 2;
                } else if (Key.isDown(82) && Key.isDown(74)) {
```

# Event Handling

```
                    _rotation += 2;
            }
            treadcheck++;
        }
        if (Key.isDown(69)) {
            turret._rotation -= 3;
        }
        if (Key.isDown(73)) {
            turret._rotation += 3;
        }
        if (treadcheck>5) {
        treadcount++;
        duplicateMovieClip (_root.tread, "tread"+treadcount, (tread
        ➥ count%100)+1000);
        treadcheck = 0;
        }
    }
```

## Firing

The last segment of the controls deals with firing – another case where something is being duplicated. Unlike our other controls where all that mattered was that the key was down, the firing button needs one more constraint. This movie is optimally running at 25 frames per second. That means that at the best of times it could check 25 times per second if the key is pressed. At that rate it's pretty hard not to fire off at least two shots whenever you hit the key. To counteract this, we'll make a timer, which again we'll be going into more depth about later on. This script should mean that you'll only be able to fire another shot when the timer reaches zero:

```
        onClipEvent (enterFrame) {
            if ((Key.isDown(70) || Key.isDown(82)) && (Key.isDown(74) ||
            ➥ Key.isDown(85))) {
            if (Key.isDown(82) && Key.isDown(85)) {
                    move(1);
            } else if (Key.isDown(70) && Key.isDown(74)) {
                    move(-1);
            } else if (Key.isDown(70) && Key.isDown(85)) {
                    _rotation -= 2;
            } else if (Key.isDown(82) && Key.isDown(74)) {
                    _rotation += 2;
            }
            treadcheck++;
            }
        if (Key.isDown(69)) {
            turret._rotation -= 3;
            }
        if (Key.isDown(73)) {
            turret._rotation += 3;
            }
```

*continues overleaf*

# Flash Games Studio

```
    if (treadcheck>5) {
    treadcount++;
    duplicateMovieClip (_root.tread, "tread"+treadcount,
➥ (treadcount%100)+1000);
        treadcheck = 0;
    }
    if (Key.isDown(Key.SPACE) && shotTimer<=0) {
        shotCount++;
        duplicateMovieClip (_parent.shot, "shot"+shotCount,
        ➥ (shotCount%100)+1100);
        shotTimer = 5;
    }
    shotTimer--;
}
```

## Customizing Keys

Now that we know what the code does, let's make it so the user can pick which keys to use.

1. To start, drag the first (and only) frame of the main timeline over to frame two, leaving us with a nice empty frame – make sure you do it to both layers! Add a stop action to the second frame so that the game doesn't continuously loop between the two frames.

2. In frame one of layer one, make a dynamic textfield and name it display. None of the options (Border/Bg, HTML, Selectable) should be checked. This text box will display the key that has been assigned to a control. Make sure it's big enough to accept full words as well as single letters – we want to be able to dsplay things like "spacebar" and "shift", and the longest key name will be "right arrow":

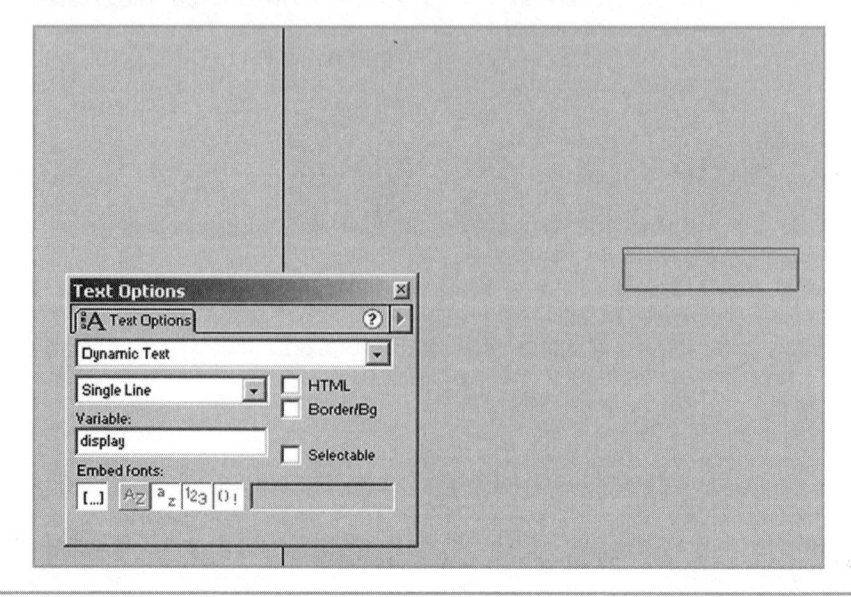

# Event Handling    4

3.  Now select your text field and convert it into a movie clip. I've called mine the key configurator. Inside the new movie clip, add a stop action to frame one, and add a blank keyframe at frame two. In frame two draw a shape the same size as the border of the text field, and add some visual cue to suggest that the space is waiting for the user to enter a key. For mine, I've chosen a thickly outlined box:

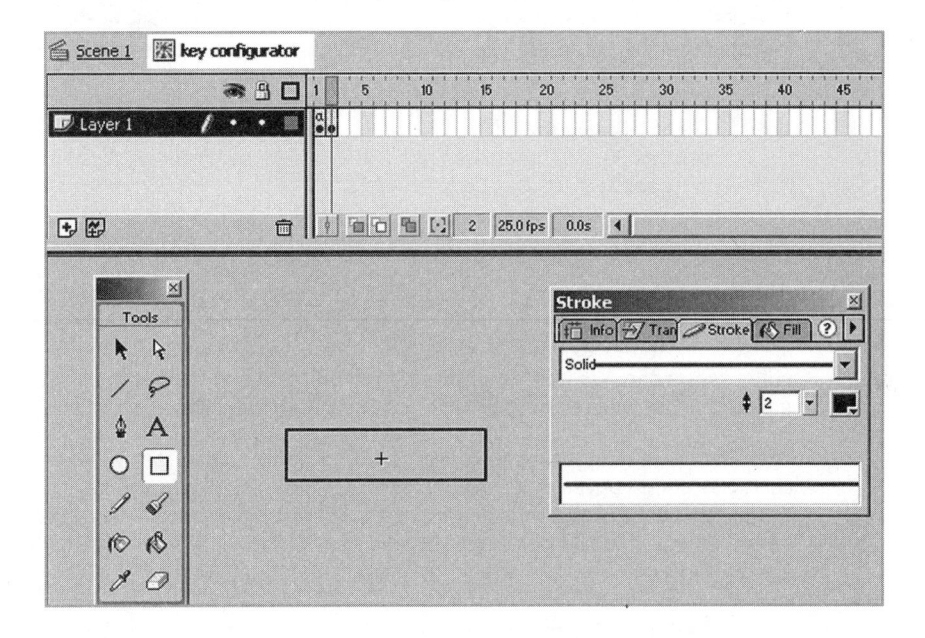

Since we haven't carried the text field over to frame two of key configurator, the yellow shape tells the user that something is still going on – that the interface element hasn't simply disappeared. I chose not to have the text field in frame two since I wanted it to look like the default control was wiped out. (In reality, the variable is still set: if the player cancels out of modifying the key, it will return to frame one, showing the previous setting).

4.  When the new movie clip is in its second frame, it needs to wait for the next key to be pressed. To do that, we can use an onClipEvent (keyDown). However, we can't place the code for this action on the outside of the key configurator movie clip because we need it to run only when it is in the second frame. That means making a new movie in frame two and adding the code onto that movie clip. The advantage of creating our yellow box then, is that we can convert it into a movie clip and use that! I've called it key editor.

5.  Select key editor and open the Actions menu. Once the user has pressed a key, we need to record it, have it displayed in the text box and finally go back to frame 1, taking us out of the control editing process:

```
onClipEvent (keyDown) {
}
```

6. Since we are going to do a fair bit with the captured key code, let's immediately assign it to a variable – `tempKey`. The letter and number keys are easier to deal with, as their characters can be accessed by scripting, so let's deal with them first.

   In order for us to determine what type of key is captured we can look at the key code. Number keys are sequentially coded 48 to 58, and letter keys are alphabetically coded from 65 to 90. None of the special keys or punctuation keys falls in the gap between the number ranges, so we can set up a check that looks to see if the key code is between 47 and 91:

   ```
   onClipEvent (keyDown) {
       tempKey = Key.getCode();
       if (tempKey>47 && tempKey<91) {
       }
   }
   ```

7. If the key falls in this range, we just need to display the character by converting the key code back to its letter or number character and setting `display` equal to it. There are two big things to keep in mind here. First, we are writing this code in the key editor movie clip. We want to display it in the display text field of the key configurator movie clip. So, we are going to have to refer out of the clip we are in using _parent.

   The second warning is that to convert a key code to a character, we'll use the inbuilt character code converter, `String.fromCharCode`. Character and key codes are not the same. Luckily for letters and numbers, there is an overlap. Any letter key is the same as the upper case character key, and the number key codes and character codes are the same:

   ```
   onClipEvent (keyDown) {
       tempKey = Key.getCode();
       if (tempKey>47 && tempKey<91) {
               _parent.display = String.fromCharCode(tempKey);
       }
   }
   ```

8. Since we have a lot more than one control to customize, it's better not to specify a particular variable inside the movie clip. Instead, we'll create a function on the outer movie clip that will set the variable. Let's plan to call it `setKey`. With that function we just need to specify what the key code is. After that, we just need to send the movie clip back to frame one since we're done with the key assignment.

   For both the function call and the `goto` line, we still need to refer to the _parent movie clip:

   ```
   onClipEvent (keyDown) {
       tempKey = Key.getCode();
       if (tempKey>47 && tempKey<91) {
               _parent.display = String.fromCharCode(tempKey);
                       _parent.setkey(tempKey);
                       _parent.gotoAndStop(1);
       }
   }
   ```

# Event Handling 4

9. If the key isn't a letter or a number, we need to come up with a way of seeing if it is an "approved" key (meaning that we have a name for it) and finding a way of accessing the name. Since the data we have is a number, it would seem to be a good place to use an array. An array is an object containing many entries that are organized by an index number. By inserting these entries at the index that matches their key code, we'll have an easy way of looking up a name.

   Arrays only need to be defined once, so we should change gears and add an `onClipEvent(load)` statement to hold our array. Add the clip event right before the `keyDown` event on the `key editor` movie clip. Inside it, we need to define the array that we'll call `keys`, and then assign the entries.

   The entries are just the text names of the special keys. I've only listed the first four here to save a bit of space, but there are 31 for your perusal in the supplied FLA file:

   ```
   onClipEvent (load) {
        keys = new Array();
        keys[8] = "backspace";
        keys[9] = "tab";
        keys[12] = "clear";
        keys[13] = "enter";
   }
   onClipEvent (keyDown) {
        tempKey = Key.getCode();
        if (tempKey>47 && tempKey<91) {
             _parent.display = String.fromCharCode(tempKey);
             _parent.setkey(tempKey);
             _parent.gotoAndStop(1);
        }
   }
   ```

10. Now that we have the array, we need to check to see if our key code falls in that list. By checking to see if the array returns a value, we can determine whether we have a name for the key code and can proceed. If both checks fail then it's an unrecognized key for our purposes, and the `keyDown` check continues. The function keys, for example, have key codes, but I haven't included them in the array. If a player picks one of these keys, then the movie simply won't react.

    We have to meddle a little more with the `keyDown` event we just created to be able to make this check:

    ```
    onClipEvent (keyDown) {
         tempKey = Key.getCode();
         if (tempKey>47 && tempKey<91) {
              _parent.display = String.fromCharCode(tempKey);
              _parent.setkey(tempKey);
              _parent.gotoAndStop(1);
         } else if (keys[tempKey] != "") {
         }
    }
    ```

# Flash Games Studio

The script to be run if the key is found in the array is very similar to the one for the regular keys. The only difference is that the display variable needs to generate the name from the array.

```
onClipEvent (keyDown) {
    tempKey = Key.getCode();
    if (tempKey>47 && tempKey<91) {
        _parent.display = String.fromCharCode(tempKey);
        _parent.setkey(tempKey);
        _parent.gotoAndStop(1);
    } else if (keys[tempKey] != "") {
        _parent.display = keys[tempKey];
        _parent.setkey(tempKey);
        _parent.gotoAndStop(1);
    }
}
```

11. The last element to put on this movie clip is a check to see if the user has clicked the mouse while in the key edit mode. If so, we need to send the movie clip back to frame one to cancel the key entry. This can be done by using a `mouseDown` event in an `onClipEvent`.

    Your final code for this movie clip should look like the following (with a few more entries in the array though!)

```
onClipEvent (load) {
    keys = new Array();
    keys[8] = "backspace";
    keys[9] = "tab";
    keys[12] = "clear";
}
onClipEvent (mouseDown) {
    _parent.gotoAndStop (1);
}
onClipEvent (keyDown) {
    tempKey = Key.getCode();
    if (tempKey>47 && tempKey<91) {
        _parent.display = String.fromCharCode(tempKey);
        _parent.setkey(tempKey);
        _parent.gotoAndStop(1);
    } else if (keys[tempKey] != "") {
        _parent.display = keys[tempKey];
        _parent.setkey(tempKey);
        _parent.gotoAndStop(1);
    }
}
```

12. There are two more elements that need to be added: the code on the outer movie clip, and a button that will actually get us to frame two.

# Event Handling 4

Back in frame one of the movie clip, where the display text field is, let's create a button on a fresh layer. Leave the up, over and down states blank, and draw a box in the hit state. Then, in the button's Object Actions window, add the command:

```
on(release) {
nextFrame();
}
```

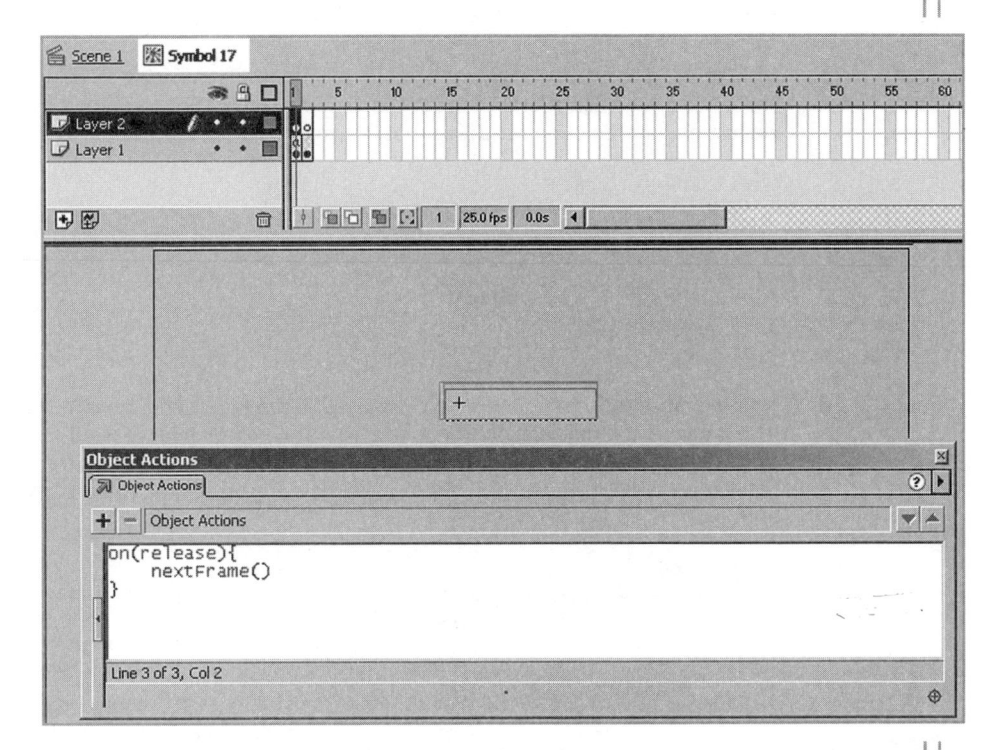

13. Now go out to the main timeline, where we'll add the last code for the key configurator. Select the movie clip and go to its Actions panel. There are a few things we need to do here. We need to define the function that will set a variable with the key code, and we also need to choose a default key setting, in case the user wants to ignore all our hard work and **not** choose keys.

   To create our function, we just need to supply a name and any arguments that the function needs to take. When we wrote the function call earlier, we called it setKey, and planned for one argument, which was the value of my chosen key. Since this code is going on a movie clip, it must be inside a clipEvent so Flash knows when to run the code. As always, functions are best put in load statements:

```
onClipEvent (load) {
    function setKey (key) {
    }
}
```

## Flash Games Studio

14. Let's make this movie clip control the firing key. To do that, we just need to set a variable up one level on the root to the key code. For the firing key, I've chosen the name fire:

```
onClipEvent (load) {
    function setKey (key) {
         _parent.fire = key;
    }
}
```

15. Now to set the default value, we need to set the display variable to show the correct character or key name, and then set the variable in the root to the right value. Since we just made a function for doing that, we might as well use it:

```
onClipEvent (load) {
    function setKey (key) {
         _parent.fire = key;
    }
    display = "spacebar";
    setKey(32);
}
```

16. Now we must place a total of seven instances of the key configurator movie clip in the first frame of the main stage, one for each of the commands we need for the tank. If the previous piece of code was in the Actions window for the fire button, the following will be in the Actions window for the **Counter clockwise turret rotation** button:

```
onClipEvent (load) {
    function setKey (key) {
         _parent.turrCCW = key;
    }
    display = "E";
    setKey(69);
}
```

...and so on for each of the buttons. As you can see, we have taken care of the function variable ("turrCCW"), the display ("E") and the setKey code ("69" – the code for E). Here is a list of the function variables I chose as the default settings:

| Variable | Control | Key | Code |
|---|---|---|---|
| turrCCW | Counter clockwise turret rotation | E | 69 |
| turrCW | Clockwise turret rotation | I | 73 |
| treadLF | Left tread forward | R | 82 |
| treadLB | Left tread backward | F | 70 |
| treadRF | Right tread forward | U | 85 |
| treadRB | Right tread backward | J | 74 |
| fire | Firing | Space | 32 |

# Event Handling

If you test the movie now, you should be able to change your character to any of the keys that we are checking for. As you'll see below, I've spruced mine up a bit with a title and captions for each box in an appropriately militaristic font, and – for good measure – an instance of the tank:

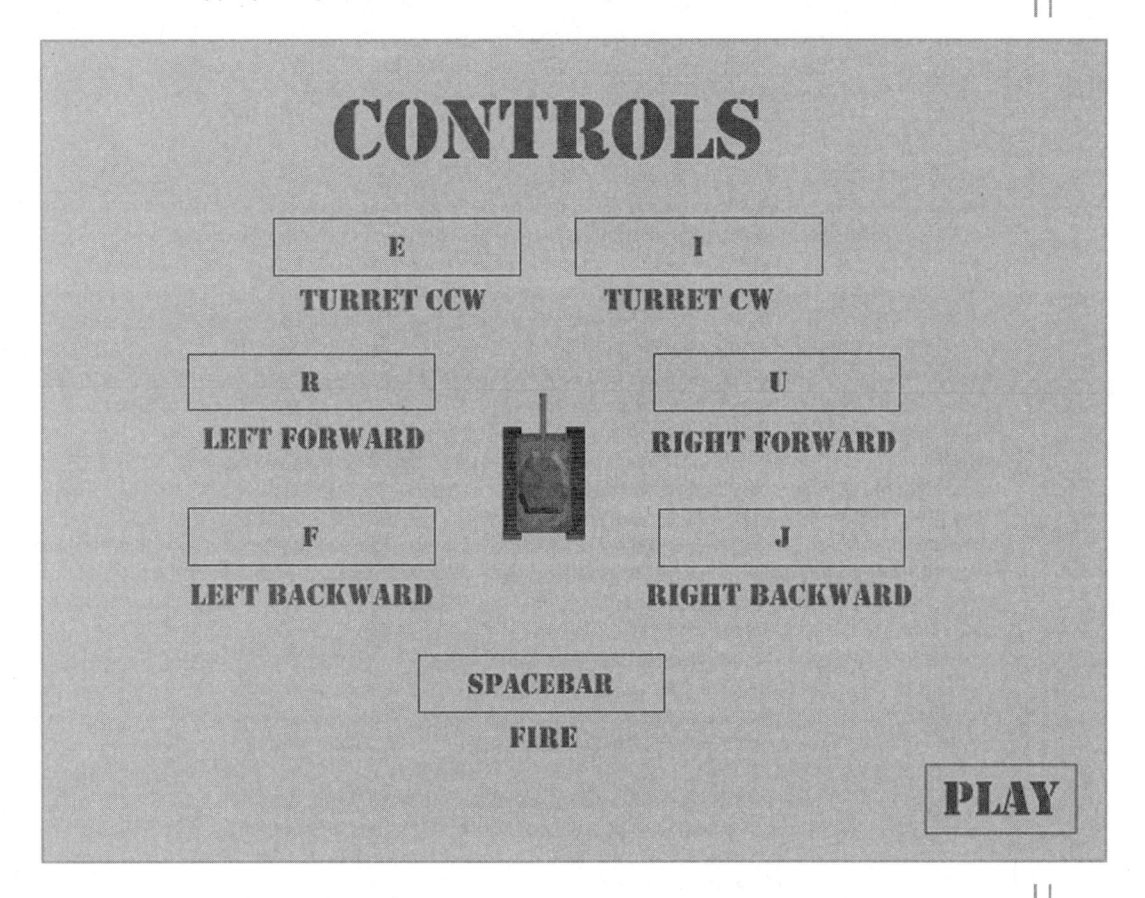

I've also created a new button symbol, called play button, which includes the code:

```
on(release) {
nextFrame();
     }
```

But we're not ready to press it yet – the game doesn't deal with the variables that we've assigned. Let's go back to frame two on the main timeline and take another look at the tank's code. All of those places that have key values statically assigned need to have the numbers replaced by the variable names above. Rather than saying "if the spacebar is pressed, start firing", the code is now saying "if the allotted firing key is pressed, start firing"

## Flash Games Studio

In that way the code can use the custom key codes in its checks. The final code should look like this:

```
onClipEvent (load) {
    this.swapDepths(100000);
    function move (distance) {
    angle = (_rotation/360)*2*Math.PI;
    _x += distance*Math.sin(angle);
    _y += -distance*Math.cos(angle);
    }
}
onClipEvent (enterFrame) {
    if ((Key.isDown(_root.treadLB) || Key.isDown(_root.treadLF))
➥ && (Key.isDown(_root.treadRB) || Key.isDown(_root.treadRF))) {
        if (Key.isDown(_root.treadLF) && Key.isDown(_root.treadRF)) {
            move(1);
            } else if (Key.isDown(_root.treadLB) &&
➥ Key.isDown(_root.treadRB)) {
            move(-1);
            } else if (Key.isDown(_root.treadLB) &&
➥ Key.isDown(_root.treadRF)) {
            _rotation -= 2;
            } else if (Key.isDown(_root.treadLF) &&
➥ Key.isDown(_root.treadRB)) {
            _rotation += 2;
            }
            treadcheck++;
    }
    if (Key.isDown(_root.turrCCW)) {
            turret._rotation -= 3;
    }
    if (Key.isDown(_root.turrCW)) {
            turret._rotation += 3;
    }
    if (treadcheck>5) {
            treadcount++;
            duplicateMovieClip (_root.tread, "tread"+treadcount,
➥ (treadcount%100)+1000);
            treadcheck = 0;
    }
    if (Key.isDown(_root.fire) && shotTimer<=0) {
            shotCount++;
            duplicateMovieClip (_parent.shot, "shot"+shotCount,
➥ (shotCount%100)+1100);
            shotTimer = 5;
    }
    shotTimer--;
}
```

# Event Handling | 4

```
onClipEvent (load) {
    this.swapDepths(100000);
    function move (distance) {
        angle = (_rotation/360)*2*Math.PI;
        _x += distance*Math.sin(angle);
        _y += -distance*Math.cos(angle);
    }
}
onClipEvent (enterFrame) {
    if ((Key.isDown(_root.treadLB) || Key.isDown(_root.treadLF)) && (Key.isDown(_root.
        if (Key.isDown(_root.treadLF) && Key.isDown(_root.treadRF)) {
            move(1);
        } else if (Key.isDown(_root.treadLB) && Key.isDown(_root.treadRB)) {
            move(-1);
        } else if (Key.isDown(_root.treadLB) && Key.isDown(_root.treadRF)) {
            _rotation -= 2;
        } else if (Key.isDown(_root.treadLF) && Key.isDown(_root.treadRB)) {
            _rotation += 2;
        }
        treadcheck++;
    }
    if (Key.isDown(_root.turrCCW)) {
        turret._rotation -= 3;
    }
    if (Key.isDown(_root.turrCW)) {
        turret._rotation += 3;
    }
    if (treadcheck>5) {
        treadcount++;
        duplicateMovieClip (_root.tread, "tread"+treadcount, (treadcount%100)+1000);
        treadcheck = 0;
    }
    if (Key.isDown(_root.fire) && shotTimer<=0) {
        shotCount++;
        duplicateMovieClip (_parent.shot, "shot"+shotCount, (shotCount%100)+1100);
```

## Spawning and Initialization

Now, there were a number of items from the tank's code I said we would get to later. To implement the firing and the mines, we will need to look at **spawning** and **initialization**, together with a **timer** to count down the life of the shot, and **collision detection** to make it explode. Let's get to it!

Spawning is when a new object is added in the course of a game. This can be any object, from the main character, to an enemy or a bullet. Here we'll look at the code in the `tankCustomKey.fla` file, checking out the process for bringing a shot and a mine into our game.

## Mines

For our tank game, the "enemies" will be small land mines that can be run over or shot. Like arcade games, a fixed number of mines can be generated at the beginning of the level, and the level will end when all of these enemies have been dispatched – or when the tank is destroyed.

# Flash Games Studio

Logically enough, the number of enemies to be created can be based on a variable like the level number – so, the higher the level number, the greater the number of enemies. In this example, we'll be simulating a level-based environment by setting a level variable which will be used by a `for` loop (in the Frame Actions panel of frame one) to create all the mines.

A `for` loop is an **iterative** loop, meaning that it repeats the code several times. The number of times it runs is determined by the **condition** – so, in this case, it will run for the amount of times specified by the level variable. In each run of the code we can use the incremented index variable to make each pass different.

```
level = 10;
for(i=1; i<=level; i++){
}
```

The code for this loop is to duplicate the mine movie clip that is sitting off the edge of the stage. When duplicating a movie clip, you need to specify the movie that is being copied (say, mine), then the name of the copy (say, mine2, mine3, mine4), and then the **depth** that it needs to exist at.

> *Depth is the stacking order in which the movie clips are rendered. Movie clips placed on the stage are rendered at the lowest depth, but can be repositioned by using* `swapDepths`. *Similarly, a duplicated movie will be assigned a depth, but this can also change through* `swapDepths`. *The higher the depth value, the "closer" the movie clip will be to the viewer. Also, note that for each depth there can only be one movie clip. If you try to duplicate a movie to a depth that is already occupied, the movie that was already there will be destroyed.*

```
level = 10;
for(i=1; i<=level; i++){
    duplicateMovieClip(mine, "mine" + i, i);
}
```

# Event Handling 4

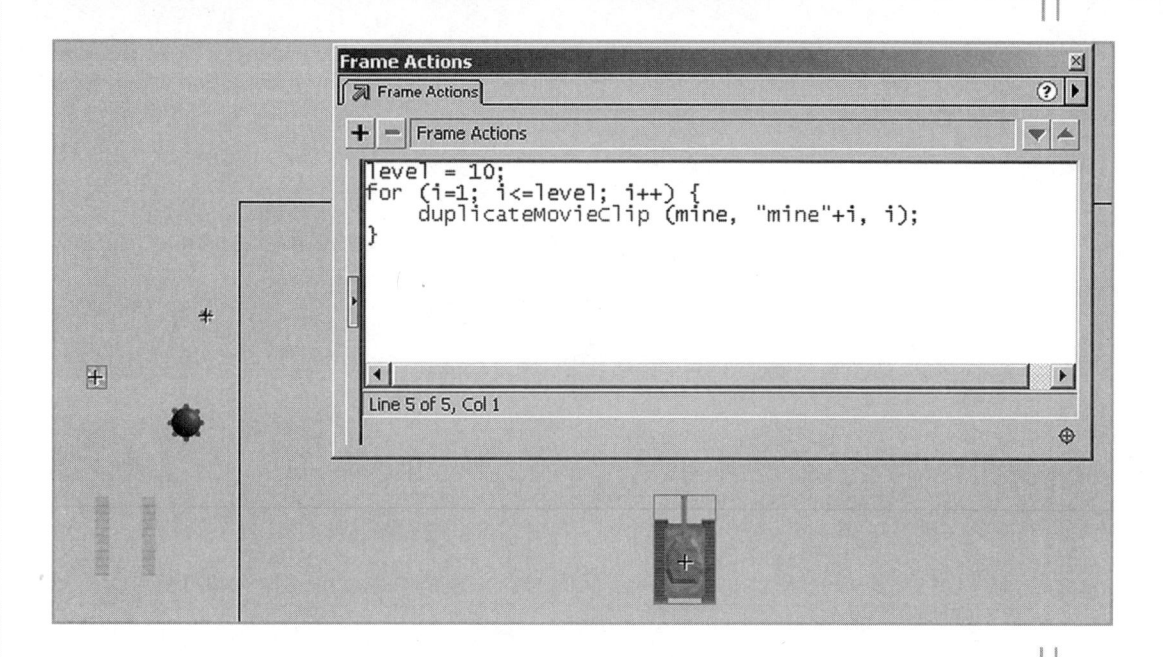

Once the mines have been duplicated, they need to be initialized. They start at frame one of the parent timeline, in the same spot as the original movie clip, which is somewhere off stage.

Initialization is easily handled by placing an `onClipEvent (load)` in the Actions window of the mine movie clip. This will position each mine at a random place on the screen.

We can specify the x and y position of the mine using the `Math.random` method, which returns a random value between 0 and 1. The range we want the mines to cover can then be used to multiply that value – in this case our range is the 550x400 pixels that go to make up the dimensions of the movie. To avoid having the mines hanging off the edge of the screen, I've taken these dimensions, chopped off 50 pixels, and then added 25 pixels onto each of the final positions, ensuring that the area where the mines can spawn in the middle of the screen:

```
onClipEvent (load) {
    if (_name != "mine") {
        _x = Math.random()*500+25;
        _y = Math.random()*350+25;
    }
}
```

As you can see, we've placed these commands inside an `if` condition that checks that the name of the movie is not equal to mine. After all, we wouldn't want our template movie out there on the screen. If it gets destroyed, we can't duplicate it any more!

# Flash Games Studio

There is another problem. What if one of the mines spawns directly under the tank? This would hardly be fair on our players! To avoid this we need to employ **collision detection**, which we will get to shortly.

## Shots

Other objects besides the main characters need to spawn. When we use the fire button, it duplicates a new shot movie clip based on the template that's sitting off the stage. The operation of this procedure is pretty similar to the mines duplication. As a refresher, here is the firing code again:

```
if (Key.isDown(_root.fire) && shotTimer<=0) {
    shotCount++;
    duplicateMovieClip (_parent.shot, "shot"+shotCount,
    ➥ (shotCount%100)+1100);
    shotTimer = 5;
}
shotTimer--;
```

Most of this code makes sure we aren't firing too many shots at once. The really important code to look at now is:

```
shotCount++;
duplicateMovieClip (_parent.shot, "shot"+shotCount,
(shotCount%100)+1100);
```

The shotCount variable is the index used for naming the duplicated shot movie clips, and is also used for determining the depth. The most noticeable difference between the duplication code for the mine and for the shot is the depth – we want them to have very different depths, to avoid crowding each other out.

It's handy to add a fixed amount to the index variable to make a depth. Another handy thing to do is to use the modulo operator.

# Event Handling 4

> *Modulo returns the remainder from a division operation. Remember the days in school before we got to long division where we could just leave it with a remainder? Who knew that would be helpful for your Flash programming needs? If you were to run 5%2 it would return 1 since 2 goes into 5 twice with one left over.*
>
> *If you know the maximum number of that object that can be on the screen at one time, then you can run the index value modulo the maximum. That way when the index exceeds the maximum, the number returned is small again. Take for instance an index at 105 and a maximum of 100. 105%100 returns 5. Even if the index should reach 1345, the returned value will be 45. The benefit of this technique is that you now have a range of 100 depths that this object could be in, and you can put your next object 101 depths above it without worrying about depth conflicts.*

As with the mines, we need to bring our spawned shot movies in from off-screen. However, this time we need more advanced positioning. We need it to come out of the cannon, and move along the appropriate trajectory – all a bit more complicated than laying mines!

Its position is going to be based on the position of the tank, but since the cannon sticks well off the tank, we have to reuse some trigonometry that takes an angle and a distance, and then returns concrete x and y distances.

The distance we need to divide is from the center of the tank to the tip of the cannon. In this case it's 44 pixels. We can set it to a variable so that if we change the tank graphics later this amount will also be easy to change.

To find the angle, we need to look at the rotation of the tank and also the rotation of the turret since it's a child movie of the tank. We take the rotation of the tank and then add to that the rotation of the turret. That composite will give us the actual angle of the cannon:

```
onClipEvent (load) {
    if (String(_name) != "shot") {
        cannonLength = 44;
        turretpoint = _parent.tank._rotation+_parent.tank.
        ➥ turret._rotation;
    }
}
```

Now that we have distance and angle, we can plug it into the trig that gives us the constituent part. By having a distance and an angle, we can imagine a right angle formed by a line going at the appropriate angle for the specified distance, and then creating the other two sides using a horizontal and vertical line:

The horizontal, which we use **sine** to figure out, is the x component and the vertical line, which we use **cosine** to find, is the y component.

Once we have the component distances, we can then place the shot at the position of the tank and finally offset it by the component amounts. This should then go in the shot movie's Actions window:

```
onClipEvent (load) {
    if (String(_name) != "shot") {
        cannonLength = 44;
        turretpoint =
_parent.tank._rotation+_parent.tank.turret._rotation;
        angle = (turretpoint/360)*2*Math.PI;
        xcomponent = cannonLength*Math.sin(angle);
        ycomponent = -cannonLength*Math.cos (angle);
        _x = xcomponent+_parent.tank._x;
        _y = ycomponent+_parent.tank._y;
    }
}
```

### Speed

The last piece of information we need to initialize is how much the bullet needs to move every frame. The component variables we just set are already in the right proportion to each other to move the bullet along the correct trajectory, but it would move it way too fast at 44 pixels per frame.

Since the proportion was what all of that trig was figuring out, it would be a shame to go through all of that again when the information is sitting right in front of us. If we take the component

# Event Handling    4

variables and divide them by the cannon length, we are down to a unit length of one pixel per frame. This is too slow for a bullet, but it is now standardized. Even if the length of the cannon should change, the fact that we are canceling out the effect of the cannon length means it will remain one pixel per frame. All we need to do is take that amount and multiply it by the actual number of pixels we want the bullet to travel per frame:

```
onClipEvent (load) {
    if (String(_name) != "shot") {
        cannonLength = 44;
        turretpoint = _parent.tank._rotation+_parent.tank.turret._rotation;
        angle = (turretpoint/360)*2*Math.PI;
        xcomponent = cannonLength*Math.sin(angle);
        ycomponent = -cannonLength*Math.cos(angle);
        _x = xcomponent+_parent.tank._x;
        _y = ycomponent+_parent.tank._y;
        xmove = (xcomponent/cannonLength)*10;
        ymove = (ycomponent/cannonLength)*10;
    }
}
```

Now that we have spawned everything that we need to spawn, we need to maintain these things and make sure they behave themselves. For the mine, this means **collision detection**, and for the bullet it means both collision detection and **a timer**.

## Collision Detection

Flash 5 has a new feature called `hitTest`. It detects when a movie clip hits either a particular point in, or the bounding box of, another movie clip. It's a feature that saves a huge amount of fuss when it comes to detecting the collision of irregular shaped objects. We'll be looking at how `hitTest` can help us begin our game properly, and how other methods of collision detection can help us when we're under way.

Basically, collision detection needs to check if the position of a movie clip is acceptable, and if not it will trigger a reaction. So, if we detect that the tank has run into a land mine, we need to have it destroyed in a spectacular fashion. Were this a game where the mines were fuel cans, and the tank was trying to pick them up rather than avoid them, we would need to detect if the tank had run into a fuel can, and bump up the fuel total if so. The principle is the same: detection > reaction:

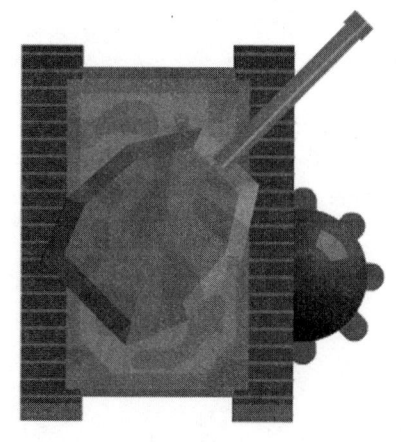

## Collision Detection for Placing Mines

Collision detection doesn't always have to be used in a black-or-white fashion. For instance, it would be very bad for our game to start with a mine under the tank. To prevent this we can use one of the aspects of the `hitTest` method to determine whether the bounding boxes for the two movie clips touch:

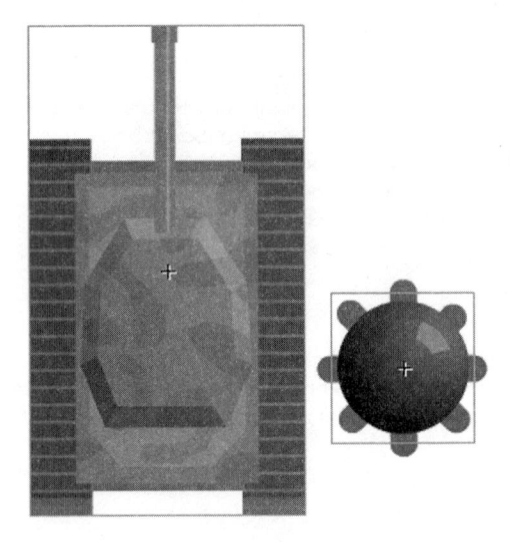

Here is how the code in the mine's Actions window last looked when we were talking about its initialization:

```
onClipEvent (load) {
    if (_name != "mine") {
        _x = Math.random()*500+25;
        _y = Math.random()*350+25;
    }
}
```

After the mine has been placed, we just need to check to see if its bounding box touches the tank's. If so, then Flash needs to try placing the mine again and re-checking. This sort of continual check until an acceptable outcome is reached is best done with a `while` loop. A `while` loop continues until its condition is satisfied:

# Event Handling 4

```
onClipEvent (load) {
    if (_name != "mine") {
        _x = Math.random()*500+25;
        _y = Math.random()*350+25;
        while (hitTest(_parent.tank)) {
            _x = Math.random()*500+25;
            _y = Math.random()*350+25;
        }
    }
}
```

## Collision Detection During Play

After the mines are successfully placed, the tank can start moving, and the game is on – and this time the mines won't be getting out of the way! Although we could use the `hitTest` method again, I thought it would be a good idea to look at a more manual way of checking. We are going to check the distance from the center of the tank to the center of the mine. If they get too close, a collision will be triggered.

This may seem a bit outdated now that we have built in collision detection, but there are still several cases where this comes in quite handy. For example, If you were making a gravity field you would still need to find the distance between the two points in order to know how much to apply the force. It is handy therefore to know the principles.

Collision detection needs to run all of the time, so we'll be placing the code in an `onClipEvent(enterFrame)` within the mine template.

The first thing we need to find is the difference in horizontal and vertical positions of the tank and the mine. Let's store these amounts in the variables `deltaX` and `deltaY`

```
onClipEvent (enterFrame) {
    deltaX = _parent.tank._x-_x;
    deltaY = _parent.tank._y-_y;
}
```

The actual distance between these two points can then be found by applying Pythagoras's Theorem. Don't worry if you can't remember your math! Think of it as Ed's Theorem and you're halfway there: it's a lot of big words to explain a simple concept.

The variables we've just calculated (`deltaX` and `deltaY`) give us the lengths of two sides of a right-angled triangle. (So, say if tank's _x position was 100 and mine's _x position was 40, then `deltaX` would be 100 – 40 = 60; a similar sum would work out `deltaY`'s length).

To work out the length of the longest side of this triangle (the hypotenuse) we must take the square root of the sum of the square of deltaX and deltaY. To find a square root, we use the Math object again, but this time with the sqrt method:

```
onClipEvent (enterFrame) {
    deltaX = _parent.tank._x-_x;
    deltaY = _parent.tank._y-_y;
    distance = Math.sqrt(deltax*deltaX+deltaY*deltaY);
}
```

All that's left is to run a check on that distance. If it's less than a certain amount, say 30, then a collision has occurred and you would put the reaction inside that if statement:

```
onClipEvent (enterFrame) {
    deltaX = _parent.tank._x-_x;
    deltaY = _parent.tank._y-_y;
    distance = Math.sqrt(deltax*deltaX+deltaY*deltaY);
    if (distance<30) {
    }
}
```

## Shot to Mine Detection

Our last collision detection example is to see if our flying bullet hits anything. In this case there are many targets that the bullet can hit. As long as it exists it needs to check against all of the mines to see if it has run into any of them.

For this check, we'll be using the other aspect of the hitTest method which is movie clip to point collision. This checks to see if a specified coordinate is within the shape of the movie clip or its bounding box. For something as small as a bullet, there is not much difference between a point and the actual shape of the bullet.

Unlike the mine, the shot has a movement script that just uses the move variables we set up in the initialization. Since this code moves the object, we need to make sure that our template shot is not moved anywhere. The same condition that checks the name of the movie clip is used:

```
onClipEvent (enterFrame) {
    if (String(_name) != "shot") {
        _x += xmove;
        _y += ymove;
    }
}
```

Now we're ready to check for the collision with the mines. Since there can be any number of mines, depending on the level, we need to write a loop to check each one. Since we can use the level variable to figure how many we need to check, this is best done with a for loop where the index can be incremented until it is greater than the value of level:

# Event Handling 4

```
onClipEvent (enterFrame) {
    if (String(_name) != "shot") {
        _x += xmove;
        _y += ymove;
        for (i=1; i<=_parent.level; i++) {
        }
    }
}
```

Inside the loop, we need to run the `hitTest` check structured to use the index variable. To do that we can use the built-in associative array for a timeline. By specifying `_parent["mine" + i]`, the object whose name is the combination of mine and the value of the index variable for one timeline up will be returned.

Also, just as a reminder, `hitTest` can only return `true` or `false`, so it must be placed in an `if` statement to be of any use. By using the third argument in `hitTest`, which is the shape flag, we are indicating that we want to check by the shape for the movie, not the bounding box.

Any code for dealing with the reaction would be placed within this `if` statement:

```
onClipEvent (enterFrame) {
    if (String(_name) != "shot") {
        _x += xmove;
        _y += ymove;
        for (i=1; i<=_parent.level; i++) {
            if (_parent["mine"+i].hitTest(_x, _y, true)) {
            }
        }
    }
}
```

## Timer

The shot movie also has one other thing it needs to do on a regular basis. It needs to count up until it reaches a certain amount. By having a movie clip increment a variable every frame, you can set a frame-based timer that allows you to time out certain objects. Shots that are fired need a timer on them to set a range. Without that range, if the shot never hit a mine, it would continue moving off the stage and off towards infinity. Even if it's not visible to the player, the code is still executing even after it is nowhere near the game area, merrily burning up your system resources. Time to stamp it out!

```
onClipEvent (enterFrame) {
    if (String(_name) != "shot") {
        _x += xmove;
        _y += ymove;
        for (i=1; i<=_parent.level; i++) {
            if (_parent["mine"+i].hitTest(_x, _y, true)) {
            }
        }
        timer++;
        if (timer>15) {
```

*continues overleaf*

```
        }
      }
    }
```

Timers are very simple to make. You just have a variable constantly incrementing and then being checked to see if it is too high. If so it falls to the next section, **death**.

## Death

When the time comes to get rid of movie clip, from either a collision, a time out, or the end of the game, you can create a death for the object that ranges from simply removing the movie to triggering all sorts of reactions before it is destroyed. To see an example of this, let's look at the two ways a shot can die.

### Death by Timeout

This is when a shot reaches the end of the line and has exceeded its time limit. We would normally just need to remove the movie clip and be done with it. For our desert scene though, I thought it would look better with a small explosion as the shot hit the sand. This explosion could be done in a few ways.

The explosion and mound of sand could be an animation inside the shot movie clip. The problem there is that the `onClipEvent` will keep moving the movie no matter what it looks like, giving us a very mobile mound of sand. We could correct it by altering the code of the clip event but, well, I'd prefer to have the explosion outside the shot anyway since I plan to recycle it for the various collisions.

So, just before the shot is removed, it needs to spawn a new explosion and move it to the right spot. We can't rely on the explosion to initialize its own location since after the next few lines of code, the clip will be removed and there will be nothing to refer to anymore.

To duplicate the `explosion` movie clip, we need to increment an index variable like we have before. This variable has to live outside the shot, owing to the fact that the movie clip and any variables inside will cease to exist soon. The duplication happens like all of the others – this object needing to be higher than mines, but lower than the tank treads and bullets:

```
timer++;
if (timer>15) {
    _parent.d++;
    duplicateMovieClip (_parent.damagedGround,
    ↪ "d"+_parent.d, (_parent.d%100)+500);
    _parent["d"+_parent.d]._x = _x;
    _parent["d"+_parent.d]._y = _y;
    removeMovieClip (this);
}
```

# Event Handling

The position for the new movie clip is dynamically created just like when we were checking for collisions with all of the mines using the associative array for the timeline.

All that's left is to remove the shot and let the explosion animation happen on its own. If you are curious and want to take a look, the explosion operates on a timer which also sets its alpha property. When its timer runs out, the movie clip is removed without any further reaction.

## Death by Collision

When a shot hits a mine, the reaction is largely the same as when it times out. This time the mine movie clip must also be removed. As you can see, the code is almost identical. I did also decide to alter the scale values of the explosion since the mine is being destroyed. Otherwise all that is left is to look up the mine that was destroyed using the index variable and remove it just before removing the shot itself. Whenever you have a script that removes the `this` object, make sure that it is the last line of code. Once the movie is removed there is no longer any code there to be processed.

```
for (i=1; i<=_parent.level; i++) {
    if (_parent["mine"+i].hitTest(_x, _y, true)) {
        _parent.d++;
        duplicateMovieClip (_parent.damagedGround,
        ➥"d"+_parent.d, (_parent.d%100)+500);
        _parent["d"+_parent.d]._x = _x;
        _parent["d"+_parent.d]._y = _y;
        _parent["d"+_parent.d]._xscale = 150;
        _parent["d"+_parent.d]._yscale = 150;
        removeMovieClip (_parent["mine"+i]);
        removeMovieClip (this);
    }
}
```

## Conclusion

Once you have digested all of this, you will hopefully have a good sense of some of the major events of a lot of games, and a notion of how to deal with them.

The event handlers we've looked at in this chapter were the `onClipEvent` used for movie clips and the `on` handler used with buttons. You should begin to feel pretty comfortable with the benefits and limitations of each, with their many events, so that you can structure your own games effectively using a combination of techniques as is appropriate for your game.

As a secondary goal, you should also now have a good working knowledge of the key object and some ideas of how the Math object works. In later chapters you'll be able to delve much more into the mathematics of games.

Now that you've been introduced to many of the general concepts of game development, its time to go on and explore them in more detail with full and sophisticated games using advanced logic, 3D and much more.

# Event Handling 4

**Introduction**
chapter 1
chapter 2
chapter 3
chapter 4
chapter 5
chapter 6
**Case Study 1**
chapter 7
chapter 8
chapter 9
chapter 10
chapter 11
chapter 12
chapter 13
**Case Study 2**
chapter 14
chapter 15
**Director Afterword**

# Chapter 5
# Turn-Based Games and Advanced Logic

# 5  Flash Games Studio

This chapter will examine the turn-based game, a particular genre of game that dates back virtually to the creation of games themselves. Although this seems perhaps the most simple of computer games to create, we will see that coding this genre unearths a specific problem – that of emulating intelligence in the computer.

After looking at methods of creating a game environment, a factor relevant to all types of computer game, we'll introduce some of the options available to the designer in terms of this emulation, discussing a variety of strategies from random to learned behavior on the part of the computer opponent.

From here, we'll move on to creating a game of tic-tac-toe, incorporating this simulated intelligence, piece by piece, and outlining all of the code involved, from creating the environment, through the production of strings, arrays and a database, to running the game and recognizing winning or endgame positions. Event and frame-based scripts are also covered, along with the advanced use of functions, so that hopefully by the end of this chapter you'll have an excellent grounding in creating your very own games.

The advantage of starting with the turn-based game is that we don't have to get involved in generating a real-time environment. The format is simple – the player takes their turn, then the computer opponent takes its turn. This pattern continues until the game is over and thus we can concentrate on the game and coding logic rather than worrying about making the graphics move continuously in real-time.

We'll consider the following issues:

**Defining the Game**

- Formulating the game environment
- Creating game rules
- Strategies for adding intelligence to game responses

**Coding the Game**

- Advanced ActionScript data structures and objects
- Use of frame based ActionScript versus event based ActionScript
- Coding strategies for readability and code re-use
- Strategies for coding intelligence
- Building up the game

Before we start working on practicalities, there is a major bit of theory we should have a look at...

# Turn-Based Games and Advanced Logic 5

## Game Definition Fundamentals

Before we can code our game, we need to tightly define it. There are a number of separate tasks a game coding plan has to cover to be well defined, and once you have written a couple you will see the following pattern occurring time and time again. Ignoring the display and animation aspects of a game, all game engines have to include these three components if they are to provide an intelligent challenge:

### 1. It Has to Create a Game Environment

This idea will be extended in the next chapter for real time environments via the concept of a *gameWorld*, but for our turn-based system it is usually much simpler. Examples include a chessboard for a game of chess, or the 3x3 grid for tic-tac-toe. In either case, the game environment is a rather simple and static structure. We don't have to worry about things like game physics, fluid motion, or anything complex such as real time 3D representations, we'll simply focus on game logic. In our example of a chess game, the game environment would also include information such as 'how big is the board' and 'where can the chess pieces move'.

The game environment also has to include information that describes where all the pieces are and what they are doing (something usually called *status*). In simple games, this information is inherent in the game graphics; you know where a space invader is by looking at the x,y co-ordinates of the Space Invader graphic.

In more complex games you sometimes can't do this and therefore have to build a **database** that includes this information. The use of such a database is usually associated with complex games such as 3D flight simulators, but there are many much simpler games that run faster if you use a simple database rather than the graphics themselves, as we shall see later.

### 2. It Has to Create and Enforce Rules

For a game of chess, this would involve checking that the player was moving his pieces correctly and removing chess pieces when they have been defeated, and so on. We can assume that the computer will never cheat or make illegal moves because it is cursed with total honesty!

# 5  Flash Games Studio

> *Surprisingly, one of the most difficult things to specify can be detecting a winning or 'end of game' condition. Although this is easy to detect in the standard space invaders game (you simply look for the players ship being hit), for complex games with several player controlled pieces and multiple outcomes, detecting an end of game can be quite difficult. This is a big problem with artificial intelligence generally; to know when a real world problem with multiple solutions has been solved. Evolutionary psychology suggests humans may have evolved possibly the most complex facility there is (consciousness and self-awareness) which allow us to recognize these states, so even nature finds this task hard. This is something to bear in mind when developing rules; for the more cerebral games, don't be surprised if the code to detect a winning position is huge.*

### 3. It Has to Include a Method of Controlling Non-Player Characters

Non-player characters (commonly referred to by the gaming community as NPCs) have to be controlled by the computer via ActionScript, which defines what they will do. An NPC can vary in complexity from an alien in a space invaders game with a simple 'move left-right and fire randomly' movement plan, right up to an enemy fighter in a 3D aircraft simulator conforming to an aerodynamics flight model, and a varied strategy depending on relative position, remaining ordnance and damage taken.

If we imagine a game of chess played by the computer against a human opponent, it is possible to comprehend the perceived intelligence necessary for the computer to perform its moves logically. It would be no good if it moved randomly, or not according to the rules, or even if it repeated the same sequence of moves in every game. We need some form of theory for the computer to simulate a thinking, worthy opponent and to approach different game situations with different strategies. As this is an important element of any game that includes an NPC (which is certainly the vast majority of games), we will look in further detail as to how this can be achieved.

There are several general NPC control strategies, and they include:

1. Random behavior
2. Goal-based behavior
3. Weighted outcomes
4. Look-ahead
5. Learned behavior

Those of you who have followed gaming through the years may even recognize the order of these strategies as an ordering of game complexity. Early games included large numbers of dumb aliens or other enemies, but the latest games (such as the recent *Black and White (EA, 2001)*, Sid Meier's *Civilization (Microprose, 1991)* strategy series and advanced third person shooters) use strategies including evaluating the results of a number of possible movements, and learning from past events.

# Turn-Based Games and Advanced Logic       5

Random and goal based behavior are the most often used strategies in current Flash games. They are the simplest strategies because neither has to evaluate the outcome of the strategy. The best way to illustrate their use is via simple examples. Because both these strategies are not usually used in turn-based games, we will dip briefly into the world of real-time in explaining them.

## Random Behavior
The first strategy is very simple; Make the NPC move in a random way. Constructing a game using random NPC control is not normally recommended because it is too obvious; the opponents will lack intelligence. More usually, only part of the NPC control is random.

In the picture below, the Galaxian invader makes its final attack on the player's ship from the point labeled *start*. Without any random element, the Galaxian would dive straight for the ship via the *target path*.

To give the attack some level of variation (and also to give the player a fighting chance!), we could make the Galaxian dive not at the ship, but at a random point to the left or right of the ship or an *offset path*. Rather than dive towards the ship's precise x,y coordinate position, we now dive towards a position x+ offset,y (where offset is something like a random number between -100 and 100 pixels). By adding a random offset, we ensure a variation of attacks *that the player cannot totally predict*. This ensures no two games are ever the same and if used correctly, may add to that elusive quality *playability*:

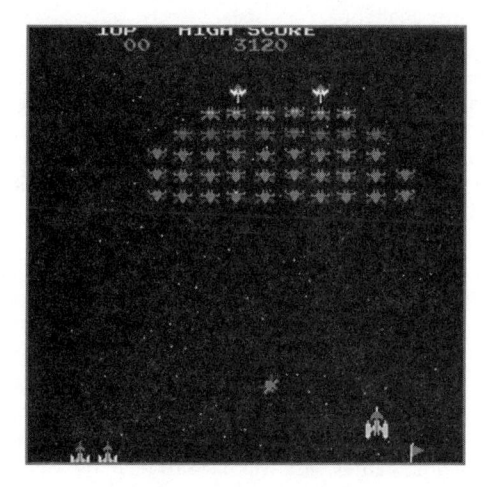

## Goal Based Behavior
The second strategy relies on NPCs having set rules that force them to work towards a certain goal.

The tennis game *Pong (Atari, 1972)* was the earliest video game. To hit the ball, the bat has to maintain a y position that is the same as the ball's position. To do this is easy in Flash; you simply have to keep the bat movie clip's _y property equal to the ball movie clip's _y property, or:

   bat._y = ball._y;

# Flash Games Studio

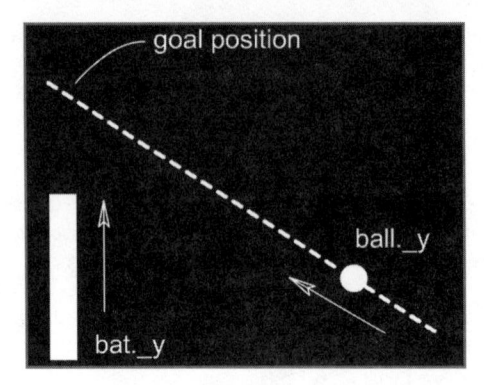

*[Figure: diagram showing goal position, bat._y, and ball._y]*

In other words, the aim of the bat is to maintain a y position that is equal to the ball's y position. This is so that when the bat and ball have the same x position (the point when the bat actually hits the ball), the two come into contact and the ball is returned. This strategy is very simple to code up (it amounts to only one line of code) and efficient. It is actually *too* efficient; the bat will never miss the ball! This is usually overcome by giving the bat a fixed maximum speed. The bat will now be limited to how quickly it can reach the goal position, and, given a good trick shot from the human player, may not make it to the goal position in time. Further, by slowly increasing the bat's maximum speed, we can make the batsmen appear increasingly skillful as time goes on, thus adding to the long-term challenge.

At the moment, there are very few Flash video games that don't use this strategy for adding intelligence. The goal-based strategy is also used in many Flash websites to emulate effects such as inertia and 'intelligent' interfaces. Anyone who implements a website interface with any of the subsequent intelligence methods discussed in this chapter will most likely be in a field of one, so they're something to consider, particularly because they allow your interface to start preempting what the user is about to do.

The goal-based strategy creates NPCs with about the perceived intelligence of those in the 8-bit game 'greats' such as *Asteroids (Atari, 1979)* and *Defender (Williams, 1980)*. Not enough intelligence to give a lasting challenge by today's standards, but resulting in a very quick game engine.

The next two strategies can give a much more intelligent opponent. They are typically used in games where there are multiple outcomes and no single 'correct move'. Games such as chess can only be implemented via these strategies, and these can be code intensive. Although they are used in some modern real-time games, you will have to have heavily optimized code if you want an efficient real time Flash game that uses them.

# Turn-Based Games and Advanced Logic

## Weighted Outcomes

When humans play games, they are not so much looking at goal based strategies, but rather 'what is the best possible move I can make, given the rules of the game and the state of play now?'. Although the aliens in a space invaders game have one goal (to hit our ship), the human player has several:

- To kill aliens

- To protect their own ship

- To get a high score

The way we play cannot be based on a single simple goal, because we have more than one, and these can even conflict with each other. As soon as I am close to the high score, I might start playing recklessly (ignoring the protection of my own ship in the search for more points). The reason why I move my ship left and not right at any instant is based not on any one single thing, but on *picking the best next move that satisfies the majority of my separate goals*. In effect, I am constantly evaluating many 'next moves' and picking the best one based on how favorable I think its outcome will be. The idea of player skill could even be defined in these narrow terms; *how quickly can I define the best next move, and how quickly can I move to this position?*

In the game tic-tac-toe below, I am playing as 'x' and it's my turn. How would I pick the best move I could make?

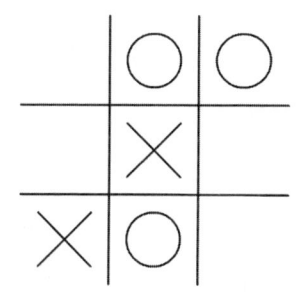

Well, if I don't put an 'x' in the top left corner, I will lose. As humans, we see this immediately, but how do we do it, and more importantly, how would we write code that would reach the same decision? One of the best ways to do it would be to define all the little sub rules we use to reach our conclusion and apply them to every possible next move. The move that meets the most sub rules is the one we take. In effect, we make every possible move, and then select the best one out of them. Possible sub rules for tic-tac-toe are:

# Flash Games Studio

For all unoccupied squares:

- If there are two 'x's already on any row, column or diagonal, then I *must* place a cross in the third free square in that line because then I will win.

- If there are two 'o's on any row, column or diagonal then I *should* place a cross in the third free square in that line or I will lose (unless of course I can win in this turn by making a row of 3 'X's as per the rule above). Remember also that each rule assumes that the preceding one *has already been applied*, so the ordering in this list is also important

- If there is at least one 'o' and no 'x' in any row, column or diagonal, then I *may* place an 'x' in the same line to prevent it becoming a row of two (because a row of two 'o's increases my chances of losing).

- If there is one 'x' in any row, column or diagonal, then I *may* place an 'x' in the same line to create a row of two because this increases my chances of reaching a winning position.

- If there is a free square, then I *could* place my 'x' in it.

So how does the computer decide which square to place its cross in? Well, we know which of the rules are the most important. I have actually listed them in the order of importance; the *must* rules are the most important because they lead to an immediate win. The *should* rules are slightly less important. Although they don't result in a win, they stop a lose position forming. The *may* rules neither result in a win nor lose position, but tend to put us in a better position. Finally, the *could* rules give us something to do if all else fails.

If we give each rule a score as follows…

Could = 1
May = 2
Should = 4
Must =8

… and then apply all the rules to each square, adding up the score for each square, we would end up with this;

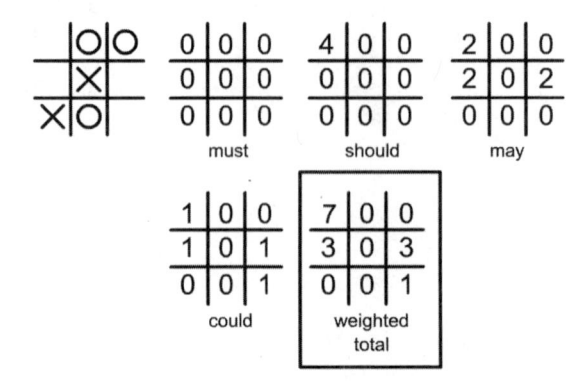

| | O | O |
|---|---|---|
| X | | |
| X | O | |

| 0 | 0 | 0 |
|---|---|---|
| 0 | 0 | 0 |
| 0 | 0 | 0 |

must

| 4 | 0 | 0 |
|---|---|---|
| 0 | 0 | 0 |
| 0 | 0 | 0 |

should

| 2 | 0 | 0 |
|---|---|---|
| 2 | 0 | 2 |
| 0 | 0 | 0 |

may

| 1 | 0 | 0 |
|---|---|---|
| 1 | 0 | 1 |
| 0 | 0 | 1 |

could

| 7 | 0 | 0 |
|---|---|---|
| 3 | 0 | 3 |
| 0 | 0 | 1 |

weighted total

# Turn-Based Games and Advanced Logic

Notice that the square we would most likely pick *has the highest score* or weighting. So if our code simply applies these rules and adds up the score (weighted outcome) of each square when all the rules are applied, the square that must be selected gets the highest weighting. Easy! This process works on a summation of outcomes. There can be (and usually is) more than one rule that is applied to a particular square to give you the final outcome. If two squares have an equal weighting the NPC's choice is likely to be based simply on the order in which it scans the matrix.

To implement this for any game, you simply form the rules, and by dry running through typical games, you assign each rule a score. Finally, your code applies the scores to each of the possible squares to select the best one.

> *An important point to notice is that if we implement this functionality, the computer can play tic-tac-toe without knowing the rules! We haven't taught it how to play, because for that to happen, the computer would have to be able to work out the weightings itself. Rather, we have told it where to place its 'x', which is a very different (and easier) thing to teach because the computer does not have to have any long-term strategy; it simply 'plays by numbers'. Many people don't appreciate it, but you don't need to build intelligence to emulate intelligent behavior.*

As well as giving a preferred turn (top left square), the weighted totals also give us a second and third choice (the two 3s and the 1). So if we implemented weighted decisions in a real-time game, we don't necessarily have to constantly work out a new set of conditions, which would be a time consuming process. We can just tell the NPC to select plan B (select one of the '3' squares) or C (select the '1' square) if plan A became too hard to follow.

Taking the theory further, the matrix can represent 'options of what to do next', and not just a board where each part of the matrix maps directly onto a board position. For example, matrix element (1,1) could represent the outcome "I am hungry", whereas matrix (1,2) could be "I feel like a fight". When the NPC has evaluated all possible game rules on the matrix, the most likely outcome specifies the final behavior, and perhaps even its urgency; the "I am hungry" weighting could be used in the "how fast to run to catch the food" formula; if the creature is very hungry, it will run faster. Also, if the "I feel like a fight" is high as well, the creature may try to eat a horse rather than a dormouse because it's feeling up for it! Weighted outcomes are great for things like this because the supposition of lots of simple rules can create some very subtle and definite behavior. I suspect something like this is used in the recent *Black and White* video game. The intelligence engine in that is considered cutting edge, but they're potentially using the same principle as the tic-tac-toe game!

Further, the weightings suggest that there is no real 'correct' answer, just ones that are more correct (the 7) or less correct (the 3). This is the basis of a branch of logic called *fuzzy logic*. In a world where real life problems have no single answer that is totally correct, fuzzy logic is useful in finding the 'most correct' or 'least incorrect' path forward.

The weighted outcome strategy is also a cool engine to develop for real time applications. For example, if used properly it could create a very intelligent, context-sensitive web site interface that presents the visitor with the options they are most likely to pursue. However, it may take some optimization to implement with the current Flash plug-in for real time operation because of speed considerations. As the Flash plug-in becomes more optimized, and processor speeds increase, it's one to consider attempting.

**Look-Ahead**

Look-ahead is very similar in implementation to weighted outcomes except that we look not only at squares in our weightings, but *outcomes*. The computer looks at all possible moves that can be made from the original position (A1) and tries each of the possible positions an 'x' can be placed on the next turn (two of the possible 4 places where the 'x' can be placed are shown, B1, B2). The computer then looks at each possible move the human can make in response to our 'x' (C1, C2, C3 in response to B1, or D1, D2, D3 in response to B2). By looking at the possible moves that the human opponent will make (via weighted outcomes or a similar strategy), the computer can decide which is the better move between B1 and B2 via an algorithm that scores the most favorable branches through our 'movement tree' with the highest scores.

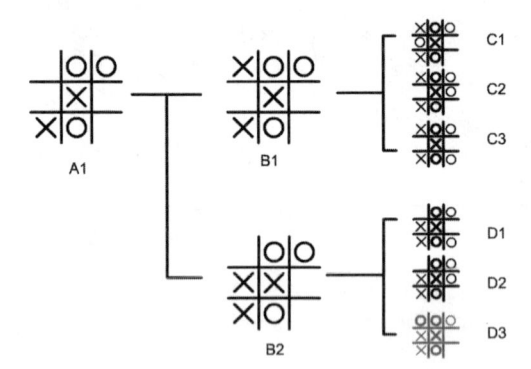

In the above example, move B2 is a bad move because when we look at the possible moves the human opponent may make in response to it, we see that one of them (D3) will cause us to lose. By looking at C1, C2, C3, D1, D2, and D3 with a weighted outcome routine where moves that tend to make us win are given positive scores, and moves that tend to make us lose are given negative scores, we can build a weighted tree of moves starting from A1, and pick from the best next move B1, B2, B3... B*n* by looking at the subsequent outcomes further down the tree.

Although at first glance this may seem similar to the weighted outcome, this strategy is more useful for games where a winning position takes more than one move to reach, such as chess. Rather than simply weighing up the advantages of a certain move over another, in this case the NPC considers all possible outcomes for each option, and as such makes a far more informed decision as to where each move will lead.

In fact, a look ahead strategy is the *only* way to code up a game of chess. Most chess intelligence engines look ahead much more than one move, and the data needed to build a tree can be huge, resulting in lots of calculations. The look ahead method is therefore not suited to real-time applications if you are using a relatively slow language such as ActionScript or JavaScript – at least, not this year, but Intel and Motorola may give us the processing power we need sooner than we think!

# Turn-Based Games and Advanced Logic

## Learned Behavior

In a previous career I met learned behavior in the form of **neural nets**. These emulate the way a real brain works by learning tasks from scratch. They are useful in building control for processes that don't follow any discernable (or mathematically predictable) rules. A couple of engineering friends I lived with at the time even developed a neural net application that took share data as input from a simple Teletext PC card and learnt how to play the stock market (all the rage in the boom years for those of us who can remember).

In the progress of a task, if a particular neural net configuration results in a 'success', that configuration is made more permanent, and given the same situation, the net is more likely to do the same thing again. If it fails, the same answer is less likely to appear again. In this way, the net learns the route to successful operation without actually needing to know anything about the logic behind the decision. In the same way a child may learn to point at things because that tends to make someone bring the object being pointed at closer. The child doesn't know *why* this happens, but soon it becomes a natural habit. This is the essential mechanism of learning without knowing what the current 'goal' actually is.

In any application, there is one major drawback in using artificial learning and one major advantage. The advantage is that you as a programmer don't have to define the solution, which is always a good thing when you don't (or can't) know it yourself. The disadvantage is that the computer has to know when it has learned something correctly. As mentioned earlier, getting a machine to detect a correct solution can be tricky if there is no true correct solution, although weighted outcomes can help by giving the machine a weighted outcome engine to fall back on when it is still learning; rather like new born babies have hard wired reflexes to help them out before their brain is sufficiently developed to take over

Another problem is that a learning strategy plays poorly when it is first started or if it meets conditions it has never seen before – such as a stock market neural net taught in boom times, but caught off-guard by a bust... watch your bank balance!

There are easier ways to implement learning in Flash than resorting to the neural net method. Looking at the tic-tac-toe game again, it's entirely possible to base learning on 'how successful was my last strategy?'. If the engine saves the position of all elements on the board after every go, it can mark each with a level of success. In the example below, A1 is the starting position. If the computer places an 'x' as per B1, this is a bad move as C1 ends with the NPC losing. If this occurred, the computer would remember B1 as a bad move by giving it a large negative score. If position A1 occurs again, the computer will recognize it and, based on its negative score, would not play position B1 again.

|O|O
X
X|O
A1

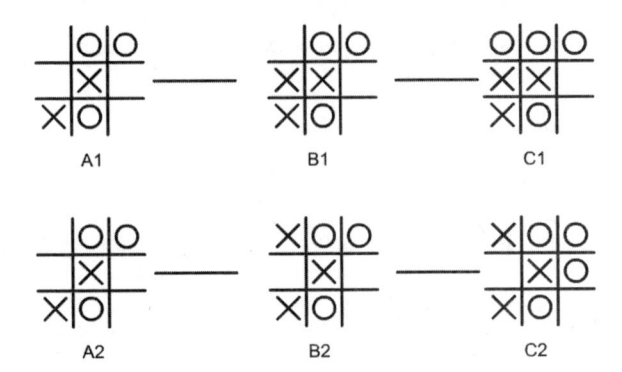

|O|O
X|X
X|O
B1

O|O|O
X|X
X|O
C1

|O|O
X
X|O
A2

X|O|O
X
X|O
B2

X|O|O
X|O
X|O
C2

If the computer instead chose position B2, then the opponent cannot make a winning position, so B2 would be remembered with a small positive score because it is a 'better than random' move (because you don't lose if you make this move). B2 is a very good position because 'x' will win in the next move wherever 'o' goes . Once a win is seen, all moves that lead up to it will have their scores raised, because they are preferable moves to make.

To make a move in the first place, the engine would make a random move (placing its 'x' in any free square) unless it recognized the last position, in which case it will make the move that has the highest score associated with it. As the program remembers more and more move combinations, it will become as good as its opponent. Those of you who are wondering if this can actually evolve true intelligence with time, the answer is no. This strategy is not based upon actually learning, but just blindly memorizing combinations.

The learning strategy can be a good one because the learning system will never be better than its opponent - it can only be as good, so after enough learning has taken place, the human player will see a well matched player that gets better as fast as they do (mainly because it has learned directly from them).

## Coding a Turn-Based Game

Okay, that's the theory done and dusted, time to get our hands dirty. I had a look at some Flash resource sites before writing this chapter and couldn't find a single tic-tac-toe game on any of them. This is odd because there's a huge number of JavaScript, Java, C++, and ASP based tic-tac-toe games on the web. I suspect that this is down to the fact that the scripts to write a decent game like this are fairly long. Although Flash 4 was up to the task, the coding environment was not really up to writing long scripts in the same way that Flash 5 expert mode now is.

Tic-tac-toe is a deceptively hard game to code up (unless of course you cheat by simply making it take predefined set moves - which is easy to code because there are only a limited number of different board configurations, but it wouldn't teach us anything about emulating an intelligent NPC), so it should give us something of a challenge for this chapter.

# Turn-Based Games and Advanced Logic 5

Our game will also include all of the common advanced ActionScript concepts you need to know to start designing games yourself, including:

- Creating structured code
- Use of event and frame-based scripts (and mixing the two)
- Use of functions
- Creating advanced data types and objects
- Duplicating and erasing movie clip instances
- Controlling game flow
- Creating custom diagnostics in your FLA

... so it forms a good beginners primer to game creation.

For those who want to see the endpoint of this journey before we start, have a look at TicTacToeFinal.fla.

There are a couple of tips to notice from the following screenshot. Firstly, the top three layers contain ActionScript only. The topmost one, actions, contains frame-based scripts, the next one down contains the function definitions, and the third one contains our event scripts. Keeping code separate from the graphics layers is always a good idea, and to enforce the difference between the ActionScript and non-ActionScript layers, I have made the layer color (the little square next to the layer title) for the top three layers black, which signifies a 'code only layer':

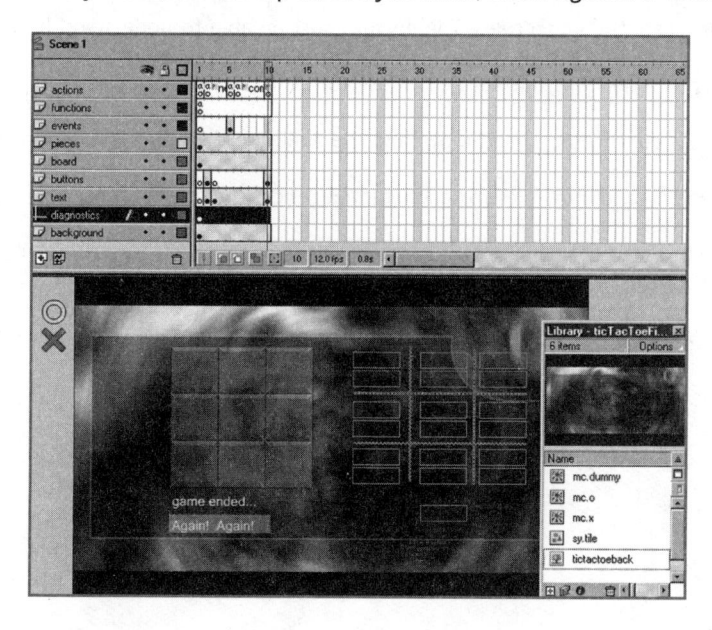

163

# 5    Flash Games Studio

> *Although the events layer does actually contain movie clips, they are purely dummy holders to attach event scripts to. So although technically the event layer doesn't only contain ActionScript, the reality is that the layer is predominantly concerned with a particular type of script.*

Secondly, the layer 'diagnostics' is currently a guide layer. If you run it with this setting you will see just the game graphics. If you now set diagnostics to a normal layer and then run the FLA, you will see some data appear to the right of the game. This lets you look into the mind of our tic-tac-toe NPC, and those of you who remember the stuff we talked about earlier regarding weighted outcomes may even have a glimmer of what is going on. The game can be beaten – there is one particular strategy I have intentionally left to the human player that is winnable, so have fun finding it.

## Game Creation from Scratch

This is the strategy we'll be following:

First, we have to formulate the game so that the engine is able to show the game environment and handle everything to make a turn. The code must have all of the data structures in place to understand what the current game status is (such as where all the pieces are), but it will do nothing with this information. We will end up with a game that understands moves but cannot make them itself.

Then, we will create the game rules. The engine must be able to understand the following:

- When a turn has started, and whose turn it is
- What constitutes a valid move and the ability to disregard invalid moves

Finally, we need to add strategies for adding intelligence to game responses.

People unused to creating complex FLAs look at other people's work and think it was all done in one go. They start thinking 'how would I ever do that - where do I start?' Most FLAs are actually created in stages, and if you keep in mind my broad-brush strategy above, you will see the underlying method to our coding route.

# Turn-Based Games and Advanced Logic    5

## Creating the Game Environment

**1.** Firstly we'll deal with the straightforward elements, the creation of the graphics and symbols. The GameSymbols.fla file contains the library we'll be using.

I wanted a simple grid as per my initial sketch for the game board:

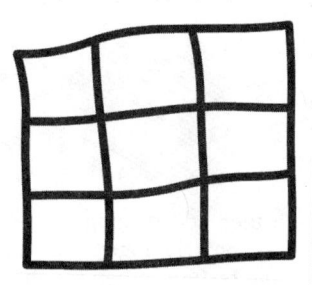

Now we'll create a simple tile symbol, sy.tile:

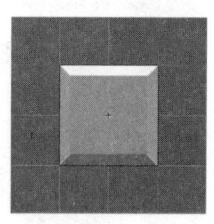

This will be used to create our faux 3D board by arranging a grid of 9 of these tiles:

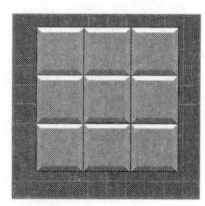

> *I always precede all symbols with a prefix describing what it is (sy: symbol, mc: movie clip, ms: smart-clip, bu: button). I find this a good idea for two reasons. The first is that the Library window lists things alphabetically, so that all the different symbol types per folder will be listed together, making for a tidier Library. The second reason is that you can add prefixes to identify variations within the standard types. For example, if you have a number of movie clips that contain ActionScript only, you could differentiate them with the prefix ma; movie clip-ActionScript.*

## 5    Flash Games Studio

Games are designed to be fun, and the standard clichéd drab black or grey background is a little counterproductive in achieving this, so a colorful background is called for. To create a simple textured background to break up all that dead space is easy in Photoshop via judicious use of filter effects.

Starting with a simple clouds filter, the texture is made more complex by repeated use of difference clouds. A radial blur followed by a blue tint gives us the final texture:

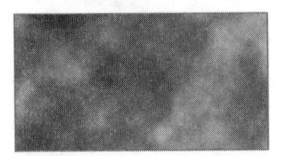

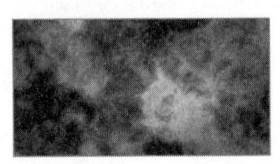

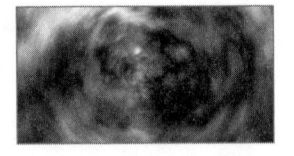

I then added samples of an ActionScript listing to the bitmap (given that this is an exercise in ActionScript logic), and also an 'x' and 'o' graphic top right. Finally, I darkened the middle area of the texture (otherwise the game graphics might get lost within the texture, especially small text) by adding a filled black shape on a new layer and giving it a 40% alpha. I then flattened the image and saved it as a JPG graphic (I find JPGs give more control of compression rates than other lossless options Flash understands):

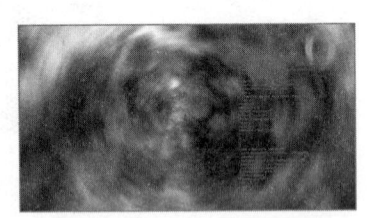

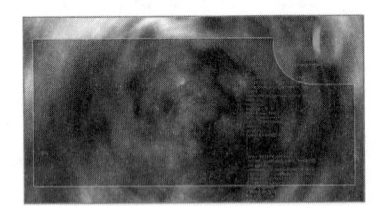

Although Flash purists may balk at using bitmaps in Flash, they can add interest to a project when used as backgrounds, breaking up the large boring expanses of solid color associated with vector-based graphics.

Now we need to create our 'x' and 'o' symbols, *mc.x* and *mc.o*. Because we'll have to move these symbols about and duplicate them, they are created as movie clips.

# Turn-Based Games and Advanced Logic | 5

> *Some designers like to create everything (including the static symbols, such as sy.tile) as movie clips. I would advise against doing this as a movie clip takes more memory to create because it has properties. A simple graphic symbol has no properties and so is easier for Flash to deal with quickly.*

If you want something a little more aesthetic than my simple 'o' and 'x' shapes, try generating extruded 3D versions in a program like Swift3D.

You may be forgiven for thinking that the creation of a background texture in game graphics is a bit of an aside, but remember that in the real world you want to sell your games, so...

- Adding background bitmaps can be one of the easiest ways to customize your game creations for the client. Bearing this in mind consider making your stage size larger than the size of the game area (as I have done) thus allowing you to add a message from your sponsor. This is very much like graphic designers who create book covers ensuring that the appropriate places for all of the client's blurb and titling are free of graphics.

- Realizing that you may have to change your game graphics in the future when it comes to a sale, make sure that your Library is organized so that all of the customizable graphics are in one folder. I've been approached in the past on a number of occasions to write 'blank game engines'. These are games with the ActionScript fully written, but the graphics replaced with placeholders ready for re-work by the design house (who will ultimately sell the whole package on to a third party). As the ActionScript required to create game engines becomes more complicated, this may become the norm - and can be quite lucrative for you because you can sell the same game engines any number of times!

    Finally, there are two symbols I tend to create as a matter of course in advanced Flash FLAs: mc.dummy and bu.invisible.

mc.dummy is simply an empty movie clip. It's used to attach *onClipEvent* code to where you don't want to attach the event to any particular instance. bu.invisible is the ubiquitous invisible button, which is a standard button with only its hit state defined. This means that you can't see the button, but can click or roll over it. This button overlays various sections of text and thus eliminates the need for each of these bits of text to be created as buttons, another cunning production tip:

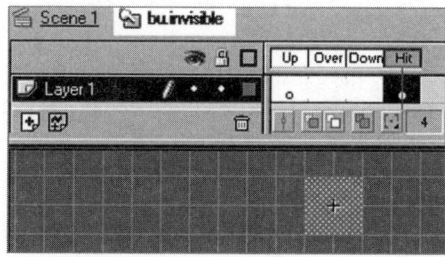

# Flash Games Studio

The next step is putting all this together so that we create our game environment and then the code that can handle all the logic to make a turn, as well as being able to track where everything is. This step is included as the simple file *ticTacToe0.fla*.

The timeline of this FLA now looks like this:

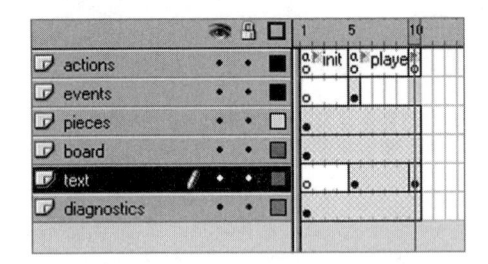

## A Three Stage Game-Plan

**Initialization** occurs at frame 1, labeled *init*. This frame creates our data and initializes it.

**Play** occurs at frame 5, labeled *player*. The game stays at this frame, responding to player requests to make a move until all 9 moves have been made.

**Endgame** is the last frame, and is labeled *endgame*. The game jumps to this frame when all 9 moves have been made.

However, at this point there is no game as such. All we can prove with this FLA is that moves can be made, and that's the first step in our strategy.

## The Stage

The main stage consists of a number of symbols and dynamic text:

To the top left sit our 'o' and 'x' movie clips that will be duplicated and moved onto the board every time a move is made. They have instance names 'o' and 'x' respectively. The game board is made up of a stack of 9 tile symbols *sy.tile* as described earlier. To the right is our diagnostic text. Right now, this text is on a normal layer *diagnostics*, but in the final game we will stop this text being exported to the SWF by making this a guide layer.

# Turn-Based Games and Advanced Logic

Although we now have the debugger window to help us, sometimes it's better to do it this way because (a) the diagnostic data is presented in exactly the way we want to see it and (b) the debugger can be a little, well... temperamental when showing certain data.

The dynamic text fields have the following variable names associated with them:

| d1-00 | d1-10 | d1-20 |
| d2-00 | d2-10 | d2-20 |
| d1-01 | d1-11 | d1-21 |
| d2-01 | d2-11 | d2-21 |
| d1-02 | d1-12 | d1-22 |
| d2-02 | d2-12 | d2-22 |

As you can see, this table contains two pieces of data for each of the tic-tac-toe board squares. During development, it was used as a view into my weighted outcomes engine to allow me to see what it was thinking. I have left it in the game so that you can see what the game is 'thinking' at every move. There are, in fact, a number of different pieces of information relating to each square: x position, y position, state, and weight. Of these, only two properties are essential to our diagnostics grid, namely state and weight, so we allow for these two variables to be recorded within the square with the variable names shown in the screenshot.

There's probably some serious shrieks of dissention from the back regarding these variable names; a name with a '-' in it is usually not a valid name (d1-10 could be taken to mean 'd1 minus ten'), but the way we will use this table doesn't fall foul of this trap (because we will be using string concatenation to form the variable names). The variable names work perfectly, as you will see in a moment.

## Building the Database

An easy way to track our game is via a mini database. We can't use the _x, _y properties of our 'o' and 'x' movie clips because for our weighted outcome intelligence emulation to work, it needs to actually dry run through all of the possible moves and weight them, and it needs a data structure to do this in. With that in mind, let's look at building a simple database:

1. Our database is created at the frame labeled *init*, on the actions layer. The first few lines make our x and o movie clips invisible. We don't strictly have to do this (they are off the edge of the stage anyway), but depending on how we embed our final SWF into HTML, they may become visible within the browser window, so better to solve the problem before it occurs:

   ```
   // Make the dummy "o" and "x" movie clips invisible...
   o._visible = false;
   x._visible = false;
   ```

# Flash Games Studio

We'll be duplicating instances of these movie clips later. Because the copies we make will not have their visibility property inherited from these instances, we don't have to worry further about _visibility.

For each tile on the board we need to know the following pieces of information:

- Where the tile center is (x,y) – Flash needs to know this so that it can place an 'x' or 'o' symbol in the right place

- What is on that tile at the moment ('x', 'o', or nothing) otherwise known as its state

So for each tile in the board we need to know 3 properties

x – The tile's x coordinate
y – The tile's y coordinate
state – x, o, or blank

We need a way of easily defining all 5 pieces of data for the 9 available tiles. One way of representing each square is by its (x,y) position in a 3x3 grid:

| (0,0) | (1,0) | (2,0) |
|-------|-------|-------|
| (0,1) | (1,1) | (2,1) |
| (0,2) | (1,2) | (2,2) |

> *Using an array, tile[0] to tile[8], could also have been used, but is not as useful given that we will be sorting the board positions in rows and columns rather than sequentially from top left to bottom right*

Thus, the top left corner is tile[0][0] and the bottom right corner is tile[2][2], noting that we are using the Flash (and print based) convention of y going in a downward direction.

# Turn-Based Games and Advanced Logic

We can now enter these co-ordinates as they stand as an index into a 2-dimensional array of the form tile[x][y], giving us array elements tile[0][0] to tile[2][2]. Each array element will represent the tile position shown below. By giving our array the x, y and state properties, we have our data in a form that Flash can use to quickly read and write data on each tile:

| tile[0][0].x<br>tile[0][0].y<br>tile[0][0].state | tile[1][0].x<br>tile[1][0].y<br>tile[1][0].state | tile[2][0].x<br>tile[2][0].y<br>tile[2][0].state |
|---|---|---|
| tile[1][0].x<br>tile[1][0].y<br>tile[1][0].state | tile[1][1].x<br>tile[1][1].y<br>tile[1][1].state | tile[2][1].x<br>tile[2][1].y<br>tile[2][1].state |
| tile[2][0].x<br>tile[2][0].y<br>tile[2][0].state | tile[2][1].x<br>tile[2][1].y<br>tile[2][1].state | tile[2][2].x<br>tile[2][2].y<br>tile[2][2].state |

As good practice, you can also investigate this data structure by running the FLA in test mode and looking at the debugger Variables tab for _level0.

The *x* and *y* properties of tile contain the (x, y) position of each tile in the board as per this diagram:

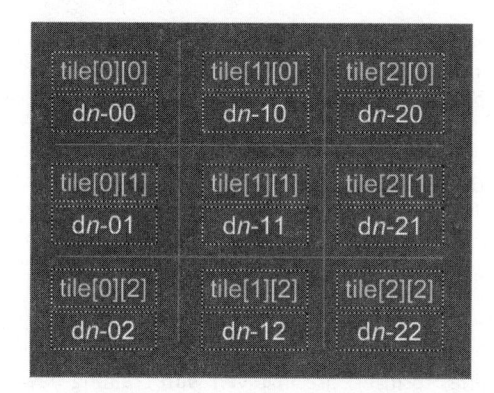

| tile[0][0]<br>d*n*-00 | tile[1][0]<br>d*n*-10 | tile[2][0]<br>d*n*-20 |
|---|---|---|
| tile[0][1]<br>d*n*-01 | tile[1][1]<br>d*n*-11 | tile[2][1]<br>d*n*-21 |
| tile[0][2]<br>d*n*-02 | tile[1][2]<br>d*n*-12 | tile[2][2]<br>d*n*-22 |

Note where the variable names come from: d1-xy and d2-xy are equivalent to array element tile[x][y], Incidentally, in the code x and y are represented by loop counter variables, i and j, (an old programming convention).

The state property will be used in a later script to keep track of what is currently on each tile.

171

# Flash Games Studio

Now we can insert the following code into the init frame of the actions layer:

```
// Initialize the tile array object of data objects...
//
// Defines new 2 dimensional array object
// of the form tilePos[i][j], with properties
// .x : the tile X position
// .y : the tile Y position
// .state: the state (blank, x, o) of the tile
//
tile = new Array(2);
for (i=0; i<=2; i++) {
    tile[i] = new Array(2);
    for (j=0; j<=2; j++) {
        tile[i][j] = new Object();
        tile[i][j].x = 130+(i*50);
        tile[i][j].y = 105+(j*50);
        tile[i][j].state = "blank";
```

The outer loop will run through 3 times (i=0, 1, and 2), and for each iteration, the inner loop will also run through 3 times giving us i,j pairs 0-0, 0-1, 0-2, 1-0, 1-1, 1-2, 2-0, 2-1, 2-2. These loop variables are used to create our array tile[0][0] to tile[2][2].

We can now add the last few lines of the initialization loop in order to output some diagnostic information to our text fields, which tell us the position of each tile in row, column and (x,y) pixels respectively. This information was used previously to prove that the array matched our board:

```
        // --diagnostic lines--
        _root["d1-"+i+j] = "("+i+", "+j+")";
        _root["d2-"+i+j] = tile[i][j].x+", "+tile[i][j].y;
        // ---------
    }
}
```

The last couple of lines to insert are involved with creating new 'x' and 'o' symbols on our board, and we'll look at them in greater detail when we review how the engine draws onto the board when moves are taken:

```
// initialize counters for duplicateMovie command
// and turns taken.
depth = 1;
turn = 0
```

For those of you who have got lost in all this, take a look back at our initial coding strategy:

# Turn-Based Games and Advanced Logic 5

> *'First, we have to formulate the game so that the engine is able to show the game environment and handle everything to make a move. The code must have all of the data structures in place to understand what the current game status is (such as where all the pieces are), but it will do nothing with this information. We will end up with a game that understands moves but cannot make them itself'.*

All that remains to be done is to code up the ability for the player to make a move and the engine to validate it as correct.

## Player Input

For the player to make his move, the traditional solution would be to add buttons over each tile. There are a number of reasons why this method would require a lot of code (not least because the player's inputs would then be coming in via 9 separate button scripts, and it'd be necessary to differentiate between them all). We *could* go down this route, (there is a rather elegant solution that reduces the amount of code required using smart clips) but I have chosen a buttonless method using mouse position and tile position. I have done it this way because we need to know the tile position anyway for when we place the symbols on the tiles:

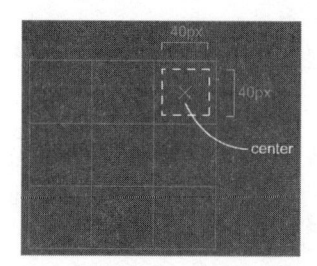

Each tile has a center point, and we need to know this position when we want to place an 'x' or an 'o' over it. This position is stored as tile[0...2][0...2].x and tile[0...2][0...2].y already. The tiles are each 50x50 pixels, so if we use our tile[0...2][0...2].x and y properties, and detect whether the mouse is within 20 pixels of either side of this x,y co-ordinate, we will then get a *true* if the mouse is within the dotted zone in the picture.

# Flash Games Studio

## Using Event Scripts

The player move script uses this system, and you can see it attached to a blank movie clip in frame 5 of the Events layer. The main timeline is halted at this frame via a stop action on the main timeline.

The first thing to notice about this script is that it uses a clip event. By triggering the script on a *mouseDown* event, the script only runs when it's needed, and this is a major advantage of using an event driven script rather than one attached to a frame based loop. This is something to bear in mind when we come to create real time games - event driven scripts are much more efficient than frame based polling loops for detecting inputs.

The only other issue to bear in mind is that an event script attached to a movie clip affects the movie clip timeline. In this case we want to affect the root, so all global variables referred to in our event script (and instances on the root timeline) have to be preceded by _root.

### Creating the Facility for Player Moves

1.  Firstly, we require a few lines to capture the mouse position and set the Boolean variable `goTaken` to `false`. This will become true later on in the script only if a valid turn has been made:

    ```
    onClipEvent (mouseDown) {
        xmouse = _root._xmouse;
        ymouse = _root._ymouse;
        goTaken = false;
    ```

    The next part of our code is the detection loop. This looks at each tile position in a turn, and whether the mouse is within the middle 40 pixels of the tile center (or rather, within 20 pixels either side of the tile center). Notice that I have used *Math.abs* to detect whether the mouse is within either +20 or -20 pixels of the center of an axis in just one line of code:

    ```
    for (i=0; i<=2; i++) {
        for (j=0; j<=2; j++) {
            if (Math.abs(xmouse-_root.tile[i][j].x)<20) {
                if (Math.abs(ymouse-_root.tile[i][j].y)<20) {
    ```

# Turn-Based Games and Advanced Logic

However, just checking for a tile hit is not quite enough, the tile also has to be empty. This check is made by looking at tile[0...2][0...2].state. If this is blank, then we know that this tile is not yet occupied, and a correct turn has been made. We can therefore set goTaken to true:

```
if (_root.tile[i][j].state == "blank") {
    goTaken = true;
```

Using the same methods as we did in the last chapter, we then duplicate the 'x' or 'o' movie clip at a specified depth:

```
name = "symbol"+_root.depth;
_root.o.duplicateMovieclip(name, _root.depth);
_root.depth++;
_root[name]._x = _root.tile[i][j].x;
_root[name]._y = _root.tile[i][j].y;
```

The action _root.o.duplicateMovieclip(name,_root.depth) copies our o instance, but the copy is at the same place as the original. The lines _root[name]._x = _root.tile[i][j].x and _root[name]._y = _root.tile[i][j].y are therefore used to move our o copy over the correct tile center.

We have to make a note of which tile we have now occupied with a 'o', and the next line does this by setting the chosen tiles *state* to 'o' (it was previously "blank"):

```
_root.tile[i][j].state = "o";
```

Finally, we have to update our diagnostic information. This sets the d2 field to our new state so that we can confirm that the right tile is being updated.

```
// diagnostic code
_root["d2-"+i+j] = _root.tile[i][j].state;
```

> *The code between the two comments can be removed in the final file once you no longer need the diagnostic text, and is a good way forward for developing complex code where you need to keep a lot of diagnostic feedback in the file until it is completed. In this case, I have just made the diagnostic text sit on a guide layer in the final FLA, so that the reader can re-instate the diagnostics by returning the* diagnostic *layer to a normal layer.*

# 5  Flash Games Studio

We want to keep running this script until all 9 turns have completed and the game is finished. If this is not the case, we simply stay at the current frame, allowing the mouseDown to be triggered again to force additional turns to be taken. If all 9 goes have been taken, we want to jump to the last frame (where our event script is no longer on the timeline, so no more turns can be taken).

We can do this via a simple set of if statements:

Here's how this is done in ActionScript:

*If this turn was valid and a new o symbol has been placed on a  
  previously blank frame (so goTaken==true)*  
*Then we increment the turn*

*If all 9 turns have been taken (_root.turn==9)*  
*Then we jump to the end of the game*  
*Otherwise we stay at the current frame*

```
if (goTaken) {
    _root.turn++;
    if (_root.turn==9) {
            _root.gotoAndStop("endGame");
    }
}
```

## Final Player Script

This is quite a heavily nested script, so for those of you who want to see it in its entirety, here it is:

```
// This event handles the players turn.
// On a mouseDown event, the code first
// looks to see where on the board the mouse
// is, and then if there is not already a
// symbol on that tile, it adds a "o" on
// that tile...
//
onClipEvent (mouseDown) {
  xmouse = _root._xmouse;
  ymouse = _root._ymouse;
  goTaken = false;
  for (i=0; i<=2; i++) {
    for (j=0; j<=2; j++) {
      if (Math.abs(xmouse-_root.tile[i][j].x)<20) {
        if (Math.abs(ymouse-_root.tile[i][j].y)<20) {
          if (_root.tile[i][j].state == "blank") {
            // This bit draws the "o" on the board.
            goTaken = true;
            name = "symbol"+_root.depth;
```

# Turn-Based Games and Advanced Logic

```
                _root.o.duplicateMovie clip(name, _root.depth);
                _root.depth++;
                _root[name]._x = _root.tile[i][j].x;
                _root[name]._y = _root.tile[i][j].y;
                _root.tile[i][j].state = "o";
                // diagnostic code
                _root["d2-"+i+j] = _root.tile[i][j].state;
                   // ————-
              }
            }
          }
        }
      }
      // if players turn has finished,
      // check for a completed game
      if (goTaken) {
        _root.turn++;
        if (_root.turn==9) {
        _root.gotoAndStop("endGame");
        }
      }
    }
```

We now have our game environment. The code understands our board and where the individual tiles are. It understands how to change the board and its own data model of the board when we take a turn, and it knows when the game is finished.
It still doesn't know how to play though...

## Creating a 'Dumb' Computer Opponent

The next FLA in our route is, unsurprisingly, TicTacToe1.fla, and it contains the code which we will later replace to allow the NPC to make more 'intelligent' moves. If you run this FLA, you will see that the computer knows how to take turns, but it isn't trying to win. The game doesn't detect a winning or losing position, and the NPC is making totally random moves. This may sound like a useless state of affairs for our newly created NPC, but it *does* have some useful features already:

- It knows about taking turns

- It knows where to place its 'x' and what constitutes a valid move

- It knows when the game has started and when it has completed

The timeline for this new FLA is identical to TicTacToe0.fla except for new keyframes at frame 2 (labeled 'startGame') and 6 (labeled computer) of the actions layer:

# Flash Games Studio

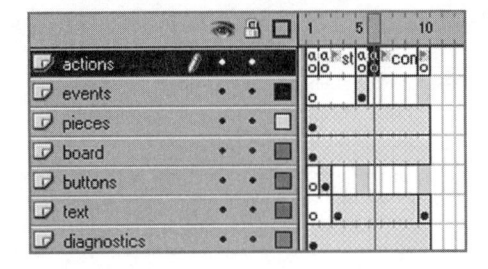

This NPC player script can be found attached to the frame labeled computer:

The first few lines select the NPC's next move. Lines 2 and 3 (listed below) randomly select the tile we want to move to. Because this tile may be occupied, we have to make sure that this is not the case. This is performed by our do... while loop, which makes us loop back and pick another tile if the tiles status property is not blank:

```
do {
    i = Math.round(Math.random()*2);
    j = Math.round(Math.random()*2);
} while (_root.tile[i][j].state != "blank");
```

As you can see, i and j will both be a random number between 0 and 2, so the actual square can be any of the square indexes between tile[0][0] and tile[2][2].

> do.. while *and the related* while... *loops are not used that often in website design logic, but you will find yourself relying on them a lot in game logic. Unlike the* for... *loop, the* do... while *and* while... *loops are useful if you don't know how many times the loop will repeat. There are some subtle differences between these two conditional loops, and these decide which one is most appropriate.*

- The do...while will run through at least once (because the condition is checked at the end of each loop), whereas the while... can loop zero times if the condition is false on the first loop.

- If the loop condition is calculated by the loop itself (as is the case in our loop; the values of i and j we want to check are defined in the loop), then you *must* use a do... while because the loop has to run before the loop condition can be tested.

The next chunk of code draws the 'x' symbol at the chosen tile position and updates our diagnostic text. It's very similar to our 'o' drawing routine, so we'll skip over it as it doesn't introduce anything new:

# Turn-Based Games and Advanced Logic

```
name = "symbol"+_root.depth;
_root.x.duplicateMovie clip(name, _root.depth);
_root.depth++;
_root[name]._x = _root.tile[i][j].x;
_root[name]._y = _root.tile[i][j].y;
_root.tile[i][j].state = "x";
_root.turn++;
// --diagnostic lines--
for (i=0; i<=2; i++) {
    for (j=0; j<=2; j++) {
        _root["d1-"+i+j] = tile[i][j].state;
    }
}
```

The final bit of code takes us back to the player frame (which is frame 5 - the one with our mouseDown event script, allowing the human player to take another turn). If all of the goes have taken place, then the game again goes to the endgame frame, signifying that the game has ended:

```
if (_root.turn<9) {
    gotoAndStop ("player");
} else {
    gotoAndStop ("endgame");
}
```

The only other addition to this FLA is at the startGame frame. We've now got a couple of buttons on the stage (implemented via invisible buttons over static text), which direct us to the frame labeled 'player' (human player takes first turn) or computer depending on which button we press. During this frame, the timeline is halted via a stop action on the main timeline:

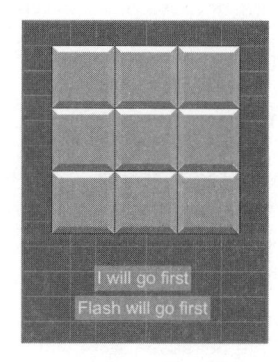

# 5   Flash Games Studio

No rocket science here, the two button scripts are simple goto commands of the form:

```
on (release) {
    gotoAndPlay ("player");
}
```

And we have a playable game!

OK, so our game may feel pretty unfinished, but there is now actually only one thing missing: *intelligence*. As you can see, the NPC cannot yet even recognize a winning position, and refuses to end the game until all nine squares are occupied. The inclusion of intelligence is the thing that will make our game playable for as long as tic-tac-toe remains interesting...

Our use of a dumb 'random', or other simplistic intelligence, is a good technique when developing games until we have worked out the game environment. It allows us to flesh out our game and build in the features that may have an impact on our intelligence engine, such as usability and the interface, handling and validating user responses, and setting up the internal game tracking database (if any). Now though, we need to take it a step further.

## Emulating Simple Intelligence

Our game will use the weighted outcomes method, following the theoretical discussion of this technique described at the beginning of this chapter. The completed game is included as TicTacToeFinal.fla.

Complex logic is best separated out into individual well-defined sections and coded separately as *functions*. Coding logic in this way has several advantages:

- Code is well defined – By looking at small parts of the entire problem we can make it easier to code and focus on the crux of the current problem

- It is easier to test functions because of their self-contained nature – By plugging in dummy values you can test each one individually, also bugs and mistakes can be contained within a function

- You can call the same function at several places in the FLA – Reduces code and therefore the number of errors

Looking at the requirements for a weighted outcome tic-tac-toe NPC, you will remember that we wrote:

For all unoccupied squares:

- If there are two 'x's on any row, column or diagonal, then I *must* place a cross in the third free square in that line because then I will win.

- If there are two 'o's on any row, column or diagonal then I *should* place a cross in the third free square in that line or I will lose.

# Turn-Based Games and Advanced Logic

- If there is at least one 'o' and no 'x' in any row, column or diagonal, then I *may* place an 'x' in the same line to prevent it becoming a row of two (because a row of two 'o's increases my chances of losing).

- If there is one 'x' in any row, column or diagonal, then I *may* place an 'x' in the same line to create a row of two because this increases my chances of reaching a winning position.

- If there is a free square, then I *could* place my 'x' in it.

So what do we have to do to implement this? Well, we first have to know how many 'x' or 'o' symbols there are in each winning line...

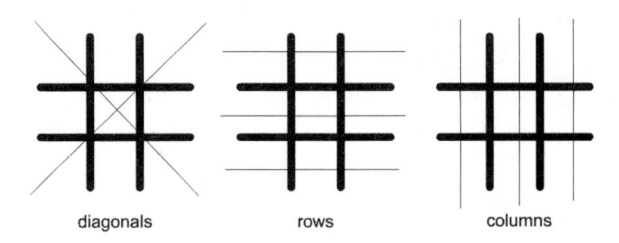

diagonals          rows          columns

So we need to write something that can count the number of symbols in each possible winning line. If that number happens to be three, then someone has won the game, and we need to detect this. If not, then a separate function is to add weightings to each tile in the current line being looked at, based on the number and combination of 'o's and 'x's in our line.

Having established this, we have two main functions to write;

1. One that looks at the board and counts the number of symbols in each row, column or diagonal. It should also look for a win (line of 3).

2. Another gives each tile in the line a weighting. Based on these weightings, the NPC will make its move.

Function 1 is actually required twice:

Once after the human player has taken his turn (to detect if the player has won)
Once after the NPC has taken its turn (to detect whether the NPC has won)

... so making it a function has the added advantage of reducing our code.

In TicTacToeFinal.fla, function 1 is called update (because amongst other things, it updates t)he game engine's internal database) and function 2 is weight (because it calculates the weightings.

# 5 Flash Games Studio

This FLA has a modified player move script that looks like this:

```
// PLAYER TURN HANDLER
// ******************************
//
// This event handles the players turn.
// On a mouseDown event, the code first
// looks to see where on the board the mouse
// is, and then if there is not already a
// symbol on that tile, it adds a "o" on
// that tile...
//
onClipEvent (mouseDown) {
    // This bit works out which tile was clicked on...
    xmouse = _root._xmouse;
    ymouse = _root._ymouse;
    goTaken = false;
    for (i=0; i<=2; i++) {
     for (j=0; j<=2; j++) {
        if (Math.abs(xmouse-_root.tile[i][j].x)<20) {
          if (Math.abs(ymouse-_root.tile[i][j].y)<20) {
             if (_root.tile[i][j].state == "blank") {
                 // This bit draws the "o" on the board...
                 goTaken = true;
                 name = "symbol"+_root.depth;
               _root.o.duplicateMovie clip(name, _root.depth);
                 _root.depth++;
                 _root[name]._x = _root.tile[i][j].x;
                 _root[name]._y = _root.tile[i][j].y;
                 _root.tile[i][j].state = "o";
             }
          }
        }
        // ---diagnostic line---
        _root["d1-"+i+j] = _root.tile[i][j].state;
        // ----------
     }
    }

    // if players turn has finished,
    // advance the main timeline.
    if (goTaken) {
       _root.winner = _root.update();
       if (_root.winner == "o") {
          _root.turn = 9;
       } else {
           _root.turn++;
       }
       if (_root.turn<9) {
```

# Turn-Based Games and Advanced Logic

```
            _root.play();
        } else {
            _root.gotoAndStop("endGame");
        }
    }
}
```

The only change here is the last set of highlighted *if... else* commands. Let's break them out in detail:

```
    if (goTaken) {
```

root.winner is given a value of either o, x, or none depending on whether x, o or neither have achieved a line of 3 (we'll look at the update function that defines root.winner presently):

```
        _root.winner = _root.update();
```

If update returns an 'o', we know that the player has won, and we end the game prematurely by setting _root.turn to 9:

```
        if (_root.winner == "o") {
            _root.turn = 9;
```

Otherwise no winner has yet been found, and we simply increment the turns taken so far:

```
        } else {
            _root.turn++;
        }
```

Finally, we check how far we are into the game. If we have not completed the game (all 9 turns not yet taken), we just continue the game via the play action. If we have reached turn 9 (either by taking 9 turns or the game being prematurely incremented to turn 9 by step 2 above), we go to the endGame label:

```
        if (_root.turn<9) {
            _root.play();
        } else {
            _root.gotoAndStop("endGame");
        }
    }
```

# 5  Flash Games Studio

> *Notice that the function* update *is called* by `_root.update()`, *and this is for the same reason that all variables in this event script are preceded by* `_root`. *The event is attached to our dummy movie clip and all actions refer to the dummy unless we specify otherwise. Because we want to work with the root timeline, we have to say so explicitly with the correct path.*

## A More Advanced NPC Routine

This FLA has a modified NPC move routine (frame 6) that looks like this:

```
if (turn<=1) {
    do {
            moveI = Math.round(Math.random()*2);
            moveJ = Math.round(Math.random()*2);
    } while (tile[moveI][moveJ].state != "blank");
} else {
    // otherwise pick best move based on weighting...
    moveI = 0;
    moveJ = 0;
    bestScore = 0;
    for (i=0; i<=2; i++) {
        for (j=0; j<=2; j++) {
                if (tile[i][j].weight>=bestScore) {
                        moveI = i;
                        moveJ = j;
                        bestScore = tile[i][j].weight;
                }
        }
    }
}
name = "symbol"+_root.depth;
_root.x.duplicateMovieclip(name, _root.depth);
_root.depth++;
_root[name]._x = _root.tile[moveI][moveJ].x;
_root[name]._y = _root.tile[moveI][moveJ].y;
_root.tile[moveI][moveJ].state = "x";
// check whether a win has occurred...
winner = update();
if (winner == "x") {
    turn = 9;
} else {
    turn++;
}
if (_root.turn<9) {
    gotoAndStop ("player");
```

# Turn-Based Games and Advanced Logic

```
        } else {
            gotoAndStop ("endGame");
        }
```

The differences between this logic and the previous, 'random move' one are highlighted. So what do these differences mean?

If this is the first or second turn in the game (that is the first turn the NPC makes, which is turn 0 if the NPC goes first, or turn 1 if the player went first), then the engine still makes a random move. Like the space invaders game we looked at earlier, this little bit of randomness is there to create some variation in game-play that keeps the human player on his toes. If we didn't include this element of random behavior the computer would *always* try to make the same opening move if it went first. This would always be the center tile, as it gets the highest weighting because more winning lines go through it than any other square thanks to the diagonal winning lines:

```
        // if this is one of the first two goes, pick a random move...
        if (turn<=1) {
            do {
                moveI = Math.round(Math.random()*2);
                moveJ = Math.round(Math.random()*2);
            } while (tile[moveI][moveJ].state != "blank");
```

If the first set of moves have been completed (both NPC and player have made one move) then the NPC starts to use its weighted table method to select the best move:

```
        } else {
            // otherwise pick best move based on weighting...
            moveI = 0;
            moveJ = 0;
            bestScore = 0;
            for (i=0; i<=2; i++) {
                for (j=0; j<=2; j++) {
                    if (tile[i][j].weight>=bestScore) {
                        moveI = i;
                        moveJ = j;
                        bestScore = tile[i][j].weight;
                    }
                }
            }
        }
```

# Flash Games Studio

The last few new lines of the script again look for a winning position, but this time for the NPC, who is playing as "x". The code again uses update to tell us if a row of three "x"s has been detected:

```
winner = update();
if (winner == "x") {
    turn = 9;
} else {
    turn++;
}
if (_root.turn<9) {
    gotoAndStop ("player");
} else {
    gotoAndStop ("endGame");
}
```

The real meat of the change between the previous FLA and ticTacToeFinal.fla are our functions. These are attached to frame 1 of the new layer functions.

## The Use of Functions in the Game

Some of you may have noticed that our weight function is not called from the main scripts. It's called from our other function update. Applying the rule that a function must be defined before it is called, the definition of weight must be made before the definition of update otherwise it won't work:

### The Weight Function

```
function weight (xNumber, oNumber) {
    var xNumber, oNumber;
    if ((xNumber == 2) && (oNumber == 0)) {
            // high chance of winning, so weight = high
            return 10;
            // low Chance of winning, so weight = low
    } else if ((oNumber == 1) && (oNumber == 0)) {
            return 3;
            // chance of losing on next go so weight = highest
    } else if ((xNumber == 0) && (oNumber == 2)) {
            return 4;
            // low chance of losing so weight = low
    } else if ((xNumber == 1) && (xNumber == 0)) {
            return 3;
    } else {
            // else we must return a value >0 otherwise Flash may
            ➥ chose
            // an occupied tile...
            return 1;
    }
}
```

# Turn-Based Games and Advanced Logic

Weight takes two arguments: xNumber and yNumber. These are the number of 'x' and 'o' symbols that were found in the current line that update is evaluating. Weight returns a weighting depending on the 'x'-'o' combinations as discussed in the theory of the weighted outcomes method. Notice that there are multiple *return* actions. This is perfectly legal; as soon as the first return is seen, the function will return the specified weighting and halt further execution of the function. The fact that you can have multiple exit points from a function, anytime the return is used to return the data from the function call, can be very useful in complex logic implementations, and is another reason for using functions.

**Our Update Function**

Our second function, update, looks like a bit of a monster, but is actually very simple, if a little repetitive.

The first thing that our function does is to define some variables, xWin, oWin, and noWin. This is done because of a quirk of functions – they can't return a literal string, which is what we want to do – so I've simply equated "x", "o" and "none" to these variables:

```
function update () {
    var i, j, k, l, xWin, oWin, noWin, win, xTotal, oTotal;
    xWin = "x";
    oWin = "o";
    noWin = "none";
```

The code then looks at each possible winning line in turn, starting with the columns, then the rows, and finally each of the two diagonals.

Depending on whether the current tile contains an "x" or "o" (which is deduced by looking at our game data via tile[0...2][0...2].state, xTotal and oTotal are incremented. The way this is done is a little novel:

xTotal += (tile[i][j].state == "x");

This will give us false on the right hand side of the equation if tile[0..2][0..2].state is not equal to "x", and true if it is. Because false is 0 and true is 1, adding all the Boolean results gives us the number of trues, or the number of "x" symbols seen in the line.

Now let's break down exactly how we'll do our searching, and apply our simulated intelligence.

# 5 Flash Games Studio

## Coding Our Weighted Intelligence NPC

1. The first thing we need to do is to work out the number of 'x' and 'o' symbols in each column:

   ```
   // DO COLUMNS
   for (i=0; i<=2; i++) {
         xTotal = 0;
         oTotal = 0;
         for (j=0; j<=2; j++) {
               xTotal += (tile[i][j].state == "x");
               oTotal += (tile[i][j].state == "o");
         }
   ```

2. At the end of the inner `for` loop, we have the number of "x" and "o" symbols in the current column (via variables xTotal, and oTotal). To convert the number of "x" and "o" symbols into a weighting, we call our previous function weight. The value that this returns is only used if the current tile is empty (and so tile[i][j].state == "blank").

   ```
   for (j=0; j<=2; j++) {
      tile[i][j].weight = weight(xTotal, oTotal)*(tile[i][j].state == "blank");
   }
   ```

   The above line in the loop is a shorthand way of saying:

   ```
   if (tile[i][j].state=="blank"){
         tile[i][j].state = 0
   }else{
         tile[i][j].state = weight(xTotal, oTotal);
   }
   ```

   The shortened line works because the condition (tile[i][j].state==blank) gives either 0 (false) or 1 (true), and multiplying this by our expression gives us either the expression, or zero. This shorthand way of implementing if logic can be much faster than using *if...* actions, and I used it here to show you a clever way of optimizing time critical logic as good shortcut practice when we come to real-time games.

3. The next chunk of code looks for a win condition (a line of 3). If this is true, update will return the name (either "x" or "o") of the winning side:

   ```
   // win?
   if (xTotal == 3) {
         return xWin;
   } else if (oTotal == 3) {
         return oWin;
   }
   }
   ```

# Turn-Based Games and Advanced Logic

**4.** The rows are implemented in exactly the same way as the columns, except the loop nesting is different so that we are now looking across the board (rows) rather than down it (columns):

```
// DO ROWS
for (j=0; j<=2; j++) {
        xTotal = 0;
        oTotal = 0;
        for (i=0; i<=2; i++) {
                xTotal += (tile[i][j].state == "x");
                oTotal += (tile[i][j].state == "o");
        }
        for (i=0; i<=2; i++) {
                tile[i][j].weight += (weight(xTotal,
oTotal)*(tile[i][j].state == "blank"));
                // ---diagnostic line---
                _root["d1-"+i+j] = tile[i][j].state;
                _root["d2-"+i+j] = tile[i][j].weight;
                // ------------
        }
        // win?
        if (xTotal == 3) {
                return xWin;
        } else if (oTotal == 3) {
                return oWin;
        }
}
```

Now, the two diagonals are also done in much the same way, except this time there are no loops because there is only one line of each type to evaluate.

This section checks the left diagonal:

```
// DO LEFT DIAGONAL
xTotal = (tile[0][0].state == "x")+(tile[1][1].state == "x")+(tile[2][2].state == "x");
oTotal = (tile[0][0].state == "o")+(tile[1][1].state == "o")+(tile[2][2].state == "o");
for (k=0; k<=2; k++) {
        tile[k][k].weight += weight(xTotal,
oTotal)*(tile[k][k].state == "blank");
        // ---diagnostic line---
        _root["d1-"+k+k] = tile[k][k].state;
        _root["d2-"+k+k] = tile[k][k].weight;
        // ------------
}
// win?
if (xTotal == 3) {
        return xWin;
```

```
        } else if (oTotal == 3) {
                return oWin;
        }
```

...and this section checks the right diagonal:

```
// DO RIGHT DIAGONAL
    xTotal = (tile[2][0].state == "x")+(tile[1][1].state == "x")+(tile[0][2].state == "x");
    oTotal = (tile[2][0].state == "o")+(tile[1][1].state == "o")+(tile[0][2].state == "o");
    for (k=0; k<=2; k++) {
            l = 2-k;
            tile[l][k].weight += weight(xTotal, oTotal)*(tile[l][k].state == "blank");
            // --diagnostic line--
            _root["d1-"+l+k] = tile[l][k].state;
            _root["d2-"+l+k] = tile[l][k].weight;
            // ----------
    }
    // win?
    if (xTotal == 3) {
            return xWin;
    } else if (oTotal == 3) {
            return oWin;
    }
```

6. Finally, if we haven't returned an "o" or "x" win so far, we'll reach the end of the function where we signify no-one has won yet by returning "none":

```
        return noWin;
}
```

## Hours of fun!

So now we have all the components for the finished game! If you wish you can follow through the logic by running through typical games with the diagnostic text visible (make layer diagnostics a normal layer), and you may also want the theory of how weighted outcomes work close to hand.

After playing the game for a while you'll soon see that the intelligence engine is fallible; it can be beaten by strategies that will result in a win not in the next turn but the turn after. This is because the computer only looks at the current turn, making it open to wrong footing. For a real time game this isn't that much of a problem because the computer will typically know what it wants to do faster than the human player. If you add the logic for the NPC to look for three corner tiles or two adjacent corner tiles and the middle tile being occupied by the same symbol, you can create an engine that will never lose. Although I added this enhancement in a subsequent version of the game, I didn't like it as much as the one you see – I like to win occasionally!

# Turn-Based Games and Advanced Logic

For those of you who want to take this game and make it more intelligent still, you may consider converting it so that it uses look ahead or learned behavior. The second of the two is actually the easiest to implement, but the first one is the real goal. Once you've worked out how to do it, you'll have all the basic code to create a Flash chess game, and from there... who knows?

## Parting shots

Tic-tac-toe is not the most long-term game, but the code we've generated contains the basis of emulated intelligence. By creating real time games with the same sort of game awareness, rather than the brute force strategies such as "we may be dumb but there's a lot of us", or "blindly follow the ball", add a new dimension to your games. This will contribute to overall longevity because your game can now react to the player in an intelligent way, and this will create variation in gameplay.

We've also gone through all of the game strategies you can use to create the illusion of an intelligent opponent. To do this requires a good understanding of generating ActionScript logic and intelligence engines.

Some of the more complex strategies are a little too intensive for the Flash plugin at the moment, but that doesn't mean you shouldn't know about them. Within a year or so of this book coming out, the hardware and software may be efficient and fast enough to allow us to incorporate advanced real-time emulated intelligence in our games and web site interfaces, and hopefully you'll be ready for it.

As with all early adopters, the trick is to learn these techniques and become familiar with them first. Not only do emulated intelligence routines add an extra input to your game designs, they also require a thorough knowledge of turning complex requirements into ActionScript logic, which is an invaluable skill.

# Flash Games Studio

## Summary

This chapter has moved us swiftly on through the actual creation of a simple game against our beloved computer opponent. Although you may be glad to have reached the end of this section, a look back now will confirm that this has taught us a great deal. We have managed to cover:

- Defining a game environment, be it a chess or tic-tac-toe board, or an entire game world
- Different strategies of adding intelligence to our NPC's responses, and the weighted outcome strategy in practice
- The advanced use of functions and the creation of databases
- The utilization of advanced structured code in ActionScript
- The entire process of producing an intelligent tic-tac-toe game
- Our ability to control game flow

In the next chapter we'll start to bring our emulated intelligence to life by looking at some real-time gaming strategies, I'll see you there.

# Turn-Based Games and Advanced Logic

5

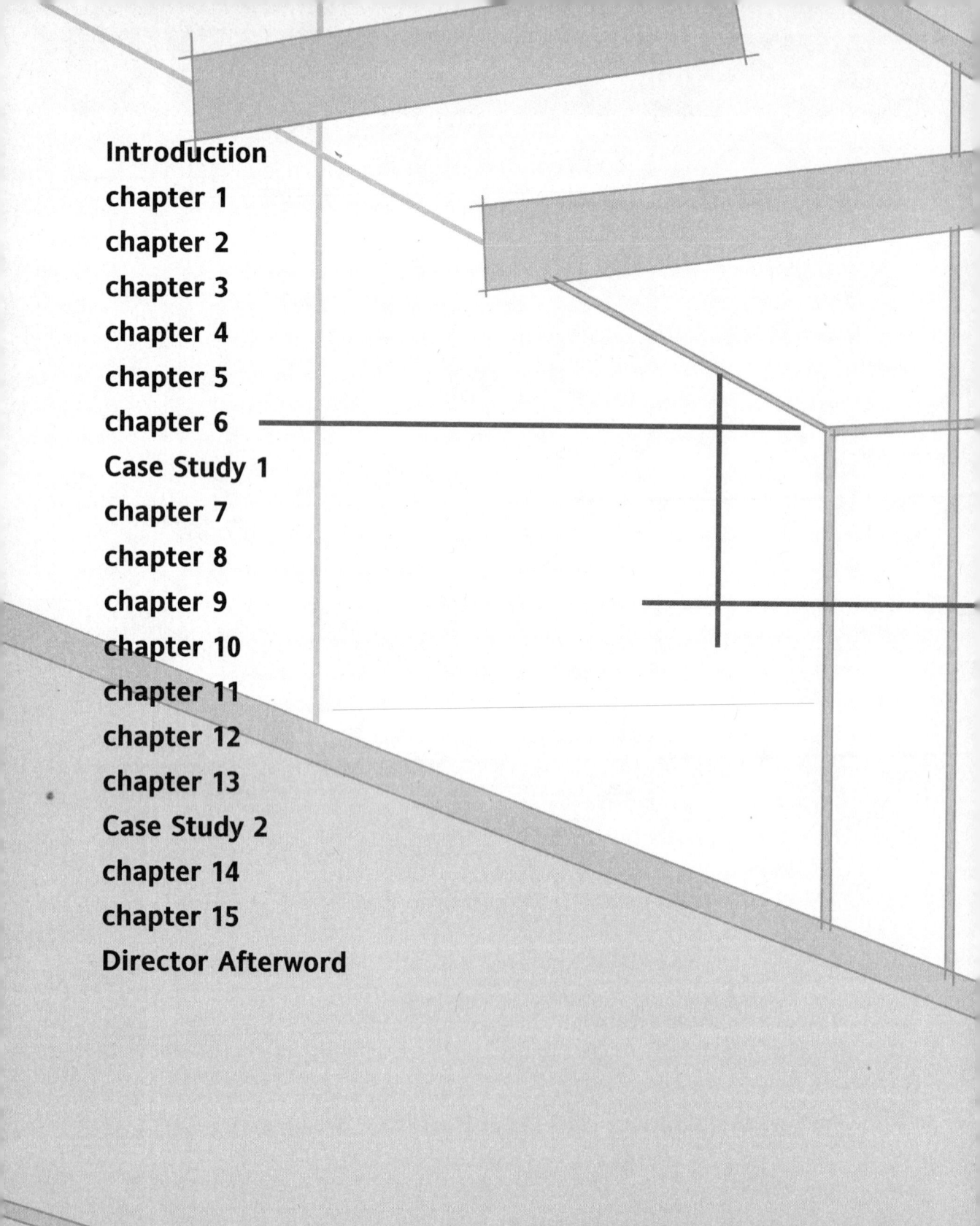

**Introduction**
chapter 1
chapter 2
chapter 3
chapter 4
chapter 5
chapter 6
Case Study 1
chapter 7
chapter 8
chapter 9
chapter 10
chapter 11
chapter 12
chapter 13
Case Study 2
chapter 14
chapter 15
**Director Afterword**

# Chapter 6
# Structured Real Time Programming

# 6    Flash Games Studio

## Structured Real-Time Programming

In this chapter we'll introduce the necessary principles for real-time game coding, and ramp up the difficulty a little from what we've done so far. For starters, the actual coding is more onerous. We're trying to build a real time animation with lots of things moving at the same time, and our code needs to be written using structures that can support this.

Later in the chapter we'll look at a general structure that allows real time animation with multiple sprites, but first, we need to talk about the most pressing concern when moving from turn based to real time – code optimization.

## Getting Ready for Real Time

### The Flash 5 Plug-in

There's been a large amount of discussion regarding the nature of the Flash 5 plug-in in relation to Flash 4. Initially, it was found that the Flash 5 plug-in was significantly faster. Early adopters were testing using old Flash 4 FLAS compiled in Flash 5. Later, when the same people were using true Flash 5 ActionScript, occasionally a *reduction* in speed was seen (you can see for yourself using `getTimer`) and this could be due to a number of reasons, the most likely of which is that some parts of Flash 5 functionality are simply the Flash 4 plug-in with a conversion wrapper around them. The most notable thing is that Flash 4 slash notation can be much faster than dot notation.

For more advanced Flash 5 notation, the equivalent Flash 4 scripts can be much longer however, and development time is vastly reduced in the Flash 5 environment. The advice at the moment is to write the code in Flash 5 and, if the game runs slow, consider converting critical portions to Flash 4 code (if you select Flash 4 for the Version in the File>Publish Settings>Flash, all non Flash 4 compatible commands will be highlighted). This may be resolved by the time of the Flash 6 plug-in, but worth keeping in the back of your mind until then.

The second thing to realize about the Flash plug-in is that it's an interpreted language. The SWF is a compressed version of the FLA (the actions are compressed to a series of individual bytes called *byte-code*) rather than a compiled language. This means that the SWF isn't converted to a computer friendly language (such as machine code), but is read instruction by instruction at run time. This is necessary for streaming to be able to take place.

### The Need for Speed

Our goal is to ensure that we minimize the number of bytes that Flash has to read during critical loops (because they will be parsed anew on every loop iteration!) by using as few separate commands as possible. Although using commands like `var` (which defines local variables on function blocks then deletes them at the end of the function) makes for structured code, their use can slow down performance if we're calling many functions in a single loop.

# Structured Real Time Programming    6

## Flash Bottlenecks

There are a few things that Flash is particularly slow at, and we should avoid doing these things in our game code if we can help it;

- Updating text fields. Surprisingly, Flash is *very* slow at doing this, and constantly updating text fields in a loop can make other animations grind to a halt. For games then, don't update an on-screen high score unless it actually changes, and use simple fonts. You may also consider the staggered redraw method described below to update the score once every few seconds.

- String editing (processes like concatenation) is traditionally a slow process, so avoid it during critical loops unless it's a turn based game.

- One of the biggest hits comes from moving graphics with alpha properties that aren't 100%. This is particularly an issue if there are other graphics behind the alpha effect. If you are using a solid background, consider using brightness or tint instead, as it's considerably faster.

- Certain math functions, particularly trigonometric ones are very slow (because they use a rather long winded binomial series in their evaluation), and we should avoid their use during run time. This doesn't mean that real time 3D in Flash is a big no-no, because a solution to this problem is shown in the form of look-up tables later in the chapter.

## Shorthand Coding

Writing games can result in lots of code and, as a rule, this involves scripting in Expert mode. One of the biggest reasons for errors in this mode is not having the correct number of {} brackets in loops and conditional statements. However, a good way to get round this is to simply not add them. Flash doesn't need the {} delimiters for simple actions.

So instead of writing:

```
if (x==1){
    test = 50;
}
```

...we can simply write:

```
if (x==1) test = 50
```

... and Flash will accept it, adding the correct indentations, semi-colons, and {} brackets itself, which we can see if we jump into Normal mode.

## Optimizing Code

There are many tricks we can use to get the zippy performance we need. This is vital for successful games programming, and is also a must if we want to create complex website navigation systems. Taken with the tips on graphic optimization given earlier in the book, the following techniques will give you a good idea on how to write efficient scripts.

### Optimizing Conditional Logic

Many of the commands in non-linear real-time applications are decision commands. We're constantly setting things based on particular circumstances, or jumping to new frames because something has happened. A little thought in optimizing this conditional logic can work wonders with performance because a typical game continually performs so many of them...

Booleans are a good way to quickly write conditionals without having to resort to large `if` statements:

```
if (x==1){
   if (test>40){
      y = 3;
   }else{
      y = 0
   }
}
```

...can be written by the quicker shorthand single line:

```
y = 3 * (x==1) * (test>40);
```

...because if any of the conditions are false, then the formula will multiply by 0, thus giving an answer of 0.

Both of the two representations have advantages. If both `x==1` and `test>40` are likely to be *true*, then the second representation is better because it's shorter and will contain slightly fewer bytes. If one of the conditions is more likely to be *false*, then the `if` is a better bet. If (`x==1`) is likely to be false, then placing it as the first thing to be tested has the advantage that the `if` will not evaluate the subsequent conditions (such as `test>40`).

`if... else if... else` structures can be very efficient. Placing the conditions most likely to be *true* first ensures that the `if` doesn't have to plough through the whole thing:

```
if (x==1){
    //do this
}else if (x>1){
    //do this
}else if (y=0){
    //do this
}
```

# Structured Real Time Programming

The code above will only evaluate the first line if it's highly likely that x is equal to 1. It's surprising how much we can increase performance if we take care to place the expressions most likely to be *false* at the bottom of an if... else tree. By doing so, we can reduce the average loop time of our major logic loops considerably, making them much leaner in readiness for real time applications.

Another good timesaving logic construction is to place mutually exclusive conditionals in the same if... else if action. For example, if we wanted to keep a movie clip between the left and right of the screen extents we *could* do this:

```
if (_x < left){
    // bring me back on screen from the left
}
if (_x > right){
    // bring me back on screen from the right
}
```

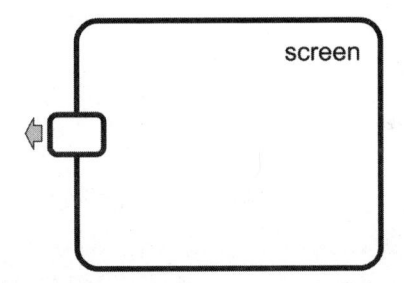

The diagram shows our movie clip going beyond the left end of the screen. Obviously, when it does this, it *can't* also be about to go beyond the right end as well. So rather than do both tests, if the first test is true, we know we don't have to perform the mutually exclusive second one, because both can't occur at the same time. Thus, taking this on board and using the structure below is twice as efficient.:

```
if (_x < left){
    // bring me back on screen from the left
}else if (_x > right){
    // bring me back on screen from the right
}
```

In most cases, *neither* of our two boundary conditions will be true, as our movie clip will be somewhere part way between the two edges. The second if structure is twice as efficient as the first in these majority cases because it only tests half of the conditions.

# 6 Flash Games Studio

**Event-Driven Interfacing**

Event-driven code can be much more efficient than frame-based code, particularly for user input and graphic control actions. By attaching code that handles user input and the subsequent graphic movements to events that are fired only when either the keyboard or mouse is pressed, we run scripts only when they are absolutely needed. Better still, detecting when scripts are required to run requires no additional calculations on our part; as soon as the event script runs, we know something is required. The following simple skeleton code illustrates this...

This code will only animate if the mouse is actually moving:

```
onClipEvent (mouseMove) {
    // do mouse animations
}
```

This code will make sure that the player's graphic only moves when a key is pressed:

```
onClipEvent (keyDown){
    // do key input handling
    // and then either perform the animations
    // or flag up that they need to be done
}
```

> *Sometimes a key press or other input starts a sequence of animation, and this needs to carry on after the key is no longer being pressed. This is what the flag in the last example does; it signifies something has to start, but doesn't specify when the animation should stop. This would be done by the animation code itself via a bit of code of the form*

```
if (flagSet){
    //do animation routine
    if (animation halt conditions are met) {
        flagSet =false;
    }
}
```

This will only carry out the animation so long as there's still a need to do so. Also, bear in mind that the Key clip events (`keyUp` and `keyDown`) can't detect for particular keys being released, which makes these events useful for only detecting a single key press and subsequent release. For games, where the player may release one key (such as the fire key) whilst keeping one or more direction key pressed, the key clip events become much less useful and we have to instead look at `Key.isDown(keycode)` polling within an `enterFrame` event script. We saw this in action in the *Event Handling* chapter earlier in the book.

# Structured Real Time Programming

## Staggered Update

One of the biggest performance hits for graphics is caused by attempting to alter too much on the stage in a single frame. By staggering the update, we can considerably lighten the animation load that our code is imposing, and this prioritizing is just as relevant on complex web sites as it is in games.

A nice little trick when moving lots of NPC graphics in real time is to not move them on every frame. For example, the following script will execute our main code only every other frame:

```
onClipEvent(load){
     flag = Math.round(Math.random());
}
onClipEvent(enterFrame){
      flag = !flag;
      if (flag){
           //do main code
      }
}
```

This gives flag a starting value of either 1 (true) or 0 (false). At every subsequent frame, the flag is toggled between true and false (!flag is true if it was previously false and vice versa). The main code only runs if flag is true, in this case on every other frame. For a large number of instances using this code, the actual frame that the main code runs at will be random, and because the human player sees movement all the time, he may not see the trick. Further, by making the player's graphic move every frame, the player sees the smoothest movement at his focus of attention, and is fooled into believing that everything is this smooth! For 3D and other intensive applications, a really nice trick is to base the update frequency on how far away the item is from the player. Not only does it give a performance enhancement, it also adds to the parallax effect for some applications.

We can also vary the redraw period on a time-based condition by using getTimer or the Time object.

## Look-up Tables

Another option to consider is to pre-calculate everything that may result in a performance hit before the game starts. This is particularly useful for working with real time trigonometry-heavy engines. By pre-calculating all the trig values (sine, cosine and arctangent are usually the ones we need) and placing them in an array (called a **look-up table**), we don't have to work them out for real during game execution. Look-up tables are used for more complex calculations in real-time physics models. For example, working out the drag on a virtual fighter traveling at a certain velocity in a flight simulator would be difficult, but by using the velocity as an index into an array, the complex physical model that produces this answer can be found with no calculations at all!

The following snippet of code sets up a fast look-up table for `sine(x)`. Although it can only return the sine of integer angles (so `sine(30.5)` can't be evaluated by this method), it's accurate enough for most gaming and real time applications. Of course, we could always use `sin(Math.round(angle))` to round the angle to the nearest integer if we were adding this look up table to existing code that expects floating point numbers:

```
// create and populate sine lookup array object.
sin = new Array(360);
for (i=0; i<=360; i++) {
   radian = (i/360)*2*Math.PI;
   sin[i] = Math.sin(radian);
}
function sine (x) {
   // Returns cos(x) via a look-up table.
   // Angle must be an integer between 0 and 360.
   return sin[x];
}
// Main Trig code uses look up table here...
sineLookUp = sine(20)
```

If we debug this movie we'll see a sine look-up table built up:

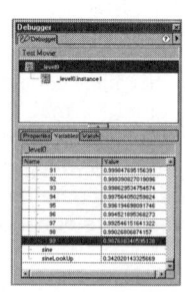

Calling `sine(20)` from here would return the 21$^{st}$ element in the series. Those of us who know a little about sines may want to consider reducing the look-up table so that it only stores data for the angles between 0 and 90 degrees, as the sines of all other angles can be calculated from these values.

## Adaptive Degradation

In traditional video games, one of the favorite tricks is to substitute far off or small graphics with low detail easy to draw versions. We can apply this to Flash very easily. For example, we can look at the actual time Flash is taking to render a single frame (via `getTimer`). If it's running fast we can add more graphics (or graphical detail) to the screen, if it's running slow, we can take some away. Both of these can be achieved via the `duplicateMovieClip` and `removeMovieClip` commands, or by making some embedded graphics in a movie clip appear or disappear by altering the `_visible` property. Simpler still, we can just create two frame movie clips that contain high and low resolution versions of our game graphic, and switch between them simply by `gotoAndStop` commands.

## Structured Real Time Programming  6

Taken together, these little techniques can be used to optimize our code as we move from turn based to real-time games. There's one problem though, and that's that we want lots of things to happen at the same time within the game. We want all of our NPCs to move at the same time as our player graphics at the same time as our logic and scorekeeping is evaluated. To write such Flash FLAs (which can be either games or complex web site interfaces), we have to look at particular structures that support this kind of requirement.

## The Power of Hierarchy

One of the features of advanced ActionScript is that it uses relative hierarchies. When using standard ActionScript and the old-fashioned `tellTarget` mindset, we reference a movie clip from scripts in one place (usually the root timeline) and, using the instance name of a movie clip `myName`, we control it using commands like:

```
myName._x += 5;
```

... which would move `myName` 5 pixels to the right. The problem here is that we have to know that the movie clip is called `myName`, and we can't use the same line to control another movie clip. Our solution can't be applied globally because it isn't general. This is bad programming, as shown by the diagram on the left:

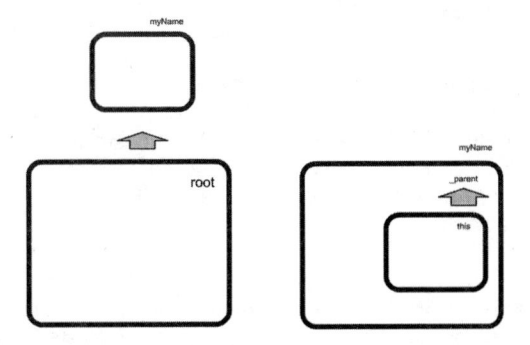

The diagram on the right shows a slightly different situation. Here we're controlling `myName` again, but this time we're doing so from a movie clip that's on the timeline of `myName` and not outside it. This time we could use the action above, but we can also use this:

```
_parent._x += 5;
```

...or:

```
_x += 5;
```

...depending on whether I want to control `_parent` or `this`.

203

The advantage here is that we don't need to know the name of the movie clip. Further, we can even take our ActionScript and put it in another movie clip, and that movie clip will also move 5 pixels to the right. Our solution can now be considered good programming because it's general, and it can be applied to any movie clip, rather than referring to a definite named instance.

When we need to control many instances at once in an efficient way, using a general name such as _parent or this has several advantages, the most important of which are:

- We don't have to use string concatenation within long loops to create unique names (such as alienName = "alien"+name). The fact that string commands are rather slow means that this isn't a performance efficient route, more so because we also have to store all those new instance names somewhere. Using an instance name such as _parent ismuch cleaner. Not only does it run faster but as long as we set up our hierarchy correctly, we can reference any movie clip without having to know its instance name.

- Our code isn't specific to any movie clip, and we can therefore use it to control any movie clip without making any code changes.

There are a number of more complex reasons for wanting to use relative paths via a hierarchy, but they won't become apparent until we've seen the method itself.

## GameWorlds and GameSprites

The method we're going to use to create our games may seem a little bizarre and impractical at first, but by the end of the chapter its virtues will be apparent. We create a 'universe' in which our game resides called the **gameWorld**. Within this world lie one or many autonomous elements, which we'll call **gameSprites**. Sprite would be simpler, and it's often used in this context, but we want to differentiate our term from Macromedia's use of the word 'sprite' in Director to refer to anything on the stage.

This method has been described previously in this book's sister publications **Foundation ActionScript** and **Flash 5 Studio**, although neither of these integrated it with a discussion on performance issues, as we'll be doing here when we come to design the second game. Because this is also a more advanced book than either of the other two, we'll move rather more quickly through the theory as well, which will hopefully please more of you than it dismays!

We've already discovered that the secret to making a good game engine is the ability to reference movie clips via relative paths. Anything else will either be too specific, slow or unwieldy to build into large scale ActionScript heavy control structures. We *can* do it from code that sits on the root timeline and controls instances by naming them explicitly, but it may not be as fast or as quick to develop. Because of the requirement for relative paths, the gameWorld will physically be either the root timeline or a movie clip that contains everything else. Each gameSprite is a movie clip on the gameWorld timeline, and so it has the gameWorld as its parent timeline.

A Metaphor for the gameWorld

Although the structure of the gameWorld and the control and interaction of gameSprites within it may seem a little odd at first, it's fundamentally very similar to how things occur in real life.

# Structured Real Time Programming            6

In real life we move around within our environment, and we're aware of images, sounds, emotions and sensations around us, which we react to. If we take the quantum step and decide that all of these elements around us are simply a form of information (albeit in some cases a high level sort that has physical form), then we can see how the gameWorld – gameSprite set-up is much the same.

As we see information in our world, the gameSprite sees information in the gameWorld. This information describes the gameWorld it inhabits. This is a good job because unlike us, the gameSprite is a software object, so has no senses to speak of except one: the ability to 'see' and react to data. It moves around within its gameWorld, taking care not to exceed any of the gameWorld limits, such as going outside the screen area or exceeding the gameWorld physics and traveling faster than it should:

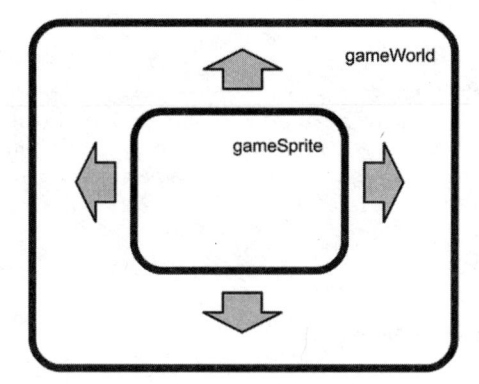

The gameWorld itself isn't as complex as ours (it has to be modeled in a computer after all), but it is very *precise*. Its world is defined by a series of numbers.

An important point to realize is that although the gameSprite moves within the gameWorld, there's nothing preventing the gameWorld from also moving. This is a very useful feature, because it allows us to quickly implement things like scrolling:

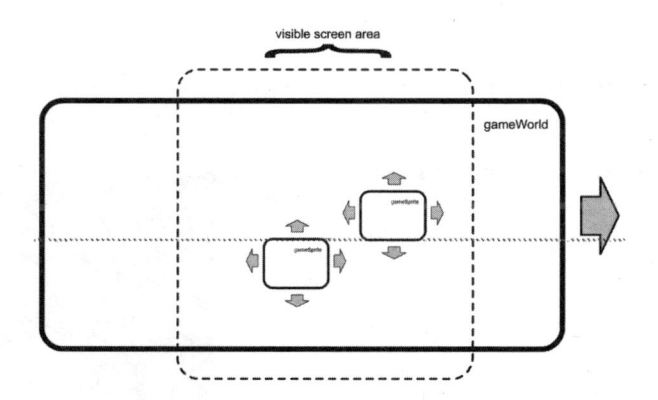

205

# Flash Games Studio

If we have a gameWorld that's bigger than the screen area, then by moving it in any direction, the contents of the world will also move. Not only will they move in the same direction as the world they are in, but any motion that they carry out as the world moves will also still work within the gameWorld itself, without the individual gameSprites having to know that their world is moving. It's rather like you within planet earth at this moment. You are possibly sitting somewhere reading this book, and you believe you aren't moving. But the planet is rotating at thousands of miles per hour, and you are rotating with it! You can also add other effects to the gameWorld timeline, and everything else inside it will follow suit: rotation, tint, scaling, whatever.

This relative hierarchy concept behind the gameWorld system may seem like a silly little structural concept, but it throws up all sorts of graphic niceties the more we use it. All those weird and wonderful scroll/rotation/zoom engines that arcade games of the late eighties had can be implemented easily within Flash as long as we're aware of the power of the gameWorld hierarchy.

> *If you ever decide to use the scrolling system, remember that you don't really want to draw things that aren't currently in the visible screen area, otherwise Flash will struggle. By simply setting the* _visible *property of all* gameSprites *outside the screen to false, you'll save all the unneeded (and unseen) re-draws.*

## Examples of Our gameWorld

The best way to show the gameWorld method being used to create games is to go ahead and build them. The first example will recreate the game Pong, a simple tennis game with only three gameSprites, designed to familiarise ourselves with the new structures being introduced. Once we've got through that, we'll look at something a little more complex with a greater level of gameSprite – gameWorld interaction – a side scrolling shooter.

## Tennis

Tennis, or Pong, is a good game to start off with because it has a simple structure and rules, allowing us to concentrate on the game creation method. In this case we'll have only three gameSprites, namely the two bats and the ball.

Tennis is a well-known game, and you can pick up the rules of the video game simply by playing it. Have a look at the completed game, `tennisFinal.fla`:

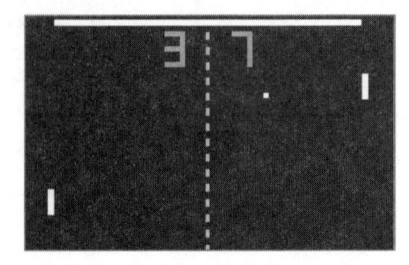

# Structured Real Time Programming 6

To create a game, there are a number of steps to be taken. We need to:

- Define the rules
- Define the game elements and their relationship
- Build the gameWorld
- Build the gameSprites

## Defining the Rules

Firstly, we need to know what we want to create. Tennis is a game with fairly easy rules, and the rules for video tennis are even easier:

1. One player starts by serving, meaning that the ball starts from the server's side of the court and moves towards the opponent's side at a constant speed.

2. If the ball hits the court top and bottom, it should bounce back into the court.

3. If the opponent misses, then the player wins a point, and the game continues from 1.

4. If the opponent hits the ball, then the ball returns back across the court.

5. If the player subsequently misses, the game continues from step 1, except that the opponent is now the 'player', and he serves the ball.

6. Steps 1 to 5 continue until either one or the other player achieves a certain score.

A couple of things to notice in our rules:

- The 'rules' not only specify the rules of the game, but also how things should behave; the fact that the ball should bounce is a rule. Computers have no knowledge of reality, and we need to also define *physical rules* – otherwise they won't be included!

- As with most games, our tennis game is a simplified version of the real thing. This is necessary in many cases, and always with Flash – we have to approximate to get a decent frame rate in our final game.

## Defining the Game Elements

When defining the game elements, most people count three things: the player's bat, the opponent's bat, and the ball. In the real world that would be okay, but in a virtual world there's one other vital component that we should always define first, namely our gameWorld. The gameWorld consists of two things; a definition of the game physics and limits and, more subtly, a means for gameSprites to talk to each other in an efficient way.

# 6  Flash Games Studio

**The gameWorld**

So what does a tennis gameWorld look like? Something like this:

Because the ball can bounce off the top and bottom of the screen, we've drawn lines there. The central dotted line represents the net. Although it serves no purpose in the game, it makes the game look a little more like real tennis.

In terms of our gameWorld, we haven't even started on our definition. We need to define a number of things:

- Limits to tell us when the ball is inside and outside the court.

- Attributes of our world that affect the ball:
  - The maximum ball speed.
  - The amount a ball bounces

- Attributes that affect our bats:
  - The maximum bat speed
  - The relationship between the bat position and the angle at which a ball bounces off it.

The best way to define all this information is to think of the gameWorld (and in fact everything) as a **software object**. Don't confuse this with object-oriented programming: we're only thinking of our game planning in object terms, and we may or may not come to follow the actual coding design in the same way (although conceptualizing in object terms is a good start to coding in the same way). To see all this in terms that we as Flash designers understand, the easiest way forward is to show it graphically via **object block diagrams**.

# Structured Real Time Programming    6

## Object Block Diagrams

An object block diagram (**OBD**) shows us a software object and its interfaces. It's rather like a flowchart, except that rather than tell us about logic flow, the OBD shows us *code structure* in the form of object interfaces and relationships. Again, the best way to show this is to see one, so here's the OBD for our gameWorld:

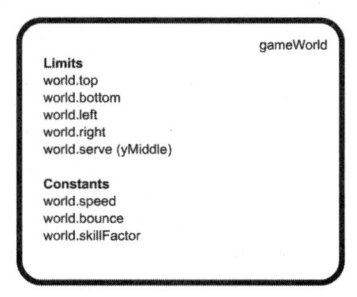

```
                                              gameWorld
       Limits
         world.top
         world.bottom
         world.left
         world.right
         world.serve (yMiddle)

       Constants
         world.speed
         world.bounce
         world.skillFactor
```

The big square represents our gameWorld object, and the list is our gameWorld's attributes (in real object terms they are its *properties*).

The value of using OBDs will become apparent as we work through this chapter. Listed below are the elements that went into the creation of the OBD for our tennis game.

## Creating this OBD

I started with a blank piece of paper and drew a big square in the middle. I then thought about what my game needs to know about itself. The gameWorld is essentially a tennis court, so I need to know its edge limits (top, bottom, left, right). In real tennis, there's also a position that the players take during serves. In my simplified world, I took this point simply to be the center of the court, so the players will serve from the center of the left or right edge:

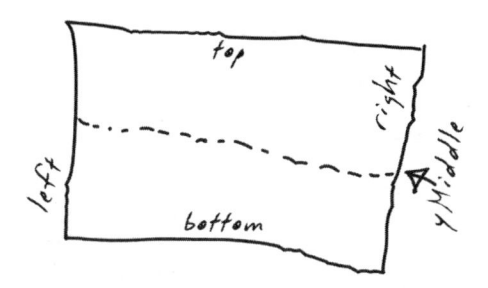

[Hand-drawn sketch of a tennis court labeled "top", "bottom", "left", "right", with an arrow pointing to "yMiddle" on the right edge]

I then drew another square on a different sheet and thought about constants and physical properties. The player's bat on the left will have some sort of speed or skill factor associated with it, and the ball will have a bounce property. The ball speed will be defined by some sort of speed constant (there's no acceleration in this game) and this may also relate to the player skill factor as you can see on the next page.

# Flash Games Studio

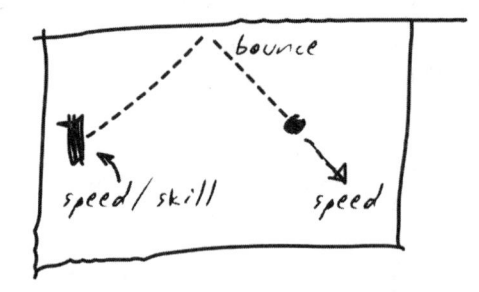

Picking out all of the pertinent properties of my world from my sketches and listing them on a third piece of paper gave me the gameWorld OBD that we saw earlier. The ability to pick out the important factors that will make up our gameWorld comes with time, and it's rare to come up with all the factors at the first attempt, but once you've built a few games you'll start to see that there's a pattern. First, we need to define our limits and boundaries, and then our game physics.

## Our gameSprites

The gameSprite objects sit inside the gameWorld (that is they are on its timeline) and read all the gameWorld limits and physical parameters (something that we'll call **configuration**):

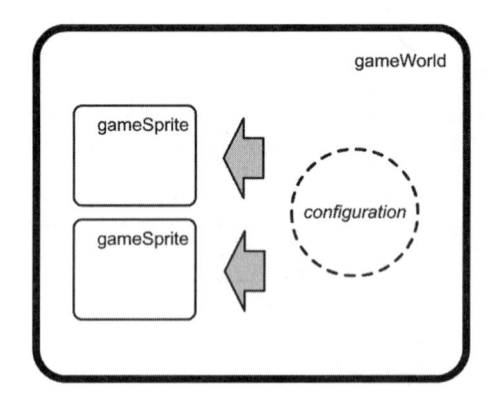

### Communication between gameSprites

The gameSprites will each be controlled by their own script, and this is the best way that I know of to build games. The scripts have to be de-centralized because too much needs to happen at the same time for control to be bunched in the root timeline. We'll look at writing these scripts for real in a moment.

This de-centralization does however throw up one additional problem – how do the gameSprites talk to each other? The answer is simple – they don't! The generalized way to accomplish this is that all communication goes through the gameWorld, and not between individual gameSprites.

The fact that this is the only way forward becomes obvious if we need multiple gameSprites talking to each other. A mess of communication lines builds up between all our information channels, slowing our movie down to a crawl as shown in the diagram opposite:

# Structured Real Time Programming

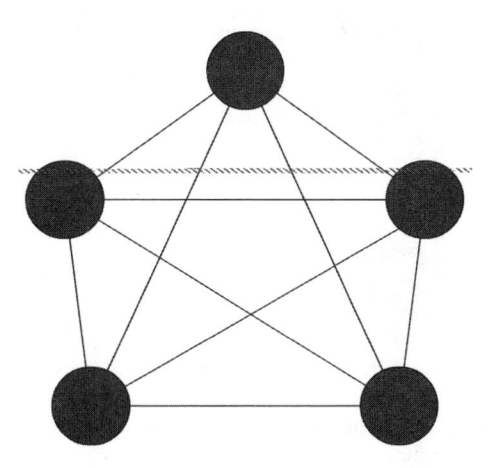

The only neat way to do it is for each of our gameSprites to leave data for whoever wants to read it, and the best place to leave them is the common area that all gameSprites inhabit – the gameWorld:

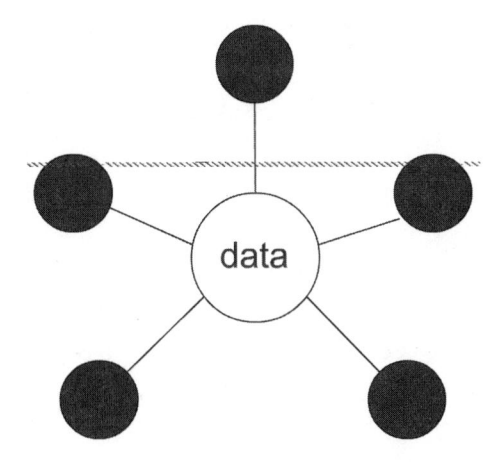

If any gameSprites contain data that they need to broadcast, they don't simply send it to the gameSprite that needs to get it, but instead make it available to a central common area, the gameWorld (usually `_parent` or `_root`). Then if any other gameSprite needs to see the information, it simply goes to the gameWorld and retrieves it. The good thing about this is that the sender gameSprite doesn't have to know who the recipients are, and the recipient doesn't have to know who sent the information. No instance names are therefore required, and the method becomes general. The only thing the gameSprites need to know is the name of the variable containing the data, `dataName`.

# Flash Games Studio

So, in terms of our object block diagrams, the setup is like this

The gameSprites sit inside the gameWorld and send data to the gameWorld or read data from it. To send data, a gameSprite simply uses this action:

```
_parent.dataName = data;
```

This creates a new variable on the gameWorld timeline, or more correctly, a **global variable,** and to read it the receiving gameSprite does this:

```
dataName = _parent.dataName;
```

This creates a new variable with value data on the gameSprite timeline, which as you may have guessed, is a variable local to the gameSprite timeline. We've all done this before in Flash, but perhaps not realized that this passing of variables can provide a general way of creating inter-object communications.

The shared data created by gameSprites tells other gameSprites what the originator is doing or its **status**, so we'll give this form of data the same name:

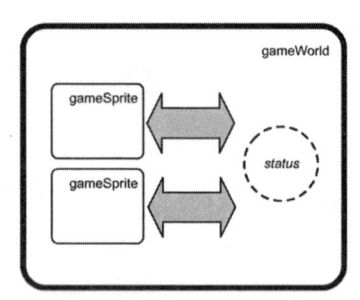

You'll notice that the only difference between **status** and **configuration** is that status comes from gameSprites, and configuration comes from the gameWorld itself. There's another more subtle difference: status data changes as the game progresses, so therefore needs to be communicated regularly because of this. Configuration, on the other hand, stays the same or changes rarely, and so only needs to be read at the start of each game, or sometimes at the beginning of each level.

## Our Tennis gameSprites

So, in our tennis game we need to define what status data each gameSprite will need to broadcast. The way to think about this is to see each gameSprite as a blindfolded person. The only thing they can use is data or 'information cues' from the other gameSprites, and the question to consider is what information does this gameSprite need to see the world around it?

# Structured Real Time Programming

## Player Bat gameSprite

**Configuration**: The player's bat is on the left of the court, so it will need to know where left actually is. To make sure it doesn't run outside the court, it will also need to know top and bottom. To serve, it will need its serving position, `serve`. To move around, it will need to know how quickly it should react to the user, `skillFactor`.

**Status**: The player's bat only interacts with the user's inputs and doesn't need to know anything else. Some of us may be a little bemused as to how the player's bat can get by without knowing the location of the ball. When considering collisions (such as the one between our bat and the ball), there are always two ways to make the collision detection. We can detect the collision from either gameSprite, but the easiest way to do it is to keep all the collision detection code in the same place. If we put the detection scripts in the bats, then *both bats have to check for a collision*, but if we put the detection in the ball then it's the only thing that needs to make the check.

## NPC Bat gameSprite

**Configuration**: the NPC needs to know everything that the player bat knows, except that it's on the right side of the court, so it needs to know right instead of left.

**Status**: The NPC bat needs to move like a real player to be believable. A real tennis player moves towards the ball when the ball is moving towards the player, and moves towards the center of the court in readiness for the next volley if the ball is moving away. Therefore, all the NPC really needs to know is the direction the ball is going and where the ball is. The NPC doesn't really need to know the ball's x coordinate, but rather just needs to keep itself in line with the ball's y coordinate (as discussed in the last chapter) so that it's in a position to force a 'hit'.

## Ball gameSprite

**Configuration**: The ball needs to know all of the world limits because it's able to move to any part of our gameWorld. It therefore needs to know `left`, `right`, `top`, `bottom`, and `serve`. It also needs to know how to bounce and how fast to travel, so it needs `speed` and `bounce`.

**Status**: The ball needs to know two things; the position of the player's bat and the NPC's bat. The bat x positions are irrelevant (because the bats don't move in the x direction, so their positions in this respect are configuration data rather than status. The bats simply stay at the far left and far right of the court, so the ball can be programmed to 'know' this by assuming that the bat positions are left and right).

# Flash Games Studio

**Our gameSprite OBDs**

This information gives us a rather important ability; the ability to show the relationships within our gameWorld:

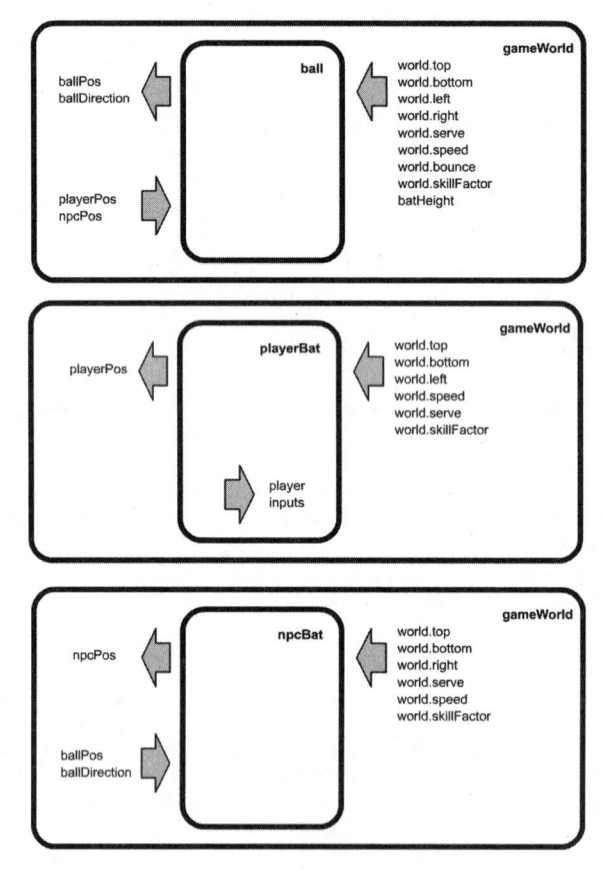

```
                                                                gameWorld
                        ┌──────────────┐
                        │     ball     │
    ballPos      ⇐      │              │   ⇐    world.top
    ballDirection       │              │        world.bottom
                        │              │        world.left
                        │              │        world.right
                        │              │        world.serve
                        │              │        world.speed
                        │              │        world.bounce
    playerPos    ⇒      │              │        world.skillFactor
    npcPos              │              │        batHeight
                        └──────────────┘

                                                                gameWorld
                        ┌──────────────┐
                        │   playerBat  │
    playerPos    ⇐      │              │   ⇐    world.top
                        │              │        world.bottom
                        │              │        world.left
                        │              │        world.speed
                        │              │        world.serve
                        │              │        world.skillFactor
                        │              │
                        │      ⇒       │
                        │   player     │
                        │   inputs     │
                        └──────────────┘

                                                                gameWorld
                        ┌──────────────┐
                        │    npcBat    │
    npcPos       ⇐      │              │   ⇐    world.top
                        │              │        world.bottom
                        │              │        world.right
                        │              │        world.serve
                        │              │        world.speed
                        │              │        world.skillFactor
    ballPos      ⇒      │              │
    ballDirection       │              │
                        └──────────────┘
```

We can actually code our world up directly from these diagrams, and the only other thing we might end up needing is the odd flow chart to sort out some tricky logic. Each diagram shows one of the three gameSprites in this game and its interfaces with the gameWorld timeline that it's placed on. To the left we see the configuration data that it needs to initialize itself, and to the right we see the status information that it's required to broadcast and retrieve from the gameWorld. Finally, inside the gameSprite we see inputs (such as user actions) that the gameSprite must retrieve itself from outside of the gameWorld.

Because each gameSprite is shown in terms of just itself and its interfaces to the gameWorld, what we have here is a path to something that's both a **modular** software definition and conducive to an object-oriented implementation if we wished to go down that path.

The diagrams give us a visual means of checking that our gameWorld – gameSprite relationship is well defined, and that the interfaces are all working. Data that's required by one gameSprite is provided by another one somewhere else along the line.

# Structured Real Time Programming    6

## Our Flash Timelines

Have a look now at the `tennisfinal.fla`. The main timeline is a simple three frame construction, consisting of a 'gameWorld initialization' frame (frame 1) a 'game start' frame (frame 2, labeled startGame) and finally a 'game in progress' frame (frame 3). Only frame 2 has a label because it's the only one that's referenced by other frames:

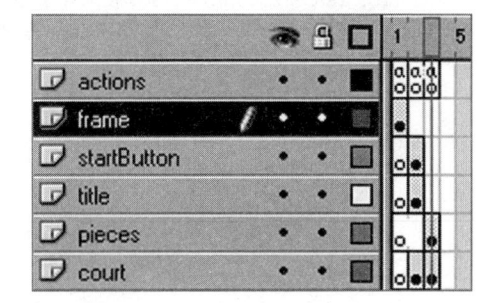

- actions is the ActionScript layer. Although you may not see this in the some of the later timelines, this has

    a layer color of black. I try to use this color as often as possible to differentiate layers that contain only ActionScript, events (event scripts attached to dummy movie clips) or function definitions. I tend to be a little creative with my layer names at times, but I can differentiate between scripting and graphical layers easily ten years from now because of this color-coding.

- frame contains some graphics that are used in the game initialization. More on this in a moment.

- startButton and title are just a (very) simple splash screen and button to get into the main game.

- pieces and court hold the gameSprites and court background graphics respectively.

Now that we know what each layer and frame represents, let's take a look at what they actually hold.

215

# 6 | Flash Games Studio

## Coding our Game

### Frame 1: Initialization

The actions layer provides the initialization script to create the gameWorld data. We'll be using an object called world to hold the main gameWorld data. There's no technical reason to do this (we can use simple variables instead), but in complex worlds this can provide a structured programmer-friendly naming convention for our data. Within the FLA, you'll see that the code is quite heavily commented. Here's the Frame 1 code in full:

```
// INITIALIZE WORLD
// ─────────────
//
//
world = new Object();
//
// define world boundaries
world.left = bounds._x;
world.right = bounds._x+bounds._width;
world.top = bounds._y;
world.bottom = bounds._y+bounds._height;
world.serve = (world.bottom-world.top)/2;
//
// Define world constants
world.speed = 20;
world.skillFactor = 1.5;
world.bounce = 1;
//
// define global bat parameters
batheight = bat._height/2;
//
// Define Sounds
batBounce = new Sound();
batBounce.attachSound("batBounce");
WallBounce = new Sound();
wallBounce.attachSound("wallBounce");
miss = new Sound();
miss.attachSound("miss");
miss2 = new Sound()
miss2.attachSound("miss2")
gameOver = new Sound();
gameOver.attachSound("gameOver");
// Blip to signify start of game...
batBounce.start(0,1)
```

# Structured Real Time Programming 6

1. We need to use the first part of our script to implement our gameWorld OBD shown previously. This is created simply by defining data to implement the diagram. There are references to an instance called `bounds` and another called `bat`. These both live on the frame layer:

   The rectangle `bounds` is used to define the boundaries of our gameWorld. Although we could have just defined it via literal numbers, it's preferable to use a frame-shaped movie clip, which is placed visually around the area we want to define. This makes sense because if we ever need to change the stage size, all we have to do is resize the frame and the graphics, and everything will still work. This is a nice little tip for web site design as well. As the Flash plug-in and hardware get faster we can make our site pages physically bigger. Using frame movie clips to define our stage coordinates makes them easier to scale up in the future.

2. There's also a bat shape in the top left corner, which is referenced in the action:

   ```
   batheight = bat._height/2;
   ```

   This is done for the same reason as we've used `bounds`. If we decide to change the size of our bat graphics the bat dimensions are also updated by this line automatically, and I like an easy life littered with little shortcuts rather than having to think too hard when the client comes knocking at the door with a sheaf full of 'minor changes' to the job. We divide the height by two because we'll want to know where the center of the bat is later on.

3. Although `bounds` and `bat` stay on the timeline during initialization, we don't want them to appear at all, so we need to add the following script to both of them to make them invisible to the user:

   ```
   onClipEvent (load) {
   _visible = false
   }
   ```

4. The next part of our script defines the sound objects associated with the retro tennis game console beeps. The sound samples were created via a Korg Electribe analog synthesizer. Sounds so retro that they probably transcend the term and, like the lava-lamp, have become techno-kitsch.

217

5. The final line in this script is just a little personal touch. The first video game console I ever owned sounded a little beep on power up (and went to a very similar splash screen as the movie we're creating). Its almost twenty years later, and about the only thing it does now is the beep, so it's a pretty darned authentic touch.

## Frame 2: Splash Screen

In frame 2 we simply create a splash screen:

6. The blocky 'Tennis' logo is covered by an invisible button that has to be clicked to enter the game proper on frame 3. The button also serves the dual purpose of hiding/revealing the mouse pointer. Frame 2 of the actions layer reveals the mouse with this little script, as well as stopping the main timeline until the button is pressed:

```
// START GAME SCREEN
// ————
//
Mouse.show()
stop()
```

7. The button then hides the mouse and sends us on to frame 3 with this:

```
on (release) {
Mouse.hide()
play ();
}
```

Ok, that little exercise has got everything prepared. We're now ready to proceed to Frame 3, where our game itself lies.

# Structured Real Time Programming

## Frame 3: The Game

Frame 3 is where our gameWorld strategy really starts to make coding easier. Each script in this frame is based on one of the OBDs defined earlier, and once the OBDs were designed properly and all of the interfaces on them were consistent with each other, then the code creation was foolproof.

Frame 3 contains an odd looking little icon at the top left area of the stage. This is actually our two bats and our ball as shown:

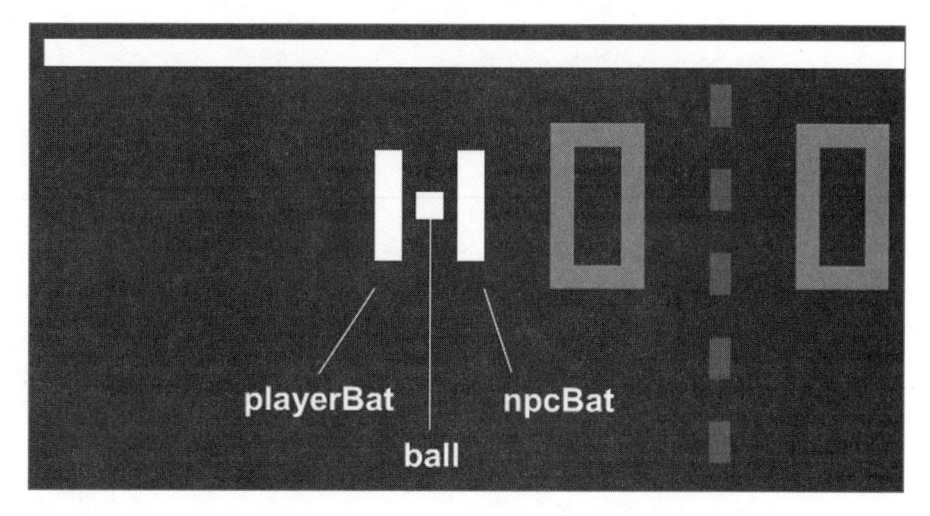

playerBat    npcBat
ball

The first gameSprite we'll look at is the player bat.

> *The human player's gameSprite is usually the simplest to implement and as a rule should be the first one we create the ActionScript for. Because it relies on the user to give it intelligence, it has a very simple set of scripts (it usually just looks for user inputs and maybe a couple of other general housekeeping tasks like collision detection or working out if it's dead or not). Also, because its main input is the user, it can animate itself without the other gameSprites broadcasting to the gameWorld.*

# 6  Flash Games Studio

## The Player Bat Script

Here's our player bat script in full:

```
onClipEvent (load) {
    // COPY WORLD CONFIGURATION
    left = _parent.world.left;
    top = _parent.world.top;
    bottom = _parent.world.bottom;
    serve = _parent.world.serve;
    speed = _parent.world.speed;
    skillFactor = _parent.world.skillFactor;
    // SET MY INITIAL POSITION
    _x = left;
    _y = serve;
    // DEFINE LOCAL DATA
    myPos = _y;
    myTarget = myPos;
}
//
onClipEvent (enterFrame) {
    // USER INPUTS
    myTarget = _root._ymouse;
    // CALCULATE NEW POSITION
    myPos -= (myPos-myTarget)/skillFactor;
    // ANIMATE ME
    _y = myPos;
    // BROADCAST GLOBALS TO GAMEWORLD
    _parent.playerPos = myPos;
}
```

We'll now break the code down and explain it. To assist in the understanding of our gameSprite functionality, we'll dissect this first example of coding to enable us to obtain a greater insight into its individual features and the code it uses. This will be of benefit when we come to coding the gameSprites for our second game which, although more complex, use the same basic principles.

1. We begin with an onLoad event. This is our initialization. During this event the gameSprite is accessing the global data that defines the gameWorld and creating a local version of this configuration. We don't have to do this (we can just keep referring back to the gameWorld global data), but it does make for gameSprites that are autonomous from the gameWorld once they've been initialized. This is useful in debugging, because errors tend to be contained in the individual gameSprites themselves (or their interfaces) once initialization has been seen to proceed successfully (which we can do by making sure that the local data matches the global data, via the debugger window):

# Structured Real Time Programming

```
onClipEvent (load) {
    // COPY WORLD CONFIGURATION
    left = _parent.world.left;
    top = _parent.world.top;
    bottom = _parent.world.bottom;
    serve = _parent.world.serve;
    speed = _parent.world.speed;
    skillFactor = _parent.world.skillFactor;
```

> *A point to note here is that although we're not using 'structured' actions like* function *or* var*, our gameSprite still contains local data and is a self standing object-like structure, complete with localized data and well-defined interfaces. Because our structure here is implicit rather than being forced via additional scripting, our system is fast, efficient and easy to set-up and debug.*

2. After setting the bat's initial position we then set up the gameSprite's own local variables `myPos` and `myTarget` based on this initialization from the gameWorld:

```
    _x = left;
    _y = serve;
    // DEFINE LOCAL DATA
    myPos = _y;
    myTarget = myPos;
}
```

In fact, it's handy to remember these three stages, as you'll find that they can be used almost universally at the beginning of any gameSprite code. The gameSprite needs to:

- Acquire gameWorld configuration

- Create local variables and initialize them based on the gameWorld configuration

- Move to initial starting position

The process of taking our configuration from our main gameWorld timeline has distinct advantages. If we want to change our game, we only have to change it in one place - the gameWorld timeline. Changes we may make in things like difficulty level, gameWorld size, gravity and inertial constants automatically feed through the hierarchy, and each gameSprite will automatically see the new data and behave differently based on these values. We can even create new worlds with a different set of configuration values, and the gameSprites will automatically reflect this in their behavior. Our code is standardized within the gameSprite structure.

3. The main script runs via the next event, the `enterFrame` script. This again has a well-defined structure and order of actions:

   ```
   onClipEvent (enterFrame) {
       // USER INPUTS
       myTarget = _root._ymouse;
       // CALCULATE NEW POSITION
       myPos -= (myPos-myTarget)/skillFactor;
       // ANIMATE ME
       _y = myPos;
       // BROADCAST GLOBALS TO GAMEWORLD
       _parent.playerPos = myPos;
   ```

   The bat takes the mouse y position as its input, and then **calculates** the new position for the gameSprite. If the gameSprite needs to read information from other gameSprites it will do it here by referring to `_parent`. The player bat calculates this new position using an inertia equation, which is usually smoother than a linear `keyPress` based motion.

   Following this, it **animates** the gameSprite to the new position (in this case using the implicit `this` path to refer to itself and move itself autonomously). This causes the bat to change its _y property to the newly calculated position.

   Next, the gameSprite **propagates** the new status information back to the gameWorld so other gameSprites can see the changes that have just taken place. The bat's y position is needed by the bat gameSprite (as per the OBDs shown previously) so its value is updated to the gameWorld timeline: `_parent`.

Although this is a fairly trivial movement script, its structure is generic for the sort of things that we want to do in games (and complex interfaces). Remember it because if you get stuck with any other method, this one is a good one to try out.

## The NPC Bat

The NPC bat has a very similar script to the player bat. This isn't surprising really as its OBD is also similar to the player bat's. Here's the NPC bat script in full:

```
onClipEvent (load) {
    // COPY WORLD CONFIGURATION
    right = _parent.world.right;
    top = _parent.world.top;
    bottom = _parent.world.bottom;
    serve = _parent.world.serve;
    speed = _parent.world.speed;
    skillFactor = _parent.world.skillFactor;
    // SET MY INITIAL POSITION
    _x = right;
    _y = serve;
    // DEFINE LOCAL DATA
```

```
            myPos = _y;
            myTarget = myPos;
    }
    //
    onClipEvent (enterFrame) {
            // CALCULATE NEW POSITION
            if (_parent.ballDir>0) {
                    myPos -= (myPos-_parent.ballPos)/skillFactor;
            } else {
                    myPos -= (myPos-serve)/20;
            }
            // ANIMATE ME
            _y = myPos;
            // BROADCAST GLOBALS TO GAMEWORLD
            _parent.npcPos = myPos;
    }
```

The only real difference is the `if` statement. If the ball is coming towards it, then our NPC bat will try to match the ball's y position via the `ballPos` status data (which looking at the OBDs, comes from the ball gameSprite). If the ball is moving away, then the NPC bat moves slowly to the center position of the court (as tennis players do in an attempt to be in the best position to return the next volley). The ball direction is retrieved via another bit of status data that comes from the ball: `ballDir`.

The speed at which the NPC moves towards the ball position is governed in our inertia equation (`myPos -= (myPos-_parent.ballPos)/skillFactor`) by `skillFactor`, which allows us to control the level of 'inertial sluggishness' that the bat shows in its motion. Set this value higher in frame 1 of the actions layer for an easier game.

Finally, the NPC bat broadcasts its position (`npcPos`) to the rest of the world via the last command.

## The Ball Script

The final script is in our ball. As mentioned earlier, the ball is actually the most important gameSprite. Not only does it create its own motion, it also controls the game scoring, handles the collision detection and creates the sound effects. The script is rather long so it's been broken down. The full script is shown again at the end of this section.

# Flash Games Studio

The `load` event script is really no different to the other two gameSprite scripts. Again, all the `load` script is doing is pulling in the global gameWorld configuration needed by the `enterFrame` script to run, and defining local variables. The only slightly new feature is that the ball gameSprite has to move in x,y space, as opposed to the bats which move only in the y direction. I have therefore defined a couple of objects `myPos` and `mySpeed` whose x and y properties will hold the x and y components of speed and position:

```
onClipEvent (load) {
    // COPY WORLD CONFIGURATION
    left = _parent.world.left;
    right = _parent.world.right;
    top = _parent.world.top;
    bottom = _parent.world.bottom;
    serve = _parent.world.serve;
    speed = _parent.world.speed;
    bounce = _parent.world.bounce;
    batHitWidth = _parent.batWidth+_width;
    batheight = _parent.batHeight;
    // SET MY INITIAL POSITION
    _x = left;
    _y = serve;
    // DEFINE LOCAL DATA
    myPos = new Object();
    myPos.x = left;
    myPos.y = serve;
    mySpeed = new Object();
    mySpeed.x = speed;
    mySpeed.y = 0;
}
```

The `enterFrame` script appears to be fairy complex, but its really only a string of simple decisions. Although it looks like it's processor intensive, careful use of `if` statements means that very few lines of code are ever actually executed at the same time. The gameWorld system doesn't help in actually defining our logic, but it does mean that we already know what the data we have to work with is.

The new ball position is simply calculated by adding the x, and y speed components in `mySpeed` to the last ball position `myPos`:

```
onClipEvent (enterFrame) {
    // CALCULATE NEW POSITION
    myPos.x += mySpeed.x;
    myPos.y -= mySpeed.y;
```

# Structured Real Time Programming

## Detecting Key Ball Positions

Now we next need to check if the ball has hit any parts of the gameWorld that require a change of behavior:

- Has the ball hit the top or bottom edges of the court?
- Has it hit the left or right edges, and if so, has it also hit the bat, or has it missed the bat?

The first if looks at whether we've hit the top or bottom part of the court. If the ball's y position is less than top or greater than bottom, then we need to alter the y component of our speed to make it 'bounce back' off the top or bottom of the court. The easiest way to do this is to change the sign (direction) of the y speed component. To simulate a 'bounce', all we have to do is reverse the y component of the ball speed whenever it hits the top or bottom edges of the court:

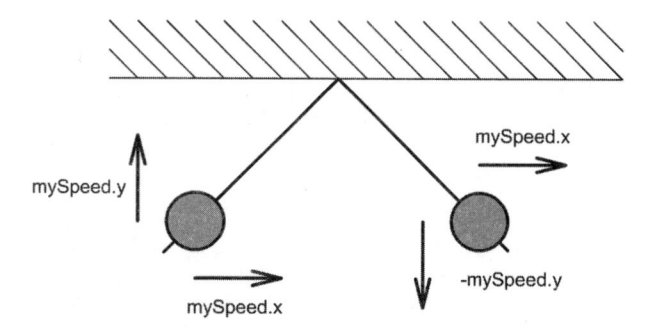

Before the collision, the ball is moving towards the wall in the y direction. Following the bounce, it should now be moving in the opposite direction. To change the direction of the speed, we simply multiply it by -1 to change its sign. The following `if else` action does this. The script also starts the appropriate 'bounce off walls' beep:

```
// IF I HIT TOP OR BOTTOM OF COURT,
// BOUNCE ME.
if (myPos.y<top) {
    myPos.y = top;
    mySpeed.y = -mySpeed.y;
    _root.wallBounce.start(0,1);
} else if (myPos.y>bottom) {
    myPos.y = bottom;
    mySpeed.y = -mySpeed.y;
    _root.wallBounce.start(0,1);
}
```

2. Next, we need to check if we've reached the extreme left or right sides of the court. If we're at this position, then either the ball is overlapping the bat (and so the ball has hit the bat), or it isn't overlapping (the bat has missed the ball):

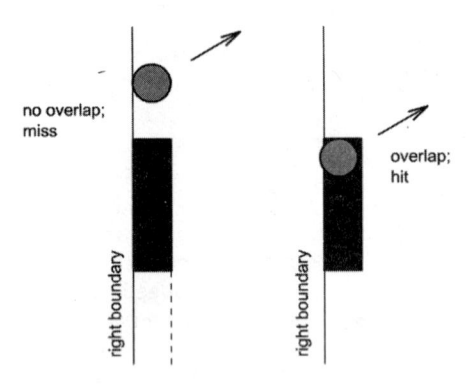

Since the bat's registration point is at its y-center point, we know if overlap has occurred because if the ball's position is less than batHeight (which is actually the height counted from the registration point of the bat, or *half* its _height property) away from the bat's center, then we know there's overlap:

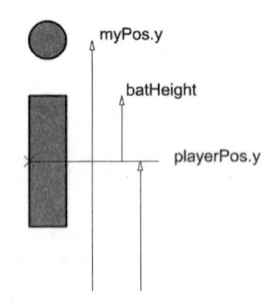

If there is overlap (worked out by Math.abs(_parent.playerPos-myPos.y)<batHeight), then we simply reverse the x component of the ball speed, mySpeed.x to get the ball to bounce back in the direction it has come from. That's not too great though because the ball would always bounce from the bat surface at 90 degrees

3. Since we want the ball to bounce off at different angles depending whereabouts on the bat it hit, we use the code:

```
mySpeed.y = (_parent.playerPos-myPos.y)/bounce;
```

# Structured Real Time Programming

This makes our ball bounce at increasingly large angles the further away from the center of the bat that collision occurs. This gives us:

```
        // HAVE I REACHED THE EXTREME LEFT OF COURT?
        if (myPos.x<left) {
                // HAS THE PLAYER BAT HIT ME?
                if (Math.abs(_parent.playerPos-myPos.y)<batHeight) {
                        // YES, BOUNCE ME
                        mySpeed.x = -mySpeed.x;
                        myPos.x = left;
                        mySpeed.y = (_parent.playerPos-myPos.y)/bounce;
                        _root.batBounce.start(0,1);
                } else {
                        // NO, NPC SERVES.
                        mySpeed.y = 0;
                        myPos.x = right;
                        myPos.y = serve;
                        _parent.npcScore.play();
                        _root.miss2.start(0,1);
                }
        // HAVE I REACHED THE EXTREME RIGHT OF COURT?
        } else if (myPos.x>right) {
                // HAS THE NPC BAT HIT ME?
                if (Math.abs(_parent.npcPos-myPos.y)<batHeight) {
                        // YES, BOUNCE ME
                        mySpeed.x = -mySpeed.x;
                        myPos.x = right;
                        mySpeed.y = (_parent.npcPos-myPos.y)/bounce;
                        _root.batBounce.start(0,1);
                } else {
                        // NO, PLAYER SERVEs
                        mySpeed.y = 0;
                        myPos.x = left;
                        myPos.y = serve;
                        _parent.playerScore.play()
                        _root.miss.start(0,1)
                }
        }
```

Note that if the ball misses the bat, the npcScore and playerScore movie clips are advanced. These two movie clips are the scoreboards, and you might want to have a look at them in the final FLA. Their job is to cause the game to end once the score on either one reads 9.

# Flash Games Studio

**4.** Once these tests are performed for the player's bat and the NPC's bat, all that remains is to animate the ball at its new position, and broadcast the `ballPos` and `ballDir` variables as used by the NPC gameSprite:

```
    // ANIMATE ME
    _x = myPos.x;
    _y = myPos.y;
    // BROADCAST GLOBALS TO GAMEWORLD
    _parent.ballPos = myPos.y;
    _parent.ballDir = mySpeed.x;
}
```

And that's our full game finished. So, our script in its entirety should look like this:

```
onClipEvent (load) {
    // COPY WORLD CONFIGURATION
    left = _parent.world.left;
    right = _parent.world.right;
    top = _parent.world.top;
    bottom = _parent.world.bottom;
    serve = _parent.world.serve;
    speed = _parent.world.speed;
    bounce = _parent.world.bounce;
    batHitWidth = _parent.batWidth+_width;
    batheight = _parent.batHeight;
    // SET MY INITIAL POSITION
    _x = left;
    _y = serve;
    // DEFINE LOCAL DATA
    myPos = new Object();
    myPos.x = left;
    myPos.y = serve;
    mySpeed = new Object();
    mySpeed.x = speed;
    mySpeed.y = 0;
}
//
onClipEvent (enterFrame) {
    // CALCULATE NEW POSITION
    myPos.x += mySpeed.x;
    myPos.y -= mySpeed.y;
    // IF I HIT TOP OR BOTTOM OF COURT,
    // BOUNCE ME.
    if (myPos.y<top) {
        myPos.y = top;
        mySpeed.y = -mySpeed.y;
        _root.wallBounce.start(0,1);
    } else if (myPos.y>bottom) {
        myPos.y = bottom;
```

# Structured Real Time Programming

```
                mySpeed.y = -mySpeed.y;
                _root.wallBounce.start(0,1);
        }
        // HAVE I REACHED THE EXTREME LEFT OF COURT?
        if (myPos.x<left) {
                // HAS THE PLAYER BAT HIT ME?
                if (Math.abs(_parent.playerPos-myPos.y)<batHeight) {
                        // YES, BOUNCE ME
                        mySpeed.x = -mySpeed.x;
                        myPos.x = left;
                        mySpeed.y = (_parent.playerPos-myPos.y)/bounce;
                        _root.batBounce.start(0,1);
                } else {
                        // NO, NPC SERVES.
                        mySpeed.y = 0;
                        myPos.x = right;
                        myPos.y = serve;
                        _parent.npcScore.play();
                        _root.miss2.start(0,1);
                }
                // HAVE I REACHED THE EXTREME RIGHT OF COURT?
        } else if (myPos.x>right) {
                // HAS THE NPC BAT HIT ME?
                if (Math.abs(_parent.npcPos-myPos.y)<batHeight) {
                        // YES, BOUNCE ME
                        mySpeed.x = -mySpeed.x;
                        myPos.x = right;
                        mySpeed.y = (_parent.npcPos-myPos.y)/bounce;
                        _root.batBounce.start(0,1);
                } else {
                        // NO, PLAYER SERVEs
                        mySpeed.y = 0;
                        myPos.x = left;
                        myPos.y = serve;
                        _parent.playerScore.play()
                        _root.miss.start(0,1)
                }
        }
        // ANIMATE ME
        _x = myPos.x;
        _y = myPos.y;
        // BROADCAST GLOBALS TO GAMEWORLD
        _parent.ballPos = myPos.y;
        _parent.ballDir = mySpeed.x;
}
```

This tennis game is reasonably easy to create without using a gameWorld system, and we could also make the code easier by using the new `hitTest` actions rather than my faster relative coordinate based comparisons. The next FLA is slightly more complex in that it uses many gameSprites, all moving at once.

## Example 2: Building a Scrolling Shoot 'Em Up

The last example was fairly easy and got us into the sort of structure that we have to adopt if we wanted to build large games. Tennis isn't a large game however, and there are shorter coding routes we could take to reach the same conclusion. This is entirely due to the small number of gameSprites involved so, the 'why don't I just code it all up as I go along' programming style (a style known as 'hacking it' in coding circles) could have also produced a working tennis game.

However, the gameWorld method works much better when there are many gameSprites to handle, where the alternative coding philosophies just break down under the strain. To conclude this chapter, I'll show you the basis of a complex game. Hold on to your hats, it's a long journey.

I suppose the first issue we need to resolve is the choice of game. Well, I have an all time personal favorite, and it's my chapter so that's the one we'll do. More importantly, it has several features that make it a good bet for a difficult game to code:

- It has two representations for each gameSprite: a local screen and a long-range radar. Because of this, we can't just use the gameSprite x and y coordinates to track our gameWorld), it would be far too slow. Instead, we'll have to implement a database that contains the real gameWorld, and use this to feed the two different graphical representations of the gameWorld. This is logically equivalent to the same thing we did in the tic-tac-toe game with our weighted outcomes matrix, in that we had a database and represented it graphically on the screen rather than just place things on the screen directly, so we'll be moving from the turn based data driven engine to a true real-time implementation of the same concept.

- It includes scrolling, so we'll need a little more than left, right, and fire for the controls, as well as handling the actual scroll and making sure that the background scroll effects don't detract from our main show (the epic battle between the player and the enemy gameSprites).

- It has many gameSprites on screen at the same time. For the game I have in mind we'll need to control up to 40 or so gameSprites being tracked and displayed at the same time, and it doesn't slow down much if you go to full screen on my development machine (a lowly P3 600).

I want a good Flash version of this game so I can run it on my laptop when I've got 5 (or even sometimes slightly more!) minutes to play around. There's some emulator versions out on the net, but they require you to use keys, and I've already popped two on the QWERTY, because laptop keyboards are just not designed for industrial strength video gaming (and the manufacturer is getting sick of me sending it back for repair).

# Structured Real Time Programming        6

Recognize it yet? Here's the original game, the Williams 1981 classic:

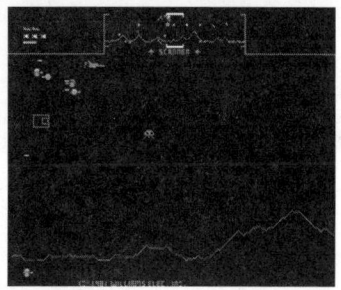

For those who haven't seen the original game running, the screenshots don't really give an indication of the motion and noise. Unlike modern games, *Stargate* screenshots don't transfer well into print. Just like the similarly frenetic game *Robotron (Williams, 1982)* you have to see it moving and hear it to understand it. I remember doing a presentation at a recent FlashForward conference, and putting *Stargate* on the big display screen as part of my talk. Needless to say, it got much bigger applause from the clued up web design crowd than I did.

What I want to do is to create the same game, complete with the cool radar and scrolling landscape, and of course the multitude of aliens lurking just off screen. The game will be different from *Stargate* in that it won't consist of levels, but of a number of missions that you must complete.

# 6 Flash Games Studio

## Game Background

The game, called *Dante (Savior part 2)*, is set soon after a previous Flash game, *Savior* (see the *Flash 5 Studio* book if you have it). The aliens have won the war and the player's now stranded on the remote and barren planet Dante. Our aim is to get off the planet by completing a set of missions and then get back to Earth. We start from the polar region, gradually making our way to the launch pad on the equator, where we'll repair our war torn *Savior Mk 1* attack fighter and make for earth... ready for part 3 no doubt.

## Game Graphics

I've always believed, at the risk of sounding patronizing, that "If you're going to do something, you should do it properly". The classics had a look and feel that's relatively easy to recreate in Flash, but it's always nice to be authentic and do your research (like searching out only one of two synthesizers that can adequately recreate the blips from *Pong* in the last section). Games that are just thrown together tend to show it.

The old games used a standard bright palette that consisted only of the primary and secondary colors (the same colors you see on a television test card).

Use the Mixer panel to mix these values if you want to see them. They are also included as preset swatch colors on the color pop-up window if you click on the fill or stroke color on the palette:

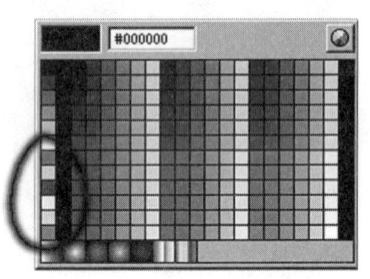

Also, the old games had a really distinctive font. This took ages to find, but the search is over:

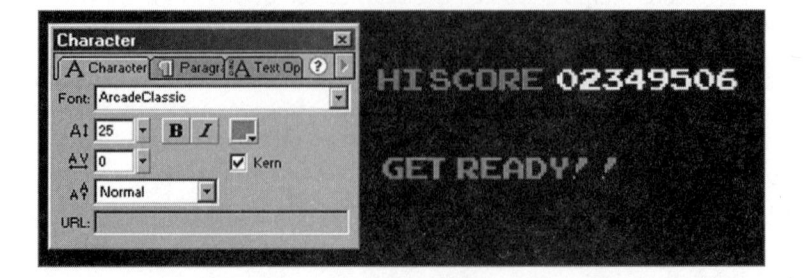

# Structured Real Time Programming 6

The font ArcadeClassic is a must for the Flash game creator, and you can get a PC or Mac version of it from *PizzaDude* at www.pizzadude.dk. Best of all, the font is freeware. If we use this font in the colors listed above, we can't help but start creating an authentic video game graphic appearance.

Having said all that, the old and classic games should only be a starting point. Take your references sure, but Flash is a different beast, and there are many innovations that we can add to the mix, like mouse control, multiplayer options and the advantages of a smoothing vector engine with lots of tween transition effects.

Back to our game. First, I set about creating some in-game graphics. Here's my players ship and the alien BomberCraft..:

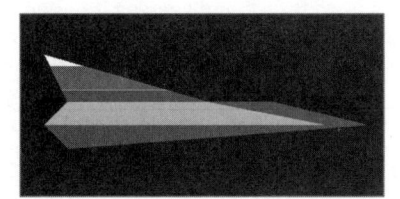

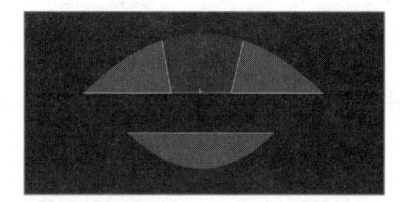

As mentioned in previous chapters, we need to keep the use of complex shapes and unnecessary strokes to a minimum if we want something that will run well in full screen, and avoid alpha in the images totally. Anyway, it's usually an unnecessary effect and a real performance killer when we move from turn based to real-time dynamic animation.

Unless we're creating a cartoon or manga style game, there's rarely any need for gradients either because the sprite graphics will be small anyway. Another important thing to consider when building large games is that although the individual graphics may look a bit sparse, when there are 40 or so of them moving about on the screen the overall effect will look very busy, so bear in mind the numbers game, and have a look at how much you can get away with downgrading the individual graphic complexity.

Many people use stand-in graphics when designing the basic engine. This is a good idea but I prefer not to do it. Although its logical when working in a team, for a sole programmer/designer the game creation is much more organic. The look and programming style tend to grow together and leaving one in search of the other may result in an unbalanced approach. Many people would disagree however, so take that as just a personal opinion.

# Flash Games Studio

## Gameplay

The FLA we'll be discussing contains the basic world setup and engine, `scrollerDemo.fla`. You may need to have a look at the included `scrollerD.swf`, if you don't yet have the ArcadeClassic font installed because the FLA uses it as the main font. scrollerDemo is a cut down version of mission 3 of *Dante*. In this mission, we're at the start of the game (at the polar region of *Dante*) and must clear the level of the alien bombers before a time limit (1 minute) otherwise the alien Executioner ship (a large 'boss' alien) will warp in and come after us, depleting a large amount of our shield energy in the ensuing battle.

Use the mouse to control the ship. Moving the mouse to the extreme edges of the screen (the areas that are under the red line at the top) causes us to thrust, and keeping it under the scanner area stops the thrusting. Moving the mouse up and down makes the ship follow suit, and best of all, pressing and holding the mouse button gives us a saucy blast of plasma death to rain down on anything that looks at us in a funny way.

To make for an understandable gameWorld however, I've stripped out the level information and mission specific game database elements as they make the code around twice as big as it already is and take up far too much room in the chapter. I've also taken out much of the pyrotechnics, sound and the attractor movie clip as they make the game FLA a massive download. So what's left? Well, the basic game engine is in there, complete with scrolling, a long range radar scanner, multiple bullets, a fast collision detection system that can handle a large number of gameSprites, and an enemy that requires a variable number of hits. It's a good example of a structured gameWorld system:

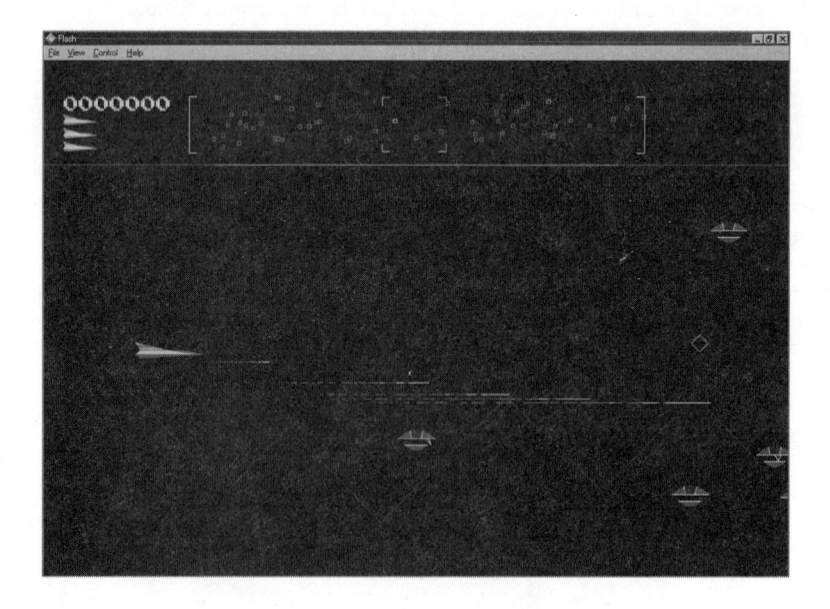

# Structured Real Time Programming    6

## Identifying the Components and Workflow

When designing a game with many components it's almost impossible to code it all in one go, so we need to identify not only the game components, but also the order in which we can implement them. Remember the first component is always the gameWorld itself, but after that, we need to start adding elements whilst keeping the overall game working. That's the only way I know of to avoid painting yourself into a corner with a complex FLA that for some reason doesn't work. If you take things one step at a time, then there's less to debug when something goes wrong.

To achieve this incremental building does of course involve some paper planning first, and the best way is to create our object block diagrams and then decide on a route that allows us to test workable FLAs at frequent steps along the journey. Here's an image and a list of the objects that we'll be using:

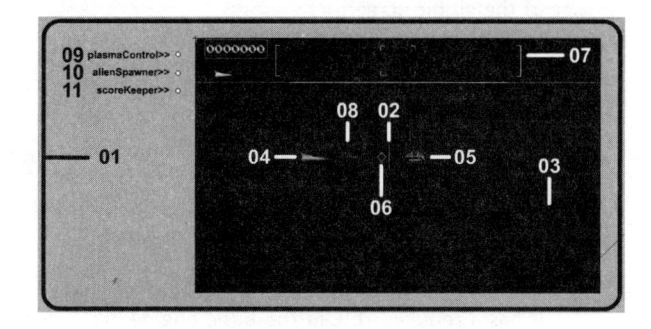

## The Object Definitions

1. GameWorld  The gameWorld object is the movie clip timeline that all other gameSprites and global variables sit on. It has four main components:

    - The gameSprites
    - The global configuration object world
    - The individual status variables transmitted between the gameSprites
    - The game database object: database. This contains structured data controlling the duplicated movie clips of type Alien (06) and the single Player Ship (04)

2. Star  The star is a member of the star field that scrolls in the background. It interacts with the gameWorld only and does not interact with any other gameSprites.

3. Terrain  The terrain object is the mountain profile that scrolls in the middle ground. It interacts with the gameWorld only and does not interact with any other gameSprites.

235

# Flash Games Studio

| | | |
|---|---|---|
| **4.** | Player Ship | The player ship is the user's ship. It takes its inputs from the Cursor (05) so the player does not actually control it directly, but through the interfacing between objects 04 and 05. |
| **5.** | Cursor | The cursor is the little caret that follows the mouse position and creates the acceleration, positioning and orientation associated with 04. It takes inputs from the users mouse and after processing this position, makes data available to the Player Ship (04) |
| **6.** | Alien | The alien is... um... the alien. Amongst other things, it decides when it has been hit by the LaserBeam (08) and when it has hit the Player Ship (04). |
| **7.** | Radar | The radar object is a movie clip that sits at the top of the game area. It includes the little blips that signify the extended game area outside of the visible screen |
| **8.** | LaserBeam | The laser beam is the series of shots that comes out of 04. The laser beam's direction is defined by 04, and its position by 04/05. |
| **9.** | PlasmaController | The plasma controller handles the creation of the laserbeam instances. It controls the auto-fire function (pressing and holding the mouse button results in a burst of laser beams (08). The plasma Controller does not appear on the screen in the game. |
| **10.** | AlienSpawner | The alien spawner handles the creation of the gameSprites. Although it has a reduced role in the basic engine, it's fundamental to creating the missions in the final game* |
| **11.** | scoreKeeper | The scorekeeper keeps a record of the player's score and uses it to update the displayed score every so often. The need to do this arises because Flash takes a surprisingly high-performance hit if we make it constantly update a text field. We can lose up to 50% of the available performance just by constantly updating a couple of text fields every frame. |
| **12.** | SYSTEM | The SYSTEM isn't really a gameSprite, it's the timeline that the gameWorld sits on, and physically it's the _root timeline. The reason for having this layer can be a little subtle so we shall consider its use when we look at the code and detailed game design later. |

# Structured Real Time Programming 6

> *\*If you're curious – it decides on the number and type of each different gameSprite that should be created based on a mission-list, and it assigns individual gameSprites as killGoals (the mission succeeds when all killGoals are destroyed), protectGoals (the mission fails if any protectGoal is destroyed), or neither (the gameSprite isn't part of the mission objective but may help or hinder us in achieving it) respectively. These flags are included in the database described as part of the gameWorld (which we'll learn about later) as database.killGoal[n] and database.protectGoal[n] respectively.*

The list is important because it gives us an early insight as to how games like *Dante* are initially planned. Not all the gameSprites were defined from the outset (08, 09 and 10 were defined to fill specific needs partway through the actual coding), but the list already begins to show that we're making a quantum leap from seeing the gameWorld as not a collection of sprites moving around on a screen, but a collection of software objects with well-defined interfaces between each other.

## Object Relationships

We then need to fix the relationship between the above objects. At this stage we need to keep away from thinking things like '*when I press the fire button on the mouse, I want this really cool wall of laser beams to come out from the spaceship, and lots of big meaty bass sounds as the gun fires*'. Remember that we're thinking objects and interfaces – the wow factor comes later. Right now, we're building a software framework. First we need to draw out the object block diagrams as we did before. Mine are just 12 pieces of paper (one per object) with a few lists, lots of crossing out, and several hastily scribbled arrows. I've included all of the OBDs as FLAs so you can load them up in Flash and print them. They are danteOBD01.fla to danteOBD12.fla respectively.

## The Individual Objects

The remainder of the chapter will be spent looking at each of our components individually. Each section has its own OBD, the code attached to it, a description of its fundamental operation, and an outline of any specific sections of code used to create new or idiosyncratic effects and features. When reading through the following sections, try not to concentrate too much on the specific code of each of our objects, but instead try to get a feel for the overall design and structure. This will assist you in learning how to design your own game using the same basic principles. The code is also quite heavily commented within the FLA, so take a look at that for another aid to understanding. Without further ado, let's get to it.

# 6    Flash Games Studio

## 1. The gameWorld

Continuing our good programming practice, we'll begin with the gameWorld itself, as this can be considered our central object, upon which all other objects depend:

**Object Block Diagram**

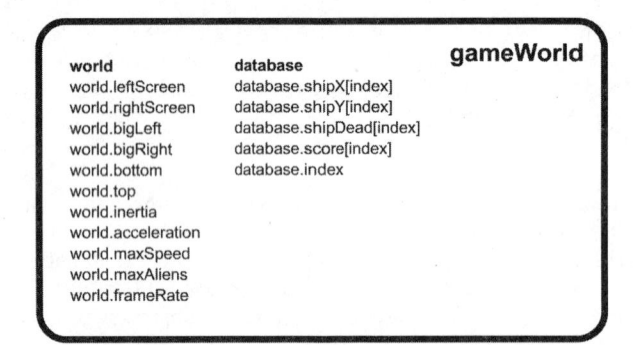

```
                                                              gameWorld
    world                      database
    world.leftScreen           database.shipX[index]
    world.rightScreen          database.shipY[index]
    world.bigLeft              database.shipDead[index]
    world.bigRight             database.score[index]
    world.bottom               database.index
    world.top
    world.inertia
    world.acceleration
    world.maxSpeed
    world.maxAliens
    world.frameRate
```

**Attached Code**

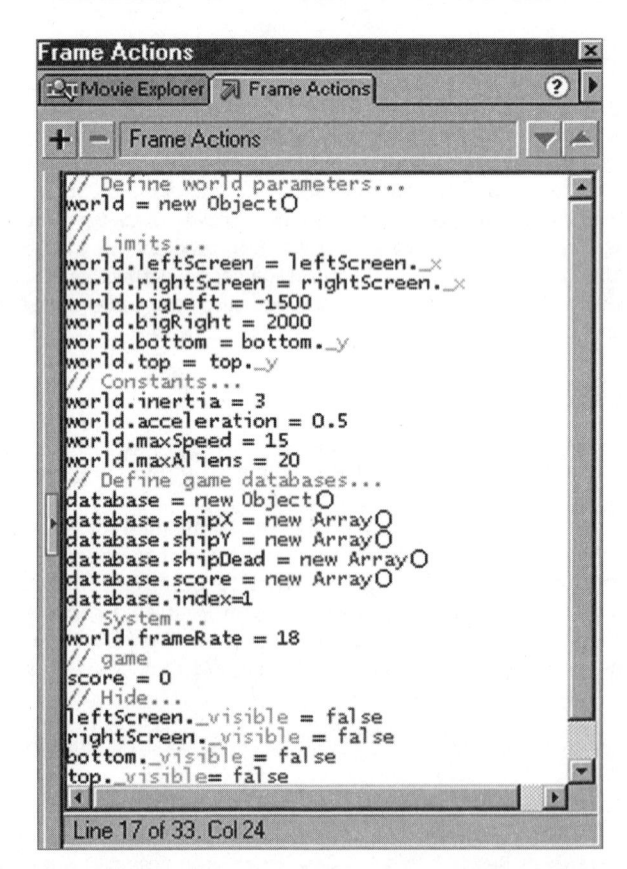

```
// Define world parameters...
world = new Object()
//
// Limits...
world.leftScreen = leftScreen._x
world.rightScreen = rightScreen._x
world.bigLeft = -1500
world.bigRight = 2000
world.bottom = bottom._y
world.top = top._y
// Constants...
world.inertia = 3
world.acceleration = 0.5
world.maxSpeed = 15
world.maxAliens = 20
// Define game databases...
database = new Object()
database.shipX = new Array()
database.shipY = new Array()
database.shipDead = new Array()
database.score = new Array()
database.index=1
// System...
world.frameRate = 18
// game
score = 0
// Hide...
leftScreen._visible = false
rightScreen._visible = false
bottom._visible = false
top._visible= false
```

Line 17 of 33. Col 24

# Structured Real Time Programming 6

## Features

The gameWorld consists of two objects, world and database, which between them define the gameWorld configuration. Although using objects in our tennis game seemed a little like overkill, in this game it's absolutely necessary. There'll be lots of status information flying about in the gameWorld, and adding the dot notation to identify configuration data from status data is a big plus in understanding.

inertia, acceleration and **maxSpeed** are gameWorld physical constants that define motion in the game. inertia is a measure of how quickly the player's ship follows the mouse. acceleration is how quickly the ship reaches its maximum speed, and maxSpeed is the maximum speed the ship can accelerate to.

The second object, database, contains all of the information needed for the player's ship and alien ships. shipX and shipY are the x,y coordinates of ship[index], and shipDead[index] is the status of the gameSprite – it can be either true (I am dead), false (I am alive), or "" (I have been removed from the game). score[index] is the number of points that the player gets for shooting the alien.

A particularly important index is zero: shipX[0], shipY[0] are the coordinates of the player's ship, and the rest of the indices are taken up by the aliens.

Having seen the general structure of the gameWorld, you may already have an inkling of how the game works when you play it. The gameWorld tends to be like that. It may just be a list of data, but that data has structure and this is very important. Although there are no words to define it, the data *strongly implies a programmatical solution for this game*. This is a feature of OBDs that make them much better than flowcharts. Flowcharts are too slow to write and sometimes too specific. OBDs look like they should be only useful for defining interfaces between objects and they don't tell anything about how to actually *code* the game, but to an intuitive coder, they speak reams of information about how the game must be coded if all the data is to mesh together. Given practice, OBDs are really all we need!

## Screen Extents

leftScreen, rightScreen, top, and bottom are our screen extents. Because the gameWorld physically extends much further off screen (as shown by the scanner) there are also two other extents that delimit the full scrollable area, bigLeft, and bigRight:

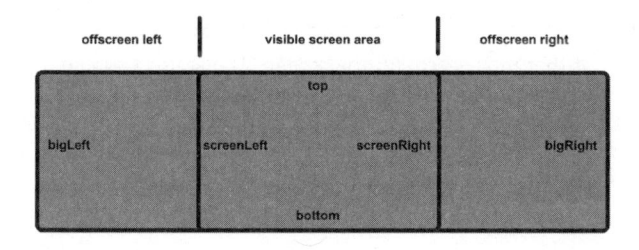

```
       offscreen left      visible screen area      offscreen right
                                  top
        bigLeft           screenLeft    screenRight        bigRight
                                bottom
```

You can see the timeline for the gameWorld by looking inside mc.world from the Library (look in the world folder, or use the Movie Explorer):

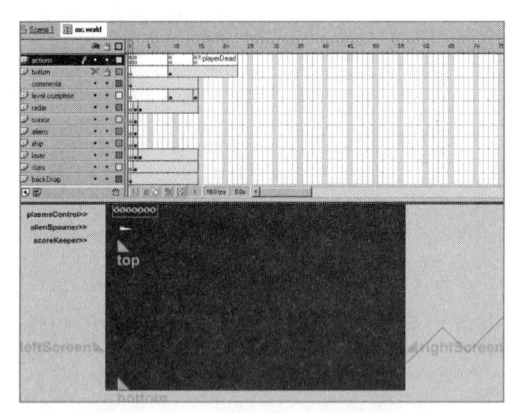

Notice the top, bottom, leftScreen, and rightScreen text. These are movie clips whose positions define our world.top, bottom, left, and right world extents. This is much easier than giving the extents numerical values, because we can now define our gameWorld extends simply by dragging a label around. I like to think in graphical terms despite being an ActionScript addict, so it's a useful technique (I also use this system in web sites to define the screen area when building whiz-bang swish action script interfaces). If you look at frame 1 of the actions layer you can see the code defining the gameWorld, and notice how much it looks just like our OBD.

> *A word of warning: the* Debugger *doesn't seem to like displaying the data for this game as there's an awful lot of it – for 30 gameSprites, the* gameWorld *consists of around 130 separate pieces of data, plus around 300 variables spread around the individual* gameSprite *timelines. The* Debugger *seems to be designed to show web sites with 20 or so variables and tends to die when asked to show this amount of data!*

## 2. The Star

The star is simply a dot that moves around the screen. The status variable viewSpeed is the rate at which the main viewable screen is scrolling, and moving at the same speed but opposite direction to this value gives the impression that the star is moving across the viewPort (rather like trees moving across a train window in the opposite direction of the train. There are a number of them in the stars layer of mc.world:

# Structured Real Time Programming 6

## Object Block Diagram

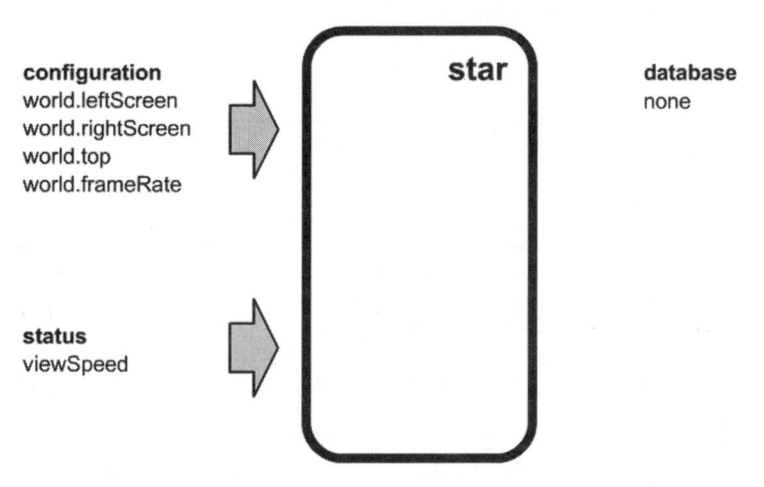

**configuration**
world.leftScreen
world.rightScreen
world.top
world.frameRate

**status**
viewSpeed

**star**

**database**
none

## Attached Code

Select one of the star movie clips and you'll see the following script:

```
onClipEvent (load) {
    left = _parent.world.leftScreen;
    right = _parent.world.rightScreen;
    top = _parent.world.top;
    bottom = 100+top;
    updateRate = Math.ceil(_parent.world.frameRate/4);
    update = Math.round(Math.random()*updateRate);
    myPosX = left+Math.random()*(right-left);
    myPosY = top+Math.random()*(bottom-top);
}
onClipEvent (enterFrame) {
    update++;
    if ((update %= updateRate) == 0) {
        myPosX -= _parent.viewSpeed/4;
        if (myPosX<left) {
            myPosX = right;
            myPosY = top+Math.random()*(bottom-top);
        } else if (myPosX>right) {
            myPosX = left;
            myPosY = top+Math.random()*(bottom-top);
        }
        _x = myPosX;
        _y = myPosY;
    }
}
```

**Features**

Because the stars are far away, they move at a fraction of the `gamePort` speed:

`viewSpeed/4`

An important trick here is that the stars are only updated every quarter second. The line:

`updateRate = Math.ceil(_parent.world.frameRate/4);`

...defines our update rate – a quarter of the number of frames per second, or every quarter of a second. In the `enterFrame` event script, you can see that the main code is enclosed in this `if` statement:

```
update++;
if ((update %= updateRate) == 0) {
<code>
}
```

`update` is essentially the number of frames that have been run through. The expression `update%=updateRate` is a modular expression, and it gives the remainder when we divide `updateRate` into `update`. Because `updateRate` is around a quarter of `update`, the division will give a remainder of 0 four times in every second's worth of frames. Therefore, the main code runs every quarter of a second. This is a *very* useful trick for animating gameSprites at different rates. The star is a background gameSprite so we don't want to squander valuable performance on it.

The concept of tailoring event execution periods is one key feature in building fast game engines. We're updating the main gameSprites (the player's ship and the aliens) every frame. Because these gameSprites are the user's main focus, they'll think that everything is running this smoothly, but things not in their immediate attention (such as the stars) are actually being updated at a much slower rate. The fact that the stars are moving slowly tends to hide this little trick as well unless you are specifically looking out for it. Sly eh?

This gaming trick is really useful in interface design. If we keep the interface elements that the user will be interacting directly with moving very quickly (every frame), and the stuff that the user isn't directly interacting with moving at a fraction of the frame rate (typically every half to a ninth of a second for an 18 frames per second SWF), the areas of main user focus give the illusion that the whole site is very quick. The user won't notice the areas of slowness because they aren't directing attention to them. This trick really makes the Flash plug-in feel like it's running much quicker, and it allows us to build more intricate games and web site interfaces than the competition.

# Structured Real Time Programming 6

## 3. The Terrain

The terrain is the little jagged blue line in the game representing mountains in the background. You can find it on the backdrop layer of movie clip mc.world. It works by being exactly two screen widths of the viewable screen, or the viewPort if we're using authentic game programming terms. The two half lengths of the terrain are identical, and when the terrain has moved half its length, it flicks back to its original starting point, giving the impression of a continuous repeating terrain:

If you can't visualize this, try marking the beginning, half way point and end point of the terrain with some text and see what it does when you run the game.

## Object Block Diagram

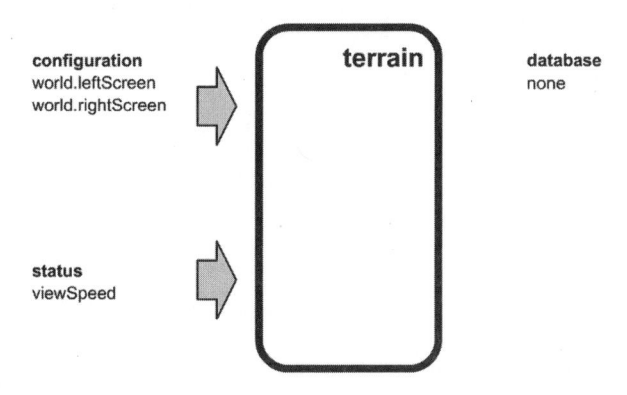

**configuration**
world.leftScreen
world.rightScreen

**terrain**

**database**
none

**status**
viewSpeed

# 6 Flash Games Studio

### Attached Code

The code for the terrain is much like that for the stars, except that it has the repeating 'flick back' functionality, implemented via the if in the `enterFrame` event script:

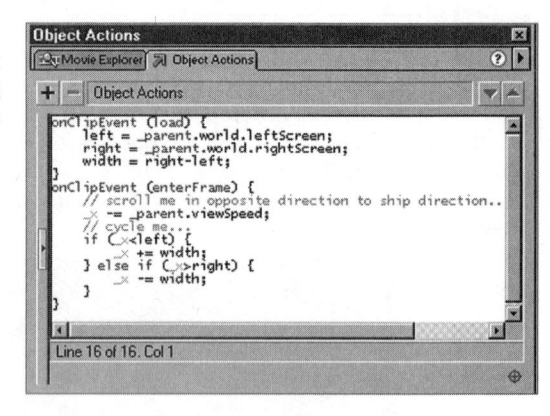

```
onClipEvent (load) {
    left = _parent.world.leftScreen;
    right = _parent.world.rightScreen;
    width = right-left;
}
onClipEvent (enterFrame) {
    // scroll me in opposite direction to ship direction..
    _x -= _parent.viewSpeed;
    // cycle me...
    if (_x<left) {
        _x += width;
    } else if (_x>right) {
        _x -= width;
    }
}
```

## 3. The playerShip

The player ship is on the ship layer of mc.world.

### Object Block Diagram

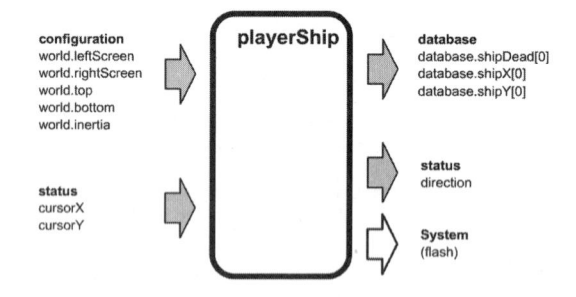

**configuration**
world.leftScreen
world.rightScreen
world.top
world.bottom
world.inertia

**status**
cursorX
cursorY

→ **playerShip** →

**database**
database.shipDead[0]
database.shipX[0]
database.shipY[0]

**status**
direction

**System**
(flash)

### Attached Code

The code for our player ship is a little longer and for this reason its operations are detailed at the side. Don't be put off however; you'll notice that it bears more than a passing resemblance to our bat script from the first game.

# Structured Real Time Programming 6

```
onClipEvent (load) {
    // Define constants
    left = _parent.world.leftScreen;
    right = _parent.world.rightScreen;
    top = _parent.world.top;
    bottom = _parent.world.bottom;
    inertia = _parent.world.inertia;
    //
    // Define local variables
    centerPos = (right-left)/2;
    leftPos = left+100;
    rightPos = right-100;
    inertiaTurn = 3*inertia;
    myTarget = new Object();
    myPos = new Object();
    myTarget.x = leftPos;
    myTarget.y = _y;
    myPos.x = _x;
    myPos.y = _y;
    direction = 100;
    _parent.database.shipDead[0] = false;
}
onClipEvent (enterFrame) {
    // Am I dead?
    if (_parent.database.shipDead[0]) {
        play ();
    // If not...
    } else {
        // Get current cursor position...
        myTarget.x = _parent.cursorX;
        myTarget.y = _parent.cursorY;
        // trace (myTarget.x);
        // trace (myTarget.y);
        // Decide which direction I am facing in...
        if (myTarget.x<centerPos) {
            myTarget.x = rightPos;
            direction = -100;
        } else {
            myTarget.x = leftPos;
            direction = 100;
        }
        // trace (direction);
        // Move towards cursor position...
        myPos.x -= (myPos.x-myTarget.x)/inertiaTurn;
        myPos.y -= (myPos.y-myTarget.y)/inertia;
        // trace (myPos.x)
        // trace (myPos.y)
        _x = myPos.x;
        _y = myPos.y;
        _xscale = direction;
        _parent.database.shipX[0] = myPos.x;
        _parent.database.shipY[0] = myPos.y;
        _parent.direction = direction;
    }
}
```

## Features

The player's ship takes the world extents from the gameWorld. It also needs to know about the world inertia value because this defines how quickly it follows the mouse cursor. The cursor position, cursorX, cursorY is taken from the gameWorld. cursorX and cursorY are placed in the gameWorld by the cursor object. The ship uses the database entries to tell the rest of the gameWorld where it is. The player's ship is actually taken to be alien zero in the gameWorld. The ship also tells the rest of the gameWorld which direction it's pointing in through the direction variable:

A strange variable used by the player ship is `system.flash`. This isn't really a variable but a call (or interface) to the `_root` timeline. When the ship explodes, there's a screen flash that is created by altering the RGB value of a square on the root timeline. The reason for placing things like this on _root (or the system level) is that it isn't really a part of the gameWorld, but part of the hardware that the game runs on. In true game hardware, the stuff that controls the joysticks and other inputs, as well as the low-level generic code such as DirectX or OpenGL that interfaces with our hardware drivers to give maximum support between the physical hardware and operating system, would be part of the system level because it's hardware specific.

I use a system level where I believe that a particular functionality would have to be implemented differently if I ported the game to a different platform (such as Director). It's also a place for things that don't really fit in the gameWorld, and would spoil my gameWorld/gameSprite structure. The mouse properties are also part of the system level, as we'll see in the OBD for it. Having a system level allows us to conceptualize the hardware-level calls as 'existing in a distinct level in the game hierarchy', and also allows for quick localization and update if the Flash plug-in changes in the future.

The code for the player ship has no real surprises, but it does show the general structure of a gameSprite's set of event handlers. As mentioned in the tennis game there are distinct phases in the gameSprite code, and the gameSprite is actually a very structured object-like software element. Not only are its interfaces formalized, but so also are its internal components.

The structure is essentially initialize, followed by a calculate-animate-propagate cycle that occurs on every gameSprite update.

As well as the attached ship script, the ship movie clip also has an internal timeline of its own, because for some occurrences there has to be an animated response as well as a coded movement response. The player's ship explosion sequence is one example of this. Double-click on the ship gameSprite to see the internal timeline:

You may have noticed that there are a lot of commented out trace actions in the code. I decided to leave these in so that you can see the places where I needed to track what was happening. One way to experiment with the game FLA is to un-comment each in turn and run the movie, comparing the outputs with the code.

# Structured Real Time Programming  6

## 5. The Cursor

The cursor is the little yellow caret that the player ship follows. You can see it on the cursor layer of mc.world.

### Object Block Diagram

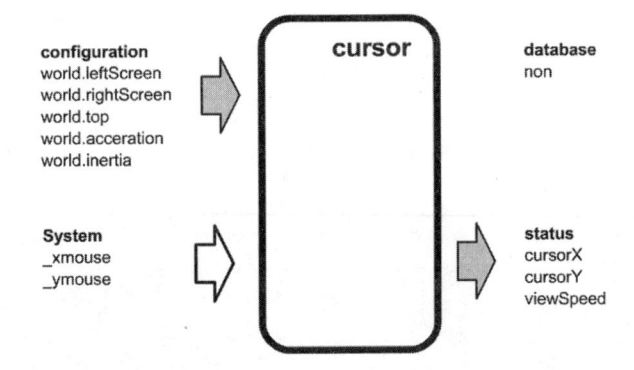

**configuration**
world.leftScreen
world.rightScreen
world.top
world.acceration
world.inertia

**cursor**

**database**
non

**System**
_xmouse
_ymouse

**status**
cursorX
cursorY
viewSpeed

### Attached Code

```
onClipEvent (load) {
    leftPos = _parent.world.leftScreen+100;
    rightPos = _parent.world.rightScreen-100;
    top = _parent.world.top;
    acceleration = _parent.world.acceleration;
    maxSpeed = _parent.world.maxSpeed;
    Mouse.hide();
    // Local variables
    viewSpeed = 0;
}
onClipEvent (enterFrame) {
    // Capture mouse position...
    cursorX = _root._xMouse;
    cursorY = _root._yMouse;
    // Use cursor position to control ship acceleration...
    if (cursorX<leftPos) {
        if (-viewSpeed<maxSpeed) {
            viewSpeed -= acceleration;
        }
    } else if (cursorX>rightPos) {
        if (viewSpeed<maxSpeed) {
            viewSpeed += acceleration;
        }
    } else {
        viewSpeed = viewSpeed*0.9;
    }
    // Range check cursor position...
    if (cursorY<top) {
        cursorY = top;
    }
    _x = cursorX;
    _y = cursorY;
    _parent.cursorX = cursorX;
    _parent.cursorY = cursorY;
    _parent.viewSpeed = viewSpeed;
}
```

# 6     Flash Games Studio

### Features

The cursor is the interface between the mouse and the game. It takes in the mouse position (which comes from the system level, _root) and various calculations are preformed on this coordinate before it's passed on to the gameWorld. As well as cursorX, and cursorY (which are range checked versions of the actual system mouse position _xmouse, _ymouse), a value viewSpeed, which is the speed at which the viewPort needs to scroll, is created. This is used by all of the displayed gameSprites in the game, because all of them need to scroll.

## 6. The Alien

The alien is one of the more complex objects in the game. Although there's only one alien, it's duplicated n times by the alienSpawner to give us the alien armada:

### Object Block Diagram

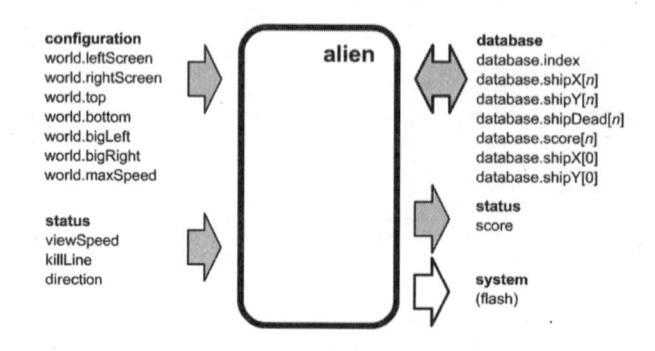

**configuration**
world.leftScreen
world.rightScreen
world.top
world.bottom
world.bigLeft
world.bigRight
world.maxSpeed

**status**
viewSpeed
killLine
direction

**alien**

**database**
database.index
database.shipX[$n$]
database.shipY[$n$]
database.shipDead[$n$]
database.score[$n$]
database.shipX[0]
database.shipY[0]

**status**
score

**system**
(flash)

# Structured Real Time Programming

## Attached Code

Our code for the alien is broken into two parts, namely the `load` script and the `enterFrame` script.

### The Load Script

```
onClipEvent (load) {
    if (_name != "alien") {
        // Define Constants
        left = _parent.world.leftScreen;
        right = _parent.world.rightScreen;
        top = _parent.world.top;
        bottom = _parent.world.bottom;
        bigLeft = _parent.world.bigLeft;
        bigRight = _parent.world.bigRight;
        maxSpeed = _parent.world.maxSpeed;
        wrapAround = bigRight-bigLeft;
        myIndex = _parent.database.index;
        _parent.database.index++;
        // Define local variables
        outLeft = left-50;
        outRight = right+50;
        myPos = new Object();
        myPos.x = _x;
        myPos.y = _y;
        mySpeed = new Object();
        mySpeed.x = Math.random()*2;
        mySpeed.y = Math.random()*2;
        // Initialize my game database entry
        _parent.database.shipX[myIndex] = myPos.x;
        _parent.database.shipY[myIndex] = myPos.y;
        _parent.database.shipDead[myIndex] = false;
        _parent.database.score[myIndex] = 230;
    } else {
        myIndex = _parent.maxAliens+1;
        _parent.database.shipDead[myIndex] = true;
        _visible = false;
    }
}
onClipEvent (enterFrame) {
```

## Features

The alien object takes the standard world extents as configuration. Because the alien can also exist in the area off screen, it also needs `bigLeft` and `bigRight`. For its movement, it needs to know `maxSpeed`, and how fast the world is scrolling so that it can scroll with it (`viewSpeed`). Status variables `killLine` and `direction` are used as part of our fast collision detection between the alien and the player's bullets.

The individual alien game data is held in a database. The alien also needs to know where the player's ship is, and this is also read from the database. The database entry `database.score` hasn't been mentioned before – it's the score that the player will get for shooting each alien. Although this isn't so useful in the demo, as all of the aliens are the same, in the full game there are different alien types. Additionally, sometimes a particular alien of a given type might have a higher score because it's a specific `killTarget` – such as in the mission "find and destroy the alien commander in this sector... he's piloting a red bomber somewhere in the landscape", in the full game.

The score status is different from the `database.score`. The score status is the player's total score that you can see at the top left of the game screen.

Finally, the alien makes calls to the system level to create a dull flash when the player vaporizes it.

Notice that a particular alien instance called `alien` isn't initialized the same way as the others. This alien is the original version on the stage. The reason for this is as follows. We can delete a movie clip that was copied with `duplicateMovieClip` (as are all the alien instances `alien1`, `alien2`, `alien3... alienn`) with `removeMovieClip`, but we can't do this with a clip that was on the stage from the start (such as `alien`). I *could* have pulled the instances in from the Library (via `attachMovie`) but this causes problems because we won't have the event scripts attached. Although we can go down this route with a little modification, I prefer just to 'kill' the original `alien` by making its `database.shipDead` database entry to `true`, and then making it invisible with its `_visible` property (it's all in the else branch at the end of the event).

**The enterFrame Script**

```
onClipEvent (enterFrame) {
    // Update my position due to speed and scrolling...
    myPos.x -= _parent.viewSpeed-mySpeed.x;
    myPos.y += mySpeed.y;
    // wraparound check for radar screen...
    if (myPos.x<bigLeft) {
        myPos.x += wrapAround;
    } else if (myPos.x>bigRight) {
        myPos.x -= wrapAround;
    }
    // top/bottom collision check...
    if (myPos.y<top) {
        mySpeed.y = -mySpeed.y;
        myPos.y = top;
    } else if (myPos.y>bottom) {
        mySpeed.y = -myspeed.y;
        myPos.y = bottom;
    }
    // if I am on the visible screen...
    if ((myPos.x>outLeft) && (myPos.x<outRight)) {
        // Have I hit the player ship?
        if (Math.abs(_parent.database.shipY[0]-myPos.y)<10) {
            // trace("hit")
            if (Math.abs(_parent.database.shipX[0]-myPos.x)<20) {
                // trace("hit")
                _parent.database.shipDead[0] = true;
            }
        }
        // Might I have been shot?
        // Do rough collision detection...
        if (Math.abs(myPos.y-_parent.killLine)<6) {
            // Do detailed collision detection...
            // Am I on the right side of the player
            // to be shot?
            if (_parent.direction == 100) {
                if (myPos.x>_parent.database.shipX[0]) {
                    // Flag me up as hit
                    play ();
                }
            } else if (_parent.direction == -100) {
                if (myPos.x<_parent.database.shipX[0]) {
                    // Flag me up as hit
                    play ();
                }
            }
        }
        // calculate my movement
        _x = myPos.x;
        _y = myPos.y;
        _visible = true;
    } else {
        _visible = false;
    }
    _parent.database.shipX[myIndex] = myPos.x;
    _parent.database.shipY[myIndex] = myPos.y;
}
```

# Structured Real Time Programming

**Features**

The code is essentially a lot of positional checks – am I in the visible screen area? Have I been hit? Do I need to wrap around the invisible screen area – but one thing to get a firm idea on is how many lines in this rather long code are actually ever executed. The reason why we can have so many aliens onscreen at any one time is because of our `if... else` logic. Very few of the `if` branches get executed for any given frame, so although the code is pretty exhaustive and looks at all conditions, only one or two of these conditions are true at any one time.

A common question when building shooting games such as this one is '"How do I get the aliens to shoot back?". The best way to do it is as follows:

Each alien has a new database entry:

```
database.shipGunX[index]
database.shipGunY[index]
database.shipGunSpeedX[index]
database.shipGunSpeedY[index]
database.shipGun[index]
```

What we could do is duplicate a gun bullet with instance name `shipGun`. This would be at the x,y coordinates (`shipGunX`, `shipGunY`) and moving at speed (`shipGunSpeedX`, `shipGunSpeedY`). Each alien can then fire a bullet at the player. For more complex games, we can even give each alien a quota of ammunition, including bullets, missiles and so on.

> *You may be thinking 'wow, that's a lot of data given that there's 30 aliens: if you give each alien 5 bullets at a time, that's 30x5x5 = 750 datapoints to track! Won't that slow the game down?' Good question. The answer is no. We do create lots of database array points for each alien, but only a few of the full 30 will be firing at any time, so most of the database isn't being used instantaneously. In general, slow engines use a little bit of data but refer to it often. Fast engines (like ours) create masses of data but only look at a little bit at any one time, if at all. The reason for this is that creating big databases at initialization time means that the datapoints are already there and structured when you need them.*

> *The memory efficient way to do it is to create a bullet instance at runtime and then create the datapoints to track it. This means you have to constantly create new variables at runtime, which can be a slow process: not only for your code but also for the Flash plug-in, which will have to internally set the memory aside dynamically. By making it do all this beforehand makes it all run faster, which is the important thing.*
>
> *And anyway, computers have 30Mb+ of RAM these days... extravagant use of about 5k worth of arrays when we could have used 50 bytes won't break the bank! Also, all this extra data is created by the SWF on the fly, so it doesn't affect download times either.*

Like the player's ship, the alien has its own timeline, which you can see by double-clicking on the alien movie clip. The alien timeline is the thing that controls how many times it's hit before it dies and creates the dull flash (via a call to the System level _root) when it finally does die.

## 7. The Radar

The radar screen is seen at the top of the game, and it shows us where the aliens are lurking off-screen. It takes the gameWorld coordinates from the gameWorld configuration and uses them to take each gameSprite's position in the gameWorld and scales it to fit into the reduced radar window, replacing each gameSprite with a colored 'blip'.

### Object Block Diagram

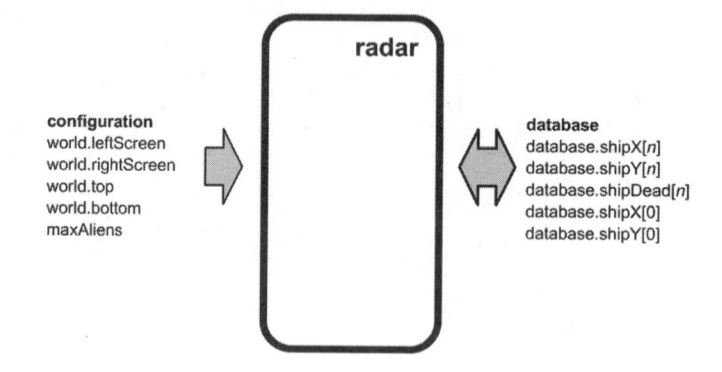

**configuration**
world.leftScreen
world.rightScreen
world.top
world.bottom
maxAliens

**radar**

**database**
database.shipX[$n$]
database.shipY[$n$]
database.shipDead[$n$]
database.shipX[0]
database.shipY[0]

# Structured Real Time Programming                                              6

The radar makes extensive use of the database. In fact, its real function is to display the individual alien's position data. In effect, it's looking at the data and plotting a visual representation of our database. The lower game screen isn't the actual gameWorld in this engine. The true 'reality' in the game is actually the database itself! Everything onscreen is really a representation of the database – the main game window is a small slice of it, and the radar is the full version:

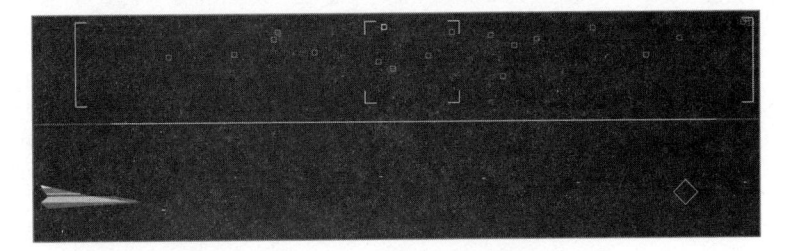

If you watch the radar, you'll see that it updates pretty slowly for the alien blips. Like the star object, it's a low priority function. The main action appears in the lower large window, and this gets the lion's share of the processing time. This is again a reason why the game runs quickly – we're concentrating processing power to where the action is. The radar actually does one blip every frame, so for 30 aliens the radar takes 30/18ths or about 2 seconds.

The player's blip (the white one) is actually updated every frame, and is much more responsive.

## Attached Code

```
onClipEvent (load) {
    // Define Constants...
    left = _parent.world.leftScreen;
    right = _parent.world.rightScreen;
    top = _parent.world.top;
    bottom = _parent.world.bottom;
    aliensRemaining = _parent.world.maxAliens;
    maxAliens = _parent.world.maxAliens;
    // Initialize local parameters...
    my = new Object();
    my.x = _x;
    my.y = _y;
    my.xScale = (right-left)/40;
    my.yScale = (bottom-top)/30;
    update = 0;
    // Duplicate blips for aliens, making the copies red
    for (i=1; i<=maxAliens; i++) {
        blip.duplicateMovieClip("blip"+i, i);
        this["blip"+i].myColor = new Color(this["blip"+i]);
        this["blip"+i].myColor.setRGB(0xFF0000);
    }
}
onClipEvent (enterFrame) {
    // Do next enemy ship in database
    update++;
    // trace(update);
    if (update>maxAliens) {
        update = 1;
    }
    // Have I just died?
    if (_parent.database.shipDead[update]) {
        // Remove my blip and update my shipDead
        // flag to "not in game"...
        this["blip"+update]._visible = false;
        _parent.database.shipDead[update] = "";
        // Reduce number of aliens by 1.
        // If I am the last alien, then level complete...
        aliensRemaining--;
        // trace(aliensRemaining);
        if (aliensRemaining<0) {
            _parent.play();
        }
    // Am I still alive?
    } else if (!_parent.database.shipDead[update]) {
        // update my radar blip position...
        blip._x = _parent.database.shipX[0]/my.xScale;
        blip._y = _parent.database.shipY[0]/my.yScale;
        // do my radar blip...
        this["blip"+update]._x = _parent.database.shipX[update]/my.xScale;
        this["blip"+update]._y = _parent.database.shipY[update]/my.yScale;
    }
}
```

# 6  Flash Games Studio

**Features**

There's not really much to see in this code. The actual scaling of the database occurs in the last few lines of the `enterframe` script (below the, "update my radar blip position", comment). Also of interest is the use of the color object to make the duplicated alien radar blips red when the original movie clip is white. A color object is created within each duplicated blip, and is then used to turn the movie clip red (hex color 0xFF0000). We can use this technique to do other things with duplicated movie clips, such as insert timelines containing ActionScript into a duplicated graphic movie clip, so not only do we duplicate a gameSprite graphic, we also insert an 'ActionScript brain' inside it! To do this, the inserted ActionScript would scope its controlling actions to _parent.

We can also insert variables within the duplicated timeline using commands such as:

```
this["blip"+i].mySkill = 10;
```

This would insert a variable `skill=10` inside the `blip` movie clip. If the scripts inside the duplicated movie clip used this to decide how fast (and also what color and shape) the copy is, we can use the `duplicateMovieclip` action to duplicate basic clones, and then configure them to act differently, rather like being born and then speed trained. It's a great technique for creating game opponents on the fly at the start of every level.

## 8. The LaserBeam (plasmaControl)

**Object Block Diagram**

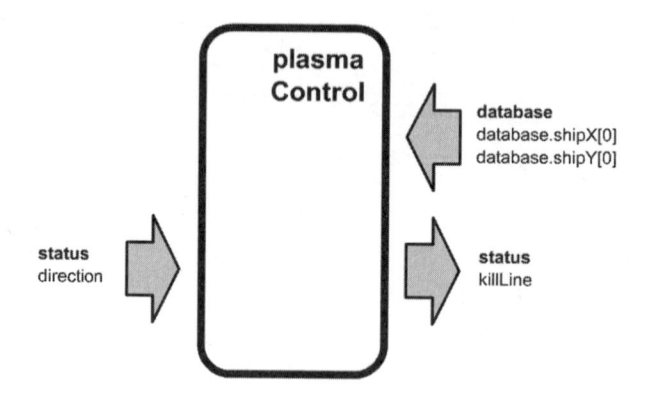

# Structured Real Time Programming    6

## Attached Code

```
onClipEvent (load) {
    // stop and hide the original laser beam
    _parent.laser.stop();
    _parent.laser._visible = false;
    // set counter for duplicates
    i = 1;
    // set starting depth past maxAliens so that
    // the aliens never get overwritten...
    startDepth = _parent.world.maxAliens+10;
    killLine = 0;
    fire = false;
    laserRepeat = 0;
    burstDuration = 2000;
}
//
onClipEvent (mouseDown) {
    if (!fire) {
        now = getTimer();
    }
    fire = true;
}
//
onClipEvent (mouseUp) {
    fire = false;
}
//
onClipEvent (enterFrame) {
    if (fire) {
        if ((getTimer()-now)>burstDuration) {
            fire = false;
        } else {
            laserRepeat++;
            if ((laserRepeat %= 3) == 0) {
                _parent.laser.duplicateMovieClip("laser"+i, i+startDepth);
                i++;
                killLine = _parent.database.shipY[0];
                frame = 10;
            }
        }
    }
    frame--;
    if (frame == 0) {
        killLine = -1000;
    }
    _parent.killLine = killLine;
}
```

Line 47 of 47, Col 1

## Features

The laser beam consists of two components: the dumb movie clip animation we see when we press and hold the mouse button, and the plasmaController movie clip on the top left corner of the mc.world movie clip that controls the mouse button events and the creation of the plasma beams. There are a group of three dummy movie clips that are just there as holders of scripts, so it's a good idea to add a guide layer with some labeling that tells us which is which. These invisible clips can be found at the side of the stage:

plasmaControl>>
alienSpawner>>
scoreKeeper>>

The plasmaController object needs to know which way the player's ship is pointing (direction) and the position that the player's ship is firing via the database. It outputs a y coordinate, killLine, which tells the game that anything on or near that line has possibly just been shot dead (the thing that works this out is the alien object, not the laser beam itself).

The script includes a timer that specifies how long each burst should last called burstDuration. This variable is the burst time in milliseconds, and is used with Flash's internal timer getTimer.

When the mouse button is either pressed or released, the appropriate mouse event scripts set a flag called fired to the appropriate state. The enterframe script also sets the flag to false if the burst duration is exceeded.

Finally, the enterframe script keeps duplicating the laser beam animation for as long as fired is true. The actual laser beam animation mc.laserBeam deletes itself when it has played once via a simple removeMovieClip action, which deletes the timeline on which the action was issued.

A point to be aware of is that the depth of a duplicated movie clip on a timeline must not be the same as an existing duplicate or it will get overwritten. This is why the load event initialization script sets our starting depth to maxAliens+10, thus keeping it well away from the depth of the duplicated aliens.

## 9. AlienSpawner

**Object Block Diagram**

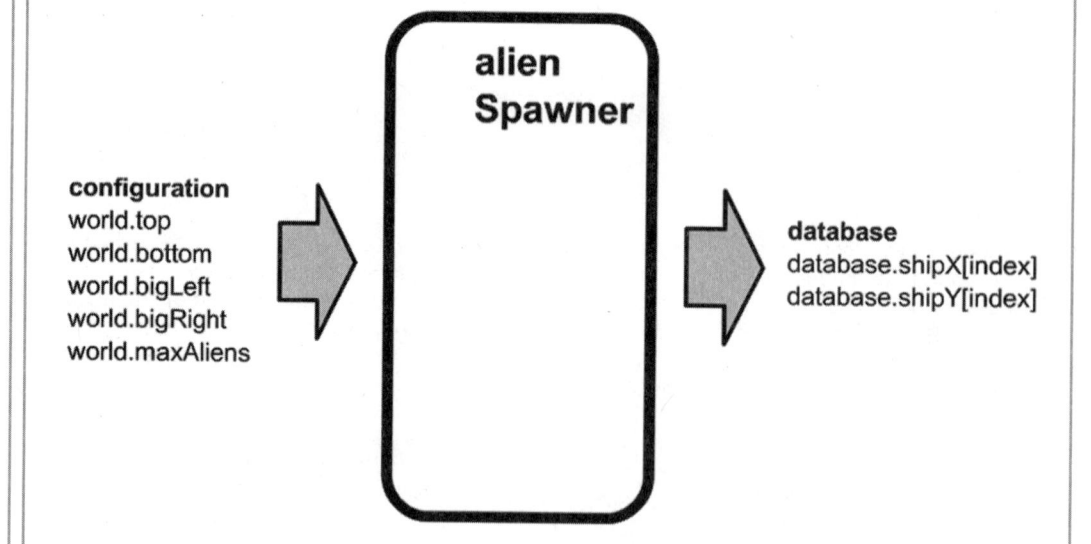

**configuration**
world.top
world.bottom
world.bigLeft
world.bigRight
world.maxAliens

⇒ **alien Spawner** ⇒

**database**
database.shipX[index]
database.shipY[index]

# Structured Real Time Programming

## Attached Code

```
onClipEvent (load) {
    bigLeft = _parent.world.bigLeft;
    bigRight = _parent.world.bigRight;
    bigRange = bigRight-bigLeft;
    top = _parent.world.top;
    bottom = _parent.world.bottom;
    yRange = bottom-top;
    maxAliens = _parent.world.maxAliens;
    // stop and hide the original alien
    _parent.alien.stop();
    _parent.alien._visible = false;
    // set counter for duplicates
    i = 1;
}
//
onClipEvent (enterFrame) {
    if (i<=maxAliens) {
        _parent.alien.duplicateMovieClip("alien"+i, i);
        thisAlienX = bigLeft-(Math.random()*bigRange);
        thisAlienY = top+(Math.random()*yRange);
        _parent["alien"+i]._x = thisAlienX;
        _parent["alien"+i]._y = thisAlienY;
        _parent.database.shipX[i] = thisAlienX;
        _parent.database.shipY[i] = thisAlienY;
        i++;
    }
}
```

## Features

The alienSpawner in the demo version simply duplicates alien objects, placing them randomly across the gameWorld (that is from bigLeft to bigRight, not just the visible screen area). It doesn't stop creating clones until it has reached the number required, maxAliens. The code also updates the database as to the starting positions of the aliens as it creates the duplicates.

# Flash Games Studio

## 10. The ScoreKeeper

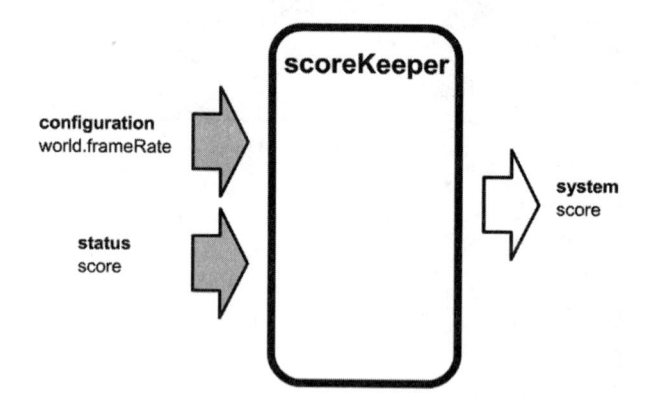

### Object block Diagram

From the diagram, it looks as though the scorekeeper doesn't do anything, it simply sends the version of score in the gameWorld down to System (or _root). That's almost all that it does, but it also does an important thing in between. It only updates System every two seconds. As mentioned before, updating dynamic text can be very time consuming for Flash, so we need to do it much less often than every frame.

### Attached Code

```
onClipEvent (load) {
    updateRate = Math.ceil(_parent.world.frameRate*2);
    update = 1;
}
onClipEvent (enterFrame) {
    update++;
    if ((update %= updateRate) == 0) {
        // trace ("updating...")
        _root.gameScore = _parent.score
    }
}
```

# Structured Real Time Programming

## Features

This is very similar code to the star object. The load event sets our update rate to once in every two seconds (`_parent.world.frameRate*2`), and the value of score is transferred to `_root`, where a dynamic text field automatically displays it.

There. Finished!

## Parting shots

Phew! That's a lot of code we flew through. Don't dwell too much on the specific code, but concentrate on how I used the gameWorld object block diagrams to set up my file structure. That's the thing that allows you to beat my engine and go on to write a cool new game of your own.

As well as see the gameWorld system used in two games of varying complexity, we've also got under the bonnet of tennis and `scrollerDemo.fla` and looked at their little coding tactics, designed to make them run at a decent speed. This is important in everything we do in Flash, not just games. In web site design, our limitation is usually the performance ceiling of the Flash plug-in rather than anything else. Hopefully, that ceiling has been raised somewhat, and our creativity has a greater number of options to play with as we find more efficient ways to implement our creative thoughts.

Now for the Big Truth. The gameWorld System isn't a new thing that I have created through trial and error. It's a standard graphical programming tool for creating an object based software specification in large-scale applications. By large scale I mean really complex. Stuff that flies, or gets really hot, or shoots down the enemy from 200 miles away.

We haven't just learned a way of creating complex multi-level gameWorlds, we've been taught a structured software definition method. Now go and create some mind-blowing stuff. Come back and tell me when you do though, I want to get my name on the high score table.

# Flash Games Studio

## Summary

In this chapter we've introduced the basics for creating real time, fully operational game engines. Through the simple tennis example, and the altogether more complex scrolling shoot 'em up, we've demonstrated the benefits of considering each component as a software object when building games. By defining each of these objects, and the relationships between objects, in advance we're able to get a valuable insight into how to actually code the game.

The value of the concepts of a gameWorld and gameSprites should now be clear and, in fact, many people see this method as the only way to go about coding up a game from scratch. When I first came across the idea of using Object Block Diagrams I could have jumped for joy, and was convinced I could hear angels singing in the background! Hopefully they will have filled you with the same confidence to go ahead and create your own real-time games. Using the techniques and optimization hints outlined in this chapter you should be able to better my examples before too long and, once you become accustomed to it and have discovered your own little coding tricks, there's no limit to what you can do.

In the next chapter we'll take time out from all this theory and have a good look at putting all of our newfound knowledge and creativity to work. The most important thing never to lose sight of when designing games is playability, and the next game has it in spades. It's an excellent example of how basic building blocks can lead on to seemingly complex games, and is a great advocate for Object-Oriented Programming. Hopefully it's also just pure, mesmerizing enjoyment.

# Structured Real Time Programming

**Introduction**
chapter 1
chapter 2
chapter 3
chapter 4
chapter 5
chapter 6
Case Study 1
chapter 7
chapter 8
chapter 9
chapter 10
chapter 11
chapter 12
chapter 13
Case Study 2
chapter 14
chapter 15
**Director Afterword**

# Case Study 1
# Turn

# Case Study 1: Flash Games Studio

This chapter is about the single player game *Turn*, which I developed shortly after Flash 5 came out. I was amazed at the major improvements in scripting that came along with the release of the latest version, and although *Turn* isn't a particularly huge-scale program, and it could probably have been designed in Flash 4, the improvements made in Flash 5 ensured that its creation was a far less painful process. Most of the ActionScript is based on functions and the decentralization of code – in other words attempting to place everything as efficiently as possible. I hope that if you're not experienced in this kind of structuring, you may learn some things that will make your life a little easier.

I'll start with how the game works from the perspective of a player, followed by an introduction into the more theoretical background, which in turn will lead on to the graphic design issues. The final part will be a walk through of the fully built file. But for now, what exactly is *Turn*?

## How it works

The easiest way for you to understand the game *Turn* would be to simply play it, but I'll attempt to define the nature of it to help you understand the design and coding issues that went into its production.

Picture a field with poles placed in a grid-like formation so that they cover a rectangular shape. In fact the field is presented isometrically but we'll come to this point later on. The poles are placed in equal rows and columns and each pole has two 'arms' placed on top at a 90-degree angle. A pair of arms can point in any of four right-angled directions, so, to explain it geographically, as the two arms are at right angles they can either point North and East, East and South, South and West or West and North. For such a simple structure, it's quite a tricky one to explain so perhaps a screenshot of the poles would help:

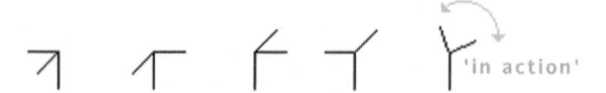

As you can see, due to the isometric nature of the game, both the 90-degree angle formed by the arms, and the direction in which they point, are skewed to comply with the faux 3D effect.

The screenshot above shows the four positions that a pole can take up, and the fifth shows a pole in action, rotating between positions. Basically, that's all that the poles do. At the beginning of the game the user clicks the pole of their choice, and this pole then rotates to one of the three other possible positions. The position the pole takes up after rotating is random, but it won't be the same as the starting position.

The space in between two vertical poles on the grid is equal to twice the length of an arm, so if the arms of two neighboring objects point to each other, their tips will slightly touch. If we think of all this in an isometric way we have the game's board:

# Turn

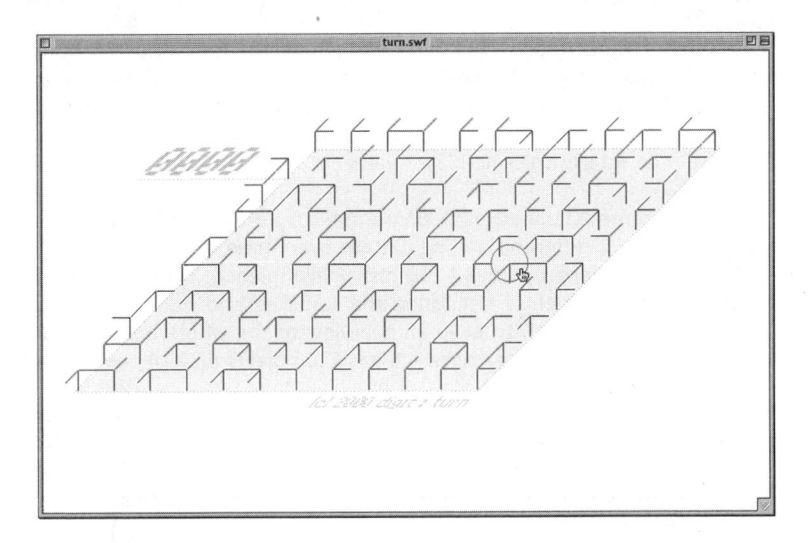

## Case Study 1

At the beginning of the game the poles all take up a random facing. The circle containing the pointer is controlled by the player's mouse and is used to select the pole that they wish to rotate. Once this pole has rotated to its new, random, position it will stop, and if one or both of its arms are in contact with a neighboring pole's arm, then that neighbor will rotate and turn its arms too until it reaches a new, again random, position. If the second pole's arms come into contact with the arm of a third pole, then this third pole will rotate, and so on. The poles can rotate either clockwise or counter-clockwise, and we'll be examining this ability later on in the chapter.

So, now we have a chain reaction of rotating poles lasting as long as their arms continue to come into contact with one another. As you play the game you'll see that this creates the appearance of a flowing motion across the grid. In the case of both a pole's arms being in contact with two adjacent pole's arms, the chain will split up and it's possible to have many poles all rotating at the same time. The aesthetic effect of this can be quite mesmerizing, as you'll no doubt notice when you start playing.

> *As you can see from the screenshot, this doesn't happen at the beginning of the game. Two adjacent poles' arms can quite happily point towards one another, and nothing will happen until the player has clicked on a pole and the game has begun.*

In order to make a game out of this movement, every turn to a new position (or every step in the chain reaction) will be added to a game score counter. Since the average chance for a rotating pole to trigger movement in another pole is far less than 100 percent, the chain reaction will sooner or later come to an end. The final score will represent the total number of turns made up until this point.

265

# Case Study 1 — Flash Games Studio

The player can also set more than one 'seed' (starting point) for chain reactions. In fact, it's possible to click on as many objects whenever and as often as is wanted, but doing so will reset the score to zero. Points are only awarded for rotations that are caused by poles coming into contact after the last mouse-click. Because of this fact Turn is open for enough diverse strategies and tactics to make it an interesting one-player game.

Immediately after the game is loaded each of the objects rotate randomly to one of the four possible positions, forming a different starting pattern every time the player loads the game. The dimensions of the grid are 10 rows with 12 objects (poles) in each. There's actually no particular reason why I chose these numbers, I just found the resulting grid big enough to allow a good amount of action, yet small enough to keep an overview of the whole board. As a result of this we get a 'pool' of 480 different initial patterns — that's 120 objects times 4 possible positions each.

There aren't any instructions available on how to play, but it's pretty simple stuff. It could even be said that Turn is more of a visual effect than a game, as the only input the user has is to select the starting point for a chain reaction. Simply place the red circle over the pole you wish to rotate first and click the mouse button. There's nothing to do after that except enjoy the hypnotic patterns and movement that the game generates:

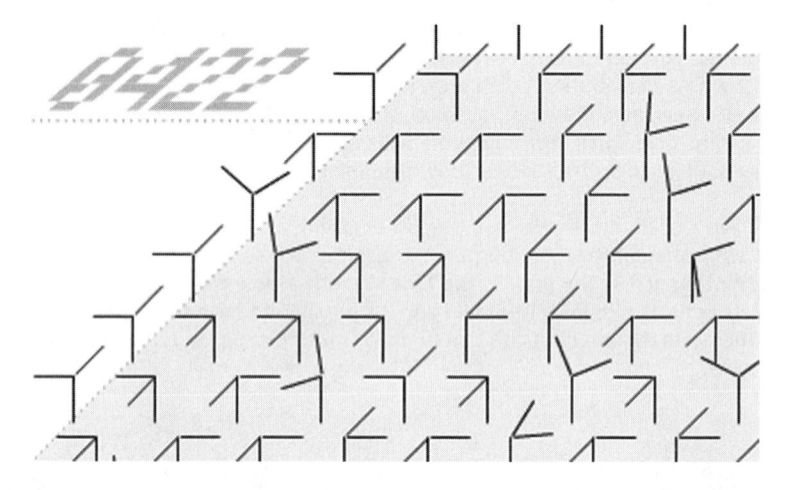

The possibility to start more than one chain reaction is something that players discover after a certain time by clicking here and there when a reaction is in motion. Once you find a nice tactic and know the places in the pattern where it's more likely for chains to split up, it's quite amazing to watch all these busy independent objects causing unpredictable chains and changes in the pattern. Underestimating the possibility for high scores, I originally designed a counter capable of only displaying three digits, but within days of the game going online, someone broke the 1000 mark, forcing me to change it. At the time of writing, the highest score stands at 1240.

There's still something missing that's holding it back from becoming an attractive online game though, the facility for direct/real-time interaction and/or the sharing of archived high scores. For single-player games like Turn, direct interaction would hardly be appropriate, so there's only the latter possibility, which isn't that hard to implement. For example, you could write a little Perl script that receives the player's name and score, opens a text file with the former scores, adds the new score to the list, sorts the list, and then saves it. As you no doubt trawl the web yourself, I'm sure that you've come across many examples of this type of worldwide competition, in which you struggle to beat the score of a total stranger – it's what gives games that elusive 'just one more go' factor.

## Background

I think i'ts safe to say that most games are born with an initial idea and a desire to create an exact effect, which is held in the creator's mind from the moment of conception until the final game production, but that's not how it happened in my case. I was actually just experimenting. While coding, testing, and generally playing around, the basic idea developed and I realized that I just needed to add a counter for the score to make it into a game. I suppose you could call it good luck, since the studies that led to the game were, in a sense, almost the game itself. I'll explain a little further what they were about.

I had in mind the notion of simulating a nice state-changing natural pattern, similar to the behavior of iron filings in a magnetic field – In fact, that's probably why the turning objects have the look and feel of compass needles, although in reality the pole arms share more with magnets with the same polarity at their tips. When a magnet gets close enough to another with the same polarity the latter one will be repelled, and you can see how this idea relates to the arms in my game.

I could have implemented this magnetic proximity-based behavior exactly in the game, but instead an arm has to actually touch a neighbor's arm to cause the rotation. This idea is much simpler, less computer intensive, and just as satisfactory in the sense that I developed a relatively complex structure based on simple objects, all of which only know, and act according to, the state of their neighboring objects. I'd advise any would-be game creators to always begin with simple ideas, as the intricate complexities can always be added later. In attempting to exactly re-create magnetic behavior, I'd have had to code a game that computed the magnetic forces between the arm shaped 'magnets' in real-time. Even if the math were simplified to the extreme, a script would still have to run the whole time, and do this for 120 objects.

## Object-oriented code

Not surprisingly these independent, similar objects can best be controlled by an object-oriented approach – a Flash 5 specialty, since you can deal with almost any physical objects in the form of movie clips. This visual object representation makes OOP much easier to get to grips with in Flash, especially in comparison to normal code-generated objects, such as `myObject = new Object`, which exist in text only. This fact makes Flash very helpful in understanding the principle of an 'object' when used in terms of object-oriented programming.

The goal of using independent objects, each with their own limited scope, is to explore huge complex systems. A manifestation of this idea that you've probably heard of is 'finite elements', a scientific method used mainly in mechanics/fluid dynamics. What this does is simplify complex systems - the ones that nobody can ever fully describe mathematically - by reducing them into easy-to-handle subparts, each with their own simple behaviors. When the system is rebuilt using these small parts, the whole should act like the original impossible-to-model real system. So more

# Case Study 1: Flash Games Studio

and more computer simulations use small objects that only communicate with their surroundings over very limited interfaces, things like 'particle systems' found in high-end 3D engines to simulate rain, snow, dust, liquids, or explosions.

*Turn* is clearly not a scientific tool, but it uses the same simulation ideas and in a way it's interesting to watch the 'chaotic' behavior in the patterns caused by just the little changes that you apply to it. You won't get any hard data for chaotic systems or pseudo-random generator theory, but it's all in there, and it's noticeable, (sometimes subconsciously) because of the game's otherwise extreme simplicity.

I was mainly interested in seeing how far a specific pattern would evolve out of the initial randomly distributed one after I'd been playing it for some time. I found that the arms tended to point to the borders of the grid, thereby bringing into question ActionScript's ability to generate a completely random number. Perhaps you can figure out the reason for this. The player nature in most of us gives us the urge to discover certain patterns in a game in order to develop strategies that lead to a high score – well, that or you can click around wildly and let luck decide, which can be fun as well.

## Design

The concept of *Turn* is absolutely two-dimensional. Every movement happens on a plane. The picture you form of a 2D concept might look flat, like a top view of a table, but when you play a board game in the real world you probably won't follow the game by looking directly from the top. Our main perceptive channel translates into a 3D understanding of the world. So 3D representations, even of 2D-only content, will feel more natural, more like real world objects than their flat projections. Unless you choose 2D for stylistic reasons or because of its simplicity, 3D environments will always be more attractive.

When you decide to build a 3D environment the idea of depth has to be visualized, which is usually done through perspective. The decision of how to achieve this in Flash depends on the graphic design and the technical specifications. In the case of *Turn* I had to spread a couple of line based objects over a plane and then place them in a geometrically clean grid.

If I worked to the 'vanishing point' perspective, each of my objects would have to appear different, according to its placement in space – for example, the objects at the back of the grid would have to be smaller than those that appear closer to us, and for this I'd have to either implement a 3D engine (which for a small amount of wire-frame objects is certainly an option), or make a different perspective drawing for each of the objects.

Fortunately, there's a satisfying alternative: the isometric view. This means giving up real perspective, but it's cheating in a fashionable way. The reason it became so popular in the early ages of computer games is that it implies a 3D look without having to do too much for it. One size (and shape) of object fits all. In sprite-based games without a 3D engine you'd need many pre-rendered views of each sprite object to show it correctly at every position in a real perspective environment, so we're talking about serious use of memory. The way around it was this pseudo 3D solution, which soon developed its own aesthetic right.

# Turn — Case Study 1

I chose the isometric view not because I was too lazy to implement a 3D engine, but because I wanted all the objects to look the same despite their position in the grid. I preferred the expression of equality to a natural perspective look:

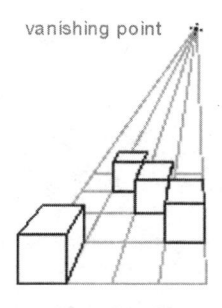

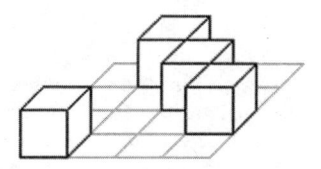

vanishing point

perspective view

isometric projection

Unfortunately, the isometric projection in my game depicts the 90 degree angle formed by the object's arms as either a 45 or 135 degree angle. This would be hard to convert into code - but hang on - Flash is a pretty good animation tool and we should use its abilities whenever possible, taking into consideration performance, development time, and also the resulting file-size. Here animation is extremely useful, because a rotation tween from start angles to end angles results in what we need. This is demonstrated later on, although I'm sure the majority of you are aware of Flash's tweening ability to perform different ranges of movement in the same amount of time.

Before I go into the details of how everything is built, I want to give you an overview of the FLA structure.

## Turn's FLA structure

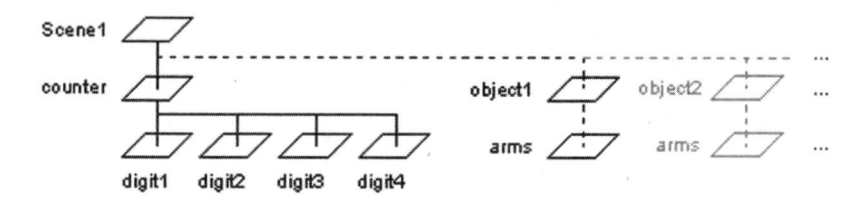

This shows the existing timelines and their content. Scene1 is the top level or main timeline. The first and only frame here contains all of the elements of the game environment, except for the objects, which will be attached from the Library and placed in a grid by the script. The counter movie clip consists of four digit movie clip instances for scores up to 9999 (reach that if you can!) and a script that controls the digits individually.

Background is just a background graphic, and it's indicative of my intention to name things sensibly for easy reference. Last but not least we have the object movie clip, the script for which controls the embedded arms clip, which contains the rotation animation.

# Case Study 1: Flash Games Studio

Since object is going to be attached, its symbol in the Library needs a linkage identifier. To set this, you have to open the Symbol Linkage Properties popup: select the symbol in the Library and choose Linkage from the option menu. In the popup, select Export this symbol and enter a name as an Identifier.

I've developed the practical habit of setting the identifier and/or instance name of an object to its name in the Library, so object has the identifier `object`.

> *Sorry to drum this in one more time, but remember that instance, function, and variable names should always have an obvious name. Don't hesitate therefore to use long names for them if it's what's necessary to explain their role. To avoid re-typing these names and generating spelling errors, copy and paste them. Especially in bigger projects it's worth knowing what a variable contains and what a function does.*

Now that you're familiar with the floor plan of the building, it's time to have a look into the rooms. The 'entrance' of *Turn* is at top level, so let's start there.

## Creating the game environment

As suggested in the chapter on Turn-based games, the first thing that we need to do when contemplating game production is to create the actual environment for our game to take place. In this case this involves setting-up the isometric columns and rows of our grid and inserting our objects, the poles, within it. Lets take a look at the code that initializes these game conditions:

# Turn

## Case Study 1

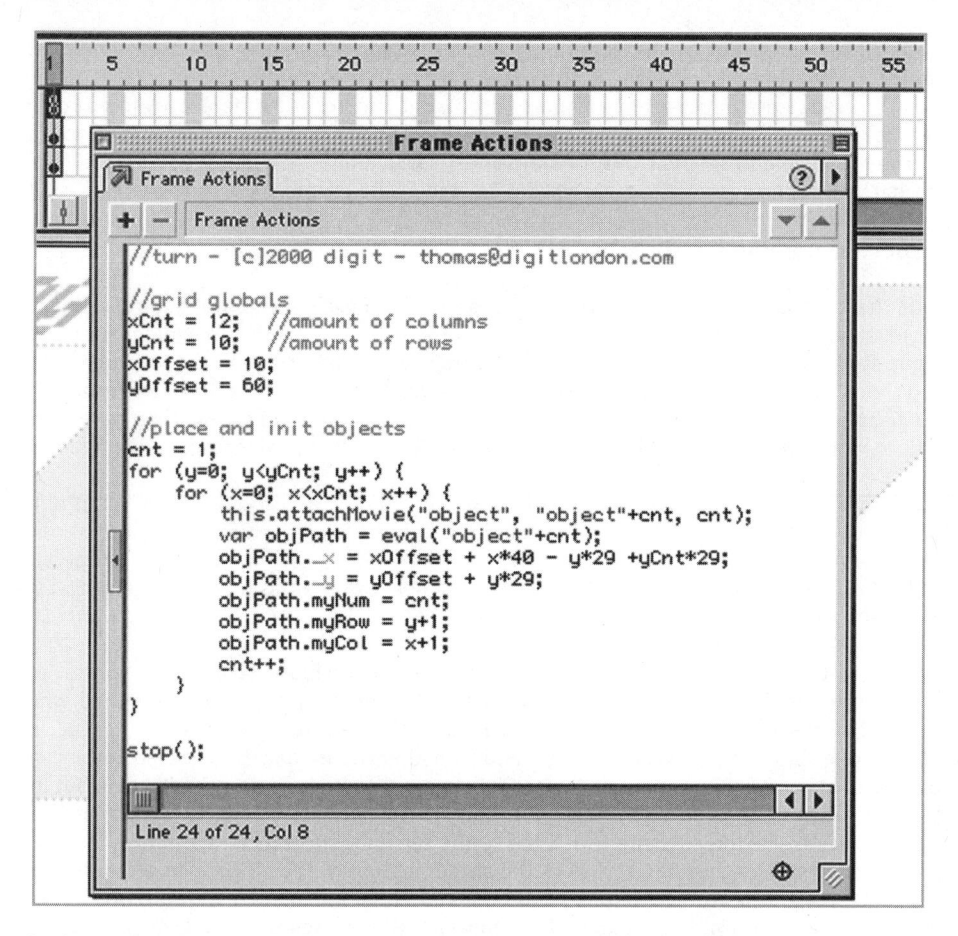

```
//turn - [c]2000 digit - thomas@digitlondon.com

//grid globals
xCnt = 12;    //amount of columns
yCnt = 10;    //amount of rows
xOffset = 10;
yOffset = 60;

//place and init objects
cnt = 1;
for (y=0; y<yCnt; y++) {
    for (x=0; x<xCnt; x++) {
        this.attachMovie("object", "object"+cnt, cnt);
        var objPath = eval("object"+cnt);
        objPath._x = xOffset + x*40 - y*29 +yCnt*29;
        objPath._y = yOffset + y*29;
        objPath.myNum = cnt;
        objPath.myRow = y+1;
        objPath.myCol = x+1;
        cnt++;
    }
}

stop();
```

At the beginning of our code some global variables have to be set. As you can see, they're also used later on in the very same script. Our object movie clips will need to be aware of, and use, the variables xCnt and yCnt, since they define the boundaries of the grid.

The main task of the script is to set object clips to certain coordinates (by setting their _x and _y properties) in the grid. I've used a common method, consisting of two loop structures with one nested inside the other. While the outer loop is responsible for the stepwise increment of one of the coordinates (in this case the y-direction), the inner loop does the same for the other: the x coordinate.

Starting on the first row, the inner loop scans along the x coordinate and sets the columns of the grid. Once a row is completed, the outer loop sets the y coordinate to the next row and the inner loop begins incrementing the columns again, until the last column in the last row is reached. This can be envisaged by picturing the grid building up like writing on a page, working from left to right until the line (or row) is completed, then beginning at the left hand side of the next line down.

# Case Study 1: Flash Games Studio

Another issue addressed by this code is creating our desired isometric effect on the coordinate settings. Setting the y coordinate is straightforward, but the x position not only considers the typical equal distance in between neighbors (x*40), but also needs a different additional offset for every row, so that it fits into the isometric projection. When you execute the loops in your mind, you should be able to see how this dynamic offset calculation works, but if you need a reminder, look back at the final isometric game engine created in the chapter: *The Third Dimension*.

## Setting specific numbers and paths

Inside the inner loop, an object movie clip gets attached to each position, and it must be given an individual name and level. Both can be done with the help of the cnt variable, since this value is unique for each position and object in the grid (cnt=1 for the first object, and increments after every one). We just set the target level to be this value, and add it to the new instance name ("object"+1 equals "object1"). Each instance of our pole in the grid will then have a specific number, which will be essential later on when we come to setting up the chain reaction movement.

Each object's path can be obtained and stored in a variable with objPath = eval("object"+cnt). An alternative would be accessing the path with the array access operator method, which would be objPath = this["object"+cnt]. If we want to set a property, set a variable, or call a function in "object"+cnt, we simply use the this path variable, which will be examined later on in the study.

In order to give the self-sufficient object movie clip a consciousness of where in the grid it's located, some global variables are given to it in a manner similar to that described when we discussed, software objects in the *Structured Real-Time Programming* chapter. Just as in that instance our gameSprites received information on themselves that they stored locally, so our poles need information, not only on their specific object number as described above, but also on their specific position or location within the grid. These variables belong to the object like DNA to a cell, and they're the only interface it has to the surrounding objects. In essence, for our poles to know when to turn they need to check the arm directions of the other poles around them. The information that we give them here on position is essential for them in knowing which poles are adjacent to them, and which will affect their movement. We'll see this when we go into detail on the arms of our objects later on.

## The object Movie Clip script – part 1

Next we will have a look into the object movie clip. You can open it with a double-click on its symbol in the Library. I've called this section 'Part 1' because we'll only deal with the first part of the object script here to ensure that we have the most logical progression through the game coding. Here's the first part of our object script:

# Turn  Case Study 1

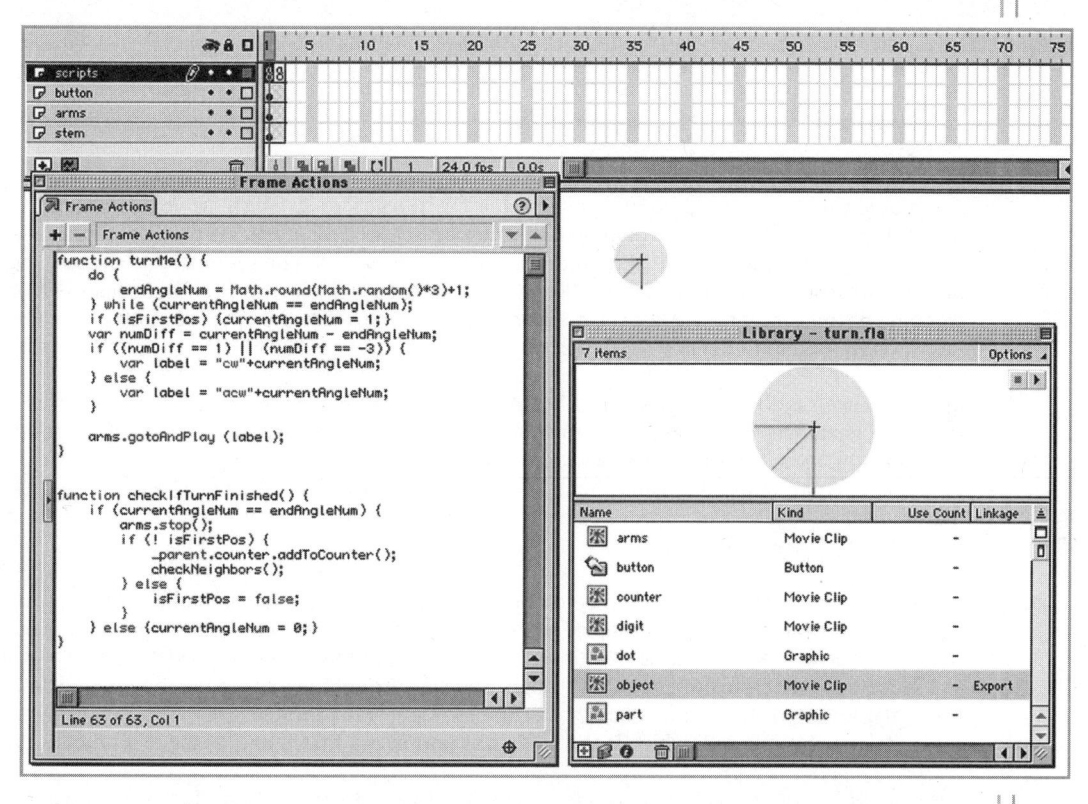

```
function turnMe() {
    do {
        endAngleNum = Math.round(Math.random()*3)+1;
    } while (currentAngleNum == endAngleNum);
    if (isFirstPos) {currentAngleNum = 1;}
    var numDiff = currentAngleNum - endAngleNum;
    if ((numDiff == 1) || (numDiff == -3)) {
        var label = "cw"+currentAngleNum;
    } else {
        var label = "acw"+currentAngleNum;
    }
    arms.gotoAndPlay (label);
}

function checkIfTurnFinished() {
    if (currentAngleNum == endAngleNum) {
        arms.stop();
        if (! isFirstPos) {
            _parent.counter.addToCounter();
            checkNeighbors();
        } else {
            isFirstPos = false;
        }
    } else {currentAngleNum = 0;}
}
```

This screenshot only shows the part of the first frame script that controls the rotation (or turn) of an object. The rest of the first frame script checks the positions of the object's neighbors to see if any of them need to rotate but, as I said, we'll get to that later.

The second frame of the object movie clip has the lines:

```
currentAngleNum = 0;
isFirstPos = true;
turnMe();
stop();
```

This script handles the initial position setting and will be executed as soon this object instance gets attached and is ready to use. It actually should be ready at the end of the first frame, but as you'll see when you start the game, it isn't. Flash often needs some time to settle everything so to compensate for this we have all of the poles spinning when the game is run, before taking up their initial random positions.

# Case Study 1: Flash Games Studio

```
                 ↗      ↑      ↖      ↱
                 ⎿      ⎿      ⎿      ⎿      Y  'in action'
currentAngleNum  1      2      3      4      0
```

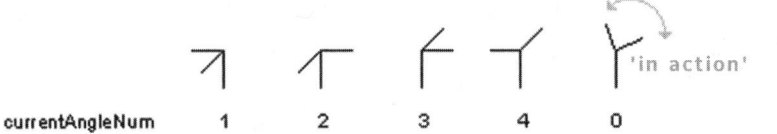

The global variable `currentAngleNum` gets the initial value of 0, which, as you can see, is also the setting while the object is rotating. Next the flag `isFirstPos` gets set to indicate that we're looking forward to the first, initial rotation. All the objects will then be set to a random start angle, but won't cause a chain reaction. We'll see why this is later on in the code that deals with the stopping of the rotation. The last thing that our code does before the timeline stops is to call the first frame's function `turnMe`.

In `turnMe` we randomly generate `endAngleNum`, which is the angle number where the arms will rotate to next. The only criteria for this generation is that the new number is different from `currentAngleNum`, hence a pole can rotate to any of the four possible positions except for the one that it was at before it began rotating. Of course `turnMe` won't only be used for initialization, it'll be used whenever this `object` needs to turn its arms (when you click on it or when its arm touches that of another pole).

Since `currentAngleNum` was set to zero above, the initial `endAngleNum` will be anything from 1 to 4. You may find this initial setting of `currentAngleNum` to zero confusing. How are we going to get the correct value for `NumDiff` (in the next line) from this? In fact, this setting is just a trick to ensure that we're outside the 1 to 4 range, making sure that any angle number can be set for the initial `endAngleNum`. Immediately after initialization `currentAngleNum` for `isFirstPos` is set to its actual value of 1, which is the angle position in the first frame of the `arms` movie clip.

The variable `numDiff` is used to decide whether to rotate the object clockwise or counter-clockwise according to the distance that the arms would have to rotate. As you can see `NumDiff` is evaluated by `currentAngleNum - endAngleNum`. As a result of this calculation we create the `label` string, which directs the engine to the relevant part of our `arms` movie clip – a rather handy bit of functionality. `arms` is just a tweened animation, and the best way to control such an animation is to send it to different labeled frames. If the labels are named with the use of numbers (cw1, cw2, ... acw4), then they're easily accessible by script. Here `cw` and `acw` stand for clockwise and anti-clockwise (counter-clockwise) respectively.

## Player Input (The Button)

Our object movie clip also has an invisible button to allow the player to select where to begin the rotation:

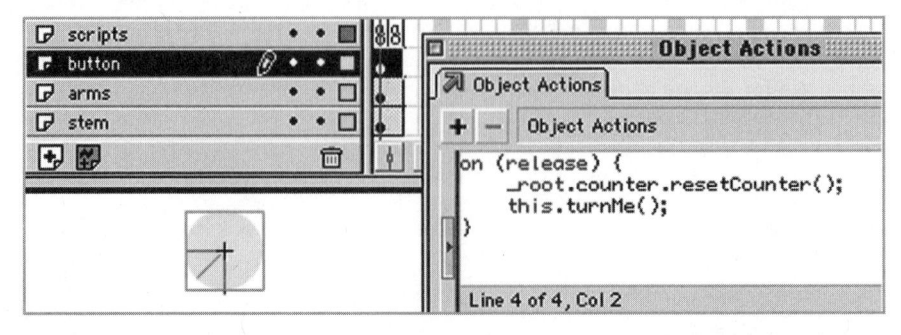

```
on (release) {
    _root.counter.resetCounter();
    this.turnMe();
}
```

# Turn

## Case Study 1

When clicked on, this resets the score counter to zero and calls `turnMe`. The Over and Down states contain a red circle stroke that marks the selected object in the grid, while the Hit state contains the circle as a filled version to define the active area of the button.

## The arms Movie Clip

OK. Now we'll take a look into the arms movie clip. This consists mainly of clockwise and counter-clockwise rotational tweens between the four different angle positions. Tweening is the perfect tool here to deal with the different rotation angles, as it automatically handles the spatial synchronization of the different rotation speeds. If you go into the arms movie clip you'll notice that one arm has to rotate faster than the other in order to have the same starting and ending time. In an anti-clockwise rotation from, for example `currentAngleNum` 1 to `currentAngleNum` 2, the isometric nature of the grid means that one arm must rotate 135 degrees, the other only 45 degrees – but both complete their movement in the same amount of time.

The first frame is simply a stop frame. The labels mark the positions from where rotations beginning with a certain `currentAngleNum` have to start playing. For example, let's assume that the current angle number is 2 and `numDiff` has decreed that the rotation should be clockwise. Therefore the right label would be cw2 and the string generated in our object movie clip code will send our animation to this point. Each time a tween ends, like in the frame selected here:

The script sets currentAngleNum in its parent object to the newly reached value and asks if this is the angle number it should rotate to (if this equals endAngleNum). The answering, handling, and reaction will take place in `_parent.checkIfTurnFinished`.

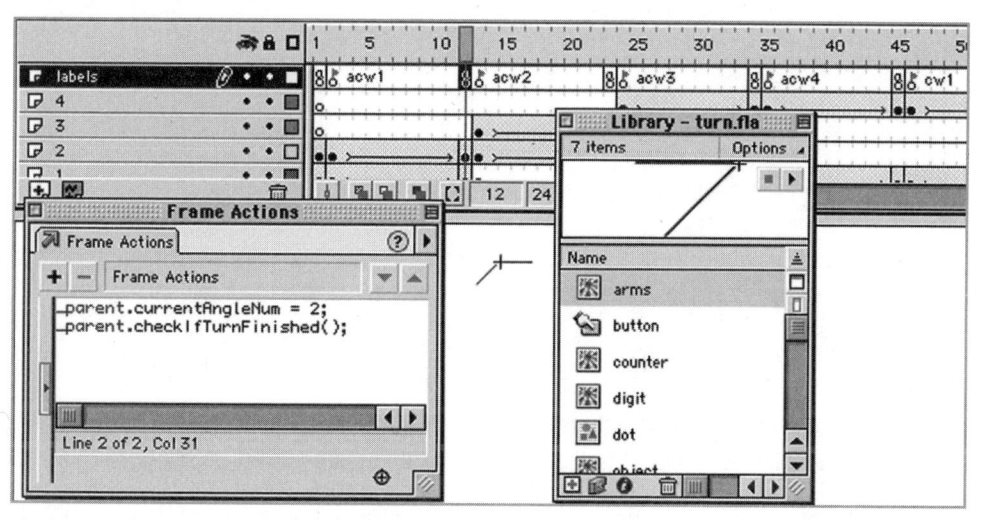

Looking back to the object script we can see how this works. If `endAngleNum` is reached, then the arm animation will be stopped. If not, then `currentAngleNum` will be set back to zero and the rotation will continue. If it reaches the end position, and it wasn't the initial turn, then a function in the counter gets called (adding to the score) and the neighbors get checked to see if they should turn. If it was the initial turn, `isFirstPos` changes to false, stopping any objects from turning or scores being added to before the player has clicked to start.

275

**Case Study 1**

# Flash Games Studio

## The object Movie Clip Script – Part 2

The `checkNeighbors` function checks to see if one or two neighbors are now touching the current object's arms, and therefore need to be told to turn themselves:

```
    } else {currentAngleNum = 0;}
}

function checkNeighbors() {
    //upper
    if ((myRow != 1) && (currentAngleNum != 1) && (currentAngleNum != 2)) {
        var neighborNum = myNum - _parent.xCnt;
        var name = eval("_parent.object"+neighborNum);
        if ((name.currentAngleNum == 1) || (name.currentAngleNum == 2)) {
            name.turnMe();
        }
    }
    //left
    if ((myCol != 1) && (currentAngleNum != 2) && (currentAngleNum != 3)) {
        var neighborNum = myNum - 1;
        var name = eval("_parent.object"+neighborNum);
        if ((name.currentAngleNum == 2) || (name.currentAngleNum == 3)) {
            name.turnMe();
        }
    }
    //right
    if ((myCol != _parent.xCnt) && (currentAngleNum != 1) && (currentAngleNum != 4)) {
        var neighborNum = myNum + 1;
        var name = eval("_parent.object"+neighborNum);
        if ((name.currentAngleNum == 1) || (name.currentAngleNum == 4)) {
            name.turnMe();
        }
    }
    //lower
    if ((myRow != _parent.yCnt) && (currentAngleNum != 3) && (currentAngleNum != 4)) {
        var neighborNum = myNum + _parent.xCnt;
        var name = eval("_parent.object"+neighborNum);
        if ((name.currentAngleNum == 3) || (name.currentAngleNum == 4)) {
            name.turnMe();
        }
    }
}
```

Line 63 of 63, Col 1

For every potential neighbor (upper, lower, left, right) there is, in principle, the same procedure. First a check to see if this object is actually a neighbor at all, then using myNum (remember: this was given to our object in the grid-placing procedure in our very first piece of code), and the global grid dimension variables in the main timeline (xCnt and yCnt), the path to that neighbor will be evaluated so that we can check its currentAngleNum. If the angle fits, then the neighbor's turnMe function will be called and it will turn.

# Turn

## Case Study 1

As an example, let's go through the upper neighbor check. If myRow is 1, then there's no upper neighbor. If none of our arms are pointing upwards (see the images of currentAngleNum that we looked at earlier), nothing is to be done either. The neighbor's number - part of its path - can be obtained by subtracting the amount of columns in a grid row (_parent.xCnt) from myNum. The path to the neighbor gets evaluated and its current angle is retrieved. This is another piece of information that each object holds about itself. If one of this neighbor's arms points downwards, then it will rotate to a new random position.

For this example, let's assume our object had 23 as myNum and 3 as currentAngleNum. myRow is 2, so we know there's an upper neighbor. One of the arms points upwards – so we now have to check the upper object's currentAngleNum. Since _parent.xCnt is 12, the upper neighbor object has 11 as myNum (evaluated by subtracting parentxcnt (12) from myNum (23)). Therefore the upper neighbor's path is _parent.object11, and we can then access _parent.object11.currentAngleNum. If this equals 1 or 2, then one of its arms must point downwards, so we call the neighbor's turnMe function.

> *This is the reason why* currentAngleNum *is set to zero while turning, because an object (here the upper neighbor) should only be able to start a turn when it sits on one of the four defined positions. It shouldn't start while its neighbor is still performing a rotation.*

## The Counter

In the end, the vast majority of games are played with one goal in mind - to get a high score. For this reason, I believe the score itself should always be nicely presented. In the testing phase, a dynamic text field served well, but now how do we integrate that into the isometrics? There are two ways:

- If you have the desired font on your computer, then you can use a dynamic text field, include the charSet (for a numeric counter select the number tab only) and skew the text field's boundary 45 degrees.

- You can use graphics or images as digit representatives, as I did in my game. The digits are then instances of one movie clip with 10 stop frames, each of which contains a digit-graphic from 0 to 9:

# Case Study 1: Flash Games Studio

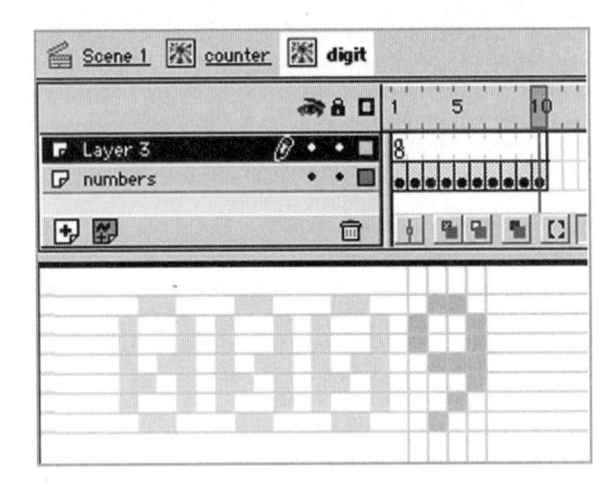

There are four of these digit movie clips embedded in the counter movie clip, which controls the digits, setting them to the appropriate frames to represent a score number:

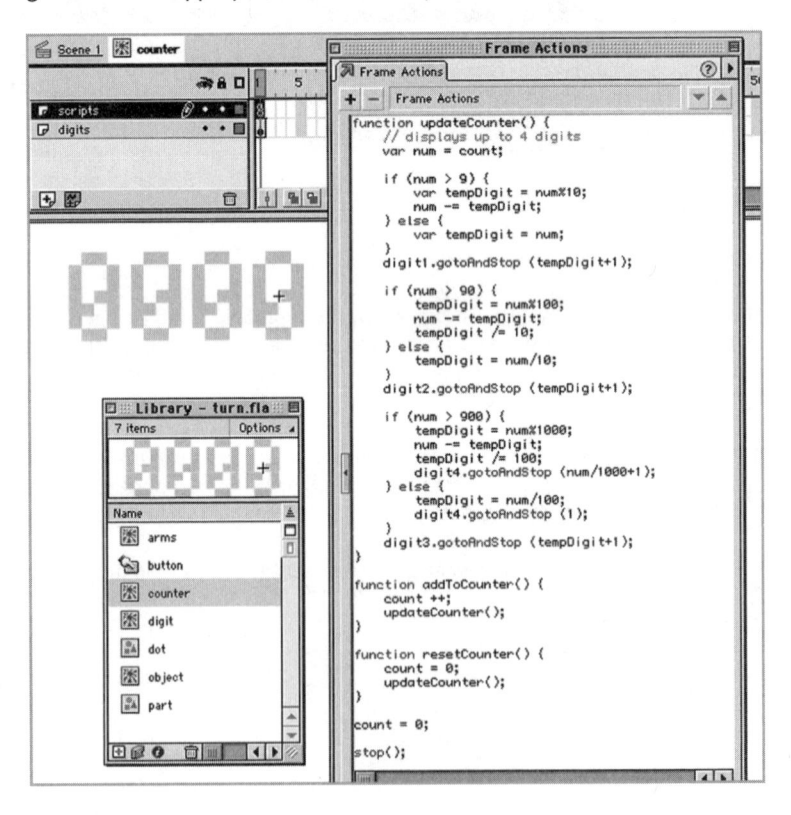

```
function updateCounter() {
    // displays up to 4 digits
    var num = count;

    if (num > 9) {
        var tempDigit = num%10;
        num -= tempDigit;
    } else {
        var tempDigit = num;
    }
    digit1.gotoAndStop (tempDigit+1);

    if (num > 90) {
        tempDigit = num%100;
        num -= tempDigit;
        tempDigit /= 10;
    } else {
        tempDigit = num/10;
    }
    digit2.gotoAndStop (tempDigit+1);

    if (num > 900) {
        tempDigit = num%1000;
        num -= tempDigit;
        tempDigit /= 100;
        digit4.gotoAndStop (num/1000+1);
    } else {
        tempDigit = num/100;
        digit4.gotoAndStop (1);
    }
    digit3.gotoAndStop (tempDigit+1);
}

function addToCounter() {
    count ++;
    updateCounter();
}

function resetCounter() {
    count = 0;
    updateCounter();
}

count = 0;

stop();
```

The global variable `count` holds the score and can be displayed by calling the function `updateCounter`. The functions `addToCounter` and `resetCounter`, are straightforward.

In the beginning of `updateCounter` the temporary variable `num` gets set to the current `count` value. It's `num` that we perform all of the following mathematical operations on – `count` will be left untouched. The rest is a cascading method to find out how many times 10, 100 and 1000 fit into our score. Let's suppose the counter is at 23. We enter `updateCounter` and `num` is set to 23 (20+3) which is bigger than 9. So `tempDigit` will be 3 (23% (modulo) 10 is equal to 3), and `num` will be 0. The lowest digit position, `digit1`, will then be sent to frame 4, which contains the graphic of a 3. Going on, we discover that our remaining 20 in `num` are not bigger than 90. As a result `tempDigit` changes to 2 (20/10) and `digit2` gets sent to frame 3, which shows a 2. `Digit3` and `digit4` will remain on frame 1 as zeroes, which is exactly how we want it. I suggest that you pick some other numbers and go through the function on your own. You'll probably even find a more elegant solution.

## And that's it!

Endgame! I hope you've enjoyed playing it and maybe even coding it. I'm sure that with your newfound game-coding ability you'll be able to make many improvements on the simple structure that I've laid out, and you'll go on experimenting and creating new games.

By now you should be brimming full of the confidence and creative energy that will allow you to create whatever form of game you wish. My code is simply an example of how you can put together the parts of your knowledge of ActionScript to form a coherent whole, a playable game to which as many, or as few, features can be added as you so desire. If you start simple and implement the basic operations first, then there's no limit to how far you can take your ideas. You may even wish to add some cool features to my game. Whatever you choose to do, I hope you have as much fun, and the same sense of fulfillment, as my creations have brought me. Maybe the next new game I play will be one of yours...

**Introduction**
chapter 1
chapter 2
chapter 3
chapter 4
chapter 5
chapter 6
Case Study 1
chapter 7
chapter 8
chapter 9
chapter 10
chapter 11
chapter 12
chapter 13
Case Study 2
chapter 14
chapter 15
**Director Afterword**

# Chapter 7
# Designing a Platform Game Construction Kit

# Flash Games Studio

One of the first things we need to learn in gaming is how to make our animated sprites intelligent. There are a number of ways to achieve this, but remember our prime objective is to keep our Flash files friendly, easy to edit and expand, and most of all small.

So, in this chapter we will examine the different ways the game sprites can interact with one another. The best way to approach this subject in a gaming scenario is by checking out the development of a platform game. This will take into account several key elements:

- **The player** – who can move left, right and jump
- **Platforms** – objects the player can jump onto, over, or run across
- **Pick-ups** – objects that the player walks through to gain specific benefits such as points, increased health, or weapons
- **Enemies** – objects that the player must avoid

Along the way we'll take in:

- How a platform game is structured and coded
- How to build, load and store level maps
- Step-by-step instructions for building a mini application to help us design our own game levels

## The Platform Game

Platform games are like soap operas. For the most part they have a fixed format, and just a little bit of tweaking here and there will get you an entirely new title. The rudiments of these games are the same, presenting a dynamic and modular structure that can be realized quite effectively in Flash.

Flash's `hitTest` method makes the detection of player collision with enemies and pick-ups straightforward and greatly simplifies the code for handling landing on platforms. It's possible to produce fast-paced platform games in Flash that look as good as platform games on hand-held devices or consoles:

# Designing a Platform Game Construction Kit

```
onClipEvent (load) {
    function reset(){
        for (var mc in this){
            this[mc]._visible=false;
        }
        this[subType]._visible=true;
        if(this._name==pickup){
            this._visible=false;
        }
        this._x=startX;
        this._y=startY;
    }

    function pickup () {
        _root.playSound();
        if (subType=="health") {
            _parent._parent.player.increaseHealth(10);
        } else if (subType=="score") {
            _parent._parent.player.increaseScore(400);
        } else if (subType=="weapon") {
            _parent._parent.player.getWeapon();
        } else if (subType=="gameEnd"){
            _root.endLevel();
        }
        this.removeMovieClip();
    }

    reset();
}
onClipEvent (enterFrame) {
    if (this.hitTest( _parent._parent.player ) ){
        pickup(); // call pickup function
    }
}
```

The game we'll be looking at is called *Rescue Run*. Its platforms are floating segments of ground, the pick-ups are health, gold, and fire extinguishers and the enemies are fires, snails and giant butterflies. But let's face it, just a few graphical and behavioral alterations will transform this into almost any platform game you can think of. At the end of this chapter we'll look at how to add features to the game that don't currently exist and discuss how changing the graphics can affect the speed of the game.

The fully commented source code for *Rescue Run* and a platform level editor are provided in the demo `rescue_run.fla`. Rather than waste time typing in the whole game and going over subjects that you'll already be familiar with, we're just going to highlight and explain some of the more intricate parts of the game, and go into detail on things that you might not have come across before. It's recommended then that you open up the Rescue Run game FLA and familiarize yourself with it, then work through it as we go through the chapter.

## How the Game Works

Most of the game code is contained either on the first frame of the main timeline or in specific functions defined within each movie clip's `load` clipEvent. The game works by the code calling the appropriate function at the appropriate time. For example when the user holds down the left arrow key the player's `moveLeft` function is called, which unsurprisingly moves the player left.

# Flash Games Studio

The functions defined within the player, enemy, and pick-up movie clips act like object methods. So, when the player walks across a health pick-up, it calls the player's `increaseHealth` function, which in turn increases the player's health by the specified amount. This object-based approach ensures that the code is easy to maintain and easy to extend.

## The Level Map

Like most scrolling platform games, *Rescue Run* is made up of a number of levels. In the sample file there are only three levels but this can easily be extended. Each level is described by a level **map**, which is a text file containing data on the whereabouts of each item in that level. At the start of each new level the data is loaded from the associated text file and interpreted within the map movie clip.

When the game starts there is only one copy of each of the pick-up and enemy movie clips. Based on the level map, these movie clips are then duplicated and moved to their appropriate x and y coordinates as needed. So, if the level map contains three pick-ups, then the pick-up movie clip will be duplicated three times. Similarly, the large and small platforms are duplicated and positioned at the associated x and y coordinates based on the level map.

A special pick-up called gameEnd is used to determine whether the player has reached the end of a level. If the players collide with a gameEnd pick-up, they have completed the level and the next level is loaded.

We'll look at the functions used to manage the retrieval and display of levels and how the level map data is stored later on. For now though, let's take a look at how the main game is structured.

## The Game Structure

Have a look at the following diagram, which I've split it into a text version and a graphic version so that you can compare it to the finished game and the finished game code. It shows how the game is structured, and what it has to do to function:

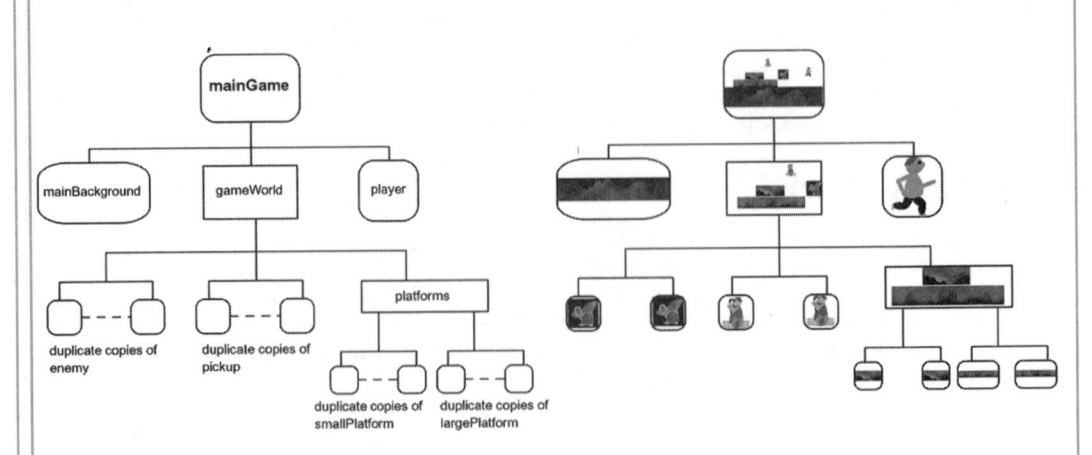

# Designing a Platform Game Construction Kit

The `mainGame` movie clip is on the main timeline. Nested within it we have three other clips:

- `mainBackground` – the scenery
- `gameWorld` – the things that the player will stand on or interact with
- `player` – that's us

You can also see a further group of movie clips nested within `gameWorld`, comprising of all the platform, enemy, and pick-up movie clips.

But why nest them in this way? Well, for starters it's going to make scrolling a whole lot easier. Imagine the difficulty of telling each platform, each enemy and each pick-up to scroll individually. So, by nesting all of these elements within the `gameWorld`, we need only worry about scrolling `gameWorld` itself. Simple.

One final layer of nesting sees the individual platform movie clips grouped together within platforms. This is done because it simplifies the platform collision detection. If we want to see if the player is standing on a platform all we need to do is use the `hitTest` function to see if the player is hitting the platforms movie clip. Again, this is a lot simpler than testing to see if the player is hitting each and every platform movie clip.

> *Throughout the code for the game we'll frequently use the `_parent` **property to refer to the movie clip that contains the current movie clip. So, if a line of code within a pick-up movie clip needs to refer to the x-position of the player it will be coded as** `_parent._parent.player._x`*

## Scrolling

In the tradition of side-scrolling platform games, players can move left or right but once they get halfway across the screen they stop moving right and the world starts scrolling to the left. To give the game a nice arcade feel the background mountains also scroll left at a half the speed of the world. This is an effect known as **parallax scrolling** and it adds a greater sense of depth to the game. We'll be looking at parallax scrolling in more detail later in the book.

So, it follows that the main reason for having the core game engine contained within the `mainGame` clip is that it allows a mask to be put over the whole game engine thus hiding the parts of the level that shouldn't yet be visible to the player.

As we've seen, the `gameWorld` movie clip contains enemies, pick-ups, and platforms. As the player moves forward the `gameWorld` movie clip is scrolled to the left giving the player the sense that they're moving through a world. The `gameWorld` movie clip can be found within the main game area movie clip.

# Flash Games Studio

To do this, the following ActionScript has been placed in gameWorld's load clipEvent.

```
function scrollLeft(speed){
  this._x-=speed;
}
```

The `scrollLeft` function simply reduces the _x position of the movie clip by however much speed tells it to.

## Pick-ups and Enemies

A pick-up is quite a simple game element. The pick-up sits within the game world doing nothing until the player collides with it, at which point something happens-typically the players score increases, The pick up then disappears.

Enemies are quite similar. Like pick-ups the enemy movie clips check to see whether they are colliding with the player. If this is true, then the player's health is reduced until the player either stops colliding with the enemy or the player dies. Different enemies decrease the player's health by different amounts.

Every pick-up and enemy movie clip has a local variable called `subType`, which is used to distinguish between different types of enemies and pick-ups. The pick-up movie clips can be one of four types: health bonuses, score bonuses, weapons, or end of level markers. So the variable `subType` is set to `health`, `score`, `weapon`, or `gameEnd`. This determines the outcome of the collision between the player and the pick-up or enemy.

Every pick-up is just a duplicated copy of the source pick-up movie clip. When a movie clip is duplicated, all of its event code is duplicated with it, so the code for the source pick-up's `enterFrame` and `load` clipEvents are duplicated for each new pick-up.

The code for the pick-up is quite straightforward. Within pick-up's `enterFrame` clipEvent we have the following ActionScript:

```
if (this.hitTest( _parent._parent.player ) ){
  pickUp();
}
```

This simply calls the function called `pickUp`, which is defined just before the enterFrame clipEvent, when the player hits the pick-up movie clip.

The image below shows the `pickUp` function and the pick-up movie clip's `enterFrame` code:

# Designing a Platform Game Construction Kit

```
function pickUp () {
    _root.playSound();
    if (subType=="health") {
        _parent._parent.player.increaseHealth(10);
    } else if (subType=="score") {
        _parent._parent.player.increaseScore(400);
    } else if (subType=="weapon") {
        _parent._parent.player.getWeapon();
    } else if (subType=="gameEnd"){
        _root.endLevel();
    }
    this.removeMovieClip();
}
reset();
}

onClipEvent (enterFrame) {
    if (this.hitTest( _parent._parent.player ) ){
        pickUp(); // call pickUp function
    }
}
```

The `pickUp` function does three things. First it plays a simple sound effect, then it calls the appropriate function based on the pick-ups `subType` and lastly it removes itself using `removeMovieClip`.

The key differences between enemies and pick-ups are that enemies don't disappear when the player collides with them, and that some enemies can move.

Moving enemies (the snails and butterflies) have their x position adjusted independently of the player's movement. The code looks to see firstly if the type of enemy is a snail or butterfly, and then if the enemy is on the viewable area of the screen. If both of these things are true then the enemy's `moveLeft` function is called which reduces the x coordinate, effectively moving the enemy left towards the player.

The enemies have an `attack` function that's called when a collision is detected between the enemy and the player:

```
// enemy.attack : call appropriate player method based on enemy type
function attack () {
    if (subType=="fire") {
        _parent._parent.player.decreaseHealth(10);
    } else if (subType=="snail") {
        _parent._parent.player.decreaseHealth(15);
    } else if (subType=="butterfly") {
        _parent._parent.player.decreaseHealth(20);
    }
}

// enemy.moveLeft : change x coord based on moveSpeed
function moveLeft() {
    this._x-=moveSpeed;
}
}

onClipEvent (enterFrame) {
    if ((subType=="butterfly" | subType=="snail") and (_parent.onScreen(this._x))){
        moveLeft();
    }
    if (this[subType].hitTest( _parent._parent.player ) ){
        attack();
    }
}
```

# Flash Games Studio

The coding is similar to the `pickUp` function mentioned previously, and it calls the appropriate player function based on the enemy's `subType`.

So why does the enemy not start moving until the player can see it? Well, this is quite a normal thing in platform games. If the enemies started moving the moment the game started, the player could just wait at the start, jump them all, and go on to finish the game without any hazards at all. Our technique makes the game more challenging and more in keeping with traditional platform games for the enemies to wait until the player can 'see' them before they start moving. And it goes without saying that no end of processing speed is saved by keeping things static until they need to move.

## Platforms

In *Rescue Run* there are two types of platform: big and small. The only difference between these is the size of the graphic. The movie clips largePlatform and smallPlatform are the source clips for all the platforms in the game. At the start of a new level, these two clips are duplicated over and over until they comply with the level map's orders.

All of the platforms are grouped together in the parent movie clip called platforms. As I said previously, there is a significant advantage in collecting together all the platforms into one movie clip. It means that we can just do one hitTest check for the platforms movie clip, which checks every platform in one go. The actual code for detecting whether the player is standing on a platform is contained within the enterFrame clipEvent of the player movie clip.

## The Player

The player movie clip contains most of the important code for the game engine. Everything that can happen to the player is defined as a function within the player movie clip including moving, jumping, health decrease, score increase and, of course, loss of life.

The player movie clip also contains a number of variables that directly relate to the player. The most important of these are:

- `score` – the player's current score
- `lives` – number of lives remaining
- `health` – value of the player's health
- `maxSpeed` – maximum speed that the player can move, measured in pixels per frame
- `deceleration` – rate at which the player slows down
- `jumpHeight` – how high the player can jump

# Designing a Platform Game Construction Kit    7

- `speedHoriz` – the current speed of the player's movement in the horizontal direction – this is a positive value if the player is moving to the right, negative if moving to the left and zero if stationary

- `speedVert` – the current speed of the player's movement in the vertical direction – this is a positive value if the player is moving down/falling and negative if moving up

The player's variables are initialized (that is, set to their start values) in one of three places. Either in the `load clipEvent` of the player movie clip, or in the player's reset function, which is called when the player loses a life, or in the player's `restart` function, which is called when the game starts.

Let's have a look at the functions that control the player.

## Increasing the Score

```
function increaseScore(incr){
    score+=incr;
}
```

This function increases the player's score. It's really quite simple: the function is passed a variable called `incr` and the variable score is increased by the value of incr. So the function call `increaseScore(20)` would increase the player's score by twenty. On the main timeline there is a dynamic text box that displays the players current score by referencing this score variable via `mainGame.player.score`.

## Decreasing the Player's Health

```
function decreaseHealth(decr){
    health-=decr;
    if (health<=0){
        endLife();
    }
}
```

This function decreases the player's health by the amount passed in the argument `decr`. If the value of `health` is zero or less the player's `endLife` function is called, because if `health` is below zero, then the player must have died.

## Losing a Life

```
function endLife(){
    lives--;
    if(lives<0){
        _root.gameOver();
    } else {
        reset();
        _parent.gameWorld.reset();
    }
}
```

This function reduces the player's `lives` variable by one. If this means that they no longer have any more lives, then the gameOver function on the main timeline is called. If the player still has lives remaining, then the player's reset function is called and the gameWorld is reset. The `player reset` function puts the player back at the start x and y coordinates, and sets `health` back to 100. The gameWorld reset function moves the gameWorld back to its start position and resets all the enemies.

### Moving to the Left

```
function moveLeft(){
    if (speedHoriz>(-1*maxSpeed)){
        speedHoriz-=incrSpeed;
    }
}
```

This function is called when the player presses the left arrow key. The function moves the player movie clip to the left by reducing its `speedHoriz` variable. In the `enterFrame clipEvent` of the player movie clip, the x coordinate is changed by the current value of `speedHoriz`. So if `speedHoriz` is minus 4, then the player's x coordinate is reduced by four, which moves the player 4 pixels to the left. The code: `if (speedHoriz>(-1*maxSpeed))` checks to see if the variable `speedHoriz` is greater than `maxSpeed` multiplied by minus 1. For example, if the current `speedHoriz` is -4 and `maxSpeed` is 8, then the code would check if –4 is greater than -8. Finding this to be true, it would then run the next piece of code: `speedHoriz-incrSpeed`. However, if `speedHoriz` were -9 then it'd be smaller than -8 and `speedHoriz` wouldn't be reduced any more. The point of this test is to ensure that the player can't move any faster to the left than the value of `maxSpeed`.

### Jumping Up and Down

```
function jump(){
    jumping=true;
    speedVert -= jumpHeight;
}
```

This function is called when the player presses the up arrow key. The function sets the variable `jumping` to true. We need this variable to ensure that player can only jump while standing on a platform and hence can't jump while in mid air. We'll take a look at how this works in just a second. The function also decreases the variable `speedVert` by the value of `jumpHeight`. In the player's `enterFrame clipEvent` the player's _y coordinate is changed by the value of speedVert.

## How The Jumping Works

The code for jumping is only a few lines but it's quite clever and worth understanding.

1. Initially `jumpHeight` equals 12, `gravity` equals 1, `maxSpeed` equals 8 and `speedVert` equals 0.

2. The player presses the up arrow key: within player's `enterFrame` clipEvent this is detected by the code:

```
if (Key.isDown(Key.UP) and jumping==false) {
jump();
}
```

...which calls the `jump` function discussed previously, as long as we're not already jumping.

3. The `jump` function reduces the variable speedVert by the value of jumpHeight, so `speedVert` is now -12.

4. Within the players `enterFrame` `clipEvent` the following code is repeated:

```
if (speedvert<maxSpeed){
  speedVert+=gravity;
}
newY=this._y+speedVert;
```

This increases `speedVert` by gravity (which is 1) with each frame loop. So `speedVert` changes to -11 then -10 then -9 then -8 etc gradually increasing until `speedVert` is no longer less than `maxSpeed`, when it is equal to 8. So the value of `speedVert` is -12 then -11, -10, -9, -8, -7, -6, -5, -4, -3, -2, -1, 0, 1, 2, 3, 4, 5, 6, 7, and finally 8.

The variable `newY` is set to the current y-coordinate of the player, plus the value of `speedVert`. We check to see if the player is not hitting a platform, (which is explained in the next section), and if that's OK then the player's y-coordinate is set to the value of `newY`.

The result of looping through this code is that the player's y-coordinate is first decreased by 11, effectively moving the player upwards 11 pixels. The y-coordinate is then decreased by 10 followed by a decrease of 9 then 8 etc until `speedVert` is 0 at which point the player is momentarily stationary in mid-air. As `speedVert` becomes positive, player's y-coordinate is increased, moving it downwards. It stops falling when it hits a platform as described in the next section.

## Player and Platform Collision Detection

The player movie clip also handles the collision detection between the player and the platforms. To give a realistic effect, such that the player appears to be walking *on* the platforms and not *in* them, we actually detect if the player is *about* to hit a platform and stop him before he hits it. The code looks to see if the player's next x or y position will result in a collision with a platform and if so, the player's movement is stopped.

# Flash Games Studio

The code that does this is within the player movie's `enterFrame clipEvent`.

First player's new x and y positions are calculated.

```
newX=this._x+speedHoriz;
newY=this._y+speedVert;
```

This is where the player will be next. We want to check that the player's next location won't be in the middle of a platform. To do this we make use of `hitTest`.

## hitTest

There are two different usages of `hitTest`. The first usage tests for a collision between the bounding boxes of two movie clips, which is what we used in the code for the enemies and pick-ups. For the platform collision detection we need to use the second version of `hitTest`, which checks for a collision between a specific point and the shape of a movie clip. In this case the specific point is the players x- and y-coordinate and the shape is the shape of all the platforms in the platforms movie clip.

We first check if the player's new x-position is within a platform:

```
if (_parent.gameWorld.platforms.hitTest( newX, this._y, true )){
  speedHoriz=0;
} else {
  if(newX<_root.scrollStart){
    this._x=newX;
  } else {
    _parent.gameWorld.scrollLeft(speedHoriz);
    _parent.mainBackground.scrollLeft(speedHoriz/2);
  }
}
```

`hitTest` is used to check if the player's current y-coordinate and new x-coordinate would mean that the player would be hitting the platforms movie clip. If the player will be hitting a platform, then his horizontal speed is set to zero, which stops him moving horizontally. If this isn't the case, then we check if the player should move horizontally or if we need to scroll the background to give the illusion that the player is moving forwards.

The variable `scrollStart` defines the x-coordinate at which the player stops moving right and the background starts scrolling left. `scrollStart` is set to be the middle of the stage, so that if the player reaches the middle he stops moving right and the background starts moving left, which gives the illusion that the player is moving forwards.

# Designing a Platform Game Construction Kit

The line: `if (newX<_root.scrollStart)` checks to see whether the player's new x-position is to the left of the scrollStart position. If this is true then the code: `this._x=newX` sets the player's current x-position to the new x-position. However if this isn't true, then the player's x-coordinate must be greater than or equal to the `scrollStart` position. In this situation instead of moving the player to the right we instead move the background to the left. This is done by the lines:

```
_parent.gameWorld.scrollLeft(speedHoriz);
_parent.mainBackground.scrollLeft(speedHoriz/2);
```

The first line calls a predefined function called `scrollLeft` that moves the gameWorld to the left by the player's current horizontal speed. The second line calls a similar `scrollLeft` function for the mainBackground, which moves it to the left by half of the player's current horizontal speed. Moving the mainBackground at half of the speed of the gameWorld results in a parallax scrolling effect that gives the game a sense of depth.

We then check if the player's new y-position is within a platform.

```
if (_parent.gameWorld.platforms.hitTest( this._x, newY, true )){
    speedVert=0;
    jumping=false;
} else {
    this._y=newY;
    if (this._y>400){
        endLife();
    }
}
```

If this is true, then we set `speedVert` to zero, which stops the player moving vertically and therefore stops the player falling. If the player won't be hitting a platform then his current y-coordinate is set to the new y-coordinate. The code also checks if the player's y-coordinate is greater than 400, which would mean that he has fallen off the bottom of the screen and hence lost a life.

## Resetting

The player, enemy and pickup movie clips all have a `reset` function defined within their load `clipEvent`. This `reset` function simply sets the movie clip to the start position determined by the game level map. For the enemies and pick-ups the `reset` function also ensures that the appropriate graphic for the clip's subType is made visible. So, if an enemy clip's subType is **snail** then the snail graphic within the enemy clip is made visible and the fire and butterfly graphics are made invisible.

The `reset` function is called when the movie clip is first loaded or duplicated and, in the case of the player movie clip, whenever the player loses a life.

# 7 Flash Games Studio

## Building Level Maps

Platforms, pick-ups, enemies and the player together form the foundation of the platform game. But a platform game is not much of a game unless it has well-designed and challenging game levels. So we need to take these building blocks of the game world and build some interesting game levels.

For each game level of the platform game we'll have a **level map** which defines the layout of the game elements for that level. The level map will store the locations (x and y coordinates) for all the platforms, enemies and pick-ups in the game level as well as where the player starts and where the level ends. As discussed previously, every pick-up, enemy and platform movie clip has a local variable called subType that defines what type of movie clip it is. So our level map will also need to store the subtype for the platforms, enemies, and pick-ups, for example saying whether an enemy is a snail, butterfly or fire.

The level maps are stored as separate text files. So we have a file called `level1.txt` that contains all the data for the first level, a file called `level2.txt` that contains all the data for the second level, and so on.

The data stored in these text files is the x-coordinate, y-coordinate, type, and subtype for each and every platform, pick-up or enemy in the level. To keep things simple we store this data as a comma separated string, so the data for an enemy snail located at x-coordinate 120 and y-coordinate 100 would be stored as 120,100,enemy, snail. For a whole level we just have a long string of text containing this data for each and every element in the game. Here's the text file that defines level one:

```
mapData=1322.45,212.4,pickup,score,263.45,226.4,enemy,fire,185.45,
224.4,pickup,score,335.45,225.4,pickup,score,721.45,148.4,enemy,bu
tterfly,569.45,190.4,pickup,score,781.45,217.4,enemy,fire,743.45,2
15.4,pickup,health,1024.45,215.4,pickup,score,1055.45,216.4,pickup
,score,1145.45,215.4,enemy,fire,1769.45,216.4,enemy,fire,1848.45,2
15.4,pickup,score,1679.45,213.4,pickup,health,2346.45,167.4,enemy,
butterfly,2223.45,198.4,enemy,fire,2375.45,167.4,pickup,gameEnd,23
74.45,183.4,platform,smallPlatform,2229.45,215.4,platform,largePla
tform,2031.45,217.4,enemy,snail,1991.45,232.4,platform,largePlatfo
rm,1796.45,232.4,platform,largePlatform,1600.45,232.4,platform,lar
gePlatform,1431.45,193.4,platform,smallPlatform,1324.45,227.4,plat
form,smallPlatform,1167.45,229.4,platform,smallPlatform,1039.45,23
0.4,platform,smallPlatform,918.45,231.4,platform,smallPlatform,749
.45,233.4,platform,largePlatform,548.45,204.4,platform,smallPlatfo
rm,310.45,241.4,platform,largePlatform,114.45,241.4,platform,large
Platform,458.45,219.4,platform,smallPlatform,72,89,player,start,
```

# Designing a Platform Game Construction Kit

This is a very simple way of storing the level data and has been used here to keep the coding as simple as possible. However there's is no reason why the game couldn't be adapted to work with level data stored in a more structured format such as XML or within a database.

The game engine `rescue_run.swf` loads each level's text file and stores the data in a custom data structure within the game. The first level map gets loaded when the game starts, and as the player completes each level the next level map is loaded, replacing the previous one.

Storing levels as separate files to the main game engine is a good programming technique and is common practice in commercial game development. It separates the game design from the game code, which makes the whole thing easier to maintain. If you want to change level three all you need to do is open up the level three text files and make the changes, without having to alter the main FLA file.

## Building a Level Editor

A level editor is a tool for building game levels. It's an additional application that enables the user to design a level and then generate a game level map that may be loaded into the main game engine.

Level editors speed up the game development process. It's much easier to design a level visually than to type out x and y coordinates. Furthermore it allows the level design process to be shared across many people, so you can get lots of levels designed simultaneously:

In this section we're going to step through building a level editor for *Rescue Run*.

We'll need to:

- Create versions of the core game elements that can be dragged around the stage in the editor window, and make it possible to scroll the editor window

- Create the core editor functions and a toolbar for duplicating the game elements

- Generate the level map data

# 7  Flash Games Studio

## The Editor Window

The editor window is where the user will be able to drag around the components of the level to create their own fantastic *Rescue Run* level.

1. To start, open the Flash file `rescuerun_editor_nocode.fla`. This is just a simple Flash file containing all the game graphics required for the editor:

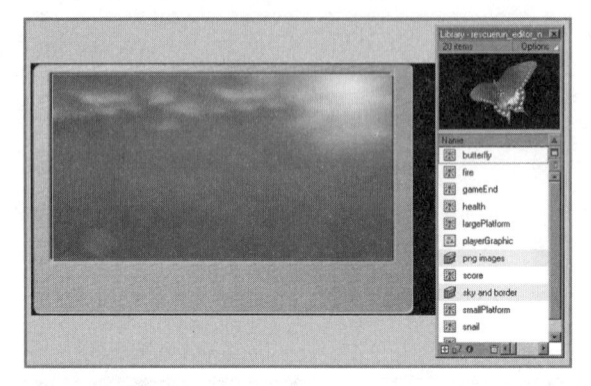

2. **The Player**
   Create a new movie clip symbol and call it player. From the Library add playerGraphic to a layer on this new movie clip and center it.

3. **The Enemy**
   Create a new movie clip symbol and call it enemy.

Within this new movie clip create three layers. From the library put the butterfly movie clip on the first layer, the snail movie clip on the second layer, and the fire movie clip on the third layer, then name the layers accordingly. Adjust these graphics so that their centers all align.

Set the instance name for each enemy to the name appropriate for its type, so the snail movie clip has the instance name snail and the fire movie clip has the instance name fire, etc.:

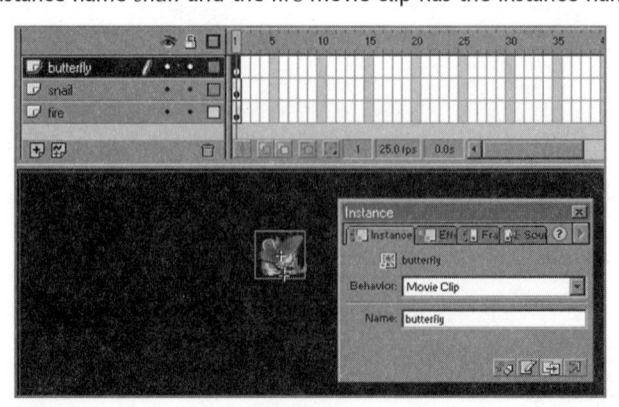

# Designing a Platform Game Construction Kit

> *It is always a good idea to re-click on a movie clip to check that Flash has registered an instance name. Believe me, it's better to find out straight away if the instance name has not been taken on by Flash!*

4. **Pick-ups and Platforms**
   Repeat the process from step 3 for the pick-ups and platforms. This produces:

   - A movie clip called pickUp which has four layers with the gameEnd, health, score, and weapon movie clips on the respective layers

   - A movie clip called platform which has two layers with the smallPlatform and largePlatform movie clips on the respective layers

5. **The Editor Movie Clip**
   Create a new movie clip symbol and call it editor. Add the player, pickup, platform, and enemy movie clips you have created to separate layers on this new movie clip. Set the instance name of the player movie clip to player, the instance name of the enemy movie clip to enemy, the instance name of the platform movie clip to platform, and the pickup movie clip instance to pickup.

6. Create a new layer on the main timeline called editor and add the editor movie clip you created in step 5. Give this new movie clip the instance name editor. Using the Info panel position the center (origin) of the movie clip at x-coordinate 0 and y-coordinate 0:

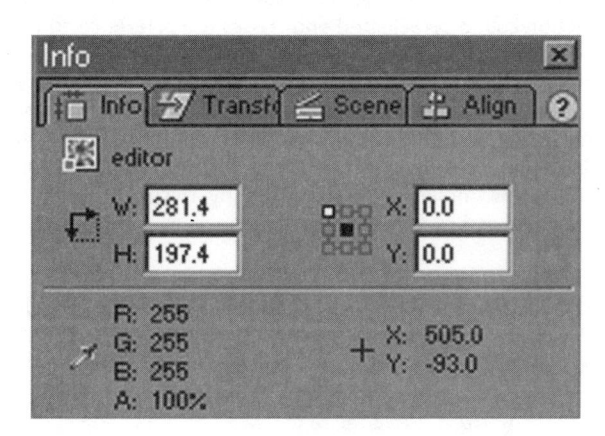

# Flash Games Studio

> *Note: We position the movie clip's center at the x and y origins because this is the where the center of the gameWorld movie clip is located in the Rescue Run game engine. For the coordinate references from our editor to make sense in the game it is necessary that the editor and gameWorld should be working from the same origin. Setting the movie clip's origin to the same as the origin for the stage also simplifies some coordinate calculations.*

7. **Draggable Clips** Open the Actions window for the editor movie clip and type the following:

```
onClipEvent (mouseDown) {
    for (mc in this) {
        if (this[mc].hitTest(_root._xmouse, _root._ymouse, true))
{
            this[mc].startDrag();
            _root.setSelected(this[mc]);
        }
    }
}
onClipEvent (mouseUp) {
    stopDrag ();
}
```

This code will let the user drag the movie clips within the editor. It also calls a global function called setSelected and passes it a reference to the movie clip being dragged.

The code for (mc in this) sets up a 'for loop' that loops through every object or variable contained within the editor movie clip. Importantly this means that as the loop executes, the reference this[mc] will reference every movie clip contained within editor. The if test in the code then checks to see if the current mouse coordinates are 'hitting' the movie clip referenced by this[mc] and if so, the movie clip is made draggable and a reference to the movie clip is passed to the setSelected function.

8. **Scrolling the Editor**
Continuing in the Actions window for the editor movie clip, type the following:

```
onClipEvent (load) {
    scrollSpeed=0;
    function move(amt){
        scrollSpeed=amt;
    }
}
onClipEvent (enterFrame) {
```

# Designing a Platform Game Construction Kit

```
          this._x+=scrollSpeed;
}
```
This code defines a `move()` function for the editor which is used to change the value of the editor's `scrollSpeed` variable. The function is passed a value `amt`, which is the amount that the editor will scroll. The clip event code just changes the x-coordinate of the editor based on the value of `scrollSpeed`.

9. Now create a new button symbol and call it scrollLeft. On the button's first frame draw a square with an arrow or triangle pointing left.

10. On the main timeline add a new layer called scroll buttons and drag a copy of your scrollLeft button from the Library to this new layer.

11. Open the Actions window for this button and type the following:

    ```
    on (press) {
         editor.move(10);
    }
    on (release, releaseOutside) {
         editor.move(0);
    }
    ```

    This code simply passes a value of 10 to the editor's move function when the button is pressed and a value of zero when released. The result is that the editor moves 10 pixels left every frame loop while the button is held down.

12. Repeat steps 9 to 11 but this time create a scrollRight button with the only difference being that the arrow should point right and the line of code:

    ```
    editor.move(10) will instead be editor.move(-10)
    ```

Now test your movie. You should find that you have four clips that can be dragged around the stage, and you are also able to use the left and right buttons to scroll the editor left and right.

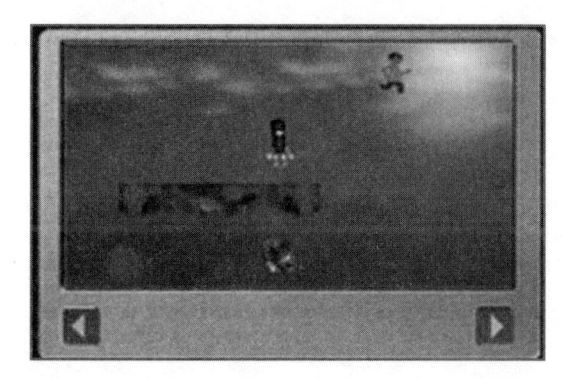

The source file `rescuerun_editor02.fla` contains all the work up to here.

299

# 7  Flash Games Studio

## Functions

If we want to add a platform to the level we're designing, we have to duplicate the movie clips we've just created. In order to do this we have to create a toolbar containing buttons representing the different platforms, pick-ups, and enemies. Clicking on one of these buttons will create a copy of that game element within the editor. Let's take a look at the main functions.

**The Functions that Do Most of the Work**

1. On the main timeline create a new layer called control. This is where most of our ActionScript will go.

2. First we're going to define a few variables and arrays. Open up the Actions window for the first frame of the control layer and type the following code:

   ```
   count=new Array();
   count["platform"]=1;
   count["enemy"]=1;
   count["pickup"]=1;
   depthCounter=1;
   tempPoint = new object();
   ```

   This defines an array in which we store a count of the number of platforms, enemies and pickups. Each of these array elements is set to 1. The depthCounter is just a counter variable that we increase every time we duplicate a movie clip and hence can be used to give movie clips a unique depth. tempPoint is a new custom object that we will use to temporarily store coordinates. We need to create this point object to use in a global-to-local coordinate conversion. Flash's globalToLocal feature, which converts coordinates from the global stage to a local movie clip, requires that we pass the coordinates as a point object and hence we need to define a point object to use for this purpose.

3. Beneath the code from the previous step type the following:

   ```
   editor.enemy._visible=false;
   editor.platform._visible=false;
   editor.pickup._visible=false;
   ```

   This code just hides the template clips for platforms, enemies and pick-ups within the editor. When the user wants to add a new element to the editor, such as a new platform, we will duplicate the appropriate template clip and make the new clip visible.

# Designing a Platform Game Construction Kit

**The Functions**

4. Below the code from the previous step, type the following: `function centerMovie(mc)`

    ```
    {   tempPoint.x=sky._x;
        tempPoint.y=sky._y;
        editor.globalToLocal(tempPoint);
        mc._x=tempPoint.x;
        mc._y=tempPoint.y;
    }
    ```

    This function takes a movie clip that is located within the editor clip and repositions it at the center of the stage. Why do we do this? Because when the user creates a new game element in the editor by clicking on the toolbar, we want to be able to position this new game element in the middle of the viewing area.

    First of all, we need to know the coordinates for the center of the stage. On the main timeline we have a movie clip called sky, which is located at the center of the stage. So this means that sky._x and sky._y happen to be the center of the stage on the main timeline, which saves us from a lot of hassle working it out another way.

    Okay, so we know the coordinates for the center of the stage for the main timeline. But we can't just use those coordinates in the editor movie clip. The main time line has its own coordinate system, and editor has its own coordinate system, and they aren't the same! With the editor clip nested in the main timeline we've got a coordinate system nested inside of a coordinate system. So how do we convert an x,y coordinate on the main time line, to an x,y coordinate within the editor clip?

    The function globalToLocal is the solution we need. It converts a global coordinate (one in the main time line) to a local coordinate (one within a movie clip). So we use globalToLocal to convert the x,y coordinates of the sky clip to the editors coordinate system.

5. Below the code from the previous step, type the following:

    ```
    functionnewGameElement(type,subtype){
       editor[type].duplicateMovieClip(type+count[type], depthCounter);
       centerMovie(editor[type+count[type]]);
       editor[type+count[type]].type=type;
       editor[type+count[type]].subtype=subtype;
       for (mc in editor[type+count[type]]){
          if (mc != subtype){
             editor[type+count[type]][mc]._visible=false;
          }
       }
       editor[type+count[type]]._visible=true;
       count[type]+=depthCounter+=1;
    }
    ```

Whew, that's quite some key work! This function creates a new game element within the editor based on the passed `type` and `subtype` arguments. A typical use of this function would be something like `newGameElement("enemy", "snail")`, which would duplicate the enemy object and hide all the internal enemy clips except for the snail.

Let's try and digest it a bit. The function basically does five things:

- The first line duplicates the appropriate movie clip based on the passed type.

- The second and third lines call the function from step four, resulting in the new duplicated clip being centered within the viewable area of the editor.

- The fourth and fifth lines give our new movie clip two new variables which store the clip's type and subtype, which will be useful to reference when we generate our level map data.

- The `for` loop simply iterates through all the movie clips contained within the new duplicated clip and hides everything except for the clip with the same name as the subtype argument. So if the type was `enemy` and the subtype was `snail` then the `fire` and `butterfly` clips will be made invisible while the `snail` clip will remain visible.

- Lastly the appropriate counters are incremented and the new duplicated clip is made visible.

6. Now we are going to define two functions to handle selection and deletion. Below the code from the previous step, type the following:

```
function setSelected(mc){
  lastSelectedClip._alpha=100;
  lastSelectedClip=mc;
  lastSelectedClip._alpha=70;
}
function deleteSelected(){
  lastSelectedClip.removeMovieClip();
  lastSelectedClip=null;
}
```

These two functions should be reasonably self-explanatory. Both functions make use of a global variable, `lastSelectedClip`, which we use to store a reference to the last movie clip that was selected (that is, the last clip that was dragged by the user. If nothing was selected then its value will be undefined or null).

The first function is called when the user drags a new movie clip. The function sets the alpha for the `lastSelectedClip` to 100% and then sets the variable lastSelectedClip to the new movie clip passed into the function and finally sets the alpha for this new clip to 70%. Effectively this means the previously selected clip has its alpha restored to normal and the clip that was just selected goes to an alpha setting of 70%.

# Designing a Platform Game Construction Kit

The second function simply removes the last selected movie clip. This is called when the user wants to delete a game element from the editor.

## *The Toolbar*

Now let's add in a toolbar with buttons that will call these new functions:

1. On the main timeline make a new layer and call it toolbar.

2. From the Library add instances of each of the different game subType movie clips (butterfly, snail, fire, largePlatform, smallPlatform, health, score, gameEnd, and weapon) to the toolbar layer. We'll be using these as the buttons for our toolbar so there is no need to give them instance names. Note: you may have to do a bit of creative resizing on the largePlatform clip to make it fall in with our plans!

3. Select the butterfly movie clip and convert it into a button, using its Behavior window on the Instance panel.

4. Open the Actions window for the button you just created and type:

   ```
   on (release)
   _root.newGameElement("enemy","butterfly");
   }
   ```

   This calls the function we defined earlier which duplicates the associated game object in the editor movie clip.

5. Repeat steps 3 and 4 for the other eight movie clips you placed on the toolbar layer, changing the function arguments to match the associated clip (namely: "enemy", "fire" / "enemy", "snail" / "pickup", "health" / "pickup", "score" / "pickup", "weapon" / "pickup", "gameEnd" / "platform", "smallPlatform" / "platform", "largePlatform")

6. **A Delete Button**
   Create a new button symbol and call it deleteButton. Draw an appropriate graphic, such as a square with an 'x' on it:

# 7   Flash Games Studio

7. From the Library add an instance of the deleteButton that you just created to the toolbar layer of the main timeline.

8. Open the Actions window for the deleteButton and type the following:

```
on (release, keyPress "<Delete>") {
    deleteSelected();
}
```

> *Pressing the delete key on your keyboard won't work when testing a movie within Flash. The delete key press is only detected in the browser or standalone player.*

This code simply calls the deleteSelected() function we defined previously whenever the user clicks the button or presses the delete key, consequently deleting the selected item. If you test your Flash file you should now be able to click on the buttons on the toolbar to create new game objects within the editor. The last selected game object should appear slightly grayed out (alpha at 70%) and you should be able to delete the currently selected object.

## Generating the Map Data

The whole point of a level editor is to create the data for a level map, so let's add that in.

1. Create a new movie clip symbol and call it mapDisplay. In this new movie clip add a Dynamic Text Field and make it a fair size (see the following image). Within the Text Options panel, set the text field's variable name to mapData and make sure that the Border/Bg, Selectable, Multiline, and Word wrap properties are all selected.

2. You may also wish to add a background graphic such as a filled rectangle behind the text box – making sure that your text is set to be a different color of course...

# Designing a Platform Game Construction Kit

3. Back on the main timeline create a new layer called map and drag a copy of mapDisplay from the Library out into the middle of the stage:

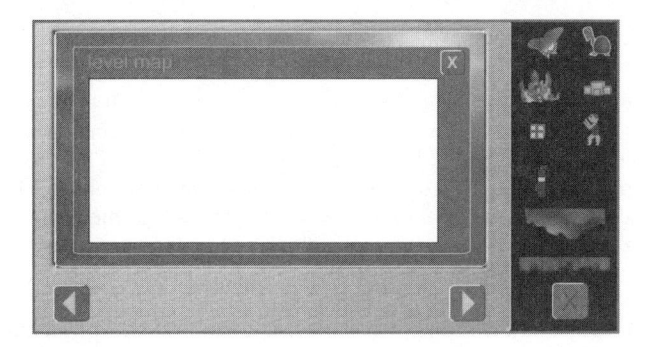

4. Give this the instance name mapDisplay.

5. Open the Actions window for the mapDisplay clip and type the following:

```
onClipEvent (load) {
    function generateMap(editorClip){
        this._visible=true;
        mapData="mapData=";
        for (mc in editorClip){
            if(editorClip[mc].subtype != null){
                mapData+=editorClip[mc]._x;
                mapData+=",";
                mapData+=editorClip[mc]._y;
                mapData+=",";
                mapData+=editorClip[mc].type;
                mapData+=",";
                mapData+=editorClip[mc].subtype;
                mapData+=",";
            }
        }
    }
}
```

This onClipEvent load code creates a generateMap function for the mapDisplay clip when it is loaded. The function is passed a reference to the editor movie clip.

The function does three things:

- The first line of the function ensures that the mapDisplay clip is visible.

- The second line of the function sets the text field to nothing.

- The remaining lines of the function are a for loop, which loops through all of the movie clips contained within the editor movie clip and appends the important properties (x, y, type, and subtype) of these movie clips to the mapData text field. Each property is separated by a comma. The if statement ensures that only movie clips with a subtype property are included which means that the properties of the template movie clips are not recorded as we didn't set subtype variables for these clips.

6. Now create a new button symbol and call it mapButton. Draw a graphic that looks like a button, such as a rectangle with the words 'Generate Map' on it.

7. On the main timeline add a new layer called map button and add the mapButton symbol from the library to this layer. Open the Actions window for the button and type the following code:

```
on (release) {
    mapDisplay.generateMap(_root.editor);
}
```

This code simply calls the generateMap function we defined in step 5 when the button is released. The function is passed a reference to the map editor movie clip.

8. Finally, open the Actions window for the first frame of the control layer on the main timeline. Just below the line editor.pickup._visible=false; and before the first function definition type the following:

```
mapDisplay._visible=false;
editor.player.type="player";
editor.player.subtype="start";
```

This code hides the mapDisplay movie clip which is only made visible when the generate map button is clicked. The second and third lines of the code set the type and subtype variables for the player, which ensures that the player's properties are included in the map data.

# Designing a Platform Game Construction Kit

You now have a fully functional level editor. It allows you to duplicate and drag around game objects to build up your own level and then click the 'Generate Map' button to create the level data:

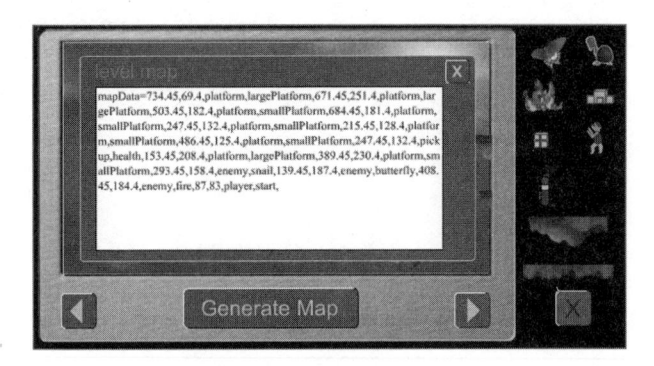

To use the level you've just created, simply select all of the data in the text field and copy and paste this text into a blank text file. Save the text file with an appropriate name (like `level1.txt`) and you'll be able to load it into the game engine and start playing your new level. We'll take a look at how you can do this directly from Flash later on when we look at ways to expand the editor. Now that we've finished with the editor, it's time to open up the game FLA again and have a look at the code behind how the level data is loaded into and stored within the *Rescue Run* game engine.

## The Data Structure for Levels

As we have already established, the *Rescue Run* game levels are stored as text files, but within the game engine itself the level data is stored in its own movie clip called map. We use a separate movie clip for the map so that we can make use of the data clipEvent when loading a new map from a text file.

Within this movie clip the level data is stored in an array of custom-defined objects. The custom defined object is called gameObject and is defined with the following constructor function:

```
function gameObject(x,y,type,subType) {
    this.x = x;
    this.y = y;
    this.type = type;
    this.subType = subType;
}
```

We have one instance of the gameObject for every platform, pick-up or enemy within the level. Using a custom object gives us a flexible way of storing the map data. If we decide that there is more information we wish to store about game elements we can easily adapt the data structure by changing the object's definition (that is, change its constructor function).

The map array is defined simply using the following code:

```
var mapArray = new Array();
```

You may have only used arrays to store variables but there is no reason why you can't have arrays of any data type including custom objects. Hence our level map is stored as an array of our `gameObject`.

The following diagram shows the structure of the `map` movie clip and the data structures within:

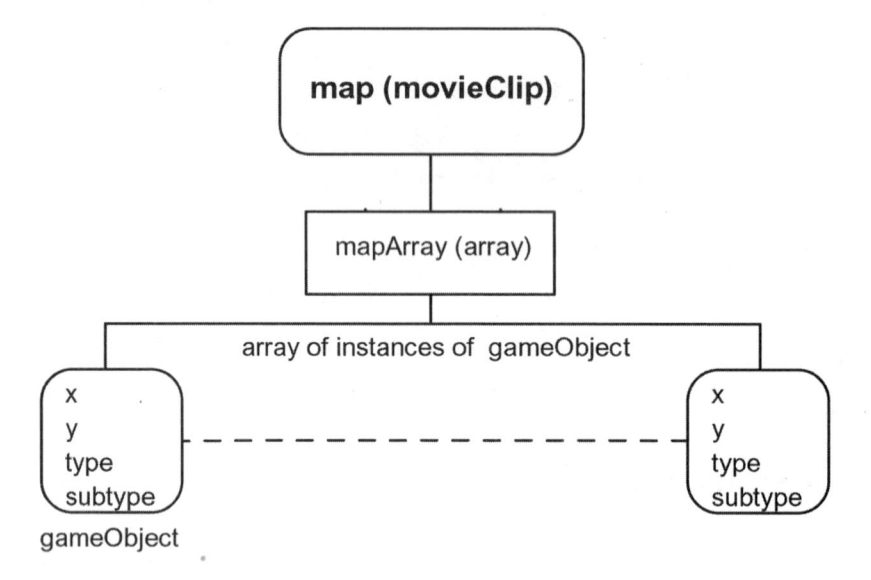

```
                    ┌─────────────────────┐
                    │   map (movieClip)   │
                    └──────────┬──────────┘
                               │
                    ┌──────────┴──────────┐
                    │   mapArray (array)  │
                    └──────────┬──────────┘
           ┌───────────────────┴───────────────────┐
           │     array of instances of gameObject  │
    ┌──────┴──────┐                         ┌──────┴──────┐
    │  x          │                         │  x          │
    │  y          │ ─ ─ ─ ─ ─ ─ ─ ─ ─ ─ ─ ─ │  y          │
    │  type       │                         │  type       │
    │  subtype    │                         │  subtype    │
    └─────────────┘                         └─────────────┘
      gameObject
```

## Loading Levels

Within the `map` movie clip we have two functions called `loadlevel` and `mapToDataStructure`, which collectively load the level map from a text file into our map data structure. The code for the loadLevel function is simply:

```
function loadLevel(){
        level++;
        mapName="level"+level+".txt";
        loadVariables(mapName, this);
}
```

This function simply increases the level variable and loads the text file specified by the `mapName` variable into the `map` movie clip.

# Designing a Platform Game Construction Kit

The text file will be loaded into one very long string called mapData. In our level editor we create a single, long, comma-separated variable to store our level map data. This is the simplest way to store and retrieve a text file in Flash but it isn't much use in our game engine, so we use the function mapToDataStructure to sort this data into our level data structure.

```
function mapToDataStructure () {
   tempArray = mapData.split(",");
   mapSize=tempArray.length/4;
   for (i=0; i<mapSize; i++) {
      tempX = Number(tempArray[i*4]);
      tempY = Number(tempArray[i*4+1]);
      temptype = tempArray[i*4+2];
      tempsubType = Number(tempArray[i*4+3]);
      mapArray[i] = new gameObject(tempX, tempY, temptype,
➥tempsubType);
   }
}
```

This function does three key things:

- The first line of the function uses the string split method to separate the mapData string, wherever a comma appears, into a temporary array of sub-strings called temparray.

- The second line sets up a variable called mapSize to store the map size which is calculated by the number of elements in the temporary array divided by four. We divide by four as that is the number of elements in the gameObject.

- Then the for loop creates the array of game objects, which is our level map data structure. With each iteration of the loop a new object is created and assigned to the current array element. The object is instantiated with the values of the previous four elements of the temporary array.

The map movie clip makes use of the data clipEvent with the code:

```
onClipEvent (data) {
    mapToDataStructure();
    unloadLevel(_root.mainGame.gameWorld);
    displayNewLevel(_root.mainGame.gameWorld);
}
```

This means that when the map movie clip detects that a new set of data has loaded into the clip it will call the mapToDataStructure function which converts the loaded data into the map data structure and the displayNewLevel function displays the new level and resets the player.

## Displaying Levels

Let's have a look at the code for displaying new levels:

```
function displayNewLevel (levelMC) {
  for (i=0; i<=mapArray.length; i++){
    if (mapArray[i].type == "player"){
      levelMC._parent.player.initalize(mapArray[i]);
    } else if (mapArray[i].type == "platform"){

      levelMC.platforms[mapArray[i].subType].
➡duplicateMovieClip(mapArray[i].type+depthCount, depthCount);
      levelMC.platforms[mapArray[i].type+depthCount].
➡initalize(mapArray[i]);

    } else {

      levelMC[mapArray[i].type].duplicateMovieClip(mapArray[i].
➡type+depthCount, depthCount);
      levelMC[mapArray[i].type+depthCount].
➡initalize(mapArray[i]);
    }
    depthCount++;
  }
}
```

This function is passed in a reference to the gameWorld movie clip. This function loops through all of the objects in the mapArray and duplicates the appropriate movie clip for each game object. The gameObject is then passed to the new movie clip's initialize function. The initialize function is a custom extension of the movie clip object that is especially useful in this case. This new function assigns local variables within the movie clip to the values contained in the gameObject. (The code for this extension is on the control layer of the main time-line along with the other object extensions.)

The code for duplicating the platform clip is slightly different, because the platforms are all grouped together in a parent platforms clip.

The displayNewLevel function works on the assumption that the movie clip passed in the function argument contains 'source' movie clips that can be duplicated and that these 'source' movie clips have instance names that match the types and subtypes defined in the map. This is of course how we set things up, so it all works nicely.

# Designing a Platform Game Construction Kit

The following function simply iterates through and removes all of the duplicated movie clips contained within the movie clip referenced in the function argument:

```
function unloadLevel(levelMC) {
        for(mc in levelMC){
                mc.removeMovieClip();
        }
}
```

You may wonder why it doesn't delete the source movie clips. This is because the `removeMovieClip` method will only remove movie clips that were created with the `duplicateMovieClip` method leaving any original clips, which is exactly what we want.

That's all the core code that's required to load and set up the level map. The level data is loaded from a text file, sorted into the level data structure and displayed in the gameWorld movie clip. Keeping all the code in a separate movie clip means that we can track the event when the data from the text file has loaded and also means that the 'map engine' is reasonably portable. We can copy the movie clip to another level based game and should only need to modify the elements of the custom object and the `displayNewLevel` function to suit the new game.

## Extending the Level Editor

You might wish to extend the editor by including a function to load in a previously designed text file or to include a test level feature, so the user can actually have a test play of their level design.

You could also put the editor online so visitors to your web site can design new levels for your platform game. To save the levels online you would need to change the generateMap function. After the `for` loop in the `generateMap` function add the following line:

`this.loadVariables( "write.asp", "POST" );`

This would send the variables to a web server script called `write.asp`. All you need to do is write a server script to write out the passed `mapData` variable to the web server as a text file.

You might also want to try adding other features to the editor, such as the ability to set the rotation or height and width of game elements. This could be achieved by adding a properties window, similar to the info and panels in the Flash development environment, which display the current selected movie clip's width, height and rotation. You could make it possible for the user to change these properties and thus open up a new range of possibilities for level design. Of course you would also need to modify the generateMap function to include these new properties in the mapData and modify the game engine's map data structure to work with these new properties.

# 7  Flash Games Studio

> *If you are working with the game level editor in the standalone player on a Windows based PC you can also save the level data directly to a text file from Flash. There is an undocumented FS command called save which will save the data from a movie clip in URL encoded format to a text file. The syntax is FSCommand("save","myLevel.txt"). However this only saves the variables from the main timeline, so to make it do something useful you will need to make the editor run within a container movie clip and then pass the mapData string back to the main timeline before calling the FSCommand. It's certainly not an elegant solution but may prove useful in some situations.*

## Adapting the Game Engine

Now we've taken a look at ways to improve the editor, let's take a look at ways to improve the actual game itself. As I said earlier, *Rescue Run* can quite easily be adapted to resemble most platform games, so now it's time to put my money where my mouth is.

### New Graphics, New Game Objects

At the simplest level you can replace any or all of the game graphics. Changing the background or platform graphics will quickly and easily give the game a very different feel.

Your new graphics can be any size or style you want but you should be aware that the collision detection between the player and the platforms won't work if the player's maxSpeed is greater than the thickness of the platforms. So if the player's maxSpeed is 20 and your platform is only 10 pixels thick then the player may fall through the platform. The player will be moving 20 pixels per frame, and the collision detection will never notice that he has collided with the platform:

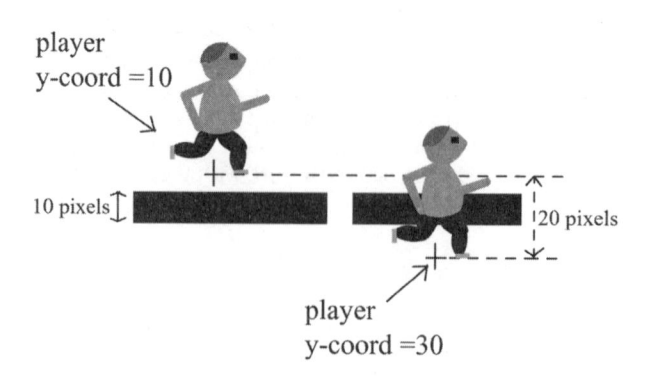

# Designing a Platform Game Construction Kit    7

You could also alter the existing graphics to change the facing of the player when he's running in the other direction. Be careful with this though, as the character may look a bit funny if you let him spin round while he's in the air, it may be better to only allow a direction change when the player's not jumping.

If you want to include additional graphics for new pick-ups, enemies or platforms all you need to do is include a movie clip for each new item within the appropriate parent clip. So if you want to include a new pick-up called goldCoin you would add the goldCoin movie clip within the `pickup` movie clip. You need to make sure you set the instance name for this new movie clip to goldCoin and include it within the definition for the `pickUp()` function. Clearly you will also need to adapt your map editor to include this new pick-up.

## Super Jumps, Springboards, and Dissolving Platforms

Another level of adaptation would be to change what the pick-ups or enemies do to the player. Everything that happens to the player is handled by functions defined within the player movie clip. So if you want something new to happen to the player all you need to do is write a new function for this new effect. For example, maybe you want the player to be able to jump twice as high after collecting a health pick-up. You could write a function defined within the player's load clipEvent like this:

```
function superJump() {
    jumpHeight*=2;
}
```

This simply multiplies the player's current `jumpHeight` by two which means the player will jump twice as high until the `jumpHeight` is reset when the player loses a life. To associate this with the health pick-up all you do is modify the pickup movie clip's pickUp() function to call the players `superJump()` function as well as increasing the player's health when the player hits a health pick-up.

This process can be used to introduce a majority of elements from platform games, it's just a case of identifying what function to write for the player and whether the new element is a pick-up or an enemy.

The trick to identifying whether something is a pick-up or an enemy is to look at how it behaves. Pick-ups happen once; the player collides with a pick-up, this calls one or more functions and then the pick-up is removed. However enemies remain on the screen until the player moves past them or they move past the player.

Think about a springboard that sends the player flying into the air. Does it disappear after the player collides with it? No! Therefore it must be an enemy. You might not think of it as an enemy as it doesn't harm the player, but for the purpose of our platform game it acts like an enemy. But what function would it call? Well its really just an involuntary jump so it would call the player's `jump` function and maybe call the `superJump` function mentioned before, to make the player fly twice as high.

How about a platform that dissolves when the player lands on it? In this case there isn't anything new happening to the player but instead something is happening to the platform. So you would need to define a new dissolve function for your new dissolving platform and call this function when the player hits the dissolving platform, using code similar to the `hitTest` check used for the pick-ups.

## A Fixed Player and a Scrolling World

What about if you want the player to be fixed in the center of the screen and the world to scroll left or right (like in many platform games)? Well it's really simple, within the code for the player's horizontal `hitTest` there is a test that checks if the player's x position is less than the `scrollStart` variable. If you remove this test the world will always scroll left or right. In this case the code will simplify to:

```
if (_parent.gameWorld.platforms.hitTest( newX, this._y, true )){
    speedHoriz=0;
} else {
    _parent.gameWorld.scrollLeft(speedHoriz);
    _parent.mainBackground.scrollLeft(speedHoriz/2);
}
```

The only other thing you need to do is to make sure the player is located in the center of the screen at the start of the game.

## Conclusion

This chapter should have given you a good deal of useful information on how to make individual game elements interact with one another, and take on the guise of intelligence. Remember, this is only the skeleton of a game, and the *Rescue Run* source file should form a good basis for building any number of different scrolling platform games. It has been structured to make adaptation and modification easy.

So what are you waiting for? Get your ActionScript hat on, and start having some fun!

# Designing a Platform Game Construction Kit

**Introduction**
chapter 1
chapter 2
chapter 3
chapter 4
chapter 5
chapter 6
Case Study 1
chapter 7
chapter 8
chapter 9
chapter 10
chapter 11
chapter 12
chapter 13
Case Study 2
chapter 14
chapter 15
Director Afterword

# Chapter 8
# Interactive Sound

# Flash Games Studio

Sound is one of the major non-visual cues we use in life, communication, and in games. Anyone who has tried to play one of the well known video games of the day without sound will quickly tell you that the gameplay just doesn't have the same feel to it and the graphics suddenly appear flat.

Although graphics are still the most processor intensive cues to the game-player, sound can reduce a surprising amount of the part of the story that would otherwise be told with bandwidth heavy graphics. For example, if we want to portray a strong heroic character and a weak cowardly one, much of this characterization can be carried across in the voices — even if the graphics to represent the two people were simple stick figures!

We tend to underestimate the power of sound even though certain games are remembered not for their graphics but for the jingles and event related sound effects they generate. Who doesn't recognize the dull heartbeat sound in space invaders or the death jingle of *Pac-Man*?

It's time to put the balance right...

## Why Games are Different

Sound in games is different from most traditional uses of sound in Flash. With Flash web design, our incidental sounds, such as button clicks or other incidental interface effects, will tend to be attached to either a button or a keyframe. We may have some ActionScript-based sound controls, but they will be relatively simple.

Sound in games is not the same. In real-time games, our sound won't usually respond to simple button or keyframe events, but rather to events that are generated by the game logic itself, such as *level completed, alien exploded* or *race won*. This means that our sound has to be much more flexible, and in many cases will be implemented at least partly using advanced ActionScript.

There are three things that we'll attempt to achieve in this chapter:

- Gain a good understanding of Flash 5's sound export options and how they do (or don't) affect game performance

- Gain a good understanding of Flash 5's basic ActionScript sound controls

- Have a look at the advanced ActionScript sound controls

To keep things practical, we'll look at adding different forms of sound to a game that we've already built in a previous chapter. We'll start with simple game event driven mono sound, and progress to building an advanced stereo image, where sound will appear to follow the position of the graphic that's making the noise. We'll also look at building user volume controls.

# Interactive Sound

## Sound File Import Options

Importing a sound file into Flash is very straightforward. Simply select File > Import, making sure that you have the Files of Type requester in the Import window set to either All Formats or All Sound Formats:

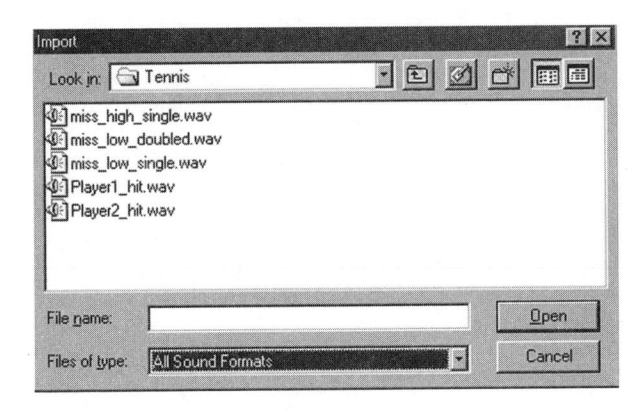

That's the easy part. The harder question for us games coders is *what effect does adding sound have to overall game performance?*

## The Implications of Adding Sound

We'll look at what all of these sound options do in the next chapter when we discuss music. For now though, I'm going to look a bit deeper into what they *really* do to your files. Before I started writing this section, I had a theory. MP3 uses a complex active digital filter in its decompression, and I figured that this might require a fair bit of processing power. The RAW sound format requires no processing (it's just sent straight to the soundcard) so it must require much less processing power. I *could* have just written some blurb like:

> "Use RAW or ADPCM in games if your sound files are small, because MP3 uses an active filter, and that will probably affect game performance, blah blah blah."

Unfortunately, my conscience doesn't allow me to tell you all to create games with bloated RAW sound files unless I can justify it, so I did some tests to see just how much having sound in your SWF affects the responsiveness of the rest of the presentation. I used a reasonably specified machine (Pentium 3,600 MHz). This is what I found:

- Choice of sound compression routine has no real effect on the rest of the SWF *unless* the SWF is already heavily loaded. There was no discernable difference in the frame duration per frame for any of the Export Settings (brought up by double-clicking on a sound in the Library).

- Choice of Bit Rate, Sample Rate, or number of bits seems to have very little effect on performance, something that I found quite surprising.

- The Fast/Medium/Best Quality setting for MP3 refers to the export compression routine from the Flash-authoring environment. It has *no effect whatsoever on run time performance*. It's there for designers exporting large sound files (which can take some time to export). In these cases, you would use the Best setting only for creating the final SWF, and use Fast for development versions. It beats me what Medium is there for.

- Another surprise is that the number of different sounds playing seems to have little effect, again unless the SWF is already heavily loaded.

- If you do start to overload the plug-in with sound, it only seems to affect the sound portion of the plug-in. The frame rate seems to play at the required speed regardless.

- The biggest hit seems to be if an already moderately loaded plug-in is streaming at the same time as playing content that has already loaded. Streaming sounds are thus something you want to be careful of using whilst a game is running through performance critical sections.

This overall favorable performance drops down significantly if your machine is closer to the minimum specifications recommended by Macromedia. If your machine is likely to start struggling, this will begin to happen as you give it more to do. Sound must be used wisely in these cases. Having said that I wouldn't expect a user with a Pentium 133 and 16 Mb of RAM to see many Flash sites playing quickly, let alone Flash games.

> *I tend to assume a minimum specification of around a two-year-old computer when designing Flash games. A computer of this pedigree can easily handle sound.*

In addition, having a high frame rate can cause small glitches in your animation, as the plug-in is momentarily overworked at times. Keeping your frame rate between 12-18 fps can significantly reduce this occurrence.

Flash 5 allows us to have up to eight sounds playing at the same time (irrespective of whether they are mono or stereo). It doesn't let us access these sound channels directly, but instead assigns them dynamically itself. If we exceed this limit we won't see errors occurring – Flash will simply drop sounds beyond the eight channel limit.

For a heavily loaded plug-in, the additional overhead caused by a large amount of sound (running all eight available sound channels simultaneously throughout the game) is approximately a 10% increase, and this doesn't seem desperately excessive.

In essence, if our game works well without sound, we'll see little difference in performance once we add it, irrespective of our sound files and how we're exporting them. The state of our FLA *before* we start adding sound is more important to overall performance.

# Interactive Sound   8

## Basic Sound Scripting Actions

Sound is an object and, as such, can take different methods. The basic methods that we can apply to our sound are:

```
new Sound()
sound.start()
sound.stop()
sound.attachSound()
```

Although many of you will already feel comfortable with your knowledge of the sound object, and be ready to skip a few pages, hold on. There is a rather subtle issue regarding **targeting sounds** that can be easy to miss. We need to know about this issue if we want to create dynamic multi-channel sound.

Before we can do anything with the sound object, we have to create it with either of two methods: **linkage** and **targeting**. For now, we'll look at the easiest method, linkage. Targeting will be covered later in the chapter.

### Linkage

Linkage is just the process of linking a sound file in the Library to an ActionScript sound object. Here's how it works:

1. First, import your sound file with File > Import.

2. You will see your sound file appear in the Library. By either selecting Options > Linkage… from the Library window drop-down menu, or right clicking on the sound file and selecting Linkage… from the pop-up menu, you should see the Symbol Linkage Properties window appear:

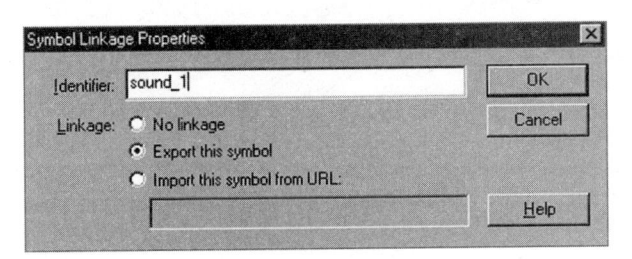

# Flash Games Studio

3. Enter a name for your sound file. This name should be unique from any other sound linkage identifiers you may already have defined in your FLA so far (but Flash won't tell you if it isn't, so be careful!). This identifier is the name that your ActionScript will use to refer to the sound file.

4. You then need to write a sound object definition in your code that creates a new sound object and links itself to the sound file like so:

```
mySound1 = new Sound();
mySound1.attachSound("sound_1");
```

Notice that the linkage identifier is written as a literal string (it's within "" marks). This allows Flash to differentiate between a simple linkage and our next sound creation method.

## Simple Sound Objects

So far we've set up our sound object, but haven't yet heard it. To stop and start a sound we use the `start` and `stop` sound object methods. The use of these two actions may at first look as if it should be very straightforward. In fact it isn't, because Flash has a very precise (and not very well documented) way of accessing individual sounds. If you use just `start` and `stop` on their own you may find that you end up stopping all the sound in your game when you merely wanted to stop a single sound.

## Controlling Linkage Sounds

Linkage sounds are easy to start, but can be difficult to stop individually. The following script defines and starts two sounds (don't forget to define your linkage identifiers):

```
mySound1 = new Sound();
mySound1.attachSound("sound_1");
mySound2 = new Sound();
mySound2.attachSound("sound_2");
mySound1.start();
mySound2.start();
```

This will only play each sound once, we'll look at looping sounds in just a second, first let's see how to stop them.

## Stopping Individual Sounds

So how do we stop our sounds? Well, adding a simple `stop` at the end of our script should stop each sound in turn, but if you try adding this action to the end of the script you won't get the desired effect:

```
mySound1.stop();
```

# Interactive Sound

After a slight delay, this stops *both* sounds! To stop a sound object created via linkage, you have to state the linkage name as well as the sound object, like this:

```
mySound1.stop("sound_1");
```

This subtle twist has fooled many people trying to understand Flash 5 ActionScript-driven sound. The `mySound1.stop` action doesn't stop the sound attached to `mySound1`, it stops *all sound in the SWF!* The `mySound1.stop("sound_1")` form is the only one that will work with multi-channel sound, so it's an important (if rather odd) syntax to remember when designing sound for games.

## Offsets and Looping

To create repeating sounds, we can add arguments to the `start` method as follows:

```
start(offset, loops);
```

Here, `offset` is how far into the sound we want it to start playing (in seconds) and `loops` is the number of times we want to repeat the sound. Each loop will start from the `offset` position.

For games, one of the main reasons we would need to use the offset value would be if we had sampled our game sounds – legally of course! – and needed to get rid of a small amount of space leading into the sample. The best way to find out what our offset will be is to use the legacy Flash 4 Edit Envelope window. To do this, temporarily attach the sound in question to a keyframe, then from the Sound panel press the Edit... button to bring up this window:

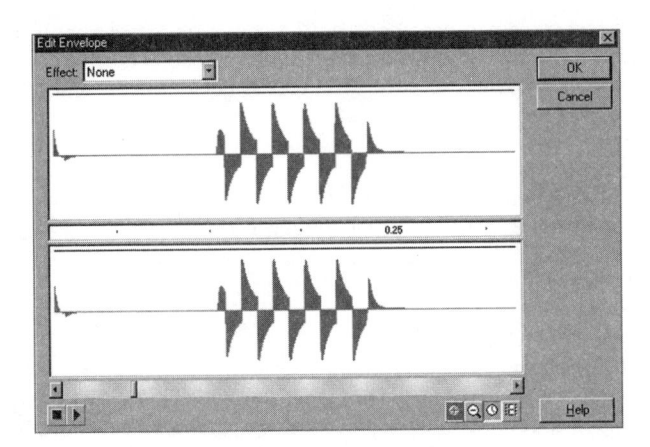

The sample here has been recorded from an arcade cabinet. As you can see there's not only a slight 'blip' at the beginning of this sample, there is also a large amount of clear space before the proper sound starts. Although I could get rid of this leading space using professional editing software (such as Sonic Foundry's SoundForge), I don't want to go to the trouble for such a short sound. By zooming into the sound waveform via the bottom right magnify icons, I can home into my sound start point and read what my offset should be from the scale, which handily enough, is also given in seconds.

> *If we ever need to know how long a sound lasts in terms of frames, we can also change the scale to show frames by clicking the far right icon in the Edit envelope window.*

The number of loops can have a maximum value of 214748, although 999 is usually enough if we want a sound that effectively loops forever. Remember though, that any offset value we've applied will be subtracted from the loop time, so we may have to increase the number of loops accordingly.

As a quick example, here's our original script, modified so that it continually cycles our sounds rather than just playing them once:

```
mySound1 = new Sound();
mySound1.attachSound("sound_1");
mySound2 = new Sound();
mySound2.attachSound("sound_2");
mySound1.start(0, 999);
mySound2.start(0, 999);
```

The example above uses no offset and loops 999 times.

### Using the Root Timeline

Another important fact to remember about Flash 5 sound objects is that if the timeline they're defined on disappears, we can no longer access the sound objects, and no sound will play. For example, if we added a movie clip with instance name myMusic, with the following script attached to it:

```
onClipEvent (load){
    mySound1 = new Sound();
    mySound1.attachSound("sound_1");
    mySound2 = new Sound();
    mySound2.attachSound("sound_2");
}
```

this would create two new sound objects, namely myMusic.mySound1 and myMusic.mySound2. If we now move to another frame in our timeline that doesn't have the myMusic instance on it, no sound will occur whatever command we use because the sound objects have been lost along with the myMusic timeline.

Unless you have a good reason to create your sound objects within a movie clip timeline (and there are a couple of good reasons to do this as we shall see later), and particularly if you are new to ActionScript based sound control, you are advised to always define your objects in the _root: The only timeline that you won't lose by accident.

# Interactive Sound 8

## Applying Sound to a Game

Okay, lets go through how we'd hook up sound to a simple game. The game I have chosen to look at is the **Tennis** one that we created in the *Structured Real-Time Programming* chapter, because the game itself is pretty simple. This is also a good candidate for the addition of sound because we can start simple, with mono beeps, gradually adding more complexity until we end up with a true stereo sound that appears to follow our graphics across the screen.

Have a look at `tennisMute.fla`. This is the basic tennis game without any sound.

## When to Add Sound

Ideally, before you start adding sound to a game you should have reached the same sort of position as `tennisMute.fla`. That is you've built a basic game and are happy with its performance and logic.

Whatever you do, don't add sound before this stage. Cool sound can easily hide a bad game design to the creator – and a game with cool sound and great graphics but poor gameplay underlying it all is known as 'eye candy'.

There are also a few good technical reasons for adding sound this late:

- One of the things that you play around with when designing the initial game engine is the frame rate. Adding sound before you start changing frame rate can mess up the sound because the game will now run quicker, possibly necessitating changes to sound sample durations.

- You need to be certain that you have a game engine that's running at an acceptable speed before you start adding sound. Although many game designers blame sound for slowing down their games, it's more often than not due to inefficient coding. You should resolve all your bottlenecks before adding sound, because although sound does slow your game down slightly, you need to get a feel for how much it's doing so. By completing the fundamental game before adding any sound you can get a much better view on when the sound-performance balance has been reached.

- By waiting until this stage to add the sound, you can get a much clearer picture of exactly where sound is needed.

I've seen a few games on the Web where the game designer has spent weeks trying to get it running at an acceptable frame rate and is about to give up, citing the Flash plug-in as 'being no good for games, so it's time to go learn Java'. After having a quick look at these games, it soon becomes apparent that the coder hasn't designed in performance at all, they've just got a few sprites running about on the screen to start off with, then added some sound and numerous other bells and whistles, and went on in that fashion until they broke the poor plug-in's performance! You have been warned...

## The Sound-building Process

Okay. Now we have our basic game, we need to do three things:

- Decide what game events should trigger sound
- Build or acquire those sounds
- Import the sounds, and cause them to trigger on the game events

> *Notice that I haven't gone down the most common route of getting lots of sounds and then just adding them where I please in the game. We have to chose the places in our game that we want sound with care, because if we don't, we'll end up with a 300k game download – fun with a very small 'f' for the discerning web games player!*

In the case of Tennis we're lucky, as we already know more or less where the sounds go because it's a simulation of an existing game. Weed:

- A blip when the ball hits either bat
- A blip when the ball hits the top or bottom wall
- A blip to signify the human player has missed the ball
- A blip to signify the computer has missed the ball
- A series of blips to signify 'game over'

There is a tendency amongst Flash games designers to say things like 'Ah, the game is still running well, how about I add some crowd noises and some sampled umpires and stuff'. This again is the route to 'bloatware'. Sound may not affect performance as much as we might have first thought, but it does affect download time significantly. Gameplay and addictiveness on the other hand add no additional download time. Need we say more?

# Interactive Sound 8

## Our Sample File

Have a look at `tennisMute2.fla`. This is the same as the previous version, except that I have imported our tennis blips into the Library (they're in a folder called sounds). Each sound has also been given a Linkage name that's the same as its Library name (a good structure to follow because it avoids confusion):

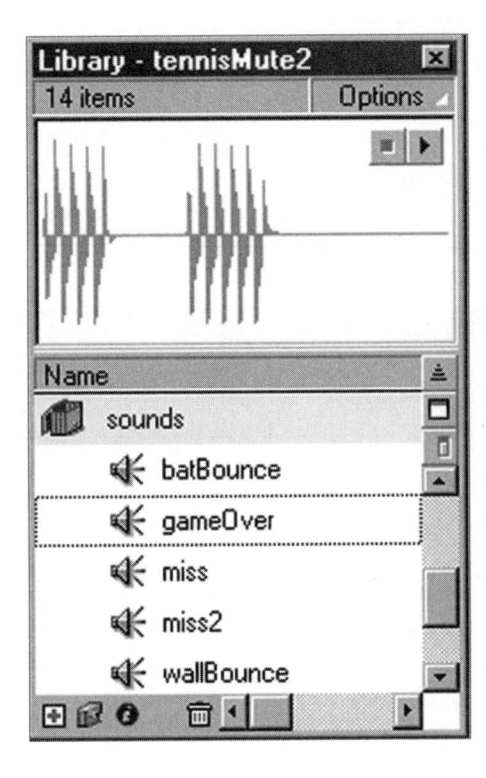

### A Quick Reminder of Our Game

So far, the main timeline of `tennisMute2.fla` looks like this:

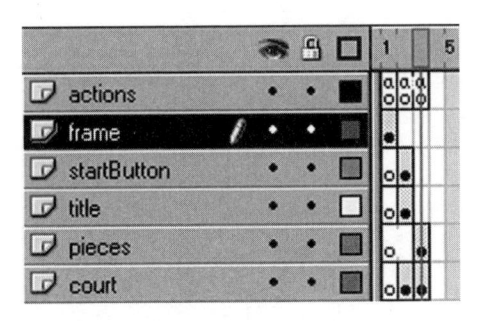

## 8    Flash Games Studio

Frame 1 is our SWF initialization, frame 2 is our game initialization, and frame 3 is our game proper.

During runtime, the timeline starts by initializing via frame 1. It then goes to frame 2, which displays a simple splash screen, and then, after the player presses an invisible button on frame 2, they're taken to frame 3 where the game starts. When the game is completed, the timeline returns them to frame 2 ready for another game.

### Attaching our Blips

Okay, let's have a go at getting these simple sounds into our tennis game.

1. To initialize our sound objects, we have to simply tack our sound object definitions onto the end of the games existing initialization script. This is on frame 1 of the actions layer. The existing script looks like this:

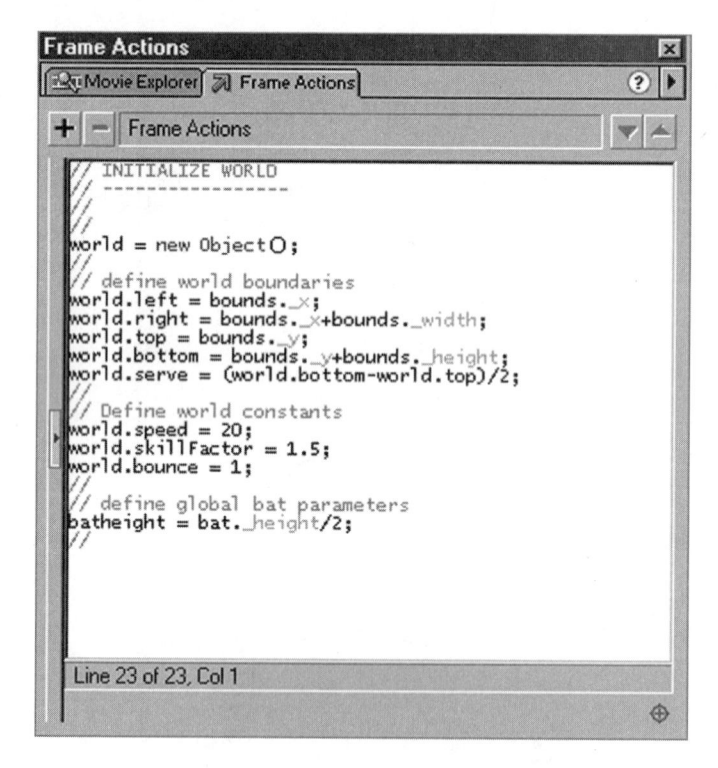

```
// INITIALIZE WORLD
// -----------------

world = new Object();

// define world boundaries
world.left = bounds._x;
world.right = bounds._x+bounds._width;
world.top = bounds._y;
world.bottom = bounds._y+bounds._height;
world.serve = (world.bottom-world.top)/2;

// Define world constants
world.speed = 20;
world.skillFactor = 1.5;
world.bounce = 1;

// define global bat parameters
batheight = bat._height/2;
```

# Interactive Sound

2. All we need to do is add our sound object definitions to the end of this script. They look like this:

   ```
   // Define Sounds
   batBounce = new Sound();
   batBounce.attachSound("batBounce");
   WallBounce = new Sound();
   wallBounce.attachSound("wallBounce");
   miss = new Sound();
   miss.attachSound("miss");
   miss2 = new Sound()
   miss2.attachSound("miss2")
   gameOver = new Sound();
   gameOver.attachSound("gameOver");
   ```

3. Next, we need to identify the places in our code where our sound needs to be triggered. There's actually only one thing that makes noise in the tennis game (jokes about racquets aside), and that's the ball.

   The ball's script can be seen on frame 3 and it is, of course, attached to the ball (pointed out by the arrow):

4. With the ball selected, bring up the Actions window to see the script. We need to identify all the events in this script that should cause sound effects. We're only interested in the `enterFrame` script, since the `load` script just deals with initialization and therefore won't be concerned with generating sounds. The script you see on the next page has been marked with all the events that should generate sound.

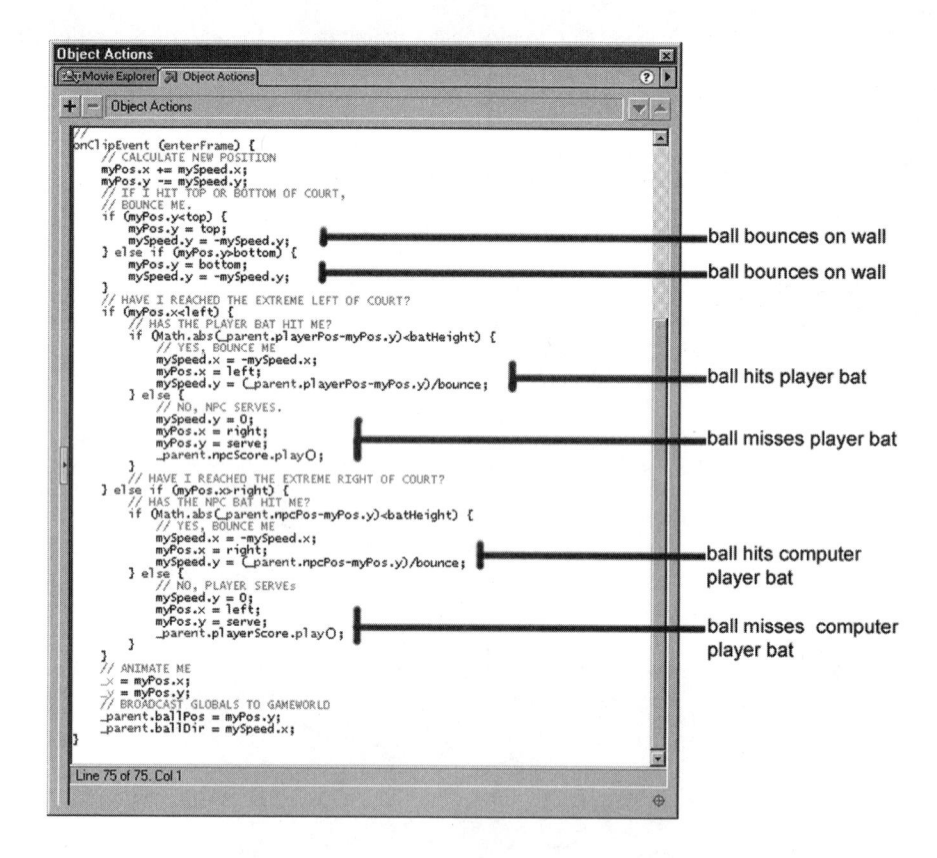

# Flash Games Studio

```
onClipEvent (enterFrame) {
    // CALCULATE NEW POSITION
    myPos.x += mySpeed.x;
    myPos.y -= mySpeed.y;
    // IF I HIT TOP OR BOTTOM OF COURT,
    // BOUNCE ME.
    if (myPos.y<top) {
        myPos.y = top;                                    // ball bounces on wall
        mySpeed.y = -mySpeed.y;
    } else if (myPos.y>bottom) {
        myPos.y = bottom;                                 // ball bounces on wall
        mySpeed.y = -mySpeed.y;
    }
    // HAVE I REACHED THE EXTREME LEFT OF COURT?
    if (myPos.x<left) {
        // HAS THE PLAYER BAT HIT ME?
        if (Math.abs(_parent.playerPos-myPos.y)<batHeight) {
            // YES, BOUNCE ME
            mySpeed.x = -mySpeed.x;
            myPos.x = left;
            mySpeed.y = (_parent.playerPos-myPos.y)/bounce;   // ball hits player bat
        } else {
            // NO, NPC SERVES.
            mySpeed.y = 0;
            myPos.x = right;
            myPos.y = serve;                              // ball misses player bat
            _parent.npcScore.play();
        }
    // HAVE I REACHED THE EXTREME RIGHT OF COURT?
    } else if (myPos.x>right) {
        // HAS THE NPC BAT HIT ME?
        if (Math.abs(_parent.npcPos-myPos.y)<batHeight) {
            // YES, BOUNCE ME
            mySpeed.x = -mySpeed.x;
            myPos.x = right;
            mySpeed.y = (_parent.npcPos-myPos.y)/bounce;  // ball hits computer
        } else {                                          //       player bat
            // NO, PLAYER SERVEs
            mySpeed.y = 0;
            myPos.x = left;
            myPos.y = serve;                              // ball misses computer
            _parent.playerScore.play();                   //      player bat
        }
    }
    // ANIMATE ME
    _x = myPos.x;
    _y = myPos.y;
    // BROADCAST GLOBALS TO GAMEWORLD
    _parent.ballPos = myPos.y;
    _parent.ballDir = mySpeed.x;
}
```

The script consists of a lot of if... statements, each looking for a particular ball position corresponding to a collision or miss event and these will determine the sounds that we use.

**5.** The first 'ball bounces off wall' events are detecting a ball bounce off the top or bottom of the court:

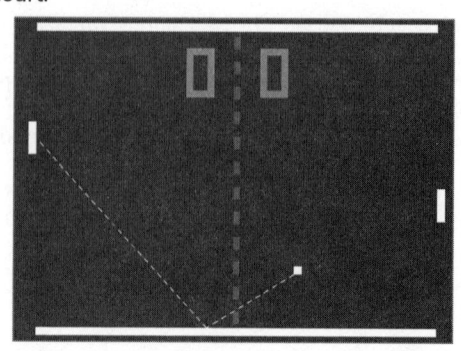

# Interactive Sound  8

For this game event, we want to use the wallBounce sound:

```
_root.wallBounce.start(0,1);
```

**6.** The next game event is the ball hitting the player's bat and bouncing off it:

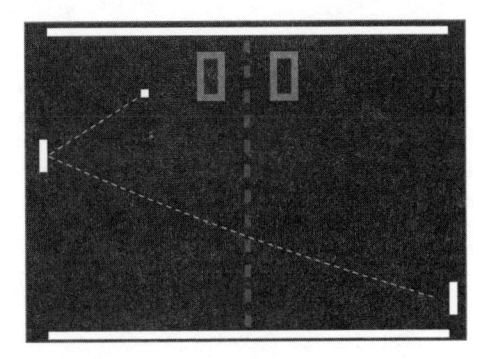

Here, we want to play the batBounce sound:

```
_root.batBounce.start(0,1);
```

**7.** If the player misses the ball rather than hitting it, we see the next game event. The sound we want to hear when this occurs is the miss2 sound:

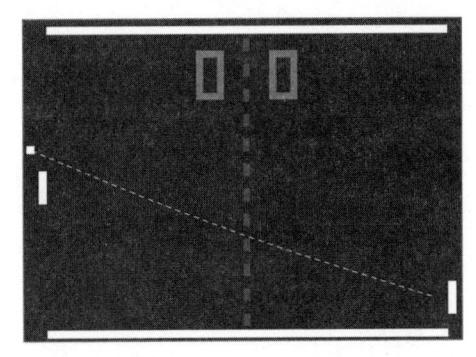

```
_root.miss2.start(0,1);
```

**8.** The final two events are identical to the last two we've looked at, but concern the computer-controlled bat. When the computer bat hits the ball, we want to hear the same sound as before (batBounce) but if the computer controlled bat misses we want to hear a different miss sound (miss instead of miss2).

# 8 Flash Games Studio

> *Finding the events in a game engine's code that should generate sound is always considerably easier if you wrote the code! Don't worry too much if you wouldn't have found the events in the tennis game straight away, it's much easier if you try it in FLAs that you know personally!*

9. All we have to do now is add the sound `start` actions at the appropriate events. The following listing shows the ball `enterFrame` script with all the correct sound actions inserted as text:

```
onClipEvent (enterFrame) {
      // CALCULATE NEW POSITION
      myPos.x += mySpeed.x;
      myPos.y -= mySpeed.y;
      // IF I HIT TOP OR BOTTOM OF COURT,
      // BOUNCE ME.
      if (myPos.y<top) {
            myPos.y = top;
            mySpeed.y = -mySpeed.y;
            _root.wallBounce.start(0,1);
      } else if (myPos.y>bottom) {
            myPos.y = bottom;
            mySpeed.y = -mySpeed.y;
            _root.wallBounce.start(0,1);
      }
      // HAVE I REACHED THE EXTREME LEFT OF COURT?
      if (myPos.x<left) {
            // HAS THE PLAYER BAT HIT ME?
            if (Math.abs(_parent.playerPos-myPos.y)<batHeight) {
                  // YES, BOUNCE ME
                  mySpeed.x = -mySpeed.x;
                  myPos.x = left;
                  mySpeed.y = (_parent.playerPos-myPos.y)/bounce;
                  _root.batBounce.start(0,1);
            } else {
                  // NO, NPC SERVES.
                  mySpeed.y = 0;
                  myPos.x = right;
                  myPos.y = serve;
                  _parent.npcScore.play();
                  _root.miss2.start(0,1);
            }
            // HAVE I REACHED THE EXTREME RIGHT OF COURT?
      } else if (myPos.x>right) {
            // HAS THE NPC BAT HIT ME?
```

# Interactive Sound

```
                if (Math.abs(_parent.npcPos-myPos.y)<batHeight) {
        // YES, BOUNCE ME
        mySpeed.x = -mySpeed.x;
        myPos.x = right;
        mySpeed.y = (_parent.npcPos-myPos.y)/bounce;
        _root.batBounce.start(0,1);
} else {
        // NO, PLAYER SERVEs
        mySpeed.y = 0;
        myPos.x = left;
        myPos.y = serve;
        _parent.playerScore.play()
        _root.miss.start(0,1)
}
}
        // ANIMATE ME
        _x = myPos.x;
        _y = myPos.y;
        // BROADCAST GLOBALS TO GAMEWORLD
        _parent.ballPos = myPos.y;
        _parent.ballDir = mySpeed.x;
}
```

There's also a final sound that occurs to signify game over, and this isn't related to the ball position, but instead to the score. As soon as one or other player has reached a score of 9, then the game is over. If you look at the mc.score movie clip, you'll see that it's simply a set of keyframes showing the numbers 0 to 9. As soon as this reaches 9 the game is over, so all we have to do is attach our 'game over' sound to the frame that shows a '9', which is in fact frame 10:

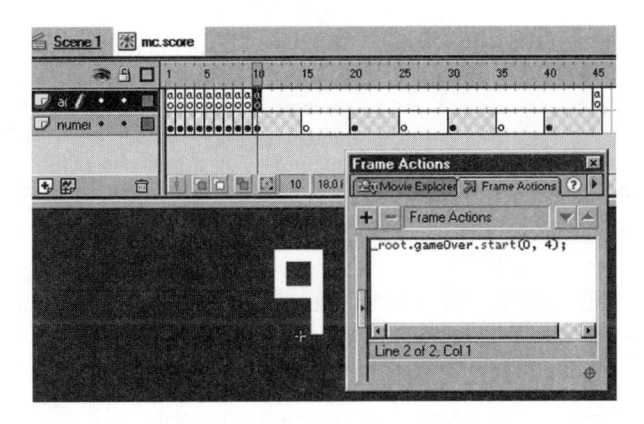

Our game now has its basic sound. As you can see we've followed our basic premise of simply identifying events in the game logic that require us to start a sound, and adding the appropriate sound actions to achieve this. There is a version of the tennis game with the basic event sound actions added, named `tennisFinal.fla` and this can be found in the *Structured Real-Time Programming* chapter. This file has an additional sound `start` command at the end of the initialization script (frame 1):

```
// Blip to signify start of game...
batBounce.start(0,1)
```

If you've read that chapter before this one will know that the reason for this is purely aesthetic – the early tennis TV consoles beeped once on power on, and this beep at frame 1 is purely for authenticity.

We could do with making use of the fact that most computers have a volume control, and since most computers are set up with two speakers, stereo is also possible.

Before we can look at the actions that allow us to add stereo and volume controls, we must learn about sound targeting.

## Sound Hierarchies - Targeting

As we mentioned earlier, as well as defining sounds via linkage, Flash also allows you to define a sound object via *targeting*. In this type of sound object, the controlled sound is not a simple sound file available from our Library, but rather a complete timeline. A typical targeted sound object definition looks like this:

```
mySound = new Sound();
mySound.attachSound(myTimeline);
```

Notice that this time the argument for the `attachSound` isn't in quotes. This fact tells Flash that, "this argument isn't a Linkage Identifier, it's a path to a target timeline". We can always use this rule to distinguish between linkages and target paths.

Targeted sounds aren't as simple as linkage sounds. For a start, we're not controlling a single sound, but potentially lots of different sounds that are attached to that timeline (which may include sound objects and sounds attached to frames in the old Flash 4 fashion as well as Flash 5 sound objects).

An important point to note (and one that's not well documented in the Macromedia help files) is that the `start` and `stop` methods *don't work with targeted sounds*. Although this may at first seem like an oversight or a bug, it does actually make total sense once you understand the issues:

- A timeline can issue sound `stop` or `start` commands of its own which may override our targeted sound object's `stop/start`.

- A timeline may have sounds directly attached to its keyframes. These would play as soon as they were encountered on the timeline, thus negating any previous sound `stop` actions.

# Interactive Sound 8

## Targeted Sound Methods

There are in fact only three sound methods that you should use with targeted sound:

- `setVolume (vol)`
- `setPan (pan)`
- `setTransform (transform)`

These are the 'advanced' Flash sound methods, and they allow us to vary sound volume and pan levels. Although they don't allow us to `start` and `stop` a sound, a sound with a volume of 0% can't be heard, but will still be playing when we raise the volume again, so we can control the presence of sound in this manner.

`setVolume`, `setPan`, and `setTransform` will work if applied to individual Linkage sound objects as well as targeted objects, and we'll look at this when we come to add stereo effects to our sounds.

To the games designer, the benefit of targeted sound objects is that they let us control the *global volume and pan of the whole game*. We do this by targeting `_root` within a sound object (called, say, `globalSound`). Then, no matter how many other sound objects there are in the game, all the ones attached to `_root` can be muted or given a variable volume simply by altering the controls for `globalSound`.

## setVolume

The `setVolume` control works just like a hi-fi volume control. Setting the volume hard left (`setVolume(0)`) gives zero signal (although the amplifier is still working, and in terms of the Flash player, has still been loaded by sound processing), and gradually moving the volume control clockwise results in increasing volume. When the volume is half way, you will hear 50% of the maximum volume (`setPan(50)`) and by the time you have turned the volume control as far as it will go, you will be hearing 100% of the maximum volume:

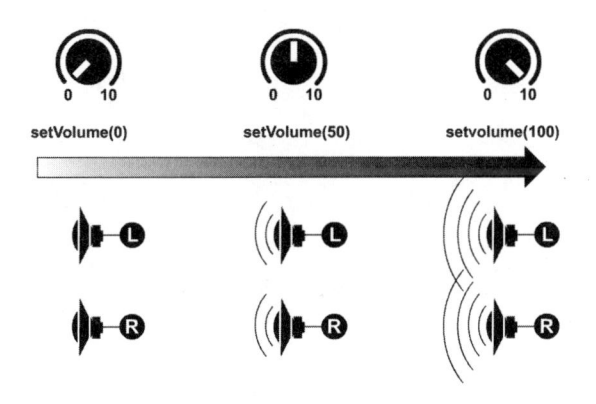

335

# Flash Games Studio

> *In fact the story doesn't end at 100% either, because* setVolume *will accept values in excess of this, and amplify the signal accordingly. This will probably result in some distortion as well if you start going much over 140%, but can be useful if you want to add some deep booming Williams style arcade cabinet shaking sounds - just make sure the user doesn't have headphones on. A negative volume gives a phase shifted (inverted) waveform that, unless you know something about sound interference, won't be something you normally want.*

## Adding global sounds to tennis

The process outlined above is actually far easier to set up than it sounds, so lets just go ahead and add a global sound control for our tennis game.

1. Either using your version of tennisMute2.fla with added sound commands, or the previously completed version tennisFinal.fla from the Structured Real-Time Programming chapter as a starting point, add the following lines at the end of the initialization script on frame 1:

   ```
   //Global volume controls
   globalSound = new Sound();
   globalSound.attachSound(_root);
   globalSound.setVolume(80);
   ```

   This creates a new sound object that targets _root, and then uses it to set the volume to 80%.

   We now need to add the controls to allow the user to set their own volume preference and for simplicity, we'll use the up-arrow and down-arrow to control the volume.

2. Create a new layer called soundControl.

# Interactive Sound

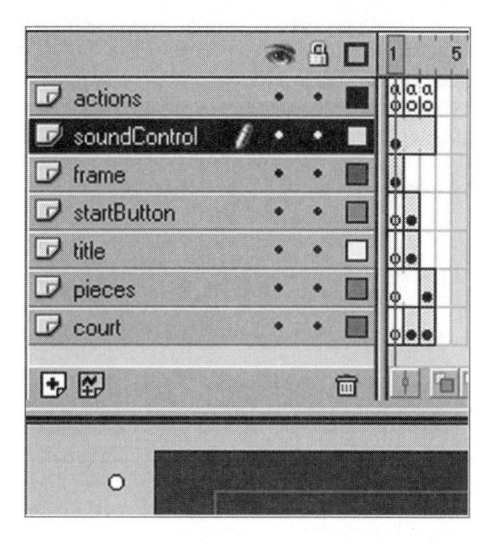

**3.** Create a new blank movie clip in the Library and call it mc.dummy, then drag an instance of it to the top left hand corner of the stage. This blank movie clip will be used to attach our sound control script to.

**4.** Now we need to compose a script for our newly dragged blank movie clip. Firstly, we need a load script to initialize our vol value to the current volume of the globalSound sound object, using the getVolume method:

```
onClipEvent (load) {
    vol =_root.globalSound.getVolume();
```

> *Some of you might have preferred to define* globalSound *in the* onClipEvent load *script. I like to keep all my sound definitions in one place (frame 1 of* _root*) so that I know where they are, but feel free to alter the script to do this if it makes more sense to you.*

# Flash Games Studio

5. Finally we need a `keyDown` event script. This event will run on every frame in which a key is detected in the down position. If a key down is detected we need to use the key object to clarify whether it's the up-arrow key or the down-arrow key that's being pressed. Then it's just a case of incrementing or decrementing our `vol` variable, and applying the new volume setting with the final `setVolume` action:

   ```
   onClipEvent (keyDown) {
       if (Key.isDown(Key.UP)) {
             if (vol<100) {
             if (vol<100) {
                   vol += 5;
             }
       }
       if (Key.isDown(Key.DOWN)) {
             if (vol>0) {
                   vol -= 5;
             }
       }
       _root.globalSound.setVolume(vol);
       //trace (vol);
   }
   ```

6. Our new movie clip should now contain the following code:

   ```
   onClipEvent (load) {
       vol =_root.globalSound.getVolume();
   }
   onClipEvent (keyDown) {
       if (Key.isDown(Key.UP)) {
             if (vol<100) {
                   vol += 5;
             }
       }
       if (Key.isDown(Key.DOWN)) {
             if (vol>0) {
                   vol -= 5;
             }
       }
       _root.globalSound.setVolume(vol);
       //trace (vol);
   }
   ```

7. If you want to see how the volume is varying numerically, simply un-comment the *trace* action and test the FLA.

   The tennis game with variable sound control is included as `tennisSound01.fla`.

# Interactive Sound  8

## Our Software Model

You'll hear the game's sound volume vary as you alter the `vol` value via the arrow keys. Although this feels like an intuitive sound control, the actual software model of what we've set up is worth a second glance:

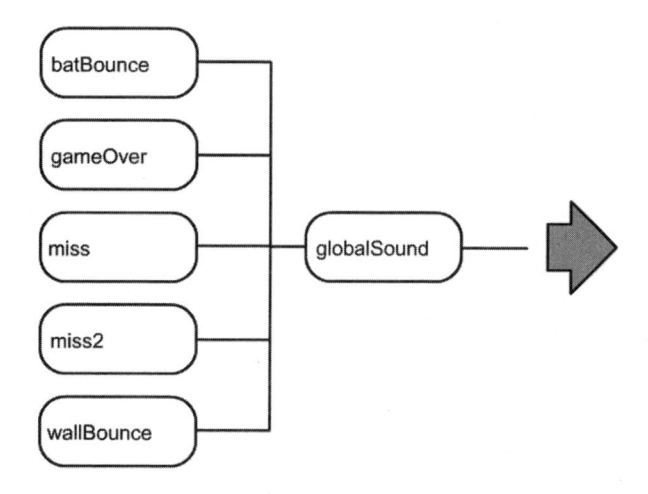

```
batBounce  ─┐
gameOver   ─┤
miss       ─┼── globalSound ──▶
miss2      ─┤
wallBounce ─┘
```

We have a whole bunch of sound objects sitting on `_root`, all doing their own thing. Each has its own separate volume control, which in our FLA is set to 100% for all of them because we've left their volume controls at their defaults. However, we could change any of these with the appropriate `setVolume` action.

Before these sound object outputs are sent to your computer sound hardware, they pass through a second sound object `globalSound`. This sound object has its sound volume altered by the user, and any sound object that passes through `globalSound` inherits this volume setting. The previous diagram shows this graphically. Those of you who know anything about electronic sound and filter circuits may see that the Flash sound objects are acting in exactly the same way as electronic audio circuits:

- The sound signal goes through one or more circuits (or sound objects) on its way to the speaker

- Any processing that any circuit (sound object) applies to the sound is **additive** – it's added on to whatever volume the sound already has at that point

## Flash Games Studio

### Combining Linkage Sounds and Targeted Sounds

Essentially, we've created a hierarchy of sound controls, where each sound object to the left is triggered on a game event. This is our lowest sound creation level for creating basic sounds. The next level is our mixing stage, the `globalSound` object, which allows the user to vary the final output in some way. This corresponds closely to real sound processing in professional music equipment, and seeing the relationship between linkage sounds and targeted sounds allows us to see how to use both together in games:

- Linkage sounds are the basic sound input. They allow us to generate sounds in response to game events such as 'shot fired' or 'ball bounced'.

- Targeted sounds are used to mix the sound inputs to the users preference.

```
( sound input ) ─── ( mixer/amplifier ) ───▶
```

Our simple sound control mixer stage has only one input, but by carefully creating our sound objects in groups in timelines above the root, we can separately mix different types of game sounds:

# Interactive Sound 8

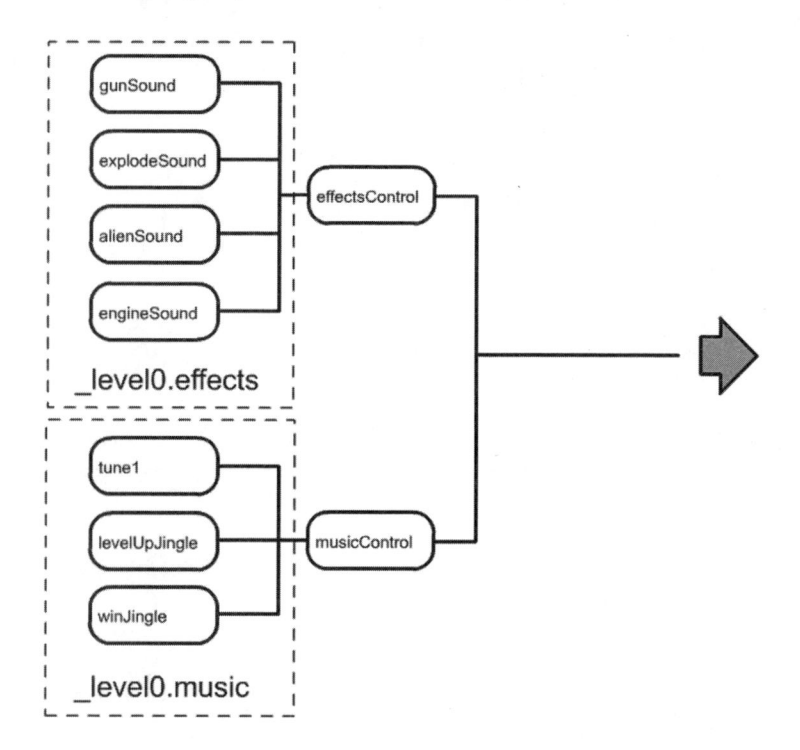

Most modern video games allow us to set the sound levels for sound effects, music and dialogue via separate controls, thus allowing us to set the overall sound levels to our own personal preference. If we want to hear the game dialogue, we may want to set it highest, but if we're more into over-the-top gratuitous violence, we might want to set the explosion effects to the max.

Using a targeting hierarchy such as the one shown above, we can create this level of sound mixing sophistication with relative ease. Here, the sound effects are all created on a timeline called effects, and this is controlled by its own targeted sound object: `effectsControl`. The same sort of setup exists for the music component below it on the music timeline and its targeted sound object: musicControl.

We've progressed from a basic game with simple sounds being generated by the game events, and fed these sounds into a user sound mixer. We're still missing the final vital component of sound though – a truly interactive *stereo* sound image.

## Adding Stereo Effects with setPan

The action to set the pan level of a sound is, unsurprisingly, setPan. This takes an argument between -100 and +100. A value of -100 gives sound from the left speaker channel only, and a value of 100 gives the right speaker channel only. The setPan action is very much like the balance control you use on a hi-fi:

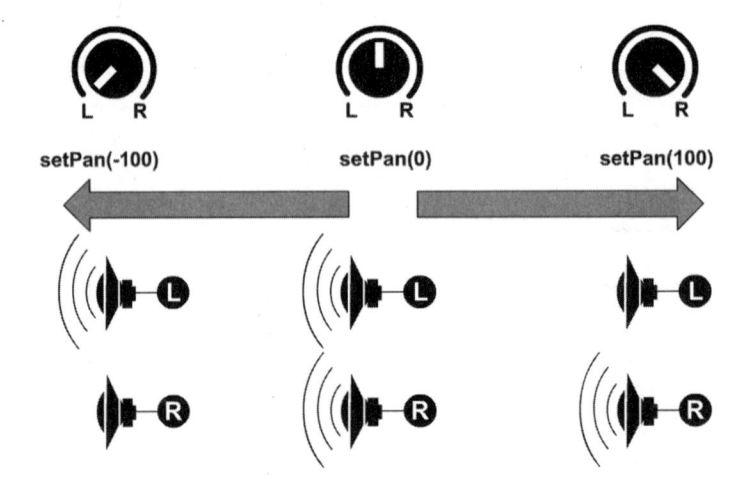

Moving the balance control from the hard left position (setPan(-100)) through to the hard right position (setPan(100)) will produce a sound that gradually moves from the left channel through to the right channel. When the balance dial is pointing straight up (setPan(0)) the sound is heard equally through both speakers.

The problem with this sort of pan control (which incidentally, also applies to hi-fis with the same balance control) is that as you move the stereo image away from the center position, you also lose signal power. At the center position you hear 2 speakers' worth of volume, whereas at the hard left and right positions you only get 1 speaker's worth, a 50% reduction.

This type of simple balance control isn't used in professional mixing equipment, where you need to be able to vary pan without losing signal power or prominence within the overall mix. There is a Flash action that can emulate this type of professional control: setTransform, but this is usually only used in true audio applications such as Flash sound mixers.

# Interactive Sound

## Producing Stereo Sound in our Tennis Game

Rather than a balance control, we have a tennis court, but the principle is the same: the position of the ball along the court can be converted to a balance control position via the `setPan` command:

1. Any sounds that occur because of events in the far left of the court (such as "ball hits the bat on the left of court") have their balance dials turned hard left via a `setPan(0)`, and any sounds that occur due to events occurring in far right of the court get a `setPan(100)`.

2. The ball can bounce anywhere along the bottom or top of the court, but since we know the length of the court and the position of the ball when it bounces, we can easily convert the position of the ball when it collides to a pan value with:

   ```
   soundRatio = ((width of stage)/100)
   pan value = ball position/ratio
   ```

3. The following additions to the ball script will give us the dynamic stereo sound image that we need. The ball bounce sounds on the two bats will always appear on the far left and right of the court, so we know that their pan values will be -100 and 100 respectively.

4. The ball pan value will be dynamic because its position changes as it moves across the court. We know from creating the game in the *Structured Real-Time Programming* chapter that the ball position is stored in `myPos.x`, and the court width is from `_root.world.right` to `_root.world.left`, so converting the equations above we have:

   ```
   soundRatio = (_root.world.right-_root.world.left)/100;
   ```

5. To set a pan value for the ball sound we use a `setPan` that uses (`myPos.x/soundRatio`) as its argument, followed by a sound `start` to actually make the sound:

   ```
   _root.wallBounce.setPan(myPos.x/soundRatio);
   _root.wallBounce.start(0, 1);
   ```

# 8  Flash Games Studio

The final ball script is given here, and included in tennisSound02.fla, and the additions to give us stereo sound have been highlighted:

```
onClipEvent (load) {
    // COPY WORLD CONFIGURATION
    left = _parent.world.left;
    right = _parent.world.right;
    top = _parent.world.top;
    bottom = _parent.world.bottom;
    serve = _parent.world.serve;
    speed = _parent.world.speed;
    bounce = _parent.world.bounce;
    batHitWidth = _parent.batWidth+_width;
    batheight = _parent.batHeight;
    // SET MY INITIAL POSITION
    _x = left;
    _y = serve;
    // DEFINE LOCAL DATA
    myPos = new Object();
    myPos.x = left;
    myPos.y = serve;
    mySpeed = new Object();
    mySpeed.x = speed;
    mySpeed.y = 0;
    soundRatio = (right-left)/100;
}
//
onClipEvent (enterFrame) {
    // CALCULATE NEW POSITION
    myPos.x += mySpeed.x;
    myPos.y -= mySpeed.y;
    // IF I HIT TOP OR BOTTOM OF COURT,
    // BOUNCE ME.
    if (myPos.y<top) {
        myPos.y = top;
        mySpeed.y = -mySpeed.y;
        _root.wallBounce.setPan(myPos.x/soundRatio);
        _root.wallBounce.start(0, 1);
    } else if (myPos.y>bottom) {
        myPos.y = bottom;
        mySpeed.y = -mySpeed.y;
        _root.wallBounce.setPan(myPos.x/soundRatio);
        _root.wallBounce.start(0, 1);
    }
    // HAVE I REACHED THE EXTREME LEFT OF COURT?
    if (myPos.x<left) {
        // HAS THE PLAYER BAT HIT ME?
        if (Math.abs(_parent.playerPos-myPos.y)<batHeight) {
            // YES, BOUNCE ME
```

# Interactive Sound   8

```
                        mySpeed.x = -mySpeed.x;
                        myPos.x = left;
                        mySpeed.y = (_parent.playerPos-myPos.y)/bounce;
                        _root.batBounce.setPan(-100);
                        _root.batBounce.start(0, 1);
                    } else {
                        // NO, NPC SERVES.
                        mySpeed.y = 0;
                        myPos.x = right;
                        myPos.y = serve;
                        _parent.npcScore.play();
                        _root.miss2.setPan(-100);
                        _root.miss2.start(0, 1);
                    }
                    // HAVE I REACHED THE EXTREME RIGHT OF COURT?
                } else if (myPos.x>right) {
                    // HAS THE NPC BAT HIT ME?
                    if (Math.abs(_parent.npcPos-myPos.y)<batHeight) {
                        // YES, BOUNCE ME
                        mySpeed.x = -mySpeed.x;
                        myPos.x = right;
                        mySpeed.y = (_parent.npcPos-myPos.y)/bounce;
                        _root.batBounce.setPan(100);
                        _root.batBounce.start(0, 1);
                    } else {
                        // NO, PLAYER SERVEs
                        mySpeed.y = 0;
                        myPos.x = left;
                        myPos.y = serve;
                        _parent.playerScore.play();
                        _root.miss.setPan(100);
                        _root.miss.start(0, 1);
                    }
                }
                // ANIMATE ME
                _x = myPos.x;
                _y = myPos.y;
                // BROADCAST GLOBALS TO GAMEWORLD
                _parent.ballPos = myPos.y;
                _parent.ballDir = mySpeed.x;
        }
```

We now have a game with a dynamic stereo sound-scape plus a user-controllable volume level. Despite this complex sound handling, the game still runs at a reasonable frame rate.

# 8  Flash Games Studio

> *One thing not touched on in the tennis game (because the sounds are all so short lived) is that varying the* `setPan` *and* `setVolume` *values whilst the sound is still playing will vary the sound volume/pan levels as the sound progresses - you don't necessarily have to set the volume/pan values before the sound is started with the* `start` *action.*

## setTransform

The final advanced sound control action, `setTransform`, has applications in Flash-based sound mixers (you can see one such FLA being built in *Flash 5 ActionScript Studio*), and other advanced audio applications, but its use in games is fairly limited given that most sound can be controlled via the easier to understand `setPan` and `setVolume`.

There are a couple of things that `setTransform` can do that the other actions cannot:

- If we want to control volume and pan at the same time (such as we would want to do in a game with a first/third person view - where we need to process the pan level as well as the 3D depth value) the use of a single action may be quicker than the `setPan`/`setVolume` pair.

- `setTransfom` allows you to convert stereo sound to true mono, something you may have to do when writing Flash games for certain wireless devices.

The `setTransform` command requires a separate object to provide control, which has properties leftleft (`ll`), rightleft (`rl`), leftright (`lr`), and rightright (`rr`). The typical definition code required to initialize a `setTransform` is as follows:

```
// set up the sound object
mySound = new Sound();
// set up the transform object
myTrans = new Object();
myTrans.ll = 100
myTrans.lr = 0
myTrans.rr = 100
myTrans.rl = 0
```

The `ll`, `lr`, `rr`, and `rl` values take some getting used to, but diagrammatically this is what we have:

# Interactive Sound 8

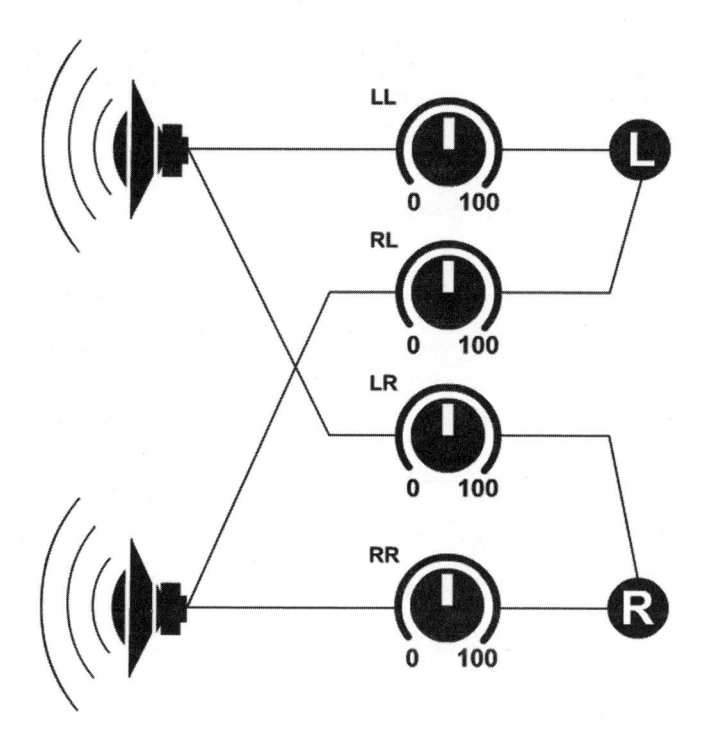

The `ll` and `rr` values correspond to the left and right stereo images of the sound signal but, unlike the other two actions, the two channels aren't connected. For example, in the `setPan` method, increasing the volume in the left channel may mean reducing the volume in the right channel, but because there is a separate control for each channel, this doesn't have to happen with `setTransform`. The listing above gives you the default setting, with 100% of the signal volume going into both speakers.

The usefulness of using `setTransform` for this isn't apparent until we want to mix sounds. If we're using normal pan controls to vary the stereo position of a sound in a composition, then we also affect its volume and therefore its prominence in the overall sound mix.

For example, if we move a drum sound from the center position (both speakers at 100 units say, giving 200 units of output) to the extreme left (one speaker at 100 units giving 100 units output) there is a loss of volume of 50%, and thus a diminishing in the prominence of the drums.

If you instead used a `setTransform`, you could ensure that the `ll` and `rr` components always add up to 200 units, thus resulting in no loss of volume (or more correctly, no loss of *power*) during the move in stereo position.

This level of sound control isn't normally required in a game (although it becomes very useful if we want to emulate certain mixing devices, such as a deejays mixing desk (sometimes called a **mixing board**) for a dance music related site.

## Flash Games Studio

This level of mixing *could* be used to create new sounds from existing samples by constantly applying complex sound envelopes to them. However the processing power required to perform this wouldn't make it a practical possibility in most applications where we're also trying to drive a real time game engine at the same time.

There are, however, two more inputs into the two speaker channels: `lr` and `rl`. These are the two 'crossover' signals:

- `rl` is the proportion of the right signal input to play in the left speaker
- `lr` is the proportion of the left signal input to play in the right speaker

By using the crossover signal values, you can feed the stereo components into both speakers, resulting in true mono sound. Effectively, you would set all the dials in the diagram above to 50%, resulting in both the left and right stereo channels being fed into both speakers.

In terms of ActionScript, the following code would give us true mono:

```
        // set up the sound object
mono = new Sound();
mono.attachSound(_root);
        // set up the transform object
myTrans = new Object();
myTrans.ll = 50;
myTrans.lr = 50;
myTrans.rr = 50;
myTrans.rl = 50;
        // apply the mono transform
mono.setTransform(myTrans);
```

Users with only one speaker (as found in many office computers) or wireless devices with only one speaker would still hear the full game sound irrespective of which speaker they had connected.

# Interactive Sound    8

## Conclusion

The Flash sound controls allow us a great deal of flexibility in the creation of dynamic sound to go with your game graphics, and if used properly, these features can enhance your game significantly. The biggest thing to watch with sound is that you get the balance right – too much and your game will take forever to load, not enough and you're missing an important cue to augment the graphics.

This chapter has concentrated on the difference between the two sound types; linkage and targeted, because this is the crucial coding concept that allows you to create hierarchical sound. Additionally, the use of `setPan` and `setVolume` can be used to add stereo effects and volume control.

Although the `setTransform` action is more useful to music mixing applications, it does have one or two applications in games, particularly in converting sound output for use on one speaker systems, something that may become more important as an increasing number of wireless devices are able to host Flash content.

In the next chapter we'll move one step on from sound and take a look at using music in games. Some of the methods for attaching and using music are similar to those used with sound, but the reasoning behind them is significantly different. People always use sound effects with their games, but why stop there? Why not go all the way and include a full score? Used in the right way, music can be the most valuable thing you can add to your game, and it doesn't have to break the performance bank.

# 8 Flash Games Studio

# Interactive Sound 8

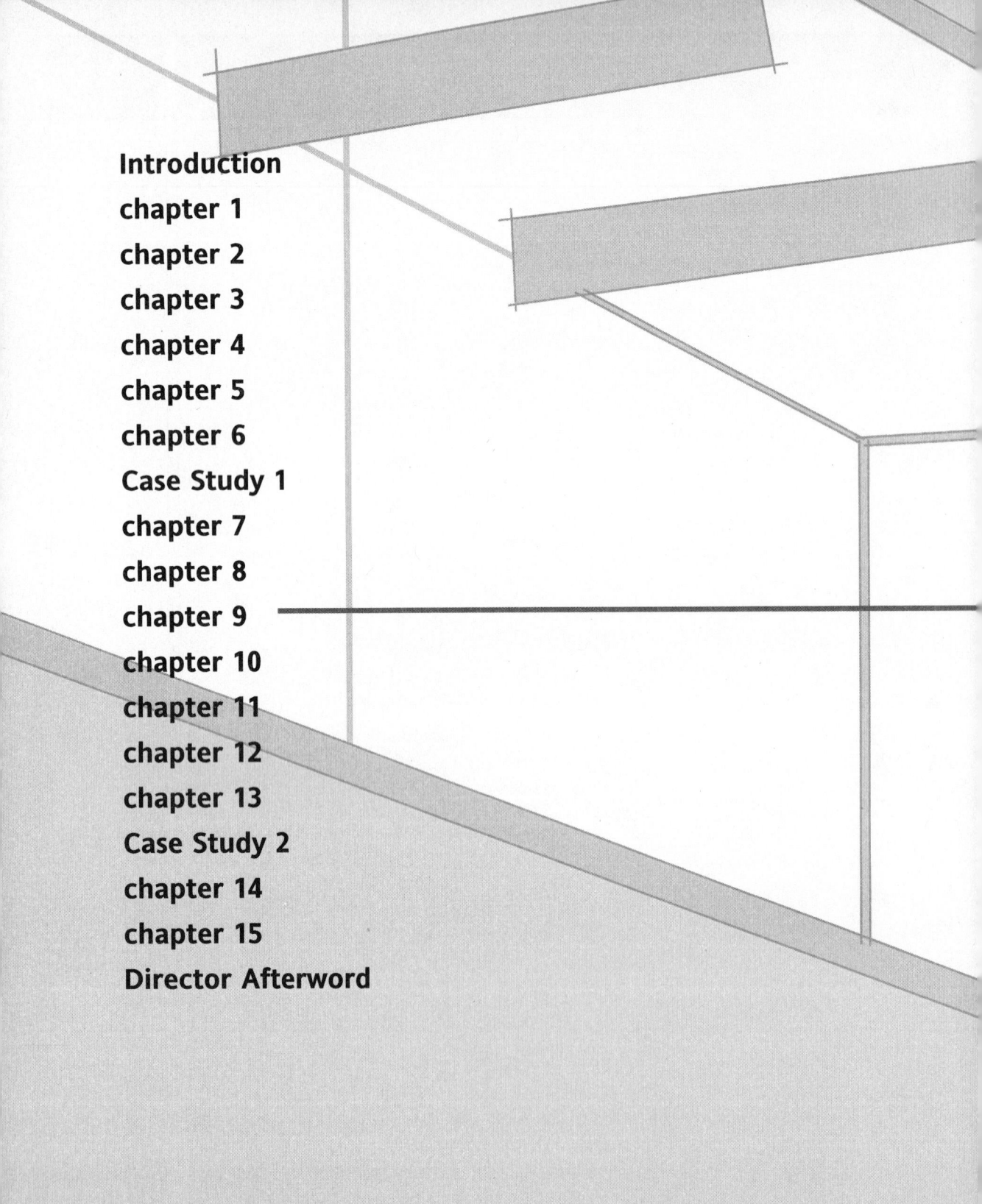

**Introduction**
chapter 1
chapter 2
chapter 3
chapter 4
chapter 5
chapter 6
Case Study 1
chapter 7
chapter 8
chapter 9
chapter 10
chapter 11
chapter 12
chapter 13
Case Study 2
chapter 14
chapter 15
**Director Afterword**

# Chapter 9
# Music in Games

# 9   Flash Games Studio

## Let There Be Music

What's so scary about music? Developers and programmers merrily build games with fantastic graphics and killer control – but then they grab a stock loop, throw it in the game, and call it music. Well, let me say this: The music in a game is as fundamentally important as control, artificial intelligence, plot, or even graphics. It is a fantastic tool. It serves as an emotional cue card, enhancing the visuals to tell players what they should be feeling at any given moment.

The perfect illustration of this is the movie. Films rely heavily on a musical score, and studios will spend millions just on the production and recording of the soundtrack. But why? Well look at the facts, the association between a killer shark and John Williams' theme for *Jaws* is unbreakable and universal. So much tension is derived from the music – face it, were you as shocked by finally seeing the fish in all its clockwork reality?

*Close Encounters of the Third Kind, Pulp Fiction, Rocky, Psycho* – hey, *any* James Bond film. They are all indebted to the composers and sound-smiths that developed little passages of music, which we indelibly associate with the action. These sorts of musical themes quickly become indispensable as they fix a moment to our minds. Indeed, technology company Intel has used the technique to enhance their brand identity. A signature jingle played every time its products are mentioned, sticks in our memory. Our brains are *branded*.

Can you imagine achieving such a profound effect on someone with a computer game? Is it possible to get the heart pumping, or the hairs rising on the back of the player's neck? Can you induce pleasure or dismay? Trust me, it can be done.

## Invisible Music

As soon as we start getting busy with the sound card, we are using a very powerful tool. Picture a scene with a tree swaying in the wind. If we overlay gentle piano and strings, then we know this is a peaceful and serene moment. However, if we overlay a dark and ominous piece of music, then we ask questions. What's with the tree? Is it evil? Is something bad about to happen?

That's our new tool at work – and the great thing is, it's practically subliminal! The audience tends to be so wrapped up in the visuals and the control of the scene, they do not think about the sneaking sounds creeping into their ears. Of course, with the wrong blend, tension is lost. Which emotion would be stimulated by a tree accompanied by a driving techno beat?

All too often, music is casually thrown into a game with the objective of fulfilling a self-imposed obligation to include a nice little ditty. This is *not* a reason to include music. Such a powerful tool can be powerfully irritating. The blend really needs to be worked at.

One particular scene can have several types of music, and each type will create a different effect and mood in the scene. Check out `demo9-1.swf` to see the effect of music on mood in a scene. Simply look at the picture, and listen to the different styles of music to see how each makes you feel differently in context to the image. The very last link is a perfect example of a *bad fit* – music that is mismatched to the scene:

# Music in Games

## Aspects of Music

I'm not going to go into a long dissertation on the theories of music – I'll leave that to the Royal Academy – but I will say a few words about the important rudiments which can make or break your game.

## Tempo

A prime factor determining the effect of a piece of music is its tempo – the measure of how fast or slow a song is. A fast driving tempo can be exciting and intense, whereas a slow tempo is more mellow and relaxed – even to the point of being leaden. Nightclubs have the tempo factor sorted. They have slapped a label on it (bpm – beats per minute) and now sell whole evenings around it. Hard-house techno reaches the high hundreds of bpm, while a chill out evening will drop below 60.

To demonstrate the effects of tempo, run the file `demo 9-2.swf` and listen to the difference when you click on the two buttons.

## Notes / Melody

Another factor that determines the impact of the music is the melody. The force of a catchy melody in games is phenomenal. *Tetris (Nintendo 1989)*, while brilliant in concept, was indebted to its Russian-style jingle, which just kept you wanting to play. In the end it was remixed and released as a single! A good melody will have the players absently humming when they are away from the game – a very good form of subliminal advertising.

Aside from full tunes, short melodies are very handy to ally with events and actions. For example, when the main character picks up a bonus, there can be a small 4 to 8 note melody that plays as a reward and as a way of instantly letting the player know what's going on. This melody will soon be gold dust to the player's brain.

# Flash Games Studio

Before you launch yourself into a composing frenzy, remember the context of the sound. Small event-related melodies are going to be heard many times. If you make your melody irritating, players will launch themselves at the mute button, and that's no good to anybody. There is of course no formula to determine whether or not a melody will be catchy or annoying. It's all about *feel*, and it's not always easy to get that balance right.

## Chords

If you're looking to get the feel right, you've got to get the chords right, because they are crucial to the overall mood of a tune. They can provide brightness and cheer or darkness and gloom, or they could blast the piece through with power and authority.

Chords come in many different styles, but the main ones are:

- Major – Typical happy chord
- Minor – Typical dark, sad chord
- Major 7th – Dreamy feel
- Suspended Chord – Anticipates resolving cleanly into a minor chord
- Diminished – Scary and uneasy

Generally speaking, one style of chord will dominate one song. For an example of what each chord sounds and feels like, run the file `demo9-4.swf`:

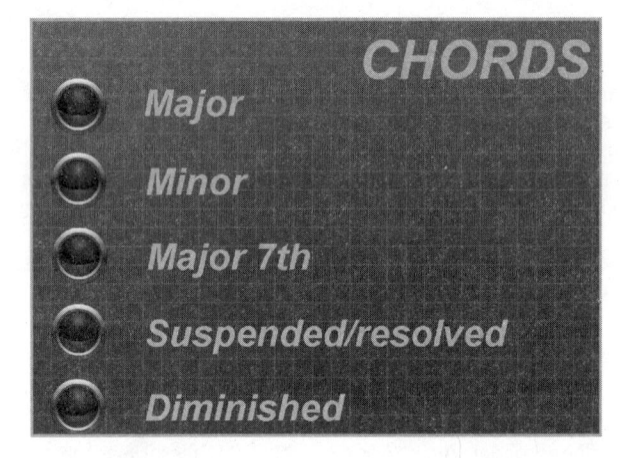

## Style

Finally, the overall type of music, or *style*, is the choice that will most affect the player's impression of your game. So what do you want? Cute and bouncy? Cinematic? Industrial? Street-wise? Then take your pick of the following – you're sure to find your mood somewhere amongst these styles:

# Music in Games

## Orchestral

Orchestral music will add immeasurable quality and professionalism to a game. These days, people associate wide and soaring orchestral scores with big budget wide screen Technicolor production. Certain styles of classical music contain the intellectual and emotional depth to give your game authority.

But don't rest your baton just yet – that's not all the classics can do. When Tom and Jerry are scurrying through their booby-trap scattered house, what accompanies them every step of the way? Music! Furiously-paced strings get that chase scene pumping, and every whack of a frying pan is accompanied by a blast of brass. Can you imagine the misery of those great scenes being left without music? If anything, the furious pace of modern gaming presents a great opportunity for this style of composition to make a return.

## Rock & Electronic

Rock music is often used to energize a scene, and to add an adrenaline push to any portion of a game. If we look back at movies, the last decade or so has seen the evolution of movie soundtracks into greatest hits collections. Really-popular songs have been used in place of the specially composed score, to guarantee a much quicker association with young, attention-deficient audiences.

In the gaming world rock music implies a coolness and confidence, and a kicking soundtrack will give players a great rush when they are trying to beat that racing or fighting opponent.

Similarly, electronic music conveys style and modern awareness better than the latest musical style. It is also very successfully used at creating a feeling of drive, power and excitement. Be warned, though. Electronic is easy to include in Flash, and has a tendency to be overused.

An excellent example of the use of rock and electronic music was *Grand Theft Auto*, which put players at the mercy of the radio of whichever car they had stolen. The slower pick-up trucks blared out country music, while the faster sports cars would crank the game up with throbbing techno beats. This, in conjunction with the speed and handling of each car, would have a profound effect on the mood of the game.

## Experimental / Ambient

Certain types of music dispense with the need for traditional form, largely ignoring tempo and tone-based harmony. They focus instead on creating the right ambience. As it's an experimental area, you can bring out whichever ideas suit you. Use realistic sounds – the seashore with birds, say – or more abstract ideas – perhaps a light pan flute, or more traumatic industrial sounds. Whatever your poison, soundscapes are perfect for adding texture to a Flash game.

## Ethnic

Ethnic music is associated with a particular geographical location or cultural reference. There are literally thousands of types of ethnic music ranging anywhere from African tribal songs, Scottish highland music to traditional Chinese opera.

Naturally, the use of ethnic music will further enhance the authenticity of your games if they are based on a specific era in a specific culture. So, when your character is running around the pyramids of ancient Egypt, then naturally, Egyptian music would round the scene. If you are based in tribal Africa, some great beats and rhythms can come to the fore. The world's music is your oyster.

## The Fundamental Truth

The elements in creating music for games are as comprehensive a subject as graphics and storyline. When you create a game, remember to think about what the music should be telling the player, and then take the necessary steps to *design* your music. After that you can find the best music for the job, no matter what it is. And remember, it's your game – so if you think it works and you have a reason for using it, then *any* music can go.

Sometimes, even a complete absence of music can create a tension. Think of Alfred Hitchcock's movie *The Birds* – it doesn't have a note in it, but creates enormous suspense through silence and ambient noise. The key point is to lead the viewer's (and player's) mood, feelings and emotions.

## What Works?

So what's good? To save us thrashing around in the silence, here are a few games that have managed to get the blend of sounds bang on.

## Super Mario Brothers

Ah, *Super Mario Brothers* (*Nintendo 1985*) can be used as the benchmark for so much that is good in games, and its sound is no exception. Most people who have played the game can hum a tune from it. For example, the music that plays at the opening level selection screen is considered the theme song. Along with that, different themes are played on different levels of the game. Underwater has one theme, while above ground uses another. So too the castles and the caves. Each theme is tailored to evoke a particular emotional response, adding to the dynamics of the level.

When you are in the underground caves, there are lot of low, rhythm-less dark tunes suggesting fear and instability, whereas up above ground you hear a nice gentle tune that suggests relaxation and freedom. As the game progresses, and the challenges become more perilous, the music develops a more minor key.

The actual technology of the music hardware in *Super Mario Brothers* was quite primitive. The designers couldn't use digital or recorded sound, rather they had to use computer generated bleeps and blips. However, they did it well and adhered to the principal of using short associative melodies. The background music, though highly synthesized, was believable because the audience understood that this was a cartoon world, and so synthesized music fit perfectly. This is proof positive that whatever your technical limitations, the musical side of games designing can be your friend.

# Music in Games

## Warcraft

Warcraft (*Blizzard Entertainment 1995*) is a real-time strategy and role playing game. You lead troops of humans or orcs into battle against each other on a mass scale. It's an overhead view where the players are small, but battles can be large.

The *Warcraft* CD came with several tracks of pre-recorded fully orchestrated music. Most of the music was of the fantasy battle genre, with dark and soaring horns and strings. The reason the music worked so well is because it was always playing, creating a sense of tension. However, when a battle started, the music fit fantastically. The orchestral shots seemed to be choreographed with orcs swinging their battle-axes, and humans swinging their swords.

Because of the CD, this music could be fully recorded and high quality. The designers used this to their advantage, and the music added a level of superiority and professionalism.

## You Don't Know Jack

*You Don't Know Jack* (*Berkley Systems*) came out in 1993, and was unique in its creative use of music. It is basically a game with many different types of trivia question, and one full game is either 7 or 21 questions.

This game's music comprised lots of manic mini-songs that were associated with different parts of the game. In between each round there was a short song that introduced the round number. Each of these songs was stylistically different (rock, country, rap, 50's TV commercial jingle, etc.) and made creative use of the number of the current round.

While the game was waiting for you to answer a question, a clock-tick-like piece of music played, and many explosive and short pieces of music played with each different question based on the content of the questions. Needless to say, each game you played was unique and different from the previous game. Consequently, the soundtrack of each game was also different. This created a very enriching and entertaining experience.

## Unreal Tournament

*Unreal Tournament* (*GT Interactive 1999*) is a first person shooter in which you are battling to the death for supremacy and victory in the "unreal tournament". *UT* is a very fast paced, intensely action-oriented game. It's set in a very dark decaying world in a bleak future.

For the most part, the music in *UT* was orchestra-based with dark melodies that echoed the eerie surroundings. The real dynamism of the *UT* soundtrack was how the music changed with the action. When you were running around between battles, the music tended to be fairly intense, but not full of action and suspense. However, when you encountered another player and the battle began, the music also picked up to match. It had the tremendous effect of creating a movie-scripted cinematic feel – even though you were controlling the action.

# 9  Flash Games Studio

## When and What to Play

When you've made a game and you want to enhance it with music, there are some common cues to be aware of.

Short melodies: These act as aural cues and are an instant way of notifying the player that a game event has occurred.

- Level Beginning
- Pick up object
- Player dies
- Points are scored
- Bonus is achieved
- A mistake is made

Complete songs: These are the songs that create the atmosphere and emotion

- Introduction
- Main selection screen/user interface
- During main game play
- Between level animations

Now we've had a look at some particular types of music, and where you might use them, let's focus on how to create this music and use it in a Flash-specific environment.

## Software

So, how do you *make* music? Well, you could grab a guitar and play some chords. But for the majority of people that would involve buying a guitar and learning to play it. That's music, but generally we want to be able to record, produce, prepare, optimize and bring it into Flash. That will require more than just a guitar. The process of full audio production is a career in itself, but there are now many tools that help speed up the process, and make it accessible to even a novice musician.

There are several types of audio software:

- Multitrack Recorders: These programs are geared towards recording source audio and creating an entire song from it. They are often accompanied by a simple studio setup that includes a microphone and sometimes a mixer and effects units. Vegas Audio and Pro Tools are just a couple of the many multitrack recording programs to choose from.

- Sequencers: For actually writing the music, there are many programs that assist you in building up songs. The standard format is MIDI (Musical Instrument Digital Interface), and it is used in conjunction with a MIDI synthesizer to create anything from piano lines, to fully orchestrated songs. There are several sequencing programs including Cakewalk, Musictime, and Encore. These programs also have the unique feature of printing out very professional sheet music.

# Music in Games    9

- Loop-based Software: One of the most popular types of software today for creating music are loop based composition programs. These programs use standard libraries of pre-recorded loops (ranging from seconds to minutes in length) that are arranged to create entire songs. They are incredibly easy, and are inviting ways to quickly produce professional sounding music. You can take a 4 bar drum loop, add a bass line, and put in a guitar and you have an entire short song that can be looped and played in any game. Loop based software includes Acid, Fruity Loops and Gigasampler.

- Wave Editors: Once your entire song is done and complete, you will often bring it into a wave editor (called wave because of the sound waves in audio) where you can perform many tasks such as shorten, crop, trim, flip, reverse, add effects and generally clean up the sound. Wave editors can also be used to record audio from the microphone or line input. There are many wave editors including Sound Forge, Wavelab and Cool Edit Pro.

- Software Synthesizers: One exciting development is the software synthesizer. These are essentially programs that are like the brains of an expensive electronic keyboard, without having to buy any hardware; they are programs that your computer runs, turning it into a state of the art synthesizer. Programs such as Gigapiano, Rebirth and Reason. Also, certain audio cards already come with a fully expandable MIDI synthesizer on board. Either way, in most cases, all you have to do is plug in a MIDI keyboard, and you're ready to start "playing" your computer.

There are several resources for downloading and ordering online sound libraries and loop libraries with which you can make high-quality professional music. These can be found in the appendix at the back of the book.

## Music in Flash

There are several approaches to putting music into a Flash game. Each has its own advantages and disadvantages, so it's important for you to know what you want out of your game's soundtrack. There are three main techniques:

- Complete soundtrack - Flash streams in a complete song, can be any particular length, and it is not based on loops.

- Simple Loop – With this method, the music is essentially one loop that plays over and over again. This loop can be anywhere from one second to one minute in length. The key objective is to create a loop that doesn't have too many major distinguishable sounds that will make the loop obvious – it should sound like one continuous song.

- Real-time mixing/layering – Individual components of a song are taken apart in separate loops, and each is controlled independently by Flash. This means that you can control bass line, guitar, drums, piano and any other intruments. all separately.

But before I go through these, let's quickly look at sound export options in Flash.

# 9    Flash Games Studio

## Exporting Music From Flash

When you have music loops loaded into the library, the way you choose to export that data will greatly affect the quality of the sound, and the size of your SWF.

- To select the export settings, go to the Library, rightclick on a sound clip and select Properties:

- In the window that opens, you can choose your export setting, weighing up what quality you would like your final playback to have:

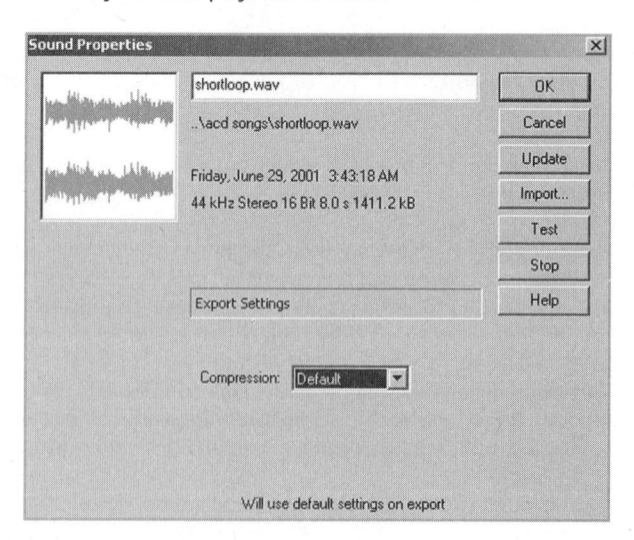

# Music in Games

- One option, Raw, is not suited for lengthy music as it maintains 100% integrity in a sound at great expense to your PC's memory. This leaves two main options for music exporting: ADPCM (Adaptive Differential Pulse Code Modulation) and MP3. So how do you choose what's right for you? Well, let's have a look at how they work.

- ADPCM works by recording the changes in sound, rather than the actual value of the samples themselves. This means that ADPCM files can have lower bit resolution than raw files because frequency changes in sound tend to be relatively small. This method is better for shorter sound loops, rarely reaching 20 seconds in length. Normally an ADPCM sound is used for small event sounds, like button clicks. In this format, you must choose a sample rate, and a bit depth:

Under Sample Rate, you can chose between 5 kHz, 11 kHz, 22 kHz and 44 kHz. Generally, the lower your sample rate, the lower the frequency range that the sound clip will be exported with – and the smaller the file size. So, if you have the sound of a full drum line, and you export it at 5 kHz, the chances are that you won't hear very much of the higher frequencies, like cymbals, at all. Anything above the frequency of 5,000 Hz will disappear.

At 5 kHz, the computer takes 5,000 distinct samples every second, however pitches that are higher than 5 kHz create their sounds at a rate that is more than 5,000 times per second – so the computer can't "hear" it.

So, for lower pitch sounds, like bass lines or bass drums, you can safely use a 5 kHz sample rate. Remember that each step you go up in sample rate doubles the size of your exported music loop. For ultimate quality (but with larger file size) choose 44 kHz. This is enough samples per second to reproduce most pitches that the human ear can hear.

Because of the fact that you'll want to use lower sample rates as often as possible, it also stands that your clearest sounds will be those that have the lowest pitch. These tend to be the most suitable for typical Internet streaming rates. So, if you set a sound at 11kHz, then consider running the sound through an 11kHz lowpass filter first. A lowpass filter is a program, or a plug-in to most major audio programs, that is responsible for scanning through a sound file and removing all high frequencies (that is the high pitched notes) and only allowing low frequencies to pass through to the final sound file. There is also an equivalent highpass filter, which is used for removing low bass sounds, things like the hum generated by electric interference, or sounds recorded on a windy day where the wind makes booming sounds on a microphone. There are hundreds of audio filter programs to be found at the websites listed in the appendix.

## Flash Games Studio

Under ADPCM Bits (bit depth), you choose the number of bits that you want to represent one sample of sound. You can choose 2, 3, 4, and 5 bits. So, a 4-bit setting will have 16 distinct levels in one sample. The more bits you use, the more detail will be preserved of your original sound. If you use a lower number of bits, you will notice what sounds like static. This is because the computer is trying to interpolate analog sound data from very limited digital information – 4 distinct levels.

Also, if you choose "Convert Stereo to Mono" then your exported size will be 50% smaller than with stereo turned on. Stereo requires the export of two separate channels of audio for one sound clip; mono only requires one.

As you're trying different settings, you can, and it's recommended that you do, press the "Test" button to see what your current settings will make your music sound like.

The MP3 format is better suited for longer sound clips as it is more efficiently compressed. The drawback with MP3 sound is that it requires a lot of overhead for the computer to play at run-time because of the complex mathematics it utilizes. MP3 saves music as a series of mathematical equations that describe the shape of the sound wave. When the MP3 format was created, one of its primary purposes was streaming audio (audio that begins playing while it's still downloading). This is why most music content on the web today is delivered via the MP3 format:

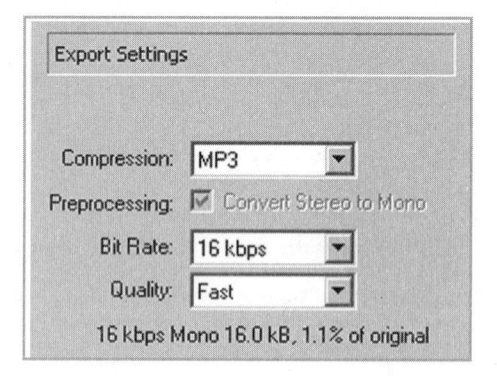

When exporting your sound loops as MP3, you have only one main setting – the Bit Rate – that affects the overall quality of the exported sound. Under Bit Rate you have several choices from 8 to 160 kbps (kilobits per second - since MP3 is designed for streaming, it's measured in bits per second, rather than just bits).

MP3 has the capacity to compress audio while still maintaining a wide range of frequencies. However, people often notice that the lower the bit rate, the stranger the sound – at low bit rates it's often described as sounding too "computerized" or "digital". This is just a result of the mathematics behind MP3. For music with lower and duller sounds (like bass, or low drums) you can choose a low bit rate; 8kbps. However, for more detailed sounds like music, you should try to stick with 24 kbps, 32 kbps or 48 kbps. If the file size is too large, try reducing its length, or making it loop.

# Music in Games

The Quality setting is a way of telling Flash how much effort to expend in preserving the quality of the original sound, at the current bit rate. You can choose Fast, Medium or Best. Best is the highest quality sound, but it will also take the longest to export when you publish or test your movie. When you have many sounds, this setting can potentially add minutes to your export time. Fast will export quicker but the quality will be lower. While developing, use Fast, and then when you're finished and you're doing a final publish, change the quality to Best.

With either export format, choosing your settings is a balancing act between quality and file size. Remember to take your time **testing** and **listening** as you're making your choices – you will thank yourself in the long run.

Now, let's look at each of the types of soundtrack in detail.

# Complete Soundtrack

The idea behind a complete soundtrack is to have a game in which an entire song plays in the background. This is accomplished by placing your full song in its own SWF file and then streaming that into your game at runtime. This has the distinct advantage of allowing you to have a fairly small main game SWF, yet have a long soundtrack. Once the game has loaded it will begin playing, and afterwards you can initiate the background loading of your song.

Take a look at `demo 9-8m.fla/swf` (the FLA file is quite big – holding the full, uncompressed song):

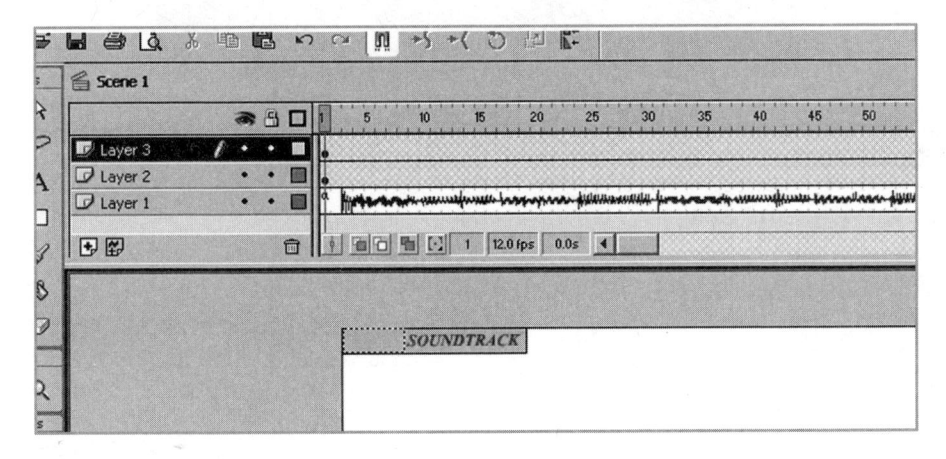

As you can see, the entire song is sitting on its own layer, and it has been placed in streaming mode:

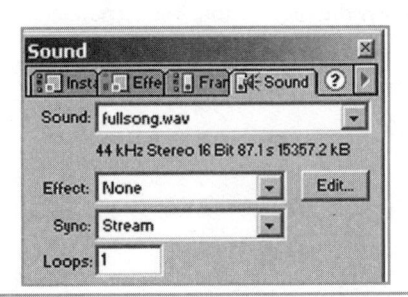

## Flash Games Studio

I've also placed a small preloader on the main timeline so I can see how the streaming process is progressing. On frame one of the main timeline is a `stop` command so that the soundtrack will be stopped, or parked, when it's loaded into our game.

Now, take a look at **demo9-8.fla**, and you'll see the layout for our "game". This is really nothing more than soundtrack player, and a way for me to clearly illustrate how the process is happening:

The **NO SOUNDTRACK** box is actually a movie clip named soundtrack. This is the target into which we will load the soundtrack SWF file (**demo9-8m.swf**).

Attached to the Load button is simply the following ActionScript:

```
on (release)
{
    loadMovie("demo9-8m.swf", soundtrack);
}
```

This will begin the loading process, and the soundtrack will start to stream into our main SWF. Once the soundtrack has been loading for a few seconds, or has completely loaded, then we can press the play button. The ActionScript for the play button consists simply of:

```
on (release)
{
    soundtrack.gotoAndPlay(2);
}
```

This will simply tell the soundtrack movie clip to jump to frame 2 and play, which will move it past the stop on frame 1, and start playing/streaming the song. If the loadMovie has not yet been initiated, the Play button will simply do nothing.

Using this technique you can have several different full songs in a game; only one being loaded at a time. This will allow you to have lots of variation in soundtrack without needing to have a large download time, which would interfere with the game.

> *It can be considered inefficient to always stream the music we want to hear if it has already been loaded. So, if you wanted to add on to this example, you could create several soundtrack movie clips (soundtrack1, soundtrack2, etc) on the main timeline, and once a soundtrack has been loaded in, attach a flag to the movie clip and set its value to true. If the flag is not set, then you load the soundtrack in. If the flag is already set, then you need not initiate the* loadMovie *again.*

The following code, attached to the Load button, would achieve the desired result of only loading in our music once.

```
on (release)
{
    if (soundtrack.loaded != true)
    {
        soundtrack.loaded = true;
    loadMovie("demo10-8m.swf", soundtrack);
    }
}
```

Now that we've seen how to use a complete soundtrack, let's take a look at another option: making one out of the same small piece of music repeated over and over again.

## Simple Loop

The idea behind simple loop music is to have one short sound clip that loops over and over, creating the effect of a long soundtrack. In a game menu screen, or even a loading screen, you can have these small songs playing to fill the silence, and they give you a quick and easy method of having full background music.

These are, however, very limiting because they have little or no variation and consequently their emotional effect is also very limited.

The most effective way to create a simple loop like this is to include it in your master SWF file, exported with linkage. In demo10-9.fla, you'll see this in action. Once you've imported your loop, simply open the library, and right-click on the sound loop and choose Linkage. Next, choose Export this symbol, and enter shortloop as the identifier:

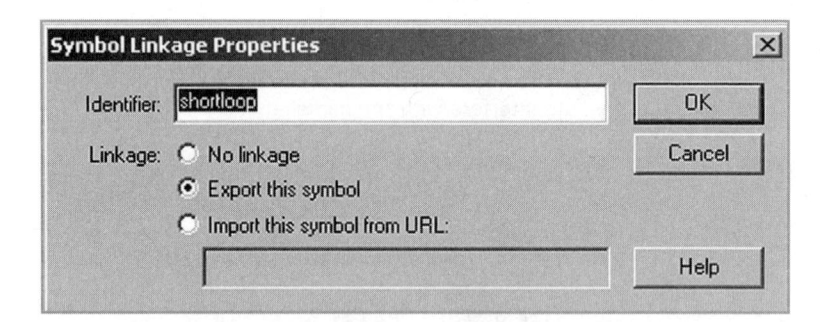

Finally, in the main movie, you need to initialize a sound object that is linked to shortloop. To accomplish this, create an empty movie clip on the main timeline, and call it controller.

In the demo, attached to controller I have the following code:

```
onClipEvent(load)
{
    _root.loop = new Sound;
    _root.loop.attachSound ("shortloop");
}
```

This simply defines a new sound object called loop, and for simplicity I've placed it on the _root timeline. If you wanted to, you could attach it to an actual movie clip, which would allow you to control its sound and volume separately to any other loaded and playing sounds. (More on this later in the music mixing example). Finally, I attach the linked sound shortloop to it. Now, all we need to do is play it by attaching the following to a play button:

```
_root.loop.start();
```

However, this will only play the loop once, so you must indicate how many times you want it to loop, as in:

```
_root.loop.start(0,100);
```

Which means it will loop 100 times – which will be quite a long time. You can choose almost any number there.

***The 0 before the ",100" is an offset; the number of seconds into the sound file at which it will begin playing – 0 is the beginning of the sound.***

Finally, to stop the sound you simply say:

```
_root.loop.stop();
```

# Music in Games    9

I've attached all this code to a play and a stop button on the main timeline, as can be seen in `demo9-9.swf`:

## Real-time Mixing/Layering

This is potentially the most exciting soundtrack method for Flash because of its versatility. With it you can create *intelligent* soundtracks that seamlessly rise, fall and change intensity as the player enters different areas of the game. For example, as you're walking through the grass fields the music is simple and free. Once you approach the dark castle the music can gradually become more suspenseful. Finally, once you enter the castle and start battling with evil monsters the music can be downright scary. All of these transitions are seamless, thus creating a soundtrack that is totally customized to that particular game.

To accomplish this, you must create a series of simple loops, but there are a few points to remember:

- All the music loops should have exactly the same tempo, otherwise they will not fit together and will sound a mess

- All the music should be in the same key, preferably following the same chord progression so that they mesh well together

Try to avoid having more than three distinct loops playing at once. You may have to record parts together: For example, rather than each loop being a distinct instrument, create loops that consist of combined instruments of a similar frequency. So, one loop could be drums and bass, another loop could be piano and guitar while another loop could be flute and violin.

# 9  Flash Games Studio

First, you must create your loops. I've made two demos, `demo9-6` and `demo9-7` which both demonstrate real-time mixing and layering:

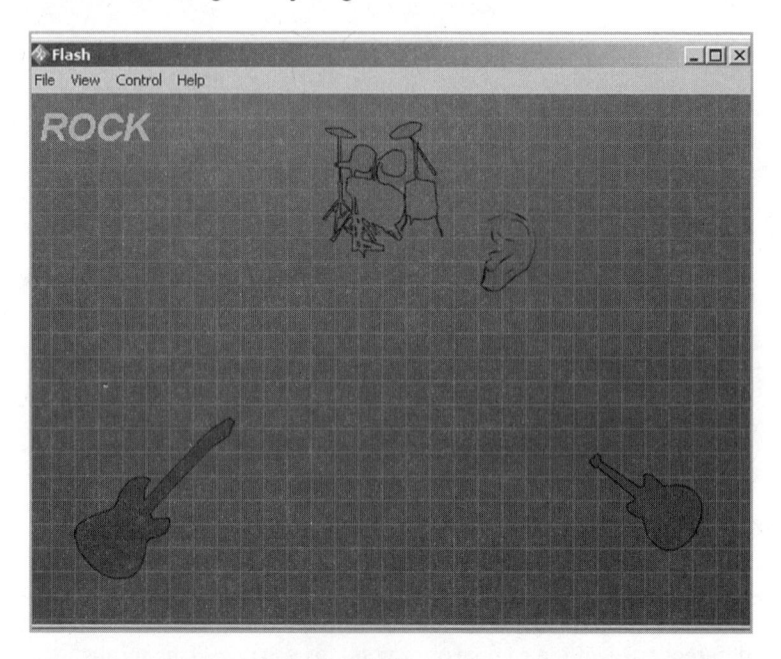

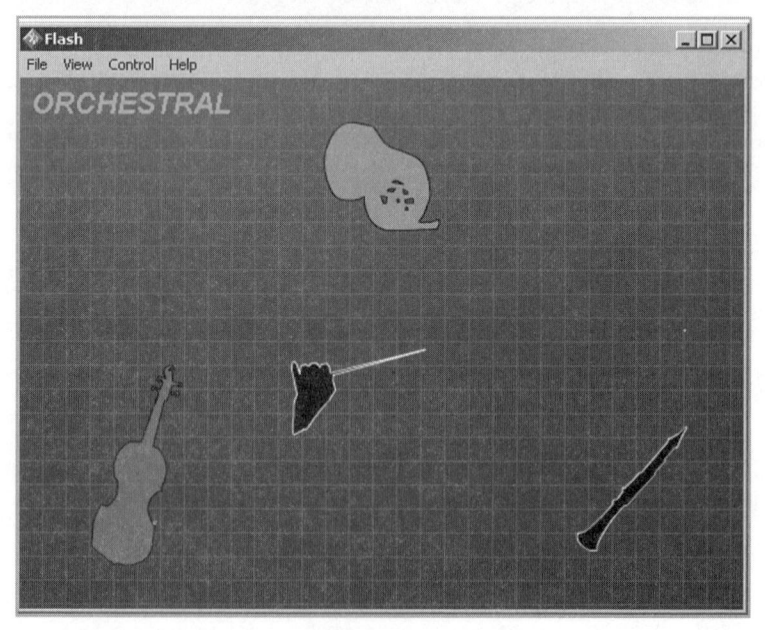

# Music in Games

In both of these demos, you simply move the mouse around the screen, and wherever the cursor is (an ear in the rock demo, and a conductor's hand in the orchestral demo) then that part of the music will be brought to the forefront. As you move around you can raise and lower the intensity, mood and feeling of the music by emphasizing different parts of it.

Since both demos are structurally the same, I'm going to use the orchestral demo (demo9-7) to illustrate the process. Let's see how it works.

## How to Mix and Layer

1. First, I created a woodwind part, a brass part, and a string part, all in the same key and at the same tempo. I imported the sounds into Flash as separate loops. Finally, I set up linkage for each loop, calling them flute, brass and strings. I've chosen to use three sound loops because that creates the most variation with the least hit on the processor, since all of Flash's mixing is done via software, and it doesn't make use of specialized sound hardware:

2. Next, I created three movie clips on the stage, one called brass, one called flute and one called strings. Inside each movie clip I created an image to be representative of the sound. Finally, I placed the movie clips in a triangle around the screen, keeping them at least 300 pixels apart. The size of the triangle is important, in order to allow the volume of each object to reach its full potential. I gave each movie clip an instance name that matched the clip name (So, strings was called strings and so on.)

3. Then I created another movie clip on the main timeline and called it conductor. In this I created the graphic of a conductor's hand holding a baton. This will be our mouse cursor. It's really just an aesthetic thing, but I like it. I gave it the instance name conductor.

# Flash Games Studio

4. Next, I created a blank movie clip on the main timeline, called it controller, and gave it the instance name controller as well. I attached the following ActionScript to it:

   ```
   onClipEvent(load)
   {
           // Create new sound object called clip in
           // each orchestra section movie clip.
           _root.brass.clip = new Sound(_root.brass);
           _root.flute.clip = new Sound(_root.flute);
           _root.strings.clip = new Sound(_root.strings);

           // Attach the linked sounds from the library.
           _root.brass.clip.attachSound("brass");
           _root.flute.clip.attachSound("flute");
           _root.strings.clip.attachSound("strings");

           // counter used in synchronization
           synch = 0;

           // replace the cursor with the conductor's hand
           startDrag (_root.conductor, true);
           Mouse.hide();
   }
   ```

5. By using clip = new Sound (clipname), Flash creates the sound object within a specific movie clip (clipname). I do this so I can control the volume of each clip independently. If you don't specify a clip name, Flash assumes that you are attaching the sounds to the main timeline, and then any action you perform on one clip is also performed on the others – turn down the volume of one, and you turn down the volume of the rest!

6. I attach the sounds that are linked in the Library, to the newly created sound objects. I also create a local variable called synch that I will explain in a minute. Finally, I attach the conductor movie clip to the mouse, and hide the mouse cursor.

7. Next, I add the following ActionScript to each of the three instrument movie clips (brass, flute, and strings)

   ```
   onClipEvent(enterFrame)
   {
           // Compute distance between mouse and current position
           distx = _root._xmouse - _x;
           disty = _root._ymouse - _y;

           // Calculate the distance between the two
           // using standard pythagorean/triangle math
           dist = Math.sqrt ((distx * distx) + (disty * disty));
   ```

# Music in Games

```
        // Cap the distance. 300 is the farthest you can
        // be.
        if (dist > 300) dist = 300;

        // Calculate a volume from 0 to 100,
        // based on dist
        vol = (100 - (dist / 3));

}
```

This simply creates a variable called `vol` in each movie clip, which is based on the position of the mouse. Nothing happens with `vol` just yet – it's simply a variable that's local to the movie clip, which we'll use in a second.

8. Finally, I add the following code to the controller movie clip:

```
onClipEvent (enterFrame)
{
        // To synchronize loops, you must stop and start them twice

        if (synch < 2)
        {
                synch++;
                _root.strings.clip.stop();
                _root.flute.clip.stop();
                _root.brass.clip.stop();
                _root.strings.clip.start(0, 999);
                _root.flute.clip.start(0, 999);
                _root.brass.clip.start(0, 999);
        }

        // Which instrument has the highest volume?
        max = 0;
        if (_root.strings.vol > max) max = _root.strings.vol;
        if (_root.brass.vol > max) max = _root.brass.vol;
        if (_root.flute.vol > max) max = _root.flute.vol;

        // Calculate the relative volumes.
        stringsRel = (_root.strings.vol / max) * 100;
        brassRel = (_root.brass.vol / max) * 100;
        fluteRel = (_root.flute.vol / max) * 100;

        // Set the volumes.
        _root.strings.clip.setVolume(stringsRel);
        _root.brass.clip.setVolume(brassRel);
        _root.flute.clip.setVolume(fluteRel);

}
```

# Flash Games Studio

That's it! Let's just identify in detail what each piece of this final section of the script has done. Here's a diagram to help you visualize the relationship between the position of the mouse and the volume of each sound:

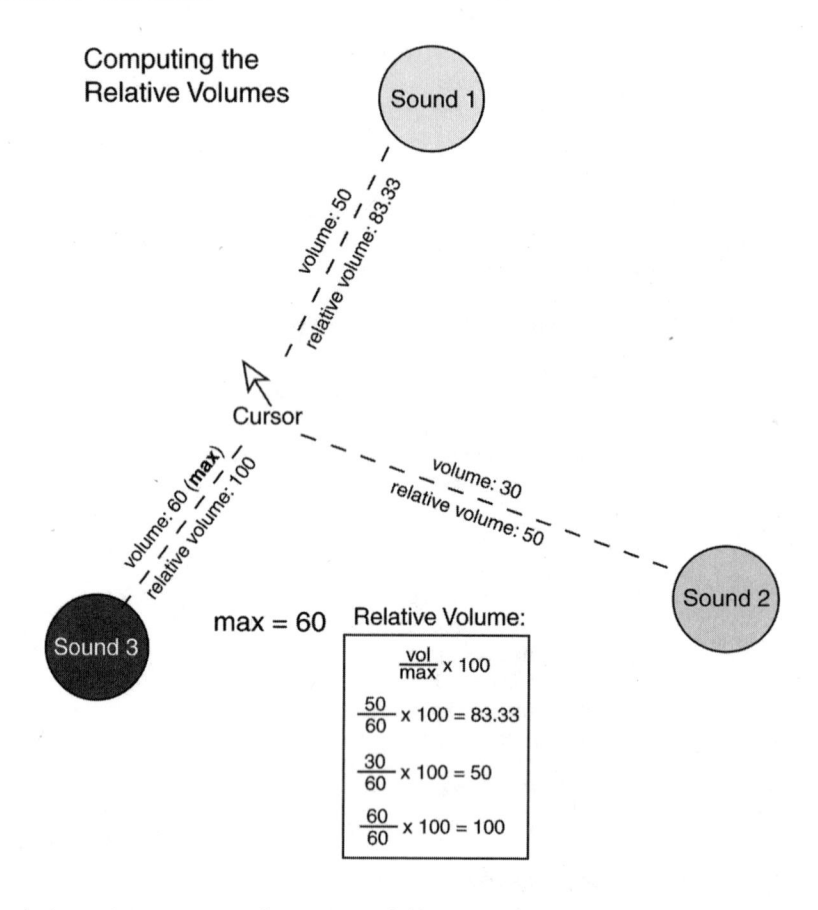

**Computing the Relative Volumes**

Sound 1
volume: 50
relative volume: 83.33

Cursor

Sound 2
volume: 30
relative volume: 50

Sound 3
volume: 60 (**max**)
relative volume: 100

max = 60

Relative Volume:

$$\frac{vol}{max} \times 100$$

$$\frac{50}{60} \times 100 = 83.33$$

$$\frac{30}{60} \times 100 = 50$$

$$\frac{60}{60} \times 100 = 100$$

Flash's desire to just pump out frames as quickly as possible means it pays little attention to the synchronization of sound. So, we sensitive designers must take this into account and perform a little jiggery pokery to get the sound loops to be perfectly in synch:

```
if (synch < 2)
{
        synch++;
        _root.strings.clip.stop();
        _root.flute.clip.stop();
        _root.brass.clip.stop();
        _root.strings.clip.start(0, 999);
        _root.flute.clip.start(0, 999);
        _root.brass.clip.start(0, 999);
}
```

# Music in Games 9

This trick simply stops and starts the loops twice. The `synch` variable keeps track of how many times the sound has been reset, and if it needs to, it will stop all three loops, and start them. After doing this once, and then again, `synch` will be equal to 2 and it will never run this ActionScript again. After the second time, I've set each loop to play 999 times, which will be a very long time. Each clip is 9.1 seconds, so that's well over 9000 seconds, or 150 minutes.

Next, I find which movie clip has the highest `vol` – or, which is closest to the conductor's hand:

```
max = 0;
if (_root.strings.vol > max) max = _root.strings.vol;
if (_root.brass.vol > max) max = _root.brass.vol;
if (_root.flute.vol > max) max = _root.flute.vol;
```

And then `max` will be set to the value of that `vol`. Next, I calculate the relative volume of each movie clip as a percentage by comparing it to the clip with the highest volume:

```
stringsRel = (_root.strings.vol / max) * 100;
brassRel = (_root.brass.vol / max) * 100;
fluteRel = (_root.flute.vol / max) * 100;
```

I do this because I always want to have at least one of the volumes at 100%. Let's say that the following are the values of each movie clip's `vol`:

```
strings.vol = 60;
brass.vol = 50;
flute.vol = 30;
```

If I were to use those numbers directly, then the whole thing would be pretty quiet. So, I figure out that `strings.vol` has the highest volume, so max gets set to 60. The relative volumes (stringsrel, brassrel, and fluterel) are set as follows:

```
stringsRel = (_root.strings.vol / max) * 100;
```

Which breaks out as:

```
stringsRel = (60 / 60) * 100;
```

Therefore...

```
stringsRel = (1) * 100;
```

Therefore...

```
stringsRel = 100;
```

375

## Flash Games Studio

That is correct-as our maximum volume instrument, it is 100. I do this for each movie clip:

```
brassRel = (50 / 60) * 100;
brassRel = (0.8333) * 100;
brassRel = 83.33;
```

And...

```
fluteRel = (30 / 60) * 100;
fluteRel = (0.5) * 100;
fluteRel = 50;
```

And voila, we have our three relative volumes:

```
stringsRel = 100
brassRel = 83.33
fluteRel = 50
```

Using this technique of creating relative volumes, it's possible to place the conductor's hand equidistant from each movie clip and get a value of 100 for each relative volume:

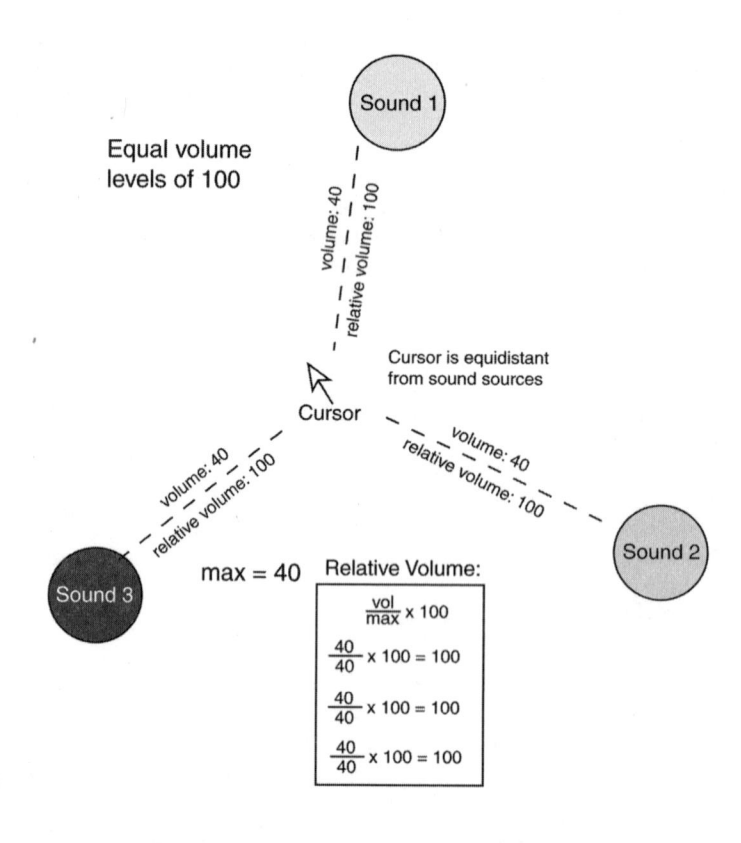

Equal volume levels of 100

Sound 1

volume: 40
relative volume: 100

Cursor

Cursor is equidistant from sound sources

volume: 40
relative volume: 100

volume: 40
relative volume: 100

Sound 3

Sound 2

max = 40

Relative Volume:

$$\frac{vol}{max} \times 100$$

$$\frac{40}{40} \times 100 = 100$$

$$\frac{40}{40} \times 100 = 100$$

$$\frac{40}{40} \times 100 = 100$$

This is the most mathematically sound technique for getting properly balanced mixing of volumes.

Finally, the volumes of each of the sound loops are set:

```
_root.strings.clip.setVolume(stringsRel);
_root.brass.clip.setVolume(brassRel);
_root.flute.clip.setVolume(fluteRel);
```

In this demo, the balancing of the sounds is based on the mouse cursor, but used in a full game you can base your balance on factors such as health level, number of monsters present, current game level, difficulty settings, running speed or just about anything you can think of. Bear in mind that the maximum number of samples Flash can play at any one time is eight, and they soon fill up.

The key objective is to change the music depending upon the scene. The goal, with this method of soundtrack creation is to base your music on numerical parameters, thus creating an *intelligent* soundtrack that will, in essence, be different every time the player plays the game. The music will respond to the player's actions. The game will act like a conductor, telling the orchestra what to play, and when to play it.

## Finale

The greatest composers, writers, rockers and virtuosos have been using the power of music to enhance our experiences for centuries. Whether it's *Firestarter, Candle in the Wind, Jerusalem,* or *Supercalifragilisticexpialidocious,* music moves us and heightens our emotional responses. Graduations, weddings, and even funerals are set against a backdrop of music to move and inspire us by making things more poignant.

In games, much emphasis has been placed on creating beautiful graphics, but that's only half the thread in the tapestry, music is just as important, and we must use it to deepen and strengthen our games.

"Music expresses that which cannot be said and on which it is impossible to be silent."
Victor Hugo

**Introduction**
chapter 1
chapter 2
chapter 3
chapter 4
chapter 5
chapter 6
Case Study 1
chapter 7
chapter 8
chapter 9
chapter 10
chapter 11
chapter 12
chapter 13
Case Study 2
chapter 14
chapter 15
**Director Afterword**

# Chapter 10 Understanding Artificial Intelligence

# Flash Games Studio

## A Being of Your Own

No sooner than you start getting into game design, you encounter the problem of action and reaction. The preceding chapters have been littered with examples of how to make game characters perform certain actions. But how do we make a reaction? Moreover, how do we create a *complex* reaction?

The most heart- (and gut-) wrenchingly sensitive entities to have come out of the entertainment world in recent times are virtual pets. They mewl and puke until we treat them right, and then they simper and purr. And what is it that makes them such delightful little creatures? What, on the other hand, can make something inanimate **irritating?** The answer is Artificial Intelligence.

Our relationship to pets is a symbiotic one; the better we take care of them, the happier they are and the happier they are, the more joy they bring to our lives. So far, so good — direct, causal functions are easy to translate into code. In the simplest of terms, they take on the form of:

```
if x satisfies y then assign a the value of b.
```

In other words, the fundamental `if/then` statement is executed in one of two ways based on a condition being either `true` or `false`. It would be nice if the rest of this exercise were as straightforward. But it isn't.

Armed with a handful of `if-then` statements, we bring into the world the most perfect pet. It does everything just the way we like it and when we like it. We know for certain that, say, given the yellow milkbone it will fetch us the stick in exactly 30 seconds, whereas the red one will result in a 12.5 second dash. Great. How many times do you suppose you'll click on each of the two buttons? Twice? Once to see that it works and once to show your housemate? Yes, we have just created a sweet, charming and perfectly obedient...robot.

But we can fix that, can't we? We'll just throw a random number into the equation and we'll never know how long it takes it to get the stick. What fun, I say — I think I'll press the button 10 times now. Our pet has just become predictably unpredictable. But is it intelligent? Does it have personality? Can you earn its trust?

**Trust**. Now, there's an interesting idea. Can we really say that trust is true or false? Personally, I find myself saying I trust one client's taste in design *more* than that of another, just as often as I hear myself proclaim complete and unconditional trust or the absence thereof. I also think that a new acquaintance's pet might be willing to let me feed it, once I've earned *enough* of its trust. I don't expect it to happen overnight, but given a week or two, I suspect that it will *grow* to trust me.

All this is fine, but how does one represent *more* and *less* within the binary universe of 1's and 0's ,where the lines of delineation are precisely defined? If we assign a 1 to *complete* trust and a 0 to *no* trust, we suddenly find ourselves without any resources to describe what is happening in between. Where does one draw the line between *near* and *far* when the horizon dividing them is best described as **fuzzy**?

# Crisp vs. Fuzzy Logic

The vast majority of computer technology in existence today, relies on what is variably referred, to as standard, classic, or more recently, in the advent of its fuzzy counterpart, **crisp** logic. Within the realm of crisp logic, membership functions have only two possible values, but the shortcoming can be compensated for by complex mathematical formulae. Where, given the nature of its usage, the average Flash ActionScript may employ grammar school level math, it is possible to apply advanced calculus and trigonometry to crisp logic and control the most complex of processes. But neither higher math, nor crisp logic, are very good about describing our pet's trust. This is where we start cultivating **fuzzy logic**.

The concept of many-valued logic reached maturity in the mid 1960's on the desk of Lotfi Zadeh, a professor of computer science at the University of California in Berkeley. The inventor of fuzzy logic was the first to propose a set theory, which operated on an inclusive **range** from 0 to 1, rather than on the two binary values alone.

In order to explore the idea of a range, let's set the issue of our pet's trust aside for a minute and look at the concepts of **young** and **old** instead. The line dividing the two extremes is just as fuzzy as in the case of trust, but as we all share general notions on age, the example may more effectively illustrate the difference between crisp and fuzzy logic.

If we were to assume, for the sake of the argument, that anyone under 18 is definitely young, anyone over 40 is clearly old and everyone else is somewhere in between, then we'd find ourselves at a loss trying to describe all those between 18 and 40 while relying on crisp logic. Its two-value system would force us to define all ages as either *old*, 1, or *not old* (young), 0. As a result, somewhere at 26 we might find ourselves proclaiming that anyone over that age is *old* and anyone under is *young*. Not exactly a comfort for those of us who didn't make the cut, not to mention grossly inaccurate as a definition.

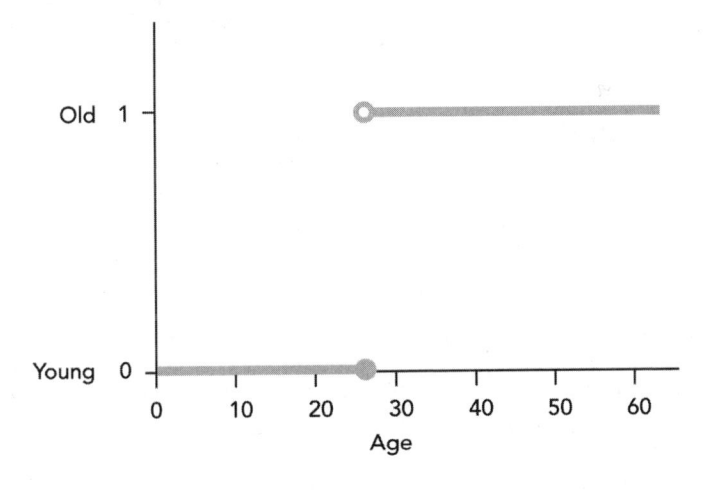

The same concept of age makes a lot more sense if illustrated with the aid of fuzzy logic.

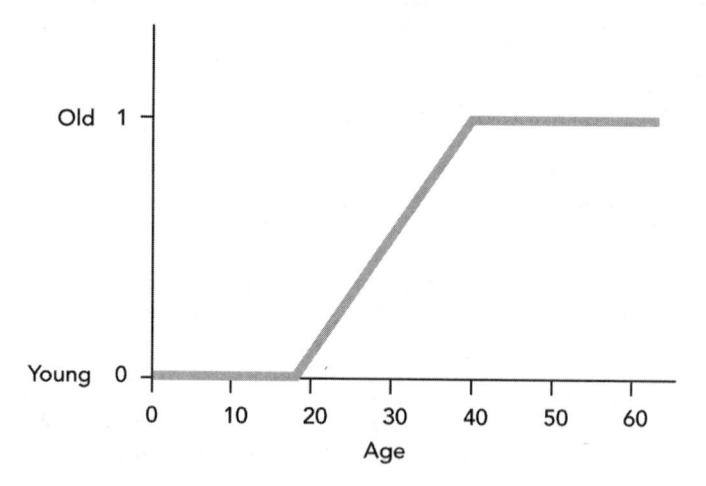

All those in the 18 to 40 age group, crudely designated as either young or old before, can be now described with such precision as 0.217 old or 0.793 young depending on which end of the spectrum you want to assign 1 and which 0. You might argue about the shape of the curve, saying that people below 26, age slower than those over 35, in terms of our common perception of the term *old* and you could convert the straight diagonal into ? of a cosine curve to describe the nuance more accurately, but you are no longer limited to placing people in groups to which they do not comfortably belong.

## Artificial Intelligence

As daunting as it sounds, your first, very basic application of artificial intelligence in Flash is a short hop away once fuzzy logic is introduced into the picture. This is due to the fact that fuzzy logic begins to resemble the way we think. Where crisp logic is very efficient at replicating our thought process in deciding whether something is or is not, say, an orange, fuzzy logic allows us to look at a nectarine and decide how closely it resembles an apple or how distant it is from being a peach.

Let's return to our virtual pet. With fuzzy logic at hand, we are suddenly in possession of a toolkit capable of conceiving a complex, semi-organic organism. The four-legged creature we brought to life earlier is no longer either happy or sad, but somewhere in between and, hmm, let's say, given the near perfect weather, a 0.9 on account of the two stray clouds to the north, as well as a chance of encountering our neighbor's cat, we're likely to have a very pleasant and possibly eventful walk together indeed!

In fact, with the three variables interacting with one another as they do, you're looking at a very modest beginning of what some refer to as a neural network. Who knows, given a couple billion of such fuzzy, interdependent sets your creature may even become self-aware!

# Understanding Artficial Intelligence  10

## Your First Virtual Pet

As I've hinted leading up to this point, the building of an intelligent virtual being consists of setting up a network of fuzzy membership sets. A more complex network will lead to greater non-linear behavior of your creature – more fuzz! I have chosen to illustrate it with a very simple example that will hopefully make you comfortable with the method and perhaps even inspire you to take the idea much further by designing a unique pet of your own.

Let us begin by establishing the premise for our game and defining its rules. The title of our game is *Sugar Monster*. The interface below may help you conceptualize the rules. You may also want to play the game `sugarmonster.swf` to get an even better idea for the relationships we're about to establish.

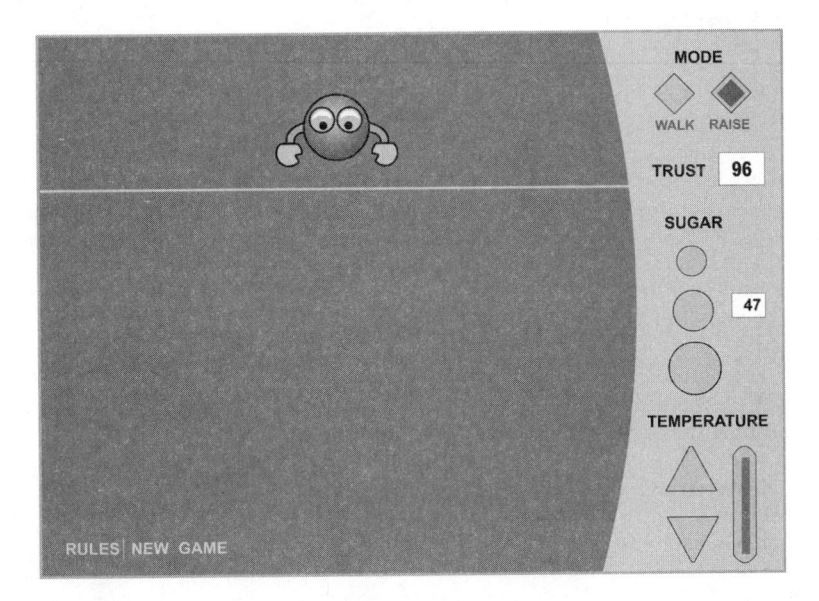

Our first assumption is that, being a pet, the sugar monster acts like one, with the player acting as master. To simulate the act of caring for our little monster, I've made it dependent on high temperature and large doses of sugar, both of which are under the control of the player. The object of the game is to take care of the pet properly and earn its trust so as to be able to take it for a walk and be rewarded by the pet staying close to you, jumping wherever you point your mouse.

The application of master-pet interdependence lies in the fact that in order to earn its trust, players need to make the monster happy. To make it happy, they will need to provide it with the right combination of sugar and temperature. The player will know whether the monster is content, if it jumps above the yellow line drawn horizontally across toward the top of the screen. Each such jump is worth trust points. Each jump that peaks below the line signifies the player's failure to attend to the pet's needs, and reduces the sugar monster's trust.

To complicate matters further and add variation to the game, the temperature is dropping constantly and the height of each jump determines the rate of sugar consumed. The higher the jump the greater the consumption. So as not to make the game too easy for players by allowing them to overfeed the pet, too much sugar can cause the monster to jump so high that it hits its head, so to speak, as it travels beyond the top of the screen. The consequence of such an event is the complete loss of sugar followed by a nearly immediate loss of all trust thus bringing the player perilously close to losing the game.

In the most significant implementation of fuzzy logic in the game, we'll allow the player to try to take the pet for a walk at any time, determining the likelihood of the pet following or abandoning its master based on the trust earned. We'll reward complete trust with absolute fidelity of the pet, while likening the game to real life by still requiring the master to feed it, punishing the failure to do so with a loss of trust, pet and game all in a very quick succession.

## Some Gaming Principles

Next, let us begin assembling the game with an explanation of its setup and structure, as well as the principal mechanics of its engine.

One of the very first aspects of this game that struck me as important is our pet's animation. The monster should not only come alive through interaction with its master, but it should give the appearance of being so at all times. The consequence of failing to provide our creature with a steady heartbeat, as any animator will tell you, is **screen death**. We don't want our little creature to be a corpse. We want to be assured that if we don't look after it, it will clear off and find something better to do of its own accord.

The subject and nature of the animation will dictate much of the structure of the AI engine that will bring our creature to life. The three distinctions between games which became apparent to me while building the sugar monster are games where:

- all movement is pre-animated
- some movement is pre-animated and some created via ActionScript, and
- all movement is created via ActionScript.

If the approach you choose is the first one (a good example being a crying baby made happy with a toy or a bottle of milk), then you know that your engine will consist of a mechanism manipulating either entire movie clips or the position of the playhead in one or multiple timelines.

The opposite of this would be a simple interpretation of a bee which flies around the screen without flapping its wings, where user interaction causes the calculation of different flight paths or subtle changes in the current one. As it stands, sugar monster falls into the second of the above distinctions, with a slight twist of its own.

# Understanding Artficial Intelligence

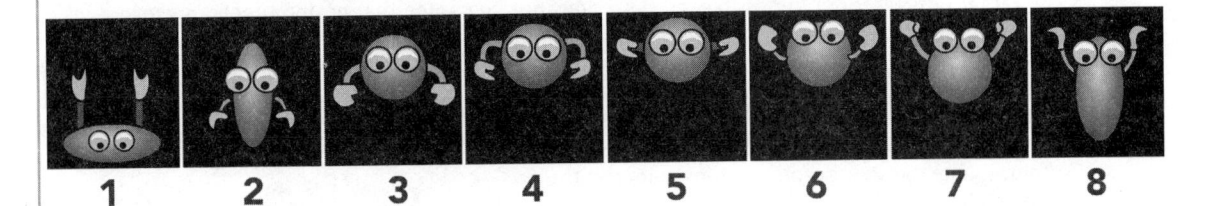

If you look at our pet's animation strip above, you'll notice that the entire animation consists of 8 frames. If you also have had the chance to play the game, you'll know that the strip does not account for the height of the monster's jumps or for the many variations in its horizontal displacement. Both of these factors are animated using ActionScript.

My initial instinct for setting up this game was to create a number of distinct, nested animations placed in separate frames of another movieClip that I'd use as my source for all animated behavior. As I began drawing the second animation, however, I quickly realized that it could be superfluous – after all, to make the game work, I only needed to vary the monster's destination in _x and _y. Subtle differences in the timing of an animation can make a big difference in the end so I tested my idea first.

As I suspected, the best results were to be obtained if each frame's position was calculated separately, stretching the ascent and descent over the total distance traveled. To do so effectively, however, one would have to preserve the ease in and ease out inherent in the original by applying some sort of higher math, perhaps no more complicated than a sine curve. To simplify this example and save myself the headache of arriving at the perfect, but possibly cumbersome solution, I decided to *cheat*.

By sending the whole animation into the orbit of the stage and back again at a couple of well chosen points in the strip, I quickly determined that the illusion of the animation could be well preserved as long as I sent mrGreen, a movie clip instance of the entire animation, to its destination at Frame 2 and brought it back on the ground at Frame 8.

With the key points in the animation identified, the issue then became *how* to control mrGreen. It is easy to send a movie clip to a particular destination on the stage, but much more complex to send it there at a particular time. Since we want the sugar monster in constant motion, in an effort to preserve the illusion of it being alive, the control would have to occur while mrGreen is cycling through its animation.

Under different circumstances, where the animation cycle could be interrupted at any point, any button containing instructions for affecting the environment of the game could be used to pass instructions for relocating our pet. A button for increasing sugar, for instance, could also execute a command calculating mrGreen's new position. Doing so here, however, would disrupt the animation. To preserve it, all actions must take place at the same time as the occurrences of Frames 8 and 2.

One approach, then, would be to match the cycle of the animation to another cycle in which calculations and instructions are executed at the same time. This could be done using timers via a combination of several Date methods or by employing a code loop. The problem with this approach is that to synchronize the events in one timeline with those of another would be still be rather difficult if not impossible, as Flash does not guarantee that nested timelines execute in a timely fashion.

To bypass this shortcoming, I reached for a very simple but effective solution, which relies on mrGreen's own timeline (the second picture below) and the key events in it to relocate the movie clip's position on the stage.

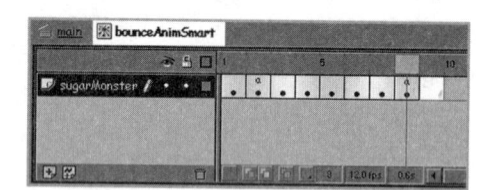

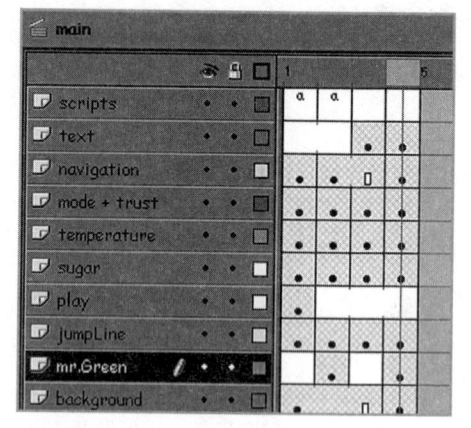

The way I put this method to work is as follows. Rather than constructing a setup in which the main timeline, `_root`, contains the entire game engine and mrGreen becomes its passive puppet, I spread the responsibilities between the two.

Once translated into code, the relationship between the movies can be compared to that of a gun and its trigger. The `_root` is home to 95% of all code necessary to make the game function, while mrGreen simply triggers the execution of that code at strategic moments in its own timeline. Frame 2 in the mrGreen timeline for instance triggers the main engine by calling on the function `adjustSpring` within `_root`, just as the sugar monster leaves the ground. The function calculates the monster's new destination and moves the movie clip, which contains it to that location. Frame 8 also calls on a function within `_root`, called `hitGround`, which ensures that the mrGreen movie clip is returned to the position in `_y` designated throughout the game as the ground.

MrGreen's convenience as a trigger, however, goes well beyond its execution of the function that determines the animation's new destination. Of great use to us is also its timeline's length. Movie clips in Flash cycle automatically unless told to behave otherwise. At only 8 frames long and the frame rate set to a very low 12, the mrGreen cycle executes once every 2/3 of a second. This means that not only can we exploit the interdependence between the two movies to keep the game going through perpetual execution of the animation itself, but that we can assign other cyclical work to the key events such as continuous evaluation of user input and the update of the status displays.

Combined with whatever behavioral algorithms we may wish to assign to various conditions, we bring the game to life and keep it in motion until the occurrence of an event that would stop it such as the player's failure to attain a given number of sugar points or a particular level of trust. At 2/3 of a second, the cycle may be very slow by some standards, impeding high levels of user interactivity, but proves sufficient to make our sugar monster acceptably lively and the user's control effective.

# Understanding Artficial Intelligence

Moving on to the details of _root, the main timeline consists of the four frames, shown. The introductory screen allows users to choose their skill level. The rules screen makes sure we all know what's going on. The game screen gives us the space to play, and the end-of-game screen shows us how unsuccessful we have been!

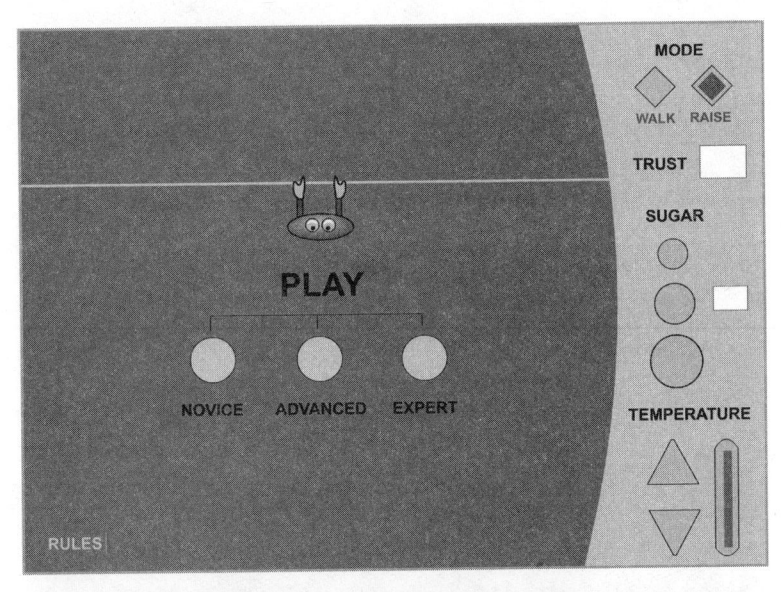

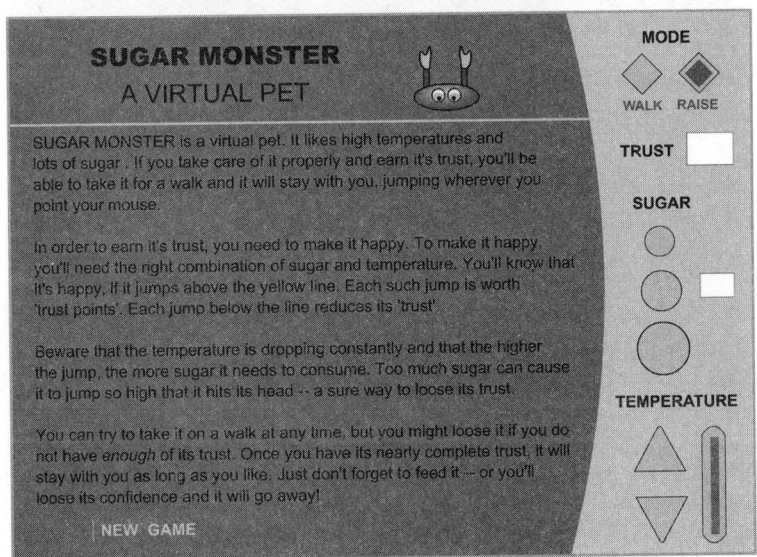

# Flash Games Studio

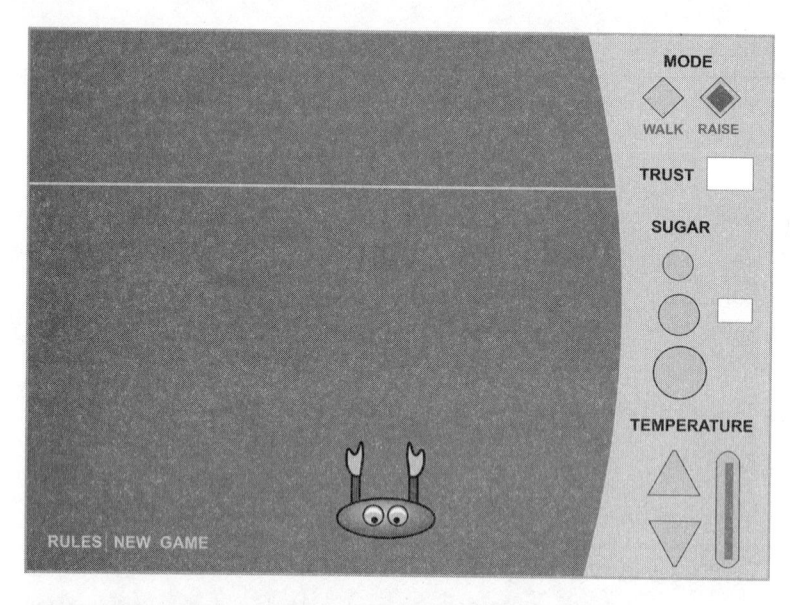

All of these frames could be combined into one with various elements defined as movie clips, and presented on the screen by means of programming, but in some instances, such as this one, this approach may introduce unnecessary levels of complexity and would take longer to set up.

Frames 3 and 4 contain only informational graphics and the player's access to them is facilitated via a `gotoAndStop` command embedded in the web style section navigation on the bottom left of the screen.

# Understanding Artficial Intelligence

Frame 1 contains all of the function definitions and most of the variable initializations, which, once interpreted, are accessible throughout the main timeline, but require a path to _root of the form: `_root.functionName()` if called from another timeline such as the sugar monster's animation. Present in Frame 1 are also 3 simple buttons, which allow the player to choose the level of difficulty by internally setting values for a number of variables, which are then plugged into the game engine at the time of play. The buttons begin the game by advancing our position in the main timeline to *Frame 2*.

Once in the game frame, the program executes a couple of simple clean up commands, ensuring that we start the game in the correct mode, and updating appropriate elements of the status display.

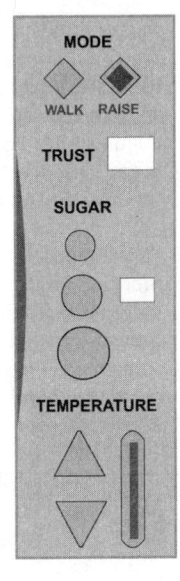

Next, a word about the status display and the user interaction elements of the interface (shown above). The game interface can be divided into 5 areas: the game arena, where our pet leads its quiet albeit exuberant existence, and 4 sets of controls on the left side of the screen used by the player to affect and monitor the pets environment.

All of the controls and status displays operate on that same cycle that we put to use keeping the game in motion in the first place. In other words, all of the variable values, whether generated for the purpose of calculating our pet's behavior or supplying us with information regarding its environment are tabulated once every 2/3 of a second. This translates to a delay of 0 to .666 seconds depending on when in the cycle the particular piece of information is actually stored.

Proceeding from top to bottom of the control strip, we first come across the mode switch used to alternate between the raise mode, in which the pet is first taken care of and where the player acquires trust points, and the walk mode, which enables the player to take the pet for a walk and experience first hand just how much obedience can be coaxed from it. The mode variable stores the two states as either 1, for raise, or 2, for walk, which are then passed on to the function `adjustSpring` where the characteristics of our pet's behavior are determined accordingly.

The mode buttons themselves function in a similar way to radio buttons with the *on* state of one button preempting that of another. The small, darker shaded square (rotated 45 degrees) used to mark the *on* state is a movie clip with an instance name of diamond, and the action of clicking either the raise or walk buttons has the effect of changing its position in _x so as to match the state chosen by the player.

Directly below mode is the trust display, which makes use of a simple dynamic text box to display the value of a variable by the same name. Flash makes this action very easy by allowing us to make the text box dynamic through the Text options dialog window. Changing the text type to **dynamic** from the default **static** and typing in the name of the variable, the value of which we want to appear in the FLA file at runtime, is all that is required.

Most of the user interaction actually takes place over the interface for sugar and temperature. This area contains buttons with corresponding variables in the code named `food` and `temp`. To facilitate a quick method for feeding our pet different doses of sugar, I have equipped this section with three, variably sized round buttons, each containing `on (release)` code instructing it to augment the `food` variable by a different amount. The larger the button, the greater the dose of sugar. The `food` variable, rounded off to the nearest integer, `rndFood`, is displayed in a dynamic text box to the left of the sugar buttons.

The temperature control employs a slightly more complex status display technique in that the mercury inside the thermometer is a movie clip. As the arrows add or subtract from the variable `temp`, the resulting value is then converted into a percentage of the total height of the `merc` movie Clip and its size is adjusted accordingly via `merc._height`. The one trick here is to make sure that the center of the `merc` clip is at the bottom of the strip, otherwise the scaling will occur from the middle giving the impression that the mercury is migrating from both top and bottom at the same time.

The interaction between `food`, `temp` and `trust` in `sugarmonster.fla` is moderately complex as almost every one of the elements participates in determining the value of all others. The rules for this behavior, minus a few exceptions, are generally the same as those described at the outset of this exercise with the equations regulated by the most basic operations of algebra including multiplication, division, subtraction and addition.

At the core of the equations is empirical data I gathered as I wrote the code. The creature I'm about to bring to life, after all, is my own and so the only real rule to defining our pet's behavior ought to be our own imagination coupled with, hopefully, making the game playable by someone other than ourselves. The latter of the two is accomplished through testing high, low and zero values for any variables we may wish to include in our equations in addition to any other limits set by the conditions described in our `if-then` statements.

The last issue I wanted to touch upon before jumping on to code is the application of fuzzy logic. Although the potentials for its usage in this example are many – we could easily take advantage of it to describe our pet's behavior in terms of both sugar consumption and temperature levels – I apply the concept, in its purest form, only in the case of trust, identified as a problem area at the very beginning. To do so, I recruit the services of two variables: `trust` and `fuzzyTrust`.

The first of the two refers to the number of trust points earned by the player. The minimum value for it is 0, the maximum 100. In terms of our earlier example on age, think of `trust` in terms of people's ages. `fuzzyTrust`, on the other hand, has the values of a typical *fuzzy set*, i.e. [0,1] or an inclusive range from 0 to 1. The relationship between the two is very similar to that between age and the term *old* described earlier, where 0 `trust` points corresponds to a `fuzzyTrust` value of 0. 94, or more points translates to a `fuzzyTrust` of 1 with anything in between 0 and 94 `trust` points being partial `fuzzyTrust` somewhere within the 0 to 1 range.

The application of `fuzzyTrust` comes in the way of determining the relative fidelity of the pet. In contrast to crisp logic, where we would have one behavior for the pet with its master's complete trust and one for its lack, `fuzzyTrust` provides for both of these situations as well as a *range* of possibilities inherent in the scale of values from 0 to 1. A `fuzzyTrust` of 1 causes the pet to accompany the player wherever the mouse may be placed, a `fuzzyTrust` of 0 precipitates the end of the game, and a value from 0 to 1 causes the pet to behave with various levels of unpredictability. The closer the player is to a `fuzzyTrust` of 1, the more consistent the behavior.

## Code

The techniques and methods I chose to use in writing the code for this game are very simple. The chances are that if you are even moderately familiar with ActionScript, you won't be surprised by anything you see. But as I see it, there is no reason to complicate things at the possible expense of a misunderstood concept, especially one that you can so easily expand upon on your own.

A couple of other general notes I wanted to mention before getting into the code are the physical location of the code and programming style. The important point in the first case is the practice of gathering all code in the top layer of any frame. By default, Flash draws its layers and interprets the code from top to bottom. The topmost layer takes precedence over the one below it, which itself is interpreted before the one below it and so on. This means that if, for example, you spread out your code over a number of layers and the top layer executes a `gotoAndPlay`, none of the rest of the code sees the light of day.

I am far from saying that you should never place your code in any layer except the top one, merely that you should be aware of what might happen if you do. To avoid any confusion, I usually designate the top layer of any timeline as the script layer and that's where I store all the code.

Somewhat related to the last point is the issue of programming style. Given the simplicity of the program we are about to write, a number of lines of code could have been eliminated for the sake of efficiency still yielding the same numerical results. To do so, however, we'd have to abandon fuzzy logic and solve the problem using one or more elements of what is collectively known as **games theory**, a close relative.

In the most basic terms, the difference between the two approaches consists of the fact that while both begin with multiple membership sets and both end up with multiple values, only the results of fuzzy logic produce fuzzy values or an inclusive range from 0 to 1 that, subsequently, can be combined with other such sets to form a neural network. The good news is that our engine makes use of both methods and you'll be able to see the difference first hand.

From here onwards, the code is presented the same way as you will find it in the example file with all formatting and indentations left intact and annotated by my explanations in the form of expanded code comments.

## _root, Frame 1

We initiate the variables used to display status to fill out the corresponding information in the interface even before the game is begun. `trust` holds trust points, distinct from `fuzzyTrust` explained later, and `rndFood` is the integer version of `food`, used to keep track of sugar levels.

```
trust = 100;
rndFood = 100;
```

The next line initiates the variable used for storing the value of sugar monster's jump in _y. Failure to initialize it here would result in infinity in one of the calculations further down the line.

```
springHeight = 400;
```

These two statements set the temperature level and execute the function adjustTherm responsible for adjusting the level of mercury in the thermometer. I call it here in order to prepare the display while we wait for the player to select a level of difficulty.

```
temp = 100;
adjustTherm();
```

The stop action pauses the playhead until the player selects a level of difficulty thus commencing the game.

```
stop ();
```

adjustSpring is the heart of the game. It determines the values of most of the variables and controls the behavior of the core of the program. It is executed by the second frame of mrGreen, placing the movie clip in its new destination and updating the status display. Argument mode passes the value of the variable mode initialized in Frame 2. The two possible values for the variable are 1, for raise and 2, for walk.

```
function adjustSpring (mode) {
```

Here's where we define the nature of our pet's fuzzyTrust based on a set of numbers collected by the variable trust. For the purpose of this program, I decided to equate any number of trust points equal to or higher than 94 to complete trust, or fuzzyTrust of 1. Any non-inclusive number of these same points between 0 and 94 has the value of trust/94 whereby the division has the function of defining a range from 0 to 1. Finally, 0 trust points amount to a fuzzyTrust of 0.

```
if (trust >= 94){
        fuzzyTrust = 1;
}else if (trust < 94 and trust > 0){
        fuzzyTrust = trust/94;
}else{
        fuzzyTrust = 0;
}
```

As adjustSpring is executed in a cycle, the statement defining the end of the game could go anywhere within the function definition. This particular placement is therefore arbitrary. The method I used for ending the game takes advantage of mrGreen's position in _x to determine whether the game should continue or not. Conditions defined later in the function set up the rules for when mrGreen might find itself thrown beyond one of the two limits stated here, at which point the play head advances to Frame 3 where the game is declared to be over.

```
if (mrGreen._x<-100 or mrGreen._x>500) {
        gotoAndStop (3);
}
```

# Understanding Artficial Intelligence

Trust depletion is a good example of a simple application of *games theory* mentioned earlier. Throughout the game, different factors affect its rate to various degrees and combined they result in something of a matrix of values where a grid of decisions results in a number of possibilities. In this particular instance, I have set up the `trust` points and thus as a consequence, `fuzzyTrust`, to reduce dramatically once the level of `food`, or sugar, falls below 6. The rate of this depletion is also affected by the `gameLevel` i.e. level of difficulty. I round off the result for the purpose of interface display in the end.

```
if (food<6) {
        trust = Math.round(trust/(gameLevel*3));
}
```

pol, short for polarity is just a quick switching device. I apply it later as I build random numbers in order to alternate between positive and negative values.

```
if (pol == 1) {
        pol = -1;
} else {
        pol = 1;
}
```

genRandom constitutes yet another step in my preparation of a random integer. I make use of Math.random in lieu of the random available in Flash 4 and deprecated in version 5 to come up with a decimal between 0 and 1.

```
genRandom = Math.random();
```

The two statements that follow lower the temperature in the sugar monster's environment by multiplying `genRandom` by `gameLevel`, the level of difficulty, and subtracting the result from `temp`'s current value. Executed once every cycle, this has the effect of the temperature constantly falling, with the rate being greater for an expert player than an advanced, which in turn is greater than that of a novice.

```
temp = temp-genRandom*gameLevel;
adjustTherm();
```

This set of `if-then` statements adjusts the rate of food depletion based a number of circumstances. The first branch set tests if we are currently *raising* the pet, `mode == 1` or have less than its perfect `trust`, `fuzzyTrust != 1`. This allows us either to continue the regular rate of depletion or to slow it down to reward the player with complete `fuzzyTrust` with a less troublesome walk.

```
if (fuzzyTrust!=1 or mode == 1) {
```

A subset of the above condition, the next `if-then-else` statement sets a constant for the rate of depletion based on level of difficulty.

```
if (gameLevel>1) {
        rate = .1;
} else {
        rate = .03;
}
```

energyCoeff, short for energy coefficient, combines the rate of depletion with the height of the previous jump springHeigh subtracted from 400, or the _y value for the ground, to produce the grand total of the amount of food to be subtracted from the current value of food.

```
energyCoeff = rate*(400-springHeight);
food = food-energyCoeff;
```

Closing the food depletion set of conditions is the else matching the first test explained earlier where the rate of food reduction is reduced for a trustful master on a walk.

```
} else {
        food = food-1;
}
```

This next collection of conditions means to punish the player for providing the pet with too much sugar by bringing the level to 0 if the amount goes over 100. It also safeguards the food variable from falling below zero.

```
if (food>=0 and food<=100) {
        food = food;
} else {
        food = 0;
}
```

By testing a number of conditions in one statement, the code below manages to accomplish several steps in one. This approach is possible because the conditions share the same results: if found to be true, they all need to set the next springHeight to 400, the ground level, and the food variable to 0. The first condition tests for food being below 1 in order to quickly bring an end to depletion calculations, which might have continued, indefinitely in attempt to reach zero through repeated division.

The remaining two conditions test for mrGreen being either sent too high, as it might happen if the player combines high doses of sugar with high temperature or too low, as it is likely to occur when high variable values in expert mode result in a springHeight below 400.

```
if (food<1 or (springHeight<100 or springHeight>400)) {
        springHeight = 400;
        food = 0;
}
```

Barring the occurrence of one of the exceptional events above, springHeight is calculated using the current temperature and sugar level. The number 25 in the equation just happens to yield good results when combined with the two variables. The idea is to make the variables interdependent and the range of results appropriate for the game. Should you choose to rewrite this equation or create others like it, the key is to test the arbitrary value throughout its range of possibilities. In this instance, for example, you'd want to know what happens when temp and food are both at their lowest and highest values.

```
else {
        springHeight = 400-(temp*(food/25));
}
```

# Understanding Artficial Intelligence     10

The food variable is rounded off to the nearest integer for interface status display.

```
rndFood = Math.round(food);
```

This statement sets the rules for acquisition and depletion of trust. As evident in the first test, trust is calculated under all condition except when the player is in the walk mode with `fuzzyTrust` at a perfect 1. Next, we test for mrGreen having gone over the yellow line: `springHeight<175`. As the _y values in Flash are calculated from the top of the stage, we are in fact testing if mrGreen has gone *below* 175. A positive answer results in trust being raised by 20 with a limit set at 100 by automatically converting any successful jump while the current trust equals or exceeds 80 to the cap. A jump below 175 costs the player one point: `trust = trust-1`, preceded by a provision for keeping trust from falling below 0.

```
if (mode == 1 or (mode != 1 and fuzzyTrust < 1 )) {
    if (springHeight<175) {
        if (trust<=80) {
            trust = trust+20;
        } else {
            trust = 100;
        }
    } else if (trust>=1) {
        trust = trust-1;
    }
}
```

Having plugged `genRandom` into the equation, which lowers `temp`, I reuse the value without a repeated call on `Math.random` in order to come up with the number of pixels by which sugar monster will deviate in _y and, in one particular instance, in _x, each time it jumps. The purpose of this is twofold: it makes the sugar monster appear a little more organic and allows us to relate the level of trust to its on-screen fidelity, in other words, how closely he is going to follow the mouse. We begin the setup by testing the current food level for 5 or above, thus keeping the random behavior out of the calculations if things become critical. We then generate two random numbers for two distinct situations.

```
if (food>5) {
```

First, there is the low random number, `myRand`, to be used if in raise or in walk under a relatively high level of trust: `fuzzyTrust > .8`. Notice also the presence of `pol`, or polarity, which alternates between the number being positive and negative.

```
if (fuzzyTrust>.8 or mode == 1) {
    myRand = pol*(2000*genRandom)*(1/trust);
```

395

# Flash Games Studio

Then, we generate a high random number for *walking* the sugar monster under a low level of `trust`. In practical terms, depending on the exact level of `trust`, this will cause the sugar monster to behave more or less erratically, resulting in the end of the game should the value of the random number place it outside of the end-of-game test boundaries: `_x < -100 or _x > 500` established at the beginning of this function.

```
    } Else {
        Myriad = poll*(20000*Fernando)*(1/trust);
    }
}
```

With the random number generated, we proceed by setting the _y value for `mrGreen` jump. If the jump occurs under walk with `fuzzyTrust == 1`, then we send mrGreen to a loyalHeight or the height where it will meet the cursor of its worthy master. To make certain that mrGreen does not go below the ground level, we set _y to 400 under all circumstances when it might attempt to do so due to a low position of the cursor.

```
if (fuzzyTrust==1 and mode != 1) {
    loyalHeight = _ymouse+50-myRand;
    if (loyalHeight <= 400){
    mrGreen._y = loyalHeight;
    } else {
    mrGreen._y = 400}
```

In all other cases, we set _y to `springHeight` generated earlier.

```
} else {
    mrGreen._y = springHeight;
}
```

Finally, we arrive at the end of `adjustSpring` where we provide mrGreen with an _x value as well as a way of escaping a negligent master. We begin by testing for negligence by asking if fuzzyTrust>0.

```
if (fuzzyTrust>0) {
```

then, if in walk,

```
if (mode != 1) {
```

we place the destination of sugar monster's jump at a random number of pixels away from the cursor in _x, but always away from the interface on the right. The `Math.min` method accomplishes this task for us very conveniently without any `if` statements. Anytime the result of adding _x of the mouse to myRand exceeds 375, the left boundary of the control strip is automatically capped at 375. We also don't need to worry about myRand being the larger or the smaller version as its value was determined earlier based on the current conditions.

```
mrGreen._x = Math.min((_xmouse+myRand), 375);
```

# Understanding Artficial Intelligence

If in *raise*, we simply instill a little life in our pet by varying its position in _x by a small random value also determined beforehand.

```
} else {
        mrGreen._x = Math.min((mrGreen._x+myRand), 375);
}
```

When `fuzzyTrust` falls to 0, a distraught situation indeed, sugar monster leaves its master exit stage left, at the rate of 40 pixels per jump.

```
    } else {
        mrGreen._x = mrGreen._x-40;
    }
}
```

The next function ensures that the sugar monster always hits the ground on the way down from its jump. The function is called from within the `mrGreen` movie Clip, at frame 8, or right at the frame before the sugar monster is shown on the ground.

```
function hitGround () {
    mrGreen._y = 400;
}
```

`adjustTherm` updates the temperature level display by adjusting the `height` of the movie clip `merc` embodied by the red strip of mercury. 71 is the original height of the movie clip and so the function basically calculates its current percentage.

```
function adjustTherm () {
    merc._height = (temp/100)*71;
}
```

Located in this frame, but in object scripts rather than the frame script above, is also the code for the three levels of difficulty buttons. All three take on the form:

```
on (release) {
    gameLevel = 4;
    temp = 70;
    food = 50;
    trust = 50;
    gotoAndStop (2);
}
```

with the variables adjusted accordingly.

## _root, Frame 2

Even though the actual game takes place in this very frame, what little code there is to be found here has to do with housekeeping. The first line makes certain that we start in *raise* in case *walk* was the last mode used, whereas the second line places the mode indicator plate contained in the movie clip diamond on top of the raise button.

```
mode = 1;
diamond._x = 510;
```

stop pauses the playhead leaving the mrGreen movie clip to roam freely and call upon functions defined in _root.

```
stop();
```

## mrGreen, Frame 2

As mentioned before, this is where mrGreen, about to leave the ground, triggers a complete cycle of the game engine determining, among other things, mrGreen's new _x and _y coordinates.

```
with (_root) {
    adjustSpring(mode);
}
```

## mrGreen, Frame 8

And here's where mrGreen is safely returned to the ground.

```
with (_root){
hitGround ();
}
```

# Conclusion

Well, that pretty much wraps it up for our sugar monster. If you play the game you will find him quickly throwing a tantrum at your inadequacies or – if you're really lucky – sucking up to you like a star pupil. More importantly, you hopefully now have a grasp on what it takes to create an artificially intelligent being. From here you can work on developing its personality, and encouraging it to threaten your gameplaying authority!

# Understanding Artficial Intelligence

**Introduction**
chapter 1
chapter 2
chapter 3
chapter 4
chapter 5
chapter 6
Case Study 1
chapter 7
chapter 8
chapter 9
chapter 10
chapter 11
chapter 12
chapter 13
Case Study 2
chapter 14
chapter 15
**Director Afterword**

# Chapter 11
# The Third Dimension

# 11    Flash Games Studio

In this chapter we'll learn how to create the appearance of 3D perspective in our games, to equip them with an added element of depth. This will include advice on achieving illusions of depth, from **parallax scrolling** to the **inverse-square law.** This will all be demonstrated through exercises of extremely playable and aesthetically pleasing games that you can build yourself, without the need for too much processor-intensive math. All the necessary code is included, and explained thoroughly to give you a grounding in producing three-dimensional game worlds in Flash.

## Demand for 3D

For years, the greatest aspiration in the game industry was to take games into the third dimension. People had played enough side-scrollers and top-down games, and they wanted to do more: they wanted to go *in* to the screen. However, the problem was simply the mathematical intensity of fully simulating a 3D world.

Human beings have always longed for the freedom of three dimensions. Yes, I know that we live in a 3D world, but we are still limited in some aspects. For instance birds have total freedom over 3D space. They can go left, right, up, down, forward and backward, making our human movement seem rather limited. As the human mind is not one to graciously accept limitations, we invented ways of leaving the ground and mastering the third dimension of our world. It's this same notion of total freedom of movement that makes 3D so attractive in the context of games.

So, people found ways of making things *appear* to be 3D – a sort of faux 3D. This 3D didn't involve fancy things like axis rotation or a specific z-coordinate (depth) so the techniques had the added bonus of not being very processor intensive, and the math was fairly rudimentary. What are these techniques? This is what we're going to look at in this chapter.

## Minimizing the math

The entire reason that there is such a thing as faux 3D is because real 3D is often too computationally intensive. If you have objects that are pre-drawn to *look* 3D, and in a sense **emulate** 3D, then you have eliminated the math that would actually be required to *render* the objects in real-time. True 3D requires several factors including **scaling**, **rotation**, **translation** and **projection** in order to make them appear correctly on screen.

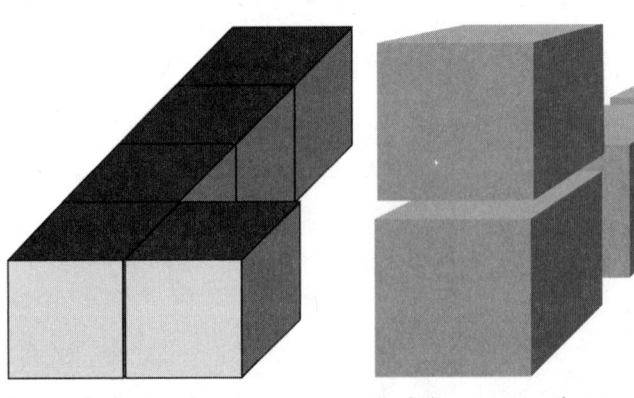

Isometrically pre-drawn          Real-time perspective rendered

# The Third Dimension    11

On the other hand, if you use a graphic that is simply a flat image of an isometric 3D shape then you can copy and position it many times over to produce the effect of a 3D world. Isometric 3D shapes are as simple as merely duplicating a movie clip, and modifying its depth to make it appear in front of, or behind other isometric 3D shapes. More on isometric 3D later.

## Faking it

Let's be clear on one thing first of all: All 3D graphics on a computer screen are "fake". This is simply because the surface of you monitor is flat – a 2D surface. So, any 3D graphics you see on screen are merely representations of objects in 3D space. Technically, the only "real" 3D objects lie in the physical world, and can be viewed only by eye.

Top-down imaginary view of 3D objects inside of screen

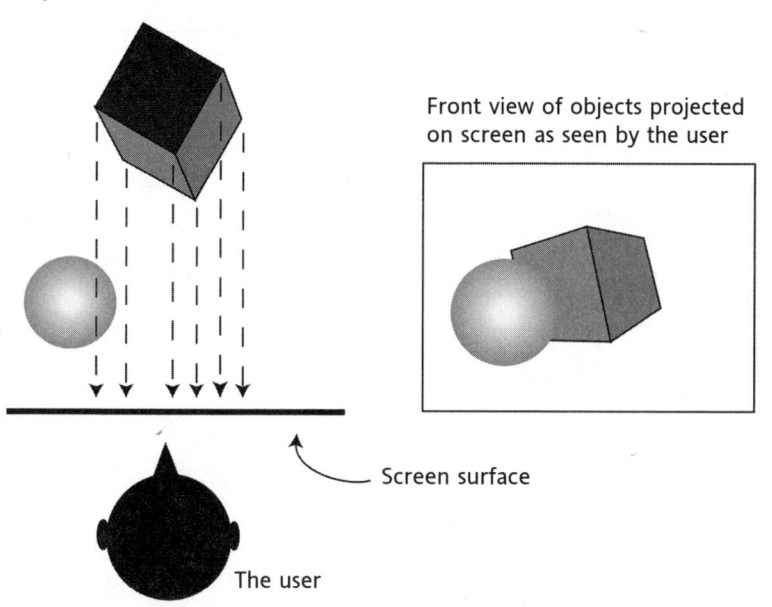

Front view of objects projected on screen as seen by the user

Screen surface

The user

In fact, even our eyes are basically flat surfaces, upon which the images we see are projected. There are three reasons why objects may appear 3D to the eye.

1. **Stereoscopic vision**. Each eye sees a slightly different image because of the fact that they're an inch or so apart. Your brain uses the slight difference between the images to extrude depth – the third dimension.

2. **Focus**. Our eyes are like camera lenses that focus differently on light coming from different distances. This creates an effect known in photography as **depth of field**; objects in front of and behind your area of focus appear blurry. This is another means of measuring the third dimension.

# Flash Games Studio

3. **Perspective**. Objects in the distance appear to be smaller, and move slower than objects in the foreground, which move faster and are larger.

Of course, blurring and perspective can be achieved on a flat screen, but stereoscopic vision requires a more hands-on approach. There are a few systems in existence designed to accomplish this. For example, virtual reality goggles; VR goggles are worn on your head, and consist of two screens – one for each eye. As you play a 3D game, the computer renders a minutely different image in each eye, and your brain believes it is 3D. The greater the difference between the two images, the more pronounced the depth (and hence the 3D) is. Old 3D movies did the same thing with red and blue lenses in a pair of glasses. The image for your left eye was projected on screen in one color, and the image for your right eye in another color. Then, each eye in the glasses would filter out the image that was the same color as the lens, and voila, your eyes would see two different images.

## Layering and Parallax Scrolling

This is all great in theory, but not very practical for making games in Flash. So how else can we accomplish faux 3D? Well, we can always use the principal of farther objects moving slower (and being smaller) than closer objects.

This is a technique known as **layering** or **parallax**. To accomplish this you must create several layers of graphics, and then move each at a different rate.

In `demo11-1.swf`, you will see that I've created a simple parallax demonstration that utilizes the following techniques to create the impression of depth:

- Objects get relatively smaller as they get farther away.

- When the screen is scrolling, the objects that are farther away move much slower than the objects that are up close.

- Objects get darker, or dim, as they get farther away.

# The Third Dimension     11

There are five layers of depth in this demo,

- The closest and largest layer of trees
- The middle layer of trees. Slightly darker, moving slightly slower.
- The back layer of trees. These are the darkest and they move the slowest
- The clouds. This layer moves the slowest.
- The mountains in the background. This layer does not move.

> *Be sure not to get layers in this demo confused with Flash's concepts of levels and depths – they're different things altogether.*

To operate the demo, simply move the mouse around. The white circle (the eye) will move around the small image that depicts the mountains (called the *navbox*). This is the navigation window and as you move the eye the whole scene will scroll in full parallax.

This is quite effective at creating depth, and it is easy to accomplish. The main stage consists of several layers of objects, called layer_1 to layer_4. The background image is stationary.

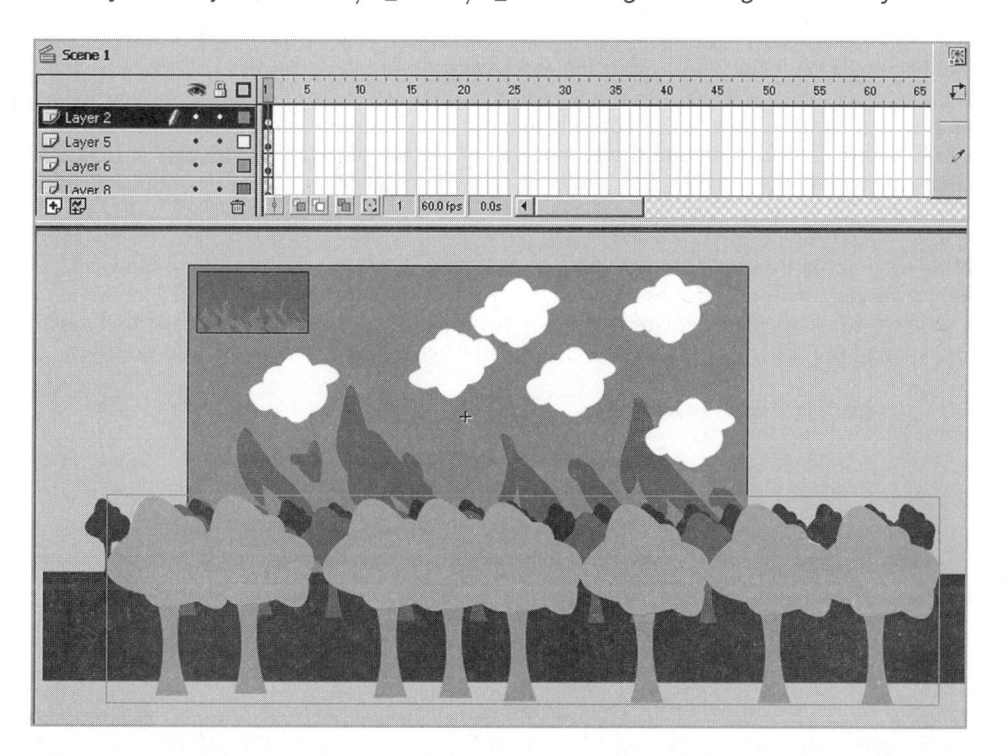

405

# 11  Flash Games Studio

There is a movie clip on the main stage called controller, which simply initializes the following code on load up:

```
onClipEvent(load)
{
        // Set the width of the navbox mini window
        _root.navbox._width = 110;
        _root.navbox._height = 60;

        xoff = _root.navbox._x;
        yoff = _root.navbox._y;

        // Start dragging the eye.
        startDrag(_root.eye, true, xoff, yoff, _root.navbox._width +
        ➥ xoff, _root.navbox._height + yoff);

        // To help the fullscreen graphics
        _quality = "MEDIUM";

}
```

The main thing this code does is start the mouse dragging the eye, set the _width and _height of the navbox, and constrain it to the area of the navbox. The size of the navbox is important because it determines how far we'll be able to move around our imaginary world. In this example, 110x60 allows us to pan around pretty much all of our world. Because the graphic changes are almost full screen, the program sets rendering to medium quality mode to allow the computer to draw a little bit faster.

Inside each of the tree layers (layer_1, layer_2 and layer_3), are several instances of the tree movie clip, and each of these movie clips contains another movie clip called treeframe. This is simply a two-frame movie, which consists of a different type of tree on each frame. At the beginning of the program, the following code (attached to each tree movie clip) executes:

```
onClipEvent(load)
{
        // Grab a random frame from 1 or 2
        fm = Math.floor(Math.random() * 2) + 1;

        // Go to that frame (choose between the 2
        // available trees)
        gotoAndStop(fm);

}
```

This randomly chooses the tree on frame 1, or the tree on frame 2. Using the Math.random command, we're creating a random number between 0.0 and 1.99, so by flooring it we force it to be *either* 1 *or* 0, and then we add 1 to the total to make it 1 or 2 – it's a frame number after all,

# The Third Dimension

and there is no such thing as frame 0. I'm doing this to create some variation in the forest. You can add as many different types of tree as you want, and just change the 2, to another number – if you had 10 choices of tree, you would simply write:

```
fm = Math.floor(Math.random() * 10) + 1;
```

When you draw your layers for parallax scrolling, it's important that you keep the center points of the layers lined up. If you don't do that, then some pretty strange parallax scrolling can occur. This is because when you run the program, the layers will be scrolled relative to the position that you placed them on screen. Also, in this example the only thing that made the distant trees smaller was my hand. I drew them smaller as they got farther away. In the next chapter, I will talk about how this scaling is accomplished via ActionScript, in true 3D.

Finally, the most important piece of code is attached to the eye movie clip:

```
onClipEvent(enterFrame)
{
    // Translate the eye's position into a world
    // coordinate for parallax scrolling.
    cx = _x - (_root.navbox._width / 2) - _root.navbox._x;
    cy = _y - (_root.navbox._height / 2) - _root.navbox._y;

    // Tree layer 1
    _root.layer_1._x = (-cx * 5) + 225;
    _root.layer_1._y = (-cy * 5) + 150;

    // Tree layer 2
    _root.layer_2._x = (-cx * 3) + 225;
    _root.layer_2._y = (-cy * 3) + 150;

    // Tree layer 3
    _root.layer_3._x = (-cx * 2) + 225;
    _root.layer_3._y = (-cy * 2) + 150;

    // The clouds
    _root.layer_4._x = (-cx * .5) + 225;
    _root.layer_4._y = (-cy * .5) + 150;
}
```

Simply put, this looks at the position of the eye relative to the navbox, and from that it calculates the relative positions of all the layers. Then, it adds 225 to each _x and 150 to each _y. This simply moves the layer to the center of the screen, because everything is centered around (0, 0), which is the upper left corner of the screen. We want (225, 150) to become the actual center of the screen.

You'll notice that each layer's position is being based on the cx and cy variables. In fact, to be more specific, they're being based on –cx and –cy. This is because we want the screen to scroll the opposite direction of the eye. So, when you move the eye to the left, the layers should move to the right. Finally, in each layer -cx and -cy are being multiplied by a specific number from 5

# 11  Flash Games Studio

(layer 1) to 0.5 (layer 4). It's this number that determines our parallax. The lower the number, the slower the layer will move, hence the further away it will appear.

That's it! Move the mouse around and your whole screen will move in a very impressive display of parallax scrolling.

## Pre-rendering

There are many software packages out there today that excel at creating 3D graphics and animation. These programs can do anything from design cars to make full feature length Hollywood movies. How do we take advantage of their power and versatility in Flash? Well, we simply pre-render our 3D images and then bring them into Flash. Using this method, we can give Flash the appearance of having full 3D support – meanwhile our images are merely 2D vector representations of a 3D image.

There are several ways to use pre-rendered 3D images in Flash:

1. Rendering a single image of a 3D object. Using this method, we simply create a sprite that is clearly a 3D object. This would be used like any other image in Flash.

2. Rendering several snapshots of an object that is animated doing a specific action, like rotating. Using this method, we can place an object on screen and it will appear to be 3D as it rotates in place, or we move it around the screen.

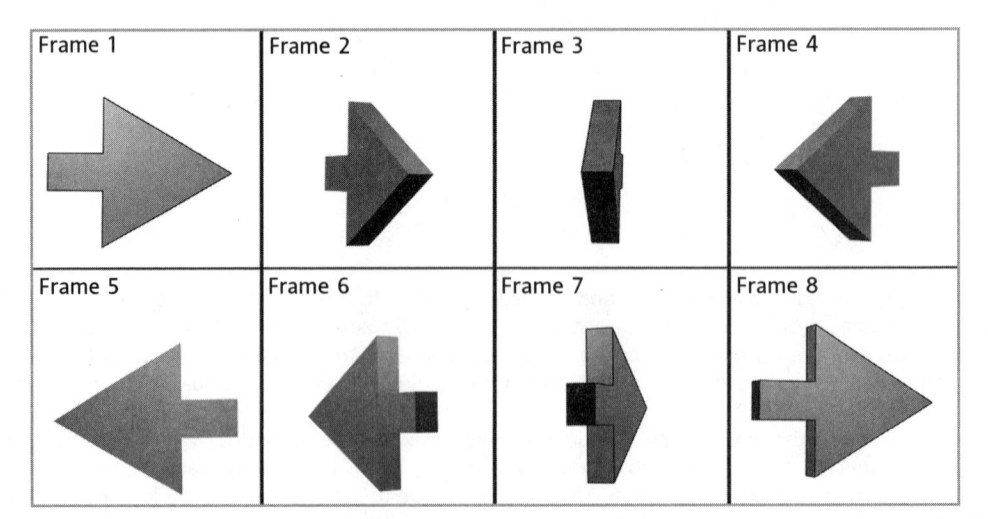

# The Third Dimension

3. Carefully rendering many different angles of an object across a logical number of frames to correspond to an angle. For example, if you rendered a cube from every angle around 360 degrees, then you could use the actual frame number to correspond to an angle. If you were looking at the cube from a 45-degree angle, then you'd set the cube to frame 45. This form of rendering is somewhat like the arrow shown previously, except with much more minute differences and with many more frames.

4. Another method, which is a very simple form of pre-rendering, is to use gradients. Take for example a circle with a radial gradient applied to it;

    This circle takes on the appearance of a 3D sphere simply because of the lighting tricks that are played.

## Getting it into Flash

There are several ways of bringing pre-rendered 3D images into Flash. What we choose depends entirely on the complexity of the task, and the desired file size. Some of it can be done without the aid of external software, and some is better done with it. Either way, you can mix and match to what which results you prefer.

## Keeping it Simple

You can simply draw your 3D image straight in Flash. This requires a good visual sense of how 3D objects look, but it can usually be done quite adequately with shading and perspective.

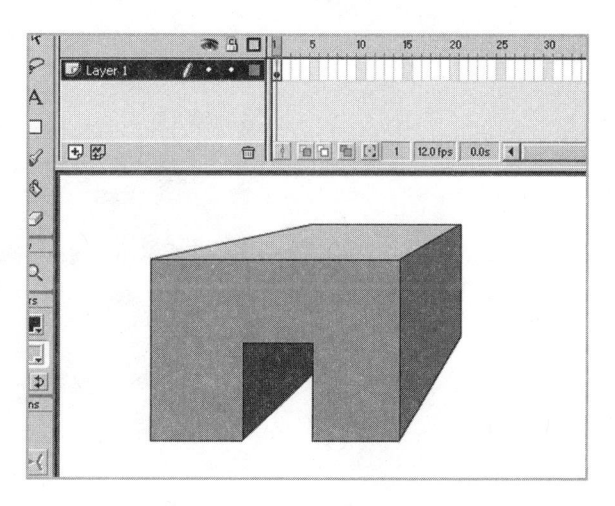

# 11   Flash Games Studio

The problem with drawing 3D objects by hand is that it becomes quite tedious to draw enough frames to create a sustained animation.

If you have a 3D bitmap image, you can bring it into Flash and trace it – effectively convert it into vector line data. You might want to do this if you have rendered your images in a 3D software package that can only export bitmaps.

There are two ways of tracing an image in Flash:

- **By hand**. This means we simply lock your image on one layer and draw over the top of it on another layer, carefully recreating the image in a vector form. This method is good because it allows you to control the complexity of the final vector image, thus saving memory and increasing processor speed.

   This method is also good if you can't draw the objects yourself from scratch. However, it can be extremely long and tedious, as I proved to myself by tracing the truck below.

# The Third Dimension 11

- **Trace Bitmap. Using Flash's** Trace Bitmap can be effective at converting a 3D bitmap into a 3D vector image. The only tradeoff is that the trace tool is not as intelligent as a hand trace, so it tends to produce more curves, a larger file size and slower performance. My manually traced image of the truck was 400 curves; Flash's automatic trace produced over 5,000 curves.

## More Complicated Methods

By far the best solution available is to use a 3D program that has the ability to output a vector version of your final rendered 3D image. While most large-scale rendering packages like **3D Studio Max**, **Lightwave**, **Maya** and **Strata 3D** output their images as pixel-based bitmaps, programs like **Swift3D**, **Vecta3D**, **Amorphium** and **Xara 3D** can output images that are rendered not as pixels, but as vector line information (in the form of an SWF) that can be pulled directly into Flash.

The spaceship below is shown in its initial 3D environment (here, in Swift 3D), and then in its Flash-imported state.

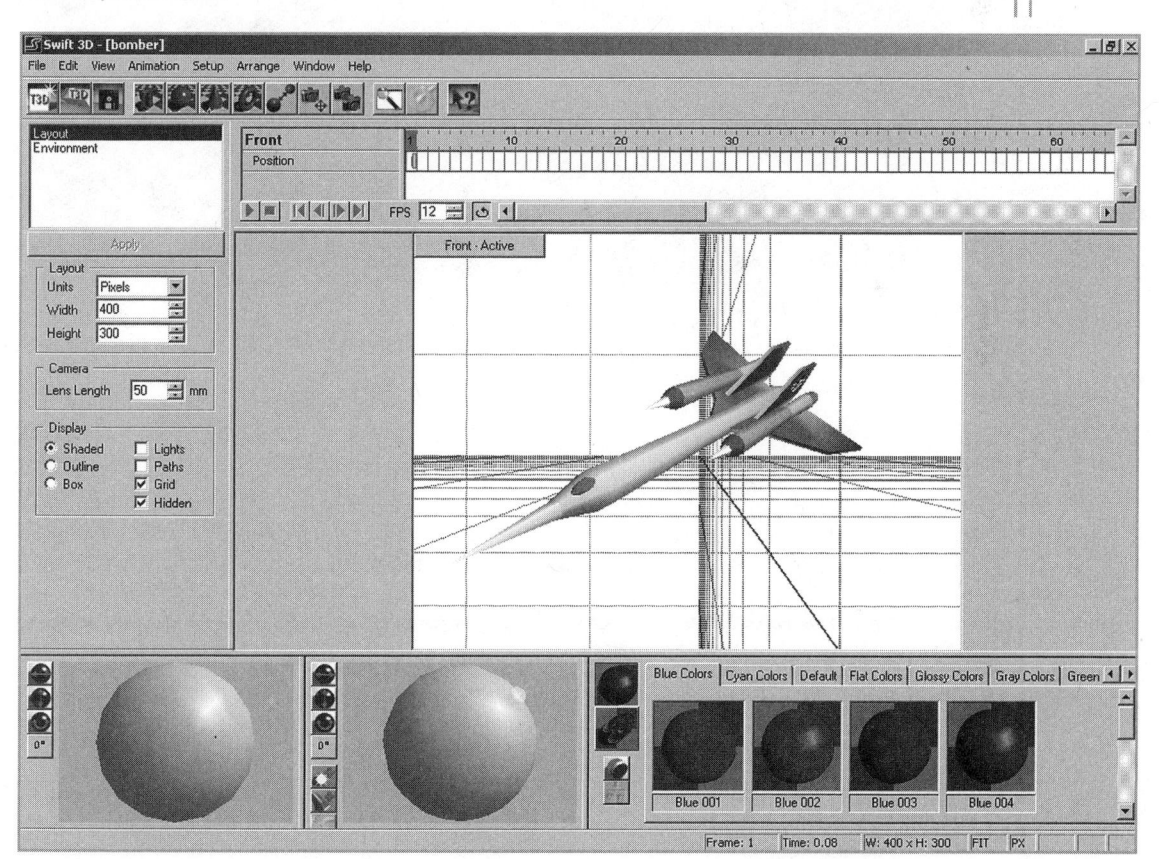

# Flash Games Studio

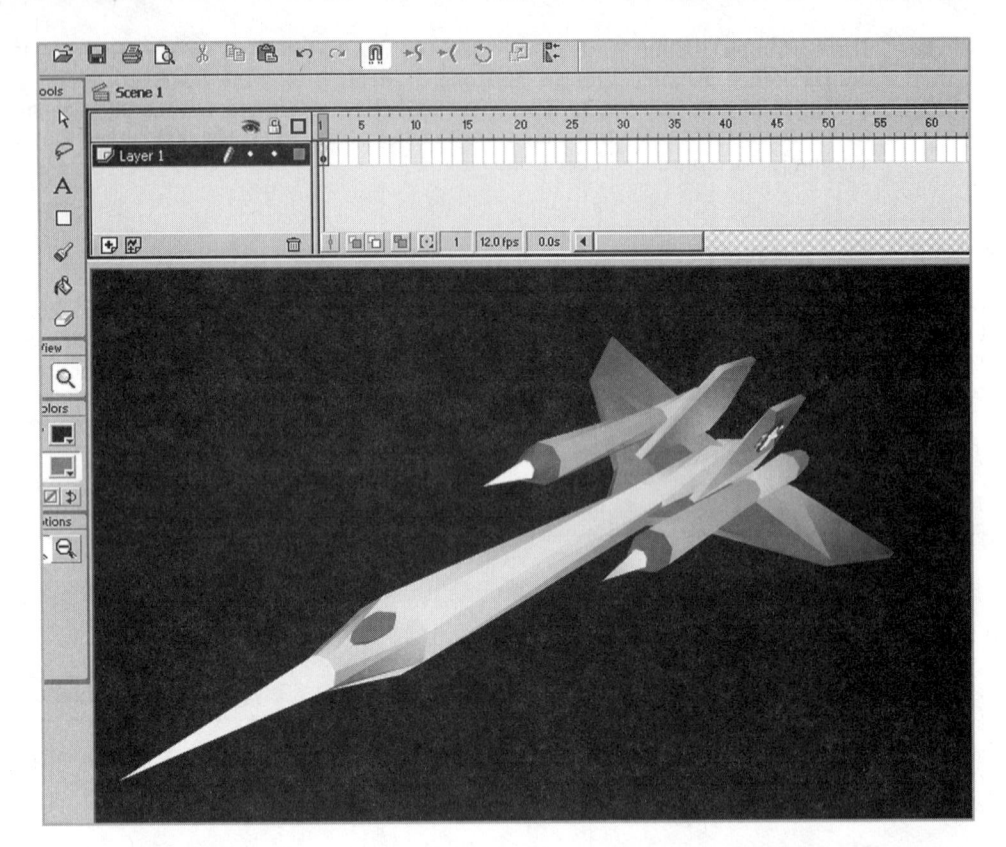

As you will be aware by now, the vector-based method has the advantage of being highly efficient, as the render engine is good at including only necessary lines and information, producing the best looking results.

## Lighting and shadow

One of the most effective techniques for creating the illusion of 3D is to use lighting and shadows. More specifically, this includes the use of less than 100% alpha black shapes to produce shadows, and less than 100% alpha white shapes to produce highlights.

Light and shadow is extremely effective in producing depth because of the fact that things get darker as they get further away. Shadow is also used to make an object look like it is part of a 3D scene by making it cast shadows on the ground.

### Shine and flaring

Take a look at `demo11-5.fla` and you'll see how easy it is to produce dozens of cool effects that add professional lighting touches to any scene. In this demo, the scene is built of up several objects that are all responding to the sun, through a series of mathematical conjuring tricks. We'll convince them of 3D yet!

# The Third Dimension    11

When you run the demo, you'll see the sun rise and set on a continuous arc. As this happens, all the different lighting and shadow effects will happen based on the sun's position. You can also click on the sun and start dragging it around to any position on screen. Clicking again will start it back on its arc.

The light from the sun produces a lens flare (which is a simulation of how light hits the various lenses in a camera), changes the color of the sky, brightens and darkens the ground and casts a shadow of the tree. A lens flare effect is achieved by simple creating a semi-transparent circle, which follows a mirror image copy of the central light source's location.

## Creating our movie

So, in our example, let's look at the code attached to one lens flare circle. To help you find items on the stage, try clicking on the outline view square – it's at the top of the timeline next to the lock layers icon. Here's the code:

```
onClipEvent(load)
{
    // A random scale value from -1 to 1
    scale = (Math.random() * 2) - 1;

    // Scale the circle in size by s
    s = (Math.random() * 90) + 10;
    _xscale = s;
    _yscale = s;
}
```

*continues overleaf*

# Flash Games Studio

```
onClipEvent(enterFrame)
{
    // Calculate the sun's distance from
    // the centre of the screen
    sunoffx = 275 - _root.sun._x;
    sunoffy = 200 - _root.sun._y;

    // Move the flare to the opposite
    // side of screen centre, multiplied
    // by a scale
    _x = (sunoffx * scale) + 275;
    _y = (sunoffy * scale) + 200;

    // Is the sun behind an object? If so
    // Hide the lens flare
    if (_root.sun.hitting)
         _visible = false;
    else
         _visible = true;
}
```

So, let's take that apart.

1. The first thing we do is randomly calculate a number called `scale`, which ranges from −1 to +1. This number determines how far along the reflecting axis the circle will sit, as demonstrated in the screenshot. A value of 1 will place the circle an equal distance from the screen center as Sun . A value of −1 will be directly over top of Sun. Any other value in between will place the circle a percentage of the way along the reflecting axis.

2. Next, we randomly resize the circle.

3. Within the `onClipEvent(enterFrame)` we simply calculate the position of the circle relative to the position of the sun, multiplied by our scale. If the sun passes behind an object (like a tree) then the lens flare disappears, as would real life lens flare.

Lens Flare Lighting Effect

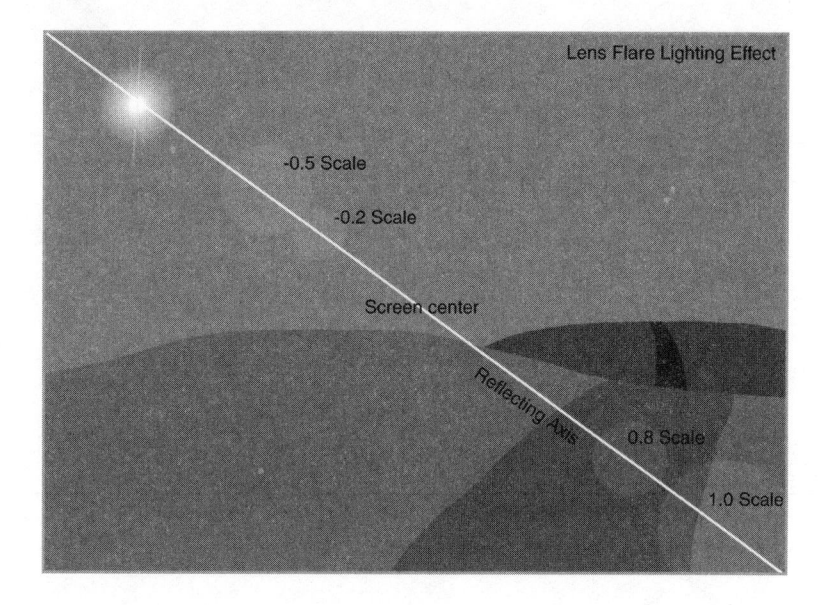

-0.5 Scale
-0.2 Scale
Screen center
Reflecting Axis
0.8 Scale
1.0 Scale

4. The next lighting effect is the shadow of the tree. To compute this we simply take the angle of the tree/shadow base and the sun. The following code is inside the `enterFrame clipEvent` of the shadow movie.

```
dx = _root.sun._x - _x;
dy = _root.sun._y - _y;

ang = Math.atan2(dy, dx);

_rotation = (ang * (180 / Math.PI)) + 270;
```

This simply makes the shadow face the opposite direction of the sun (270 degrees from the angle *to* the sun – 90 degrees to make the shadow lay sideways, and then 180 degrees to make it opposite the sun), making the light source appear to move.

The shadow is a solid black shape that has a low percentage alpha. This way, the ground is still seen through it, but it can be moved freely. We use the `Math.atan2` function to return the angle between two sides of a right-angled triangle, where `dx` is the base and `dy` is the height. By looking at the x distance and the y distance between the shadow and the sun, we have the bottom and side of a triangle. Then, the returned angle (which is measured in Flash's preferred unit of **radians**) is converted to degrees and the `rotation` property is set.

## 11  Flash Games Studio

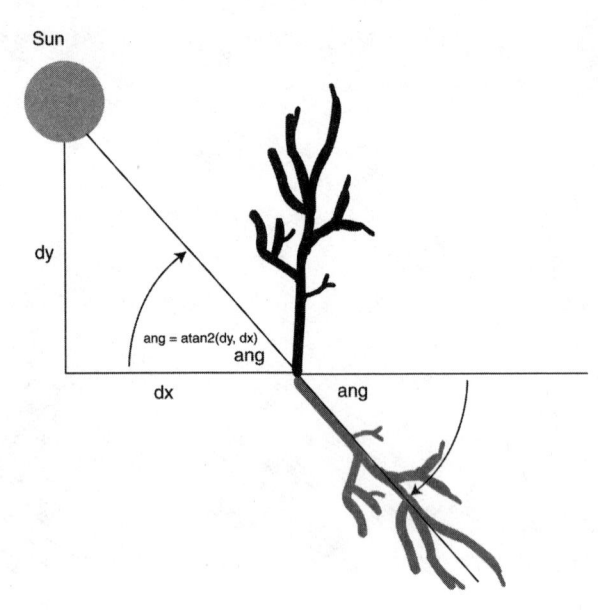

*[Diagram: Sun casting shadow on tree, with labels "Sun", "dy", "dx", "ang", and formula "ang = atan2(dy, dx)"]*

5. Once the `rotation` is set, the `yscale` of the shadow is set with:

   ```
   _yscale = _root.sun._y;
   ```

   The line above makes the shadow grow longer, as the sun lowers across the screen, just like in real life where the setting sun makes the shadows long and thin.

6. The tree is created as a movie clip, called `object` in our demonstration. Obviously you don't have to draw a tree if you have a particular aversion to them, or would simply prefer something else. However, the tree produces some impressive lighting effects.

7. Now, the cool thing is how the shadow is done: The shadow is simply another instance of `object`, which is rotated, and the color object is used to make it solid black, with a low `alpha` setting. The shadow is colored using the code below:

```
onClipEvent(load)
{
    cl = new Color(this);

    colorTrans = new Object();
    colorTrans.ra = 0;
    colorTrans.rb = 0;
    colorTrans.ga = 0;
    colorTrans.gb = 0;
    colorTrans.ba = 0;
    colorTrans.bb = 0;
    colorTrans.aa = 30;
```

```
            colorTrans.ab = 0;

            cl.setTransform(colorTrans);

            b = 100;

            // Reverse the reflection so the shadow matches
            _xscale = -50;

    }
```

What we are doing here, aside from correctly setting the parameters, is simply making the color black, and setting an alpha of 30%. With this, our object will automatically cast an accurate shadow of the tree in the appropriate direction, and on the same axis as the sun and the object. This means that no matter what you draw in object, it will cast a realistic and correct shadow on the ground. Now that's impressive!

Our line _xscale = -50; is also an important addition in the code above. This will reverse the horizontal direction of the shadow so that it matches the tree. The fact that I've used the number 50 is because I want the shadow to be only 50% as wide as the tree. This is simply an aesthetic choice, and I feel it looks convincing.

# Manic Bounce

After that example, let's look at how pre-rendered 3D images can be seamlessly used in Flash in the context of a game. I've created a simple game called *Manic Bounce*. The complete game can be found in demo11-4.fla or demo11-4.swf.

# 11    Flash Games Studio

The object of our game is to keep the bouncing ball from falling off the bottom of the screen. There are three blocks on the screen that can be dragged either up or down with the mouse. Simply click on the box, drag it, and let go. The purpose of the blocks is to provide solid ground upon which the ball can bounce. The longer you keep the ball alive, the more points you get. Sounds easy, doesn't it?

There must be more to it than that, and there is…

Firstly, each block will very slowly sink once you let go of it. This means that you can't place them and leave them, you must keep them from sinking off the bottom of the screen otherwise you'll lose them. The more successful bounces you get, the faster the blocks sink, so keeping an eye on all three becomes quite a challenge. Combined with this is the fact that the more successful bounces we achieve, the faster the ball will bounce. This makes things increasingly challenging!

The 3D effect here has been achieved with the use of pre-rendered 3D blocks, and a gradient-filled sphere. I have also used colored lighting to give vertical sense of depth. Everything appears to be lit from the bottom with a red glow – as if a fiery pit lurks below, awaiting the unsuccessful player.

## Game creation

1. To begin with we must produce the necessary game components, and in this case our first task is to render the block. As our block is to appear 3D we must create several images of it at different angles, to enable us to achieve the effect of the screenshot. Try creating about eleven images of it (our example used 3D Studio Max, but any other 3D package would provide an accurate rendering), starting at a -25 degree angle, and rotating the block by 5 degrees until we have an image of the block at +25 degrees.

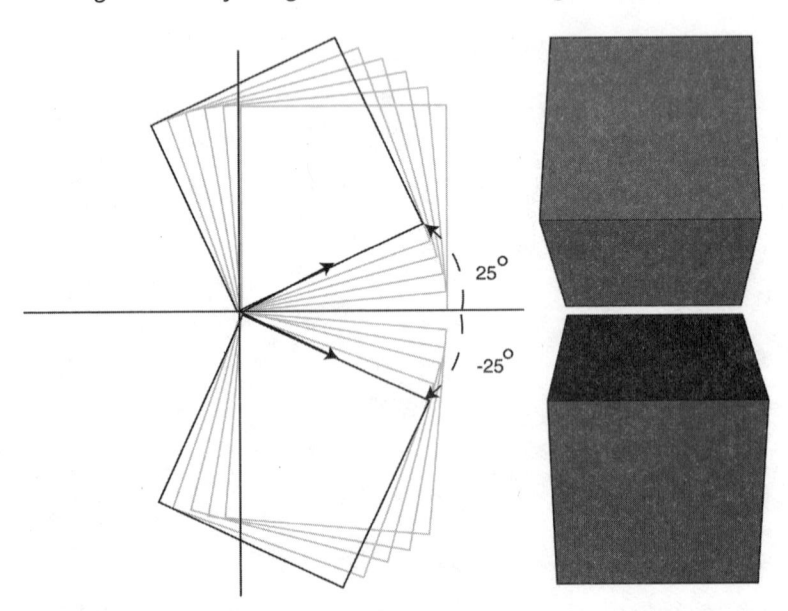

# The Third Dimension | 11

2. Next, bring the block into Flash (our demonstration used a series of bitmaps, exported from Studio Max as .PNG images) and place each bitmap in a separate frame. Because of the simplicity of the images, it is possible to use Flash's bitmap trace tool and still achieve very simple graphics. Make this 11-frame animation into its own movie clip called 3dbox.

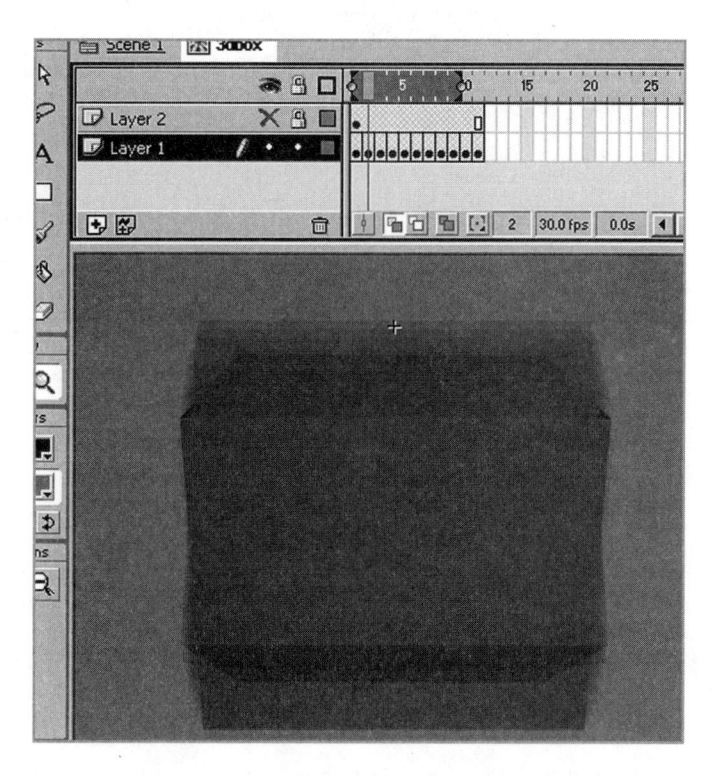

3. Next, create a ball on the stage, filled with a gradient to make it look 3D. Convert this ball into a movie clip and call it (you guessed it) ball. Place it on the stage and name its instance ball as well. Create two **text fields** on the main timeline, making them **dynamic text**, and give them the names lives and score.

4. Now, in order to take advantage of the 3D effect on the box, we have to create some code that uses a logical way to set the current frame of the box, based on its _y location on screen. The higher up on screen it is, the more of the bottom you want to see; the lower on screen it is, the more of the top you want to see. This is achieved with the following lines of code:

```
offy = (_y / 400) * 11;
frm = Math.floor(12 - offy);
gotoAndStop(frm);
```

As you can see, because the screen is 400 pixels in height, we can divide _y into 400, and get a percentage. Multiplying that by 11 gives us a number between 0 and 11. The computer then subtracts that number from 12, rounds down and is left with a frame number from 1 to 11. Though this all sounds a little complex mathematically, all it achieves is to select the appropriate image of our 3D block. We tell the computer to `gotoAndStop` on that frame. This method could work with any number of frames.

5. Place an instance of the movie clip 3dbox on the stage, and call it box1. Attach the following code to it:

```
onClipEvent (mouseDown)
{
    // Check to see if the mouse was pressed down over
    // this cube, if so, start dragging it

    // drag is restrained to vertical strip at _x
    if (hitTest (_root._xmouse, _root._ymouse, true))
        startDrag (this, false, _x, 0, _x, 400);
}

onClipEvent (mouseUp)
{
    // Mouse is released
    stopDrag ();
}
```

This will allow the user to click on the block and drag it to a new location. When they press the mouse button, Flash checks to see if the cursor is over the block, and if it is, begins dragging the block along a strict vertical line. This line ranges from 0 to 400 along _y, which is the height of the screen, though the _x position of the block stays constant. When the mouse button is released, the dragging stops.

6. Finally, add the following code to box1:

```
onClipEvent (enterFrame)
{
    // Calculate which frame of the square to display
    // from 1 to 12;
    offy = (_y / 400) * 11;
    frm = Math.floor(12 - offy);
    gotoAndStop(frm);

    // We must move the box forward in front of the ball if we
    // are looking at the box from the bottom, behind the ball
    // if we are looking at it from the top. This is vital for 3D
    // depth.
    if (frm <= 5)
        this.swapDepths(9);
```

## The Third Dimension

```
         else
                this.swapDepths(99);
        // Check to see if the cube hit the ball
        // by looking at the collisionbox object on the cube
        if (_root.ball.hitTest(collisionbox) && _root.ball.dy > 0)
        {
                // Move the ball to the top of the box
                _root.ball._y = _y - (_root.ball._height / 2);

                // Change the ball's y velocity (dy) to go upwards
                _root.ball.dy = -Math.abs(_root.ball.dy);

                // Add score based on ball's x velocity
                _root.myscore += Math.round(Math.abs(_root.ball.dx)
                ➥ * 10);
                _root.score = _root.myscore;

                // Increase the ball's x velocity
                _root.ball.dx *= 1.2;
        }

        // Make the block slowly sink
        // sinks faster as the ball speeds up
        // careful not to lose the block!!
        _y += Math.abs(_root.ball.dx) / 15;

}
```

This is all the code required to make the block work in our game, and we'll come back to it shortly when the rest of our components have been created. If you look at it, you'll see that it's checking for collision with the ball using something called `collisionbox`.

7. To create `collisionbox`, we must edit the 3dbox movie clip by adding another layer above the 3D images. In this layer, place a rectangle that covers the upper part of the square, as shown overleaf:

# Flash Games Studio

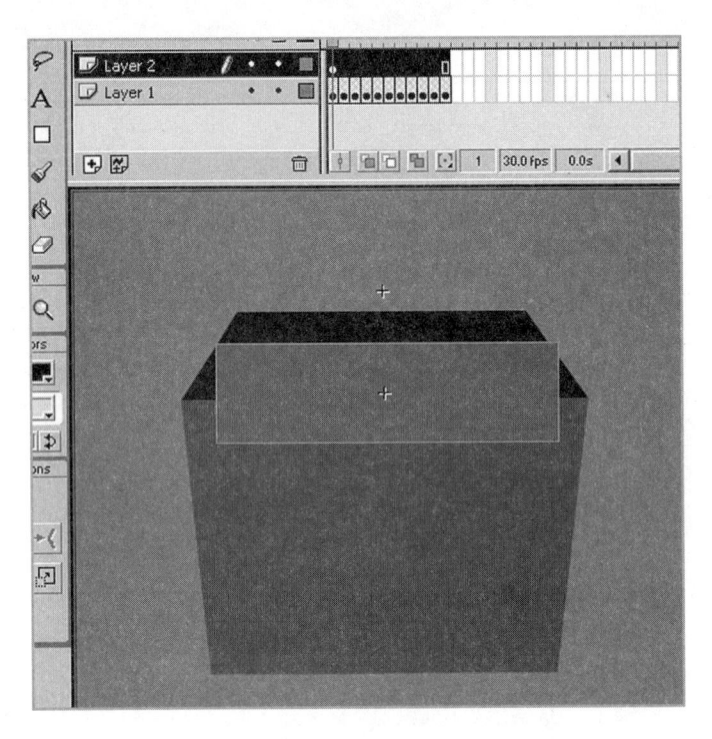

The rectangle in this image is simply a movie clip with the instance name `collisionbox`. Flash will check to see if the ball has collided with our 3dbox by performing a `hitTest` with `collisionbox`. This is necessary because the entire 3dbox is too inaccurate for collision detection; we only want the ball to bounce off the top of the box, not the sides.

8. We also need to add the following code to `collisionbox`, simply to ensure it is not visible during the game.

```
onClipEvent(load)
{
     _visible = false;
}
```

9. If we look at the code again we can see that a lot of reference is made to `_root.ball`. This is, of course, the ball we drew earlier. Go back to the stage and add the following code to `ball`:

```
onClipEvent (load)
{
     // Set up stuff, score, lives, etc.
     dx = 3;
     dy = 0;
```

```
        livesleft = 5;
        _root.lives = livesleft;

        _root.myscore = 0;
        _root.score = 0;

        // Place in middle depth.
        this.swapDepths(50);
}

onClipEvent (enterFrame)
{
        // Move by dx and dy
        _x += dx;
        _y += dy;

        // Gravity, increase dy
        dy += .1;

        // Hit the edge of the screen and bounce
        if (_x > 550)
        {
                _x = 550;
                dx = -Math.abs(dx);
        }
        else if (_x < 0)
        {
                _x = 0;
                dx = Math.abs(dx);
        }

        // Ball falls off bottom of screen
        if (_y > 410)
        {
                // Any lives left?
                if (livesleft > 0)
                {
                        // Decrease lives
                        livesleft --;
                        _root.lives = livesleft;

                        // Give ball new location and trajectory
                        dir = Math.floor(Math.random() * 2);
                        if (dir == 0)
                                dx = -3;
                        else if (dir == 1)
                                dx = 3;
```

*continues overleaf*

# Flash Games Studio

```
                dy = 0;
                _x = (Math.random() * 300) + 100;
                _y = 0;

                // Move the boxes back on screen
                _root.box1._y = 200;
                _root.box2._y = 200;
                _root.box3._y = 200;
            }
            else
                _root.lives = "GAME OVER";
    }
}
```

The ball moves every frame. The amount that it moves is stored in the variables dx (added to _x) and dy (added to _y). If dx is a negative number, then the ball is moving left, if it's a positive number then the ball is moving right. When the ball hits the edge of the screen, dx is reversed, and hence the ball changes horizontal direction. dy operates somewhat the same way, except along the vertical axis. When dy is negative, the ball moves up, and when dy is positive the ball moves down.

> *You may notice that there's one difference between dy and dx, implemented by the following line of code:*
>
> ```
> dy += .1;
> ```
>
> *This means that dy increases marginally on its own every frame. Because this increase is positive, dy is increasing in the downward direction. Does that sound like anything from everyday life? Yes, we've created gravity (of sorts). By increasing dy each frame, the ball will drop faster and faster. It also means that the ball will bounce and arc, because even when dy is negative (and the ball is flying upward) we're still increasing dy each frame so eventually it will reach 0, a static position. From this point dy will begin to increase positively and the ball will start to fall. This is the constant force of gravity.*

**10.** Finally, we check to make sure the ball hasn't fallen off the bottom of the screen. If it has, then we check to make sure that the user hasn't lost their last life. If they haven't then the following things occur:

- The ball is returned to the top of the screen (_y = 0)
- dy is set to 0, so the ball will not start out with too much downward velocity

# The Third Dimension

- The ball is given a dx of -3, or +3, meaning that it will start off moving either left or right.
- The _x location of the ball is decided randomly between 100 and 400
- The variable `livesleft` is decreased by 1.
- The three boxes are returned to the middle of the screen, handy if you've lost any of them off the bottom of the screen.

However, if it was the last life, then the text field lives on the main timeline is simply filled with the words "GAME OVER".

OK. Now that our basic game components are established we'll take a look back at the code that we attached to the block.

```
if (_root.ball.hitTest(collisionbox) && _root.ball.dy > 0)
{
    // Move the ball to the top of the box
    _root.ball._y = _y - (_root.ball._height / 2);

    // Change the ball's y velocity (dy) to go upwards
    _root.ball.dy = -Math.abs(_root.ball.dy);

    // Add score based on ball's x velocity
    _root.myscore += Math.round(Math.abs(_root.ball.dx)
    ➥ * 10);
    _root.score = _root.myscore;

    // Increase the ball's x velocity
    _root.ball.dx *= 1.2;
}
```

Here, we're simply testing to see if the ball has hit the `collisionbox` and that its dy is greater than 0 (in other words, the ball is moving down). We don't want collision happening if the ball is moving back up after a bounce.

If there is a collision, the first thing we do is move the ball up to the top of the block, and then we reverse its dy so that whatever downward velocity it had will be instantly converted into upward velocity – the ball will bounce. We then take the ball's dx and use that to compute a score. The faster the ball is moving on _x, the more points the players gets. Finally, we increase the ball's dx, thus speeding it up. We want the game to get more challenging.

The block has one more line of code after that which says:

```
_y += Math.abs(_root.ball.dx) / 15;
```

This simply moves the block down each frame. However, the movement is based on the ball's dx again. Meaning, the faster the ball flies, the faster the block sinks. This is to add challenge to the game.

# 11  Flash Games Studio

Now we need to create our additional blocks.

**11.** Copy the `box1` movie clip twice, to create two more 3dbox objects on screen. Name them `box2` and `box3` accordingly. Now, in `box2` find the following code:

```
if (frm <= 5)
        this.swapDepths(9);
else
        this.swapDepths(99);
```

and change it to

```
if (frm <= 5)
        this.swapDepths(10);
else
        this.swapDepths(100);
```

**12.** Do the same for `box3`, but this time change it to:

```
if (frm <= 5)
        this.swapDepths(8);
else
        this.swapDepths(98);
```

This code simply ensures that the box appears in front of the ball (which is at `depth 50`) when we're seeing the bottom of the box, and behind the ball when we're seeing the top of the box. This is necessary to create the 3D effect of the box and the ball. We must put each box on different depth levels (10 and 100, 8 and 98, 9 and 99) because no two movie clips can sit on the same depth level.

If you test this movie, your game should run! Although you'll notice that when the ball moves off the top of the screen it can be hard to tell where it has gone and where it is going to appear again. To round off our game we'll create an indicator arrow

**13.** Simply draw an arrow on the main timeline pointing up.

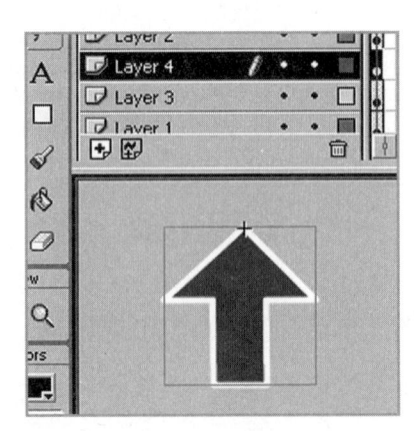

# The Third Dimension 11

14. Now, convert the arrow to a movie clip, and then edit this movie clip so that the center point is at the tip of the arrow, as seen in the image above.

15. And finally, attach the following code to the arrow:

```
onClipEvent(enterFrame)
{
    // this arrow helps locate the ball's
    // position off screen.

    // put arrow at the top of the screen
    // horizontally lined up with the ball
    _y = 0;
    _x = _root.ball._x;

    // Only visible if ball is off the top of
    // the screen.
    if (_root.ball._y < -15)
        _visible = true;
    else
        _visible = false;

}
```

This will simply follow the ball horizontally at the top of the screen, and only appear when the ball has flown off screen. The rest of the time it is invisible.

That's it! Have fun playing the game. My high-score is about 1,800 points without letting the ball drop. As a challenge, try adding a second ball to the game. You will need to make the blocks test for collision with both balls.

**So what have we got so far?** Well, we've examined a couple of elements that demonstrate exactly what effects Flash can generate to improve the aesthetics and 'feel' of our games.

**Parallax scrolling:** We've seen that an impressive 3D effect can be obtained with the use of multiple layers moving at different rates.

**Pre-rendered 3D graphics:** By using images that are rendered from various angles, we can smoothly create the effect of 3D – or, faux 3D.

Let's put it all together, and see what we can come up with!

# Star Cruiser

In *Star Cruiser* we're going to take pre-rendered 3D graphics and parallax scrolling stars to create a full game. The object of the game is to get our ship safely from the left-hand side of the screen to the right hand side of the screen. In our crossing we must avoid the energy orbs, which will electrocute us and deplete our life. Once our life has been completely depleted our craft will

# 11 Flash Games Studio

explode, and the game will be over. The complete game can be found in `demo11-3.fla` and `demo11-3.swf`.

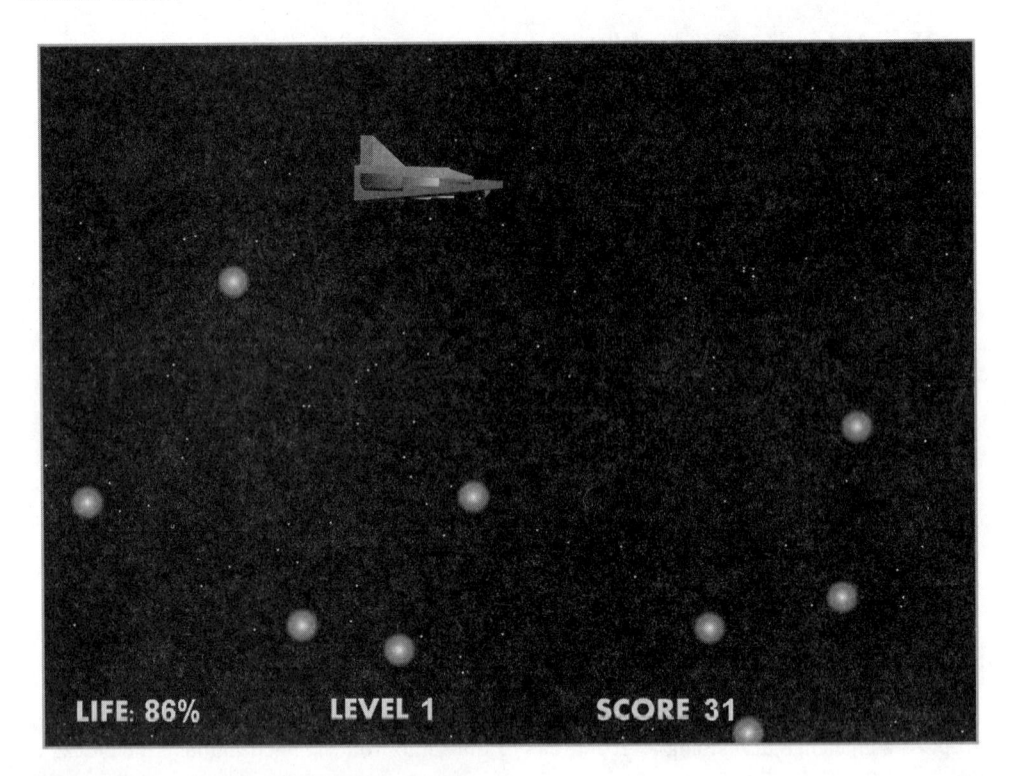

## Creating the star field

First, let's look at how we would create a parallax scrolling star field. Much like in `demo16-1`, the star field works on the principal of layers scrolling at different rates. In the case of our stars, the only difference is, we don't pre-draw all the stars in a self-contained movie clip layer, rather the stars are individual objects that are assigned to move based on their layer.

Let's build a parallax scrolling star field. You can see this in `demo11-2`.

# The Third Dimension — 11

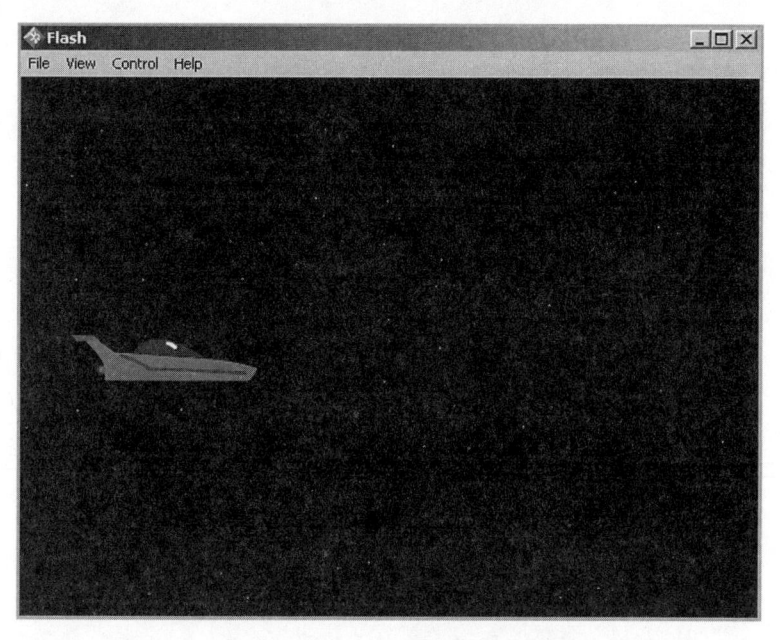

1. Create a new movie with a black background and place a single white dot on the screen. Convert this dot to a movie clip and give it the instance name star0.

2. Create another movie clip on the main timeline called controller. Attach the following code to it:

```
onClipEvent(load)
{
      // Produce 100 stars
      for (i = 0; i < 100; i++)
      {
            nm = "star" add i;
            if (i > 0) duplicateMovieclip("_root.star0", nm, i);

            // Give each new star a random location
            _root[nm]._x = Math.random() * 550;
            _root[nm]._y = Math.random() * 400;

            // Place each star on a random depth level
            _root[nm].depth = Math.floor(Math.random() * 3);

      }

}
```

# 11 Flash Games Studio

This will make 100 copies of star, and move them to random locations on the screen. It will also create a variable called depth in each star movie clip and this depth will be set to 0, 1 or 2 with a random statement. Using the Math.floor command, these random depths will be rounded *down* to the nearest integer. Thus 1.3 becomes 1; 2.93 becomes 2; 0.33224 becomes 0.

3. Now, attach the following code to star0:

```
onClipEvent(enterFrame)
{
        // Depending on the star's depth, move it at
        // one of 3 speeds -2, -4 or -6
        if (depth == 0)
        {
                _x -= 2;
        }
        else if (depth == 1)
        {
                _x -= 4;
        }
        else if (depth == 2)
        {
                _x -= 6;
        }

        // Star has left the screen? Move it back off-screen
        // to the right of the stage.
        if (_x < 0) _x += 550;

}
```

This simply makes the star move. Depending on its depth, it will move either –2 pixels per frame, –4 pixels per frame or –6 pixels per frame, meaning it will move to the left, and create a parallax effect of varying distance from the craft. Finally, when the star has left the screen via the left edge, it will be placed just off screen by the right edge. Essentially, the star will reappear from the right, and scroll again.

4. Run this movie and you'll see an impressive looking star field effect, with a great sense of depth. For reference, I've placed another movie clip of a spaceship on another layer. This fully completes the appearance of movement, as the ship appears to be zooming along through space.

5. Attach the following code to the spaceship movie clip:

```
onClipEvent(load)
{
    sy = _y;
    ang = 0;
```

# The Third Dimension | 11

```
        // Place the ship in front of the stars
        this.swapDepths(100);
}

onClipEvent(enterFrame)
{
    // Bob up and down smoothly
    _y = sy + 4 * Math.cos(ang+=0.2);
}
```

All that really matters here is the `swapDepths`, which brings the ship in front of the stars, since all the stars are presumed to be far in the background. The other bit of code...

```
        _y = sy + 4 * Math.cos(ang+=0.2);
```

creates the effect of making the ship move up and down slightly. This is simply a neat trick that adds to the appearance of movement.

So, now we've got our stars. Let's see what we can do with them in a game.

## Creating the components of our game

1. The first thing we need to do is get our main character, the star cruiser, ready. In this example, I used Swift3D and prepared a 28-frame animation where frames 1 to 13 show more of the top of the ship, frame 14 is straight from the side, and frames 15 to 28 show more of the bottom. It looks approximately like this:

   Frame 28

   Frame 21

   Of course, there are frames between each of these images, but you can get the basic essence of the animation here. The ship itself is just a simple 3D Studio model courtesy of Dave's 3D Studio, whose site you will find in the appendix at the back of this book.

   Frame 14

2. Next we create a blank movie clip called craft on the main timeline. Give it the instance name craft as well. Within it, create another movie clip called shipframes with the instance name shipframes. Within this movie clip, import the ship animation.

   Frame 7

   So, basically we have craft on the main timeline, which contains shipframes,

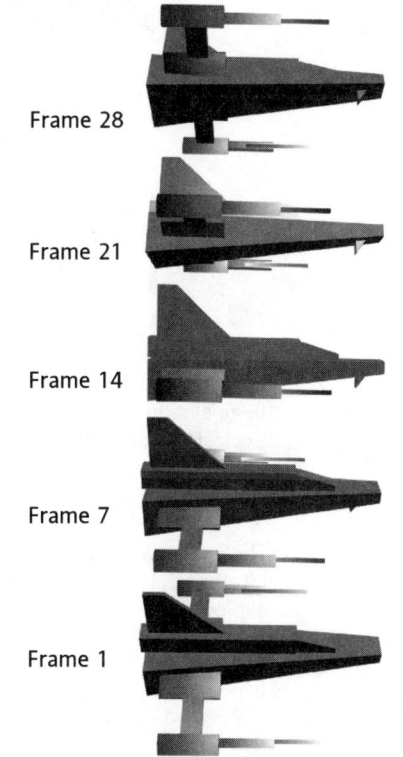

   Frame 1

# 11  Flash Games Studio

consisting of a 28-frame animation of a ship rotating about 45 degrees in either direction.

3. Frame 1 of craft should contain shipframes. For simplicity, call this layer shipframes as well. Insert another layer above this layer, and call it explosion. You should now have something like this:

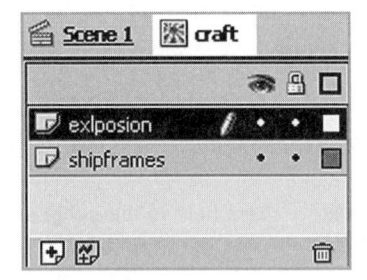

4. On the explosion layer, draw or import a 16 to 20 frame explosion starting on frame 2. This will be played when your ship is destroyed. Also, make the shipframes visible all the way out to about frame 7 so that the ship will not disappear until the explosion fully engulfs it. You whole layout should look something like this:

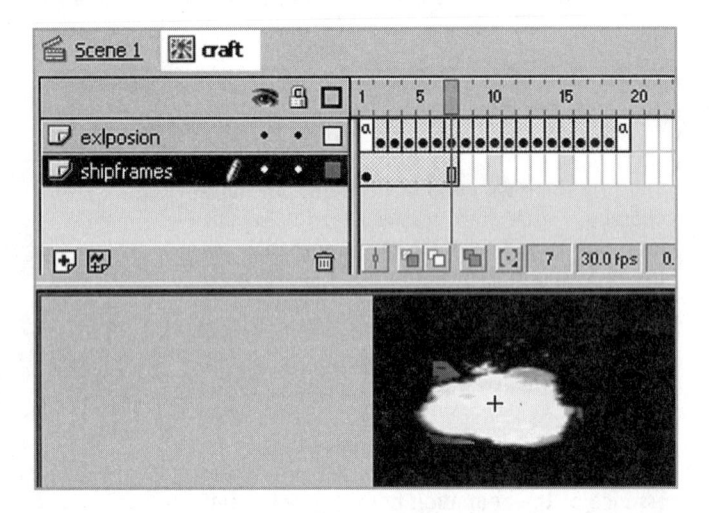

5. Add a stop command to the first frame of the explosion layer (before the explosion begins) and the last frame (after the explosion ends). This will ensure that the explosion does not occur until we tell it to; it will be parked at a blank frame.

Now let's create a bad guy.

The enemies in this game are basically energy orbs that sizzle with electricity when you hit them. This electricity saps your health, and when your health reaches 0, you explode and die.

6. On the main timeline, draw a circle of about 20 pixels in width and height, and convert it to a movie clip called orb. Give it the instance name orb0.

# The Third Dimension    11

**7.** Within the orb movie clip extend the orb so it takes up 2 frames, and call its layer orb. Create another layer above the orb layer and call it lightning. Leave the first frame of the lightning layer blank, and in the second frame place a movie clip called lightning that contains (you guessed it!) a lightning animation. Make sure the lightning is lined up with the image of the orb. Phew! This is how it should look:

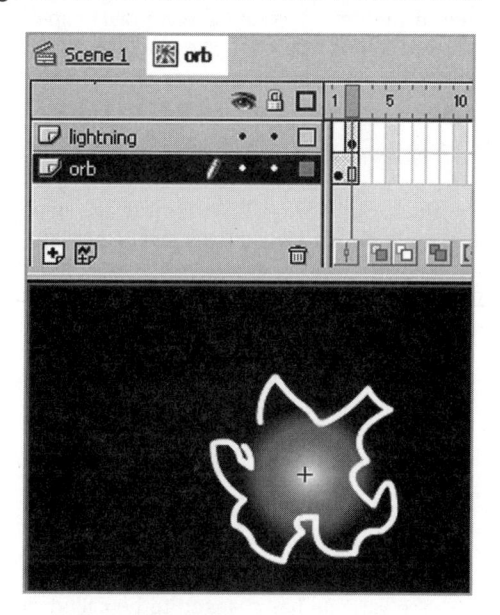

The lightning animation should simply be 6 or 7 frames of random lines that approximately encompass the ball, like so:

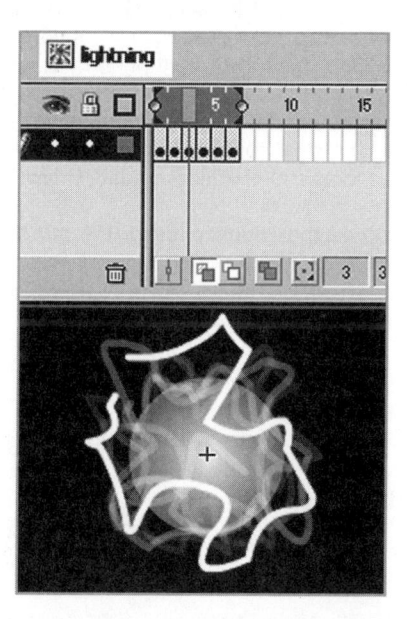

# 11    Flash Games Studio

8. Now you should have one star, one controller, one craft and one orb on frame 1 of the main timeline. Create 3 dynamic text boxes at the bottom of the screen with the variable names life, currentlevel and score. Draw in the words "Life", "Level" and "Score" next to each of these to provide a label.

9. In the middle of the screen, create a new movie clip called status that simply contains the words "GAME OVER". Give this the instance name stat.

## Dabbling with the Z Co-ordinate

Let's change something about our star field. We'll make the depth level of the stars different to just 0, 1, and 2 – we'll allow a star to exist on any level from 0.01 to 2.

1. Edit the ActionScript for the controller, so that the code

    ```
    // Place each star on a random layer
    _root[nm].depth = Math.floor(Math.random() * 3);
    ```

    becomes...

    ```
    // Random z (depth level)
    _root[nm].z = (Math.random() * 2) + 0.01;
    ```

    Notice the depth variable has changed to be called simply z. This is a very important step in the direction of 3D. Simply put, z is the third axis after x and y. More on this in the next chapter, but what we're doing here is making the stars actually exist in 3D space. We have removed the Math.floor so that z can be anything from 0 to 1.9999999. Since Math.random returns a random number from 0 to 1 (well, more precisely 0.99999999) then if we multiply it by 2, we'll get 0 to 1.9999999.

    You'll notice that we add 0.01 to the final number – this is because we don't want to have a z of 0, or too close to 0 because the way the stars move has also been changed (as we'll see in a moment) to follow actual 3D laws and principals of light.

2. OK, we need to edit the ActionScript for the star movie clip. Find the following code:

    ```
    // Depending on the star's depth, move it at
    // one of 3 speeds -2, -4 or -6
    if (depth == 0)
    {
            _x -= 2;
    }
    else if (depth == 1)
    {
            _x -= 4;
    }
    else if (depth == 2)
    ```

# The Third Dimension

```
        {
                _x -= 6;
        }
```

And change it to this:

```
        // Move based on z value
        _x -= 1 / z;
```

Yep, that's it. Why did it get so short and simple? Because we're using a `z` value, which is mathematically based on our distance from the object, so all we need is the property of light known as the inverse square law.

> *Everything we see is light. Even if it is not self-illuminating like a star, it is still reflecting light, like the ground reflects the sun and the moon's light into our eyes.*
>
> *The inverse-square law simply says that as you get farther away from a light-source, its brightness dims at a rate of 1 / d2 – where d is your distance from the light. This is how vision works in general. Objects that are far away appear exponentially smaller and dimmer than objects that are up close. So, objects far away will move slower and be smaller, as we discussed early in the chapter, and also appear dimmer than objects up close.*
>
> *Now, for the purposes of this example, we can ignore the processor intensive square calculation (d2) and simply look at d – or, in this case, z (which represents our distance). The square does not make much difference because it's still an inverse relationship (1/ z). So depending on the z value, the star moves left at a rate of 1 / z. This means that stars that are nearby will really whiz past, while stars that are farther away will move quite slowly. The effect is fantastic and, because it obeys true physics, our eyes accept it because that's how we're used to seeing real life behave. You'll notice that the star field appears much more 3D now than it did with simply the three layers of the first star field.*

3. So now our entire `star0` code looks like this:

```
onClipEvent(enterFrame)
{
        // Move based on z value
        _x -= 1 / z;
```

*continues overleaf*

## Flash Games Studio

```
        // Star has left the screen? Move it back off-screen
        // to the right of the stage.
        if (_x < 0) _x += 550;

}
```

Add the following code to the controller movie clip's `onClipEvent(load)` function:

```
// Health level
_root.craft.health = 100;
// Current game level - can go indefinitely.
_root.currentlevel = 1;

// Duplicate 10 Energy Orbs
for (i = 1; i < 10; i++)
{

        nm = "orb" add i;
        duplicateMovieclip("_root.orb0", nm, i + 100);

}

// Called when player reaches edge of screen.
function reset_orbs()
{
        for (i = 0; i < 10; i++)
        {

                nm = "orb" add i;

                // Random locations (+500 to start offscreen)
                _root[nm]._x = Math.random() * 550 + 500;
                _root[nm]._y = Math.random() * 350;
                _root[nm].z = (Math.random() * 0.3) + 0.1;

        }
}

reset_orbs();
```

All of the above code should be below the star duplication code. You'll notice that we're making nine copies of the orb object, to create a total of 10 orbs. We're also declaring a function called reset_orbs which is basically responsible for clearing the orbs off the screen, placing them off the stage to the right, and giving them new _x, _y and z coordinates. You'll also notice that the orbs are also using a z value, however they are much closer than the stars, ranging from 0.1 to 0.4.

Obviously, the stars are not actually huge items that are far away, they are merely single pixel dots which are relatively close, but because they're so small, we don't have to accommodate for their size. In truth, if the stars were accurately scaled and moved to a proper z value to make them that

# The Third Dimension | 11

small, then they would be billions of miles away, and they certainly would not zoom past the screen as they do. Such is the nature of dramatic space!

The last line of the controller script makes a call to reset_orbs so that all the orbs are in position.

Now, we almost have a game, except for two more sections of code: The craft and the orb. So, let's look at those now.

## The orb code

Let's have another look at those evil electrical orbs. Add the following code to orb0:

```
onClipEvent (enterFrame)
{
        // Move each orb left, based on their z
        // and the currentlevel - the orbs move faster
        // as the difficulty level increases
        _x -= (1 / z) + _root.currentlevel;

        // If they leave the screen, wrap them around to
        // the right side, and move them to a new random _y
        if (_x < -20)
        {
                _x += 590;
                _y = _root.craft._y + Math.random() * 80 - 40;
        }

        // See if they hit the craft
        hit = hitTest(_root.craft);

        // Make sure they weren't hitting last frame
        if (hit != lasthit)
        {
                // There's a hit, go to the lightning frame
                if (hit)
                        gotoAndStop(2);
                else
                        gotoAndStop(1); // no longer hitting, stop
                        ➥ lightning

                // set the current hit state
                lasthit = hit;
        }

        // While a hit is taking place, deplete the health level
        // of the craft (faster as the level is higher)
        if (hit) _root.craft.health -= (0.5 * _root.currentlevel);

}
```

This code is pretty straightforward. We're doing two things

- Moving the orb
- Testing for collision with the ship

Moving the orb is very much based on the same code that moves the stars. The only difference is that the orb's speed is increased in relation the game level we're on. This means that the orbs will move faster as we get further into the game, thus increasing the challenge.

When the orb leaves the left-hand edge of the screen, it is moved back off the right-hand edge. In this case, I've chosen to then give the orb a new random _y value that is based on the position of the craft. This is simply so that the orb doesn't appear to be running on a track along the same vertical strip across the screen. Once it leaves the screen, it is moved to a new height and then re-enters the screen.

The collision code is based simply on a `hitTest`, but you'll notice that I'm storing the results of the `hitTest` in a variable called `hit`.

```
hit = hitTest(_root.craft);
```

Usually, you might think of `hitTest` being used in an `if` statement, like this:

```
if (hitTest(movie clip))
```

But in fact, all that `hitTest` does is return `true` or `false`, so that the if statement is actually like this:

```
if (true)
```

or

```
if (false)
```

So, when we assign the results of `hitTest(_root.craft)` to `hit`, then it is our intermediary variable `hit` that will be set to either `true` or `false`. I'm also using another variable called `lasthit`, which is simply a way of checking if the state of `hit` has changed since the last frame. We don't want the `gotoAndStop` action to happen every single frame, so we only do it if there's a change in `hit` state.

If the `hit` state becomes `true`, then we `gotoAndPlay(2)`, which is the frame with the lightning overlaid (arrgh – the ship is suffering!). If the hit state becomes false, then we `gotoAndPlay(1)`, and the lightning disappears (phew!).

Finally, if a hit is occurring, then we want the player's life to be depleted, so we accomplish this with:

```
if (hit) _root.craft.health -= (0.5 * _root.currentlevel);
```

We decrease the amount of health they have by an amount based on 0.5 times the current game level. So, on level 1, every orb that's hitting you removes 0.5 health points from you. On level 2,

## The Third Dimension    11

it's 1 health point, etc. By the time you get to level 10, each hit is worth 5 points of damage. Therefore, again we're following a golden rule of games – increase the challenge and difficulty level as the player progresses.

# The full craft script

Finally we attach the following code to the craft:

```
onClipEvent(load)
{
    // Keep track of the starting y position
    sy = _y;

    // the variable used in creating the bobbing motion
    ang = 0;

    // No score to start
    score = 0;

    // Not dead to start
    dead = false;

    // Bring craft to front
    this.swapDepths(200);
}

onClipEvent(enterFrame)
{
    // Only do stuff if the player is alive
    if (!dead)
    {
        // Set the ship's frame based on its _y speed
        frm = Math.floor(15 - dy);
        shipframes.gotoAndStop(frm);

        // hide the Game Over display
        _root.stat._visible = false;

        // Creates a slight bobbing motion
        _y = sy + 4 * Math.cos(ang+=0.2);

        // Test the status of the arrow keys
        kd = Key.isDown(Key.DOWN);
        ku = Key.isDown(Key.UP);
        kl = Key.isDown(Key.LEFT);
        kr = Key.isDown(Key.RIGHT);
```

## Flash Games Studio

```
// If pressing up, accelerate up
if (ku)
      dy -= 0.7;

// If pressing down, accelerate down
if (kd)
      dy += 0.7;

// If not pressing up or down, slow down vertical motion
if (!kd && !ku)
      dy *= 0.8;

// If pressing left, accelerate left
if (kl)
      dx -= 0.6;

// If pressing right, accelerate right
if (kr)
      dx += 0.6;

// If not pressing left or right, slow horizontal motion
if (!kl && !kr)
      dx *= 0.8;

// Move the craft by the acceleration amounts
_y += dy;
_x += dx;

// Display health
if (health > 0)
{
      _root.life = Math.round(health) add "%";
      // Just for staying alive, some points
      score += 0.1;
      _root.score = Math.round(score);
}
else
{
      // You have died
      _root.life = "0%";
      health = 0;
      // Show death explosion
      gotoAndPlay(2);
      dead = true;
}

// Did player reach the edge of the screen?
if (_x > 620)
{
      // Increase the score
```

# The Third Dimension

```
                    score += (_root.currentlevel *
                    ➥ _root.currentlevel) * 100;

                    // yes, so increment the level
                    _root.currentlevel ++;

                    // Move player to left hand side of screen
                    _x = _width / 2;
                    sy = 200;
                    _y = 200;
                    dx = 0;
                    dy = 0;

                    // Move the orbs to new locations, so you dont
                    // respawn right on top of an orb, potentially
                    // killing you
                    _root.controller.reset_orbs();
            }

            // Stop player from flying off the
            // left, top and bottom of the screen
            if (_x < 20)
            {
                    _x = 20;
                    dx = 0;
            }
            if (sy < 10)
            {
                    sy = 10;
                    dy = 0;
            }
            if (sy > 350)
            {
                    sy = 350;
                    dy = 0;
            }


      }
      else
            _root.stat._visible = true;

}
```

# 11  Flash Games Studio

## Breaking this code down

As this is a long section of code, it is broken down on the following pages to demonstrate that it's still fairly simple and straightforward!

1. The first thing we do is initialize some variables with the `onClipEvent(load)` method. We set the player's score to 0 and we set a flag (true/false variable) called `dead` to false. This is used later to determine a game state based on the player's health. We also set the `ang` and `sy` variables, which are used to create the slight bobbing of the craft. Finally, `swapDepths` is used to bring the ship forward – in front of the stars and the orbs.

   ```
   onClipEvent(load)
   {
       // Keep track of the starting y position
       sy = _y;

       // the variable used in creating the bobbing motion
       ang = 0;

       // No score to start
       score = 0;

       // Not dead to start
       dead = false;

       // Bring craft to front
       this.swapDepths(200);
   }
   ```

2. Next we start the main game loop which is in `onClipEvent(enterFrame)`. The first thing we do in here is check to see if the player is alive or not. This is important because we don't want any of the player's game code to be carried out if they're dead. We say:

   ```
   if (!dead)
   ```

   Which is exactly the same as

   ```
   if (dead == false)
   ```

   Remember the ! symbol means "not". So, we're saying "if not dead".

3. Following this we have:

   ```
   frm = Math.floor(15 - dy);
   shipframes.gotoAndStop(frm);

   // hide the Game Over display
   ```

# The Third Dimension 11

```
            _root.stat._visible = false;

            // Creates a slight bobbing motion
            _y = sy + 4 * Math.cos(ang+=0.2);
```

Here we decide which frame of the shipframes pre-rendered 3D image to display, based on the craft's current _y velocity, dy. This frame will be a number from 1 to 28. The faster we are ascending, the more of the bottom of the ship we will see. Conversely, the faster we descend, the more of the top of the ship we will see. This creates the appearance that the ship is banking. We also create the slight bobbing motion on the craft, and set the movie clip called stat (with the "GAME OVER" text in it) to be invisible.

4. Next, we assign four variables:

   ```
   kd = Key.isDown(Key.DOWN);
   ku = Key.isDown(Key.UP);
   kl = Key.isDown(Key.LEFT);
   kr = Key.isDown(Key.RIGHT);
   ```

   ...in order to check the current state of the keyboard. Each variable of kd, ku, kl and kr will be set to either true or false by the Key.isDown method, based on the state of the up, down, left and right arrow keys.

5. We then use those four values to affect the motion of the craft. Since the ship's motion is based on dx and dy, we want the keys to have an effect on dx and dy, not on _x and _y directly. We are only changing the craft's movement with the key's, not its position. The position will change automatically as the movement variables (dx and dy) change. If you press up or down, the ship will move up or down. If you press left or right, then the ship will move left or right.

   If you release both vertical keys (ku = false, kd = false) then the ship will slow to a stop, as seen here:

   ```
   if (!kd && !ku)
         dy *= 0.8;
   ```

   What happens is, when those keys are not pressed the ship will slow down by 80% each frame. This only takes a few seconds to completely stop the ship. The same logic is applied to kl and kr – the horizontal movement variables.

6. Next, the ship is actually moved:

   ```
   sy += dy;
   _x += dx;
   ```

   This is based on the values of dx and dy. Notice that _y is not being changed, but rather sy is being changed. This is because earlier, we wrote:

   ```
   _y = sy + 4 * Math.cos(ang+=0.2);
   ```

   ...which is essentially like saying _y = sy but with a slight modulation of 4 pixels up or down along a cosine wave.

## Flash Games Studio

7. We then check the player's health level. If they have more than 0 health, then we update the screen display with their score and health level. We also give them some free points just for staying alive. 0.1 is added to the score, which means, every 10 frames 1 point will be added.

   If, however, the player's health is 0 or less, then we update the display to say "0%" life, and we start the explosion animation playing. If you recall, once the explosion has reached its final frame, it will `stop`; and the player will not be visible. We also set the `dead` flag to be true.

   ```
   // Display health
           if (health > 0)
           {
                   _root.life = Math.round(health) add "%";
                   // Just for staying alive, some points
                   score += 0.1;
                   _root.score = Math.round(score);
           }
           else
           {
                   // You have died
                   _root.life = "0%";
                   health = 0;
                   // Show death explosion
                   gotoAndPlay(2);
                   dead = true;
           }
   ```

8. Next, we check to see if the player has reached the right edge of the screen. If they have, then we add the square of the current level times 100 to their score. This means that on level 1 you get (1 x 1 x 100) 100 points, level 2 you get (2 x 2 x 100) 400 points, level 3 (3 x 3 x 100) 900 points, etc. The higher you get, the more points you get - Level 20 would get you (20 x 20 x 100) 40,000 points.

   ```
   // Did player reach the edge of the screen?
           if (_x > 620)
           {
                   // Increase the score
                   score += (_root.currentlevel *
   _root.currentlevel) * 100;
   ```

9. This achieved, we advance them one level. This has the ripple-down effect of making the game more difficult because many different elements of the game are based on the `_root.currentlevel` variable. We then move the player to the left edge of the screen, halfway between the top and the bottom. We also clear their dx and dy variables so that they don't start off moving. Finally, we clear the orbs off the screen so that the player doesn't reappear inside an orb and potentially be harmed – that wouldn't be at all fair!

```
            // yes, so increment the level
                _root.currentlevel ++;

                // Move player to left hand side of screen
                _x = _width / 2;
                sy = 200;
                _y = 200;
                dx = 0;
                dy = 0;

                // Move the orbs to new locations, so you dont
                // respawn right on top of an orb, potentially
                // killing you
                _root.controller.reset_orbs();
        }
```

10. With the code below, we are checking to make sure that the player is not trying to fly off the top, bottom or left hand side of the screen – something they'll surely try in an effort to escape from the orbs! When the player flies off screen, we simply return them to the edge of the screen and remove any momentum they may have.

```
        if (_x < 20)
        {
                _x = 20;
                dx = 0;
        }
        if (sy < 10)
        {
                sy = 10;
                dy = 0;
        }
        if (sy > 350)
        {
                sy = 350;
                dy = 0;
        }
```

11. Finally, we have the alternative to the main loop – what will happen if dead is true: We simply make the movie clip stat, the "GAME OVER" image, visible.

That's it! That's our full game using 3D parallax scrolling, and pre-rendered 3D images.

# Flash Games Studio

## Suggested modifications

As with any game, *Star Cruiser* has lots of improvements and modifications that can be made. Here are a few to start off the top of my head:

- Bonus objects that increase score and refill your health
- The ability to shoot and destroy the orbs
- Smart orbs that follow you and you must get to the edge of the screen before they touch you
- An introduction screen / difficulty setting

Try flexing your coding muscles to make the game even more impressive!

## Isometric 3D

One of the easiest and most processor-undemanding methods for creating 3D is the use of isometric 3D graphics. These are simply pre-drawn graphics that have been skewed along a set angle (usually 45 degrees) to create the illusion of depth.

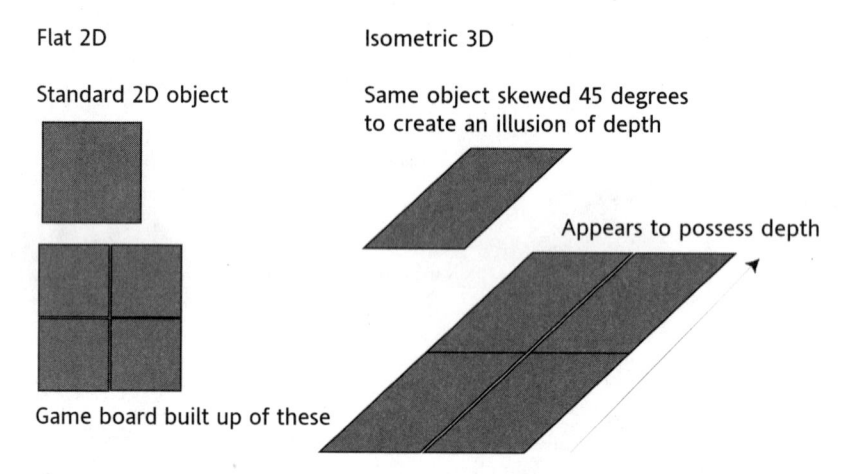

Flat 2D

Standard 2D object

Game board built up of these

Isometric 3D

Same object skewed 45 degrees to create an illusion of depth

Appears to possess depth

One of the easiest ways to implement this in practice is to use **tiles**. Tiles are simply shapes that can be repeated and used over and over to create a screen's worth of graphics. Most modern platform games are made up of tiles, and tiles allow your game worlds to be much bigger than if you had hand drawn the entire map.

# The Third Dimension | 11

When you lay a series of isometric 3D tiles next to each other, you get the appearance of a 3D world, like this:

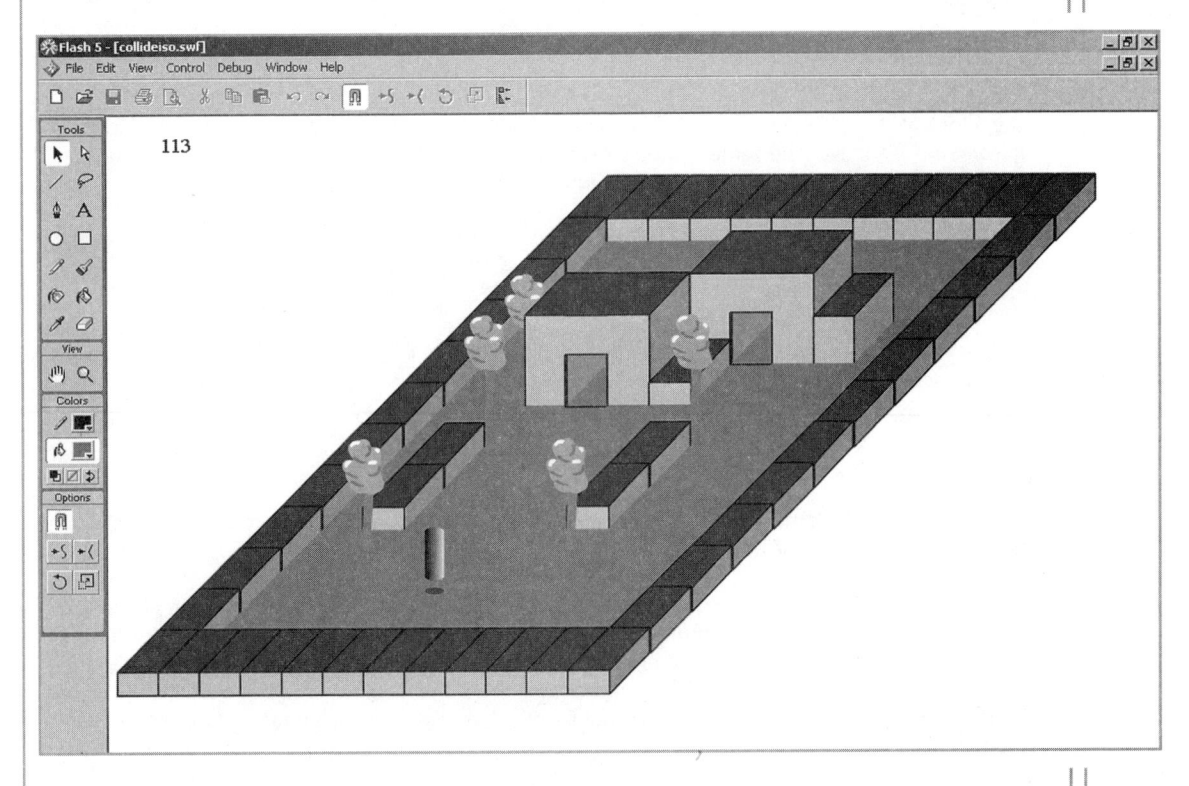

Now, the key thing that must be remembered is that isometric is *not* actually 3D, it only appears that way. In actuality, isometric images are based on a 2D world, which is simply then skewed along the x-axis to create an illusion of depth.

Let's say we're looking at a character from overhead. On our 2D map we will store that character's position using sx and sy coordinates. Now, normally, if we wanted to display him on screen, we would simply do this by putting in the character's onClipEvent handler the following code:

```
_x = sx;
_y = sy;
```

However, in an isometric setting, the standard method for putting him on screen would be:

```
_x = sx - sz;
_y = sz;
```

The only thing we're doing that's important is **changing his horizontal position on screen based on his vertical position**. In this case, it's best to think of it in terms of sx and sz, since z usually indicates depth – into the screen. So, we're saying that for every z that we move into the screen, let's add 1 to the x coordinate to show that. We're simply cheating! We're saying that we're on a 2D game board, but lets make it *look* 3D by moving things horizontally as we move vertically.

## Putting it into practice

Take a look at `demo11-6.fla`. This is a mini game that takes place on a 2D map, which is shown in an isometric 3D image. The game is simply made up of a 12 x 12 tiled map, which consist of several different types of tile. Each tile is built to fit into an isometric setting. Here's a look at the tiles:

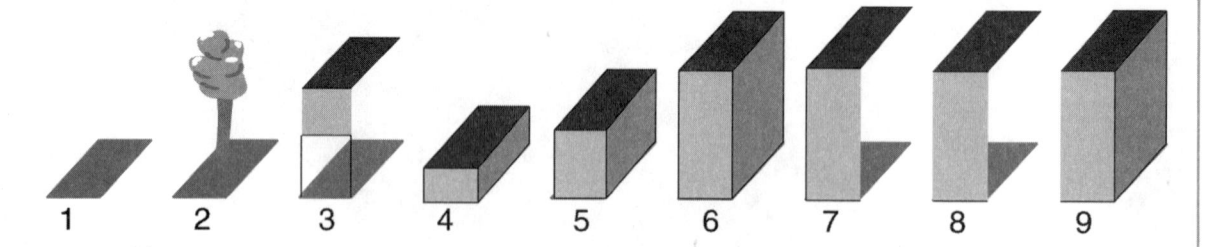

When you play the demo, you can move the mouse around and click on the grid surface to change the appearance of the tile.

Each tile is on a separate frame of a movie clip called `object`, which is inside a movie clip called `quad0`. A full game could have hundreds of tiles, but we're only using nine in this example. Placing these tiles next to each other, we can create a whole 3D world, as seen in the completed scenario pictured towards the start of this section. For example, tiles 7, 8 and 9 are placed together to create a large block. There are endless combinations that can produce a huge array of scenes and settings.

When the game first starts, a grid of 12x12 tiles is created, by copying one movie clip over and over, positioning it, setting its `depth`, and then setting its current frame to choose the tile to display. There's an object called `controller` sitting on the main timeline with the following code attached to it:

```
onClipEvent(load)
{
        // The width and height of the base of each tile
        w = 22.4;
        h = 22.4;

        // Dimensions of board
        cols = 12;
        rows = 12;

        // Starting screen position of first tile
        offx = _root.quad0._x;
        offz = _root.quad0._y;
```

# The Third Dimension   11

```
_root.quad0.w = w;
_root.quad0.h = h;

for (i = 0; i < rows; i++)
{
        for (j = 0; j < cols; j++)
        {
                n = (i * cols) + j;
                nm = "quad" add n;

                if (n > 0)
                {
                        duplicateMovieclip (_root.quad0, nm,
                        ➥ n * 2);
                }

                // Calculate x and z coordinates for each tile
                x = (j * w);
                z = (i * h);

                // Place on screen, based on isometric
                projection
                _root[nm]._x = (x - z) + offx;
                _root[nm]._y = (z) + offz;

                // Create a border around the map
                if (j == 0 || i == 0 || j == (cols - 1) || i
                ➥ == (rows - 1))
                        _root[nm].object.gotoAndStop(4);
                else
                        _root[nm].object.gotoAndStop(1);
        }
    }
}
```

As the tiles are copied, they are actually copied in a 1-dimensional array of objects called quadN, where N is a number. So, quad0 is the first tile, quad1 is the second tile, etc. N is calculated with this formula:

```
n = (i * cols) + j;
```

This simply takes the row, times the total number of columns per row, and adds the current column. This formula works well to create a linear sequence.

449

When the tiles are positioned on screen, they are set according to the isometric formula:

```
// Place on screen, based on isometric projection
_root[nm]._x = (x - z) + offx;
_root[nm]._y = (z) + offz;
```

This places them according to their z and x values. Also, `offx` and `offy` are added to each tile's position so that we can decide where the whole board will appear, by placing `quad0` at design time on the stage. Without `offx` and `offy`, the game board could run off the screen because of the fact that the board is not square, but diagonal.

As the tiles are being duplicated, their depth is also being set within the `duplicateMovieClip`. We're simply setting the depth to n * 2, which means that every tile is on its own depth, on an even number (0, 2, 4, 6, 8, etc). This way we are leaving all the odd numbers to insert other objects (namely, the player) at a later time. As the numbers increase, we draw from left to right, top to bottom, which means that the correct layering of tiles will occur.

## Player position and movement

Because this is basically a 2D grid, the game collision and navigation is very easy. We keep track of the player's position using a simple two coordinate system. In most 2D games we call this x and y, but in this game we're going to call it x and z. We have a game grid of 12x12 tiles. Each tile has a width and a faux-depth. Knowing this, we can easily find out which tile the player is in with the following formula:

```
axtile = Math.floor(x / _root.quad0.w);
aztile = Math.floor(z / _root.quad0.h);
```

This simply takes the player's position and divides it by the width of the tile on x and the height of the tile on z.

To move the player around, we simply read the keyboard and set two values, `dx` and `dz`, based on the keys that the player is pressing. If the player is pressing up or down, then we set `dz` to be +2 or −2, and if the player is pressing left or right then we set the `dx` to be +2 or −2. This can be seen in the following code, which is attached to the player's `enterFrame` clip event.

```
// Test keys
kl = Key.isDown(Key.LEFT);
kr = Key.isDown(Key.RIGHT);

ku = Key.isDown(Key.UP);
kd = Key.isDown(Key.DOWN);

// Pressing Left?
if (kl)
{
        dx = -2;
}
```

# The Third Dimension 11

```
            // Pressing right?
            if (kr)
            {
                    dx = 2;
            }

            // Pressing up?
            if (ku)
            {
                    dz = -2;
            }

            // Pressing down?
            if (kd)
            {
                    dz = 2;
            }

            // Not pressing a particular axis key,
            // then stop moving
            if (!kl && !kr)    dx = 0;
            if (!ku && !kd) dz = 0;
```

If neither key on a particular axis is being pressed, then we set that axis' speed to 0. If we didn't then the player would keep going in that direction until they hit a wall.

## Collision testing

Before we actually move the player however, we want to test for collision. For collision, we want to look at the player's *next* position, and see if it's going to be hitting a solid object. Therefore, we get two sets of coordinates with this code in the player's enterFrame clip event:

```
            // Compute collision information.
            // Check next tile along the x axis
            nxxtile = Math.floor((x + dx) / _root.quad0.w);
            nxztile = Math.floor(z / _root.quad0.h);
            nx = nxztile * _root.controller.cols + nxxtile;

            // Check next tile along the z axis
            nzxtile = Math.floor(x / _root.quad0.w);
            nzztile = Math.floor((z + dz) / _root.quad0.h);
            nz = nzztile * _root.controller.rows + nzxtile;

            // Store the value of those tiles in stx and stz
            stx = _root["quad" add nx].object._currentframe;
            stz = _root["quad" add nz].object._currentframe;

            // Was collision detected along the x-axis?
            // (if tile type >= 4)
            if (stx >= 4)
            {
```

# 11 Flash Games Studio

```
                    // if so, zero the x velocity, dx
                    if (dx < 0)
                    {
                            // Move the player flush with the edge of the
                            // tile
                            x = nzxtile * _root.quad0.w + 1;
                            dx = 0;
                    }
                    else
                    {
                            // Move the player flush with the edge of the
                            // tile
                            x = nxxtile * _root.quad0.w - 1;
                            dx = 0;
                    }
            }

            // Was collision detected along the z-axis?
            if (stz >= 4)
            {
                    // if so, zero the z velocity, dz
                    if (dz < 0)
                    {
                            // Move the player flush with the edge of the
                            // tile
                            z = nxztile * _root.quad0.h + 1;
                            dz = 0;
                    }
                    else
                    {
                            // Move the player flush with the edge of the
                            // tile
                            z = nzztile * _root.quad0.h - 1;
                            dz = 0;
                    }
            }
```

By looking at the next tile in each direction, we can tell if the player is going to hit anything solid. We test each axis independently so that we can keep the player moving in the direction that they are allowed to go, and stop them from moving in the direction that creates a collision. This will create the effect of making the player *slide* along any surface, without stopping them dead.

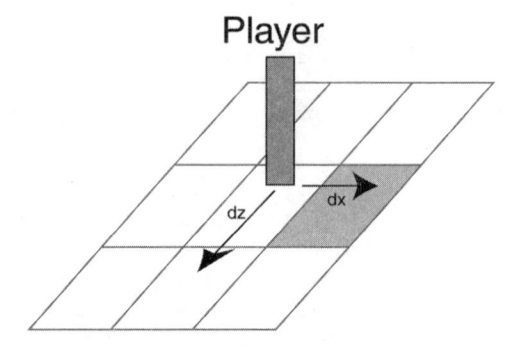

# The Third Dimension    11

If a particular direction does lead to a collision, then we set that movement variable (dx or dy) to 0, and then we move the player flush with the edge of the tile, thus moving them as far as they can go.

## Depth perspective

Once we've made our modifications to dx and dz then we must also compute depth. One of the challenges with isometric 3D is that the player must appear behind some objects, yet in front of others. This is accomplished with the following code:

```
// Get the player's current tile for depth sorting
axtile = Math.floor(x / _root.quad0.w);
aztile = Math.floor(z / _root.quad0.h);

// Compute the tile number from the two coordinates
st = ((aztile) * _root.controller.cols + axtile);

// Place the player behind lower on-screen objects,
// but above higher on-screen objects.
this.swapDepths((st * 2) + 1);
```

Here, we're simply calculating the player's current tile and then going to a particular quad based on that position. The formula to calculate the player's quad is the same as the formula used to duplicate and name the quads earlier.

Also, we set the player's depth in the same manner as the quads, however in this case we add 1 to the depth, so that the player is always on the odd numbers for depth (1, 3, 5, 7, etc.) This creates the effect of placing the player properly behind objects to the right and below on screen, and in front of objects to the left and above on screen.

Finally, the player has the following code attached to the enterFrame event:

```
// Move player
x += dx;
z += dz;

// Project player on the the actual screen
_x = (x - z) + _root.controller.offx;
_y = (z) + _root.controller.offz;
```

We're simply moving the player along x and z by the determined dx and dz. Then, what we're doing is the heart of isometric 3D – we're projecting the conceptual x and z, into an actual, on-screen _x and _y. We use the standard isometric formula, except we add _root.controller.offx and _root.controller.offy to get the game board on to the center of the screen based on where quad0 was initially placed on the stage.

This is the foundation to making a great 3D isometric game. There are a few more small items that you can explore yourself. For example, the code for clicking on the tiles is simply attached to an invisible button that is overlaid on top of each tile. The basic premise is to get the feel for creating faux 3D.

# Flash Games Studio

## Summary

What we've seen in this chapter has been 3D at its simplest. There hasn't really been too much actual 3D math, apart from our minimal use of z in the last demo, yet we have discovered many means of creating the appearance of realism in our images. For the most part, we have seen faux 3D – graphics that are specifically designed in a 2D manner, to appear 3D.

We've also discovered how to

- create parallax scrolling
- set depths to make objects appear in front of one another
- create collisions
- import and adjust 3D images in Flash
- create realistic movement

...along with picking up many cool effects for games possible through Flash!

This is, however, a preview into the wonderful world of true 3D, as we blast off into the third dimension in the following chapters. The math for this stuff is going to get a bit more involved, but the results are going to be fantastic.

# The Third Dimension

11

**Introduction**
chapter 1
chapter 2
chapter 3
chapter 4
chapter 5
chapter 6
Case Study 1
chapter 7
chapter 8
chapter 9
chapter 10
chapter 11
chapter 12
chapter 13
Case Study 2
chapter 14
chapter 15
Director Afterword

# Chapter 12
# Real 3D

# 12    Flash Games Studio

In the previous chapter, we looked at the different techniques used to simulate 3D effects – ways of cheating at 3D. Well, the logical question is, what is it we were cheating against? What were we trying to avoid?

Very simply: **Real 3D**. It's the holy grail of games programming. As we have seen, designers have been on its trail for years, trying to pin it down to a simple, effective, speed-efficient process. In this chapter we're going to take a look at Flash's 3D capabilities, and provide a straightforward guide to the principles of 3D creation.

The reason designers tend to avoid real 3D is because of the math they think is involved. However, given a firm grounding and a little bit of careful logical deduction, 3D need not be a complex mathematical monster at all. It's really as easy as x, y, z!

Over the following pages we will talk about:

- How to construct a 3D object
- How to create a really useful line engine in Flash
- The ups and downs (and ins and outs) of rendering a 3D object on screen
- The math involved in generating a cube, plus a look at sprites
- How to put it all together in a game

## Square One

Okay, so let's start at ground level here. We all know that when you want to convey a position in 2D, you simply detail its x and y coordinates, like so:

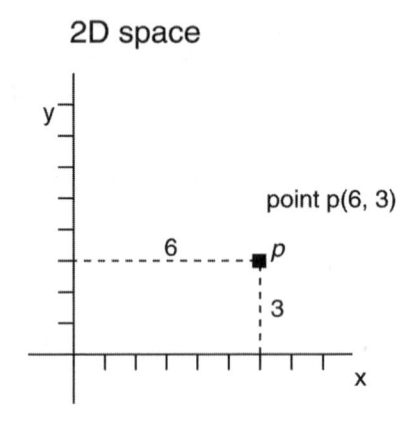

### 2D space

point p(6, 3)

They represent its position in terms of width (along the x axis) and height (along the y axis). When we bring things into the third dimension, all we're doing is adding another axis called z, which represents depth. It goes **in** and **out**, like so:

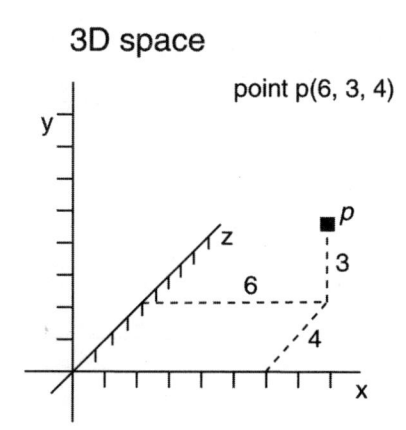

### 3D space

point p(6, 3, 4)

The image displayed here is an **isometric** display (we covered isometric images in the last chapter), and as you can see, it's very much like our isometric demo. In that demo, we had x and z as a flat surface, whereas here we have reintroduced y.

Any location in space can be described using these three coordinates and, as before, all the locations are relative to the **origin**. The origin is the point where all the axes cross – the coordinates x, y and z being (0,0,0). When we start shoving objects around in 3D space the origin becomes very important, so we would do well to bear it in mind early on.

## Defining Shapes

Let's look at how a 2D object is defined in a 2D coordinate system. Take for example, a simple square:

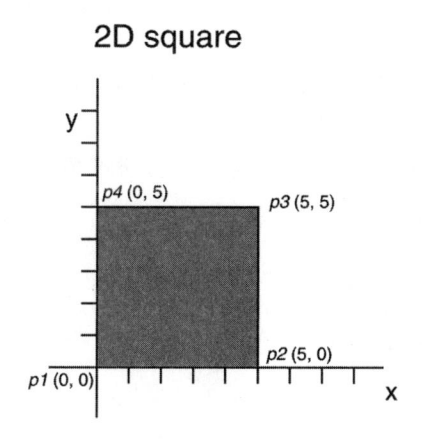

### 2D square

p4 (0, 5)  p3 (5, 5)

p1 (0, 0)  p2 (5, 0)

There are four points (p) that make up a square. These points are known as *vertices* (plural for *vertex*), and they go counterclockwise around the square. With these four pieces of information, this square can be reconstructed easily and this, as you will recall, is the way in which vector images are generated.

So, how do we now go on to define a 3D shape? Well, it's a simple task – we merely need to extend the 2D coordinate system. So, let's define the vertices of a cube.

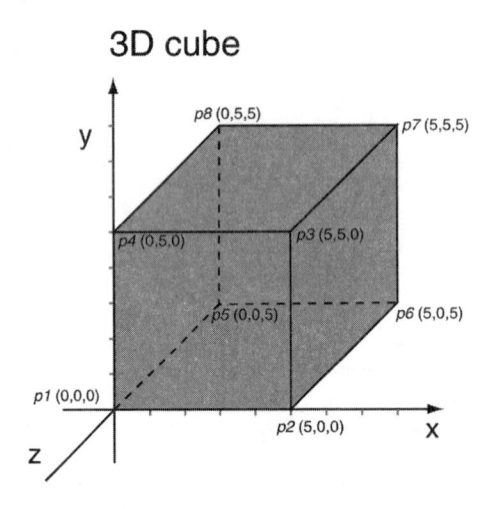

### 3D cube

Notice that we need eight vertices to describe this shape, rather than the previous four, plus we've added a third number to our bracketed point definition to refer to the z coordinate. Point 6 for example is now described as p6 (5,0,5).

This, at its core, is all the information we require to generate things in 3D. How we *interpret* that information is another matter because all we have is a series of points. If we put these into a Flash game, Flash would not know how to connect them – it would be like a join-the-dots picture with no numbers! So, we need to come up with a logical way of defining our 3D objects for our 3D renderer to know how to draw them.

## Object Definition

To properly render a 3D shape, we need to look at its individual components.

- **Points**: We know that any 3D object is defined by a number of points, as illustrated in the above example.

- **Lines**: The next logical constituent is to join those points with a line. In 3D of course this is also known as an **edge**. When a 3D image is made up entirely of lines, it is known as a **wireframe**.

- **Surface, Faces, Polygons**: These are the actual flat surfaces that make up the shape. The cube in our above example is made up of 6 polygons. Polygons are the building blocks of 3D games – they are used to build up entire scenes. Often, the performance of a 3D rendering engine is measured by how many polygons it can handle in one frame before performance starts to dwindle.

- **Shapes, Objects**: This is are the highest level of 3D definition, effectively comprising each of the above elements. Objects are simply a series of polygons – like the cube in our example.

In this chapter, I'm going to focus mainly on a straight wireframe vector engine, so our objects of choice are going to be lines and points. In the next chapter, I'll look at **quads** (polygons with 4 edges).

## Point

A point is the simplest of our data objects, consisting only of the (x,y,z) coordinates. The best way of approaching how to plot a point is to create a **constructor function** (in my example I have called it point3d). This function can be called by us at a later point, and it will assign the values we give it to the x, y, and z coordinate of a point. The code to create a function looks like this:

```
function point3d (x, y, z)
{
    this.x = x;
    this.y = y;
    this.z = z;
}
```

Later on in our script, if we want to generate a point object we simply name it, call the point3d function, and feed it the values, like so:

```
point1 = new point3d (3,4,5);
```

This would create a point called point 1 and fix its coordinates to (3,4,5), as illustrated below:

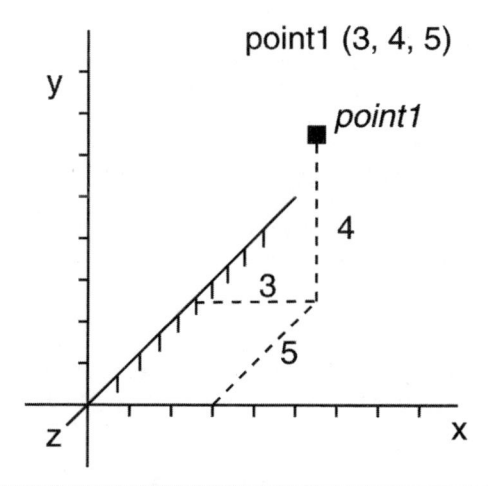

This means that you can now find the value of the point at `point1.x`, `point1.y` and `point1.z`. That's it! It's very simple.

### Line

The next data object in the hierarchy is the line. A line object consists of two point objects, p1 and p2. Once again, we can create a constructor function, here called `line3d`, to carry out all the labor for us:

```
function line3d (p1, p2)
{
    this.p1 = p1;
    this.p2 = p2;
}
```

So, if you wanted to create a line object, that spanned from a point at (0,0,0) to a point at (6,5,4) you would do the following:

```
point1 = new point3d (0,0,0);
point2 = new point3d (6,5,4);
line1  = new line3d (point1, point2);
```

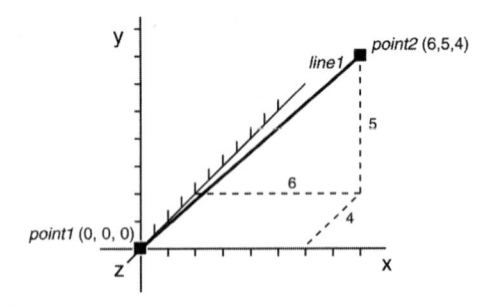

To access the value of the first point of the line, you would (quite logically) refer to `line1.p1.x`, `line1.p1.y` and `line1.p1.z`. It follows then, that the second point is at `line1.p2.x`, `line1.p2.y` and `line1.p2.z`. Note that they're called `line1.p1` and not `line1.point1`. Although the points are defined as `point1` and `point2` outside the line, once they're part of the line object they take on the names that are in the constructor function, p1 and p2.

To further reduce our typing, we could take it down some more. Once again, we just name the line, call the `line3d` function, and feed the values:

```
line1 = new line3d ( new point3d(0,0,0), new point3d(6,5,4) );
```

When we use this method, we are creating local point objects, and not global point objects. This saves on memory, which is at a premium when we're dealing with 3D.

## Quad

As we're going through the hierarchy, let's touch on quads for a moment. A quad is a special type of polygon that only has four edges. In the context of games, most 3D shapes use quads. The quad is created with the following constructor function:

```
function quad3d (p1, p2, p3, p4)
{
    this.p1 = p1;
    this.p2 = p2;
    this.p3 = p3;
    this.p4 = p4;
}
```

This takes the four points and keeps them in one structure known as a quad. So, let's create a 5x5 quad that is aligned with the z-axis, and has an x coordinate of 3. Remember, all quads are simply 2D objects positioned in 3D space.

```
point1 = new point3d (3,0,0);
point2 = new point3d (3,0,5);
point3 = new point3d (3,5,5);
point4 = new point3d (3,5,0);
quad1 = new quad3d (point1, point2, point3, point4);
```

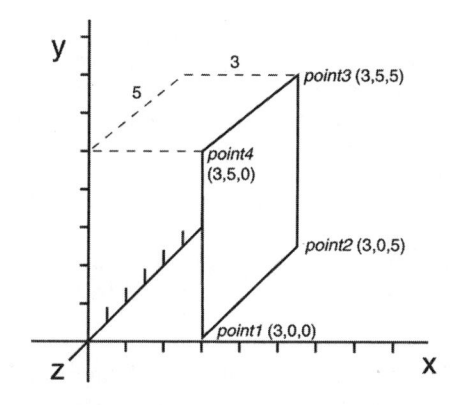

Now, you would refer to each point like `quad1.p1`, or `quad1.p2`, or `quad1.p3` or `quad1.p4`. Logically enough, if you want to refer in greater detail to the positioning of the points, you could write `quad1.p1.x`, or `quad1.p2.z`, etc.

You can also create a quad with local points using the following line of code:

```
quad1 = new quad3d (new point3d (3,0,0), new point3d (3,0,5),
↪new point3d (3,5,5), new point3d (3,5,0));
```

Another important thing to pay attention to is the order in which the points are passed. The quad is drawn from `point1` to `point2` to `point3` to `point4`. Earlier, I mentioned the fact that the points go around the square. This is true for our polygons. What would happen if we didn't put the points in clockwise or counterclockwise around the polygon? Let's say we created the polygon with:

```
quad1 = new quad3d (point1, point3, point4, point2);
```

Our quad would end up looking like this:

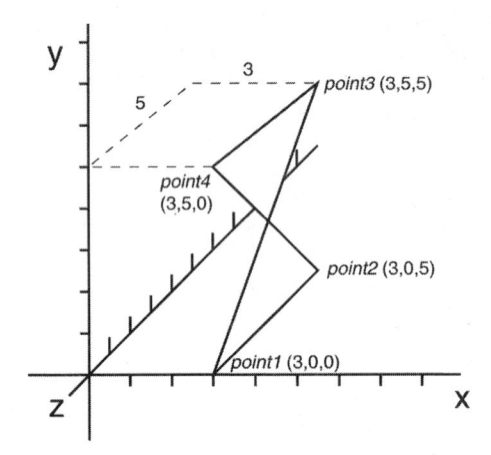

This is known as a bowtie, because the order of the points is incorrect (as you can see, the line starts at `point1`, goes to `point3`, then to `point4` and finally to `point2`). A quad like this can wreak havoc on a game – especially when you are performing calculations that are dependent on the direction that the quad is facing.

## Wireframe

The next data structure we're going to look at is the wireframe object. Once again with this, we write a constructor function, called `wireframe3d`. It will take the values we give it and assign them to the wireframe.

However, whereas with a line you can say that it will go from p1 to p2, or with a quad it will go from p1 to p2 to p3 to p4, you simply *don't know* how many points there will be in a wireframe. There may be hundreds! So too with lines. Who's to say how many there will be? Who knows? Well, something that is going to want to know is the `wireframe3d` constructor function.

What we're going to have to do is create the `wireframe3d` function with space for a variable number of points. The best way to do all of this is to create an array inside it. Let's have a look at how to do this, plus how to declare some other functions to bring it all together. The following is the ActionScript, but I'll provide explanations along the way.

# Real 3D

## Scripting the wireframe3d Function

1. First we need to state what the function is going to do:

   ```
   function wireframe3d (x, y, z, rx, ry, rz, sx, sy, sz)
   {
   ```

   This declares that the `wireframe3d` function will have nine parameters: three for the positioning of each point, three for its rotation (r) and three for its scale (s). The scale will become important because an object's points have to be in a certain numerical range in order for them to be visible on screen. Note that even though all the points of an object already have x, y, and z coordinates, these will end up being relative to the entire object's x, y, and z coordinates. This way, we can move the object around the screen, and all its points and lines will move with it, rather than breaking apart.

2. Next, we set the variable `pointlist`. It stands by to receive an array of `point3d` objects:

   ```
   this.numpoints = 0;
   this.pointlist = new Array();
   this.tpointlist = new Array();
   ```

   As you will have noticed, under `pointlist` we have another array called `tpointlist`. It is identical to `pointlist`, except that the points are in their manipulated (rotated, scaled and translated) state. More on this later.

3. Just as we have prepared the function to receive a bunch of `point3d` objects, we need to prepare it to receive an array of `line3d` objects.

   ```
   this.numlines = 0;
   this.linep1 = new Array();
   this.linep2 = new Array();

   this.linename = new Array();
   ```

   `linep1` and `linep2`, represent the two points at the end of the line. This array will store numbers, which act as indexes into the `pointlist` array. In this way we can avoid having redundant points – lines that share points will use the same `point3d` in `pointlist`. This also means that we will not be performing redundant math on the same point twice.

4. The array called `linename` is simply going to be used later in addressing an instance of a movie clip that is the actual graphic of a line. This is followed by the familiar list of settings:

   ```
   this.x = x;
   this.y = y;
   this.z = z;
   this.rx = rx;
   this.ry = ry;
   this.rz = rz;
   this.sx = sx;
   this.sy = sy;
   this.sz = sz;
   }
   ```

5. Another piece of code will follow this, to declare another two functions, `addpoint` and `addline`, which are actually methods of the `wireframe3d` object.

   ```
   wireframe3d.prototype.addpoint = function (point)
   {
   this.pointlist[this.numpoints] = point;
        this.tpointlist[this.numpoints] = new point3d(point.x, point.y, point.z);
   this.numpoints++;
   }

   wireframe3d.prototype.addline = function (p1num, p2num)
   {
   this.linep1[this.numlines] = p1num;
   this.linep2[this.numlines] = p2num;
   this.numlines++;
   }
   ```

   Okay, so that's our new function defined. Now we have to put it into practice, which means we have to think up a wireframe to draw!

   Let's invent some facts about our wireframe: it's a cube that is 5x5x5, it sits at position (0,0,0), with a rotation of 0 on all axes and a scale of 40. That should do it.

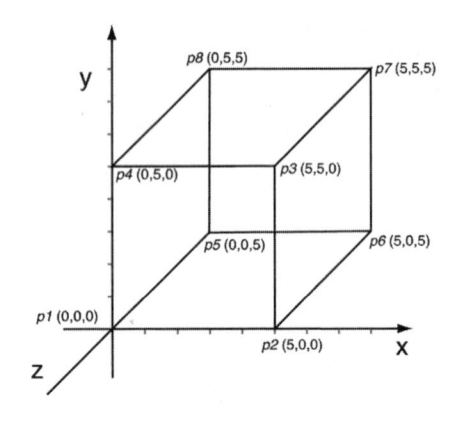

# Real 3D

So where do we begin?

**6.** Well, first let's create the cube object. As with all the other objects, we name it, call the function, and feed it the values.

```
cube = new wireframe3d(0, 0, 0, 0, 0, 0, 40, 40, 40);
```

That's simple enough.

**7.** Next we have to create the 8 points that define the vertices of the cube:

```
cube.addpoint (new point3d (0,0,0));   // p1
cube.addpoint (new point3d (5,0,0));   // p2
cube.addpoint (new point3d (5,5,0));   // p3
cube.addpoint (new point3d (0,5,0));   // p4
cube.addpoint (new point3d (0,0,5));   // p5
cube.addpoint (new point3d (5,0,5));   // p6
cube.addpoint (new point3d (5,5,5));   // p7
cube.addpoint (new point3d (0,5,5));   // p8
```

So you see what's happening: we're adding points to our wireframe, and the `pointlist` variable we created in the `wireframe3d` function will be gobbling them up. Now, let's make the lines use the correct points. We pass the indexes of the created points to the `addline` function:

```
cube.addline (0, 1); // Near lines
cube.addline (1, 2);
cube.addline (2, 3);
cube.addline (3, 0);

cube.addline (0, 4); // Middle lines
cube.addline (1, 5);
cube.addline (2, 6);
cube.addline (3, 7);

cube.addline (4, 5); // Far lines
cube.addline (5, 6);
cube.addline (6, 7);
cube.addline (7, 4);
```

That's it, now we've completely defined a 3D wireframe cube, and it all exists within the object named `cube`. We have all the information we need to render the cube on screen in wireframe.

# 12    Flash Games Studio

## Drawing Things

Okay, so we've got our data structures neatly defined, and we can see how to create a 3D object – *in code*. What about actually getting it on screen? That's our next objective.

One of the greatest disadvantages with Flash is that there's currently no way to modify the individual vertices of a shape at runtime. For example, if you draw a square on screen, there's no easy way for you to use ActionScript to move one of the vertices to a new position, thereby changing its shape.

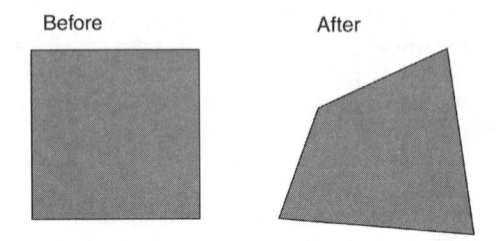

Sure, you can use shape tweening to change the shape of an object like this, but that's not done with ActionScript. Ideally, we would have complete control over each vertex in the shape. Yes, we can freely scale and rotate any object, but that's still not the same as actually changing individual vertices.

So, what can we do? Well, we have to find a way to work around it. The polygon problem is a particularly tough one, so let's look at lines. In Flash, there is also no way of arbitrarily setting the two points of a line, but luckily, there is a fairly easy way of creating a dynamic line renderer.

## Line engines

In order to make our 3D wireframe images happen, we first have to come up with a way of drawing an arbitrary line in Flash. This is a problem that was cracked long ago by the many Flash masters out there. Let's look at two of the solutions here:

### Line engine #1

Line engine #1 has the goal of creating any arbitrary line between any two screen points (x1,y1) and (x2,y2). With this method, you must figure out the angle and the distance between the two points. The line is a movie clip called line1, and it contains a horizontal straight-line graphic that is arranged so that its left vertex is on the center point of the movie clip, with the line itself exactly 100 pixels in length.

# Real 3D

**Line Engine #1**

straight line from (0, 0) to (100, 0)

Simple *line* MovieClip

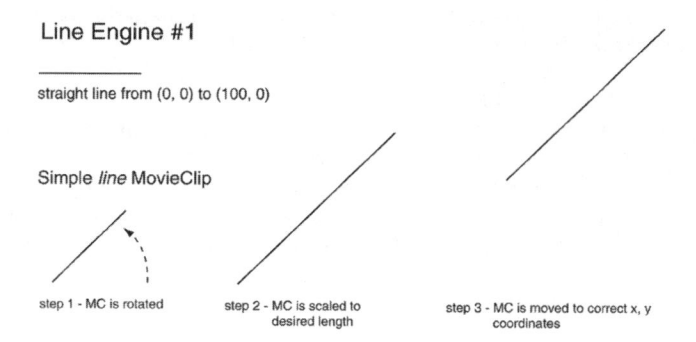

step 1 - MC is rotated    step 2 - MC is scaled to desired length    step 3 - MC is moved to correct x, y coordinates

To calculate the length of the line, you must do the following:

```
dx = x2 - x1;
dy = y2 - y1;
len = Math.sqrt((dx * dx) + (dy * dy));
```

And then to calculate the angle of the line, you must add this:

```
ang = Math.atan2(dy, dx);
```

This takes the two distances between the two x coordinates and two y coordinates and figures out the resulting angle. This will return the angle in Flash's preferred unit of circle measurement, **radians**.

Next, you must set the line to be the desired length, move it to the correct location on screen (x1,y1), and rotate it so its other end meets (x2,y2). In order to do this, we firstly use the _xscale (we want to make it longer on its own x axis) to set the length, then we use _x and _y to set the position, and finally _rotation to set the angle, like this:

```
_xscale = len;
_x = x1;
_y = y1;
_rotation = ang * (180 / Math.PI);
```

That's it, you'll have a line on-screen between (x1,y1) and (x2,y2). You'll notice that I'm multiplying the angle by 180 / PI. This simply converts radians to degrees, since the _rotation property requires degrees as its unit.

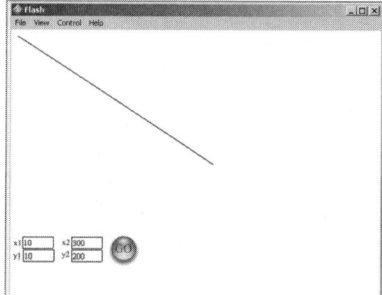

To play with this line engine, take a look at `demo12-2.fla` and experiment with different settings in the dynamic text boxes in the bottom left hand corner.

There are two problems with this approach for rendering a line, namely the Math.sqrt() function and the Math.atan2() function. These functions are both extremely processor intensive to execute, and cannot be relied upon much past a simple demo like this one.
So, although this method works well for a few lines, once we have thousands of lines all moving around, then we'll be performing far too many slow calculations in ActionScript which will slow the game. So, we'd better seek out an alternative.

### Line engine #2

This line engine eliminates the use of any math functions, and simply uses _xscale and _yscale to achieve the desired line.

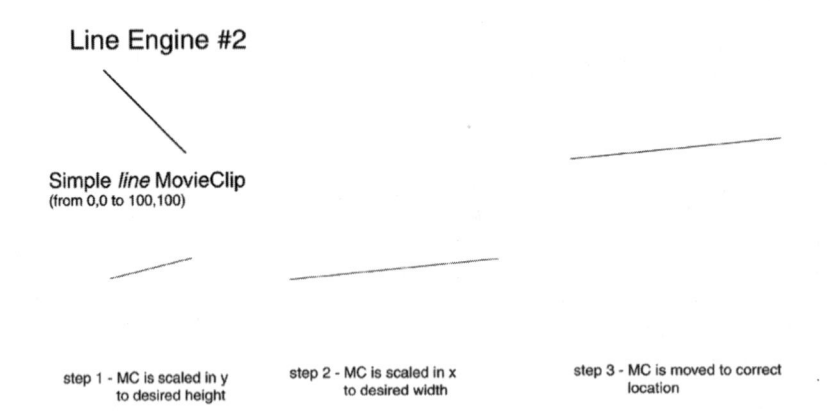

**Line Engine #2**

Simple *line* MovieClip
(from 0,0 to 100,100)

step 1 - MC is scaled in y to desired height

step 2 - MC is scaled in x to desired width

step 3 - MC is moved to correct location

By creating a line that goes from (0,0) to (100,100) within its local coordinate system, we have a movie clip that can simply be scaled in x and y to create the desired height and width of the line. For example, if we want a line from (40,40) to (60,70) we know that the distance in x is (60 – 40) 20, and (70 – 40) 30 in y.

# Real 3D | 12

This means that we simply set the `_xscale` of our movie clip to 20 and the `_yscale` of our movie clip to 30, and it will be the correct angle and length. All we need to do then is move it to the correct starting point. Look at the following ActionScript to see what I mean.

```
dx = x2 - x1;
dy = y2 - y1;

_xscale = dx;
_yscale = dy;
_x = x1;
_y = y1;
```

The magic of this line engine is that no Math functions are used, and hence it is very fast. Much faster than line engine #1, and therefore it is the only one I would recommend that you use.

Take a look at `demo12-3.fla` to see this line method in action. You shouldn't see much of a difference between this and the previous demo, but the inner workings are very different.

> *It's best that you use a hairline for your line, otherwise you'll notice the line thickness changing as you scale it in x and y.*

## Rendering a Shape

Okay, so now we've got a way to define and keep track of 3D shapes, and we also have a nice way of drawing any arbitrary line – let's take a look at how we actually go about making our shape appear on screen.

### The Concepts

Getting an object onto the screen is a multi-staged process that basically consists of carrying out all of the instructions in that nine-parameter list we defined earlier. These numbers dictate how we manipulate the points of the 3D object, before we render them on screen.

As we established, the manipulations we must perform on the object are as follows:

- **Translation** – The object is moved in 3D space to a new location.

- **Scaling** – The object is increased or decreased in size.

- **Rotation** – The object is rotated around any of the axes, thus adjusting its orientation and direction.

# Flash Games Studio

So let's have a look at each of these and see what they're going to do to our object.

**Translation**

Translation is simply the act of moving something from one location to another. When you translate an object, you move all the points of that object at once to a new location. Take a look at the diagram below and see how we have translated this 3D cube:

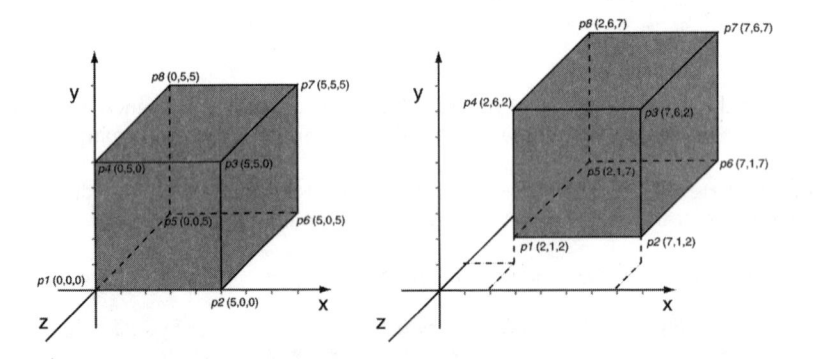

So, relative to the point of origin (0,0,0), the cube has been translated by 2 along its x-axis, 1 along the y and 2 along the z. This is referred to as a translation of (2,1,2).

In the data structures that we defined earlier, this translation is also known simply as the object's position, and it is defined when the object is defined. In our object definition, the above translation is defined like this:

```
cube = new wireframe3d(2, 1, 2, 0, 0, 0, 1, 1, 1);
```

While a game is running, moving the object around the screen is simply a matter of changing its position...

```
cube.x += xtranslation;
cube.y += ytranslation;
cube.z += ztranslation;
```

...or just setting the position like this:

```
cube.x = newx;
cube.y = newy;
cube.z = newz;
```

This is just the principle now, we'll get into the details when I explain the actual rendering engine.

# Real 3D    12

## Scaling

Scaling means making an object larger or smaller on screen. Scaling can be different for each axis, so you can stretch an object lengthwise, but shrink its height. The most common use for scaling is to make an object look correct in proportion to everything else in the game.

**Scaling** (object scaled by 2 in x, 1/2 in y, 1 in z)

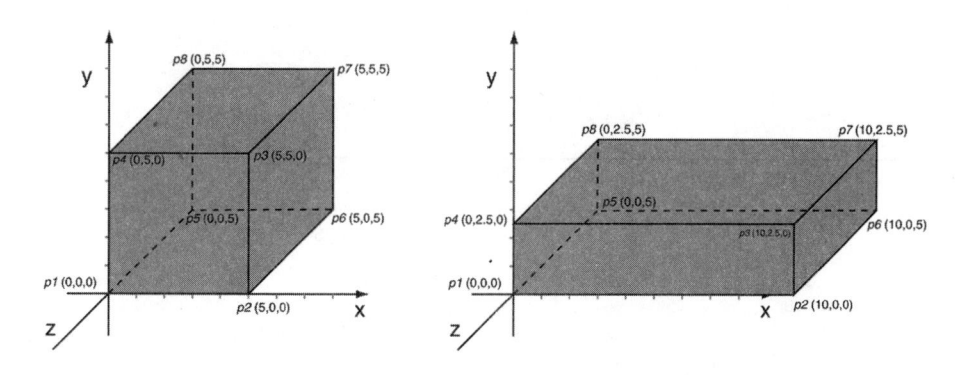

The above example would be defined like follows:

```
cube = new wireframe3d(0, 0, 0, 0, 0, 0, 2, 0.5, 1);
```

You'll see when we get to the renderer that this doesn't actually modify the points as they're stored in the data structure, it simply performs a multiplication to the points as they're being drawn. The object data itself remains untouched.

To increase or decrease the scale of an object, you would simply modify the scale like this...

```
cube.sx += xresize;
cube.sy += yresize;
cube.sz += zresize;
```

...or just set the scale like this:

```
cube.sx = newxscale;
cube.sy = newyscale;
cube.sz = newzscale;
```

All scaling is made relative to the origin (0,0,0). More on the actual details of the functionality in a little bit.

## Rotation

Rotation is the manipulation that makes objects truly come to life in the third dimension. It's with this that objects can be seen from different angles, producing 3D freedom of movement. If your object were an airplane, then rotation would be the act of turning rolling, banking and pitching through the air. There are three directions of rotation, one around each axis.

**Yaw Rotation** (object rotated by 45 degrees around y-axis)

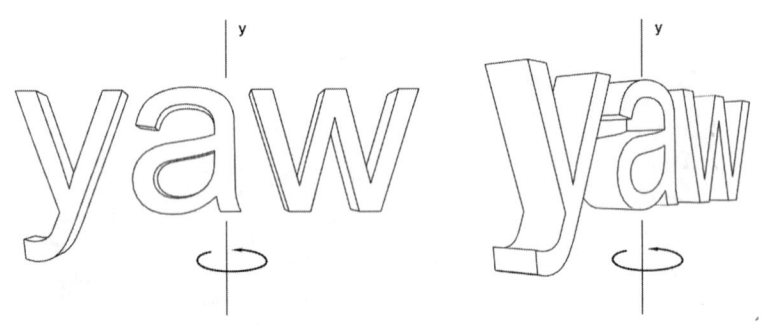

**Roll Rotation** (object rotated by 45 degrees around z-axis)

**Pitch Rotaion** (Object Rotated by 45 degrees around x-axis)

When it comes time to render an object, all its points are first rotated around the three axes, and then the modified points are projected onto the screen. In our object definition, the three rotations are defined as follows:

```
cube = new wireframe3d(0, 0, 0, pitch, yaw, roll, 1, 1, 1);
```

And let's say that during the game, you wanted to yaw a player around a left hand corner (change its direction by yawing to the left) then you would change the yaw as follows:

```
cube.ry += yawchange;
```

Or of course you would use "-=" to yaw to the right. Similarly, you could set the rotation by assigning any value to the three rotations, as follows:

```
cube.rx = pitchamount;
cube.ry = yawamount;
cube.rz = rollamount;
```

As I have tried to stress all along, any calculation – translation, scaling, or rotation – takes place around the origin (0,0,0). With rotation these manipulations can make your 3D objects move all about in space, turning, zooming, flipping, squashing and spinning!

## Ordering

So why has it been important to stress the point of origin? Well, our final consideration in 3D manipulation is that of **order**. Think about it; if you translate your object to a new location and then rotate it, it will rotate relative to the origin and could move quite far from your desired destination. Let's say we want to have a box spinning on the spot at position (5,0,3). If we translate then rotate, our box will misbehave and fly all over the place! This effect can be seen below in the sample overhead view.

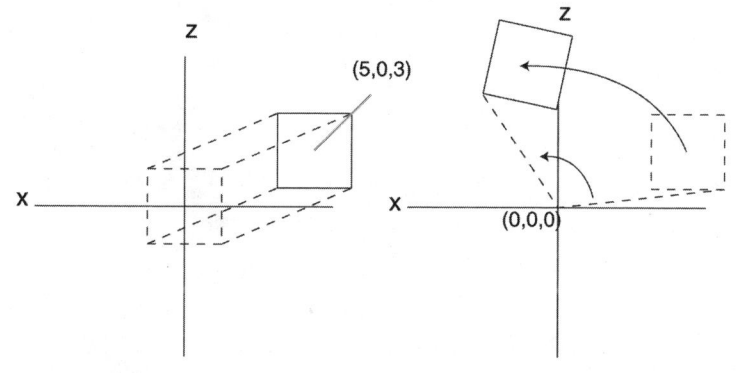

1. Object is translated to new position

2. Object is rotated around (0,0,0)

# 12    Flash Games Studio

Now, let's try it the other way and take the same box, rotate it first and *then* translate it to (5,0,3):

Rotation followed by Translation

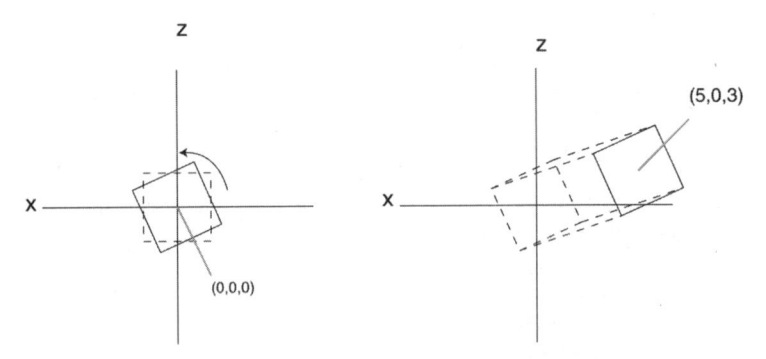

1. Object is rotated around (0,0,0)

2. Object is translated to new position, correctly rotated

This doesn't appear obvious when you're first getting into 3D so it can often be a source of much frustration. You must always remember the effect that order can have on 3D manipulations. The same rules apply with scaling; you should always scale at the origin, and then translate the objects.

However, in some circumstances, you want to translate and then rotate. Let's take an example of a situation where you have a parking lot with four cars all aligned the same direction and you want to be able to walk around them in 3D. This situation ideally would look something like this:

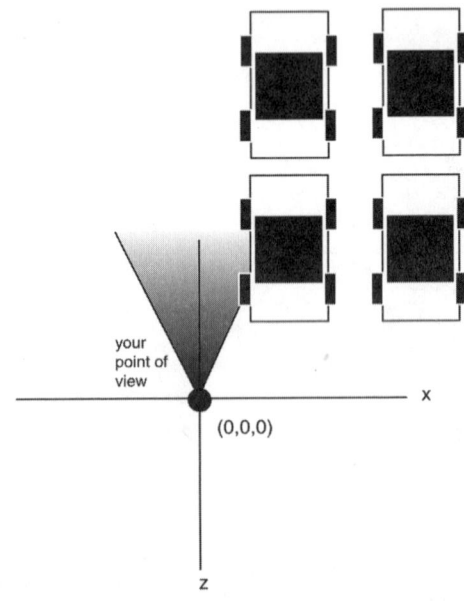

**Top View**

# Real 3D    12

The player is always at the origin (0,0,0) looking forward in z, and everything is merely rotated and translated *around* the origin to give the effect that you are walking around. In essence, you are not moving – instead the whole world is translated (by your position) and rotated (around your position) – *that order is vital*.

These are 3D cars that you need to be able to walk around to view. So, let's say the players control their view by yawing left or right as they walk (the typical first person shooter view).

If we were to rotate the vehicles in the order previously described (rotating and then translating), the cars will be dutifully spinning on the spot – on their *local coordinates*. This is not quite the first person effect we were going for!

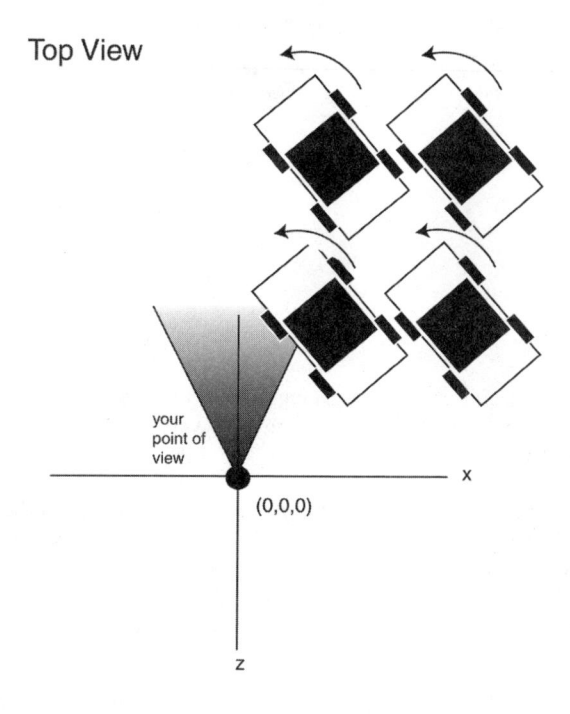

How about the other way – translate and *then* rotate:

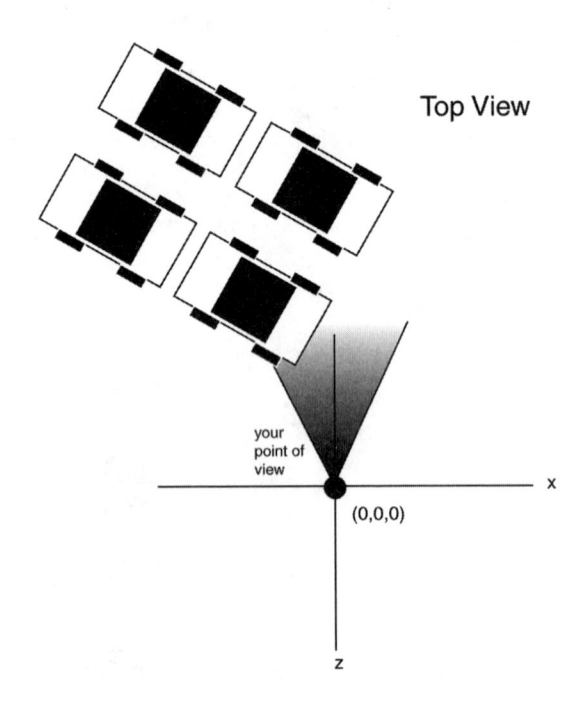

Top View

your point of view

(0,0,0)

x

z

Now you can see that the point of view has changed, but the cars have stayed in the same relative position. This is the desired effect, and now you can walk freely around the cars – or, more accurately, the cars will move around you.

Now, what happens if you want to walk around a car that is spinning on the spot? Oh, come on, use your imagination – it's on a turntable at a trade show or something! It's both rotating in its own coordinate system, and also rotating relative to you as you walk. The answer would be to adopt the order *rotate > translate > rotate*. Simple really, isn't it? As with all of the 3D concepts, it can be daunting to get your head around, but once you've got it, it's a piece of cake.

## Projection

The last stage in 3D imaging is to get the images on screen. It's all well and good to rotate, translate and scale your objects in 3D space but it's all numbers until something actually appears on screen! That's where projection comes in.

Projection is the act of taking your points in 3D space, and somehow getting them on screen in such a way as to make them appear 3D. When we're creating a 3D wireframe object, you'll also want to connect the points with on-screen lines.

# Real 3D | 12

## Parallel Projection

So, how do you take a single point located at x, y and z and bring it on the screen (s) as `sx` and `sy`? Well, what if you simply took x and y (and ignored z) and mapped those directly onto the screen? It *can* be done this way. Very simply, you would retain no depth information and your objects would appear the same no matter how near or far they were! Let's look at a `point3d` object called p1, and see how we would map a movie clip called pointMC onto the screen.

```
pointMC._x = p1.x + screencenterX;
pointMC._y = p1.y + screencenterY;
```

That's it! Notice that we're completely ignoring z. Also, since everything is around (0,0) our objects would appear in the upper left hand corner of the screen – which is also (0,0). In order to get our 3D space nicely centered on the screen, we must add the screen center to each point. We're only looking at one point here, but in order to project an object on screen you just do this with each point in the object.

This type of projection is called **parallel projection** and it has the potential to confuse us because of its lack of z. Take a look at this example:

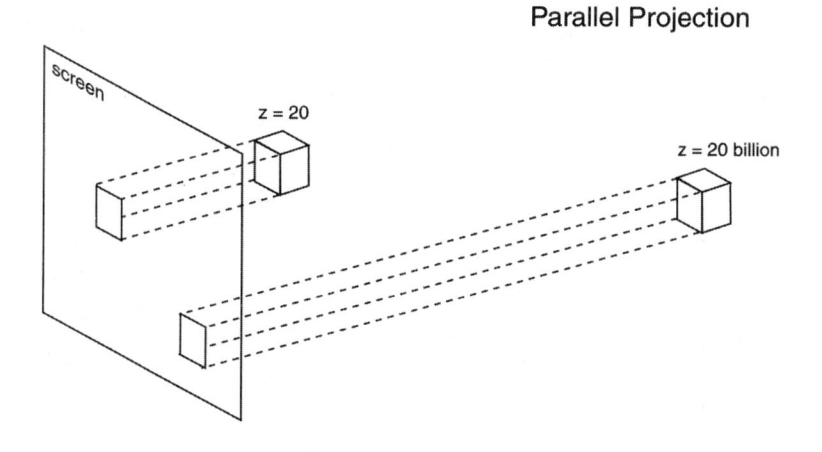

Parallel Projection

In this total exaggeration you can see that although the far cube is ridiculously farther away than the near cube, they both appear the same size on screen! That far cube should be so miniscule – pretty much invisible – because it's so far away. This is the effect of parallel projection – it squashes the third dimension.

479

## Perspective Projection

This method of projection is the true-to-life form of projection. Using perspective projection, objects appear smaller as they recede into the distance. Obviously then, we have to make use of z somehow. How would we make x and y appear smaller as they have higher z values? Simply by dividing the x and y by the z, like this:

```
pointMX._x = (d * (p1.x / p1.z)) + screencenterX;
pointMX._y = (d * (p1.y / p1.z)) + screencenterX;
```

The higher the z value, the closer the x and y values will be to screen center, which is the way perspective works – all points converge towards (screencenterX, screencenterY) as they recede.

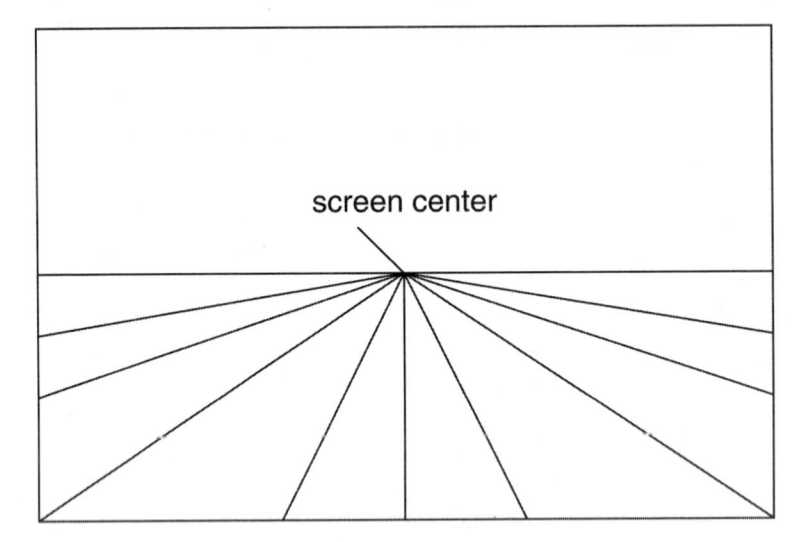

You'll notice in the above code that I'm using a variable called d as well. This is known as the **view distance** and it is an easily-changed variable – handy to accommodate scale differences between object space and screen space.

So, if we were to define a cube that was 5x5x5 sitting at (0,0,1) and then project it on screen, it would only be 5 pixels in size – not very big. If we were to move it back to (0,0,10), then based on the fact that all the points were divided by z, then our square would be 5/10 or 0.5 pixels in size! That's very small!

So, we pick a d that has the effect of making our object appear the most naturally sized on screen (d is therefore related to screen resolution). Most commonly, a d value of 250 to 400 will suit best. This number really depends on the scale of your movie, and therefore you should always play around with different values when you first start creating your 3D engine.

# Real 3D

When we do this to all our rotated/scaled/translated points, and then connect the on-screen points with lines, we will have brought our 3D world to life!

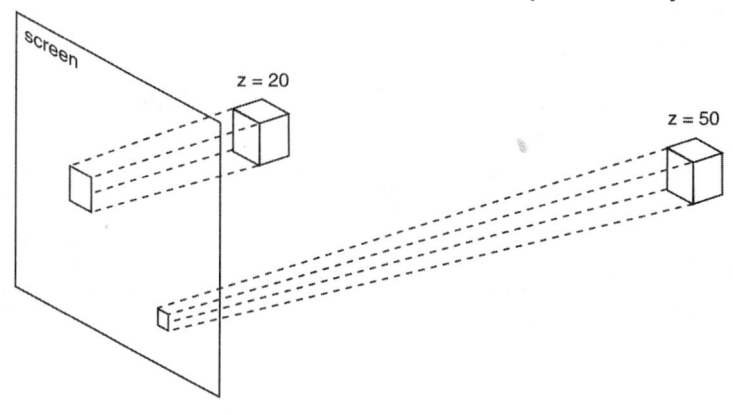

**Perspective Projection**

## The Math In Action

Okay, now that we know all the fundamentals, let's take a look at the actual renderer in action.

**1.** Open `demo12-4.swf`, and you'll see it going through its paces.

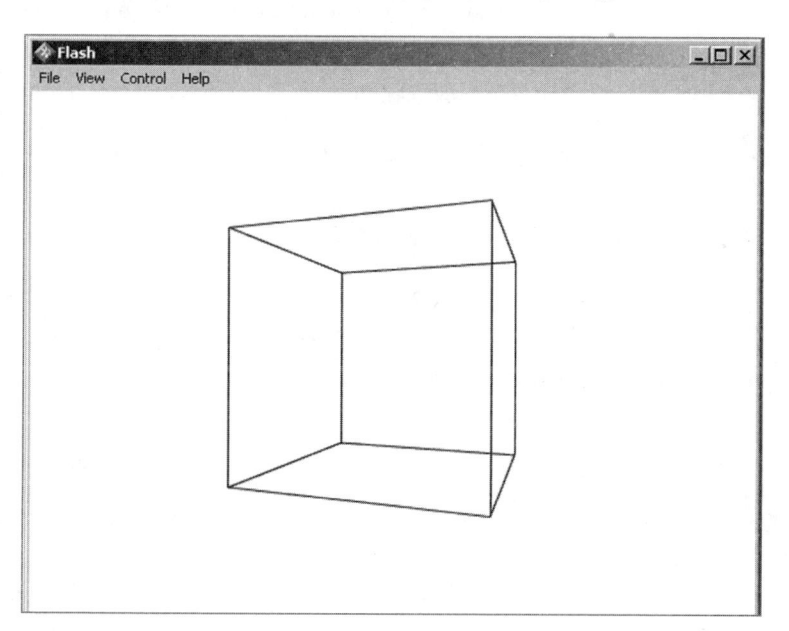

2. On the main timeline, I have a movie clip called line. It's exactly the same line used in line engine #2, except it now actually has its controlling ActionScript attached to it, using the wonderfully versatile `onClipEvent (load)` function. So now we don't need to use line engine #2's button to run the code!

```
onClipEvent (load)
{
    function drawline (sx1, sy1, sx2, sy2)
    {
        dx = sx2 - sx1;
        dy = sy2 - sy1;

        _xscale = dx;
        _yscale = dy;
        _x = sx1;
        _y = sy1;
    }

}
```

3. In order to make a line movie clip with the instance name happyline drawn from (10,0) to (300, 200) we would simply say:

```
happyline.drawline(10,0,300,200);
```

Most of the magic in this demo is performed in a movie clip on the main timeline called controller. This movie clip contains all of the **object definition** code (within the `onClipEvent(load)`) that was outlined earlier, with one addition to the wireframe3d addline function.

4. The new addline function looks like this:

```
wireframe3d.prototype.addline = function (p1num, p2num)
{
    this.linep1[this.numlines] = p1num;
    this.linep2[this.numlines] = p2num;

    duplicateMovieClip (_root.line, "line" add lnum, lnum);
    this.linename[this.numlines] = "line" add lnum++;

    this.numlines++;
}
```

# Real 3D

When a new line is added to the object, a new instance of the line movie clip is also created, thus conveniently giving us the graphic that we will use to draw the `line3d` object. The line's instance name is created and stored in an array of the object called linename. The global variable `lnum` is incremented at the end.

5. I've also added the following code to the beginning of the controller's `load` clip event.

```
// counter for duplicating the line graphics
lnum = 1;

// Screen center
screencenterX = 275;
screencenterY = 200;

// For perspective projection
d = 350;

// World's overall relative position
offx = 0;
offy = 0;
offz = -140;

// World's overall relative rotation
playerrx = 0;
playerry = 0;
playerrz = 0;

// Cos and sin look-up table
mycos = new Array;
mysin = new Array;

for (i = 0; i < 3600; i++)
{
        mycos[i] = Math.cos (i * (Math.PI / 1800));
        mysin[i] = Math.sin (i * (Math.PI / 1800));
}
```

In this code I'm initializing some data that I'm going to use later. `lnum` is simply a counter that is used in the `line3d` constructor to create the instance name of our next line. The `screencenterX` and `screencenterY` are set based on the mid-point of my stage. The variable `d` is set to 350 for this demo. Through trial and error, this seemed to be the optimum value for making realistic 3D projections.

# Flash Games Studio

Finally, I create two arrays, `mycos` and `mysin`. These arrays each contain 3600 numbers, which are the cos and sin values of 3600 units around a circle. I've chosen 3600 because it neatly divides each degree of a 360 degree circle into 10 angles, thus giving us 10 times more accuracy than if we had just stored one angle per degree. By using this array later when we want a sin or cos, we avoid the computer having to perform the `Math.cos` and `Math.sin` (which are slow) while the game is running.

To get the sin of 180 degrees we simply look at `mysin[1800]`. The cos of 72 degrees is `mycos[720]`. In this way you can go all the way around the circle. For this demo, we're going to create a 50x50x50 cube, that is centered around the origin (0,0,0).

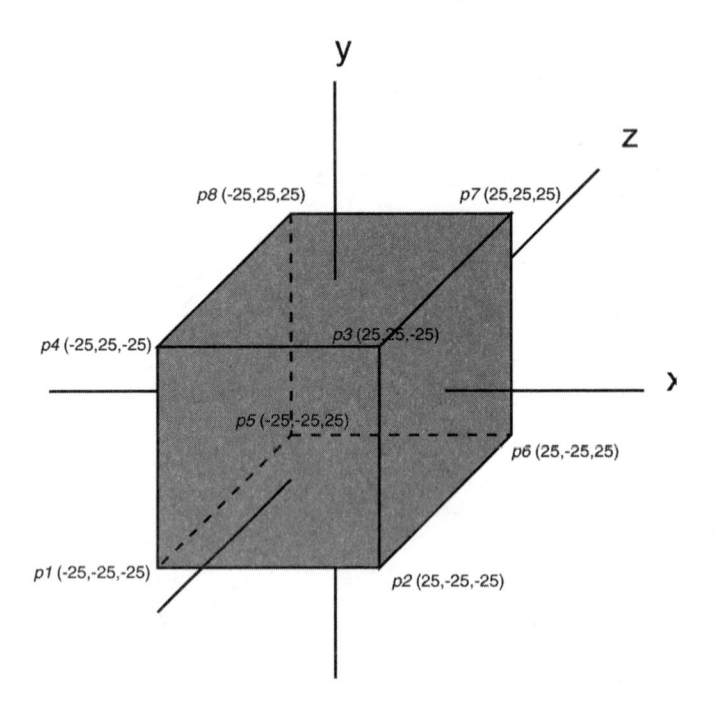

6. The cube is defined with the following ActionScript at the bottom of the controller's `load` clip event:

```
cube = new wireframe3d(0, 0, 140, 0, 0, 0, 1, 1, 1);

cube.addpoint (new point3d (-25,-25,-25));  // 0
cube.addpoint (new point3d (25,-25,-25));   // 1
cube.addpoint (new point3d (25,25,-25));    // 2
cube.addpoint (new point3d (-25,25,-25));   // 3
cube.addpoint (new point3d (-25,-25,25));   // 4
cube.addpoint (new point3d (25,-25,25));    // 5
```

# Real 3D

```
cube.addpoint (new point3d (25,25,25));    // 6
cube.addpoint (new point3d (-25,25,25));   // 7

cube.addline (0, 1); // Near lines
cube.addline (1, 2);
cube.addline (2, 3);
cube.addline (3, 0);

cube.addline (0, 4); // Middle lines
cube.addline (1, 5);
cube.addline (2, 6);
cube.addline (3, 7);

cube.addline (4, 5); // Far lines
cube.addline (5, 6);
cube.addline (6, 7);
cube.addline (7, 4);
```

This cube is sitting at (0,0,140) and it has a yaw, roll and pitch of 0, and its x, y and z scale are all 1 – the cube is neither stretched nor squashed.

## Drawing It

Now that the object itself is defined, we have all the necessary components required to draw the object on the screen. We have the mathematical data, and we also have the line movie clips ready. Let's see how the object renderer does its work. Here's the main body of the code, and I'll go through it step by step in a moment.

```
function drawobject (obj)
{
  for (i = 0; i < obj.numlines; i++)
  {
    p1ind = obj.linep1[i];
    p2ind = obj.linep2[i];

    newx1 = obj.tpointlist[p1ind].x;
    newy1 = obj.tpointlist[p1ind].y;
    newz1 = obj.tpointlist[p1ind].z;

    newx2 = obj.tpointlist[p2ind].x;
    newy2 = obj.tpointlist[p2ind].y;
    newz2 = obj.tpointlist[p2ind].z;

    // is line behind me?
    if (newz1 > 0 && newz2 > 0)
    {
    // Perspective project both points into screen coordinates
        sx1 = (d * (newx1 / newz1)) + screencenterX;
        sy1 = (d * (newy1 / newz1)) + screencenterY;
```

# 12 Flash Games Studio

```
            sx2 = (d * (newx2 / newz2)) + screencenterX;
            sy2 = (d * (newy2 / newz2)) + screencenterY;

            avez = (newz1 + newz2) >> 1;

            // draw the line
            _root[obj.linename[i]]._visible = true;
            _root[obj.linename[i]].swapDepths(100000-Math.floor(avez));
            _root[obj.linename[i]].drawline(sx1, sy1, sx2, sy2);
        }
        else
            _root[obj.linename[i]]._visible = false;
    }
}
```

To draw the cube, we would simply do the following:

```
        drawobject(cube);
```

That's it done. But what exactly is that renderer doing? Let's look at it piece by piece:

```
        for (i = 0; i < obj.numlines; i++)
        {
```

Here we're going through an iteration loop of all the lines in the wireframe object.

```
        p1ind = obj.linep1[i];
        p2ind = obj.linep2[i];
```

What we're doing next is getting the two point indexes and storing them in two temporary variables `p1ind` and `p2ind` for convenience.

```
        newx1 = obj.tpointlist[p1ind].x;
        newy1 = obj.tpointlist[p1ind].y;
        newz1 = obj.tpointlist[p1ind].z;

        newx2 = obj.tpointlist[p2ind].x;
        newy2 = obj.tpointlist[p2ind].y;
        newz2 = obj.tpointlist[p2ind].z;
```

Here we're getting the actual x, y and z coordinates of the endpoints of the line, and storing them in temporary variables. We're getting our points from `tpointlist` instead of `pointlist`. That's because we're only interested in the final position of the points in world space, not the local position of the points that define the object.

# Real 3D

You may be wondering how we can use `tpointlist` when no manipulation has yet been performed – well, we can't. In a moment I'll be going over the manipulation. But, for now...

```
// is line behind me?
if (newz1 > 0 && newz2 > 0)
{
```

Next we take a look at the z value of both points. If either of them is less than 0 (behind the player's point of view) then there's no reason to draw the line. However, assuming the line is valid, we next do the following:

```
sx1 = (d * (newx1 / newz1)) + screencenterX;
sy1 = (d * (newy1 / newz1)) + screencenterY;

sx2 = (d * (newx2 / newz2)) + screencenterX;
sy2 = (d * (newy2 / newz2)) + screencenterY;
```

That is our simple perspective projection, as discussed earlier. We're creating two screen coordinates: (sx1,sy1) and (sx2,sy2) – These coordinates are the two endpoints of the line. Next, we quickly compute the average z value of the line's two points with the following code:

```
avez = (newz1 + newz2) >> 1;
```

We're using a special operator called a bitshift.

> *Bitshift operators are tricks of the trade for game programmers because they're incredibly fast. What exactly does a bitshift do? Well, it moves the bits of a number depending on the direction of the bitshift. Numbers are stored in a computer in a binary (1's and 0's only) form like so:*
>
> *11010*
>
> *is the number 26, for example. When we shift the bits of a number, we are moving the bits left or right.*
>
> *So, bitshifting left (<<) will turn 11010 into 110100 because we're moving all the other bits to the left, and creating an empty space, where we place a 0.*
>
> *It turns out that 110100 is equal to 52 – exactly two times 26.*
>
> *If we bitshift our 11010 to the right (>>) we get 1101, which is 13 – exactly half of 26. What's the moral of the story? Bitshifting left will double a number, bitshifting right will halve a number – and it's very, very fast – much faster than actually using the \* 2 or \* 0.5 instructions. It's an optimization trick used to speed up games.*

Finally, we draw our line:

```
_root[obj.linename[i]]._visible = true;
_root[obj.linename[i]].swapDepths(100000-Math.floor(avez));
_root[obj.linename[i]].drawline(sx1, sy1, sx2, sy2);
```

We use the built in drawline function of the line movie clip. Here we use the linename array to address the proper line movie clip instance. We're also doing a simple form of depth sorting (making farther objects appear behind closer objects) by using a `swapDepths` command that is based on the average z (avez) of the line. The use for this is not so obvious with wireframe lines, but it will be later when we introduce sprites.

We're also setting its visibility to `true` just in case it had been made invisible previously by the `_root[obj.linename[i]]._visible = false;` command when the line was behind the viewer.

That's all there is to the wireframe shape drawing function. This will draw any shape we define using the `addpoint` and `addline` functions.

## Adding More Math

Okay, now comes the advanced stuff. We're going to talk about the math involved in manipulating our 3D points to create the correctly modified, and renderable version of our cube.

All the work is done in a function called `manipulateobject`, which is called with the following syntax:

```
manipulateobject(cube, playeroffx, playeroffy, playeroffz,
playerrx, playerry, playerrz);
```

Basically, we're passing our location and rotation to the function, and it is going to perform all the necessary manipulations to get it into the correct location in 3D space. Within the function itself, the object is also going to be rotated, scaled and translated by its own internal settings as defined in `cube.rx`, `cube.ry`, `cube.rz` (rotation), `cube.sx`, `cube.sy`, `cube.sz` (scale), `cube.x`, `cube.y` and `cube.z` (translation).

Let's look at `manipulateobject` now. Once again this is a whole list of ActionScript, broken down by my explanations.

# Real 3D    12

1. First, we take all the rotation angles and making sure that they fall within a valid range:

   ```
   // fix object angle so it's between 0 and 3600
   obj.rx = (Math.floor(obj.rx) % 3600);
   obj.ry = (Math.floor(obj.ry) % 3600);
   obj.rz = (Math.floor(obj.rz) % 3600);
   if (obj.rx < 0) obj.rx += 3600;
   if (obj.ry < 0) obj.ry += 3600;
   if (obj.rz < 0) obj.rz += 3600;

   // fix player angle so it's between 0 and 3600
   xrot = (Math.floor(xrot) % 3600);
   yrot = (Math.floor(yrot) % 3600);
   zrot = (Math.floor(zrot) % 3600);
   if (xrot < 0) xrot += 3600;
   if (yrot < 0) yrot += 3600;
   if (zrot < 0) zrot += 3600;
   ```

   Remember, we're not using actual angles here, but rather we want numbers that can be used as indexes into the `mysin` and `mycos` arrays we created earlier. So, we're rounding the angle to the nearest whole number and then using the modulus operator (%) to calculate where in the 3600 we are.

2. Next, we assign 12 temporary variables that will be used in a few moments:

   ```
   // Look up the trig
   yawsin = mysin[obj.ry];
   yawcos = mycos[obj.ry];
   rollsin = mysin[obj.rz];
   rollcos = mycos[obj.rz];
   pitchsin = mysin[obj.rx];
   pitchcos = mycos[obj.rx];

   pyawsin = mysin[yrot];
   pyawcos = mycos[yrot];
   prollsin = mysin[zrot];
   prollcos = mycos[zrot];
   ppitchsin = mysin[xrot];
   ppitchcos = mycos[xrot];
   ```

   These contain the sin and cos of yaw, roll and pitch for both the object's rotation and the player's rotation. These are, of course, using the `mycos` and `mysin` arrays to look up the results, *not* calculating sin and cos on the fly.

## Flash Games Studio

3. Then we start stepping through the points one at a time.

   ```
   // Manipulate the points
   for (i = 0; i < obj.numpoints; i++)
   {
   ```

4. The first thing we do is scale the points on x, y and z and store the results in `x1`, `y1` and `z1`. This is the first of our manipulations.

   ```
   // Scale the point
   x1 = obj.pointlist[i].x * obj.sx;
   y1 = obj.pointlist[i].y * obj.sy;
   z1 = obj.pointlist[i].z * obj.sz;
   ```

5. Next, we rotate the points:

   ```
   // Rotate point
   tx = (yawcos * x1) - (yawsin * z1);
   tz = (yawsin * x1) + (yawcos * z1);
   newx = (rollcos * tx) + (rollsin * y1);
   ty = (rollcos * y1) - (rollsin * tx);
   newz = (pitchcos * tz) - (pitchsin * ty);
   newy = (pitchsin * tz) + (pitchcos * ty);
   ```

   Notice that we're rotating the point first before translating it. This is because here we're rotating the object by its own local rotation. This is the same concept as I illustrated earlier in manipulation ordering.

   > *Note: These formulae are simply the result of matrix multiplication. I'm choosing not to go into a full explanation of matrices because the topic is long and involved, and we're only really interested in these final results. I also want to approach it from an optimized route, and multi-staged matrix math can introduce too much overhead. If you want to find out more details about matrix math, take a look at Flash 5 ActionScript Studio, there's a great description in there.*

6. Next, we translate the point (which is now a work in progress) to its x, y and z location – relative to its own local origin. Then we also translate it based on the `xoff`, `yoff` and `zoff` – the distance from the world's origin. This offset is used as the player's position in a 3D game.

   ```
   // Translate point
   newx += (obj.x - xoff);
   newy += (obj.y - yoff);
   newz += (obj.z - zoff);
   ```

# Real 3D

**7.** Now we perform a totally new rotation on the points around another set of rotations. Although, this time, because the points have been translated, this will have the effect of rotating around the world's origin. The player will control these rotation values, and this will allow them to walk around the objects, like our earlier parking lot example.

```
// Rotate point around player
tx = (pyawcos * newx) - (pyawsin * newz);
tz = (pyawsin * newx) + (pyawcos * newz);
newx = (prollcos * tx) + (prollsin * newy);
ty = (prollcos * newy) - (prollsin * tx);
newz = (ppitchcos * tz) - (ppitchsin * ty);
newy = (ppitchsin * tz) + (ppitchcos * ty);
```

**8.** Finally, we each freshly manipulated point, and store it back in the tpointlist array of the object. It's funny really – all that math just to (ultimately) move a bunch of 3D points from one (x, y, z) location to another (x, y, z) location, with some very specific parameters.

```
// Store manipulated point
obj.tpointlist[i].x = newx;
obj.tpointlist[i].y = newy;
obj.tpointlist[i].z = newz;
```

**9.** To render the cube, simply add the following ActionScript to the controller movie clip:

```
onClipEvent(enterFrame)
{
manipulateobject(cube, offx, offy, offz, playerrx, playerry,
playerrz);
        drawobject(cube);
        cube.ry += 10;
}
```

**10.** If you run your movie, you will see a cube spinning in the center of the screen.

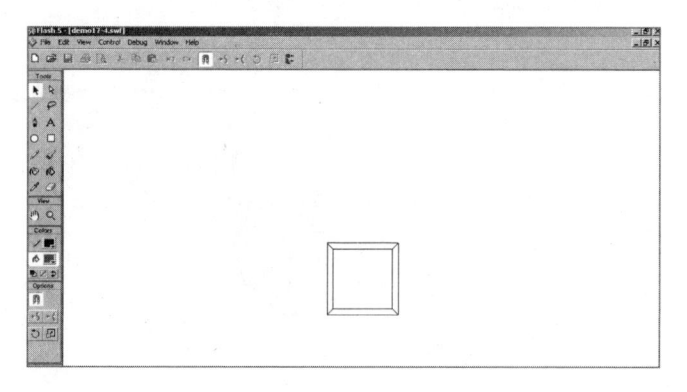

That's all there is to the wireframe renderer (`demo12-4.swf`). Before we get to the game, I have to introduce one more concept.

## Sprites

Some of the most important aspects of a 3D game are objects that are not actually rendered in real-time, but instead are merely moved and scaled in 3D. In the context of this rendering engine, a sprite is simply a pre-drawn image. Take a look at this image of `demo12-5.swf`.

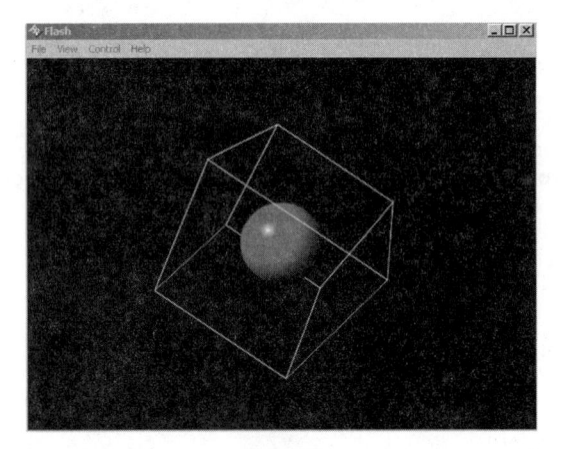

The ball in the center of the square is a **sprite**. It's merely a pre-drawn movie clip image that is moved and scaled according to standard 3D rotation and projection. It is actually a flat 2D image, which we bring into the third dimension with our sprite renderer. The sprite will always be facing us, no matter where it is in 3D space, so for this reason it's best suited for symmetrical objects, like the ball in this example.

# Real 3D

To hold the sprite, a new object type called `sprite3d` has been created. Here is its constructor function (from the controller's `load` clip event)

```
function sprite3d (x, y, z, scale, source)
{
    this.x = x;
    this.y = y;
    this.z = z;
    this.scale = scale;

    duplicateMovieClip (source, "image" add lnum, lnum);
    this.name = "image" add lnum++;
}
```

This is quite similar to the `point3d`, except we have the addition of scale and an image. Realistically, the sprite object only possesses one 3D point, and that will be wherever the actual center point on the sprite image's movie clip is. Looking at the above, you can see that the center point (the small "+") is in the middle of the ball sprite. Consequently, this will be treated as the center point of the object when placed in 3D.

Rather than an x, y and z scale, there is simply a single `scale`. This is a number that represents the relative size of the sprite in 3D. If you pass in 1 as the scale, then the object will be sized as you designed it. 2 will make it twice as big, 0.5 will make it half size, and so on. Note: This scale is in addition to the natural scaling that will take place as the object moves into the distance. No matter what `scale` you put here, the sprite will still shrink as it gets farther away.

There is one more parameter passed to the constructor function, and that is `source`. This is the name of a movie clip instance that will be duplicated and used as the image for the sprite.

This is the syntax to create a `sprite3d` object:

```
ball = new sprite3d(0, 0, 140, 2, "_root.ballimage");
```

In this example, we're saying that the `sprite3d` called ball will be sitting at (0,0,140), it will be scaled 2x, and the movie clip to use as the source image is `_root.ballimage`.

The code to render a `sprite3d` onto the screen is quite similar to the code required to render a wireframe object, with just a couple of differences:

- We only need one point: the sprite's 3D position, not several points/vertices as in a wireframe object.

- There is no rotation that can be applied to a sprite. It is always facing directly towards us.

# Flash Games Studio

To draw a sprite, we simply make a call to a single function `drawsprite3d`, which takes the player's position and rotation as parameters, and moves and scales the sprite according to these. The call looks like this:

```
drawsprite3d(ball, offx, offy, offz, playerrx, playerry, playerrz);
```

And the actual `drawsprite3d` code (which is also in the controller's `load` clip event), looks like this:

```
function drawsprite3d (obj, xoff, yoff, zoff, xrot, yrot, zrot)
{
    // fix angle so it's between 0 and 3600
    xrot = (Math.floor(xrot) % 3600);
    yrot = (Math.floor(yrot) % 3600);
    zrot = (Math.floor(zrot) % 3600);
    if (xrot < 0) xrot += 3600;
    if (yrot < 0) yrot += 3600;
    if (zrot < 0) zrot += 3600;

    pyawsin = mysin[yrot];
    pyawcos = mycos[yrot];
    prollsin = mysin[zrot];
    prollcos = mycos[zrot];
    ppitchsin = mysin[xrot];
    ppitchcos = mycos[xrot];

    // Translate object
    newx = obj.x - xoff;
    newy = obj.y - yoff;
    newz = obj.z - zoff;

    // Rotate object around player
    tx = (pyawcos * newx) - (pyawsin * newz);
    tz = (pyawsin * newx) + (pyawcos * newz);
    newx = (prollcos * tx) + (prollsin * newy);
    ty = (prollcos * newy) - (prollsin * tx);
    newz = (ppitchcos * tz) - (ppitchsin * ty);
    newy = (ppitchsin * tz) + (ppitchcos * ty);

    // is object behind me?
    if (newz > 0)
    {
    // Perspective project the object into screen coordinates

        sx = (d * (newx / newz)) + screencenterX;
        sy = (d * (newy / newz)) + screencenterY;

        // draw the object
        _root[obj.name]._visible = true;
```

# Real 3D

```
            _root[obj.name]._x = sx;
            _root[obj.name]._y = sy;

            scale = ((d * 100) / newz) * obj.scale;

            _root[obj.name]._xscale = scale;
            _root[obj.name]._yscale = scale;

            _root[obj.name].swapDepths(100000-Math.floor(newz));
        }
        else
            _root[obj.name]._visible = false;
    }
```

This is quite similar to the `manipulateobject` and the `drawobject` functions. We still check the range of the angles (from 0 to 3600) and then lookup the pre-computed `sin` and `cos` values at the beginning.

We're missing the step of rotating the sprite before translating it, but that's because the sprite is not actually 3D, so rotating it in its own local 3D coordinates would produce no change – it would rotate around its center.

So next we translate it out to its correct 3D position and then we rotate it around the player (this rotation *is* necessary because it has the effect of moving the sprite to a new location on screen).

```
            sx = (d * (newx / newz)) + screencenterX;
            sy = (d * (newy / newz)) + screencenterY;

            // draw the object
            _root[obj.name]._visible = true;
            _root[obj.name]._x = sx;
            _root[obj.name]._y = sy;
```

Next, the sprite's manipulated x, y and z is perspective-projected onto the screen, and then its \_x and \_y coordinates are set to that screen projection.

There is one significant difference between the sprite renderer and the wireframe 3D renderer, and that is here:

```
            scale = ((d * 100) / newz) * obj.scale;

            _root[obj.name]._xscale = scale;
            _root[obj.name]._yscale = scale;
```

# Flash Games Studio

This bit of ActionScript is responsible for resizing the object itself based on its z coordinate. It's almost identical to the standard perspective projection, except it doesn't use x or y, but rather (d * 100), which is the d as we defined earlier, multiplied by 100. This 100 is simply required to make the object appear 100% correctly sized on screen. Finally, the whole scale is multiplied by obj.scale (the scale value we set when we created the sprite), to shrink or grow the sprite overall in 3D space.

Lastly, using the sprite's manipulated z value, we can set the graphical depth of the sprite movie clip instance, and make it appear behind closer objects, and in front of farther objects.

```
_root[obj.name].swapDepths(100000-Math.floor(newz));
```

This type of depth sorting is essential in creating a believable 3D effect.

Congratulations! If you've gotten this far, then you are truly a brave soul, and are ready to take on the challenges of applying 3D to a game!

## Fancy a Game of 3D Pong?

Everyone has played the classic game, *Pong*. Well, now we're going to bring it into the exciting third dimension with action-packed angles and smooth camera moves. In 3D Pong, you control a single paddle, which moves around in a circle while the ball floats along. Your mission is to keep the ball from flying off into space. This game can be seen in demo12-6.swf.

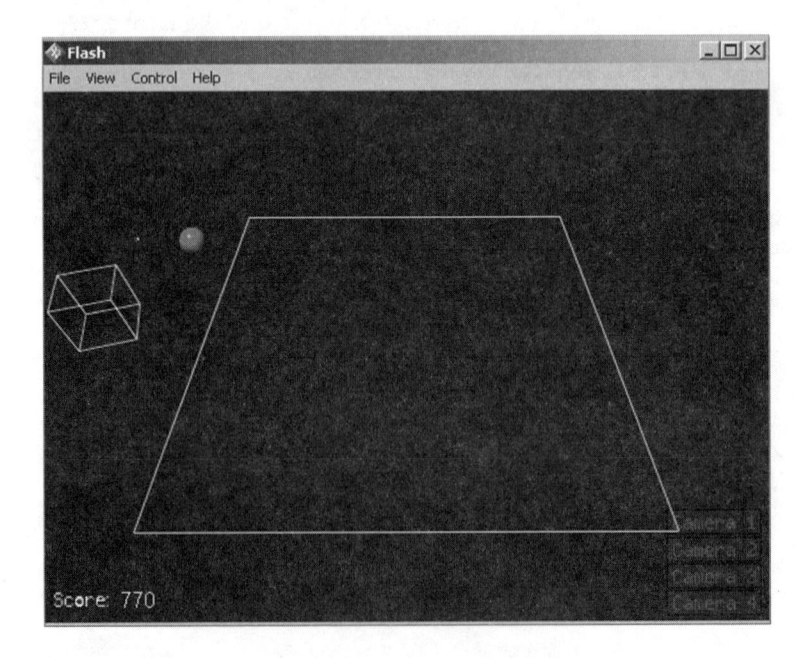

# Real 3D | 12

Controlling the paddle is fairly straightforward: Move the mouse left and right, and the x location of the cursor determines the angle and location of the paddle.

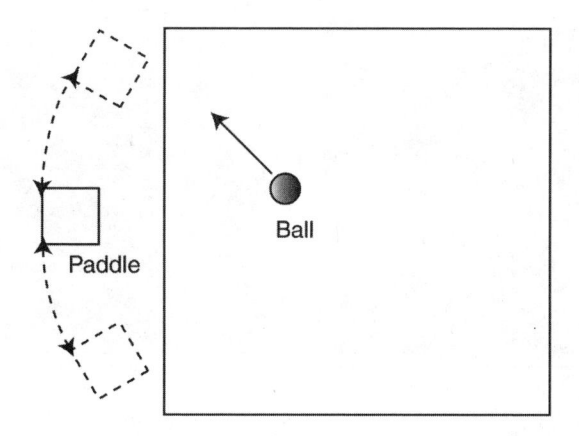

## Cameras

1. A "camera" is simply a **view** – a preset x, y, z location and yaw, roll and pitch angle. When we are looking at the world through a specific camera, then that camera's attributes are applied to the current view translation and rotation. We have to create a new data structure and constructor function to accommodate our cameras. Here's the constructor function (within the `load` event of the controller):

    ```
    function camera3d (x, y, z, rx, ry, rz)
    {
            this.x = x;
            this.y = y;
            this.z = z;
            this.rx = rx;
            this.ry = ry;
            this.rz = rz;
    }
    ```

2. This is very basic, and a camera itself doesn't do anything, it's just a convenient way of holding data and information about a particular view of the game field. At the bottom of the `load` event, we define four cameras like so:

    ```
    cam1 = new camera3d (0, -300, -400, -500, 0, 0);
    cam2 = new camera3d (0, -600, 0, -900, 0, 0);
    cam3 = new camera3d (0, 90, -500, 100, 0, 0);
    cam4 = new camera3d (-300, -90, -500, -220, 400, 320);
    ```

# Flash Games Studio

These values were arrived at through some trial and error, and they provide four very distinct views of the play field:

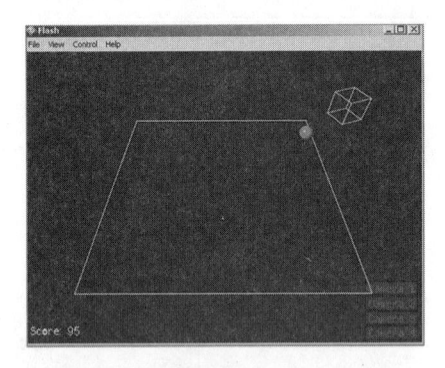

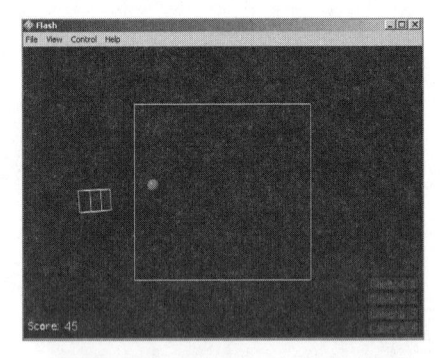

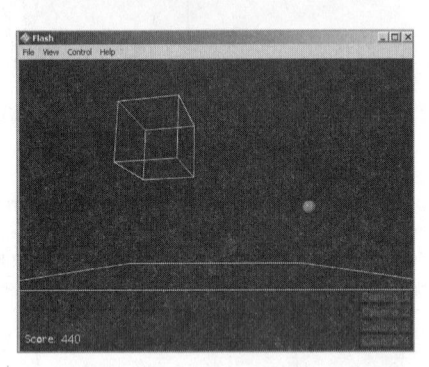

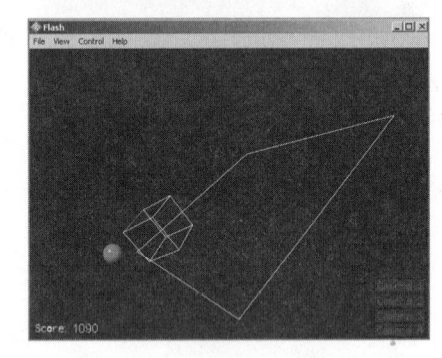

3. We have a function called `setcam`, which is responsible for designating the active camera.

   ```
   function setcam(cam)
   {
           playerdestrx = cam.rx;
           playerdestry = cam.ry;
           playerdestrz = cam.rz;
           destoffx = cam.x;
           destoffy = cam.y;
           destoffz = cam.z;
   }
   ```

   This takes a single parameter, a camera object, and from that it sets six **destination** variables, which are used to make the camera move smoothly to its new location. At the end of the `load` clipEvent of the controller, you'll see the following line:

   ```
   setcam(cam1);
   ```

   This simply makes camera 1 the active camera.

# The Objects

4. This game has 3 objects in the 3D world:

   - The paddle
   - The ball
   - The ground (the flat surface)

5. The paddle is simply the same cube as created in demo13-4, and the following line of code is the actual object creation line:

   ```
   cube = new wireframe3d(0, 0, 0, 0, 0, 0, 1, 1, 1);
   ```

   Notice that we're setting its location and rotation to zero, and its x and y scale to 1.

6. As for its points and lines, they're all identical to the cube in demo13-4, so let's not waste space reprinting it here. As in the previous demo, the ball is simply a movie clip with an image in it, and it is defined in the controller's load event with the following code:

   ```
   ball = new image3d(0, 0, 0, 1, "_root.ballimage");
   ball.speed = 4;
   ball.ang = 1;
   ```

   We're creating two new variables in the ball object, speed and ang. These are used in the main game loop, which I will be showing you shortly. We are allowed to easily attach any variables to an object that we've created. This is the beauty of ActionScript.

7. The ground is basically the top surface of a cube. The object is defined like so:

   ```
   ground = new wireframe3d(0, 140, 0, 0, 0, 0, 10, 1, 10);
   ```

   We're stating here that we want it to be sitting centered on position (0,140,0), which is 140 units down. We're also stating that it has 0 rotation on all axes, and finally we're saying that it is going to be scaled by 10 times along x and z. This is what gives us the size of the box, because it is actually initialized to be the same dimensions as the main paddle cube, like this:

   ```
   ground.addpoint (new point3d (-25,-25,-25)); // 0
   ground.addpoint (new point3d (25,-25,-25));  // 1
   ground.addpoint (new point3d (25,-25,25));   // 2
   ground.addpoint (new point3d (-25,-25,25));  // 3
   ground.addline (0, 1); // Top lines
   ground.addline (1, 2);
   ground.addline (2, 3);
   ground.addline (3, 0);
   ```

   But, because we are scaling ground by 10 in width and depth, it will be much larger than the paddle. We are also only creating this object with one surface (4 points, 4 lines).

## The Game Loop

All of the handling for the game takes place in the `enterFrame` clip event of the `controller` movie clip. The game is quite simple. When you manage to bounce the ball, your score is increased by 10 times the ball's speed (the faster the ball is going, more points you get), and every time you successfully deflect the ball, it speeds up. If you miss the ball, and it floats away, then it's returned to the center of the playing field, and most of its speed is removed.

On the main stage, there are four buttons, each corresponding to a camera:

8.  Each button has a variation of the following code attached to it:

    ```
    on (release)
    {
         _root.controller.setcam(_root.controller.cam1);
    }
    ```

    This simply tells the game to move to the camera that corresponds to the button you've pressed. The above code is for camera 1, but the only difference for each other camera is the `_root.controller.cam1` becomes `_root.controller.cam2`, `_root.controller.cam3` or `_root.controller.cam4`.

    I have a dynamic text box sitting on the main stage, and its variable is called *points*. In the load event of the controller, I simply say `_root.points = 0` to set the score back to 0 before the game begins.

# Real 3D    12

9. Now, let's go through the heart of the game. The code is located in the `enterFrame` clip event of the controller. The first thing we do is manipulate and draw the cube (paddle) and the ground.

   ```
   onClipEvent(enterFrame)
   {
     manipulateobject(cube, offx, offy, offz, playerrx, playerry,
   ➥playerrz);
     drawobject(cube);

     manipulateobject(ground, offx, offy, offz, playerrx, playerry,
   ➥playerrz);
     drawobject(ground);
   ```

   This is the same as in the previous demo.

10. Next, we render the ball with:

    ```
    drawimage(ball, offx, offy, offz, playerrx, playerry, playerrz);
    ```

    This too, is fairly straightforward.

11. The next line controls the rotation of the paddle based on the horizontal position of the mouse, _xmouse.

    ```
    cube.ry = (Math.floor((_root._xmouse / 500) * 3600)) % 3600;
    if (cube.ry < 0) cube.ry += 3600;
    ```

    This rotation is used to determine the look of the paddle, the position of the paddle around its circle, and the angle at which the ball is deflected once contact is made We're also checking to make sure that the angle is between 0 and 3600, and that it's a whole number with no decimal places (so we can use it as an index into the `mysin` and `mycos` in a minute).

12. Take a look at the following

    ```
    cube.x = 300 * mycos[cube.ry];
    cube.z = 300 * mysin[cube.ry];
    ```

    What we're doing here is setting the position of the paddle at the edge of a circle with a radius of 300. Where on the circle the paddle will be, is determined by the cube's `ry` rotation (yaw).

13. Next we determine the ball's speed along the x and z axis, based on its `speed` and its `angle`.

    ```
    balldx = ball.speed * mycos[ball.ang];
    balldz = ball.speed * mysin[ball.ang];
    ```

14. This simply converts a radial coordinate (direction and velocity) and turns it into two rectangular velocities (`balldx` and `balldz`). This is to determine how far to move the ball this frame. Next, we want to see if the ball has made contact with the paddle.

    ```
    // Did the ball hit the cube?
    diffx = Math.abs(ball.x - cube.x);
    diffz = Math.abs(ball.z - cube.z);

    if (diffx < 40 && diffz < 40)
    {
            // Hit cube.
            ball.ang = (cube.ry + 1800) % 3600;
            balldx = ball.speed * mycos[ball.ang];
            balldz = ball.speed * mysin[ball.ang];
            ball.speed += 0.5;
            _root.points += ball.speed * 10;
    }
    ```

    Here we're performing 3D collision detection. It's very simple because it's based on bounding boxes. The first thing we do is check to see how close the ball is to the paddle by comparing their x and z coordinates. We don't need to worry about y in this game because they're both in the same plane (with the same y value). However, testing for a y coordinate, should we need to, is very easy – it's just a matter of adding a `diffy` calculation just like `diffx` and `diffz`, and then determining if `diffy < 40` as well.

    If it's determined that both the x and the z values of the ball and the paddle are less than 40 units, then we perform the collision.

15. First thing in the collision is to set the ball's angle to be 180 degrees plus the angle of the paddle (completely away from the paddle's direction), and then once we've got that, we recomputed `balldx` and `balldz`. Then we increase the speed of the ball by 0.5 and then award the points based on the ball's speed times 10. Finally, we move the ball:

    ```
    // Move the ball
    ball.x += balldx;
    ball.z += balldz;
    ```

16. This is used to move the ball by the computed `balldx` and `balldz`. This line is what gives the ball its life. The next thing we must do, is see if the ball has left the playing field (through the player having missed it):

    ```
        if (ball.x > 350 || ball.x < -350 || ball.z > 350 || ball.z
    ➥< -350)
        {
                ball.x = 0;
                ball.z = 0;
                ball.speed = 4;
        }
    ```

Since the paddle's radius around its play circle is 300, then we know that when the ball gets more than 350 units away in any direction that it is lost and unreachable. When this happens, the ball is brought back to the center of the playing field, and its speed is reduced back to 4.

17. Finally, we perform our camera magic:

```
// Move camera into position
deltarx = playerdestrx - playerrx;
deltary = playerdestry - playerry;
deltarz = playerdestrz - playerrz;
deltaoffx = destoffx - offx;
deltaoffy = destoffy - offy;
deltaoffz = destoffz - offz;

playerrx += (deltarx * .1);
playerry += (deltary * .1);
playerrz += (deltarz * .1);
offx += (deltaoffx * .1);
offy += (deltaoffy * .1);
offz += (deltaoffz * .1);
}
```

Imagine that you are 10 feet from a wall. You decide to jump exactly half that distance to the wall. So you make a 5-foot jump, and now you're 5 feet from the wall. You decide to do the halving trick again, and you step 2.5 feet forward, and now you're 2.5 feet from the wall. Each step you take will be exactly half the remaining distance. If you keep doing this, will you ever actually reach the wall? Yes, eventually, because you're not infinitesimal in size.

This is a popular trick that is often used to make an object move smoothly into place on screen. It works by figuring out how much distance there is between the current position and the destination – and then it moves a certain percentage of that distance. Each frame, it recalculates the remaining distance, and then moves a percentage of that.

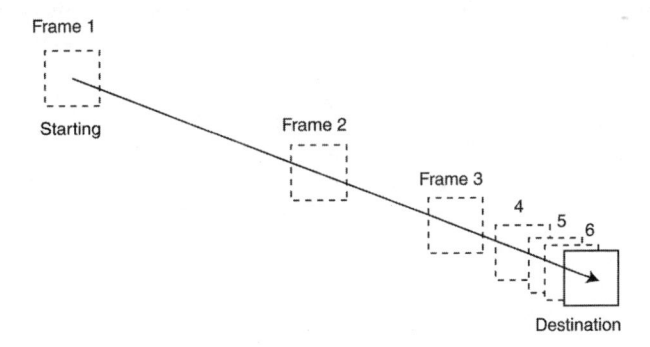

This style of movement has the effect of creating a nice, smooth decelerating motion. Just as this can be done with `_x` and `_y` coordinates, this technique can actually be done with any numerical value. All we need to know is our desired destination number, and our current number, and then we add a fixed percentage to our current number – thus bringing us closer to our destination.

In the case of our camera, this is what we're doing with its position and its rotation, so that when the `setcamera` routine is called, which changes the destination camera coordinates, the above code will immediately send us towards the destination, and it will take several frames to settle into position. The effect is a transition between camera positions that particularly emphasizes the 3D engine, and how everything works seamlessly together. We have objects moving around and rotating in 3D, within their own coordinate systems, while at the same time the overall global system is panning and rotating too. The effects, and the potentials are boundless.

## Final Thoughts

There are a few ways that you could improve upon this game.

- It could use a limit on the number of lives you have.
- Perhaps as the game increases in difficulty, you could introduce a few more 3D balls on screen.
- Different camera angles

With the engine there the possibilities are limitless. However, there are a few optimizations that could be made to the rendering engine that would speed it up, because right now, if you add too many more objects (especially wireframe objects), the game will slow down visibly.

I'll be talking about several important optimizations next chapter that involve only performing math when necessary (as the math is one of the killers on performance) and knowing when and when not to draw certain things.

In programming technologies like this, we will always run into the limits of what a computer is capable of. In this case, we see the limitations as soon as we add too many objects. But that's okay, because today's limitation is tomorrow's standard. Hardware is always improving.

The vector 3D engine I've outlined in this chapter is Flash based. However, the concepts and fundamentals are not specific to Flash. The math is universal, and the data structures transfer easily into any programming language. The 3D math in here is exactly the same kind of 3D math that makes today's hottest games come to life. Object rotation, scaling, translation, and camera rotation and translation are the keys to taking anything into the 3D realm. Once you have mastered these concepts, then you are on your way to becoming a 3D game master.

# Real 3D

Introduction
chapter 1
chapter 2
chapter 3
chapter 4
chapter 5
chapter 6
Case Study 1
chapter 7
chapter 8
chapter 9
chapter 10
chapter 11
chapter 12
chapter 13
Case Study 2
chapter 14
chapter 15
Director Afterword

# Chapter 13
# Ultimate 3D

# Flash Games Studio

In recent years, as computers have become faster and more capable, it's become common to see images that obtain near total realism. In our wireframe examples, our 3D scenes were built up of several lines, and that's all. In typical 3D games like *Half-Life*, *Quake*, and *Tribes*, the scenes are built up of what is essentially a wireframe world, that's been made solid by stretching skins between the wireframe mesh.

Take a look at the following image to see what I mean:

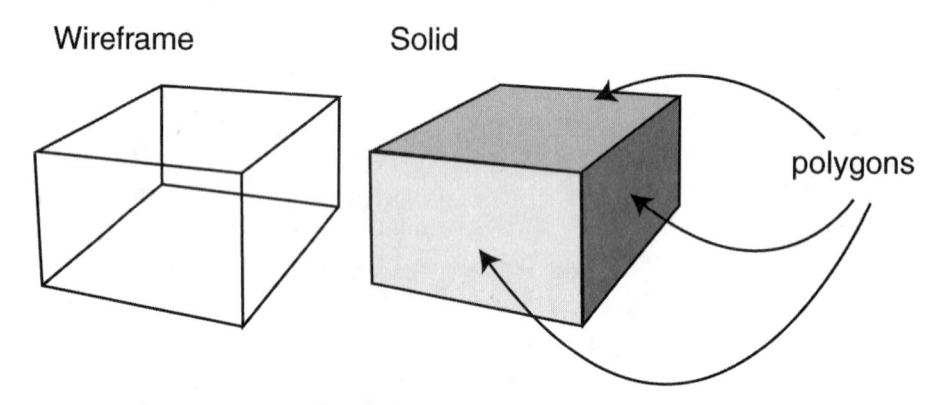

These solid areas are known as polygons. A polygon is defined as an area that's enclosed within three or more lines. In the context of games, there are usually two types of polygon that are used to create 3D scenes – triangles and quadrangles (or quads, as they're usually called). Quads tend to be the polygon of choice in most games. Triangles are used more often in 3D movies and television when more detailed shapes are needed. A triangle allows you to have twice as much 3-dimensional detail as a quad:

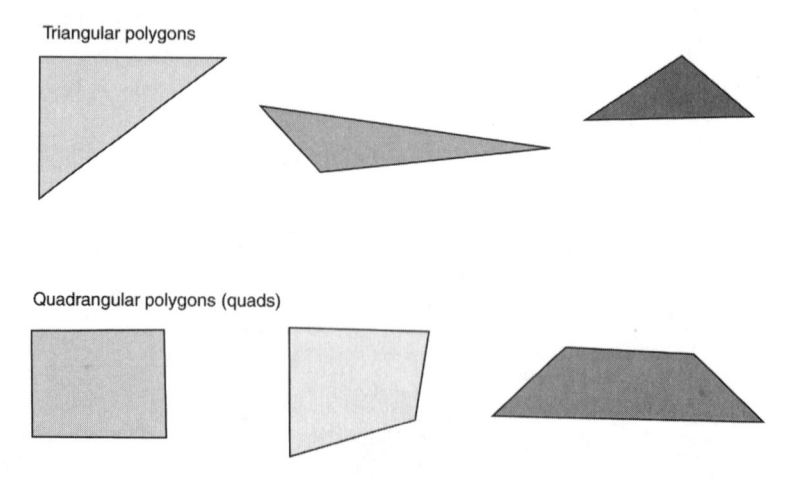

# Ultimate 3D

Most of the 3D gaming world is made up of polygons, and indeed polygons have become the benchmark for measuring a game's performance; polygons per second rendered is a way of telling how powerful a 3D system is.

Now, with modern 3D games, most of the polygons are usually textured – the skin surface is a bitmap picture itself. The bitmap is squashed, rotated and scaled with perspective depending on the orientation of the polygon, to create the illusion that this object is an actual real-world 3D object, with surface texture and character:

Texture Mapped Solid

In this texture mapped polygon, you can see that the surface bitmap has been rotated, skewed, scaled and stretched so that the top and side surfaces look like they're receding into the distance – it's been **mapped** onto the polygons. There are three polygons in this image, and in actuality, they're simply 2D screen objects. It's because of the way our eyes perceive them pieced together as a whole that we believe this object is completely 3D.

A game can have thousands of polygons on screen at once. A 3D CGI movie like *Toy Story (Disney-Pixar, 1995)*, *Final Fantasy (Square Pictures, 2001)*, or *Shrek (Dreamworks SKG, 2001)* can have hundreds of millions of polygons at once, but in Flash – how do we even create one polygon?

# 13  Flash Games Studio

## Limitations of Flash

In the last chapter, I mentioned that Flash causes the annoying limitation of not being able to arbitrarily move vertices in a polygon. We saw how it was possible to move end points of a line (by moving the starting point, and stretching the line), but how do we take a solid shape with four vertices and move those vertices around to change the shape of our quad at runtime? Looking at this image, you can see the desired effect:

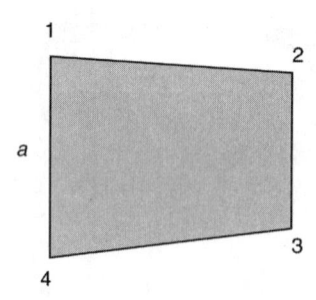

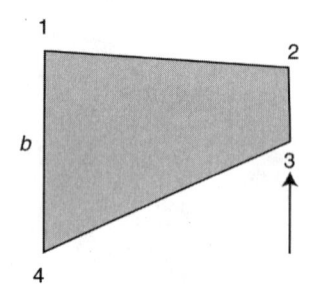

We want point 3 on the polygon to move, but we want points 1, 2, and 4 to remain in the same spot. How can we do this in an environment like Flash, where there are so few shape manipulation options available to us? Let's say that our polygon a is its own movie clip, how can we modify this movie clip to make it look like polygon b?

It's certainly possible to turn polygon a into our desired polygon b, at **design** time when you're building your FLA in Flash – all you have to do is drag that corner, simple, but what we're after is a way of converting polygon a into polygon b at **runtime**, using ActionScript. We're not talking about drawing a 4-sided **wireframe** square, we're talking about a **solid** shape made up of four lines and four vertices.

In pseudo-code we want to be able to draw our polygon on screen by providing four points to a polygon engine, like so:

```
draw_polygon (point1, point2, point3, point4, color);
```

In a programming language like C it's quite easy to do. And if you are using a programming library like DirectX, you can simply specify your points, specify your texture, and the perfect polygon will appear on screen exactly as you want it. However, in ActionScript – it can't be done that way.

In fact, can it be done at all? Well, it's a long shot, but it might just work.

# Ultimate 3D     13

## The Flash Polygon Engine

We've seen how it's possible to create a great 3D wireframe game, but to a large extent, wireframe went out with the 80s. It's so retro! 21st Century gamers want **solid**. So, we have to come up with a solution in Flash for drawing arbitrary solid shapes on screen that don't need to be pre-rendered, rather they can be drawn as required at runtime, just like our wireframe images of the previous chapter.

This is where we have to be sneaky. After much head scratching, I have produced a basic polygon engine. However, since this is a considerably restricted and difficult thing for Flash to do, these are a few limitations that I must first mention:

The side edges must be completely vertical.

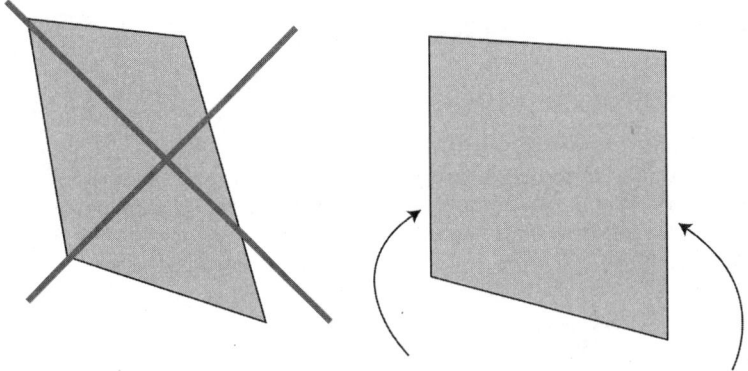

*left and right edges must be vertical*     This is an acceptable limitation however, because we plan on using this polygon engine for creating objects like walls that we can walk alongside.

The polygons cannot be texture mapped with detailed bitmaps. These polygons are going to be solid filled. Later, I'll show you how we can in fact make a few simple textures on the surfaces to give them a little bit of detail, but unfortunately we can't do detailed textures like modern commercial games. We just don't have the speed.

These things aside, we're still going to have a 3D world where solid polygons obscure other polygons in an arbitrary fashion. In a normal, unrestricted polygon, the information for its shape is contained as four distinct points. Let's look at a normal screen polygon:

# 13  Flash Games Studio

## Screen Space

**Polygon Coordinates**
p1 (2, 1)
p2 (6, 2)
p3 (7, 7)
p4 (2, 5)

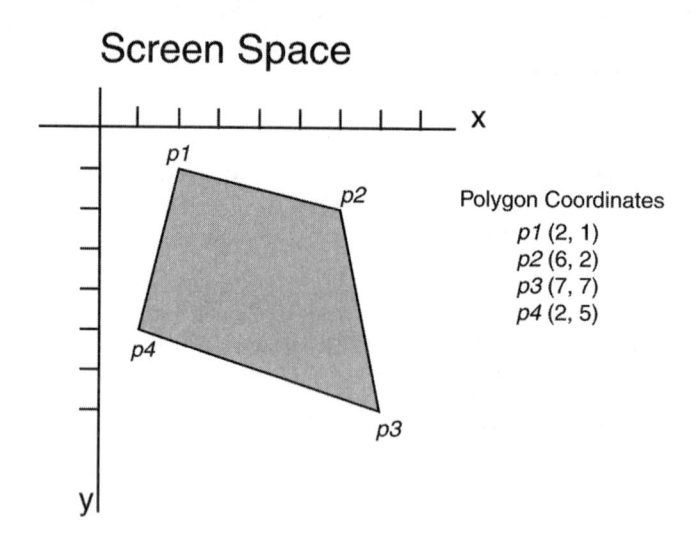

This polygon could be created with the imaginary function:

```
draw_polygon (2, 1, 6, 2, 7, 7, 2, 5, RED);
```

Here, each point in the polygon is passed in order of x, y from point 1 to point 4, followed by the desired color. This would, of course, create a red quad. This function takes eight distinct numbers (x1, y1, x2, y2, x3, y3, x4, and y4), but as I said, Flash can't do this at runtime so we need to find a way of reducing the information it needs to take in. Let's take a look at our polygon, and how we could represent it:

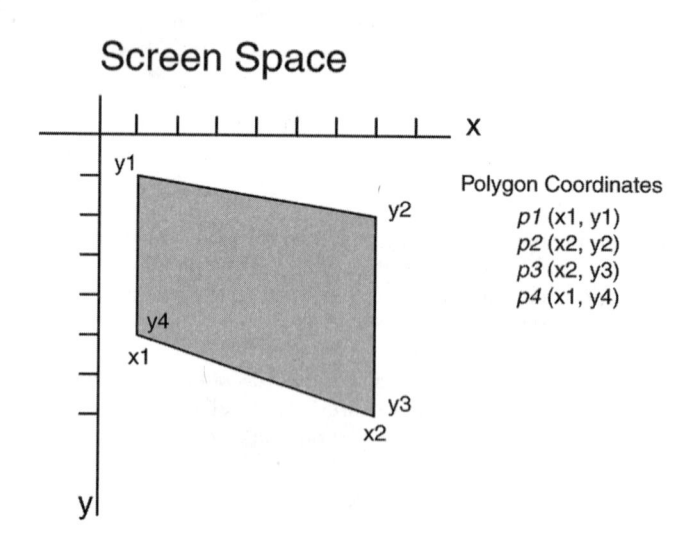

## Screen Space

**Polygon Coordinates**
p1 (x1, y1)
p2 (x2, y2)
p3 (x2, y3)
p4 (x1, y4)

# Ultimate 3D

As you can see I've chosen to use variables instead of numbers because I want to illustrate the fact that we have only *six* distinct variables. While we do have four y values (y1, y2, y3, y4), we only have two x values, left edge and right edge (x1, x2).

Now, for the purposes of making things clearer, I'm not going to refer to the y variables as simply y1, y2, y3, and y4. From now on I'm going to call them y1t and y1b for the top and bottom y values at x1, and y2t and y2b for the top and bottom values at x2.

So, if we wanted to draw a polygon using this variable structure, we simply pass our x variables, and top and bottom y variables, like so:

```
draw_polygon (x1, y1t, y1b, x2, y2t, y2b, BLUE);
```

Using this, we could easily draw simple wall polygons, mapped from a 3D coordinate system. Now that you understand how the data is represented, let's take a look at how the graphics are actually drawn – the big secret.

## Abracadabra

Our answer comes in the form of finding an **arbitrary polygon**. Remember how we solved our wireframe problems by using a single line movie clip and then scaling it to create any line? Well, we're going to do the same thing here, but with a polygon instead of a line. We're going to base everything on the fact that a polygon with a vertical left and right edge is basically made up of three objects: one square and two triangles, like so:

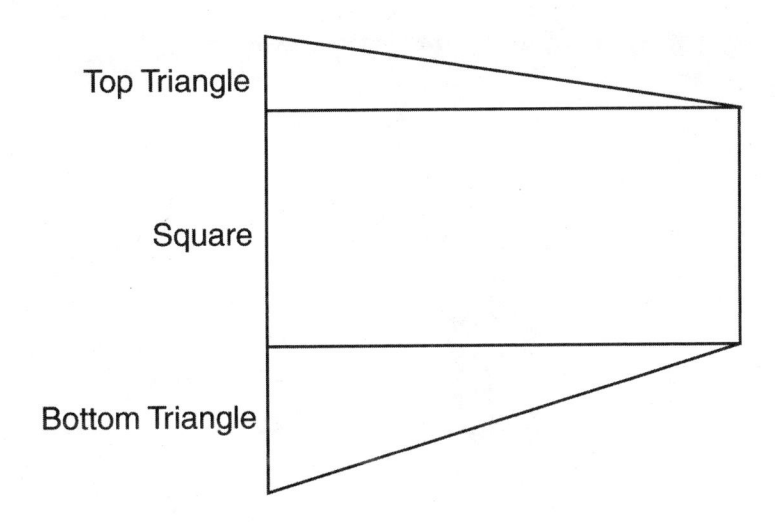

# 13 Flash Games Studio

When the lines are removed, and the three shapes are filled in, we get this:

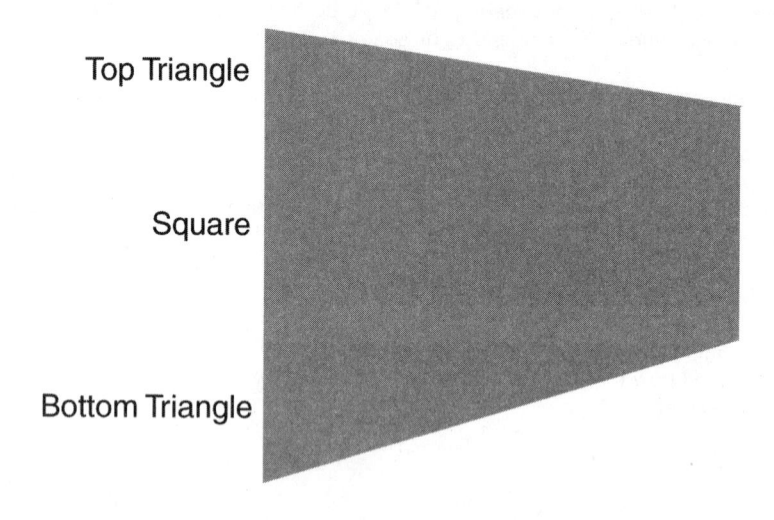

Top Triangle

Square

Bottom Triangle

Our solid polygon! Remember that we can easily scale things in Flash using the `_xscale` and `_yscale` properties. What we're doing is scaling the two triangles and the square based on the information provided (x1, y1t, y2b, x2, y2t, y2b).

Let's take a look at the polygon engine running. Check out `demo13-1.fla`.

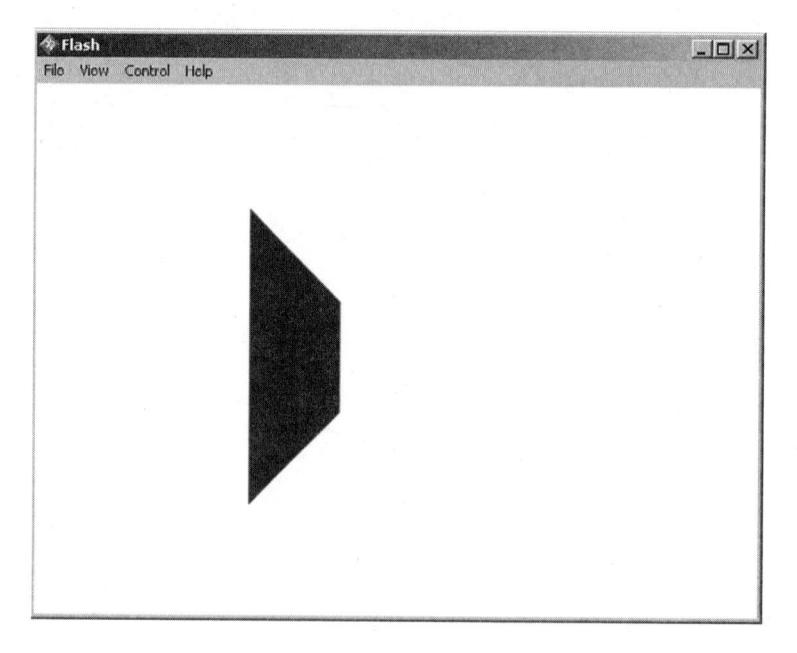

# Ultimate 3D

The key object in our movie is a movie clip on the main timeline called polygon, with the instance name poly0. It's this object that contains our three sub-objects, the top triangle, the square and the bottom triangle, each with a corresponding instance name of top, mid, and bottom:

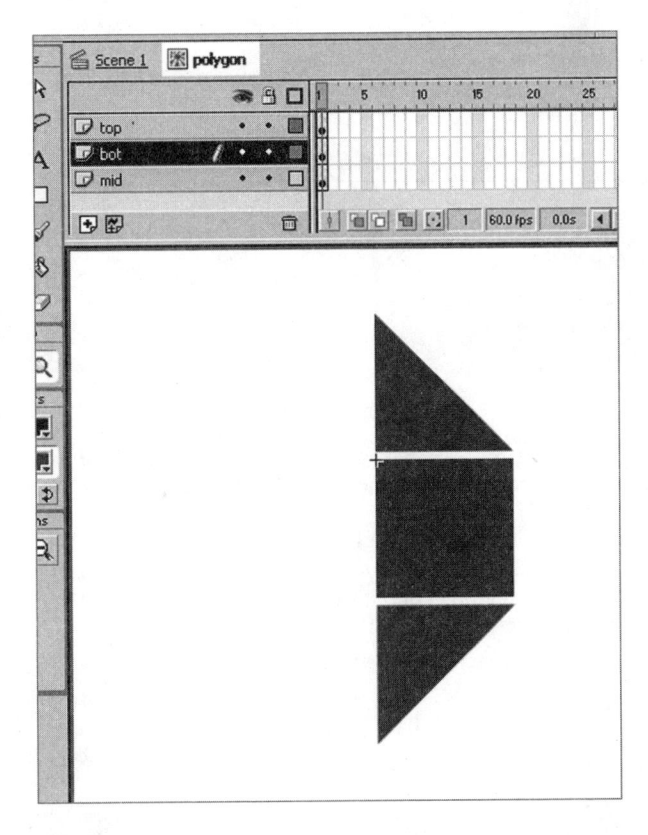

All three of the sub shapes are based on the size of 100x100. For example, the middle box is exactly 100x100 in size, while the top triangle is 100 along the base and the left side. It's almost like our line renderer from the previous chapter, except the triangle is filled in below the line.

We can use the _xscale and _yscale properties of mid to squash and stretch the middle rectangle easily to any width or height. Also, when we squash and stretch the top triangle, we can get many variations, like so:

# 13  Flash Games Studio

Top Triangle

All this is achieved by setting the _xscale and _yscale of top. Of course, the bottom triangle can also be squashed and stretched to produce similar versions of the top triangle, just upside down.

There is one more thing, while the mid movie clip is only one frame, the top and bottom movie clips are both two frames. Frame one contains the triangle going from left to right, and frame two contains the triangle going from right to left, like so:

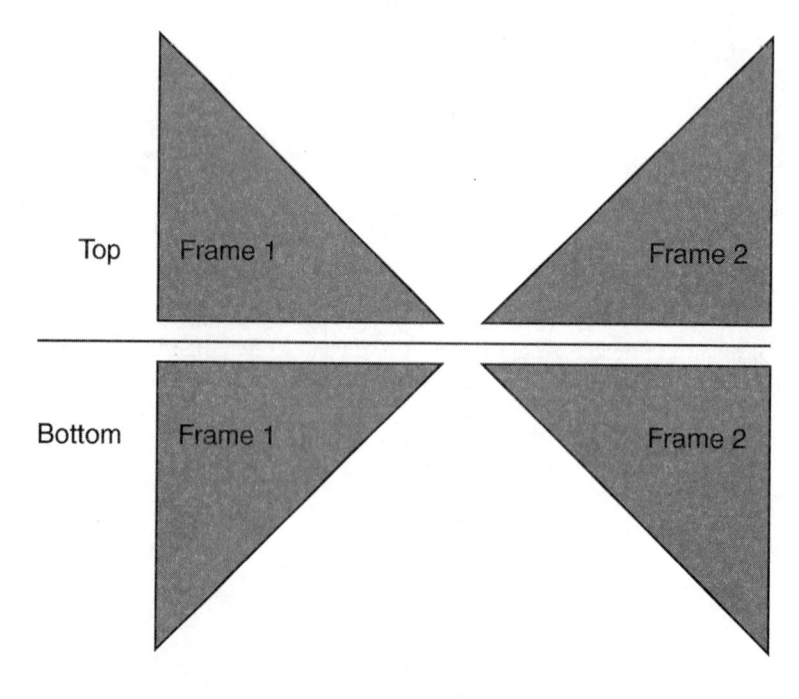

Top — Frame 1 | Frame 2

Bottom — Frame 1 | Frame 2

# Ultimate 3D 13

So, now you can see exactly how our polygon is defined and laid out, let's take a look at the actual code required to make it appear anywhere on screen. Let's assume that the instance name of our polygon movie clip is contained within a variable called `obj`:

```
eval(obj).mid._x = x1;
eval(obj).mid._xscale = x2 - x1;
eval(obj).mid._y = y2t;
eval(obj).mid._yscale = y2b - y2t;

eval(obj).top._x = x1;
eval(obj).top._y = y1t;
eval(obj).top._xscale = x2 - x1;
eval(obj).top._yscale = y2t - y1t;

eval(obj).bottom._x = x1;
eval(obj).bottom._y = y2b;
eval(obj).bottom._xscale = x2 - x1;
eval(obj).bottom._yscale = y1b - y2b;
```

Remember, x1, y1t, y1b, x2, y2t, and y2b are our six variables as defined earlier. That's all we need to make the polygon appear on screen correctly:

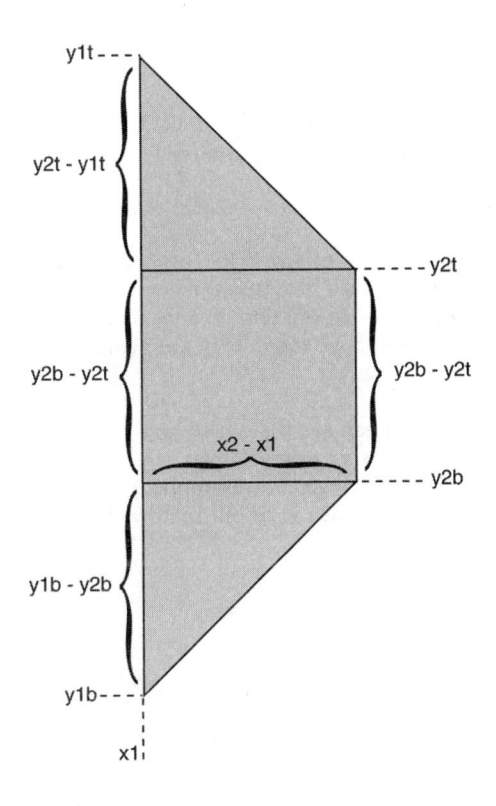

# Flash Games Studio

We do have to take a few other things into consideration. If it happens that y2t is more than y1t (the top slopes up and to the right, instead of down to the left), then we must switch `top` to frame 2. Correspondingly, if y1b is less than y2b, then we must switch `bottom` to frame 2. This is handled with the following code:

```
if (y1t <= y2t)
{
        eval(obj).top.gotoAndStop(1);
        ry1t = y1t;
        ry2t = y2t;
}
if (y1t > y2t)
{
        eval(obj).top.gotoAndStop(2);
        ry1t = y2t;
        ry2t = y1t;
}
if (y1b > y2b)
{
        eval(obj).bottom.gotoAndStop(1);
        ry1b = y1b;
        ry2b = y2b;
}
if (y1b <= y2b)
{
        eval(obj).bottom.gotoAndStop(2);
        ry1b = y2b;
        ry2b = y1b;
}
```

This means that we can have polygons of any shape, as long as the left and right edges are both perfectly vertical. Finally, we must make sure that the center point of poly0 is sitting at (0,0) on the main timeline. This is because we're working on a local coordinate system to move `top`, `mid` and `bottom` around, and when we move them, they are being moved relative to the location of poly0.

Looking at the previous code, you can see that we're reassigning the six passed screen variables x1, y1t, y1b, x2, y2t, and y2b into six new variables rx1, ry1t, ry1b, rx2, ry2t, and ry2b if we need to play frame 2 of either triangle. For example, if y1t is more than y2t then we must set ry1t to y2t and ry2t to y1t so that all of our math will work correctly.

# Ultimate 3D

The whole polygon rendering routine looks like this:

```
function renderpoly(x1, y1t, y1b, x2, y2t, y2b, avez, obj)
{
    // Takes a poly movie clip and makes it appear on screen
    // this is the magic routine.  It takes 6 screen coordinates
    // Left edge, Right edge, and top and bottom at both edges

    // Figure out which top point (near or far) is the highest
    if (y1t <= y2t)
    {
        _root[obj].top.gotoAndStop(1);
        ry1t = y1t;
        ry2t = y2t;
    }
    if (y1t > y2t)
    {
        // flip to frame 2, the triangle facing left
        _root[obj].top.gotoAndStop(2);
        ry1t = y2t;
        ry2t = y1t;
    }

    // Figure out which bottom point (near or far) is the lowest
    if (y1b > y2b)
    {
        _root[obj].bottom.gotoAndStop(1);
        ry1b = y1b;
        ry2b = y2b;
    }
    if (y1b <= y2b)
    {
        // flip to frame 2, the triangle facing left
        _root[obj].bottom.gotoAndStop(2);
ry1b = y2b;
        ry2b = y1b;
    }

    rx1 = x1;
    rx2 = x2;

    // adjusted values now in rx1, rx2, ry1t, ry1b, ry2t, ry2b

    // Scale middle square of the polygon based on screen values

    _root[obj].mid._x = rx1;
    _root[obj].mid._xscale = rx2 - rx1;
    _root[obj].mid._y = (ry2t - 1);
    _root[obj].mid._yscale = (ry2b - ry2t) + 2;
```

```
            // scale the top triangle based on the screen values
            _root[obj].top._x = rx1;
            _root[obj].top._y = ry1t;
            _root[obj].top._xscale = rx2 - rx1;
            _root[obj].top._yscale = ry2t - ry1t;

            // scale the bottom triangle based on the screen values
            _root[obj].bottom._x = rx1;
            _root[obj].bottom._y = ry2b;
            _root[obj].bottom._xscale = rx2 - rx1;
            _root[obj].bottom._yscale = ry1b - ry2b;

            // Set the depth level of the polygon based on avez,
            // The average z depth of the poly (passed in from renderer)
            _root[obj].swapDepths(Math.round(10000 - avez));

    }
```

That's the magic routine that makes our solid polygons happen in Flash. You'll notice that we're passing in `obj`, which is just the name of the movie clip instance containing our polygon.

Also, since this polygon is actually going to be in 3D space, we're passing in another variable called `avez`. This is the "average z" of the polygon. You'll see how we get this later, but it's basically the z value that's calculated when the z value at both ends of the polygon are averaged. This is used to order our polygons on screen so that they are rendered the correct distance from the viewer.

## Making it 3D

If you look at `demo13-1.swf` you'll see a single polygon on screen, moving around in 3D. How do you make the polygon into something that's 3D? Well, to be perfectly honest, you don't. The polygon render engine knows nothing about 3D (except for the `avez`, but that's only for layering). The polygon engine is brought into action only *after* any 3D walls/quads/polygons have been translated, rotated and then projected into screen space. Our polygon engine only creates 2D representations of 3D objects, just like our wireframe engine from the previous chapter.

# Ultimate 3D

Looking at the demo, you'll see a movie clip on the main timeline called controller. Attached to this movie clip, on the `load` ClipEvent, you'll see the following code:

```
// View position
xloc = 0;
yloc = 0;
zloc = -10;
d = 200;

// Polygon information
x1 = 0;
y1t = -100;
y1b = 100;
z1 = 100;

x2 = 0;
y2t = -100;
y2b = 100;
z2 = 400;
```

For this demo, we're defining one 3D polygon. You can see that we've added variables called z1 and z2. This is how we're giving our polygon its third dimension. Attached to the controller movie clip's enterFrame ClipEvent, you can find the following code:

```
onClipEvent(enterFrame)
{

    nm = "poly0";

    // Translate polygon into world space, relative to
    // view (xloc, yloc, zloc)
    wx1 = x1 - xloc;
    wy1t = y1t - yloc;
    wy1b = y1b - yloc;
    wz1 = z1 - zloc;

    wx2 = x2 - xloc;
    wy2t = y2t - yloc;
    wy2b = y2b - yloc;
    wz2 = z2 - zloc;

    // Project all 3D points onto the screen
    // to determine our 2D screen points - move to
    // screen center (275, 200)
    sx1 = (d * wx1 / wz1) + 275;
    sy1t = (d * wy1t / wz1) + 200;
    sy1b = (d * wy1b / wz1) + 200;

    sx2 = (d * wx2 / wz2) + 275;
```

*continues overleaf*

```
            sy2t = (d * wy2t / wz2) + 200;
            sy2b = (d * wy2b / wz2) + 200;

            // If the left edge is greater than our
            // right edge, then the polygon is backwards
            // so we must swap left values and right values
            if (sx1 > sx2)
            {
                    tsx1 = sx1;
                    tsy1t = sy1t;
                    tsy1b = sy1b;

                    sx1 = sx2;
                    sy1t = sy2t;
                    sy1b = sy2b;

                    sx2 = tsx1;
                    sy2t = tsy1t;
                    sy2b = tsy1b;
            }

            // Render the 2D polygon we've come up with
            renderpoly(sx1, sy1t, sy1b, sx2, sy2t, sy2b, 0, nm);

            // Move the camera around in smooth circles
            xloc+= 3 * Math.cos(ang+=.005);
            zloc-= Math.sin(ang+=.005);
    }
```

We're simply taking our previously defined 3D polygon, translating it by `xloc`, `yloc`, and `zloc`, and then perspective-projecting it on screen. By dividing all the x and y coordinates by the corresponding z coordinate, we will create the 3D we're trying to achieve. This is the same principle we covered in the last chapter with projecting 3D points into 2D to render our wireframe images.

Remember, now that we're in 3D, the terms "left" edge and "right" edge, are not as applicable, because edges can also be "near" and "far" and be on the same x coordinate. For this reason, I will refer to them as edge 1 (x1, y1t, y1b, z1) and edge 2 (x2, y2t, y2b, z2).

# Ultimate 3D

We've still got one more thing to do though; we want to check whether or not we're looking at the back of our polygon. The following code ought to do the trick, by checking to make sure that edge 1 hasn't somehow actually moved right of edge 2 on screen:

```
if (sx1 > sx2)
{
        tsx1 = sx1;
        tsy1t = sy1t;
        tsy1b = sy1b;

        sx1 = sx2;
        sy1t = sy2t;
        sy1b = sy2b;

        sx2 = tsx1;
        sy2t = tsy1t;
        sy2b = tsy1b;
}
```

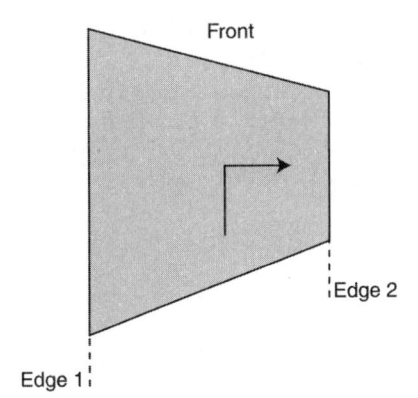

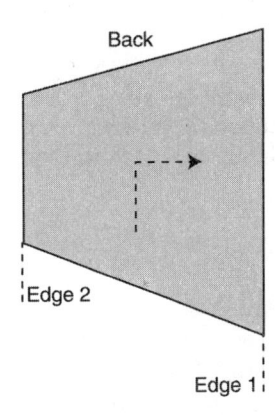

Front | Back
Edge 2 | Edge 2
Edge 1 | Edge 1

This check is useful in determining the visibility of polygons when we're rendering solid objects. Take a cube for example – any of the surfaces facing away from us (backfaces) will have their edge 1 to the right of their edge 2 on screen. This little piece of logic means that the edge is facing away from us, and we may not want to draw it.

In the above piece of code however, what we're actually doing is checking to see if edge 1 has surpassed edge 2, and if it has, we're swapping all the sx and sy values of both edges, flipping the polygon to face us, without changing the way it looks.

We could change the logic like this:

```
offscreen = false;

if (sx1 > sx2)
{
        if (culling)
                offscreen = true;
        else
        {
        tsx1 = sx1;
        tsy1t = sy1t;
        tsy1b = sy1b;

        sx1 = sx2;
        sy1t = sy2t;
        sy1b = sy2b;

        sx2 = tsx1;
        sy2t = tsy1t;
        sy2b = tsy1b;
        }
}
```

This way, we can create a flag called `culling` that's true or false. If it's set to true, then we have a variable called `offscreen` that we can use later to determine whether or not to actually draw our polygon, or hide it, like so:

```
if (offscreen)
{
        _root[nm]._visible = false;
}
else
{
        // Draw, and call renderpoly with our 6 screen
        // coordinates
        _root[nm]._visible = true;
        renderpoly(sx1, sy1t, sy1b, sx2, sy2t, sy2b, avez, nm);
}
```

You'll see all of this later in our 3D game demonstration, but I'm giving you a teaser for it now. **Backface culling** is a term used in professional 3D game and movie production. It's a form of hidden surface removal, where we're trying to cut down the amount of drawing that a computer must do, in order to make our game run faster. If you look at demo13-2.swf, you'll see the culling in action. It's exactly like demo13-1, except when the back of the polygon is facing us it will disappear.

# Ultimate 3D

It's important to make note of just which edge you define as edge 1 and edge 2. If we define out polygons in the wrong order, we could make a cube where all the edges appear to face in, instead of out, and we'd see something like this:

**Correct order**
Surfaces correctly facing out,
backfaces are hidden

Edge1 < Edge2 in both front polygons

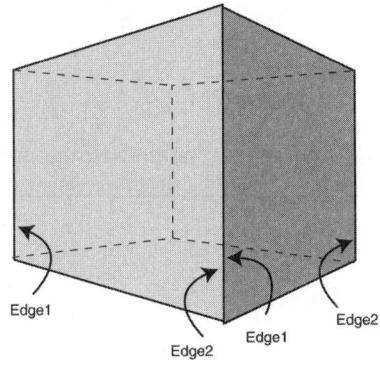

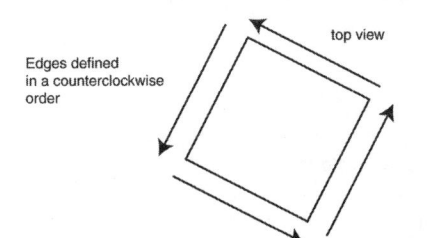

**Incorrect order**
Surfaces facing in to cube,
only backfaces are showing

Edge2 < Edge1 in both front polygons

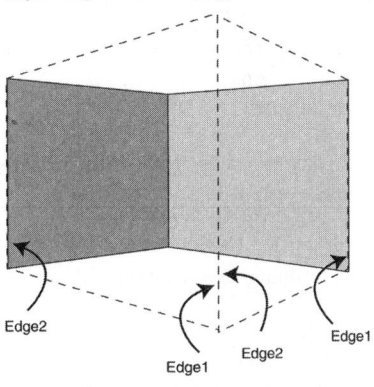

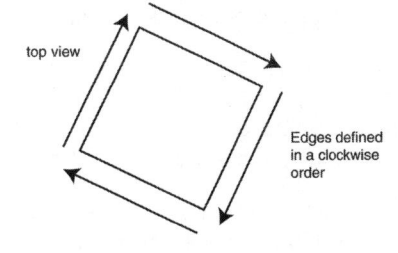

Edges defined in a counterclockwise order

Edges defined in a clockwise order

In the right hand image, the object will look quite strange as we walk around it and only the rear polygons are visible! Essentially, we want to make sure that our polygons are defined in an order that goes *around* the object – either clockwise or counterclockwise. Take a look at this polygon definition:

```
x1 = 0;
y1t = -100;
y1b = 100;
z1 = 100;

x2 = 200;
y2t = -100;
y2b = 100;
z2 = 100;
```

This is a flat polygon that's facing us, the $y$ and $z$ values of both edges are identical, however, $x1$ is at $0$, and $x2$ is at $100$. Without moving, we'll see this polygon facing us because $x1$ is less than $x2$. However, something rather different happens if we change the definitions to look like this:

```
x1 = 200;
y1t = -100;
y1b = 100;
z1 = 100;

x2 = 0;
y2t = -100;
y2b = 100;
z2 = 100;
```

Mathematically speaking, that polygon is pretty much the same as the previous, except for one key difference – $x2$ is less than $x1$ (edge 2 is less than edge 1), so the polygon is facing away from us, and we therefore won't draw it.

Because our culling check starts with this:

```
if (sx1 > sx2)
```

...we want to define our shapes in a counterclockwise direction, as in the left box in the previous image. However, if our check looked like this:

```
if (sx1 < sx2)
```

...then we would only see backfaces if they were defined in a counterclockwise direction. Therefore, using this check, we must define our objects in a clockwise direction.

It's important to remember that we're looking at polygon orientation in screen space, and not simply in world space. We only do the backface check once we've transformed and projected the polygon into screen coordinates.

## Speed Considerations for Games

There are some important things to note as we delve deeper into this type of 3D for games. We're taxing Flash just about as much as we possibly can. We're going to have graphics that are updating full screen, every frame. The more polygons we have on screen (even if they're partially hidden) the more our game's performance is going to suffer. So, we need to take a look at how we can reduce what we're demanding of Flash.

# Ultimate 3D | 13

## Limiting the Math

In the previous chapter, we showed you how to rotate the object, and rotate the world through a series of detailed and complex equations. The problem with that is that in the context of a game, we're going to find that much math slows down performance considerably. So what can we do?

Well, for a start we can make sure that our game only does what math is necessary. Let's assume that our game is made up of a series of stationary boxes. In our previous chapter, we had a function called manipulateobject, which took a 3D object and rotated it around three axes and translated it into position, then we used a function called drawobject, which rotated the object around the player's point of view:

```
manipulateobject(cube, offx, offy, offz, playerrx, playerry, playerrz);
drawobject(cube);
```

To optimize our game, we're going to eliminate the rotation in the manipulateobject step, and combine the translation relative to the player into the draw routine. This way, we only need to perform one rotation (relative to the player) and two translations (the object's position plus our position). Translations are easy because they're simply additions, but the elimination of the rotation steps is crucial. We're also going to limit the amount of rotation that the player can do to only one axis, only letting them perform a yaw around the y-axis – turning left and right.

To recap:

- We're assuming that the object won't need to rotate around its own axis – meaning that the box won't be spinning on the spot. This means we assume its coordinates are provided as-is, and do not need to be moved. **We're going to store the object in variables in its already manipulated state**.

- We're assuming that all translation will simply be relative to the player.

- We're assuming that the player will only turn around one axis (the y-axis) thus reducing the amount of math required to compute rotations.

So, now we have a grip on that, let's see if we can't just impress ourselves and put it all into a game!

**Introduction**
chapter 1
chapter 2
chapter 3
chapter 4
chapter 5
chapter 6
Case Study 1
chapter 7
chapter 8
chapter 9
chapter 10
chapter 11
chapter 12
chapter 13
Case Study 2
chapter 14
chapter 15
**Director Afterword**

# Case Study 2
# Mech Attack

**Case Study 2**

# Flash Games Studio

So now the time has come. We're going to take Flash, push it to its absolute limits, and make it do things that most people don't even realize are possible. All of the principles and practices of 3D have already been explained, so now we're left with the task of coming up with ways of improving upon the foundation that we've established. We're going to take everything that we've learned, add in some spicy new 3D tricks, and bring it all together to create the ultimate 3D Flash game. You have been warned.

## The Story So Far...

The year is 2220, and Earth has become a playground for alien races from all around the galaxy. It's quite common for the aliens to send in mechanized robots (mechs) to roam the Earth stealing artifacts and treasures, just as Earthlings once did to the ancient treasures of Egypt, the Aztec temples, and other places of interest.

In *Mech Attack*, you control a giant robot as it invades a city and tries to steal the last few remaining buildings as treasures. You have a jetpack on your back that allows you to fly until you run out of fuel. You also have a molecular disassembling laser that is used to capture the buildings, and destroy enemies. Humankind is responding to your offensive by launching helibombs. A helibomb will follow you and attempt to hit you – and when it does, it will explode.

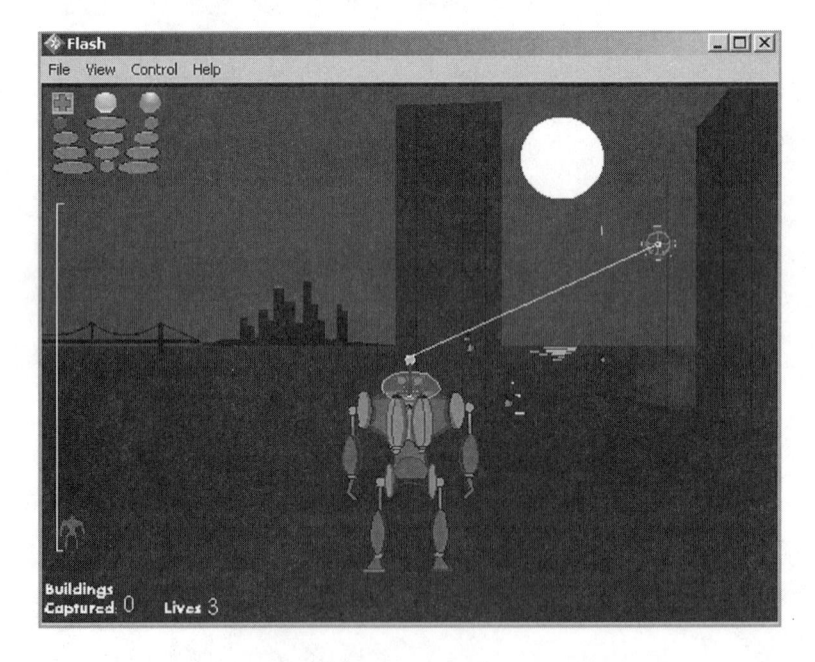

You have three resources – life, laser energy, and rocket pack fuel. When you're hit by a helibomb, or fall a long distance from the sky, your life is depleted. As you use your laser to fire at a helibomb, or capture a building, your laser's energy depletes. As you use your jetpack, your fuel decreases.

# Mech Attack

## Case Study 2

When you destroy a helibomb, it will release a power-up. There are three types of power-ups: life, fuel, and laser ammo. When a life power-up is created, it will float on the spot. When a fuel power-up is created, it will sink to the ground. When an ammo power-up is created, it will float up towards the sky. Eventually however, all power-ups will sink to the ground. When you walk over a power-up, the equivalent resource is increased.

Resource Meters

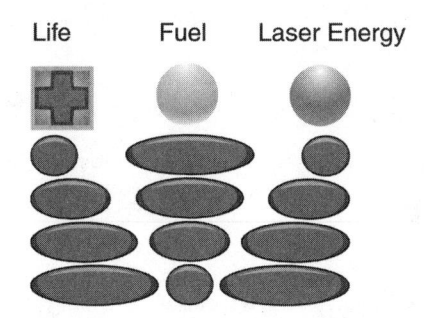

Life   Fuel   Laser Energy

Controlling the robot requires both hands. Your left hand is used to move the robot around the screen, and to fly. The keys used are the standard default configuration for most 3D games today: W – Forward, S – Backward, A – Turn left, D – Turn right, and the space bar fires your jetpack. With your right hand, use your mouse to move the aiming target around, and the mouse button to fire your laser.

When you shoot your laser at a building it takes several seconds to capture it, during which time, helibombs will be attacking you. The higher you are off the ground, the quicker your laser will able to capture buildings. Every time you capture all the buildings in a level, the next level is loaded. Note that in our example, there's only one level that is loaded repeatedly when you capture all the buildings. I'll leave it to you to design your own subsequent fiendish maps.

You must also be careful to make sure that you don't run out of fuel while you're high up in the air, otherwise you'll fall very quickly back to the ground and be badly hurt. The trick is to apply just enough rocket power to keep yourself airborne, and just before you land, apply a burst of rocket to slow down your descent (this aspect is similar to the classic Lunar Lander games). On the left-hand side of your display, you'll see the graphical altitude indicator, which will show you how far you are off the ground *(see image, left)*.

When your life reaches 0, your robot will explode. You'll then regenerate at the starting point if you have any lives left. After all of your lives have been used up, the game is over.

# Case Study 2

# Flash Games Studio

## What's Going on in the Game

Several key things are being brought into play to make this game happen. It's going to be a veritable Who's Who of 3D techniques in Flash, thus combining the last three chapters into one overall demonstration. We will have:

- **3D sprites** – The helibombs, streetlamps and power-ups are all simple sprites that are being moved and scaled in 3D.

- **3D polygons** – The buildings are made up of polygons that are created from 3D data.

- **Physics** – The game is based on a physical model that includes gravity, resistance and momentum.

- **3D movement** – Movement is based on a velocity (speed and direction).

- **Collision** – The game uses a collision engine that checks for collision with the buildings, the ground, the 'ceiling' and the sprites.

- **External level data** – The information for the layout of the level is pulled in from an external file.

- **Level editor** – There is a simple level editor used to create the game grid.

Now, are you sitting comfortably? Then let's begin piecing the game together.

## The Level Editor

Before we look at the game itself, we have to look at the level editor, which is used to create game levels. This file is called `editor.fla`:

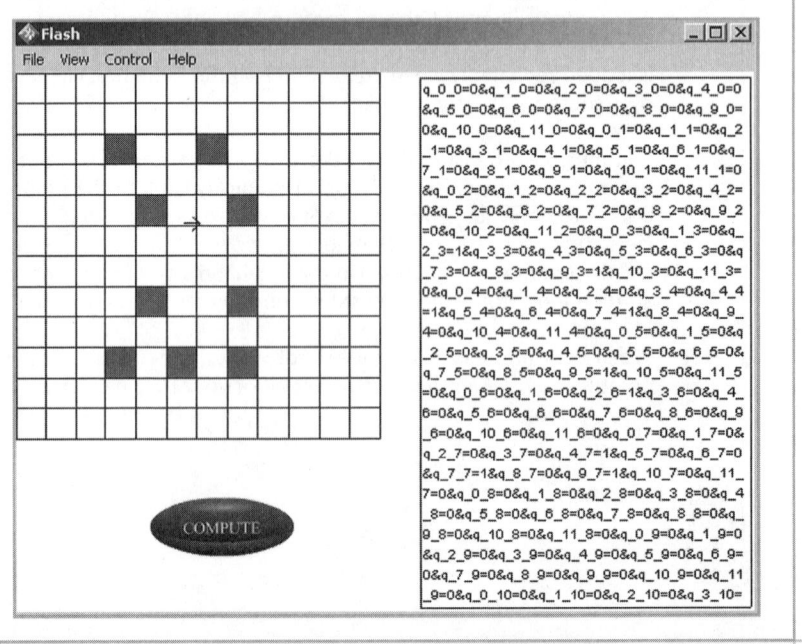

# Mech Attack

Case Study 2

In *Mech Attack*, a game level is simply a grid of buildings. The level editor provides an overhead plan of the city grid. When you click on one of the grid squares, it will toggle between on and off. When it's on (dark gray) there is a building present. When it's off (white) it means there's only road. The default level is simply four buildings arranged like so:

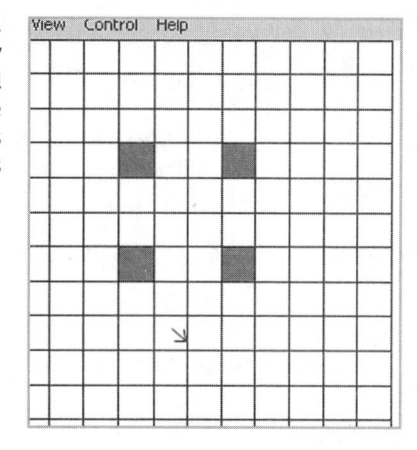

That's really all there is to making a level. Everything else – like helibombs, power-ups and building height – is determined by the game.

## How the Level Editor Works

On the level editor's stage there are only three movie clips:

- A movie clip called quad, with the instance name quad0. This is one of the squares that make up the grid.

- A movie clip called controller, with the instance name controller

- A movie clip called player, with the instance name player. This is an arrow that you can move around the screen with the cursor keys and it gives you an idea of how game collision will work.

You'll also see a large text box at the right, with the variable name output, and a button to the left of that called compute.

### quad
If you take a look at quad, you'll see that it contains two frames and two layers. The top layer is an invisible button, and the bottom layer contains the box in our two states – on or off. It looks like this:

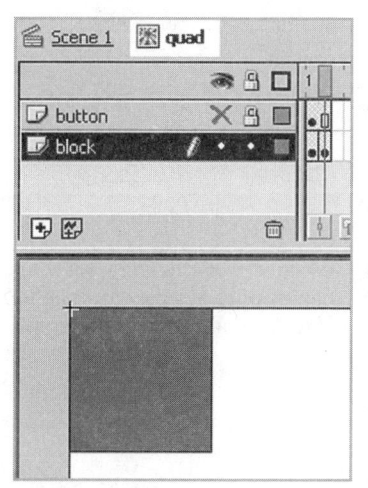

# Case Study 2: Flash Games Studio

The following code is attached to the button on the top layer:

```
on (release)
{
    // Toggles between frame 1 and frame 2
    gotoAndStop((1 - (_currentframe - 1)) + 1);
}
```

What we're doing here is simple. When you click on the button, it toggles the quad between the on and off state.

### Controller

The following code is attached to the controller movie clip on the main timeline:

```
onClipEvent(load)
{
  // Draw a grid of 12 x 12 copies of quad0
  // movieClip
  for (i = 0; i < 12; i++)
  {
  for (j = 0; j < 12; j++)
  {
    // Calculate the quad name based on i and j
    // quad1, quad2 ... quad143
    n = (i * 12) + j;
    nm = "quad" add n;

    if (n > 0)
            {
        // Don't duplicate quad0 to quad0
        duplicateMovieClip (_root.quad0, nm, n);
    }

    // Move square into location
    _root[nm]._x = (i * _root[nm]._width);
    _root[nm]._y = (j * _root[nm]._height);

    // Sit it on frame 1 (empty box, not toggled)
    _root[nm].gotoAndStop(1);
    }
  }
}
```

When we run this code, we're simply creating a 12x12 grid of quad movie clips. The quad instance names will be quad0 to quad143. Once a quad has been correctly place in position, we're telling it to stop on frame 1, the empty frame.

# Mech Attack

Case Study 2

## Compute Button

When we've drawn the map that we want to use in the game, we press the compute button and a string of variables representing our map is placed in the output text box. Within the compute button, we have the following code:

```
on (release)
{
  // Here we're creating an output of the state of the grid.
  // this will be placed in a text box on the main timeline
  // called output.  Copy this into a text file called
  // level.txt to make it play in the game

  // Clear the output
  _root.output = "";

  // Create output from quad states
  for (i = 0; i < 12; i++)
  {
      for (j = 0; j < 12; j++)
      {
       // Calculate quad name based on i and j
       n = (i * 12) + j;
       nm = "quad" add n;

       // construct a q_j_i variable q_2_2, q_2_3 etc
       // and fill it with the value of quad's _currentframe - 1
       // so it will be either 1 or 0 (on or off)
       stg = "q_" add j add "_" add i add "=" add
➥ (_root[nm]._currentFrame - 1) add "&";

       // Add it to the output box
       _root.output = _root.output add stg;
      }
    }
}
```

This parses through all of the quads, and creates a string of variables by looking at the currentframe property of each one. It looks like this:

q_0_0=0&q_1_0=0&q_2_0=0&q_3_0=0&q_4_0=0 ...and so on, up to... q_11_11=0

This string of variables is our level data, and is used by the game to construct the level on screen. Once you've built your level and computed the level data, you can take the contents of the output text box and save them in a text file. The game looks for a file called level.txt.

That's all there is to the level editor, except for one additional thing, the player code.

# Case Study 2: Flash Games Studio

### Player

You can move the player arrow around the screen with the cursor keys, and it will collide with the game grid you have created. To achieve this, the following code is attached to the player object:

```
onClipEvent(load)
{
     // Bring me in front of everything
     this.swapDepths(400);
}

onClipEvent(enterFrame)
{
     // Assign key states
     kl = Key.isDown(Key.LEFT);
     kr = Key.isDown(Key.RIGHT);
     ku = Key.isDown(Key.UP);
     kd = Key.isDown(Key.DOWN);

     // Turn me?
     if (kl) _rotation -= 10;
     if (kr) _rotation += 10;

     // Speed me forward
     if (ku)
     {
           vel++;
     }
     // Speed me backward
     if (kd)
     {
           vel--;
     }

     // Slow me down if I'm not pressing keys
     if (!ku && !kd) vel *= 0.8;

     // Put a limit on my speed
     if (vel < -5) vel = -5;
     if (vel > 5) vel = 5;

     // Convert _rotation to radians
     r = _rotation * (Math.PI / 180);

     // Figure out my x and y speed
     dx = vel * Math.cos(r);
     dy = vel * Math.sin(r);

     // Compute the next tile along x
     nxxtile = Math.floor((_x + dx) / _root.quad0._width);
```

## Mech Attack

**Case Study 2**

```
nxytile = Math.floor(_y / _root.quad0._height);
nx = nxxtile * 12 + nxytile;

// Compute the next tile along y
nyxtile = Math.floor(_x   / _root.quad0._width);
nyytile = Math.floor((_y + dy) / _root.quad0._height);
ny = nyxtile * 12 + nyytile;

// What are the tiles set to?
stx = _root["quad" add nx]._currentframe;
sty = _root["quad" add ny]._currentframe;

// Am I hitting a block along x?
if (stx == 2)
{
        if (dx < 0)
        {
                // Hitting at left of tile, stop my x movement
                _x = nyxtile * _root.quad0._width + 1;
                dx = 0;
        }
        else
        {
                // Hitting at right of tile, stop my x movement
                _x = nxxtile * _root.quad0._width - 1;
                dx = 0;
        }
}

// Am I hitting a block along y?
if (sty == 2)
{
        if (dy < 0)
        {
                // Hitting at top of tile, stop my y movement
                _y = nxytile * _root.quad0._height + 1;
                dy = 0;
        }
        else
        {
                // Hitting at bottom of tile, stop my y movement
                _y = nyytile * _root.quad0._height - 1;
                dy = 0;
        }

}

// Move me
_x += dx;
_y += dy;
```

*continues overleaf*

# Case Study 2: Flash Games Studio

```
        // Stop me if I'm almost stopped
        if (vel < 1 && vel > -1) vel = 0;

}
```

This checks the state of the arrow keys and stores the results in kl, kr, ku, and kd. Once we've got those, then we change the player's speed and rotation with:

```
        // Turn me?
        if (kl) _rotation -= 10;
        if (kr) _rotation += 10;

        // Speed me forward
        if (ku)
        {
                vel++;
        }
        // Speed me backward
        if (kd)
        {
                vel--;
        }
```

The vel and rotation variables are used at the bottom of the code to compute dx and dy – how far to move along x- and y-axis. Next, we make sure that the player isn't moving too fast, and if they are we slow them down:

```
        // Slow me down if I'm not pressing keys
        if (!ku && !kd) vel *= 0.8;

        // Put a limit on my speed
        if (vel < -5) vel = -5;
        if (vel > 5) vel = 5;
```

Next, we use the player movie clip's rotation property (which is in degrees) to determine r – the equivalent angle in radians:

```
        // Convert _rotation to radians
        r = _rotation * (Math.PI / 180);
```

And then we're using our recently computed r value, and the player's velocity to work out dx and dy – how far to move along the x- and y-axis:

```
        // Figure out my x and y speed
        dx = vel * Math.cos(r);
        dy = vel * Math.sin(r);
```

# Mech Attack

*Case Study 2*

**Figure:** Player Object with velocity vector

$dx = vel * \cos(r)$
$dy = vel * \sin(r)$

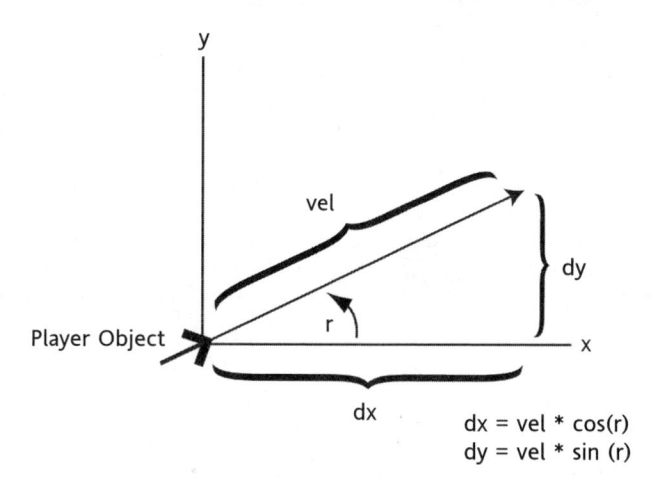

By looking at the player's next position along x (_x + dx, _y) and along y (_x, _y + dy), we can tell the tile number that the player will be in along either direction. Using this knowledge, we can check the value of each of those tiles:

```
// Compute the next tile along x
nxxtile = Math.floor((_x + dx) / _root.quad0._width);
nxytile = Math.floor(_y / _root.quad0._height);
nx = nxxtile * 12 + nxytile;

// Compute the next tile along y
nyxtile = Math.floor(_x  / _root.quad0._width);
nyytile = Math.floor((_y + dy) / _root.quad0._height);
ny = nyxtile * 12 + nyytile;

// What are the tiles set to?
stx = _root["quad" add nx]._currentframe;
sty = _root["quad" add ny]._currentframe;
```

stx and sty will contain the frame number of the tiles at those two positions (frame 1 for unblocked, frame 2 for blocked). If there's a solid object there, we stop the player from proceeding in that direction. We do this with the following code:

```
// Am I hitting a block along x?
if (stx == 2)
{
    if (dx < 0)
    {
        // Hitting at left of tile, stop my x movement
        _x = nyxtile * _root.quad0._width + 1;
        dx = 0;
    }
    else
```

*continues overleaf*

# Case Study 2: Flash Games Studio

```
                        {
                                // Hitting at right of tile, stop my x movement
                                _x = nxxtile * _root.quad0._width - 1;
                                dx = 0;
                        }
                }
```

We're simply looking at the next block on the x-axis and seeing if it's solid. If it is, then we check to see which direction the player is heading in, and then move them flush with the edge of the block, before removing all x velocity (dx). We do the exact same thing along the y-axis:

```
                // Am I hitting a block along y?
                if (sty == 2)
                {
                        if (dy < 0)
                        {
                                // Hitting at top of tile, stop my y movement
                                _y = nxytile * _root.quad0._height + 1;
                                dy = 0;
                        }
                        else
                        {
                                // Hitting at bottom of tile, stop my y movement
                                _y = nyytile * _root.quad0._height - 1;
                                dy = 0;
                        }
                }
```

Once we've adjusted the player's position, and their velocity, we can actually perform the player move instructions:

```
                // Move me
                _x += dx;
                _y += dy;
```

Finally, we just want to put a stop to the player's speed if they've almost stopped. Because we're scaling vel by 0.8 every frame that they player isn't holding down a key, it's actually possible that vel will never reach 0, only get very, very close. So we set vel to 0 like so:

```
                // Stop me if I'm almost stopped
                if (vel < 1 && vel > -1) vel = 0;
```

All of this movement code is very similar to the way our robot is going to be moved in the final game.

That's all there is to the level editor. Use this to create levels that you want to play in *Mech Attack*. Just copy the contents of the output text variable to a text file and call it level.txt.

# Mech Attack — Case Study 2

## The Game

Okay, now let's look at how the game is done. Here's a look at the `demoCs2-1.fla` on the stage:

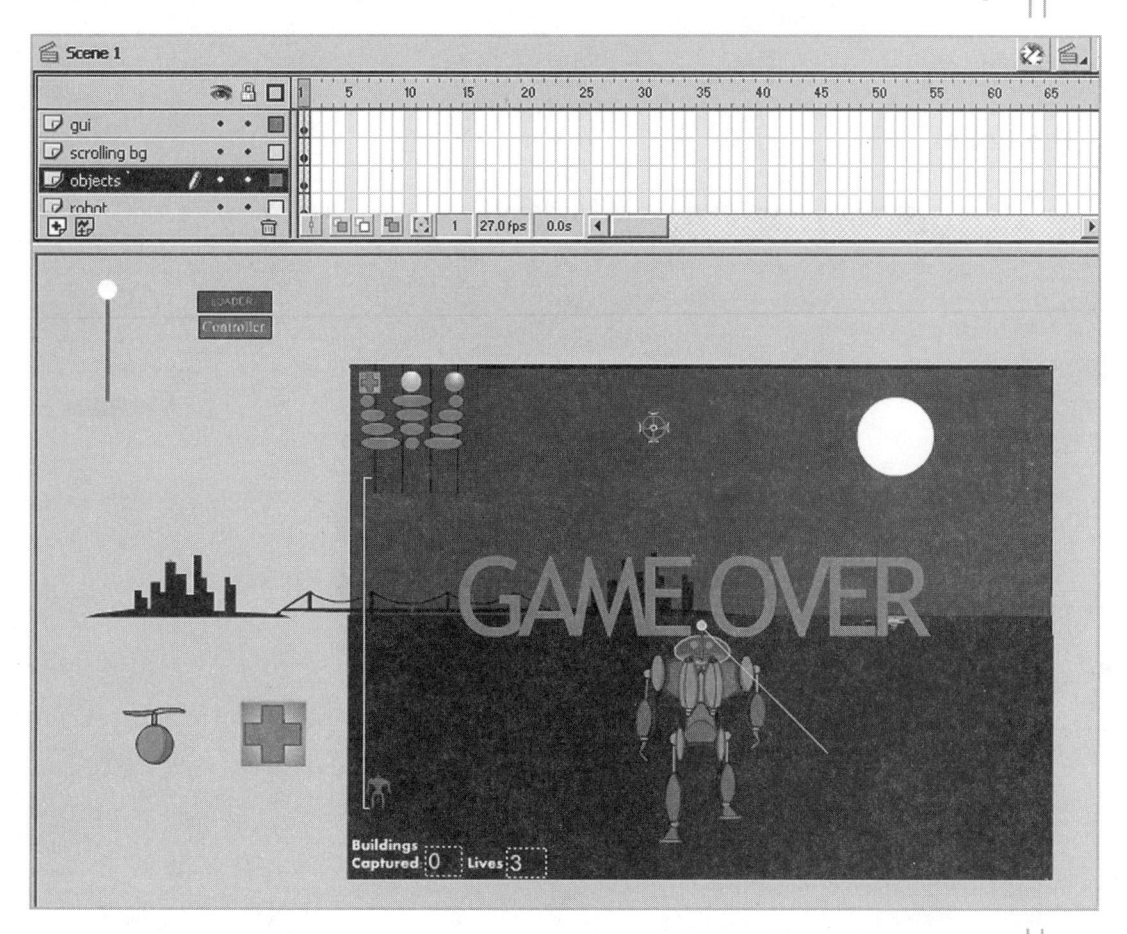

The game is made up of several key game objects sitting on the stage:

- The **robot** – This is our main character
- The **cityscape** – This is part of the background used to create a distant parallax effect, which is based on the player's angle
- The **GUI display** – All the informational display of the game
- The **crosshair** – The point in at which the laser will fire
- The **laser** – A dynamically drawn line that is the weapon
- The **streetlamp** – A sprite object as a prop in the city
- The **power-up** – Objects that you can collect to increase your life, fuel or ammo
- The **helibomb** – The enemy

# Case Study 2: Flash Games Studio

- The **polygon** object – The crucial object of the rendering engine that's responsible for creating the 3D buildings
- The **loader** – A movie clip that contains routines to handle loading in externally created levels
- The **controller** – The main ActionScript that controls scene rendering and player movement

All of these work together to make our game. Let's look at each of them in detail.

## The Robot

The robot is a movie clip on the stage with the instance name **robot**. Within the robot, we have about 70 frames of animation, showing the robot doing his different activities. The image below is the robot in his stationary frame.

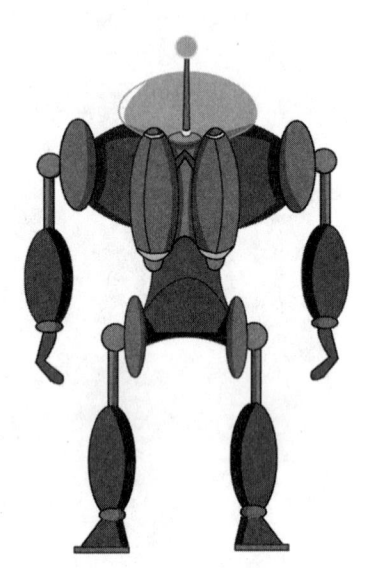

Here are some of the others:

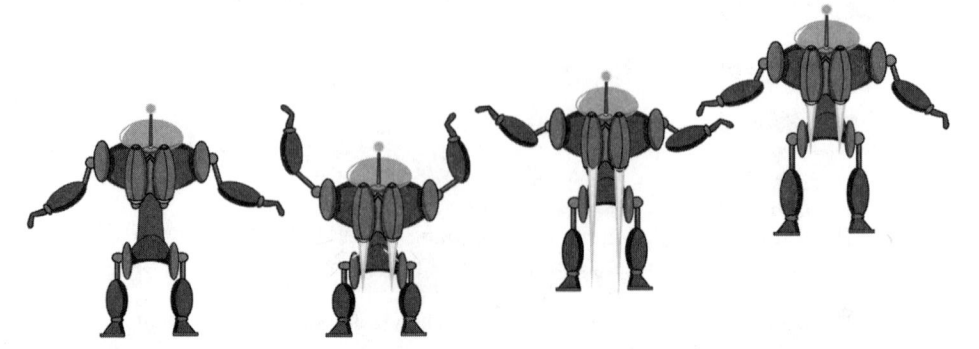

Jumping

# Mech Attack  Case Study 2

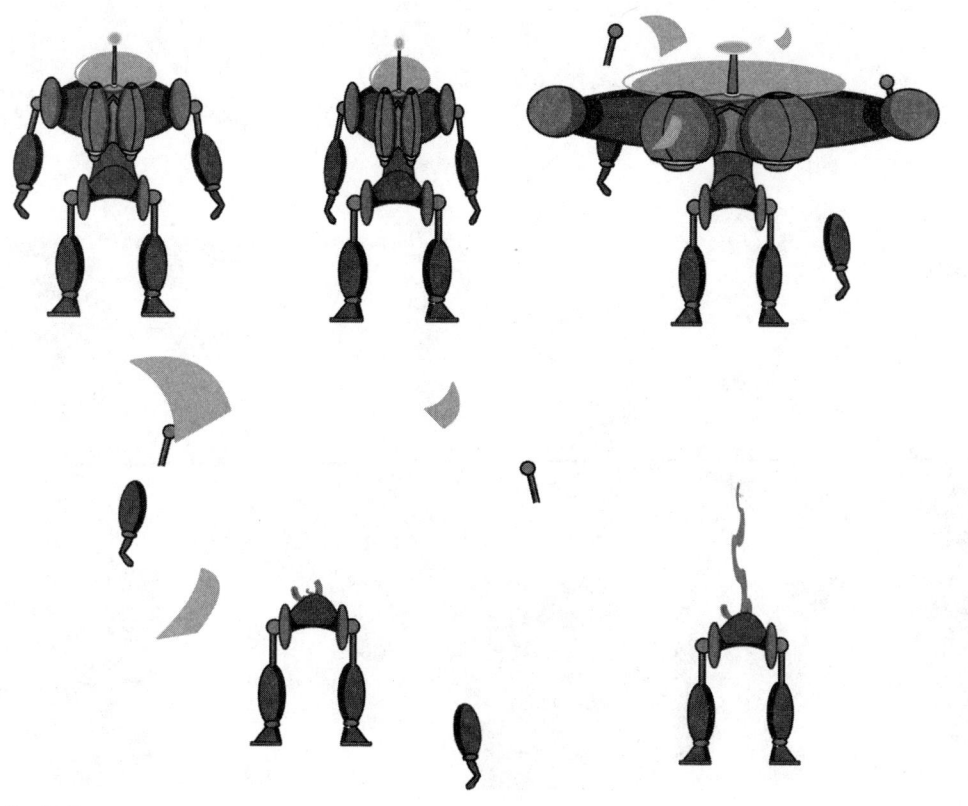

Exploding

All of these animations are arranged sequentially within the robot movie clip, so that the walk is from frames 1 to 8, stationary is frame 9, jumping is frames 10 to 17, flying is frame 18, falling is frame 19 and exploding is frames 20 to 70:

# Case Study 2 | Flash Games Studio

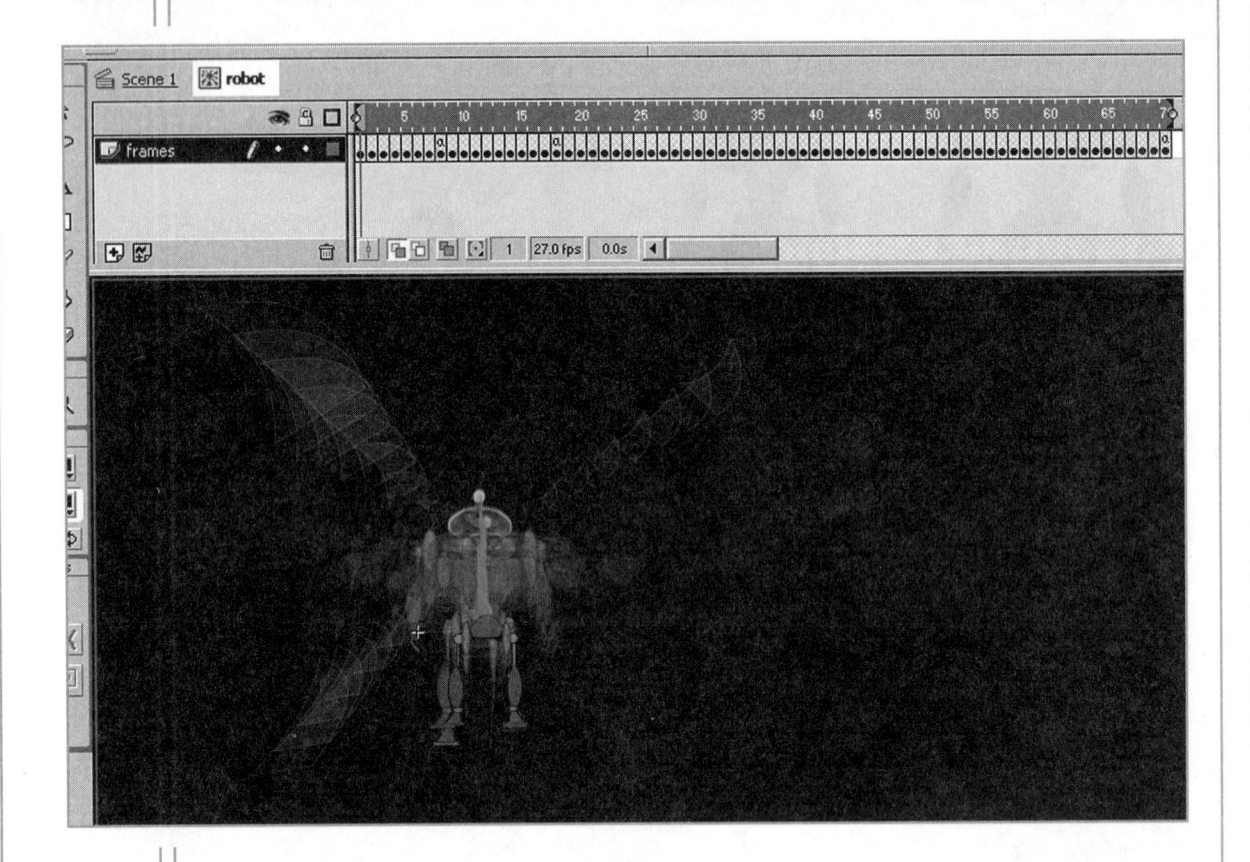

Frame 8 of the movie clip sends us back to frame 1 thus creating a walk loop. A `stop` action on frame 18 halts the robot at the end of its jump animation. It remains there throughout the time it's flying. On the very last frame of the robot's animations, at the end of the explosion, we have the following code:

```
// Any lives left?
if (_root.gui.lives > 0)
{
    // Player has died, reset them to starting position
    _root.controller.xloc = 500;
    _root.controller.yloc = 00;
    _root.controller.zloc = 500;
    _root.controller.ang = 100;
    _root.controller.dvel = 0;
    _root.controller.dy = 0;

    // return their resources to 80
    _root.controller.life = 80;
    _root.controller.fuel = 80;
```

```
                _root.controller.ammo = 80;

                // remove a life
                _root.gui.lives --;
        }
        else
        {
                // No more lives left, player is dead.
                // stay on this dead frame
                stop();

                // Game over text visible
                _root.gui.gameover._visible = true;
        }
```

Here, we're simply checking to see how many lives are left, and if we have one or more lives, then we reset the player back to their starting location, rotation, velocity and speed. We also reset their resources (life, fuel, ammo) back to full, and finally we remove one life.

If the player doesn't have any lives left we simply stop the game on that last dead frame, and make a movie clip called gameover visible. You'll see where this movie clip is situated in a moment.

## The Cityscape

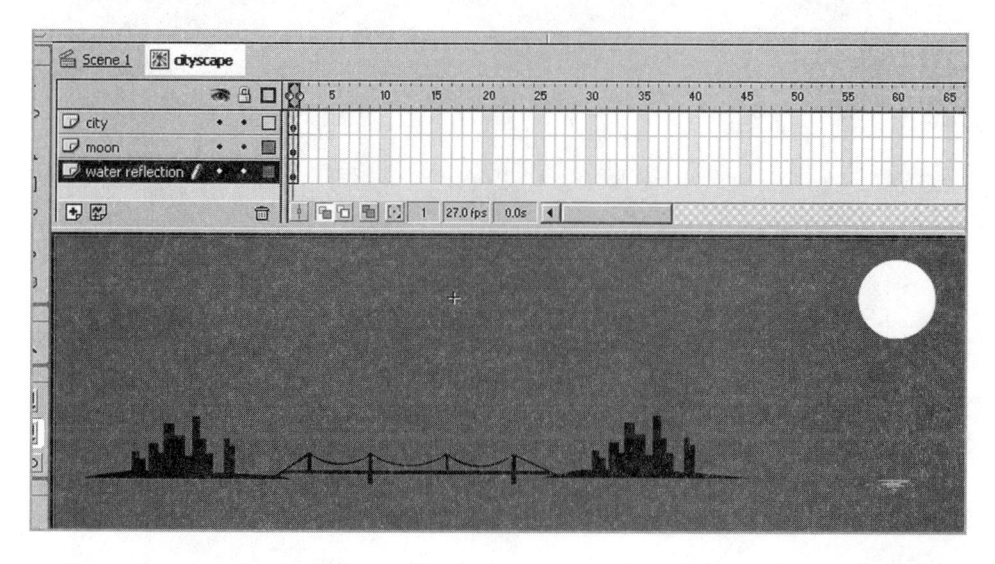

The cityscape skyline is a movie clip with the instance name cityscape. This is moved in the background to give the appearance that the player is on an island and that there's a large city in the distance.

## Case Study 2: Flash Games Studio

The location of the cityscape is based on the direction that the player is facing, and its position is set with this code:

```
// Move the background cityscape
_root.cityscape._x = 1000 - (ang << 1);
```

Here `ang` represents the player's rotation. We're bitshifting `ang` left by 1, effectively doubling it. This works well to make the background move in opposition to the direction that you're turning, mimicking a real distant background. We'll see the location of this code later, in the controller object.

### The GUI Display

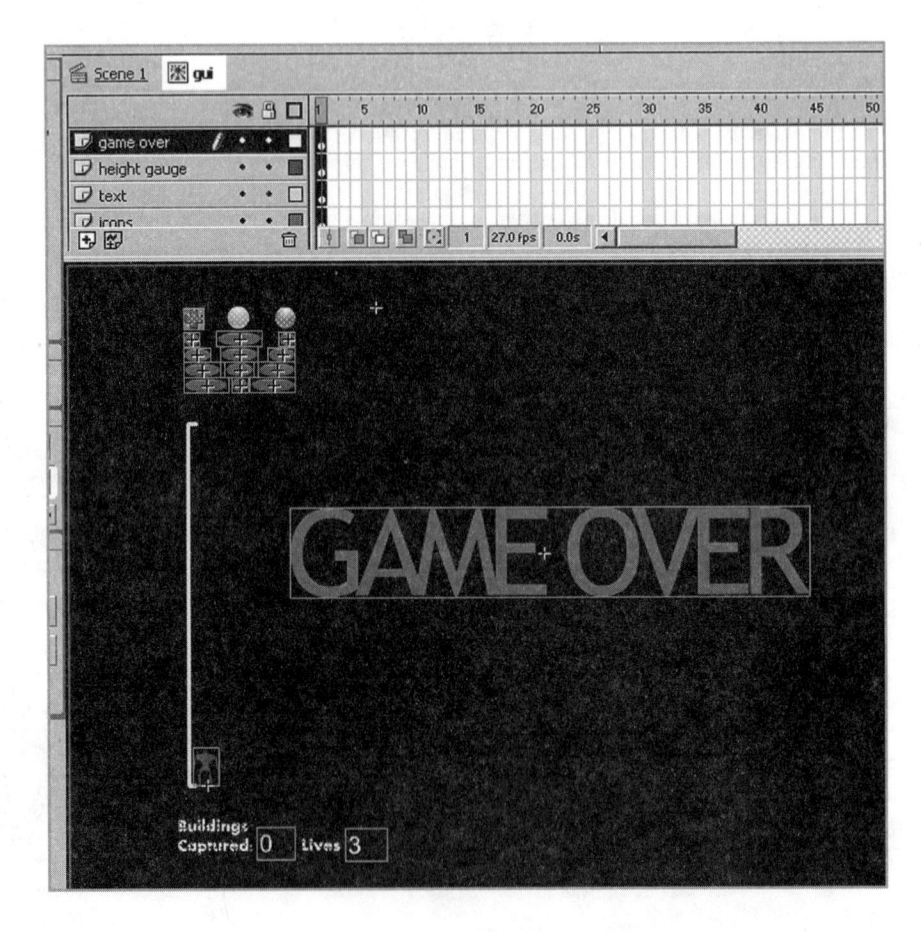

The GUI is a movie clip on the main timeline called gui, with the instance name `gui`. This contains the life, fuel, and energy meters, the graphical height indicator, the number of buildings captured, the lives remaining, and that movie clip called gameover with the words "GAME OVER" in large red text.

The two text variables, captures and lives, contain numbers that indicate how many buildings the player has captured, and how many lives they have remaining.

We attach the following code to the gameover movie clip:

```
onClipEvent (load)
{
    _visible = false;
}
```

Because we don't want the words "GAME OVER" to be visible when the game begins. At the bottom graphical height indicator is a small movie clip with the instance name, minime. This is moved up and down based on the current altitude of the player. We'll attach the following code to the minime movie clip.

```
onClipEvent(load)
{
    // Store my starting position
    sy = _y;
}

onClipEvent(enterFrame)
{
    // Where am I based on a max height of -1200
    // (negative y is up)
    myht = (_root.controller.yloc / -1200) * 250;

    // Move me
    _y = sy - myht;
}
```

This simply makes minime always check to see what altitude the robot is at (stored in yloc) and scale that down to somewhere between 0 and 250 – the height of the graphical height indicator. Then, we simply set the height of minime to that number, subtracted from sy, which is its starting position. This means that minime will move up and down on the screen perfectly mirroring the altitude of the player.

The meters in the upper left-hand corner are simply made up of twelve ovals, four for each resource. Their instance names are: life0 to life3, fuel0 to fuel3, and ammo0 to ammo3. As the player loses life, fuel and ammo the meters begin to go down, like so:

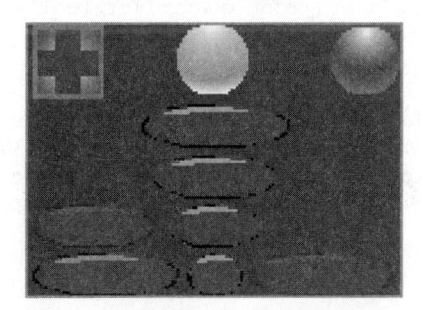

# Case Study 2: Flash Games Studio

The `alpha` property of each oval changes according to the corresponding resource level. Now, the meters themselves are intelligent in that they are self-motivated to change as the player's levels change. Attached to the master gui movie clip is the following code:

```
onClipEvent(load)
{
    // Bring this right to the very front
    this.swapDepths(11000);
}

onClipEvent(enterFrame)
{
    // Set each oval to a certain transparency based on
    // the value of 3 resources; fuel, ammo, and life.
    // Works on a scale so that the bottom oval (3) doesn't
    // dim until the resource is nearly empty, while the
    // top oval (0) dims immediately

    fuel0._alpha = _root.controller.fuel << 2;
    fuel1._alpha = (_root.controller.fuel - 10) << 2;
    fuel2._alpha = (_root.controller.fuel - 20) << 2;
    fuel3._alpha = (_root.controller.fuel - 30) << 2;

    ammo0._alpha = _root.controller.ammo << 2;
    ammo1._alpha = (_root.controller.ammo - 10) << 2;
    ammo2._alpha = (_root.controller.ammo - 20) << 2;
    ammo3._alpha = (_root.controller.ammo - 30) << 2;

    life0._alpha = _root.controller.life << 2;
    life1._alpha = (_root.controller.life - 10) << 2;
    life2._alpha = (_root.controller.life - 20) << 2;
    life3._alpha = (_root.controller.life - 30) << 2;
}
```

The first thing we're doing is bringing the whole gui movie clip in front of everything else, by setting its depth to 11000. Then, on the `enterFrame` event, we're setting the `alpha` level of each oval based on the resource level. Each meter uses the same formula to calculate the `alpha` of its ovals, so let's take a look at fuel as an example:

```
fuel0._alpha = _root.controller.fuel << 2;
fuel1._alpha = (_root.controller.fuel - 10) << 2;
fuel2._alpha = (_root.controller.fuel - 20) << 2;
fuel3._alpha = (_root.controller.fuel - 30) << 2;
```

When fuel is at 80, then all four ovals will be completely solid – `fuel0` will be 160% solid, `fuel1` will be 140% solid, `fuel2` will be 120% solid, and `fuel3` will be 100% solid. As the fuel level decreases, so too will the `alpha` of each oval. `fuel3` will immediately begin to fade, then `fuel2` once the player passes below 80% fuel, then `fuel1` will fade, and so on.

# Mech Attack

**Case Study 2**

This will create a gradual effect, like any meter should. When the fuel level reaches 30 and below, the `fuel3` will be completely gone, and will progress until all fuel ovals are completely invisible – and the player is out of fuel.

## The Crosshair

When the player moves their mouse around the screen, they'll see a crosshair that indicates where the robot's laser will fire:

The crosshair is simply a movie clip with the name crosshair. It consists of a nine frame animation where the outer arcs of the crosshair animate into the middle of the crosshair. We attach the following code to the crosshair movie clip:

```
onClipEvent(load)
{
    // Bring crosshair so it's hidden by the
    // player, yet in front of everything else
    this.swapDepths(9200);

    // Start dragging the crosshair, so the
    // mouse cursor is locked to the center
    this.startDrag(true);

    // Hide the mouse cursor (pointer)
    Mouse.hide();
}
```

All of this code is simply for aesthetics. We're attaching the crosshair to the mouse, and then hiding the mouse cursor so that when we move the mouse around in the Flash window, it will be the crosshair that we're moving. We're also using the `swapDepths` command to move the crosshair to a depth that will be hidden by the player, yet on top of all the other game objects, as you'll see in a little while.

## Case Study 2: Flash Games Studio

### The Laser

The laser is a special movie clip called line that contains a single hairline running from (0,0) to (100,100). This was used as part of the line drawing engine that was outlined in the *Real 3D* chapter. We have a line object with the instance name laser, and it's positioned so that its center point is positioned over the robot's laser emitter, as seen here:

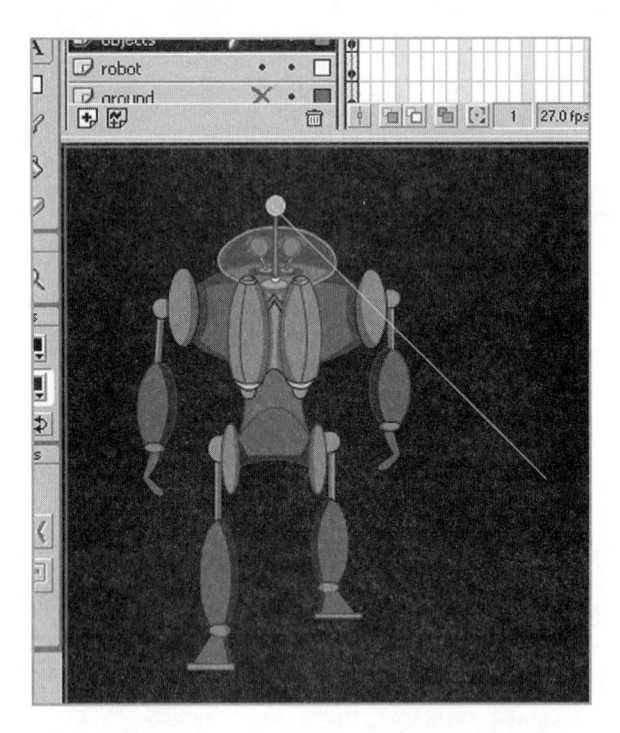

When the player moves their target around the screen, and then opens fire on an enemy or a building, the laser beam is oriented so that it traces a line between the laser emitter and the mouse cursor, thus creating the appearance that the robot is firing the laser.

We attach the following code to the laser movie clip:

```
onClipEvent(load)
{
    // In front of the player
    this.swapDepths(9209);

    // Takes two points and makes the line draw
    // between them
    function drawline (sx1, sy1, sx2, sy2)
    {
```

# Mech Attack

## Case Study 2

```
                dx = sx2 - sx1;
                dy = sy2 - sy1;

                _xscale = dx;
                _yscale = dy;
                _x = sx1;
                _y = sy1;
        }

        // hide line to start
        _visible = false;
}
```

This is simply the line drawing function from the *Real 3D* chapter, but with a few additions. First, we're setting the depth level of the movie clip to 9209, which is just obscured by the player, but on top of the crosshair. This appears correctly on screen when the laser is fired. We then hide the laser to start off with by setting its `visible` property to false. Finally we attach the following code below the `load clipEvent`:

```
onClipEvent(enterFrame)
{
        // if the hittingsomething flag has been set,
        // then make the laser and the hit sparks
        // visible
        if (_root.hittingsomething)
        {
                _root.sparks._x = _root._xmouse;
                _root.sparks._y = _root._ymouse;
                _root.sparks._visible = true;
                _root.laser._visible = true;

                // reduce ammo level
                _root.controller.ammo--;
        }
        else
        {
                // Not hitting something, laser and
                // sparks are invisible - even if the
                // player is holding the mouse button
                _root.sparks._visible = false;
                _root.laser._visible = false;
        }

        _root.hittingsomething = false;
}
```

What we're simply doing here is trying to determine whether or not the laser beam should be visible. Because there are so many different targets (enemies and buildings) that can make a laser visible, we don't want them turning the laser on and off. When the player presses the mouse button, the laser won't necessarily become visible. It will only appear if they're hitting something.

# Case Study 2: Flash Games Studio

So, we check to see whether elsewhere in the game a variable called `hittingsomething` has been set to `true`, and if it has, we can safely show the laser and the sparks. If the laser is hitting something, the small movie clip called `sparks` gives off a little action. There's also the question of ammunition:

```
_root.controller.ammo--;
```

If we are hitting something we want to deplete the player's ammo supply. If however, we weren't hitting anything, then we make sure that the laser and the sparks are invisible. We set `hittingsomething` to `false`. In doing this, we leave it up to something else in the game to set it to `true`, so that we can draw the laser again. This variable is like a signal between many different areas of the game. We'll cover how the variable is set soon.

## The Streetlamp

The streetlamp is simply a one-frame movie clip called `object`, with an instance name `streetlamp` that is an image of a streetlamp meant to be seen as if below you, as you're 200 feet tall. It's drawn in such a way that it's identical from any angle – a perfect faux 3D sprite:

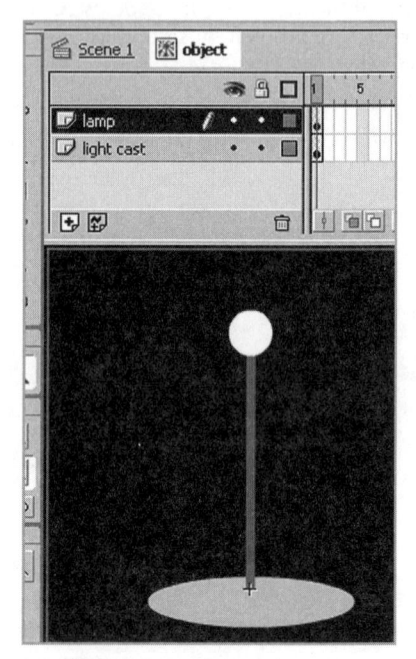

What's important about this sprite (as with any sprite) is where we have the center point of the movie clip. You'll notice that here it's at the base of the lamp's pole, somewhere near the middle of the light circle the lamp is casting.

Since a sprite is represented by a single (x,y,z) coordinate, we have to correspond this point to somewhere on the actual sprite image. What we do is render our scene so that the movie clip's center point is what is positioned at the sprite's x, y, and z location. In the case of our streetlamp, if we position it at (0,300,0), then it will truly appear to be sitting on the ground, because our ground is at y value of 300.

# Mech Attack

## Case Study 2

In this game, our eye level is at 0 on the y-axis. We want the ground to be below our eye level, so, bearing in mind that the y-axis in Flash is reversed, we say that it's 300 below our eye, which is a y value of 300. The tops of the buildings are up at -1200, and this is known as the 'ceiling'. When the player flies up, this is the point at which they are not allowed to fly any higher.

## Power-ups

The power-ups are contained in a movie clip on the main timeline called powerup with the instance name powerup. The clip consists of three frames, each one containing an icon:

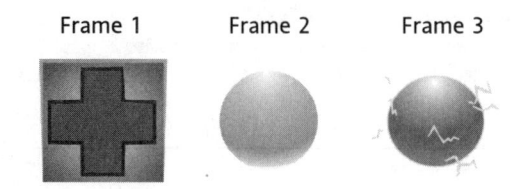

Frame 1    Frame 2    Frame 3

Unlike the streetlamp, the image on each frame has its center point directly in the middle of the icon; these will be floating objects, so the movie clip's center is the most logical position to place the icons.

Although this movie clip has the instance name powerup, it's important to note that when the game is playing, we'll actually be seeing copies of it, with the instance names obj0, obj1, obj2, and so on. I'll get into that shortly when I detail the object creation routines.

The power-ups float around in 3D, so when a power-up is created in the game, it possesses an x, y, and z location. These are stored in local variables attached to the movie clip called x1, y1, and z1. There's also another variable, dy, which is its velocity along the y-axis. This allows the power-up to float or fall. Attached to the powerup object is the following code:

```
onClipEvent(enterFrame)
{
  // Only act if the powerup isn't 'dead' (inactive) if (!dead)
  {
     // Hit the ground? stop falling
     if (y1 > 300)
     {
            y1 = 300;
            dy = 0;
     }

     // Hit the 'ceiling'? stop rising
     if (y1 < -1200)
     {
            y1 = -1200;
            dy = 0;
     }
```

*continues overleaf*

# Case Study 2: Flash Games Studio

```
            // Move me along the vertical based on
            // my vertical speed
            y1 += dy;
            // Slowly increase my downward speed
            dy += 0.01;

            // Compute my distance from the player on all
            // 3 axes
            distx = Math.abs(x1 - _root.controller.xloc);
            distz = Math.abs(z1 - _root.controller.zloc);

            // Head is at 0, feet are at 300, so we compute based
            // on yloc + 150 which is mid body
            disty = Math.abs(y1 - (_root.controller.yloc + 150));

            // Is the player on top of me, and does the player
            // have some life? (dead people can't grab powerups)
            if (distx < 180 && distz < 180 && disty < 200 &&
            ➥ _root.controller.life > 0)
            {
                    // What powerup type am i?
                    type = _currentframe;
                    if (type == 1)
                            _root.controller.life += 20; // Life
                    if (type == 2)
                            _root.controller.fuel += 20; // Fuel
                    if (type == 3)
                            _root.controller.ammo += 10; // Ammo

                    // Put limits on the resource levels - 80 max
                    if (_root.controller.life > 80)
                            _root.controller.life = 80;
                    if (_root.controller.fuel > 80)
                            _root.controller.fuel = 80;
                    if (_root.controller.ammo > 80)
                            _root.controller.ammo = 80;

                    // Deactivate me and hide me
                    dead = true;
                    _visible = false;
            }
      }
}
```

What we're doing here is giving each power-up some self-motivation. The first thing we do is check to make sure it's active. It's possible for the powerup movie clip to be inactive when the local variable dead is true.

# Mech Attack

## Case Study 2

Next, we check to see whether the power-up has hit the ground or the ceiling:

```
// Hit the ground? stop falling
if (y1 > 300)
{
        y1 = 300;
        dy = 0;
}
// Hit the 'ceiling'? stop rising
if (y1 < -1200)
{
        y1 = -1200;
        dy = 0;
}
```

We don't want the power-up to disappear into the ground, or to float away into the sky. So, if it hits the ground then we set its dy to 0 (stop it from falling) and move it to y position 0. If it has hit the ceiling we move it back to the ceiling and stop it from rising by setting dy to 0. Next we apply some physics:

```
// Move me along the vertical based on
// my vertical speed
y1 += dy;

// Slowly increase my downward speed
dy += 0.01;
```

This moves the y1 coordinate of powerup by dy each frame. Then we increase dy by 0.01 each frame, which creates a gravitational pull down on the object. No matter what dy is to start with it will eventually end up as a positive number, and thus be falling down towards the ground. Next, we figure out how far away we are from the player in each axis:

```
// Compute my distance from the player on all
// 3 axes
distx = Math.abs(x1 - _root.controller.xloc);
distz = Math.abs(z1 - _root.controller.zloc);

// Head is at 0, feet are at 300, so we compute based
// on yloc + 150 which is mid body
disty = Math.abs(y1 - (_root.controller.yloc + 150));
```

We check our distance along x (distx), along z (distz), and along y (disty). For y however, we are comparing the power-up's distance to a point about halfway down the player's body. We then check to see if the power-up is within a certain range on each axis:

```
if (distx < 180 && distz < 180 && disty < 200 &&
_root.controller.life > 0)
```

We're making sure that we are + or − 180 on x and z, and + or − 200 on y. Since we're measuring the y distance from the player's midpoint, + or − 200 will easily be anywhere from the feet to the head.

# Case Study 2: Flash Games Studio

These values are actually more than enough than for our requirements, but we want to make it relatively easy to pick up a power-up. We're also making sure that the player's life is more than 0 – we don't want them picking up power-ups and being resurrected if they're dead (in the middle of playing an explosion animation for example).

Finally we have to determine what kind of a power-up the object is:

```
// What powerup type am i?
type = _currentframe;
if (type == 1)
    _root.controller.life += 20; // Life
if (type == 2)
    _root.controller.fuel += 20; // Fuel
if (type == 3)
    _root.controller.ammo += 10; // Ammo

// Put limits on the resource levels - 80 max
if (_root.controller.life > 80)
    _root.controller.life = 80;
if (_root.controller.fuel > 80)
    _root.controller.fuel = 80;
if (_root.controller.ammo > 80)
    _root.controller.ammo = 80;

// Deactivate me and hide me
dead = true;
_visible = false;
```

We're looking at the `currentframe` of the power-up to determine its type and then increasing the appropriate resource. We also perform one more check to make sure that the player isn't carrying more than 80 in any resource, as 80 is the maximum that we're setting.

## Helibombs

The helibombs are quite similar to the power-ups, except that they have a few more variables attached to them, and a few more frames of animation. The helibomb is in a movie clip called helibomb, with the instance name `heli`. As with the power-ups, the `heli` instance will never actually be in the game – it's merely a movie clip that will be contained within the `obj#` instance name convention.

This naming convention is chosen because it's used by the sprite rendering engine (as you'll see later) to loop through all the objects and place them correctly in 3D on screen. Within the helibomb movie clip, we have one frame that contains the helibomb image, and then starting in frame 2 we have a 16 frame animated explosion. The layout should look something like this:

# Mech Attack

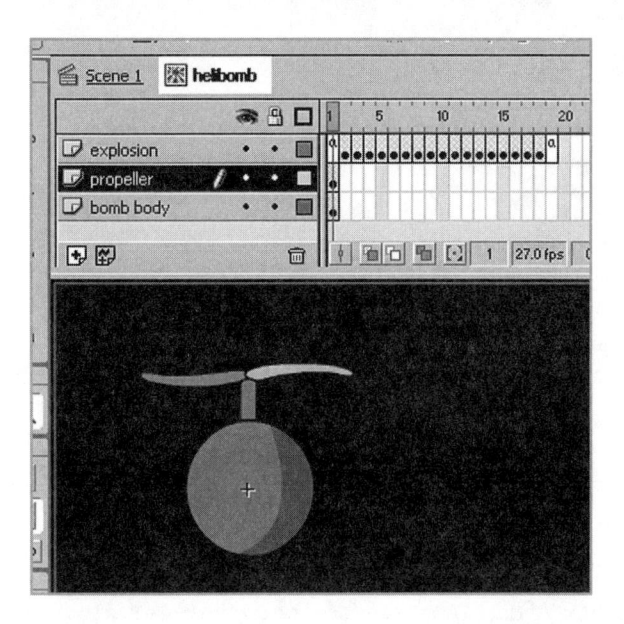

## Case Study 2

Attached to the first frame of the explosion layer is a stop command so that the helibomb won't start out its existence by merely exploding into oblivion. Attached to the main helibomb movie clip, is the following code:

```
onClipEvent(enterFrame)
{
    // Is player shooting me?
    if (_root.controller.shooting && this.hitTest(_root._xmouse,
    ➥ _root._ymouse, false))
    {
        _root.hittingsomething = true;
        play();
    }

    // accellerate along x to reach player
    if (x1 > _root.controller.xloc)
        dx -= 1;
    else if (x1 < _root.controller.xloc)
        dx += 1;

    // accellerate along z to reach player
    if (z1 > _root.controller.zloc)
        dz -= 1;
    else if (z1 < _root.controller.zloc)
        dz += 1;

    // accellerate along y to reach player
    if (y1 > (_root.controller.yloc + 50))
```

*continues overleaf*

# Case Study 2: Flash Games Studio

```
                    dy -= 1;
            else if (y1 < (_root.controller.yloc + 50))
                    dy += 1;

            // put a limit on my speed
            if (dx > 18) dx = 18;
            if (dx < -18) dx = -18;

            if (dz > 18) dz = 18;
            if (dz < -18) dz = -18;

            if (dy > 18) dy = 18;
            if (dy < -18) dy = -18;

            // Move me
            x1 += dx;
            z1 += dz;
            y1 += dy;

            // compute my distance from the player
            distx = Math.abs(x1 - _root.controller.xloc);
            distz = Math.abs(z1 - _root.controller.zloc);
            disty = Math.abs(y1 - (_root.controller.yloc + 50));

            // Am I hitting the player?
            if (distx < 180 && distz < 180 && disty < 100)
            {
                    // Yes. While player is over top of me, or my
                    // explosion, decrease their health.
                    _root.controller.life -= 0.5;
                    play();
            }
    }
```

A helibomb has `x1`, `y1`, and `z1` associated with it, but it also has `dx`, `dy`, and `dz`. You'll recognize `dy` from the power-ups, but we also have `dx` and `dz`, which are movements along the x- and z-axes. The first thing the helibomb script does is check to see if the player is shooting it:

```
            // Is player shooting me?
            if (_root.controller.shooting && this.hitTest(_root._xmouse,
            _root._ymouse, false))
            {
                    _root.hittingsomething = true;
                    play();
            }
```

This relies on a global variable called `shooting`, which is simply `true` when the mouse button is being held down, and `false` when it isn't. If the player is indeed holding down the mouse button, we take advantage of Flash's `hitTest` action. We're checking to see whether the position of the mouse intersects with the shape of helibomb. If so, we set `hittingsomething` to `true`, and then

# Mech Attack

## Case Study 2

we play, telling helibomb to start its explosion animation. The flag hittingsomething is global, and is used by the laser object to determine whether it should make itself visible or not.

Next, we move the helibomb based on the position of the player:

```
// accelerate along x to reach player
if (x1 > _root.controller.xloc)
        dx -= 1;
else if (x1 < _root.controller.xloc)
        dx += 1;

// accellerate along z to reach player
if (z1 > _root.controller.zloc)
        dz -= 1;
else if (z1 < _root.controller.zloc)
        dz += 1;

// accellerate along y to reach player
if (y1 > (_root.controller.yloc + 50))
        dy -= 1;
else if (y1 < (_root.controller.yloc + 50))
        dy += 1;
```

All we're doing is making helibomb check to see whether it's greater or less than the player movie clip on each axis. For example, if the helibomb's x1 value is less than the player's xloc, then the helibomb will increase its speed along the x-axis (dx). However, once the helibomb passes the player's xloc it will start to decrease its dx value, which will make it slow down and eventually head back towards the player:

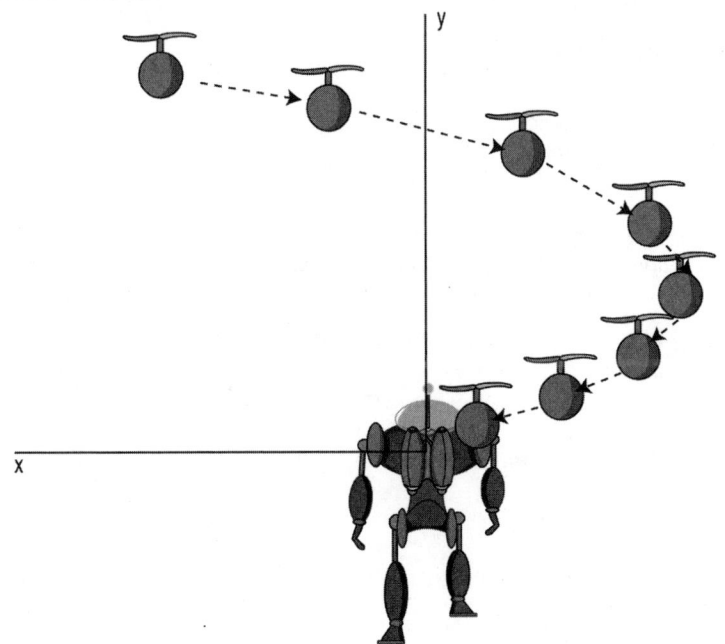

559

# Case Study 2: Flash Games Studio

The same is applied on the remaining two axes (y and z). This gives the helibomb a very natural tracking appearance since it can't simply change direction on the spot – it must slow down first. Using this tracking, the helibomb will eventually zero in on the player. We also make sure that the helibomb has a speed limit on each axis with:

```
// put a limit on my speed
if (dx > 18) dx = 18;
if (dx < -18) dx = -18;

if (dz > 18) dz = 18;
if (dz < -18) dz = -18;

if (dy > 18) dy = 18;
if (dy < -18) dy = -18;
```

We don't want the helibomb to infinitely pick up speed, because if it were far away from you, it could pick up so much speed that it would never be able to slow down to get to you, and it would zoom increasingly further and further away. To prevent this we make sure that the helibomb can't travel faster than 18 units per frame along any axis. Next, we move the helibomb:

```
// Move me
x1 += dx;
z1 += dz;
y1 += dy;
```

And then we calculate its distance from the player, just as with the power-up, but instead of rewarding the player for a hit, we punish them like so:

```
if (distx < 180 && distz < 180 && disty < 100)
{
    // Yes. While player is over top of me, or my
    // explosion, decrease their health.
    _root.controller.life -= 0.5;
    play();
}
```

While the player is colliding with the helibomb, it will remove 0.5 points of life from them. This then uses the `play` command to make sure that the helibomb explosion starts playing. The player will still take damage if they haven't moved out of the collision region while the explosion is playing.

On the very last frame of the helibomb's explosion sequence is a frame with ActionScript in it. The script is as follows:

```
// Random number between 0, 1 or 2
t = Math.floor(Math.random() * 3);

if (t == 0)
{
    // Spawn an energy that rises up
```

# Mech Attack  Case Study 2

```
            _root.controller.spawnpowerup (x1, y1, z1, 0, -6, 0, 3);
        }
        else if (t == 1)
        {
            // Spawn an fuel that sinks up
            _root.controller.spawnpowerup (x1, y1, z1, 0, 6, 0, 2);
        }
        else if (t == 2)
        {
            // Spawn a health that floats on the spot
            _root.controller.spawnpowerup (x1, y1, z1, 0, 0, 0, 1);
        }

        // Move me to a new random location in space.
        x1 = Math.random() * 3000;
        y1 = -Math.random() * 800;
        z1 = Math.random() * 3000;
        // Set my speed to 0
        dx = 0;
        dy = 0;
        dz = 0;
```

This grabs a random number between 0, 1, or 2 and stores it in t. Depending upon t, it will spawn ammo, life or fuel. Next we move the helibomb to a new random location from 0 to 3000 in x, 0 to –800 in y and 0 to 3000 in z. Finally we start the helibomb off with a speed of 0.

We also make a call to spawnpowerup, which is a function that is defined in the controller object, which we we'll be covering shortly.

## The Polygon

The polygon is simply an object on the stage called poly1 with the instance name polymast. This is the master polygon that's copied to create our game polygons (poly0, poly1, poly2, poly3, and so on), which are used by the polygon rendering engine that was detailed in the last chapter. We attach the following ActionScript to the poly1 movie clip:

```
onClipEvent (enterFrame)
{
    // In this code, the building 'heals' itself
    // If too green, resort slowly back to normal
    if (tr.ga > 40)
    {
        tr.ga --;
    }

    // If not solid, increase alpha slowly
    if (tr.aa < 100)
    {
```

*continues overleaf*

# Flash Games Studio

```
            tr.aa += 0.2;
        }
        c.setTransform(tr);
    }
```

All this does is look at an object caller `tr`, which is created when the polygon is created, and checks to see if its `ga` variable is greater than 40. If it is, then it decreases it by one. It also looks to see if the `aa` variable of `tr` is less than 100, and if it is, it increases it by 0.2.

This probably seems like gibberish at the moment, but hopefully this should help demystify it:

- `tr` is an object that is being applied to `c`, which is a color object.
- `tr` represents the color transform that is used in the `setTransform` command.
- `ga` and `aa` are the green and alpha values respectively.

When the player is firing their laser at a polygon (a building) it will begin to glow green, and fade out (the `ga` will increase, and the `aa` will decrease). The above code is doing the opposite of that – it's removing the green and fading the polygon back in. What is this doing? It's simply 'healing' the polygon. All polygons do this, and the purpose of it is to restore the integrity of a building that you started to capture, but didn't quite complete (for whatever reason; maybe you died, or ran out of ammo). This adds an element of challenge to the game.

The polygon has another, greater – to be rendered and create a full 3D scene with polygons and shading, but the controller object, which we'll get to in a moment, handles the rendering.

If you look at the polygon, you can see that we've created some vertical stripes on the top, middle, and bottom shapes:

I know, I said you couldn't texture the polygons. Well, we can to a certain extent, as long as our textures are vertical, not horizontal. If you like, try some other textures on the polygon shapes and see what happens – but don't say I didn't warn you...

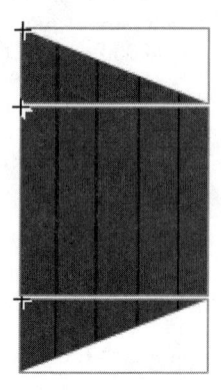

### Modifying the Robot Movie Clip

I'd like to take a minute to add the following code to the robot movie clip. We didn't cover this earlier because it wouldn't have made much sense, but now we should be equipped to handle it:

```
onClipEvent(load)
{
    // Stationary stance
    gotoAndStop(9);
}
```

This simply starts the robot in a standing position (frame 9). Continue with the following:

# Mech Attack

## Case Study 2

```
onClipEvent(enterFrame)
{
  // Is the player shooting?
  if (_root.controller.shooting)
  {
    // Go through each poly and see if we're hitting it.
    for (i = 0; i < _root.polynum; i++)
    {
      nam = "poly" add i;

      // Use the hittest to see if we're hitting the
      // polygon, and make sure it's alive already.
      if (_root[nam].hitTest(_root._xmouse,
      ➥_root._ymouse, true) && _root[nam].alive == true)
      {

        // What building is the polygon in?
        // divide the polygon by 4, giving
        // us the building
        tl = (i >> 2);

        // Increase the green value, and
        // decrease the alpha value of each
        // of the four polys in the building
        // this makes it glow green and fade out

        // Capturerate is based on the
        // player's height
        capturerate = -(_root.controller.yloc / 800) + 1;

        nm = "poly" add (tl * 4);
        _root[nm].tr.ga += capturerate;
        _root[nm].tr.aa -= capturerate;
        _root[nm].c.setTransform(_root[nm].tr);

        nm = "poly" add ((tl * 4) + 1);
        _root[nm].tr.ga += capturerate;
        _root[nm].tr.aa -= capturerate;
        _root[nm].c.setTransform(_root[nm].tr);

        nm = "poly" add ((tl * 4) + 2);
        _root[nm].tr.ga += capturerate;
        _root[nm].tr.aa -= capturerate;
        _root[nm].c.setTransform(_root[nm].tr);

        nm = "poly" add ((tl * 4) + 3);
        _root[nm].tr.ga += capturerate;
        _root[nm].tr.aa -= capturerate;

_root[nm].c.setTransform(_root[nm].tr);
```

*continues overleaf*

# Case Study 2

# Flash Games Studio

```
                    // if the poly's alpha is 0 or less
                    // then we've captured the building!
                    if (_root[nm].tr.aa <= 0)
                    {
                      nm = "poly" add (tl * 4);
                      _root[nm].alive = false;
                      nm = "poly" add ((tl * 4) + 1);
                      _root[nm].alive = false;
                      nm = "poly" add ((tl * 4) + 2);
                      _root[nm].alive = false;
                      nm = "poly" add ((tl * 4) + 3);
                      _root[nm].alive = false;
                      _root.gui.captures++;
                      if (_root.gui.captures == _root.buildings)
          _root.loader.loadVariables ("level.txt");

                    }

                    // hittingsomething flag is true, so
                    // the laser will make itself visible
                    _root.hittingsomething = true;
                  }
                }
              }
            }
```

This controls what happens when the player shoots at a building. The first thing we do is check to make sure that the player is indeed shooting, via the variable `_root.controller.shooting`. If so, then we begin a loop:

```
            for (i = 0; i < _root.polynum; i++)
```

This loop will go through every single polygon in the game. It's important to note that each building in a level is made up of four polygons – one for each side of the building. So, a map with 4 buildings has 16 polygons, and so on. Next, we store the name of the polygon that we're checking in a string called `nam`:

```
            nam = "poly" add i;
```

And then we use Flash's `hitTest` on the polygon movie clip to see if we're hitting it with the mouse cursor:

```
            // Use the hittest to see if we're hitting the polygon,
            // and make sure it's alive already.
            if (_root[nam].hitTest(_root._xmouse, _root._ymouse, true) &&
         ➥ _root[nam].alive == true)
```

We're also checking to see whether the polygon is 'alive' – quite literally whether its `alive` variable is set to `true`. This is important because once a building has been captured, the `alive`

# Mech Attack

## Case Study 2

flag of each of its polygons is set to `false`. If we're shooting the polygon, then the next thing we do is figure out which building we're looking at:

```
// divide the polygon by 4, giving us the building
tl = (i >> 2);
```

Since the polygons are created in order of building, four polygons per building, we can easily figure out which building we're looking at by dividing the polygon number by 4. In this case, I use a bitshift right by 2 to get the desired result. So, if we're looking at polygon 3, then we know it's building 0 (3 >> 2 is 0). However, if we're looking at polygon 4 then we know it's building 1, and so on. Next we compute `capturerate`:

```
// Capturerate is based on the player's height
capturerate = -(_root.controller.yloc / 800) + 1;
```

`capturerate` is used to determine just how quickly a building will fade out, and be captured. The decisive parameter is the player's `yloc` – how high they are in the air. The higher they are, the quicker a polygon will be captured. Next, we step through each polygon in the same building as `tl`, and decrease the `aa` of its `tr` color transform object, and increase the `ga`, like this:

```
nm = "poly" add (tl * 4);
_root[nm].tr.ga += capturerate;
_root[nm].tr.aa -= capturerate;
_root[nm].c.setTransform(_root[nm].tr);

nm = "poly" add ((tl * 4) + 1);
_root[nm].tr.ga += capturerate;
_root[nm].tr.aa -= capturerate;
_root[nm].c.setTransform(_root[nm].tr);

nm = "poly" add ((tl * 4) + 2);
_root[nm].tr.ga += capturerate;
_root[nm].tr.aa -= capturerate;
_root[nm].c.setTransform(_root[nm].tr);

nm = "poly" add ((tl * 4) + 3);
_root[nm].tr.ga += capturerate;
_root[nm].tr.aa -= capturerate;
_root[nm].c.setTransform(_root[nm].tr);
```

We're doing this four times (once per side). If `tl` was 0, then we would look at `poly0`, `poly1`, `poly2`, and `poly3`. Within each polygon, we're modifying its `tr` object. `tr` is simply a color transform object and then we apply its transform to `c`, which is the unique color object attached to each polygon.

## Case Study 2: Flash Games Studio

This will have the effect of making any polygons you're hitting turn green and fade away. Next, we check to see whether the polygon has faded away yet (whether its aa has reached 0):

```
if (_root[nm].tr.aa <= 0)
```

If it has, we set the alive status of each polygon to false, and then reward the player with a capture:

```
nm = "poly" add (tl * 4);
_root[nm].alive = false;
nm = "poly" add ((tl * 4) + 1);
_root[nm].alive = false;
nm = "poly" add ((tl * 4) + 2);
_root[nm].alive = false;
nm = "poly" add ((tl * 4) + 3);
_root[nm].alive = false;

_root.gui.captures++;
```

Next, we check to see if that capture was the last building left to be captured, and if so, then we load the next level with:

```
if (_root.gui.captures == _root.buildings)
    _root.loader.loadVariables ("level.txt");
```

_root.loader.bldg contains the number of buildings that were created when the level was loaded in. We load the next level into the loader movie clip, which handles the incoming level data, as we'll see shortly.

Finally, we set the hittingsomething flag to true, so that the laser movie clip will know to make itself visible:

```
// hittingsomething flag is true, so the
// laser will make itself visible
_root.hittingsomething = true;
```

### The Loader

The loader is one of two movie clips on the stage that isn't used for its visual appearance but rather for the ActionScript that is contained within it. The loader responds to the arrival of data via the onClipEvent(data) handler. It's called loader and has an instance name of loader, and it sits on the main timeline in the upper left hand corner, near the controller movie clip:

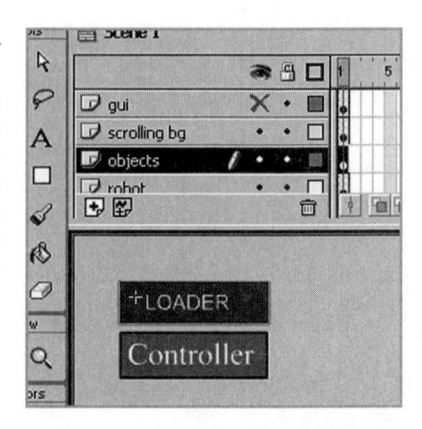

# Mech Attack
## Case Study 2

A `loadVariables` action sends data to the `loader` movie clip with this command:

```
_root.loader.loadVariables ("level.txt");
```

This would load the file `level.txt` into loader. `level.txt` should be the file containing the variables created with the level editor as outlined at the beginning of this chapter.

The following code is attached within the `loader` movie clip:

```
onClipEvent (data)
{
  // Go through the grid data in q_j_i and store it in
  // a 2-dimensional array called gamegrid
  for (i = 0; i < 12; i++)
  {
    for (j = 0; j < 12; j++)
    {
      _root.controller.gamegrid[i][j] =
      ↳ Number(eval("q_" add j add "_" add i));
    }
  }
}
```

This parses through the variables that were pulled in from the `level.txt` file, which are stored as q_0_0, q_0_1, q_0_2, all the way to q_11_11. We take each imported q value and store it in the appropriate location in the two-dimensional `_root.controller.gamegrid` array. At this point, the grid will be filled with either 1, or 0. 1 will be a building, 0 will be no building.

Beneath this, add the following code:

```
// Temporary variables
p = 0;
bldg = 1;

// Globals used in many places
_root.polynum = 0;
_root.objnum = 0;

// Starting position and velocity of the player
_root.controller.xloc = 500;
_root.controller.yloc = 0;
_root.controller.zloc = 500;
_root.controller.ang = 100;
_root.controller.dvel = 0;
_root.controller.dy = 0;

// Starting fuel, ammo and life
_root.controller.fuel = 80;
_root.controller.ammo = 80;
_root.controller.life = 80;
```

# Case Study 2: Flash Games Studio

All we're doing here is some initialization; we're setting two counters `polynum` and `objnum` to 0. We're also setting the player's starting position to (500,0,500) and giving them a rotation of 100. This rotation is based on a full circle going from 0 to 1000. We're not using degrees, we're using a slightly more accurate method, which we'll cover in the controller section.

We're also setting `dvel` to 0, which is the player's forward speed. The player's `dy` is also being set to 0, which is their vertical speed – along the y-axis. This speed is used to determine how fast they're rising or falling. Then we're setting the fuel, ammo and life to full, 80. Below this, add this ActionScript:

```
// Create powerups, create them dead - inactive
for (i = 0; i < _root.controller.numpowerups; i++)
{
    _root.controller.setupObj (0, 0, 0, 100, "_root.powerup", 0, 0);
    _root["obj" + i].dead = true;
}
```

Here we're pre-creating a certain number of powerup movie clips by calling the `setupObj` function, which I will outline shortly. We're telling them to start at position (0,0,0) with an `alpha` value of 100 (solid). We're also specifying the name of the source movie clip from which to take our image – in this case `_root.powerup`. Finally we're saying that we want `dx` and `dz` to both be 0. We're also setting the power-up's `dead` state to `true`, so it will start out inactive and invisible. Below this, add the following code:

```
for (i = 0; i < 12; i++)
{
  for (j = 0; j < 12; j++)
  {
    // Does this piece of grid contain something?
    if (_root.controller.gamegrid[i][j] == 1)
    {
      // Set up 4 corner points
      _root.controller.pointx[p] = i *
      ↪_root.controller.gridxsize;
      _root.controller.pointz[p] = j *
      ↪_root.controller.gridzsize;

      _root.controller.pointx[p + 1] = i *
      ↪_root.controller.gridxsize +
      ↪_root.controller.gridxsize;
      _root.controller.pointz[p + 1] = j *
      ↪_root.controller.gridzsize;

      _root.controller.pointx[p + 2] = i *
      ↪_root.controller.gridxsize +
      ↪_root.controller.gridxsize;
      _root.controller.pointz[p + 2] = j *
      ↪_root.controller.gridzsize +
      ↪_root.controller.gridzsize;
```

## Mech Attack — Case Study 2

```
                    _root.controller.pointx[p + 3] = i *
                    ➥ _root.controller.gridxsize;
                    _root.controller.pointz[p + 3] = j *
                    ➥ _root.controller.gridzsize +
                    ➥ _root.controller.gridzsize;

                    // Create 4 polygons to connect those points
                    _root.controller.setupPoly (p, p + 1, 30, 30,
                    ➥ 102, 100, true);
                    _root.controller.setupPoly (p + 1, p + 2, 30,
                    ➥ 30, 30, 100, true);
                    _root.controller.setupPoly (p + 2, p + 3, 30,
                    ➥ 30, 102, 100, true);
                    _root.controller.setupPoly (p + 3, p, 30, 30,
                    ➥ 30, 100, true);

                    // Create a streetlamp next to each building,
                    // near point 1 of the building.
                    _root.controller.setupObj (i *
                    ➥ _root.controller.gridxsize - 90, 320, j *
                    ➥ _root.controller.gridzsize - off, 100,
                    ➥ "_root.streetlamp", 0, 0);

                    // Change the gamegrid for this building from
                    // 1, to the actual building this is
                    // (1, 2, 3, 4, etc..)
                    _root.controller.gamegrid[i][j] = bldg ++;

                    // Increase point counter by 4
                    p += 4;
                }
            }
        }
```

In this code we're parsing through the gamegrid that was just loaded in, and allocating polygon objects based on the value at that location of the gamegrid, 1 or 0. If a 1 is there in the grid, then we must create a building.

Based on our polygon renderer, we create our four points in order around the building so that the rendering engine will properly be able to handle the backface culling as we discussed earlier. We have two variables called gridxsize and gridzsize. These are used to determine the width and depth of our buildings since each square in the actual grid data is only 1x1 and that would mean very thin buildings.

# Case Study 2: Flash Games Studio

The four points are as follows:

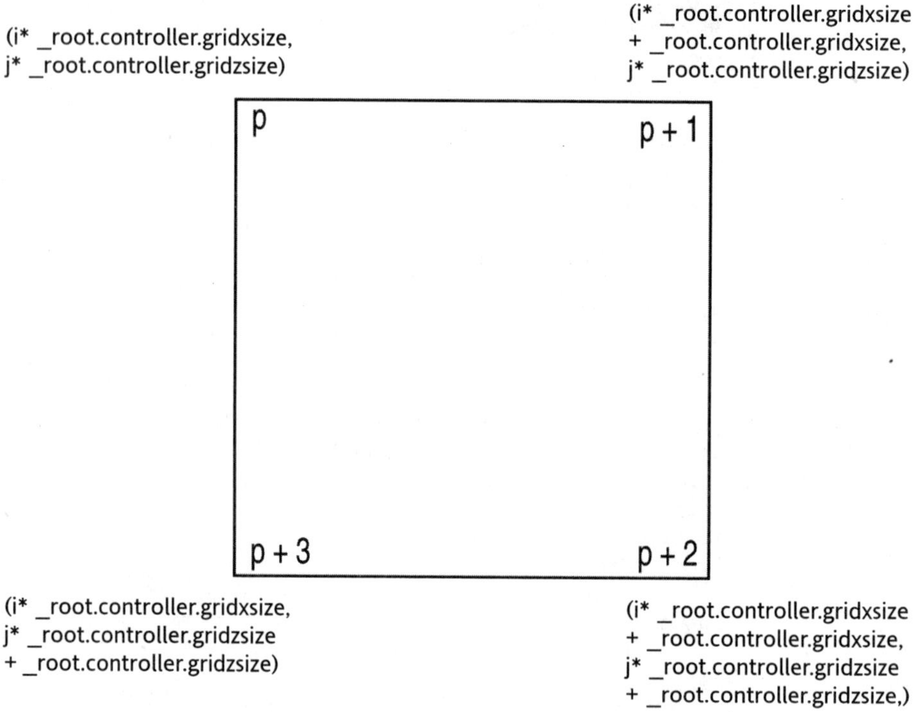

(i* _root.controller.gridxsize,
j* _root.controller.gridzsize)

(i* _root.controller.gridxsize
+ _root.controller.gridxsize,
j* _root.controller.gridzsize)

```
p                p + 1




p + 3            p + 2
```

(i* _root.controller.gridxsize,
j* _root.controller.gridzsize
+ _root.controller.gridzsize)

(i* _root.controller.gridxsize
+ _root.controller.gridxsize,
j* _root.controller.gridzsize
+ _root.controller.gridzsize,)

The points are stored in the point arrays called `pointx` and `pointz`, which are both inside the controller movie clip. Next we create our four polygon objects using the custom `setupPoly` function. This function has seven parameters: two points (which are merely indexes into the point arrays), R, G, B, A color values for the polygon's initial color, and finally a `true` or `false` which is used to state whether or not that polygon will be subject to backface culling or not. We're doing things so that the polygons facing forward and backward are colored with RGB of 30, 30 and 102, and the polygons facing sideways are colored with RGB of 30, 30, and 30. This will give the buildings some definition, because polygons next to each other will have two different shades of blue.

Next, we create a streetlamp object near the same location where point 1 was created. Then we change the value of the `gamegrid` at that location from 1 to whatever this building's number is. So, the first building we create stays as 1, but the next building will have the `gamegrid` changed to 2, the next will be 3, and so on.

Finally, we increase the point counter by 4. The next building we create should start at the next position in the point arrays, after p+3. Below this, add the final code of the loader movie clip:

```
// change bldg to reflect number of building in level
_root.buildings = bldg - 1;

// Store total points in global variable
```

# Mech Attack  Case Study 2

```
            _root.points = p;

            // Create 5 helibomb objects
            _root.controller.setupObj (0, -800, 1600, 100, "_root.heli",
            ↪ 0, 0);
            _root.controller.setupObj (440, -100, 1600, 100,
            ↪ "_root.heli", 0, 0);
            _root.controller.setupObj (2510, -800, -1600, 100,
            ↪ "_root.heli", 0, 0);
            _root.controller.setupObj (220, -800, 600, 100, "_root.heli",
            ↪ 0, 0);
            _root.controller.setupObj (10, -500, 1600, 100, "_root.heli",
            ↪ 0, 0);
        }
```

First, we're setting the global variable `_root.buildings` to be `bldg-1`. We're subtracting 1 to accurately reflect the number of buildings in the level (`bldg` was initially set to 1, not 0). Then we're setting the global variable `_root.points` to p, which is the number of points in our map. Finally, we're creating five helibombs, at various different positions in the sky, with `alpha` levels of 100. We're also specifying that the source sprite movie clip is `_root.heli`.

That's the whole loader code. Now, on to the most important part – the heart of the game – the controller movie clip.

## The Controller

The controller movie clip has the instance name `controller`, and sits on the main timeline. It has a fair bit of code, so I'm going to break it down into two subsections, the `onClipEvent(load)` and the `onClipEvent(enterFrame)`.

### onClipEvent (load)

The controller is where we hold most of our important functions including `setupPoly`, `setupObj`, `renderpoly` and `spawnpowerup`. To start with, add the following code to it:

```
        onClipEvent (load)
        {
            // For game performance
            _quality = "LOW";

            // Hide the master polygon on the stage
            _root.polymast._visible = false;

            // Number of powerups that can be in the world at once
            numpowerups = 8;

            // d value for 3D rendering
            d = 500;
```

*continues overleaf*

# Case Study 2: Flash Games Studio

```
            // The size of the gamegrid world
            gridxsize = 500;
            gridzsize = 500;
            gridheight = 300;

            // Create the 2 dimensional game grid array
            gamegrid = new Array;
            gamegrid[0] = new Array;
            gamegrid[1] = new Array;
            gamegrid[2] = new Array;
            gamegrid[3] = new Array;
            gamegrid[4] = new Array;
            gamegrid[5] = new Array;
            gamegrid[6] = new Array;
            gamegrid[7] = new Array;
            gamegrid[8] = new Array;
            gamegrid[9] = new Array;
            gamegrid[10] = new Array;
            gamegrid[11] = new Array;

            // The array of points
            pointx = new Array;
            pointyt = new Array;
            pointyb = new Array;
            pointz = new Array;

            // The temporary arrays to store the transformed 3D points
            // and screen points
            tpointx = new Array;
            tpointyt = new Array;
            tpointyb = new Array;
            tpointz = new Array;
            tsx = new Array;
            tsyt = new Array;
            tsyb = new Array;
```

This is a lot of code, but it's very simple. First we're setting the game's quality to low – this is the only way that we can get adequate performance for all that we're asking Flash to do. Next we're hiding the master polygon, which is sitting on the stage and would obscure the game if we didn't hide it.

Then, all we're doing is declaring a whole bunch of variables and initializing a few arrays that are used at different locations throughout the game. We're creating a 12x12 two-dimensional gamegrid array, and then we're creating our point arrays, pointx, pointyt, pointyb, and pointz.

Rather than use point arrays that are based on point3D objects, we're using the quicker method of storing them directly as arrays, pointx, pointyt, pointyb, and pointz.

# Mech Attack

## Case Study 2

> *Referencing a value in an array is always faster for the computer than referencing a value that is part of an object, like* `point.x` *or* `point.y`.

After this, we're creating arrays that mirror the `point` arrays, but are preceded with the letter t (such as `tpointx`, and `tpointyt`). These are for temporary variable storage of their 3D transformed counterparts. We're also creating temporary variables for the storage of our polygons' screen coordinates in `tsx`, `tsyt`, and `tsyb`.

> *Remember that we're defining edges here, so every y coordinate must have a top and a bottom – pointyt and pointyb, tpointyt and tpointyb, tsyt and tysb.*

Now we must define the routines. First, we'll add `setupPoly`. Add the following code:

```
function setupPoly (p1, p2, r, g, b, a, c)
{
        // Creates a 3D polygon, consisting of 2 points,
        // color and culling flag

        // Creates the poly movie clip that will be used on screen
        nm = "poly" add _root.polynum;
        removeMovieClip(_root[nm]);
        duplicateMovieClip(_root.polymast, nm, 10 +
        ➥ _root.polynum);

        // Create a color object that is attached to the polygon
        // to create color effects.
        _root[nm].c = new Color(_root[nm]);
        _root[nm].tr = new Object;
        _root[nm].tr.ra = r;
        _root[nm].tr.ga = g;
        _root[nm].tr.ba = b;
        _root[nm].tr.aa = a;
        _root[nm].c.setTransform(_root[nm].tr);

        // Assign the points that the polygon up,
        _root[nm].point1 = p1;
        _root[nm].point2 = p2;
        // True or False - backface culling
        _root[nm].cull = c;
```

*continues overleaf*

# Case Study 2: Flash Games Studio

```
            // Remember who I am, and set my alive (active) state
            _root[nm].whoiam = _root.polynum;
            _root[nm].alive = true;

            _root.polynum++;
    }
```

This is the function that is called by the loader to create our polygons. When this function is called, it first creates a name for itself based on the current number of polygons defined in memory. At the start there are 0 polygons defined, so the name will be poly0. What we do now, is make a duplicate of polymast (the master polygon) and call it poly0, poly1, poly2, and so on.

Next, we're creating a color object and a transform object local to the movie clip. We're setting it to the RGB and Alpha values that were passed into the function, and then using setTransform to modify the color.

The original master polygon on the stage is a medium gray, so any color we add in the transform will be directly inherited by the polygon, without adding any of its own color, just shading.

Finally we're making the newly created polygon remember its point indices and whether or not it's being checked for backface culling. It's storing the points in point1 and point2 and the culling flag in cull. Then, we assign the polygon number to whoiam, and set the alive state of the polygon to true – it will be visible to start.

Lastly, we're incrementing the polynum counter so that the next polygon we create will be the next in sequence.

No time to rest now! We're going to add the setupObj routine, as follows:

```
    function setupObj (x1, y1, z1, a, type, dx, dz)
    {
            // creates an 3D object (sprite) instance based on
            // parameters passed

            // Determine the name of the new object, and use
            // 'type' to specify the name of the source object
            // movie clip
            nm = "obj" add _root.objnum;
            removeMovieClip(_root[nm]);
            duplicateMovieClip(eval(type), nm, 100 +
            ↪ _root.objnum);

            // Sets the object's alpha level (if we want it)
            _root[nm]._alpha = a;

            // Object's speed along x and z
            _root[nm].dx = dx;
            _root[nm].dz = dz;
```

```
            // Set object to 'not dead/inactive'
            _root[nm].dead = false;

            // Set object's position in 3D space
            _root[nm].x1 = x1;
            _root[nm].y1 = y1;
            _root[nm].z1 = z1;

            _root.objnum++;
    }
```

This sets up sprite objects and is quite similar to the `setupPoly` routine except it's creating a generic movie clip instance called `objn`, instead of `polyn` where `n` will be a sequence starting at 0 going up to as high as we want.

There are a few unique differences however. First of all, in `setupPoly`, we duplicated `polymast` to create our polygons. In this routine however, the source movie clip is passed into the function in the variable `type`. Therefore, we can make *any* movie clip act as the source image for an object – it's endlessly versatile.

We're not creating color objects for the sprite objects but we are passing in `a`, which is set as the `alpha` value of the sprite should we want it to be semi-transparent. Also, we're passing `dx` and `dz` – the sprite's speed along the x and z axes. We have a `dead` flag, which is set to `false` so that the sprite starts out in an active state.

Finally, rather than passing a reference to a point in the point arrays, we're simply passing in the x, y, and z location of the sprite object directly. Since it won't be sharing its point with any other object, there's nothing to be gained by grouping it with a point array and computing it first (as we'll soon see).

Finally, we're incrementing the `objnum`, so that the next object we create will be the next in the sequence.

Now, the next function defined in the controller `load clipEvent`, is the `renderpolygon` routine. However, I've already shown you the whole `renderpolygon` routine once, in the last chapter, so we don't need to look at it again here.

# Case Study 2: Flash Games Studio

The final function is the `spawnpowerup` function.

```
function spawnpowerup (x, y, z, dx, dy, dz, frm)
{
    // Creates a new powerup object.

    // Search through all the powerups (which are from
    // 0 to numpowerups)
    for (i = 0; i < numpowerups; i++)
    {
        nm = "obj" add i;

        // is the powerup inactive? If so, activate it
        if (_root[nm].dead)
        {
            // position
            _root[nm].x1 = x;
            _root[nm].y1 = y;
            _root[nm].z1 = z;

            // speed
            _root[nm].dx = dx;
            _root[nm].dy = dy;
            _root[nm].dz = dz;

            // Type
            _root[nm].gotoAndStop(frm);
            // make it alive
            _root[nm].dead = false;

            // break out of the loop
            break;
        }
    }
}
```

This function is called every time you kill a helibomb. It loops through the power-up objects that were created when the level was loaded, and checks whether any of them are inactive (dead). It will find the first inactive power-up, and then set its x, y, z coordinates and dx, dy, dz velocities according to what was passed to the function. Finally it sets the currentframe of the reanimated power-up to frm, which was passed in to the function. The dead state is then set to false (the sprite comes to life) and then we break out of the loop because we've created our power-up. The break command simply jumps to the first statement after the end of the loop.

# Mech Attack

**Case Study 2**

Those are our functions. The remainder of the `load clipEvent` is fairly straightforward:

```
// Compute SIN and COS tables
mycos = new Array;
mysin = new Array;
for (i = 0; i < 1000; i++)
{
        mycos[i] = Math.cos (i * (Math.PI / 500));
        mysin[i] = Math.sin (i * (Math.PI / 500));
}

// Load the level
_root.loader.loadVariables ("level.txt");

}
```

We're creating two arrays, `mysin` and `mycos`, which will contain pre-computed sin and cos values. We're calculating the sin/cos at 1000 points around the full 360 degrees of the circle. The code:

```
(i * (Math.PI / 500))
```

simply converts our number to a radian.

Lastly, we load up the level, and that's it. If the level loads correctly, the game will begin. That's the whole controller `load ClipEvent`. Next, we'll take a look at the `enterFrame ClipEvent`.

### onClipEvent (enterFrame)

Every time our game enters a new frame, the `enterFrame ClipEvent` of the controller movie clip will be triggered. This code is responsible for rendering the polygons, rendering the objects, handling the player control, displaying the player animation and handling the player's collision.

Let's begin at the top. Add the following code to the controller:

```
onClipEvent(enterFrame)
{

      // Make sure the angle is between 0 and 999
      // to get a valid index of the mysin and mycos array
      if ((ang %= 1000) < 0) ang += 1000;

      // store the cos and sin of the angle
      cosang = mycos[ang];
      sinang = mysin[ang];
```

First we make sure that no matter what angle the player was facing before, we bring it to the equivalent angle between 0 and 1000. Because the 1000 angles represent a full circle we can carry on looping round, so angle 1300 is the same as angle 300, and so on.

# Case Study 2: Flash Games Studio

```
                if ((ang %= 1000) < 0) ang += 1000;
```

This line of code places the angle between 0 and 1000, by first placing `ang` between -1000 and 1000 with the `ang %= 1000` code, and then if `ang` is less than 0, adding 1000 to it so it sits nicely between 0 and 1000.

Once we have this, then we want to store the cos and sin of the player's angle in `cosang` and `sinang` for use in the following code, which we will place next:

```
        // Transform each point into 3D space
        for (i = 0; i < _root.points; i++)
        {
                // translate x by players location
                wx1 = (pointx[i] - xloc);

                // Set the tops and the bottoms of the buildings
                // top is -1200, bottom is 300
                wy1t = -1200 - yloc;
                wy1b = 300 - yloc;

                // translate the z by players location
                wz1 = (pointz[i] - zloc);

                // Rotate point based on players rotation
                wx1f = cosang * wx1 - sinang * wz1;
                wz1f = sinang * wx1 + cosang * wz1;

                // Move out 1000 so camera is behind player
                wz1f += 1000;

                // Project onto screen space - Perspective
                // and store in temporary array
                tsx[i] = (d * wx1f / wz1f) + 275;
                tsyt[i] = (d * wy1t / wz1f) + 200;
                tsyb[i] = (d * wy1b / wz1f) + 200;
                tpointz[i] = wz1f;
        }
```

This is all the math required to calculate the 2D screen coordinates of our 3D polygons. What we're doing here is looping through each point in the point arrays and then translating it based on the player's position. You can also see that we're setting the `wy1t` and `wy1b` (y top and bottom) to be −1200 and 300 respectively. This is how we set the height of our buildings.

Once all the points have been translated in `wx1`, `wy1t`, `wy1b`, and `wz1`, then we want to rotate x and z around the player's rotation (we don't need to worry about rotating the y coordinates, because our player's yaw rotation doesn't affect them – we're not pitching up and down, or rolling left and right).

# Mech Attack

## Case Study 2

Now we have our final coordinates in `wx1f`, `wy1t`, `wy1b`, and `wz1f` – but we must make one more change – we must add 1000 to `wz1f`, to push our view point 1000 units behind the player – this game is a third-person perspective after all, so we must see the player in the scene.

Lastly, we convert the world coordinates of each point into screen coordinates by performing a perspective projection, and then moving the world to the center of the screen with +275 on x and +200 on y. Now, we have each edge defined – in `tsx`, `tsyt`, and `tsyb`. We must also store the z value of each point for depth sorting later, so we store it in `tpointz`.

Once our points have been manipulated, we can then draw the polygons, with the following code:

```
// Render polygons
for (i = 0; i < _root.polynum; i++)
{
  nm = "poly" add i;

  // Make sure the polygon is not behind us, and
  // that it is still 'alive' / active
  if (tpointz[_root[nm].point1] > 500 &&
➥ tpointz[_root[nm].point2] > 500 && _root[nm].alive)
  {
    // Grab the point information from the pre
    // calculated temporary arrays
    wz1f = tpointz[_root[nm].point1];
    wz2f = tpointz[_root[nm].point2];

    sx1 = tsx[_root[nm].point1];
    sy1t = tsyt[_root[nm].point1];
    sy1b = tsyb[_root[nm].point1];

    sx2 = tsx[_root[nm].point2];
    sy2t = tsyt[_root[nm].point2];
    sy2b = tsyb[_root[nm].point2];

    offscreen = false;

    // Hidden surface removal
    // Backface Culling - if the drawing order is
    // from right to left (left edge is to the right
    // of the right edge) then we are looking at
    // the back of the polygon, and we may not
    // want to draw it.
    if (sx1 > sx2)
    {
      if (_root[nm].cull)
      {
        // cull is true, don't draw
        offscreen = true;
      }
```

*continues overleaf*

## Case Study 2: Flash Games Studio

```
            else
            {
              // otherwise, flip the edges and draw
              // the  polygon as if it were two sided
              tsx1 = sx1;
              tsy1t = sy1t;
              tsy1b = sy1b;

              sx1 = sx2;
              sy1t = sy2t;
              sy1b = sy2b;

              sx2 = tsx1;
              sy2t = tsy1t;
              sy2b = tsy1b;
            }
         }
         avez = (wz1f + wz2f) >> 1; // Calculate the depth

         // Is it completely off right hand side of screen?
         if (sx1 > 550 && sx2 > 550)
         {
            offscreen = true;
         }
         // is it completely off the left hand side of the screen?
         if (sx1 < 0 && sx2 < 0)
         {
            offscreen = true;
         }
         // If offscreen has been set to true, then don't draw
         if (offscreen)
         {
            _root[nm]._visible = false;
         }
         else
         {
            // Draw, and call renderpoly with our 6 screen
            // coordinates
            _root[nm]._visible = true;
            renderpoly(sx1, sy1t, sy1b, sx2, sy2t, sy2b, avez, nm);
         }
      }
   else
      _root[nm]._visible = false; // invisible or dead
}
```

# Mech Attack

**Case Study 2**

This is quite similar to the polygon rendering methodology from demoCs2-1, but with a few differences. First of all, we're looping through each polygon and determining first whether it's in front of us (is the tpointz of both edges greater than 500) and then is the polygon alive? We're using 500 because 0 is too close to the camera and tends to make the game difficult to play if the player turns around while near a building. By using 500, the player can safely turn around and buildings behind him will disappear and not get in the way of the camera (between our view, and the robot).

Once we've determined that the polygon could be on screen, we look up the values of its two edges by looking at the temporary coordinates for the polygon's point1 and point2 – the points that we just finished calculating. The two z coordinates for checking depth level (tpointz) are placed in wz1f, wz2f, and the screen coordinates for the two edges are placed in sx1, sy1t, sy1b, and sx2, sy2t, sy2b.

Next we perform the backface culling if the polygon's cull flag is set to true. Otherwise, we simply flip the polygon so back becomes front. In this game, we don't actually ever draw the backfaces, but it's in there for expandability.

After this, we compute the average z value for the polygon, avez. This is done simply by adding together the z value of each edge and then dividing the whole thing by 2 (bitshifting right by 1). You can see in the following image that by computing the average z of each polygon we can figure out which polygons are in front of other polygons, and we can draw our scene correctly:

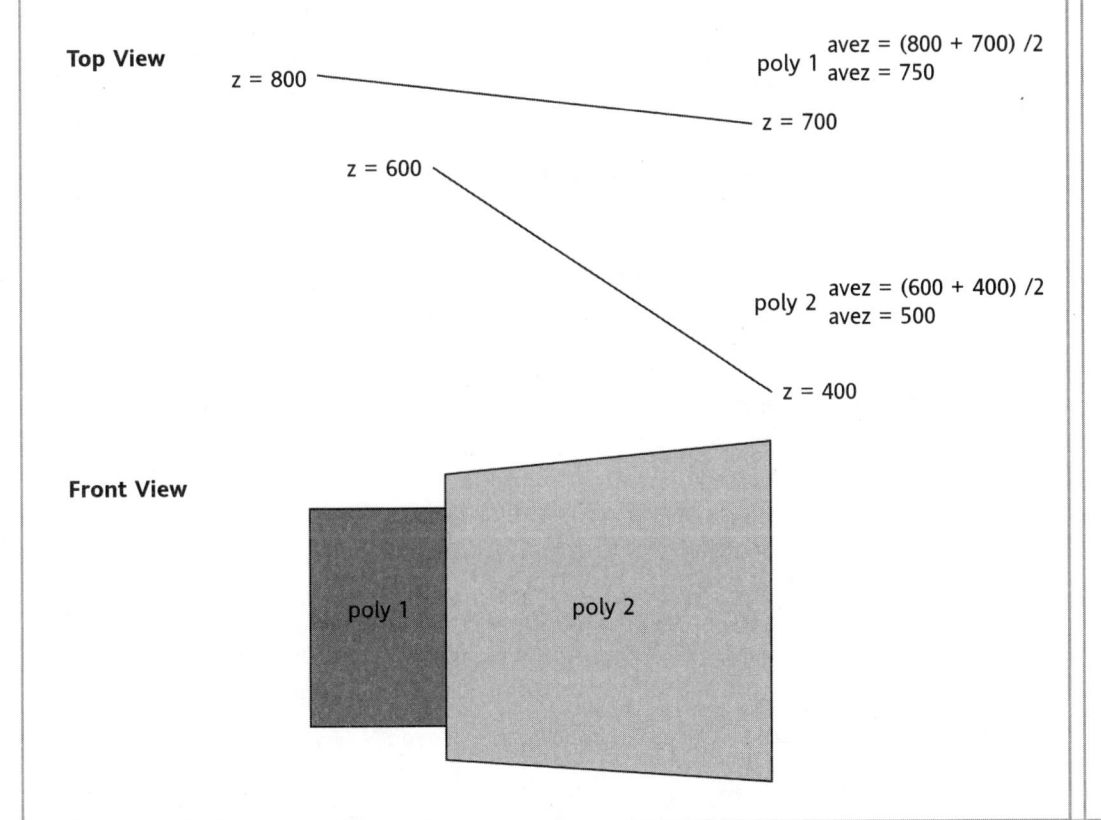

**Top View**

z = 800

z = 700

poly 1  avez = (800 + 700) /2
        avez = 750

z = 600

z = 400

poly 2  avez = (600 + 400) /2
        avez = 500

**Front View**

poly 1

poly 2

# Case Study 2: Flash Games Studio

Because poly1 has an avez of 750 and poly2 has an avez of 500, we know that poly1 is behind poly2. In the renderpolygon function, the depth of the polygon is set via the swapDepths command to 10000-avez, so the closer a polygon is to us, the higher its depth is set. That is correct for the way Flash orders things – higher depth levels are drawn in front.

Next, we perform two more checks to see if both edges are either off screen to the left (sx1 and sx2 is less than 0), or off screen to the right (sx1 and sx2 are greater than 550). If this is the case, then we set the flag offscreen to be true.

If the polygon has been deemed to be invisible (offscreen = true) we set its visible property to false, and then we're done with that polygon, otherwise we send our screen coordinates, average z value, and polygon name to renderpolygon, and it will be drawn on the screen.

If the polygon wasn't alive in the first place however, we set its visible property to false, and that's all we do with it.

Below this we have the following code:

```
// Render sprite objects
for (i = 0; i < _root.objnum; i++)
{
  nm = "obj" add i;

  // is object inactive?
  if (!_root[nm].dead)
  {

    // Move object relative to Point of view
    wx1 = _root[nm].x1 - xloc;
    wy1 = _root[nm].y1 - yloc;
    wz1 = _root[nm].z1 - zloc;

    // Perform the all important rotation around
    // the y-axis
    wx1f = cosang * wx1 - sinang * wz1;
    wz1f = sinang * wx1 + cosang * wz1;

    // move out by 1000 to move into camera space
    wz1f += 1000;

    // Project onto screen space - Perspective
    sx1 = (d * wx1f / wz1f) + 275;
    sy1 = (d * wy1 / wz1f) + 200;

    avez = wz1f; // Calculate the depth

    // set the depth level
    _root[nm].swapDepths(Math.round(10000 - avez));
```

# Mech Attack

## Case Study 2

```
            offscreen = false;

            // Is object off right hand side?
            if (sx1 > 550)
            {
              offscreen = true;
            }
            // is object off left hand side?
            if (sx1 < 0)
            {
              offscreen = true;
            }
            // Is object behind camera?
            if (wz1f < 400)
            {
              offscreen = true;
            }

            if (offscreen)
            {
              // object is offscreen - don't draw it
              _root[nm]._visible = false;
            }
            else
            {
              // object is on screen
              _root[nm]._visible = true;
              _root[nm]._x = sx1;
              _root[nm]._y = sy1;

              // Set the size of the sprite based on
              // z value
              _root[nm]._xscale = (d * 100) / wz1f;
              _root[nm]._yscale = (d * 100) / wz1f;
            }
         }
      }
```

What we're doing here is going through each sprite object and moving it into the 3D world via translations, rotation and then adding 1000 to z1 to place it in our camera space. Next we compute the screen coordinates via a perspective projection and set their depth level with `swapDepths`. The math is the same as the polygon points.

Next, we're checking to see whether the sprite is off screen to the right or left (x1 > 550 or x1 < 0) or if it's `wz1f` (transformed z1) is less than 500 (off screen behind the player). If it's off screen, we don't draw it; rather we simply set its `visible` to `false`. If it's on screen however, we set the sprite object's `visible` property to `true`, and set its `x` property to `sx1`, and `y` to `sy1`.

Finally, we perform sprite scaling based on its z value. We adjust `xscale` and `yscale` to be relative to d*100/z. This is the same sprite scaling technique discussed in the *Real 3D* chapter.

## Case Study 2: Flash Games Studio

That's it for the 3D math. With that code, our scene will fill up with polygons and sprites. Now we need to allow the player to move. Add the following code after the object-rendering loop:

```
// kd = Down key, 's'
kd = Key.isDown(83);

// ku = Up key, 'w'
ku = Key.isDown(87);

// kl = Left key, 'a'
kl = Key.isDown(65);

// kr = Right key, 'd'
kr = Key.isDown(68);

// Space bar being pressed
ks = Key.isDown(Key.SPACE);

// Put the robot at depth 9210 - behind objects that
// are between the robot and the camera
_root.robot.swapDepths(9210);

// Turning left or right? Increase the turn speed
if (kl) dang -= 4;
if (kr) dang += 4;
// Otherwise, slow down the turn
if (!kl && !kr) dang *= .7;

// Moving forward or backward? Increase the accelleration
if (ku) dvel += 3;
if (kd) dvel -= 3;
// Otherwise, grind to a halt
if (!ku && !kd) dvel *= .7;

// Put a limit on turning speed
if (dang < -8) dang = -8;
if (dang > 8) dang = 8;

// Put a limit on forward/backward speed
if (dvel < -34) dvel = -34;
if (dvel > 34) dvel = 34;
```

What we're doing here is checking for user interaction by reacting to the states of the game keys, w, s, a, and d. We're storing the values of the key-states in `ku`, `kd`, `kl`, and `kr`, as well as storing the state of the spacebar in `ks`.

We're also setting the depth level of the robot to 9210 with `_root.robot.swapDepths(9210)`. This simply places the robot correctly in correlation to the rest of the 3D world, on top of the laser beam, on top of the crosshair, but not on top of any object that happens to fly between the camera and the player (like a helibomb).

# Mech Attack

## Case Study 2

If the player is pressing 'a' left or 'd' right (kl or kr is true), then we increase or decrease dang – the rate of change of angle. We're using an accelerated turning method, rather than acting on ang directly, we act on dang, which in turn is added to ang to create a smooth turn. If the player isn't pressing a turn key, then we slow dang down by 70% each frame, until it will eventually be pretty much stopped. We do the same with dvel (change in forward velocity), which is how fast the player is running forward or backward each frame.

We then impose a few limitations on dang and dvel, making sure that the player isn't able to turn too fast, or run forward/backward too quickly. The maximum turning speed is 8 (right)/-8 (left) and the maximum running speed it 34 (forward) or -34 (backward).

Next, we handle the player's use of the rocket pack with:

```
// Pressing spacebar, and still have fuel and life left?
if (ks && fuel > 0 && life > 0)
{
    // Move player up, and diminish fuel
    if (dy > -20)
        dy -= 8;
    fuel--;
}
// Above ground, and below ceiling?
if (yloc < 0 && yloc >= -1200)
{
    // Constant downward accelleration = gravity
    dy += 2;
}
else if (yloc > 0)
{
    // yloc below 0?  Player hit the ground!!
    // if fall was faster than 40, then that did
    // some damage!  Life is decreased by speed of fall
    if (dy > 40)
        life -= dy;

    // Move player back to 0, and stop the descent
    yloc = 0;
    dy = 0;
}
else if (yloc < -1200)
{
    // Player has hit the 'ceiling' (top of building
    // height)
    // So stop climbing.
    yloc = -1200;
    dy = 0;
}
```

# Case Study 2

# Flash Games Studio

We check to see if the player is holding down the space bar, that they still have fuel left, and that they're not dead (`life > 0`). If so, then we increase `dy` in a negative direction (up, against gravity) to a maximum of -20, and then we decrease the player's fuel level. This will allow the player to fly upwards.

Following that, we check to make sure that the player is off the ground, and if they are, we add 2 to their `dy` (in a downward direction) to create the gravity necessary to bring them back down to the ground. Then we detect whether the player's `yloc` is greater than zero, it means they've hit the ground. If they hit it at a `dy` that is faster than 40, then they'll take some damage. Their life will be diminished by the value of `dy` (a fall from the very top of the sky, -1200, will cause a lot of damage to the player, probably killing them):

Ceiling   y = -1200

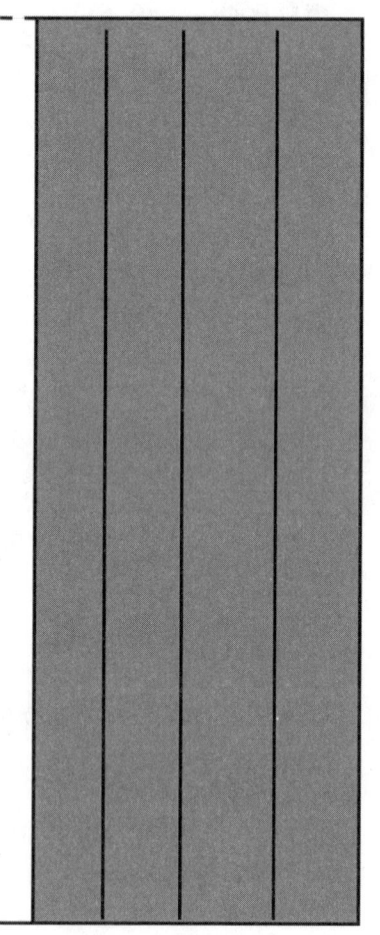

Building

Ground   y = 300

# Mech Attack

Finally, we make sure they haven't hit the 'ceiling' – if they have we move them back into the world space by setting their `yloc` to -1200, and then remove all their y velocity (`dy = 0`).

There's a good reason for imposing the ceiling limitation – the buildings have no roof polygons, so if the player flies above the tops of the buildings, they'll be able to see the backface culling in action. We can't create roof polygons because they can't follow the rule that polygons must have straight vertical left and right edges – a roof polygon would have to be arbitrarily shaped.

Okay, more code:

```
// Move the background cityscape
_root.cityscape._x = 1000 - (ang << 1);
```

We discussed this earlier – this moves the cityscape to the correct position relative to the player's rotation.

After this, we add:

```
// Spin around, increase angle by dang, but
// round it down so it can still be used as
// an index in mycos and mysin.
ang = Math.round(ang + dang);

// Figure out player's x and z speed (along the ground)
// based on forward speed and direction
dx = (dvel * sinang);
dz = (dvel * cosang);
```

This adds `dang` to the player's `ang`. It also rounds the result because `ang` can't be a fractional number – it's being used as an index into the `mycos` and `mysin` arrays. The `Math.round` function will round the number within the brackets to the nearest whole number, so 10.3 will become 10, but 10.8 will become 11, and so on.

Then we're calculating `dx` and `dz` based on the player's velocity and angle. This is the same technique that was used in the player arrow in the level editor.

Next, we have the logic to decide what state the player is in:

```
// Moving horizontally?
hmoving = false;
if (Math.abs(dvel) > 1 || Math.abs(dang) > 1)
hmoving = true;

// Rising?
vrising = false;
if (ks && fuel > 0)
vrising = true;

// Falling?
```

*continues overleaf*

# Case Study 2

# Flash Games Studio

```
        vfalling = false;
        if (ks && fuel <= 0 && yloc < 0)
        vfalling = true;
        if (!ks && yloc < 0)
        vfalling = true;

        // Dying?
        vdying = false;
        if (life <= 0)
        vdying = true;
```

We're deciding whether the player is moving horizontally (forward, backward, or turning) and if so, we set the variable hmoving to true.

Then we decide whether the player is currently rising up (jumping or flying) based on the ks (space bar) and the fuel level. If the player is pressing the space bar, and the fuel level is more than 0, then the player is moving up, and vrising is set to true.

Next, we decide whether the player is falling. If the player is hitting the space bar, but they have no fuel, and they are off the ground (yloc < 0), they are going to be falling. Alternatively, if the player isn't pressing the space bar, and they're off the ground, they'll also be falling (vfalling = true).

Finally, if they have no more life left, the player will be dying. (vdying = true).

We then take these values, and apply them to decide which animation to play:

```
        // Now we use these values and prioritize animations
        // Dying is most important.  Don't show any other
        // animation if player is in the middle of exploding
        if (!vdying)
        {
            // If player is rising, and on the ground,
            // and we're not currently watching a jump animation then
            // show the jump off
            if (vrising && yloc == 0 && (_root.robot._currentframe < 10
        || _root.robot._currentframe > 18))
                _root.robot.gotoAndPlay(10);

            // If player is rising and NOT on the ground, but we weren't
            // watching a rising animation (probably was falling)
            // then show a small burst of flame and rise up
            if (vrising && yloc < 0 && (_root.robot._currentframe < 10
        || _root.robot._currentframe > 18))
                _root.robot.gotoAndPlay(14);

            // Are we falling?
            if (vfalling && _root.robot._currentframe < 19)
                _root.robot.gotoAndStop(19);
```

# Mech Attack

## Case Study 2

```
        // Are we on the ground, not falling or rising, but not
currently
        // watching the run cycle?  Start playing the run cycle
        if (hmoving && !vrising && !vfalling &&
_root.robot._currentframe > 8)
                        _root.robot.gotoAndPlay(1);

        // Are we stationary, not rising and not falling? show the
        // stationary pose.
        if (!hmoving && !vrising && !vfalling)
                _root.robot.gotoAndPlay(9);
}
else if (_root.robot._currentframe < 20)
{
        // Otherwise, we're dying.
        _root.robot.gotoAndPlay(20);
}
```

What we're doing is looking at each type of movement, making sure that the player isn't already playing that animation, and if they aren't, sending the robot movie clip to the correct frame. This is a battle in logic, so read over the code carefully as the thought process is explained clearly in the code comments.

The next code we check is the collision with the game grid. We already have the gamegrid array, so we simply check the player's next position along the x- and z-axis to see if we're hitting anything:

```
        // Tile collision - X axis
        xtile = Math.floor((xloc + dx) / gridxsize);
        ztile = Math.floor(zloc / gridzsize);
        if (gamegrid[xtile][ztile] > 0)
        {
                tl = gamegrid[xtile][ztile] - 1;
                nm = "poly" add (tl * 4);
                // If that building has not been captured
                // then we can't walk through it.
                if (_root[nm].alive)
                        dx = 0;
        }

        // Tile collision - Z axis
        xtile = Math.floor(xloc / gridxsize);
        ztile = Math.floor((zloc + dz) / gridzsize);
        if (gamegrid[xtile][ztile] > 0)
        {
                tl = gamegrid[xtile][ztile] - 1;
                nm = "poly" add (tl * 4);
                // If that building has not been captured
                // then we can't walk through it.
                if (_root[nm].alive)
                        dz = 0;
        }
```

# Case Study 2: Flash Games Studio

This is almost like the collision from the level editor. We're taking the player's location, dividing it by the size of each grid square, flooring that and then we're left with actual `gamegrid` tile coordinates. We then take this and figure out the value of what's in that space. Remember that each `gamegrid` that isn't 0 now contains the number of the actual building that's there, so we take that number directly, look at one of its polygons and see if it's alive. If we've already captured the building, the polygon won't be alive, and we don't need to collide with it.

We do this along both the x and z axes, and when we're done, `dx` and `dz` will be adjusted to either be the same as they were before, or 0 if we can't move in a particular direction.

To round off the `enterFrame clipEvent`, add the following code:

```
// I can fall to the ground even if I'm dead
yloc += dy;

// If I'm not dying, then...
if (!vdying)
{
  // Move me
  xloc += dx;
  zloc += dz;

  // If I'm shooting, but I'm out of ammo then..
  if (shooting && ammo <= 0)
  {
    // Reset my ammo to 0, and stop my shooting
    ammo = 0;
    shooting = false;
  }

  // But, if I have ammo left, then draw the laser line
  if (shooting && ammo > 0)
    _root.laser.drawline (274, 203, _root._xmouse, _root._ymouse);
  }
}
```

First thing we do is add `dy` to the player's `yloc`. This is sitting outside of the `if (!vdying)` statement because we want the player to fall to the ground even if they died in the air. However, anything inside that `if` statement will only execute if the player is alive. What we're doing is moving the player along x and z by adding `dx` and `dz` to `xloc` and `zloc`. We're also making sure that the player can't shoot unless they have ammo. If they do have ammo and they're shooting (the mouse is held down), we tell the laser movie clip (the line object) to draw a line from (274,203) – the Robot's laser generator, to the mouse cursor location, using the `drawline` function.

That's it for the `enterFrame` event. We have two more short events to handle in the controller:

```
onClipEvent (mouseDown)
{
  // Mouse down, but Only start the shooting if I have ammo
  if (ammo > 0)
    shooting = true;
  else
    ammo = 0;
}

onClipEvent (mouseUp)
{
  // Mouse up, so stop shooting
  shooting = false;
}
```

This controls our firing of the laser. If the mouse button is pressed, and you have ammo, then we set the variable `shooting` to `true`. If you recall, `shooting` is used in several other locations throughout the game to determine whether certain checking should be performed.

When the mouse button is released, then `shooting` is set to `false`, and among other things, the laser will disappear.

Dare I say it? That's all! All this code will work together to produce a great, fun game.

# Finishing Up

Now, there are a few performance issues that must be acknowledged with this game. Because we're pressing the limits of Flash, we have to live within them, and they are:

- Too many objects will make the game slow down. The more sprite objects you have in the game at once, the slower it will run. That's why I've opted to have only eight powerups, four streetlamps and five helibombs.

- Too many polygons will make the game slow down. Though we've made our rendering engine highly efficient, we are still limited by Flash's vector capabilities, and therefore, the more buildings you have, the more polygons you have, the slower the game will perform.

I've managed to get the game running at a max of 17 frames per second as a standalone SWF file running in a window. It runs at about 10 frames per second when I test it in the Flash editing environment but that's because the screen size is much bigger. Which leads to the conclusion that one of the biggest hits on performance is the graphics. On average however, the game runs on my machine at about 14 or 15 frames per second.

# Case Study 2: Flash Games Studio

## Improvements

There are many ways this game can be improved, but remember that more improvements will equal a slow down in game performance (unless your improvements are made on the engine itself). Here are a few:

- **New enemies** – How about enemies that fire lasers back at you, or evade your fire with improved AI?

- **Difficulty increase** – Perhaps as you complete levels in the game, things can get more difficult. More helibombs, less powerups, more buildings, and so on.

- **More levels** – How about increasing the number of levels by designing a few more, or perhaps making the game randomly generate its own levels at the start of each game.

- **Sound and music** – Need I say more?

## Conclusion

Well, that brings us to the end of a very thorough and comprehensive set of chapters on 3D in Flash. I hope that I've shown you that 3D is more than just math – it's a whole type of game genre, and a complete way of designing and thinking.

With a fresh approach to 3D, and the goal of entertaining people, it's possible to create engaging 3D games in Flash that will hold the interest of your players for hours, where they'll lose themselves in a wholly immersing world of your creation. That's powerful stuff.

We'll finish up the book with two chapters essential to web-based gaming. The first is on using PHP to store high-scores and other attributes, and the second is on building real-time web-based multiplayer games. They're indispensable for online playability, they're fun, and they're a break from 3D. What more could you ask for?

# Mech Attack

Case Study 2

**Introduction**
chapter 1
chapter 2
chapter 3
chapter 4
chapter 5
chapter 6
Case Study 1
chapter 7
chapter 8
chapter 9
chapter 10
chapter 11
chapter 12
chapter 13
Case Study 2
chapter 14
chapter 15
**Director Afterword**

# Chapter 14
# Online Data

# 14 Flash Games Studio

This chapter will introduce the use of online data in Flash. We will achieve this by the creation of a game that includes a high score table and saves high scores, along with the player,s names, as these scores are attained. To perform this task we will need to use other software alongside Flash, and these applications will be examined as they are introduced.

So what nature will our game take? Well, have you ever known what's going to happen before it actually happens? What about knowing what somebody is going to say before they say it? If your answer to either of the above questions is *yes* then perhaps you have some psychic ability.

In this chapter we'll create a simple Flash 5 psychic ability testing game and, during this process, we'll be covering a number of topics and techniques that are widely used in Flash games development.

We'll be using a combination of Flash, PHP and the mySQL relational database to create a high score table for the game. Although it's a simple game, the techniques used are fairly common in the area of Flash development, and will help take your development skills to a whole new level.

Upon completion of this chapter you will be confident with the use of:

- Flash arrays, functions, and variables
- PHP database connectivity
- Integrated Flash and PHP

Since we'll be introducing a number of additional technologies during the course of the chapter, perhaps now would be a good opportunity to give you some background information on them.

## What is PHP?

PHP (officially **PHP Hypertext Preprocessor**) is a server-side HTML-embedded scripting language. The goal of developing the language was to allow web developers to write dynamically generated pages quickly.

Offering functionality previously available only to Perl, C and Java developers, PHP is causing quite a stir in the web development community. At the most basic level, PHP can do anything any other CGI program can do, such as collect form data, generate dynamic page content, or send and receive cookies.

Perhaps the strongest and most useful feature in PHP is its support for a wide range of databases. The databases PHP supports are listed below.

| | | |
|---|---|---|
| Adabas D | Ingres | Oracle (OCI7 and OCI8) |
| dBase | InterBase | Ovrimos |
| Empress | FrontBase | PostgreSQL |
| FilePro (read-only) | mSQL | Solid |
| Hyperwave | Direct MS-SQL | Sybase |
| IBM DB2 | MySQL | Velocis |
| Informix | ODBC | Unix dbm |

# Online Data

> *PHP's other greatest feature is that it is completely free open source software – visit the web site* www.php.net *for more information and to download it!*

PHP offers Flash developers a whole new lease of life by as acting as an interface between Flash and all of the above databases and services. While Flash has matured a great deal over the last few years the absence of database connectivity remains an extremely limiting factor, but PHP is doing a sterling job of bridging the gap between Flash and the database.

There's quite a lot to PHP (including support for many other services using protocols such as IMAP, SNMP, NNTP, POP3, HTTP and countless others), but what we're really interested in is what it can do for you as a Flash games designer, and that's what this chapter is about.

So, what about that database we need to connect to? Well, there is a great solution in the form of **mySQL**.

## What is mySQL?

MySQL is a relational database that has long been the database favoured by PHP developers due to its speed and functionality. Its being *free* has also undoubtedly contributed to its popularity! And the ability for PHP to talk directly with mySQL makes them the perfect partners.

If you have little or no experience in using a database from the command line then you can use the wonderful **phpMyAdmin,** a graphical user interface for mySQL written with PHP. It provides you with a friendly interface making database design with mySQL a piece of cake.

> *Check out* www.phpwizard.net *for lots more information on phpMyAdmin. For more information about mySQL see* www.mysql.com.

Now that we've looked at the main technologies, we can roll up our sleeves and get into the Flash.

## Reading Minds with Flash and PHP

The basis for our game is that the computer selects a symbol at random from a bank of symbols. The player must then try to predict what symbol has been selected by making a selection from the symbols on the screen. Matching selections score points and high scores will be recorded in a high score table.

Let's start by creating a new file in Flash. We'll need five layers for our content, so add four more on top of the default layer.

# 14  Flash Games Studio

Once created, we need to rename the layers for use within our game. Use the details below to help you with the naming of the layers.

- **Code** – This layer will hold the bulk of our game code, it's good practice to keep the bulk of the game code on its own layer where possible, as it aids development by making code easier to find when changes are required.

- **Symbols** – Here you'll find the game's symbol graphics.

- **Score** – Text and graphics relevant to the game's scoring will be stored on this layer

- **Crystal Content** – This layer contains anything and everything that may appear inside the crystal ball at some point during play.

- **Crystal Ball** – The crystal ball graphics etc are held on this layer; these are simply for display purposes and do not interact with the rest of the components in the game.

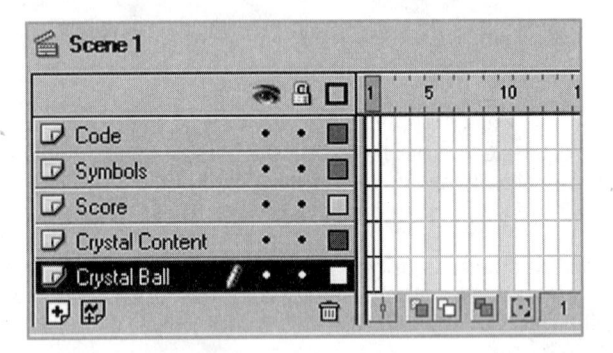

Your movie timeline should look like the above screenshot – the layer structure will aid us in the development of the game, providing logical places for the storage of our game components. We now have a starting point for our game and can begin creating our game environment.

# Online Data | 14

As the theme for our game is psychic ability we'll be using a crystal ball for our central graphic – you'll find the `crystalball.swf` graphic in the source files for this chapter. The player will make his\her selection using the extra graphics below, and these can also be found in the source folder.

A small amount of creativity and you end up with a layout similar to that shown below. The crystal ball is on the Crystal Ball layer (did you see that coming?) and the surrounding graphics should be placed on the Symbols layer.

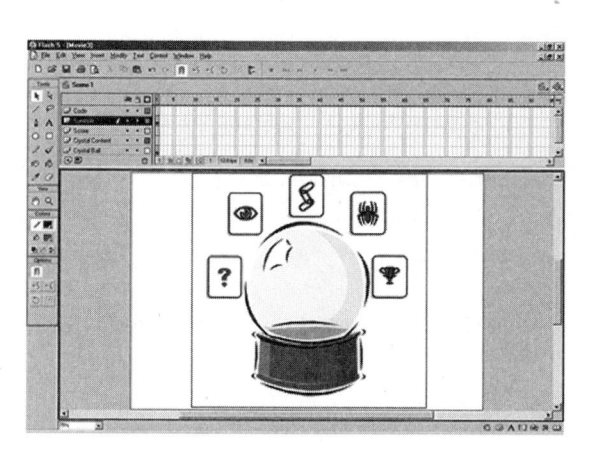

So far we've created the look and feel for the game. What we need to concentrate on next is the functionality.

## Adding Functionality

### Think of a number

We'll start by writing the function that will randomly 'think' of a particular symbol; this function will live in frame 1 of the Code layer. Select frame 1 on the main timeline and bring up the Actions panel.

# 14  Flash Games Studio

1. Enter the following code to select a random symbol:

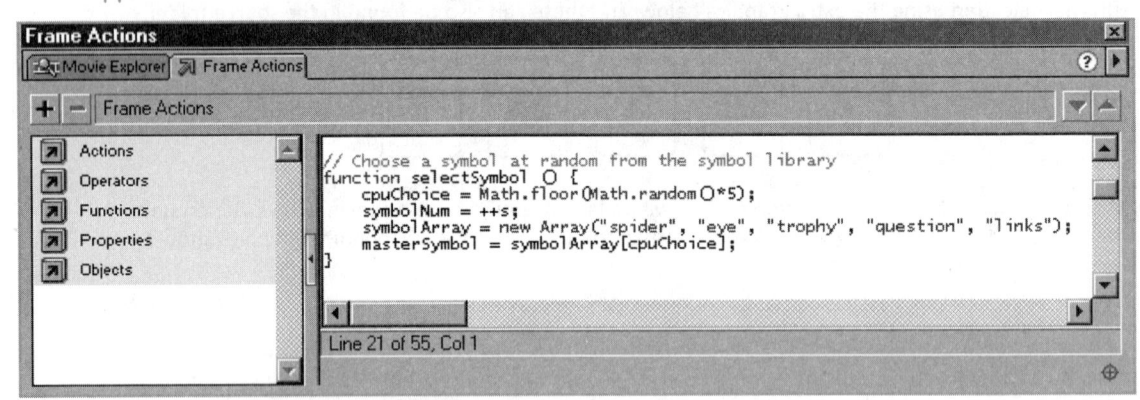

```
// Choose a symbol at random from the symbol library
function selectSymbol () {
    cpuChoice = Math.floor(Math.random()*5);
    symbolNum = ++s;
    symbolArray = new Array("spider", "eye", "trophy", "question", "links");
    masterSymbol = symbolArray[cpuChoice];
}
```

The above code is written as a function. It's good practice to use functions where possible as it reduces the amount of code you need to write. Any code that may be used repeatedly within your games should be written as a function, as this will allow you to write the code just once and then call it for every subsequent use.

Let's step through this code to get a better idea of what exactly it does.

```
function selectSymbol ()
{
```

2. The first line simply defines the function `selectSymbol()`, everything between the {...} can then be called by simply using `selectSymbol()` in your code.

```
cpuChoice = Math.floor(Math.random()*5);
```

3. This line assigns a random number between 0 and 5 to variable `cpuChoice`. We'll use this value later to select the random symbol.

```
symbolNum = ++s;
```

4. The above line of code simply increases the value of the variable `symbolNum` by 1 each time this function is run, which allows us to keep track of how many symbols we have shown to the user during the game.

```
symbolArray = new Array("spider", "eye", "trophy", "question", "links");
masterSymbol = symbolArray[cpuChoice];
}
```

5. Here we're making use of arrays. Arrays are a very important part of Flash development and are common to almost all development languages. They provide the ability to assign multiple values to a single variable in a structured way.

We assign the names of our symbols to the variable `symbolArray` using the array object.

## Online Data

The variable `masterSymbol` is then assigned the value of `symbolArray`, which is our newly created array, but notice that the index value of the array is the random number variable (`cpuChoice`) we created earlier in the function. This means that the value of `masterSymbol` is chosen at random from our array.

We'll be adding a few more lines of code to the `selectSymbol()` function a little later as the game develops but for now it does everything we need it to – it picks at random from five different options.

## Player Selection

We now have a game where the computer selects a symbol at random but we have no way of allowing the player to guess what symbol the computer has selected. Here's where we get interactive!

Remember the symbol graphics from earlier in the chapter? Well, we're going to write the code so that the player can click on one of the symbols to guess which of the symbols the computer has selected.

**6.** First we create another function in frame 1 of the Code layer on the main timeline which will handle the selection made by the player.

```
function playerSelection (playerChoice) {
    if (masterSymbol == playerChoice) {
       doCorrect();
       }
    else {
       doWrong();
       }
    selectSymbol();
}
```

Simply put, the above function takes the selection made by the player and compares it with the value of the computers symbol selection. If the selections match it calls the function `doCorrect()`. If they don't match it calls the function `doWrong()`. We'll discuss the details of both of these functions shortly.

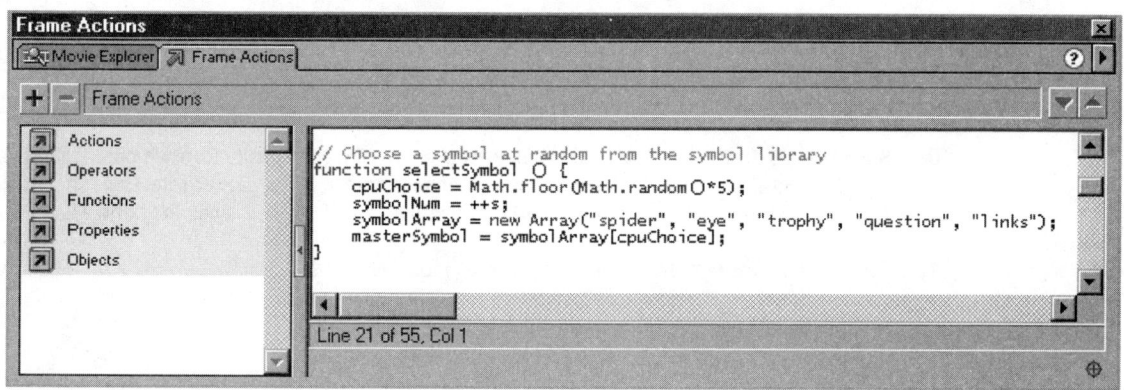

```
// Choose a symbol at random from the symbol library
function selectSymbol () {
    cpuChoice = Math.floor(Math.random()*5);
    symbolNum = ++s;
    symbolArray = new Array("spider", "eye", "trophy", "question", "links");
    masterSymbol = symbolArray[cpuChoice];
}
```

# 14    Flash Games Studio

It then calls the `selectSymbol()` function to select another random symbol and the entire process starts again.

Note that this time the function has a parameter called `playerChoice`. This parameter is set by the individual symbol buttons when each symbol button is pressed - i.e. 'spider' when the spider button is pressed.

Let's take a look at the code for the symbol buttons and perhaps it'll all make sense.

7. First convert the symbol graphics into buttons by selecting them and pressing the F8 key. Choose button as the symbol's behavior.

8. The name of the button is not important, but try to keep the names descriptive and simple.

9. Once we have converted the symbols to buttons we can add the code required for when the player makes a symbol selection. Add this code to each button instance on the main timeline:

```
on (release)
{
playerSelection ("spider");
}
```

Repeat this for all the new buttons, and remember to change the name from "spider" to "trophy", "links" etc...

What can I say, that's the wonder of functions. By creating a central function we can call it time and time again - in this case from each of the symbol buttons, changing only the value of the `playerChoice` parameter. Life doesn't get much simpler than that.

The player can now interact with the game and the game is capable of checking whether or not the player has made the correct selection. But we have not yet defined what happens when the player is right or wrong.

## Am I Right or Am I Wrong?

Remember the `doCorrect()` and `doWrong()` functions we referenced in the `playerSelection()` function? It's time to tell Flash what to do when the player answers correctly or, alternately, gets it wrong.

10. Surprise! It's function time again; below is the `doCorrect()` function which is called by `playerSelection()` when the computer selection and the player selections match (as with all the functions in this tutorial it also lives on the Code layer in frame 1).

11. Let's take a closer look at the `doCorrect()` code.

# Online Data 14

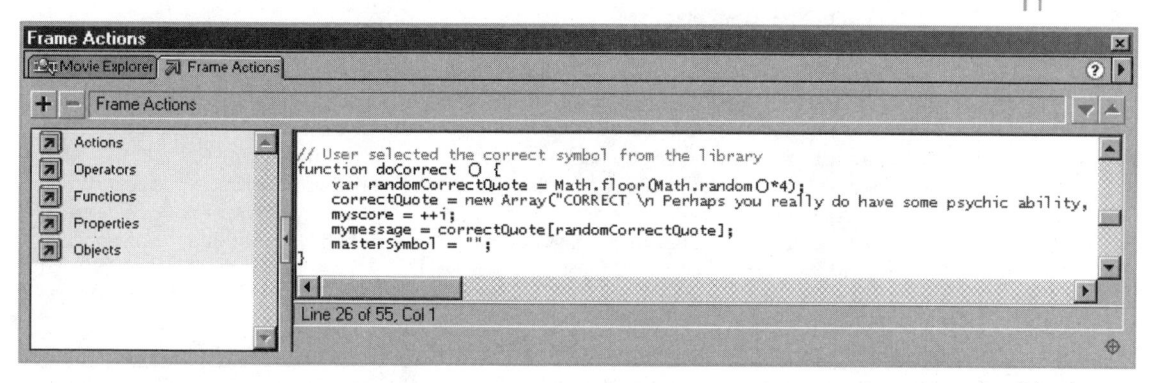

```
function doCorrect ()
{
var randomCorrectQuote = Math.floor(Math.random()*4);
```

```
// User selected the correct symbol from the library
function doCorrect () {
    var randomCorrectQuote = Math.floor(Math.random()*4);
    correctQuote = new Array("CORRECT \n Perhaps you really do have some psychic ability,
    myscore = ++i;
    mymessage = correctQuote[randomCorrectQuote];
    masterSymbol = "";
}
```

Line 26 of 55, Col 1

**12.** After we've defined the function we assign a random number between 0 and 4 to the variable `randomCorrectQuote`.

```
correctQuote = new Array("CORRECT \n Perhaps you really do have
some psychic ability, try the next one", "WELL DONE \n Great
minds think a like, can you guess which of the symbols I'm
thinking about this time?", " EXCELLENT  \n Your powers grow
stronger, don't stop now", "CORRECT \n You got that one right but
maybe you were just lucky, try the next one");
```

This part of the function requires a little explanation as it provides an important part of the games feedback.

You don't want the games to respond with a simple CORRECT comment when you match a symbol correctly, so in a bid to inject a little personality into the game we'll create an array of possible responses to a correct answer.

The value of `correctQuote` will be used during the game to display a random correct answer message where appropriate.

**13.** The following code is a simple incrementing variable, each time this code is run the value of myscore increases by 1. If you get the question right your score is increased by one point

```
myscore = ++i;

mymessage = correctQuote[randomCorrectQuote];
    masterSymbol = "";
}
```

**14.** We then assign our "You got it right" message to the variable `mymessage`. We'll see the result of this action shortly. Following the assigning of the variable we reset the `masterSymbol` ready for another go and there's where the `doCorrect()` function ends.

# Flash Games Studio

15. Ok, so we know what happens when you get the right answer but what happens when you get the answer wrong? Bring on the `doWrong()` function.

    ```
    function doWrong ()
    {
    var randomWrongQuote = Math.floor(Math.random()*4);

    wrongQuote = new Array("SORRY \nFocus your mind, I was thinking
    about the "+masterSymbol+" symbol try the next one", "WRONG \nYou
    need to concentrate much harder, the "+masterSymbol+" symbol was
    the right answer, try again", "CONCENTRATE \n Your powers are
    weak, I was concentrating very hard on the "+masterSymbol+"
    symbol and you still got it wrong, try the next one", "WRONG \n I
    was thinking about the "+masterSymbol+" symbol, try the next
    one");

    mymessage = wrongQuote[randomWrongQuote];
    masterSymbol = "";
    }
    ```

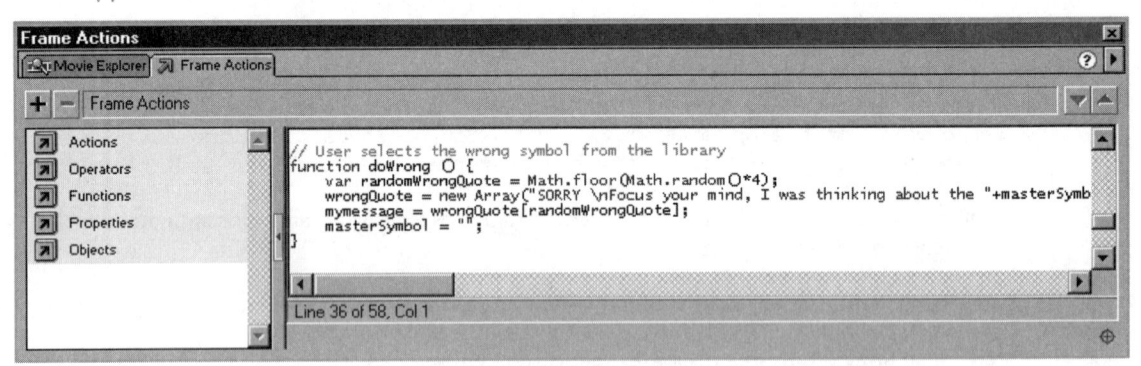

16. This should prove somewhat easier to explain as it's similar in structure to the `doCorrect()` function we've just covered; this time obviously we don't increment the `myscore` variable because the player got it wrong.

We still assign the message array to the variable `mymessage` although this time the messages are of a negative nature and also include the correct answer (+masterSymbol+) to show the player what symbol had been selected by the computer.

As with the previous function we end by resetting the value of the `masterSymbol` this ensures that a new symbol value is assigned each time.

## Looking Back and Looking Ahead...

Let's summarize what we've achieved so far:

# Online Data

- We created the interface for the game.
- The game is capable of selecting a symbol at random from those listed.
- The player can make a selection using the symbol buttons.
- We can compare the selections, made by both the player and the computer.
- We can respond appropriately to both correct and incorrect answers.

Things are beginning to come together now but without giving the players any idea of how they are doing, it's not much of a game. None of the messages or score functionality we've built appears in the screen's output yet.

As we've already done quite a bit of work behind the scenes, getting the message and score information out to the screen will be simple. We can now easily create some new dynamic text fields and by giving them the same name as the variables we have created, they will automatically display the values of the variables.

## ESPecially Nice Frills

**Displaying messages**

   1. Let's create a new dynamic text box and place it centrally in the crystal ball. This will hold all the feedback messages that are displayed to the player when they get the answer right or wrong.

By setting the variable property of the dynamic textbox to `mymessage` our `mymessage` variable value will appear in the new textbox.

When we play the game now we can see that correct and incorrect answers produce the appropriate messages inside the crystal ball.

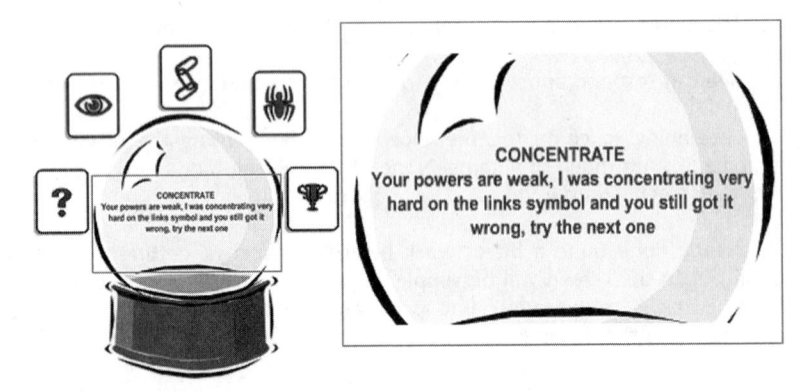

2. We can repeat this process for the other variables we created that are appropriate for output to the screen during game play. The variable `myscore` holds the value of the questions you have answered correctly and the `symbolNum` variable contains the number of symbols you have seen so far during the game.

## Psychic Ability

Now we're going to add one or two extras to our code to increase the information we output to the screen during the game.

3. Adding the following code to the `selectSymbol()` function will give us even more useful variables to play with.

```
function selectSymbol () {
    cpuChoice = Math.floor(Math.random()*5);
    symbolNum = ++s;
    symbolArray = new Array("spider", "eye", "trophy",
"question", "links");
    masterSymbol = symbolArray[cpuChoice];
    pAbility = int((myscore/symbolNum)*100);
    symbolsShown();
}
```

We'll take a closer look at the additional code.

```
pAbility = int((myscore/symbolNum)*100);
```

## Online Data    14

4. Firstly we calculate the number of correct answers (`myscore`) against the number of questions asked (`symbolNum`) as a percentage and assign the value to the psychic ability variable `pAbility`.

   We'll be using the `pAbility` value as our final score later on in the chapter. The addition of the new `pAbility` variable will give us a running score during the game by creating a dynamic text box using the same technique we used for the message variable earlier.

5. Create a new dynamic text field and place it at the base of the crystal ball (as shown in the screenshot) and set the variable property to `pAbilty`.

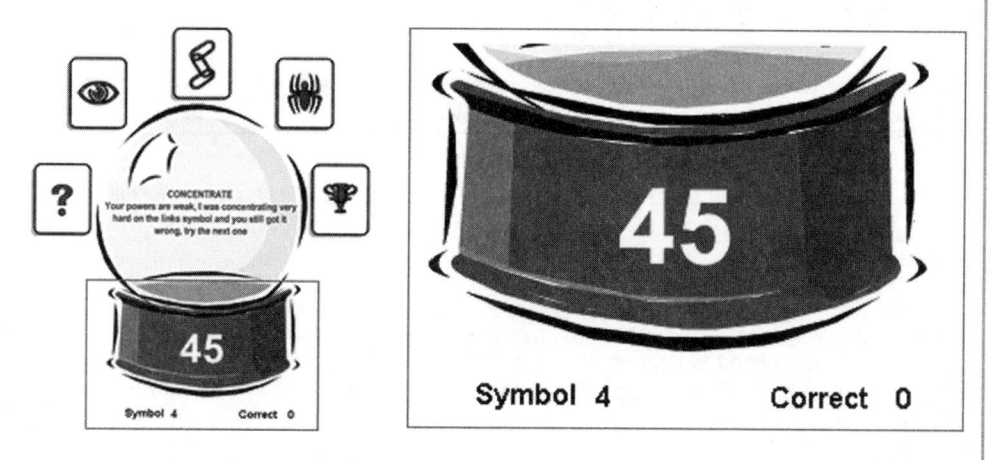

The value of `pAbility` rises and falls with the level of psychic accuracy displayed by the player. This provides additional level of interest as the player attempts to maintain a high level.

## Game Over

As the game stands you could go on forever and ever guessing the next symbol selected by the computer as there is no mechanism in place for stopping the game once a number of symbols has been selected.

6. We can create this feature with the addition of a new function. Again it will live in frame 1 of the Code layer with the others.

```
function symbolsShown ()
{
        if (symbolNum == "20")
{
                        gotoAndStop (5);
                }
}
selectSymbol();
stop ();
```

This is a simple function that checks the value of the variable `symbolNum` (the number of symbols shown so far in the game) and if it is equal to 20, it sends us to frame 5 of the movie and stops.

The final two lines of code run the `selectSymbol()` function and then stop the movie from leaving frame 1 (where the game action is) unless told to do otherwise by the code in the functions.

We now have a complete game and, once the player has guessed at twenty symbols, the game ends by going to frame 5 and stopping.

## Keeping the score

Although we have a running score during the game play, once the game has ended so too does our score. What we need is a high score table where players scores can be stored and seen by other players.

We'll add this feature to our game using a combination of Flash, PHP and a mySQL database.

### Our database

Assuming that you have access to a mySQL database we need to set up our psychic table structure. First we need to connect to the database. This can be done locally at the command line if you're running mySQL on your local machine, or you can connect to a remote database using telnet.

Once you have access to the command line on your local or remote machine we can connect to the database using the following command. In this command 'username' is the username you use to connect to your database and 'password' is the password for this username.

```
mysql -u username -p password
```

If the specified login details were correct you should now be looking at a mySQL command prompt.

```
mysql>
```

All our database commands will be typed at the command line so let's try a few basics.

```
show databases;
```

This will display all the databases available to us.

```
use databasename;
```

– where `database name` is the name of the database we want to use for our game.

```
Show tables;
```

# Online Data

This will display any tables that exist within the database we have chosen to use.

As you can see for the most part all the mysql commands are in plain English and straight forward. For our game we need to create a new table called 'psychic'.

Type the command exactly as it appears below:

```
CREATE TABLE psychic (
    id int(4) NOT NULL auto_increment,
    playerName varchar(12) DEFAULT '0' NOT NULL,
    score int(2) DEFAULT '0' NOT NULL,
    UNIQUE id (id)
);
```

> Note: Pressing the enter key does not execute the command unless the command ends with a semicolon (;) so it's perfectly safe to enter each the code line by line.

And that's it as far as our database structure goes! You can leave the mySQL environment by using the `exit;` command.

## Bring on PHP!

Okay, we have the game, we have the database, what we need now is a way of allowing the Flash game to talk to the mySQL database. Bring on PHP! Hold on though, because before we dive into PHP we need to decide how we want the game to work.

When the player finishes a game, we need to check if the players score is higher than the lowest score in the high score table. In other words is the player's score a *high score* or not? We can't answer this question without checking the scores held in the database and Flash alone cannot do this.

We can however with the `show_scores.php` script. We'll take a more detailed look at it later but to summarize, when run it outputs the following information in a format that Flash can understand.

| Variable | Value |
| --- | --- |
| lowscore | The lowest score currently held in the database. |
| lowplayer | The player that scored the lowest score. |
| scoreid | The record id of the lowest scoring record. |
| Num | The total number of scores currently in the |
| database.highscore | A list of players and scores separated by a new line (\n) |

So with this simple script we now have every piece of information we require to display, not only a high score table, but also to make the decision whether or not a players score is high enough to be added to the table.

Let's take a look at the script itself.

```php
<?php
include_once ("./db_include.php");
$sql="SELECT * FROM $table_name ORDER BY 'score' DESC";
$result=mysql_query($sql,$connection) or die("Could not connect to table while checking if score is a high score");
$num=mysql_numrows($result);

$x=0;
echo "&highscore=";
while ($x < $num):
        $player = mysql_result($result, $x, 'playerName');
        $score = mysql_result($result, $x, 'score');
        $scoreid= mysql_result($result, $x, 'id');
        echo "$player     $score \n";
$x++;
endwhile;

echo "&lowscore=$score";
echo "&lowplayer=$player";
echo "&num=$num";
echo "&scoreid=$scoreid";
?>
```

The first part of the script is an `include` command which basically tells the script, when it's executed, to include the contents of another file. In this case the file is the `db_include.php` file shown below:

```php
<?
    $db_name="NAME OF DATABASE HERE";
    $db_user="DATABASE USER NAME";
    $db_password="USER PASSWORD";
    $table_name="psychic";
    $db_host="NAME OR ADDRESS OF SERVER";
    $connection=mysql_connect("$db_host","$db_user","$db_password") or die ("I couldn't connect to mysql");
    $db=mysql_select_db($db_name ,$connection) or die ("I couldn't connect to $db_name");
?>
```

The `db_include.php` file contains the database connection information and it's wise to create an include file in this way. Using this method you need not put secure information such as usernames and passwords directly in your scripts, your include script can be kept in a secured directory, for example well away from the script that references it.

# Online Data

In addition to security advantages, it also means that all scripts that require database access can simply use the same database connection information. Changes in this information need only be made once in the include file, and the change will affect all of the scripts that use the database connection.

Let's move on to the next part of the `show_scores.php` file.

Once we have made a connection to the database we want to extract the score information from it and we do this using a query:

```
$sql="SELECT * FROM $table_name ORDER BY 'score' DESC";
$result=mysql_query($sql,$connection) or die("Could not connect to
table while checking if score is a high score");
```

The above query simply says, "fetch all the rows from the `psychic` table and put them in score order starting with the highest score first and assign them to the array `result`".

The next line (shown below) simply counts the number of rows that were retrieved by the query and stores the total in the variable `num`.

```
$num=mysql_numrows($result);
```

We now have all the score information and the number of scores held in the `psychic` table of the database but, in order for them to be accessible to Flash, we need to change their format. The next part of `show_scores.php` is responsible for this.

```
$x=0;
echo "&highscore=";
while ($x < $num) :
        $player = mysql_result($result, $x, 'playerName');
        $score = mysql_result($result, $x, 'score');
        $scoreid= mysql_result($result, $x, 'id');
        echo "$player    $score \n";
$x++;
endwhile;
```

We are currently holding the players and score in an array but we need to break them up into the format `variablename=value` so that Flash can use them.

We start by creating a `while` loop which will execute its contents while the specified conditions exist ($x<num). In this case we want to extract each player name and each score from the array until we reach the end of the array, each row being separated by \n which forces the next value onto a new line.

We know when we have reached the end of the array in this case because the variable `num` holds the value of the total number of rows returned by the query.

# 14  Flash Games Studio

An example of the output from the above script might look like similar to that shown below.

```
highscore=Kev 99 Alan 87 Steve 85 Gaddy 73
```

The final part of the script adds a few more variables to the output that we will be using shortly.

```
echo "&lowscore=$score";
echo "&lowplayer=$player";
echo "&num=$num";
echo "&scoreid=$scoreid";
?>
```

> *Note: Each variable must be separated by the '&' symbol, this tells Flash that we are now talking about a new variable. You can see this in use in the above code.*

## Tying it Together

The `show_scores.php` script gives us all the information we need within Flash to display a high score table but how do we call PHP scripts from within Flash? Let's go back to our game now and make preparations for the new high score table.

The entire game exists on frame 1 of the timeline. We're now going to expand this a little by creating the high score table in frame 20 of the timeline.

# Online Data 14

Firstly we'll copy the crystal ball from Frame 1 to Frame 20. We'll use this as backdrop for our high scores.

# 14  Flash Games Studio

To this we'll add a new multiline dynamic text field and position it centrally on the top of the crystal ball in frame 20 of the Score layer.

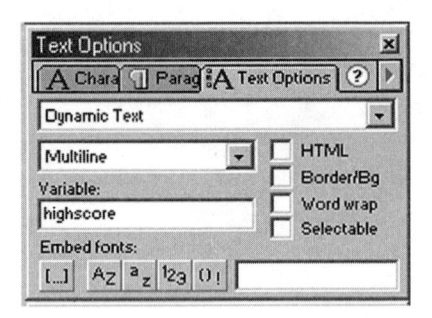

We'll set the variable value to highscore. As with our other dynamic textfields the values returned by our PHP script will be displayed inside the new textfield, giving us our high score table.

As yet we have no way of running the script and this will be our next task. For the moment, however, let's take a look at the logic of what we want to do.

When the game has finished there are two possible outcomes:

- The player's score is a high score – in this case we want to give them the opportunity to enter their name into the high score table.

- The player's score is not a high score – in this case we want to simply display the existing high score table to the player.

To make this decision we need some more code in the form of an invisible movie clip.

On frame 5 of the main timeline in the Score layer we'll create our movie clip. It's not a particularly visually exciting one!

## Integrating Flash and PHP

**1.** Create a small white square (about 1cm) and convert it into a movie clip symbol (F8) we'll call it check score. The content isn't important for this movie clip as it's really just a container for our score checking code.

## Online Data

**2.** Add the following code to the check score movie clip:

```
onClipEvent (load)
{
     this.loadVariables ("./show_scores.php");
}
onClipEvent (data)
{
     _root.lowscore=this.lowscore;
     _root.lowplayer=this.lowplayer;
     _root.num = this.num;
     _root.scoreid = this.scoreid;

if ((this.num < 10) or (this.lowscore < _root.PAbility))
     {
     _root.gotoAndStop(10);
     } else {
     _root.gotoAndStop(20);
     }
}
```

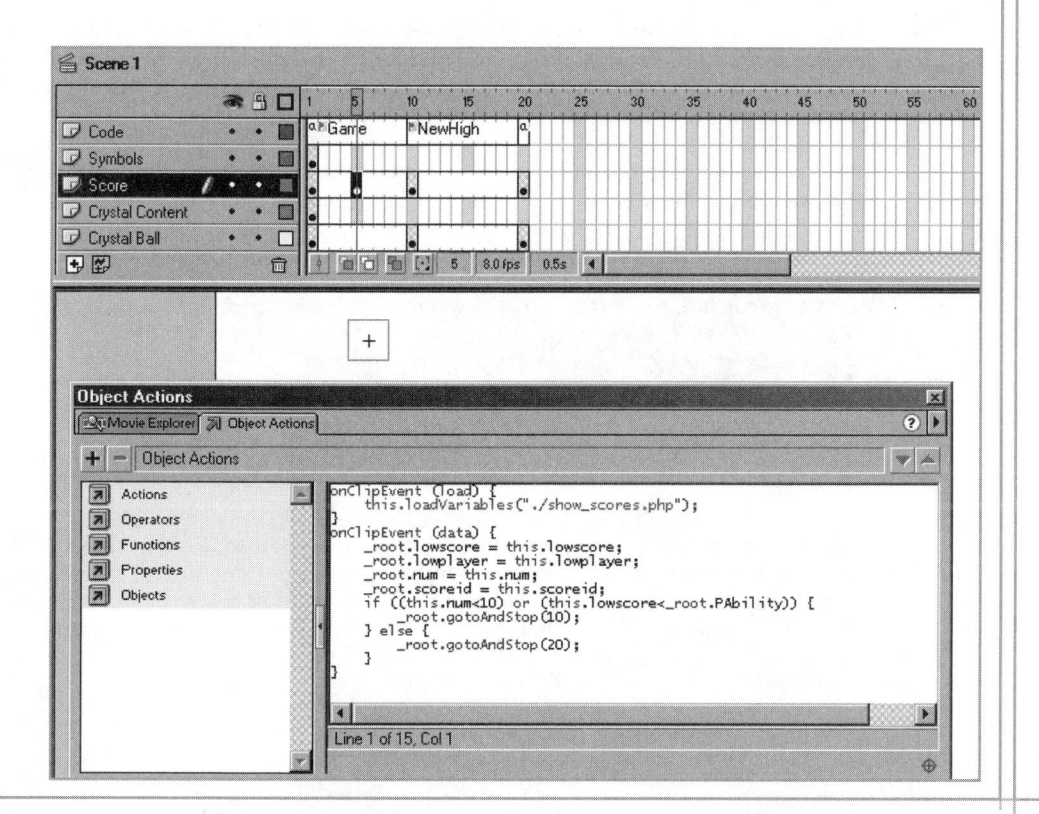

# Flash Games Studio

Let's take a step-by-step look at what this does.

```
onClipEvent (load)
{
    this.loadVariables ("./show_scores.php");
}
```

3. The above code is executed as soon as the check_score movie is loaded, and the second line executes the show_scores.php script we created earlier using loadVariables. The variables that are returned by the script (remember all those player names and score variables?) are loaded into the check_scores movie.

```
onClipEvent (data) {
    _root.lowscore = this.lowscore;
    _root.lowplayer = this.lowplayer;
    _root.num = this.num;
    _root.scoreid = this.scoreid;
    if ((this.num<10) or (this.lowscore<_root.PAbility)) {
        _root.gotoAndStop(10);
    } else {
        _root.gotoAndStop(20);
    }
}
```

4. The second portion of our code uses the onClipEvent (data) event, which is only executed once the variables from the PHP have been returned to the movie. This is extremely useful as it eliminates the need for creating loops that check for values being loaded into the movie.

    Once the values have been loaded we copy them to the _root level of our movie so that we can use them easily later in the rest of the game.

    > *It's worth noting that you can use variables that exist in other movies using the dot syntax but I prefer to keep them on the _root level so I know where they are at all times.*

    After we've copied the values to the _root the next part of the code contains an if statement.

    In simple terms the if statement says "If there are less than 10 high scores in the database or the current player's score is higher than any of those held in the database, go to frame 10 on the main timeline and stop. If the current score is not a high score then go to frame 20 on the main timeline (our show high score table frame) and stop".

# Online Data 14

5. So we now have our logic built. The check score movie clip (with help of course from our `show_scores.php` script) will ensure that the player is directed to the correct frame on the timeline depending on the score.

   What we need to concentrate on now is what the player will see when they scores a high score. Because they have achieved a high score we want to give them the opportunity to enter their name into the table with their high score.

6. Let's start by copying the crystal ball graphic from frame 1 to frame 10 as this will form the background to our "enter your name" feature.

7. We now need to create an input text field and set the variable property to newplayer.

8. Next, create an enter your name style graphic in the center of the crystal ball on frame 10 of the timeline, as shown in the image below:

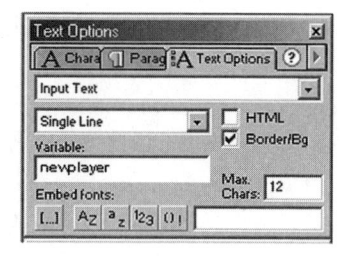

9. After adding the pAbility (score) dynamic text box again as we did earlier in the chapter, frame 10 should look something like the image above. This will provide our high scoring player with a text box that they can use to input their name.

10. We need to convert the enter graphic into a button (F8). Name this (simply enough) enter button. Select both the input box and the newly created button and convert both into a movie.

11. Name the movie new highscore then add the following code to the movie clip's Actions panel.

    ```
    onClipEvent (data)
    {
    _root.gotoAndStop(20);
    }
    ```

12. While the previous code doesn't really mean much on its own, it's used by the enter button code below to take the player to the high score table after they have entered their name and pressed the enter button.

    ```
    on (release) {
        var lowscore = _root.lowscore;
        var lowplayer = _root.lowplayer;
        var pAbility = _root.pAbility;
        var scoreid = _root.scoreid;
        var num = _root.num;
        loadVariables ("./update_scores.php", _root, "POST");
    }
    ```

13. Let's look at the above code in a little more detail. The on (release) code is executed when the enter button is released by the player entering their name. It begins by copying the variables we need from the _root layer into the movie so that they are included when the loadVariables command sends the new highscore movie clip variables to the update_scores.php for processing by PHP.

## Return to the database

Once the Flash variables are sent to the update_scores.php script the player's details are then added to the psychic table in the database.

It's time for the return of PHP; this time we'll be using it to insert our new high score details into the psychic table. Here's how it's done:

```
<?php
include_once ("./db_include.php");

if ($num < "10")
{
$sql= "INSERT INTO psychic (playerName, score) VALUES
(\"$newplayer\",\"$pAbility\")";
$result=mysql_query($sql,$connection) or die ("There was a problem
updating the database");
}
else
{
    $sql="DELETE FROM psychic WHERE id=\"$scoreid\"";
$result=mysql_query($sql,$connection) or die ("There was a problem
deleting the record");
$sql= "INSERT INTO psychic (playerName, score) VALUES
(\"$newplayer\",\"$pAbility\")";
$result=mysql_query($sql,$connection) or die ("There was a problem
updating the database");
}
?>
```

# Online Data    14

This is the `update_scores.php` script that we'll use to insert our high scores into the mySQL database. The script performs 1 of 2 roles depending on the number of scores currently held in the database.

We want to show the top 10 high scores in our table but until the game has been played at least 10 times we obviously want to store every score in the database. The script handles this by checking the value of the variable `num` which holds the total number of rows in our table.

In simple terms the script is saying the following – "If there are less than 10 scores in the database, insert the player's name and their score into the database. If however there are 10 scores already in the database, the script deletes the lowest score row from the database before inserting the new player and score details.

The `or die` function in the script writes a message out to the screen in the event that there was a problem executing any of the database commands in the script.

You'll notice that once again we use the db_include.php file to include the database connection details in our script. After the script has been executed the player is taken to frame 20.

## Running out of cache

When you visit a page with your web browser, a copy of the file is held on your hard drive. This area is known as the cache. When you return to the site at a later date, instead of having to download the page again, it can be read from the hard drive saving time and bandwidth.

This sounds like a great idea but it's a mixed blessing for Flash developers. When you're trying to build sites with dynamic content, the last thing you want to happen is for visitors to your site to see data from the last time they visited.

There are number of HTML meta tags that will help in certain cases but for your Flash projects, the only certain way to avoid having your pages cached is to make each viewing of the page unique.

Below is the code I used to ensure that the page I'm calling will not read from cache:

```
nocacheURL="./show_scores.php"+"?"+Math.floor(Math.random()*99999)
;
this.loadVariables(nocacheURL);
stop();
```

It works by appending a random number to the end of the URL; this (more or less) ensures that the URL will be unique and therefore not a cached page.

Our cache problem is solved and the results are shown below.

## Power Psychics

Kev 97
Alan 93
Steve 89
Matthew 84
Sven 80
Stef 73
Gareth 71
Pamela 69
Jake 62
Pete 60

Your Score

93

Play Again

And that just about brings our chapter to a close. All the files used for this chapter have been included in the source files downloadable from the friends of ED web site, so take a look.

I hope I've managed to give you a basic introduction to using PHP with Flash to add database functionality to your game. The things you've learned here are only the beginning of Flash's dynamic potential, so get experimenting with PHP and see what you can create!

# Online Data

14

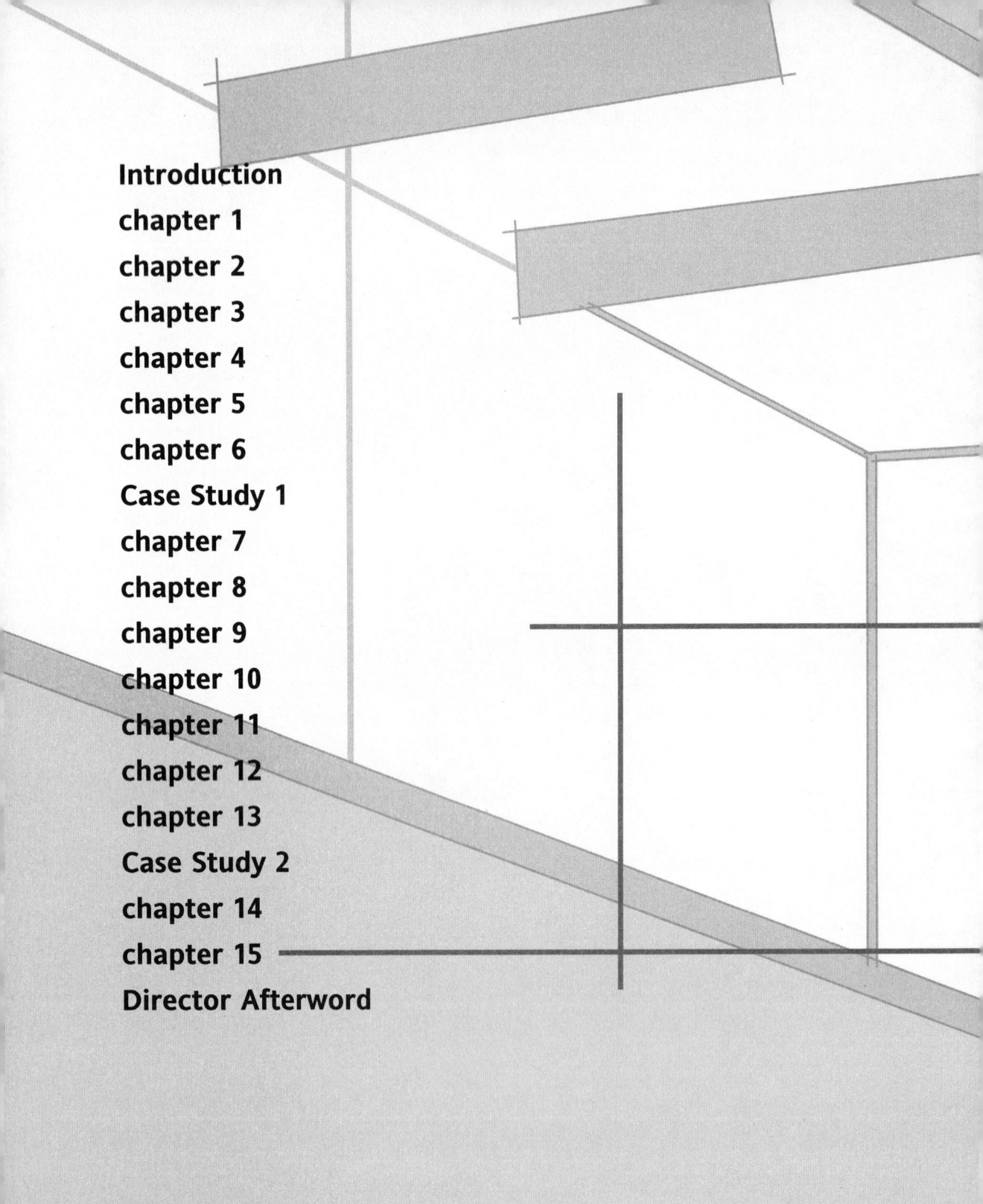

**Introduction**
chapter 1
chapter 2
chapter 3
chapter 4
chapter 5
chapter 6
Case Study 1
chapter 7
chapter 8
chapter 9
chapter 10
chapter 11
chapter 12
chapter 13
Case Study 2
chapter 14
chapter 15
**Director Afterword**

# Chapter 15
# Multiplayer Applications

# 15  Flash Games Studio

> *"The future is now. Soon every American home will integrate their television, phone, and computer. You'll be able to visit the Louvre on one channel, and watch female mud wrestling on another. You can do your shopping at home, or play Mortal Kombat with a friend in Vietnam. There's no end to the possibilities."*
>
> Jim Carrey, The Cable Guy (Columbia, 1996)

When it comes to modern technology, multiplayer is where it's at. The arrival of the Internet has brought about an opportunity for people to connect on a global scale like never before.

I remember years ago, long before Flash or the Internet, I was always trying to find multiplayer games in the stores (they were few and far between). I got a game called *F29 Retaliator* back in 1991, and it was astounding because I could fly this jet (an F29) and have dogfights against my friend. We were able to connect via our 2400 bps modems and play for hours, attacking, evading, firing missiles and just generally feeling the thrill of competition. It was then that I knew; this was the direction that games had to go. I dreamt of a game where four, or even eight players could run around in full 3D and fight against each other. Little did I know; it wasn't that far off.

*Doom* came out in 1993 and soon after its release, Id software introduced the multiplayer version of that supported up to two players over a modem or four players over a local area network (LAN), and the term "deathmatch" was coined.

My dreams have since been surpassed. Today, multiplayer games span the globe and support tens of thousands of players simultaneously. The thrill of playing against (or with) other humans is immeasurable. When battling human beings, you are no longer limited by the confines of artificial intelligence. The people you compete with will be learning and adapting just like you, increasing the challenge and the reward of playing.

Multiplayer games generally come in two types: **real-time** and **turn-based**. Real-time games are games in which the action is reflected on all players' screens and things change and move quickly (many times per second). There is no stopping to wait for other players to make their moves and the sense of being there in an alternate reality is heightened. These games have a large hardware requirement in order to make the game run quickly and smoothly over the Internet with an indefinite number of players.

A turn-based game is just the opposite. It's a game in which players wait for their turn to perform an action. Games like Chess or Risk are classic examples of turn-based games. Turn-based games require a less robust communication architecture. As you'll be aware, both of these types of games have already been discussed in this book, but here we'll see how to create multiplayer versions.

## Systems Architecture

Multiplayer games come in all shapes and sizes. From one-on-one games where two people battle it out, to full-sized persistent worlds in which thousands of people may interact in a massive multiplayer world.

# Multiplayer Applications    15

Naturally, these very different types of games have very different types of systems architecture, and it's important to understand the differences.

## Peer-to-peer

When two players play head-to-head or one-on-one, they are playing in what is known as **peer-to-peer** architecture. This is a closed system in which two computers communicate directly with each other, usually over a modem or a serial cable. Let's look at it graphically:

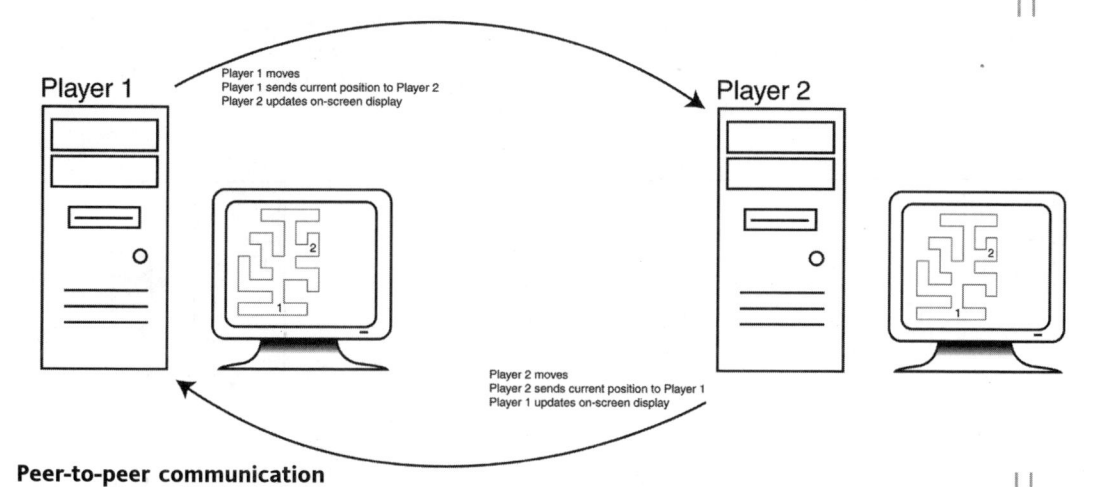

**Peer-to-peer communication**

The Player 1 computer is constantly sending information to Player 2, and Player 2 is constantly sending information to Player 1. Just what this information is will vary depending on the game. Here are some examples:

- **Player location**: When the player moves (runs, walks, flies) around the game world, the updated position is sent to the other player so it can be reflected on screen.

- **Weapons and attacks**: When a player fires a gun, launches a missile or performs any other type of attack, the specifics of that attack are sent to the other player so they are reflected in their game. If Player 1 fires a missile, then Player 2's game must generate an on-screen missile to indicate that the missile is incoming. If Player 2 shoots and hits Player 1, then Player 1 must know this and take some damage.

- **Secondary game actions**: If Player 1 destroys a bridge over the river, then player 2 must receive this information so that they no longer see an intact bridge when they reach the river. Any time a game action is performed that potentially changes the state of things in the game world, the other player must be made aware of this.

This is the simplest form of multiplayer game, and isn't widely used today. It's severely limited in use because of the fact that only two people can play. On the Internet today, even if you're playing with only one other player, most games are using a **client-serves** model of communication.

625

## Client–Server

The client-server method of connection and communication differs from peer-to-peer because it utilizes an intermediary in the communication process.

The **client** is simply an industry word that refers to the player's computer. This is the game itself, and is all the player cares about.

The **server** is a centralized computer that connects many clients together, and is often responsible for performing a great many tasks. Usually, the server is a very powerful computer that can handle things that an individual client can't. The server is responsible for telling all of the clients where each other client is. Take a look at this image:

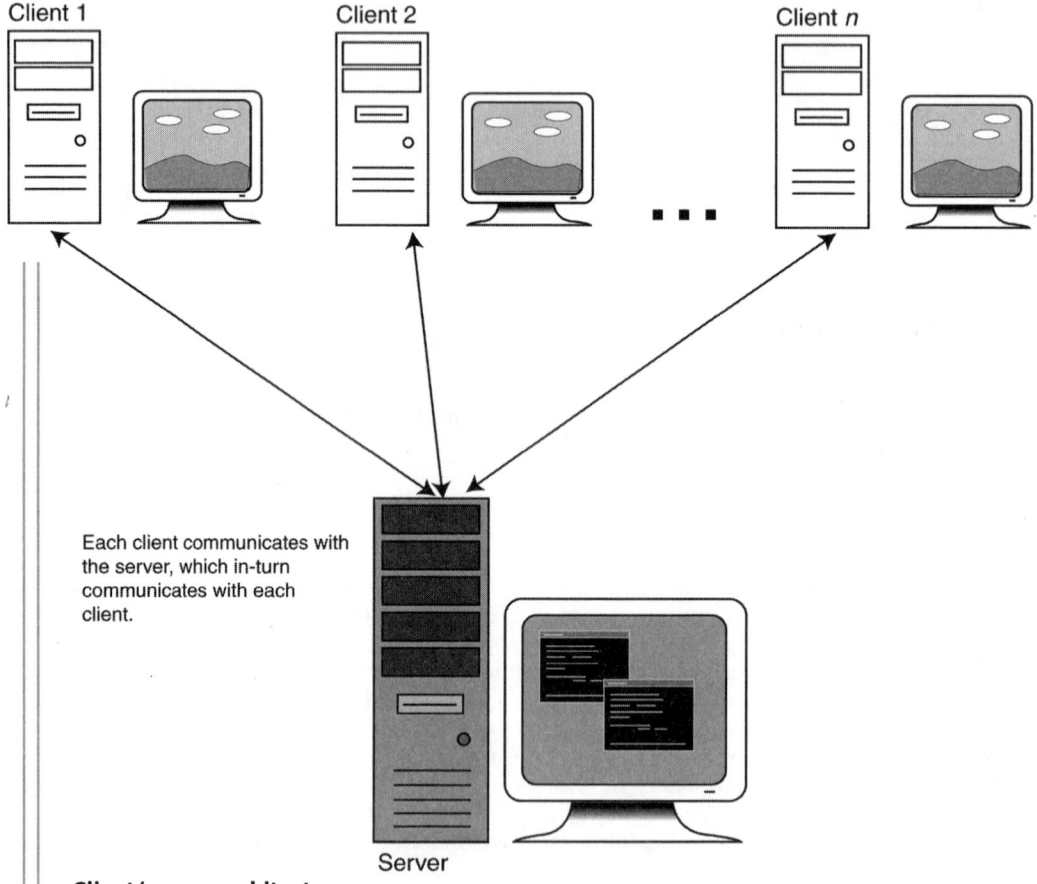

Each client communicates with the server, which in-turn communicates with each client.

Server

**Client/server architecture**
When one client performs an action, like moving or attacking, that message action is conveyed to the server, which then informs every other client of the action. This has the advantage of allowing an unlimited number of players to connect to one game. The server keeps track of the entire

# Multiplayer Applications    15

game world, allowing the players to roam freely. The server is also responsible for keeping everything synchronized between clients.

In client/server architecture, the players never directly communicate with each other peer-to-peer. Any action, like moving, shooting, or even chatting must pass through the server. There are many different types of servers, from game servers to FTP servers to HTTP servers.

## Internet Protocol Address

The standard method for addressing an individual computer on the Internet is through a number known as an IP (Internet Protocol) address. This number comes in the form of ###.###.###.###, where each number between the dots can be from 0 to 255. So a computer might have the IP address 24.133.223.211, and that computer is accessible from anywhere on the Internet, as long as you know that address.

How exactly that computer responds to incoming requests depends on the computer's setup. For example, a computer that is setup as a web server will respond to incoming requests by sending back web pages. However, a computer that is set up as an FTP (File Transfer Protocol) server will respond by attempting to create an FTP session with the incoming computer. However, it's not that simple, because a computer can be both a HTTP and a FTP server. This is accomplished with the use of ports.

## Ports

Along with the IP address, there is another number known as the port. The port is usually notated by putting a colon after the computer's IP address followed by the number, so 24.133.223.221:80, would be port 80 at that IP address. A port is like a television channel – certain types of information are transferred over different ports, though they all come from the same station (the IP address).

For example, port 80 is usually reserved for HTTP, so when you use a web browser to visit a site, your browser invisibly sends its requests to the web server through port 80. On the other side, the web server is sitting listening on port 80, and it knows that anything that arrives on port 80 is an HTTP request so it prepares to fire up a HTML page. These are some of the typical reserved port numbers:

| Port  | Item                |
|-------|---------------------|
| 21    | FTP                 |
| 80    | WWW HTTP            |
| 43/63 | Whois/Whois++       |
| 70    | Gopher              |
| 23    | Telnet              |
| 79    | Finger              |
| 101   | NIC Hostname Server |
| 110   | POP3 (E-mail)       |

# Flash Games Studio

Expect a response from an IP (on a particular port) *only* if the computer at that IP has a server running that is designed to listen on that port. So, if you find out the IP address of your friend's computer, don't expect to find an FTP server running on port 21 of it. Your friend must have an FTP server running before your FTP client will be able to connect to him.

There are many other reserved ports beyond these. When we get into socket communications for games, you'll see that they require an IP and port to transfer game information. Your choice of port is arbitrary but it shouldn't interfere with common port numbers. So, as a rule of thumb it's generally a good idea to try and use ports for your game that are above 1023.

## Firewalls

When information is passed from a client to a server on the Internet, it will occasionally pass through a firewall. A firewall is a device that is intended to stop unwanted intruders sending and receiving data to and from a computer. A firewall works by blocking certain ports from allowing data through. It creates a hardware shield that stops, for example, hackers from entering through a Trojan horse (a piece of code that installs itself on the server and sends data to the remote hacker's computer) that is listening on a given port. Many firewalls block all ports except port 80, the HTTP port, thus allowing people to surf the Web from that computer, and nothing else. However, a standard firewall will block all ports above 1023, which can pose a problem for some multiplayer games.

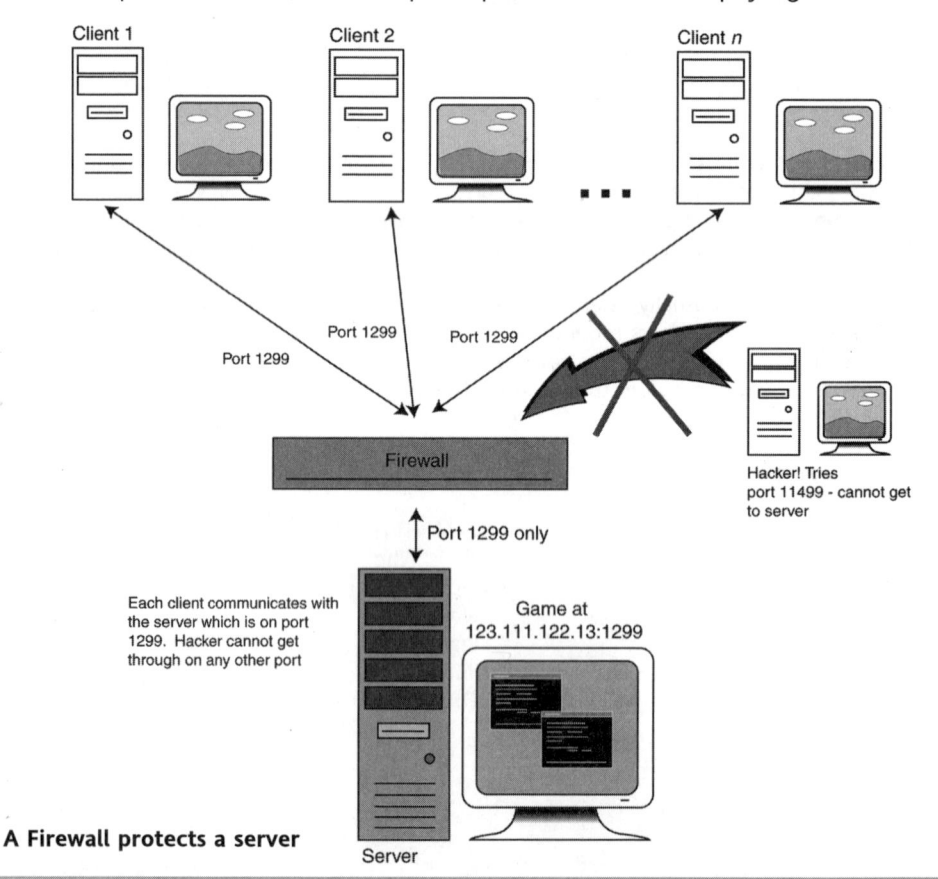

**A Firewall protects a server**

For this reason, it's important to ensure that your players aren't behind such a firewall. Sometimes people attempt to connect to game server/ports while they're sitting at work. This can pose a problem as companies often have firewalls that prevent communication to and from the company on ports other than a specified few. If this is the case the user may not be able to use the fast socket communications method and may only use the slower HTTP method for communication.

# Multiplayer Flash

Flash has two means of communicating with external resources: HTTP and Sockets. Each has advantages and disadvantages.

# HTTP

**HTTP (HyperText Transfer Protocol)** is the standard method of data transmission amongst computers on the Web. HTTP works by sending variables to an HTTP server (a web site), which performs various tasks and sends information back to Flash. An HTTP connection is opened once the data is sent, and then closed when the results are returned to Flash. This is exactly the same protocol used in web pages when you send data from an online form.

HTTP information is sent primarily with the `loadVariables` function, and it works by sending the variables that are sitting in the same object level as the call to `loadVariables`. Take a look at a the following ActionScript attached to a button that is inside a movie clip called container:

```
on (release)
{
    a = 1;
    b = "HELLO";
    loadVariables ("http://www.test.com", _root.results, "POST");
}
```

This is a very simple piece of code that creates two variables, a and b, and then POSTs them over HTTP to the HTTP server at www.test.com. When the server has performed some actions with these variables, it will return its results to a movie clip on the _root timeline called results.

> *Flash will send any variables that have been defined in the local object (from where the `loadVariables` was called), so even though we see only a and b in this example, if there were any other variables that were created in the container movie clip, then these will be sent too. The URL specified in the `loadVariables` command must begin with http:// in order to work.*

There are two methods of sending data: GET and POST. These are functionally different, and some servers expect to receive data via GET and some via POST. When information is sent via HTTP, there are several other items that Flash sends (in accordance with the HTT protocol) that increase overhead and slow down the system. Items such as the current time, the user's IP address, referrer address and browser information are all sent through with our GET/POST data.

I'm assuming that if you can make a server, you know the difference between GET and POST. This chapter is not about making servers; it's about making multiplayer games.

HTTP has one distinct disadvantage, and that is its speed and connection. Since HTTP closes the connection after data has been returned, a connection must be re-established when the next call is made and this slows things down. It also means that the server cannot talk to us unprompted. In order to get a server status update, we must send a HTTP request *asking* the server for updates and information.

Many games can be produced, however, that make use of HTTP communication, and it has the distinct advantage of being able to get past most major firewalls. Simply put, firewalls do not usually block port 80 (HTTP) so any Flash request coming via that port will not normally be blocked.

HTTP is best suited for turn-based games because of the connection and communication limitations. From a programming standpoint, this type of game is generally easier to make than a real-time game, as you may have discovered in the course of this book.

## Sockets

Socket communications are one of the most recent additions to Flash, and one of the most powerful. With a socket, it's possible to open a direct line of communication between a Flash client and a game server. This socket doesn't require a specific protocol like HTTP, so the user can specify exactly what is sent. We can send any amount of information between two computers talking on a socket port.

Generally, a socket connection is established with a socket server (a server that's set up to listen on a pre-determined port) and, when a connection request comes through, it initiates a connection. The client and the server are then *connected* and any data can be freely transferred between them. Like other objects in Flash 5, sockets have to be defined before we can perform actions with them.

In terms of gameplay, sockets are extremely useful for performing the communication updates we outlined at the beginning of this chapter. When the server decides that the client needs something updating in a game, it can simply send out the information to the client and, when the client receives this, ActionScript is automatically executed to handle the incoming data. This real-time event response means that sockets are a much faster and more stable way of communicating between a game client and server, and, because of this sockets lend themselves perfectly to the task of creating high-speed, real-time multiplayer games.

Generally, a server is located at a specific IP address, and it sits listening and waiting on a specific port. Let's say that there was a chess game server at IP 22.22.22.22 on port 15000. This would mean that when our chess client connected to 22.22.22.22, port 15000, the game server would recognize the incoming connection request and, upon acceptance of the connection, the game could begin.

## Opening and Using a Socket

Opening a socket involves the simple procedure of creating a new XMLSocket object in Flash and then assigning it some callback functions that will be automatically executed when data is received. The following code creates a new XMLSocket object:

```
sock = new XMLSocket();
```

Now, sock is an XMLSocket object, and we can assign two callback functions, onConnect and onXML. Let's say that we create two functions:

```
function myOnConnect(success)
{
    if (success)
        trace ("Connected");
    else
        trace ("Failed");
}
```

...And also:

```
function myOnXML (doc)
{
    trace (doc);
}
```

These two functions are very simple, and they merely use the trace command to display some information. The key thing is the purpose of the functions. myOnConnect is going to be the function that is called when our socket server returns a successful connection message. myOnXML is what is going to be called every time the server sends us information. It's this function that is the bread and butter of Flash socket communications, and we'll look at specific examples of it later in the chapter.

But, first we have to tell Flash what the names of our functions are, so that it knows what to call when these events occur. This is accomplished with the following ActionScript:

```
sock.onXML = myOnXML;
sock.onConnect = myOnConnect;
```

onXML and onConnect are simply properties of the XMLSocket object, and into those we assign the names of our custom functions.

When onConnect is triggered, myOnConnect is called, and it's passed a simple Boolean (true/false) variable that determines whether or not the connection was a success. In our function I've called the variable success.

When onXML is triggered, myOnXML is called and the incoming data is passed as a string. In our function I've called the variable simply doc.

# Flash Games Studio

When you wish to actually issue the connection request, you simply use the `XMLSocket`'s connect method, like so:

```
sock.connect(ipaddress, serverport);
```

Where `ipaddress` and `serverport` are going to be defined by the IP of the server and the port on which it's listening. When the server returns a successful connect, then `success` will be passed as `true` to the `myOnConnect` function.

### What to use?

Deciding which method of communications to use is entirely dependent on the type of game you wish to create. If you are creating a fast, real-time game like the racing game later in this chapter, then you must use sockets, because only they can quickly and freely send data back and forth between the server and multiple clients. However, if your players are behind a firewall, then you can create a game that doesn't utilize a real time high-speed structure (like Chess or Bingo) and perform communications over the unblocked HTTP port 80. Unfortunately because HTTP communication doesn't use callback functions, the client must be programmed to regularly send a POST or GET to the server to find out the current status.

In this chapter, we're going to focus on socket communications for making high-speed multiplayer games. This is the communication model that allows the fastest gameplay, and at the time of writing, its potentials go untapped in today's Flash games. We're really reaching the cutting-edge now!

Another point to note is that, in terms of Flash, we should use the client/server model, and not the peer-to-peer model. This is because Flash, unlike a server, can't be told to listen on a port without first establishing a connection. Two Flash peers would therefore never be able to talk to each other because, in effect, neither one would be willing to listen. We need the server to bridge this communication gap.

### XML

Looking back at our `XMLSocket` object, we see that `myOnXML` is returning something called `doc`. What is this?

Generally, `doc` is intended to be data that is formatted as XML, which stands for **Extensible Markup Language**. XML is basically a logical way of representing information in a pre-formatted, visual and intuitive manner. XML looks quite like HTML, except that in XML we define our own tags. Also, XML is intended to convey *information*, rather than documents. In HTML, we would say:

```
<B> This is Bold </B>
```

...to indicate that we want the text to be bold. The web browser will interpret the `<B> </B>` pair and draw the words as **This is Bold**. With XML, we could do something like this:

```
<Funky>This is Funky</Funky>
```

Here we're creating our own unique variable Funky and are assigning to it "This is Funky". Take a look at the following XML code:

```xml
<Person>
    <Name>Jane Doe</Name>
    <ID>122432</ID>
    <Gender>Female</Gender>
    <Appearance>
        <Height>5</Height>
        <Weight>120</Weight>
        <Eyes>Brown</Eyes>
        <Hair>Red</Hair>
    </Appearance>
</Person>
<Person>
    <Name>Glen Rhodes</Name>
    <ID>122231</ID>
    <Gender>Male</Gender>
    <Appearance>
        <Height>6</Height>
        <Weight>170</Weight>
        <Eyes>Blue</Eyes>
        <Hair>Brown</Hair>
    </Appearance>
</Person>
```

That's XML code. Think of it as information that is somewhat analogous to hierarchical data, and could be represented with dot notation like the standard Flash variables below:

```
Person1.Name = "Jane Doe";
Person1.ID = 122432;
Person1.Gender = "Female";
Person1.Appearance.Height = 5;
Person1.Appearance.Weight = 120;
Person1.Appearance.Eyes = "Brown";
Person1.Appearance.Hair = "Red";

Person2.Name = "Glen Rhodes";
Person2.ID = 122231;
Person2.Gender = "Male";
Person2.Appearance.Height = 6;
Person2.Appearance.Weight = 170;
Person2.Appearance.Eyes = "Blue";
Person2.Appearance.Hair = "Brown";
```

The difference is that the process of getting from an XML document to properly parsed variables can be a long and slow one. The following code, when attached to a movie clip, will load in an XML document and display the contents.

```
onClipEvent(load)
{
    function showresults ()
    {
        trace (this);
    }

    myXML = new XML();
    myXML.onLoad = showresults;
    myXML.load ("demo15-1.xml");
}
```

The object `myXML` is created and then the external `demo15-1.xml` is loaded into it. The function `showresults` is an automatic callback function, called when the XML document is loaded, by being assigned as the XML object's `onLoad` function.

When the function is called, the contents of the XML document (which will simply be called `this` in the context of the function) are printed out.

One fact is important to remember here: XML is a very powerful way of sending large amounts of data from a server to a client. However, there is one small problem: XML is *not* efficient – in space or in time. An XML document takes a relatively large amount of time for Flash to parse into directly usable variables, and the amount of data sent from a server is large because it contains all the `<tags></tags>`.

So what does this mean? Basically that in the context of our high-speed multiplayer Flash games, XML is *not* the route we're going to take. Yes, we're using the `XMLSocket`, but we're not sending XML data across it. We're only interested in the socket part of it, and what we're going to be sending are pieces of data called **packets**. These are much smaller, and can be anything we want them to be.

Thus ends our discussion of XML. If you want to learn about the XML or *Flash 5 XML* published soon object itself, then take a look at *Flash 5 ActionScript Studio*, Chapter 11 on the XML object. We're going to focus now on game efficiencies.

## Packets

The packet is soon to become our best friend! A packet isn't something that we can define – it is, put simply, anything we want it to be. A packet is a general term used to describe some data that is sent from one computer to another.

A packet, like its physical equivalent, will vary in shape and size depending on the information that is being sent or, in this case, transmitted. For example, a packet that sends a player's location may look like this:

```
L,p451,x200,y100
```

That's all the information that will be sent either from the client or from the server. We *make up* our own packets – *we* decide how they are going to be structured, nobody else. For us, a packet is simply a string. For example, I've decided that my packet will consist of variables and values, separated by commas. The above packet would mean:

> "This is a player's location (the L), Player number 451 is at location _x = 200, _y = 100."

If our `XMLSocket` object was called `sock` as in our earlier example, and our packet was stored in a variable called `packet`, we would send the information to the server like so:

```
sock.send(packet);
```

And that's it. Packets are short and simple, and don't require tons of overhead to dissect and interpret. A few simple string manipulations are all that are required to break the above packet apart.

Packets are usually sent every time an event occurs. Some of the events that may trigger packets are:

- **Movement**: When a player moves, the client will send through a packet indicating that movement to the server. Such a packet might include player ID, x and y coordinates, speed and direction. When the server receives this packet, it will then send out a packet to all other players, telling them that this player has moved, and where they are.

- **Firing**: When a player fires a weapon, it sends a packet to the server in the same manner, and the server tells everyone else, and determines whether someone was hurt, and if so, informs the victim's client.

- **Connection**: When someone joins the game, they will be sent a packet from the server, which indicates the location of every other player in the game. The other players in the game will also be sent a packet informing them of the new player's arrival.

- **Disconnection**: When a player leaves, the server will inform all the other players and the exiting player will disappear from everyone's game.

- **Chat Message**: When a player uses an in-game chat feature, the client will send a packet to the server that contains the chat message. This will then be sent out to the appropriate clients so that the message appears on their screen.

- **Game Restart**: When the game finishes or restarts, the server will send a restart packet to every player so that everyone's game will restart at the same point (for example, back at the starting line).

# Flash Games Studio

- **Key State**: Sometimes the simplest packet is sending the player's current key state (which keys are currently pressed) to the server, so that other clients can use this information to accurately draw the player's movement.

Packet design is a tricky process of deciding what information is needed to fully convey game events, without providing too much information and taking up unnecessary bandwidth. Remember, in a socket-based multiplayer game, bandwidth is very important because the information is coming fast and furious, so Flash needs as much help as it can get in simplifying the overall process.

## The Server

I've talked a bit about how our clients are passing information to a "server", but what exactly is this server? Well, in the case of a game server, it's simply an application that's running on a computer that has an IP address and an Internet connection.

Most servers tend to be very powerful machines with many hundreds of gigabytes of hard-drive space, and even many gigabytes of RAM. The operating system of choice for most servers is either Windows NT Server, Windows 2000, UNIX or Linux. For testing the multiplayer application in this book, however, my server was simply a Pentium III, 600MHz, with 256 MB RAM, running Windows 2000. This is because the server software is pretty simple and not very taxing on the computer. Large-scale servers, like web servers and database servers, tend to demand a lot of hardware power.

The core problem with this topic in general is the hardware requirements necessary for me to show any of it to you in action! In order for me to bring you into my multiplayer game, I require a server on a fast Internet pipe to be running 24/7. This is an expensive prospect, although the cost does seem to be falling, and not one that I personally can undertake. For this reason, virtually everything I talk about here is going to be theory; you *could* do this *if* you were running your own server.

Nevertheless, you can take my word that this stuff works – and works well. I have included the server application (which I wrote in Visual Basic) with this book, so if you are so inclined, and you have a fast Internet connection, you can run the server on your machine and play against your friends.

### Limitations

There are several limitations that have to be acknowledged and dealt with when we're creating a multiplayer client/server game.

- **Server Connection Speed**: The speed that our server connects to the outside world can make a big difference on the game's performance to people playing. For example, if we were hosting our server on a computer with only a 56k connection to the outside world, then that server would almost certainly be too slow to properly keep everyone's game synchronized (in real time). Most fast-paced game servers should have at least a cable or DSL connection. If we plan on running multiple servers to the same location, then we will probably need at least a T1 connection.

# Multiplayer Applications

- **Client Connection Speed**: On the other side, there's the client's connection speed. This will often slow down their game so much that it will be unplayable to them, though they will often blame the server, saying that it's "laggy". Lag is what happens when there is a slow-down in the connection and data takes extra time to get to the server or to the client. In this instance, the player's game will either become out of synch with everyone else's, or pause while it waits for resynchronization. In other cases, the game can be severely affected when entire packets are lost. Unfortunately, on occasion the data simply doesn't get through and gets lost somewhere in the Internet. This will cause the game to get dramatically out of synch on different machines.

- **Bandwidth**: When we're writing a game, we must keep the bandwidth in mind, that is the amount of data that is flying back and forth at any one time. If we have a game in which clients report their position to the server 60 times a second, then the bandwidth is likely to be huge. For example, let's say we have the following hypothetical packet on the players position:

    ```
    "1,p31,x200,y100,k1,k2,k3,k4,122,n40"
    ```

    ...coming and going 60 times a second - that's 35 bytes per packet, x 60 = 2,100 Bytes per second, x 2 (for it must send and receive) = 4,200 Bytes per second to one computer,

    This may not seem like a lot, but it must be maintained at a steady rate in order for the game to play properly, and modems often have trouble maintaining such a steady throughput. As more players join the game, this number will multiply.

    So, it's important to keep the bandwidth low wherever possible, and only send packets when we absolutely must.

- **Ping**: Pinging is a process by which distance is measured between two objects by sending out a signal, and seeing how long it takes to get back to you. Submarines used pinging to echolocate underwater objects in World War II. In modern terms, pinging a computer on the Internet is the process of determining how long it will take for a packet to reach the destination and for a packet to be returned. This can dramatically affect the game, as players with a high ping (or long return time) will become temporarily out of synch. Generally speaking, our ping increases the further we are (geographically) from the server. For that reason, it's a good idea to play on game servers that are at least in the same region as you (North America, Europe, Far East, etc,) and you may have seen host screens that ask you to choose your nearest server. It's a strange concept to consider when we're talking about communication over thousands of miles but it's also well worth remembering.

The bullet points above are all important things to consider. It may be starting to sound as if making a multiplayer game is more trouble than it's worth but once you have a multiplayer game up and running successfully, you'll be glad you did it. Being able to bring your audience into a real-time environment, where people will be able to meet and play your games together anytime, is a rewarding experience.

# 15 Flash Games Studio

## The Game

OK. Now we're going to look at all this principle in practice, and see how we can make a fantastic, socket-based, client/server multiplayer Flash game. This game is called *Radio Racer* and — you guessed it — it's a racing car game, in the style of the arcade classic, *Sprint*.

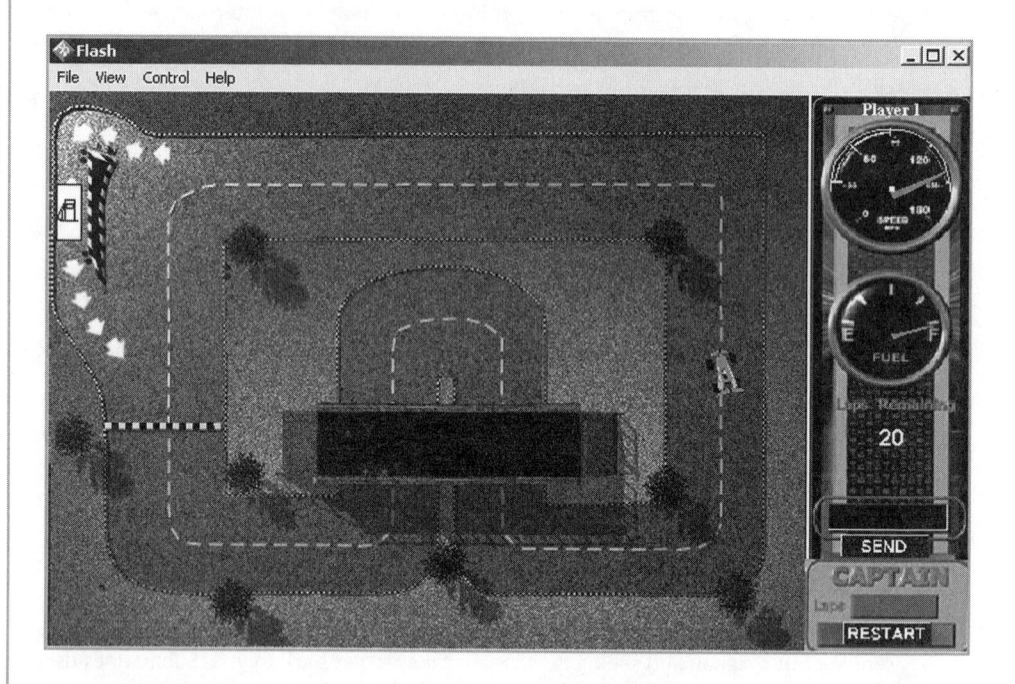

The idea behind *Radio Racer* is simple: You are driving a radio-controlled (RC) car around the track, and up to five other players can join, totaling six players maximum in one game.

The first player to join is known as the Captain and they have the power to restart the game, sending everyone back to the starting line, with a countdown in the center of the screen. As the players race, they can run out of fuel, and when they're empty, they must drive to the pit stop and fill up.

# Multiplayer Applications    15

# Game Screen

The game screen is comprises of two main areas:

- **The main game area where the actual track is located:**

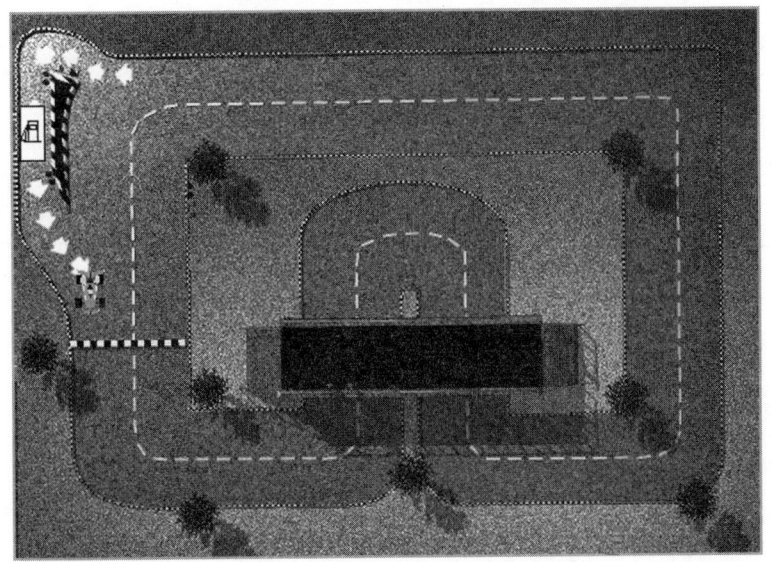

**The track**

- **The sidebar, which contains several key things:**

### The speedometer and fuel gauge:

These indicate the speed at which you are traveling, and also let you know when your car is going to run out of gas and need refueling.

### The Lap counter:

The lap counter tells you how many laps are remaining until you have completed the race.

### The chat box

In the chat box you can type messages to other players, and when you click 'send', the message will appear right next to the chatter's car, like so:

### The captain dialog box

Player 1 has the designation of being the captain, so they can start the race over when it has been won. The captain simply enters the desired number of laps in the new race, and then clicks 'restart'. This is an object with the instance name 'admin'.

## Control

The control in this game is performed with the cursor keys. The control is pretty much intuitive, and it follows the traditional overhead racing game template. The keys are:

- Up – Accelerate forward
- Down – Brake and accelerate backward
- Left – Turn/Steer left
- Right – Turn/Steer right

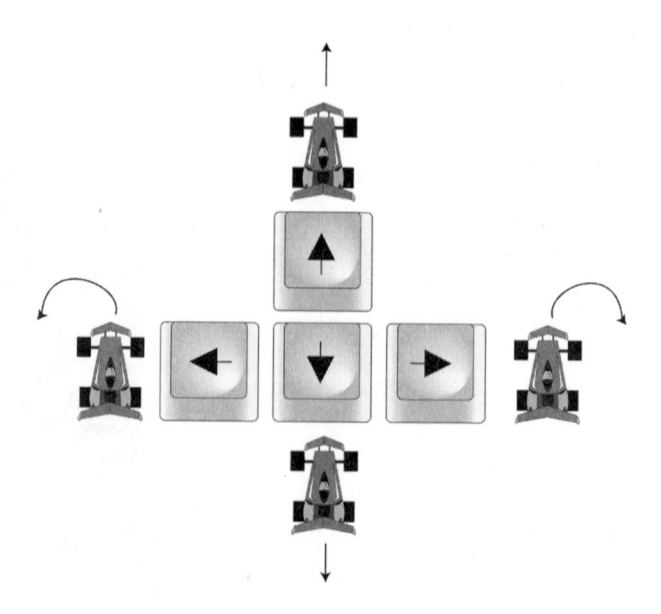

# Multiplayer Applications

As soon as a player joins the game, they are in race mode, and have twenty laps remaining. It will remain like this until the captain decides to start a new race, at which point everyone will be moved to the starting line with the same number of laps remaining. The captain decides the number of laps.

## Coding the Car Movement

Each car is controlled in an identical manner, so we'll just focus on the ActionScript for one car.

1. The movement of the car is achieved using a velocity/angle method of momentum. The player's speed and angle are converted in to x and y screen speeds, like so:

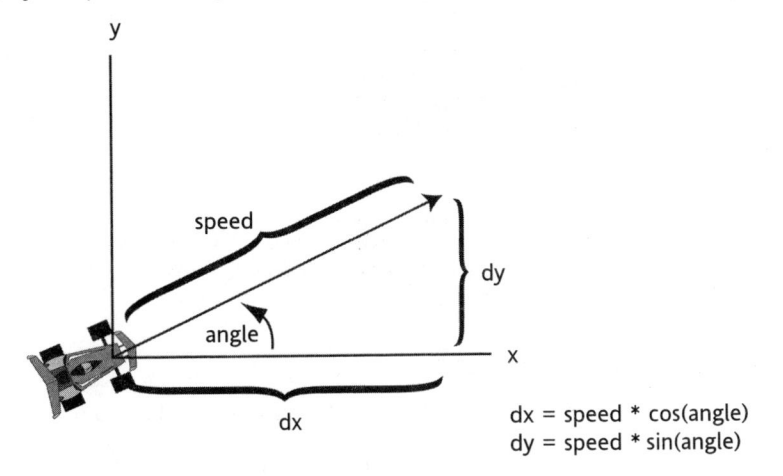

   dx = speed * cos(angle)
   dy = speed * sin(angle)

### Converting from angle/speed to square dx and dy

This is also known as converting polar coordinates to square coordinates and what it gives us is basically a vector value of the car's horizontal and vertical movement. The formula is quite simple, and each car has the following code attached to it:

```
dx = vel * Math.sin (ang);
dy = vel * Math.cos (ang);
```

2. Of course, for this to mean anything, vel and ang need to be controlled. This is done with the following code:

```
// Move if keys are pressed
if (key_Up)
{
        vel += 1;
}

if (key_Down)
{
```

# 15 Flash Games Studio

```
                vel -= 1;
        }

        if (key_Left && Math.abs(vel) > 0.1)
        {
                ang += .2;
        }

        if (key_Right && Math.abs(vel) > 0.1)
        {
                ang -= .2;
        }

        // The effect of Physics
        if (vel > maxspeed) vel = maxspeed;
        if (vel < -4) vel = -4;
```

As you can see, the arrow keys control `ang` and `vel`, which in turn are used to compute `dx` and `dy`.

3. We also make sure that the player doesn't accelerate faster than a speed called `maxspeed`. When going in reverse, we want to make sure that the player doesn't go faster than –4 (velocity of 4 in a backwards direction). In the car's `loadMovie` clip event, we set `maxspeed` to:

```
maxspeed = 12;
```

I found this to be a good speed that's neither too fast nor too slow.

4. Finally in each frame we add `dx` and `dy` to the car's current position. This means that we're controlling the car by accelerating, decelerating and steering:

```
_x += dx;
_y += dy;
```

5. Our actual checking of the keyboard occurs in the like this:

```
// Is this car me?
if (id == _root.myid)
{
        keychange = false;

        // Is key Pressed?
        if (Key.isDown(Key.UP) && key_Up == 0)
        {
                key_Up = 1;
                keychange = true;
        }
```

# Multiplayer Applications

```
    if (Key.isDown(Key.DOWN) && key_Down == 0)
    {
        key_Down = 1;
        keychange = true;
    }

    if (Key.isDown(Key.LEFT) && key_Left == 0)
    {
        key_Left = 1;
        keychange = true;
    }

    if (Key.isDown(Key.RIGHT) && key_Right == 0)
    {
        key_Right = 1;
        keychange = true;
    }

    // Is Key Released?
    if (!Key.isDown(Key.UP) && key_Up == 1)
    {
        key_Up = 0;
        keychange = true;
    }

    if (!Key.isDown(Key.DOWN) && key_Down == 1)
    {
        key_Down = 0;
        keychange = true;
    }

    if (!Key.isDown(Key.LEFT) && key_Left == 1)
    {
        key_Left = 0;
        keychange = true;
    }

    if (!Key.isDown(Key.RIGHT) && key_Right == 1)
    {
        key_Right = 0;
        keychange = true;
    }

}
```

With this code, we're simply setting flags (key_Down, key_Up, key_Left and key_Right) to 1 or 0, depending on whether the key is pressed or released. This code allows us to react only if a key has been pressed or released, and not worry about things in between.

# 15  Flash Games Studio

This way, we only need to send information to the server every time the player presses a key, which will dramatically reduce our bandwidth. As you'll see, our magic variable is `keychange`. This is a flag that tells the game that something has changed, and we must send the information to the server. You'll also see that the whole key control code is contained within `if (id == _root.myid)` but don't worry – we'll get to that later!

## Collision

We have three types of collision that can occur in this game:

- Car with grass
- Car with obstacle (tree, wall, bridge)
- Car with car

Each one, as you would expect, is done in a slightly different way.

### Colliding with Grass

When the car runs off the road and onto the grass, we want it to slow down and almost come to a stop. This is the penalty for running off the track. We include this for two reasons. Firstly to discourage cheating in the form of taking shortcuts, and secondly to reward handling skill. Our grass collision is based on the fact that the entire road is own movie clip called roadsurface.

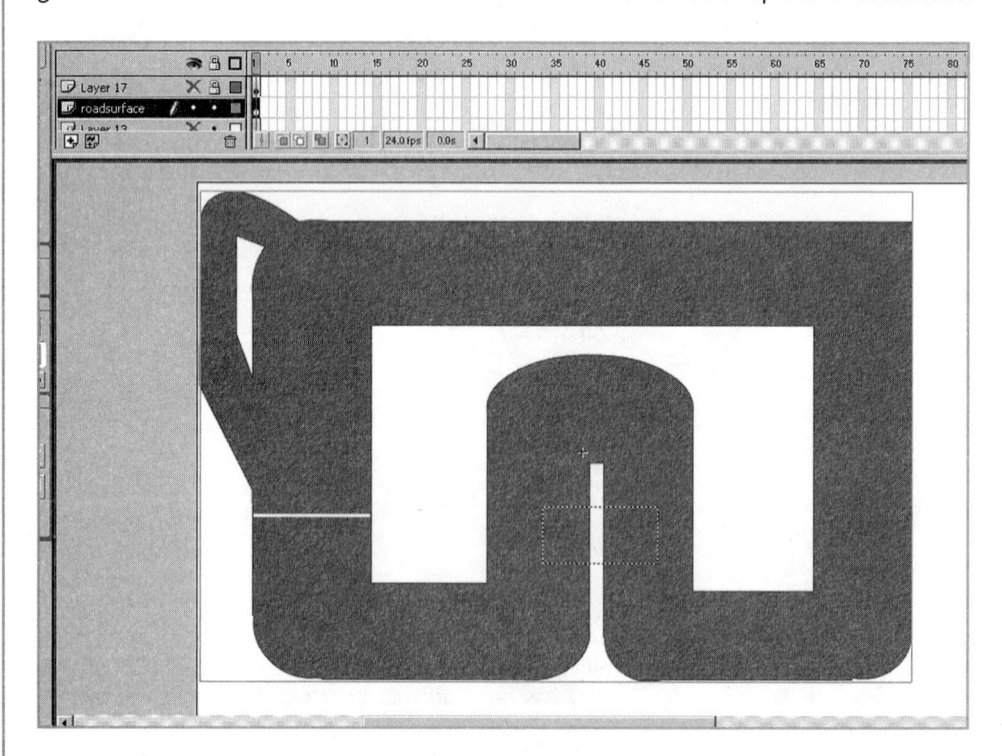

# Multiplayer Applications 15

The roadsurface movie clip simply exists for its shape – the road graphic is on another layer. In each frame, a hitTest is performed on the roadsurface to see whether the player is in contact with it or not. If the hitTest returns true, then the player may continue as planned. If the hitTest returns false, then the player has left the track and we change the maxspeed to 2. This is performed in the code below.

```
// Hitting grass?
if (!_root.roadsurface.hittest(_x, _y, true) && on_Road == 1)
{
    on_Road = 0;
    maxspeed = 2;
    keychange = true;
}

// Not hitting grass?
if (_root.roadsurface.hittest(_x, _y, true) && on_Road == 0)
{
    on_Road = 1;
    maxspeed = 12;
    keychange = true;
}
```

By issuing the command !_root.roadsurface.hittest(_x, _y, true) within the car movie clip, we are checking to see if there is *not* (the ! mark) a hitTest on the roadsurface at the car's _x and _y position (the nose of the car).

If this is the case, then we have run off the grass. The keychange flag is used to tell the game when to send a position packet to the server, but I'll get into that in a little while. We use the on_Road flag so that we only report this collision when we actually leave or enter the track – not every single frame.

## Obstacles

The track has several obstacles on it – trees, a footbridge and a wall near the pit stop. Here's a look at the obstacles layer:

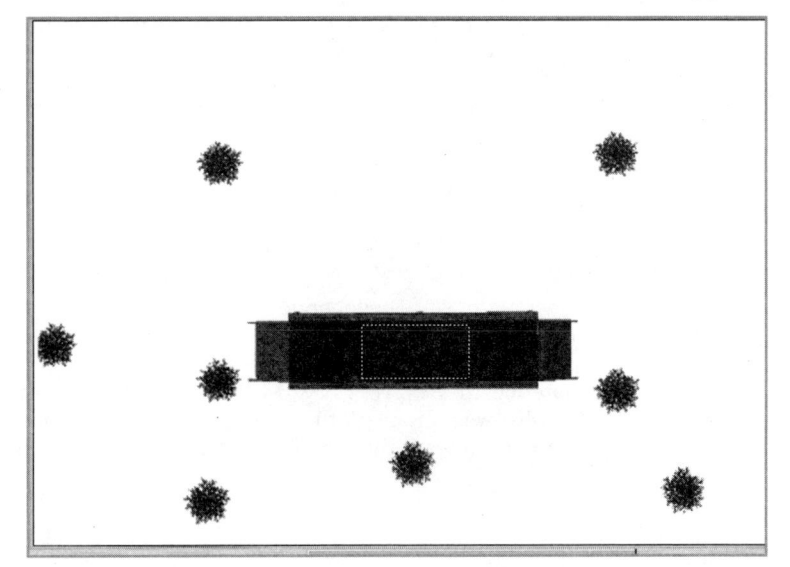

## 15　Flash Games Studio

However, these are only graphics. On a separate layer, there is another movie clip called collide and it is filled simply with solid shapes that correspond to the objects on the obstacles layer, like so:

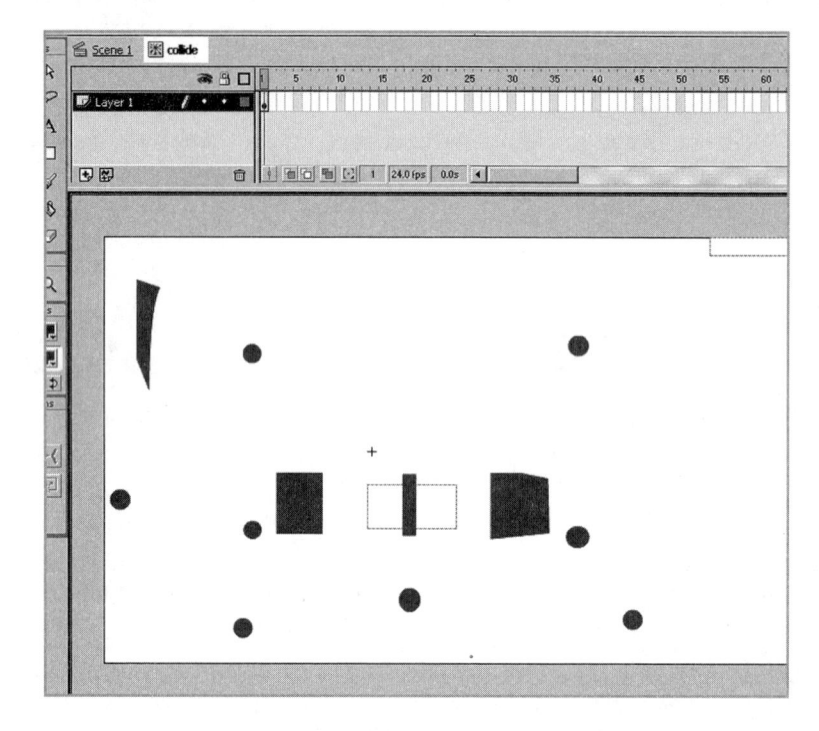

As the player drives around, we do a hitTest on the collide movie clip (often called a collision map) to see if they have hit any of the solid shapes, and therefore have appeared to hit any of the objects on the obstacles layer. The code to do this is relatively simple:

```
        if (id == _root.myid && _root.collide.hittest(_x + dx, _y +
dx, true))
        {
            key_Up = 0;
            key_Down = 0;
            vel = -2;
            dx = vel * Math.sin (ang);
            dy = vel * Math.cos (ang);
            keychange = true;
        }
```

Again, ignore the id == _root.myid for now – that's multiplayer code, and I'll be explaining it shortly. So, what we do is check to see if there's a collision, not at (_x, _y), but at (_x + dx, _y+dy). We want to see if the car will be hitting anything the *next* time we move it.

# Multiplayer Applications

If a collision is reported, we simply 'release' the up and down keys so the player won't continue to bounce into the obstacle, and then we set the `vel` to −2, effectively making the car roll backwards as if it has hit the object and bounced. Once this change has been made, we need to recalculate `dx` and `dy` based on the new `vel`. We also set the flag `keychange` to true, so this collision is sent to the server.

## Shadows

We achieve a nice effect in this game by using shadows of objects like the trees and the bridge. When a car passes into a shadow, the shadow appears *above* the player, because the shadows are simply on a higher layer.

Because the shadows are simply black with a 50% alpha transparency on them we are able to see the cars through the shadow (the shadows darken parts of the car) truly giving us the illusion that the shadows are real.

## Other Cars

When you're playing against other players, and two cars hit, we want this collision to be reflected on the screen and to send both cars off track as a penalty for not being careful. The code for this is shown in full below:

```
if (getTimer() > hitTimer)
{
    for (i = 1; i < 7; i++)
    {
        if (i != _root.myid)
        {
            xd = Math.abs(eval("_root.guy" add i)._x - _x);
            yd = Math.abs(eval("_root.guy" add i)._y - _y);
            if (xd < 20 && yd < 20 && eval("_root.guy" add i)._visible)
            {
                hittimer = getTimer() + 4000;
                vel = 14;
                ang = eval("_root.guy" add i).ang - .8;
                keychange = true;
            }
        }
    }
}
```

# 15   Flash Games Studio

Here we are looping through each car and checking to see how close they are to us. If a car is within 20 pixels on x and y then we fire off at an angle relative to them, and our speed is increased to 14.

We're also then setting a variable called `hitTimer` to `(getTimer + 4000)`. This is used to ensure that we have at least four seconds (4000 milliseconds) of invulnerability from other hits. This gives us a chance to try and get back in the game. We check for this at the beginning of the collision check with:

```
if (getTimer() > hitTimer)
```

This will be true if `getTimer` has exceeded what `hitTimer` was set to four seconds ago, which was `getTimer + 4000`. In exactly 4000 milliseconds, `hitTimer` will be equal to `getTimer`.

No Collision

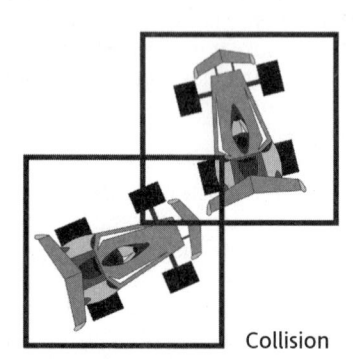

Collision

`xd` and `yd` are simply the distance between our car and the car we are checking. If `xd` is less than 20 and `yd` is less than 20, then we are assuming the cars have hit each other. We're also checking to make sure that the car is `_visible`, or in other words that the car is in the game!

We set `keyChange` to `true` so that our client will send through a new location/direction packet to the server.

## Nodes

As we navigate around the track, we must complete a full run before the lap counter decreases. This means that we must have a way of monitoring the player's progress and ensuring that they have indeed completed a lap. We do this using **nodes** – areas of collision that are used to determine the player's progress.

# Multiplayer Applications

On the main timeline, there is a layer called nodes and it looks like this:

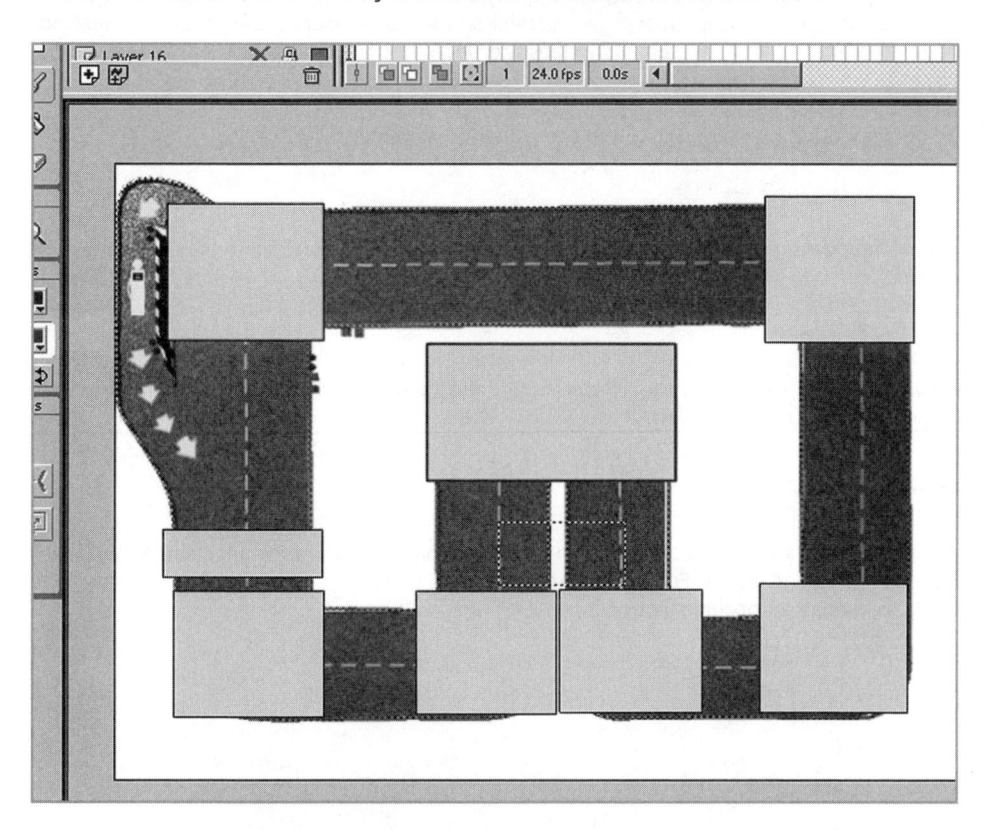

Each green square is a node – a movie clip with the instance names: node1, node2, node3, etc ... up to node8. At the beginning of the game, there is a variable called mynode, which is set to the number '1'. When we pass through the node named ("node" add mynode) then mynode is incremented, and the next node becomes the active node. Once we have passed through each node in order, we have completed a lap. Take a look at the following code:

```
if (eval("_root.node" add _root.mynode).hittest(_x, _y, false))
{
    _root.mynode++;
    if (_root.mynode > _root.numnodes)
    {
        _root.mynode = 1;
        if (—remaininglaps == 1)
            _root.stat.laps = "Last Lap";
        else
            _root.stat.laps = remaininglaps;
```

We're simply performing a `hitTest` with the current node, and if so, we increment `mynode`. If we've passed through all the nodes (`_root.mynode > _root.numnodes`) then our next node is brought back to 1, and our remaining laps are decreased. If it's our last lap, the lap counter displays the words Last Lap.

We're decrementing `remainingLaps` in the actual `if` statement itself with

`if (--remaininglaps == 1)`

Which means, "decrement `remainingLaps` and then do the `if` statement with the new value." If we said...

```
if (remaininglaps-- == 1)
```

...then we would be saying "do the `if` statement, and then decrement `remainingLaps`". So the order here is obviously important.

## Multiple Cars

On the stage, there are six identical cars, and each one has a different instance name guy1, guy2, guy3, guy4, guy5 and guy6. (Forgive the gender-biased naming; it was arbitrary and now it's too daunting to change all occurrences of it.)

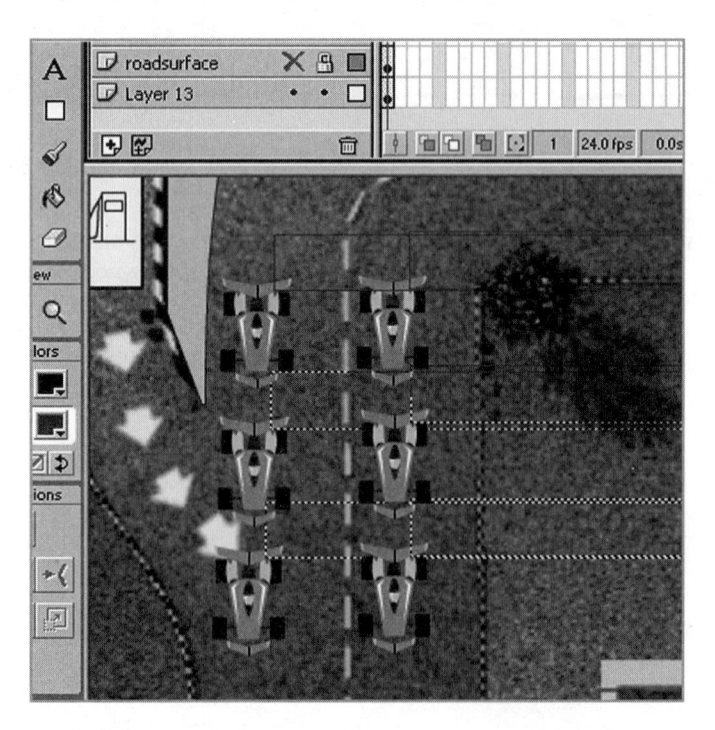

# Multiplayer Applications

Now, earlier I showed how our car simply has a speed and an angle, and that that determines our movement on each frame. Well, each car actually has identical ActionScript. They use keyboard input to determine changes in angle and speed, and these are reflected on screen.

But how do we use the keyboard to control six cars? Well, we don't. Simply put, the incoming packets from other players include the current state of their keyboard. Basically, our opponents are controlling their cars with their keyboards and this is updated on your screen, and on theirs.

So, when an opponent presses the up arrow key and begins accelerating, that key press will be sent, via the server, to you, and their car will begin to accelerate on your screen. When that same opponent releases the accelerate key, another message will be sent through to you (via the server) telling you that the player has stopped pressing the key, and then your client will make them slow down on your screen.

Each car moves identically so each client will see the cars in the same location at the same speed.

Theoretically, we could simply send each player's position to every other player 20 or 30 times per second, and not worry about key presses and acceleration. However, we want to reduce bandwidth, and we also want your opponent's car to continue moving even if we stop receiving packets from them. We don't want them to appear to freeze on screen.

There's an important global variable called `_root.myid` that I told you to ignore earlier. Well, this variable will be set to 1, 2, 3, 4, 5, or 6, and it is a number that tells your client which car is yours. This is important because that is the car that your client will direct your key presses to. However, the server must assign you this number because only the server will know which slot is free. If you were to set `_root.myid` to 2 and the server were to be sending you packets from player 2, then you and your opponent would be fighting for control of the same car!

The main key control code I showed you earlier was contained within:

```
// Is this car me?
if (id == _root.myid)
{

    ...

}
```

.....where each car contains a local variable called `id`, a number from 1 to 6 depending upon which car it is. That variable is simply set in each car's `loadMovie` clip event, like so:

```
onClipEvent(load)
{
    ...
    id = 1;
    ...
}
```

This is the code in `guy1`. It differs for each other car to be `id=2`, `id=3`, `id=4`, `id=5` or `id=6`.

# 15  Flash Games Studio

As the server sends us information about the speed, angle and key state of the other cars, our client updates the car movie clips on our screen, and they magically behave in a controlled manner – driving around the screen as our opponents control them.

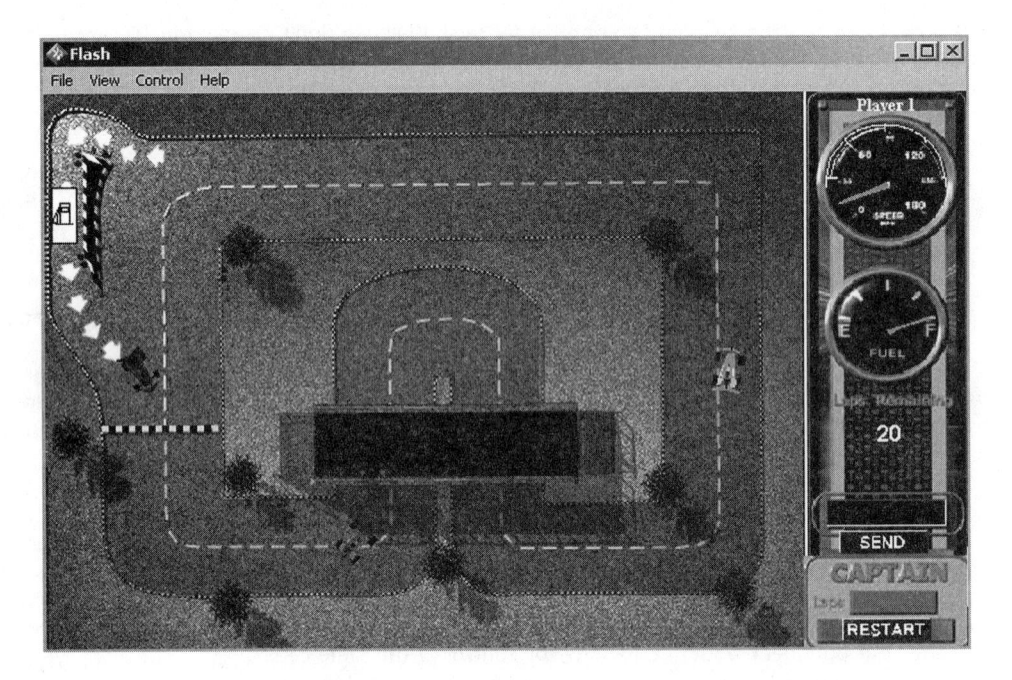

## Packets and Communication in our Game

Throughout this game, there are several occasions where the client talks to the server and vice versa. The messages will vary depending on the event. Here's the list of events:

- Login – When the player joins the game from the splash screen.

- Key Press – When the player hits up, down, left or right and changes their speed or angle.

- Player Collisions – When the player collides with the grass, a stationary obstacle or another player.

- Player runs out of fuel – When a player runs out of fuel, their `maxspeed` is set to 2, and that event is sent to the other players.

- Chat – When the player sends a chat message through to the other players.

- Captain Restart – When the captain restarts the game.

# Multiplayer Applications    15

The server will send packets to the clients based on different events as well:

- When a player logs in. Server will send new player information to every other client. Server will also send the newly logged-in player an ID number. The client will use this ID number to decide which on-screen car is their own, and hence give the player control over it.

- When a player moves or collides. Server will send new player's position, speed and key state to every other client.

- Chat message. When a player sends a chat message, the server will relay that message to every other client.

- When a player disconnects/is no longer present. The server will tell every other client that the player is gone, and the client will make that player invisible.

The communication packets vary depending on their function.

# Client Packets

Let's have a look at the actual make-up of some of these packets. Below are the packets sent from the client to the server.

**General Position Packet:**
This is triggered by up key, down key, left key, right key, collision and fuel depletion.

```
p, x location, y location, velocity, angle, key_Up, key_Down,
key_Left, key_Right, maxspeed, remaininglaps.
```

As an example, let's say a player was at position (30, 40) that they had a speed of 8, and an angle of 3. Let's also say that their max speed is 12 and that they have 9 remaining laps. This packet will be triggered by the player pressing down on the left arrow key (key_Left = 1), and also already pressing down on the accelerate key (key_Up = 1). Now we have all this information, we simply need to put it in the appropriate place in the packet. Our packet would look like this:

```
p,30,40,8,3,1,0,1,0,12,9
```

That's it! That packet will tell the server where the player is.

**Login Packet**
This is sent after a player has successfully logged in, and the server has returned an ID number to them.

```
l, x location, y location, velocity, angle, key_Up, key_Down,
key_Left, key_Right, maxspeed, remaininglaps.
```

This is identical to the general position packet, except it starts with the letter l for Login instead of p for Position.

```
l,30,40,8,3,1,0,1,0,12,9
```

### Chat Packet
This is sent after player enters text in the chat box and clicks send, or when the player completes a lap ("x laps remaining" is sent).

```
t,message
```

If a player says "Hello", then the following packet will be sent to the server:

```
t,Hello
```

### Restart Packet
This is sent by the captain, this packet makes the server tell every other client to restart:

```
r,laps
```

If the captain chooses to restart the game with 20 laps, then the following packet is sent to the server:

```
r,20
```

## Server Packets

These are the packets sent from the server to the client.

### Client Position Packets
When the server receives a position packet from a client, it sends the following packet out to each of the other connected clients:

```
P, idnumber, x location, y location, velocity, angle, key_Up,
key_Down, key_Left, key_Right, maxspeed, remaininglaps.
```

It's very similar to the player position packet, except it uses an uppercase P to indicate to us (the designer) that it is a server packet. It doesn't matter to Flash because it will never confuse incoming and outgoing packets. It also adds an idnumber to the beginning of the packet so the client knows which car to update on screen with this new position information.

### Connection ID Packet
When a client successfully uses the XMLSocket.connect command and connects to the server, the server will then send the client a connection packet, which contains an ID number for the client to use in knowing which car to control.

```
ID,idnumber
```

# Multiplayer Applications   15

When a player connects, the server checks through its list of active players and sees if any slots are free. If all six slots are full, then the connection request is simply denied. However, if it finds, for example, that the third slot is empty because someone disconnected, or it has simply not yet been filled, it will send this ID packet:

    ID,3

Immediately after the client has connected it will send a login packet to the server (see client packets), and then the server will send a client position packet to all other players.

## Disconnect Packet

When a client disconnects or drops out of the game, then the server will alert all the other clients of this by sending a disconnect packet which is simply:

    C,idnumber

So, if Player 3 leaves the game, then the server will send the following packet to each player:

    C,3

## Chat Packet

When a client sends a chat message to the server, the server will forward that message on to every other player with the following packet:

    T,idnumber,message

The server sends an idnumber so the receiving clients will know which car to draw the message next to. If Player 1 says "Hello everyone", then the server will send the following packet to each client:

    T,1,Hello everyone

## Restart Packet

When the captain tells the server to reset the game, the server will respond by sending a reset packet to every other client:

    R,laps

So, if Player 1 (the captain) restarts the game with 50 laps, the server will send the following packet to every other client:

    R,50

# 15 Flash Games Studio

## The Socket Object

On our main timeline, there is a movie clip with the instance name comm. It's this movie clip that we will be doing our socket communication through. The comm movie clip is like our dispatch – it receives messages from the server and handles them appropriately.

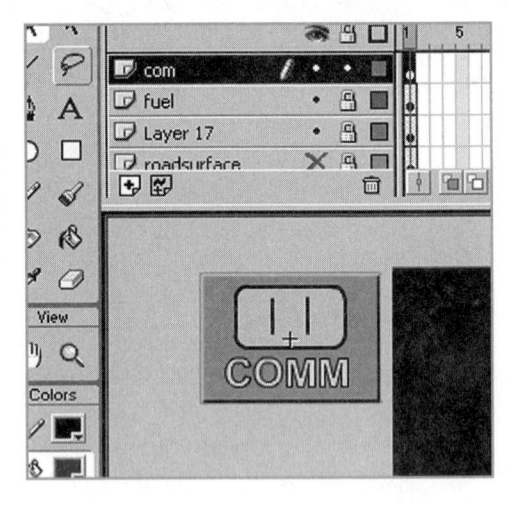

Within the comm movie clip we declare an XMLSocket object with the following code in the load clipEvent:

```
sock = new XMLSocket();
sock.onXML = myOnXML;
sock.onConnect = myOnConnect;
```

sock is our conduit to the outside world. Through it we send and receive packets. We have two functions, myOnXML and myOnConnect. They are coded as follows.

### Building the myOnConnect Script

1. The myOnConnect script consists of the following code:

```
function myOnConnect(success)
{
        // Initialize
        laps = 20;
        _root.fuel = 1800;
        _root.mynode = 1;
        _root.numnodes = 8;
        _root.stat.laps = laps;

        // Did we connect successfully?
        if (success)
        {
                _root.status = "Connected";
                _root.comm.connectstat = true;
        }
        else
```

# Multiplayer Applications

```
            {
                    _root.status = "Failed";
                    _root.myid = 1;
                    eval("_root.guy" add _root.myid)._visible = true;
                    _root.status = "Player " add _root.myid;
                    _root.stat.admin._visible = true;
            }
            eval("_root.guy" add _root.myid).remaininglaps = laps;
    }
```

Let's look at this in more detail.

2. `myOnConnect` is called only once when our `sock` object receives a `connect` event from the server, or when it times out (the server doesn't respond).

   ```
   function myOnConnect(success)
       {
               // Initialize
   ```

3. If a server doesn't respond, it could be offline, or the client's Internet connection could be down. It's important to verify that the server is running before we try to connect.

4. When `myOnConnect` is called, several variables are set including fuel level, the current node (for your progress around the track), the total number of nodes (so you know when you've completed a lap), and the total number of laps in the race.

   ```
   laps = 20;
               _root.fuel = 1800;
               _root.mynode = 1;
               _root.numnodes = 8;
               _root.stat.laps = laps;
   ```

5. Next, we check to see the value of the success variable, which is automatically passed in by the `sock` object. If success is `true` then we are connected, and we must wait for the server to send through an ID packet. A variable called `connectStat` is set to `true` – indicating that we are indeed connected. This will be used later on.

   ```
   // Did we connect successfully?
               if (success)
               {
                       _root.status = "Connected";
                       _root.comm.connectstat = true;
               }
   ```

6. If for some reason success is `false` (for example the server rejected the connection request because the game was already full), then the client will initiate a local-mode version of the game. It automatically sets `_root.myid` to 1, so that we are controlling car number 1, makes that car `visible` and updates the sidebar to say Player 1.

# 15  Flash Games Studio

```
            else
                    {
                            _root.status = "Failed";
                            _root.myid = 1;
                            eval("_root.guy" add _root.myid)._visible = true;
                            _root.status = "Player " add _root.myid;
```

7. Finally, we make the captain box (instance name `admin`) visible so we can restart the races when they're over.

```
    _root.stat.admin._visible = true;
                    }
                    eval("_root.guy" add _root.myid).remaininglaps = laps;
            }
```

That's the whole of `myOnConnect`.

Next we'll look at `myOnXML`. This is the function that is automatically called whenever a packet arrives from the server. There's the code in full.

```
            function myOnXML(doc)
            {
                    f = new String(doc);
                    j = f.split(",");

                    // ID Packet, returned after login
                    if (j[0] == "ID")
                    {
                            _root.myid = j[1];
                            if (_root.myid == 1)
                                    _root.stat.admin._visible = true;
                            eval("_root.guy" add j[1])._visible = true;
                            _root.status = "Player " add _root.myid;

                                    st = "1," add Math.floor(eval("_root.guy" add
            j[1])._x) add "," add Math.floor(eval("_root.guy" add j[1])._y)
            add "," add Math.floor(eval("_root.guy" add j[1]).vel) add ","
            add eval("_root.guy" add j[1]).ang add "," add eval("_root.guy"
            add j[1]).key_Up add "," add eval("_root.guy" add j[1]).key_Down
            add "," add eval("_root.guy" add j[1]).key_Left add "," add
            eval("_root.guy" add j[1]).key_Right add "," add eval("_root.guy"
            add j[1]).maxspeed add "," add eval("_root.guy" add
            j[1]).remaininglaps add ",";

                                    if (_root.comm.connectstat)
                                    {
                                            _root.comm.sock.send(st);
                                    }
```

# Multiplayer Applications

```
                }
                else if (j[0] == "P")
                {
                        // Player position packet
                        i = j[1];
                        eval("_root.guy" add i)._visible = true;
                        eval("_root.guy" add i)._x = j[2];
                        eval("_root.guy" add i)._y = j[3];

                        eval("_root.guy" add i).vel = Number(j[4]);
                        eval("_root.guy" add i).ang = Number(j[5]);

                        eval("_root.guy" add i).key_Up = Number(j[6]);
                        eval("_root.guy" add i).key_Down =
➥Number(j[7]);
                        eval("_root.guy" add i).key_Left =
➥Number(j[8]);
                        eval("_root.guy" add i).key_Right =
➥Number(j[9]);

                        eval("_root.guy" add i).maxspeed =
➥Number(j[10]);
                        eval("_root.guy" add i).remaininglaps =
➥Number(j[11]);

                }
                else if (j[0] == "C")
                {
                        // Disconnect Packet
                        i = j[1];
                        eval("_root.guy" add i)._visible = false;
                }
                else if (j[0] == "T")
                {
                        // Chat Packet
                        i = j[1];
                        msg = j[2];
                        eval("_root.guy" add i).chatclear = getTimer()
➥+ 5000;
                        eval("_root.guy" add i).msgmc.msg = msg;
                }
                else if (j[0] == "R")
                {
                        // Reset Packet
                        _root.comm.laps = j[1];
                        _root.restart1 = true;
                        _root.restart2 = true;
                        _root.restart3 = true;
                        _root.restart4 = true;
                        _root.restart5 = true;
```

*continues overleaf*

# 15  Flash Games Studio

```
                    _root.restart6 = true;
            }
    }
```

Pretty daunting, eh? I think we ought to break it down a little.

## Breaking down the myOnXML script

The `myOnXML` script is the meat and potatoes of the game's communication center. It's here that we handle all incoming packets. As you can see, most of the above code is in the form of `if ... else` statements that determine what type of packet has been sent and carry out actions accordingly.

1. The first thing we do is take the incoming packet, which will be in a string called `doc`, and use the `String.split` function to split it up into an array called, simply, `j`. The split function works by taking a delimiter (in this case, a comma) and breaking up a string (at the delimiter) into sub-strings in an array.

   ```
   function myOnXML(doc)
       {
           f = new String(doc);
           j = f.split(",");
   ```

   Once this is done, `j[0]` will contain the first element in our packet – the packet type. These are from the server so `j[0]` will be either ID, P, C, T, or R.

### Packet Type ID

2. If the packet is an ID packet, then the second element `j[1]` will be the actual ID number, and we assign it to `_root.myid`. This is now the car that we are controlling. We then make that car visible and write Player num in the sidebar.

   ```
   // ID Packet, returned after login
       if (j[0] == "ID")
       {
           _root.myid = j[1];
           if (_root.myid == 1)
               _root.stat.admin._visible = true;
           eval("_root.guy" add j[1])._visible = true;
           _root.status = "Player " add _root.myid;
   ```

3. Next, we put together a very long string called `st`:

   ```
   st = "1," add Math.floor(eval("_root.guy" add j[1])._x) add ","
   add Math.floor(eval("_root.guy" add j[1])._y) add "," add
   Math.floor(eval("_root.guy" add j[1]).vel) add "," add
   eval("_root.guy" add j[1]).ang add "," add eval("_root.guy" add
   ```

# Multiplayer Applications 15

```
j[1]).key_Up add "," add eval("_root.guy" add j[1]).key_Down add
"," add eval("_root.guy" add j[1]).key_Left add "," add
eval("_root.guy" add j[1]).key_Right add "," add eval("_root.guy"
add j[1]).maxspeed add "," add eval("_root.guy" add
j[1]).remaininglaps add ",";
```

This creates a login packet that contains all the necessary items about your newly created car – specifically velocity, location, key state, max speed and remaining laps.

4. Once this string has been compiled, it's sent to the server with the following code:

```
if (_root.comm.connectstat)
{
    _root.comm.sock.send(st);
}
```

We're checking to see a connection is indeed present (if `connectstat` is true) and if so, we use the `XMLSocket`'s `send` function to send the packet through the socket to the server. This command is important, and we use it in several locations throughout the game.

## Packet Type P

5. Continuing along with the packet checking – if `j[0]` is `"P"`, we know this packet is a player position packet, and that `j[1]` is the player's ID. So we set `i` to be that ID, and then we set all the various properties about the car (x, y, speed, angle, key state, max speed and remaining laps). Once all this information is set, the car will behave exactly as it is on the screen of the opponent from whom it came.

```
else if (j[0] == "P")
{
    // Player position packet
    i = j[1];
    eval("_root.guy" add i)._visible = true;
    eval("_root.guy" add i)._x = j[2];
    eval("_root.guy" add i)._y = j[3];

    eval("_root.guy" add i).vel = Number(j[4]);
    eval("_root.guy" add i).ang = Number(j[5]);

    eval("_root.guy" add i).key_Up = Number(j[6]);
    eval("_root.guy" add i).key_Down = Number(j[7]);
    eval("_root.guy" add i).key_Left = Number(j[8]);
    eval("_root.guy" add i).key_Right = Number(j[9]);

    eval("_root.guy" add i).maxspeed = Number(j[10]);
    eval("_root.guy" add i).remaininglaps = Number(j[11]);

}
```

## Flash Games Studio

**Packet Type C**

6. If we receive a C as the packet type, we know that this is a disconnect packet, and we simply make the player with the passed ID (in `j[1]`) invisible.

    ```
    else if (j[0] == "C")
            {
                    // Disconnect Packet
                    i = j[1];
                    eval("_root.guy" add i)._visible = false;
            }
    ```

**Packet Type T**

7. We receive a T as the packet type, then we know that this is a chat packet, so we handle it appropriately. The first thing we do is assign the sender's ID to `i`, and then we store the message itself in a variable called `msg`.

    ```
    else if (j[0] == "T")
            {
                    // Chat Packet
                    i = j[1];
        msg = j[2];
    ```

8. Next, we must set two variables that are local to the sender's car: `chatclear` and `msgmc.msg`:

    ```
    eval("_root.guy" add i).chatclear = getTimer() + 5000;
    eval("_root.guy" add i).msgmc.msg = msg;
    ```

    `chatclear` is a number that is used to decide how long to keep the chat message visible next to the sender's car before it vanishes. It is set to `getTimer() + 5000`, which is 5 seconds from the moment it is received.

    Attached to each car is a movie clip called `msgmc`. Inside this movie clip is a textbox called `msg`. When the chat arrives, we set this text box to equal the contents of the incoming message.

9. Inside each car's `enterFrame clipEvent`, the following code can be found:

    ```
    if (getTimer() > chatclear) msgmc.msg = "";
    ```

    This simply clears the chat message away when the `chatclear` variable has been reached – the 5 seconds have passed.

10. There's also another interesting piece of code in each car's `enterFrame clipEvent`:

    ```
    msgmc._rotation = -_rotation;
    ```

    What this does is rotate the `msgmc` to be the opposite angle of the car. This has the simple effect of always making the text appear upright, no matter what direction the car is facing.

# Multiplayer Applications

**Packet Type R**

11. Finally, the last packet type is a reset/restart packet type. Passed along with the R in `j[0]` is the number of laps to reset to, in `j[1]`. All we do is set the global lap counter, `_root.comm.laps` to this number, and then we set 6 global flag variables `restart1`, `restart2`, `restart3`, `restart4`, `restart5` and `restart6` to true.

    ```
    else if (j[0] == "R")
            {
                    // Reset Packet
                    _root.comm.laps = j[1];
                    _root.restart1 = true;
                    _root.restart2 = true;
                    _root.restart3 = true;
                    _root.restart4 = true;
                    _root.restart5 = true;
                    _root.restart6 = true;
            }
    ```

12. These variables are checked by the corresponding car each frame, and if set to true, then the car runs the following code:

    ```
    g = getTimer();

    if (eval("_root.restart" add id) == true)
    {
        _x = sx;
        _y = sy;
        vel = 0;
        ang = 0;
        _rotation = 0;
        key_Up = 0;
        key_Down = 0;
        key_Left = 0;
        key_Right = 0;
        _root.waitstart = g + 5000;
        _root.fuel = 1800;
        _root.mynode = 1;
        remaininglaps = Number(_root.comm.laps);
        eval("_root.restart" add id) = false;
    }
    ```

    This simply moves the car back to it's starting position (`sx`, `sy`), sets the velocity and angle to 0, resets all the keys, refills the fuel, resets the current node in the lap progress and resets the `remaininglaps` to equal the number that was passed by the server, and put in `_root.comm.laps`. Finally, we turn off the restart flag, by setting it to `false`.

13. There is one more thing: we have a variable called _root.waitstart. This is a counter that determines how long we have before the race begins – during this countdown the player cannot move. It's set to 5 seconds (g + 5000).

    Within the car's `enterFrame` `clipEvent`, we have the following `if` statement that surrounds the entire code:

    ```
    if (_root.waitstart < g)
    {
        ...
        ++Car control and movement code++
        ...
    }
    else
    {
        _root.countdown = Math.floor(Math.abs(_root.waitstart - g) /
    ➥1000) + 1;
    }
    ```

    This will mean that as long as `waitstart` is more than `getTimer`, we are frozen, and we should display the number of seconds remaining in a text box called `_root.countdown`. This means that the text box will display 5, then 4, then 3, then 2, then 1, and then the race will begin (`waitstart` will then be less than g).

That's it! That's our whole `myOnXML` function. Using this code, all the incoming packets are deciphered and appropriately handled. Quite a journey but hopefully you've made it in one piece.

## Login and Connection

When the player first loads the game, they are met with an introduction splash screen. On this screen are several items including:

- The title – Radio Racer
- Keyboard controls and chat instructions
- Server IP and port boxes
- Connect button
- Play Local button

# Multiplayer Applications 15

It is from this screen that we choose how we're going to play the game. If we want to play multiplayer on a server that we know of, then we enter the IP of the server and the port upon which the game is playing, and then click Connect.

## Connect Button Code

The following code is attached to the Connect button:

```
on (release)
{
    _quality = "LOW";
    _root.status = "Connecting...";
    _root.comm.sock.connect(ipaddress, serverport);
    _visible = false;
}
```

Once Connect has been pressed then we set the game visuals to low quality so that the game will run faster. We also display the words "Connecting..." in a text box on the stage called status. We then attempt to connect using the connect function of the XMLSocket object, with:

```
_root.comm.sock.connect(ipaddress, serverport);
```

# 15  Flash Games Studio

`ipaddress` and `serverport` are both the textfield variables that are on the login screen. You must set these values to match the actual IP address that your server is running on, and the port that you have selected to have the server listen on.

Once the connect request has been sent, the login screen is made invisible with the `_visible = false` command. Control is now handed off to our `sock` object, which will handle the `onConnect` response in our `myOnConnect` function outlined earlier.

## Play Local Code

If we want to simply drive around the track by ourselves as Player 1 (the captain) then we simply click on Play Local and the game will quickly begin. The following code is attached to the Play Local button.

```
on (release)
{
    laps = 20;
    _root.fuel = 1800;
    _root.mynode = 1;
    _root.numnodes = 8;
    _root.stat.laps = laps;
    _root.status = "Playing Locally";
    _root.myid = 1;
    eval("_root.guy" add _root.myid)._visible = true;
    eval("_root.guy" add _root.myid).remaininglaps = laps;
    _root.status = "Player " add _root.myid;
    _root.stat.admin._visible = true;
    _visible = false;
    _quality = "LOW";
}
```

This simply does all the same things that a failed connection would do: sets laps to 20, fills up the fuel, sets our current track node to 1, and the number of nodes to 8. We make `_root.myid` equal to 1 so that we are controlling Player 1 (the captain). Finally, we hide the login screen and set the game visuals to low quality.

## The Car Control Code in Full

We've already covered most of it, but here is the complete code for control of the cars. This code is identical for each car, whether it's yours or an opponent's:

# Multiplayer Applications 15

```
onClipEvent (enterFrame)
{

g = getTimer();

if (eval("_root.restart" add id) == true)
{

    // Reset the game
    _x = sx;
    _y = sy;
    vel = 0;
    ang = 0;
    _rotation = 0;
    key_Up = 0;
    key_Down = 0;
    key_Left = 0;
    key_Right = 0;
    _root.waitstart = g + 5000;
    _root.fuel = 1800;
    _root.mynode = 1;
    remaininglaps = Number(_root.comm.laps);
    eval("_root.restart" add id) = false;
}

if (_root.waitstart < g)
{

    // Clear the countdown text field on the stage.
    _root.countdown = "";

    // Is this car me?
    if (id == _root.myid)
    {

        // Set the speed needle to indicate my speed
        _root.stat.speedneedle._rotation = (Math.abs(vel) *
14) - 20;

        // Set the fuel guage needle to show my fuel
        _root.stat.fuelneedle._rotation =
➥(Math.abs(_root.fuel) / 10);

        // Display my number of laps remaining in the side
bar
        _root.stat.laps = remaininglaps;

        // Diminish fuel based on current speed
        _root.fuel -= (Math.abs(vel) + 1) / 10;
```

# 15  Flash Games Studio

```
                        if (_root.fuelpad.hittest(_x, _y, false))
                        {
                                maxspeed = 12;
                                if (_root.fuel < 1800)
                                        _root.fuel += 4;
                        }

                        keychange = false;

                        // Is key Pressed?
                        if (Key.isDown(Key.UP) && key_Up == 0)
                        {
                                key_Up = 1;
                                keychange = true;
                        }

                        if (Key.isDown(Key.DOWN) && key_Down == 0)
                        {
                                key_Down = 1;
                                keychange = true;
                        }

                        if (Key.isDown(Key.LEFT) && key_Left == 0)
                        {
                                key_Left = 1;
                                keychange = true;
                        }

                        if (Key.isDown(Key.RIGHT) && key_Right == 0)
                        {
                                key_Right = 1;
                                keychange = true;
                        }

                        // Is Key Released?
                        if (!Key.isDown(Key.UP) && key_Up == 1)
                        {
                                key_Up = 0;
                                keychange = true;
                        }

                        if (!Key.isDown(Key.DOWN) && key_Down == 1)
                        {
                                key_Down = 0;
                                keychange = true;
                        }

                        if (!Key.isDown(Key.LEFT) && key_Left == 1)
                        {
                                key_Left = 0;
```

# Multiplayer Applications     15

```
                        keychange = true;
            }

            if (!Key.isDown(Key.RIGHT) && key_Right == 1)
            {
                        key_Right = 0;
                        keychange = true;
            }

            // Run off the road
            if (!_root.roadsurface.hittest(_x, _y, true) &&
on_Road == 1)
            {
                        on_Road = 0;
                        maxspeed = 2;
                        keychange = true;
            }
            // On the road
            if (_root.roadsurface.hittest(_x, _y, true) &&
on_Road == 0)
            {
                        on_Road = 1;
                        maxspeed = 12;
                        keychange = true;
            }

            // Node code - for tracking our progress around the
➥track
            if (eval("_root.node" add _root.mynode).hittest(_x,
➥_y, false))
            {
                        _root.mynode++;
                        if (_root.mynode > _root.numnodes)
                        {
                                    _root.mynode = 1;
                                    if (—remaininglaps == 1)
                                                _root.stat.laps = "Last Lap";
                                    else
                                                _root.stat.laps = remaininglaps;

                                    ch = remaininglaps add " laps left";

                                    st = "t," add ch add ",";

                                    if (_root.comm.connectstat)
                                    {
                                                _root.comm.sock.send(st);
                                    }
                                    else
```

## Flash Games Studio

```
                        {
                            eval("_root.guy" add _root.myid).msgmc.msg =
➥ch;
                            eval("_root.guy" add _root.myid).chatclear =
➥getTimer() + 2000;
                        }
                    }
                }

                // Car collisions
                if (getTimer() > hittimer)
                {
                    for (i = 1; i < 7; i++)
                    {
                        if (i != _root.myid)
                        {
                            xd = Math.abs(eval("_root.guy" add
➥i)._x _x);
                            yd = Math.abs(eval("_root.guy" add
➥i)._y - _y);
                            if (xd < 20 && yd < 20 && eval("_root.guy" add
➥i)._visible)
                            {
                                hittimer = getTimer() + 4000;
                                vel = 14;
                                ang = eval("_root.guy" add
➥i).ang - .8;
                                keychange = true;
                            }
                        }
                    }
                }

                // Move if keys are pressed
                if (key_Up)
                {
                    vel += 1;
                }

                if (key_Down)
                {
                    vel -= 1;
                }

                if (key_Left && Math.abs(vel) > 0.1)
                {
                    ang += .2;
                }
```

## Multiplayer Applications

```
        if (key_Right && Math.abs(vel) > 0.1)
        {
              ang -= .2;
        }

        // The effect of Physics - limit forward and backward speed
        if (vel > maxspeed) vel = maxspeed;
        if (vel < -4) vel = -4;

        // If not pressing forward, slow the car down
        if (Math.abs(vel) > 0 && key_Up == 0) vel *= .9;

        // Set velocity to 0 if it's almost 0
        if (Math.abs(vel) < 0.1) vel = 0;

        if (id == _root.myid && _root.fuel <= 0)
        {
              maxspeed = 2;
              _root.fuel = 0;
              _key_Up = 0;
              _key_Down = 0;
        }

        // Calculate x and y speed from vel and ang
        dx = vel * Math.sin (ang);
        dy = vel * Math.cos (ang);

        // Hit a collision object?
        if (id == _root.myid && _root.collide.hittest(_x + dx, _y +
➥dx, true))
        {
              key_Up = 0;
              key_Down = 0;
              vel = -2;
              dx = vel * Math.sin (ang);
              dy = vel * Math.cos (ang);
              keychange = true;
        }

        // Move car
        _x += dx;
        _y += dy;

        // Set the car's rotation
        _rotation = (360 - (ang * (180 / Math.PI))) % 360;

        // Set the chat box (msgmc)'s rotation.
        msgmc._rotation = -_rotation;

        // Hit the edges of the screen
```

## 15  Flash Games Studio

```
            if (_x > 550)
            {
                    _x = 550;
            }

            if (_x < 0)
            {
                    _x = 0;
            }

            if (_y < 0)
            {
                    _y = 0;
            }

            if (_y > 400)
            {
                    _y = 400;
            }

            // If necessary, send through a packet.
            if (id == _root.myid && keychange)
            {
                    st = "p," add Math.floor(_x) add "," add
➥Math.floor(_y) add "," add vel add "," add ang add "," add
➥key_Up add "," add key_Down add "," add key_Left add "," add
➥key_Right add "," add maxspeed add "," add remaininglaps add
",";

                    if (_root.comm.connectstat)
                    {
                            _root.comm.sock.send(st);
                    }
            }

        if (getTimer() > chatclear) msgmc.msg = "";
    }
    else
    {

        _root.countdown = Math.floor(Math.abs(_root.waitstart - g) /
➥1000) + 1;

    }
}
```

That's a lot of code! Fortunately, we've covered most of it already, but there are a few small things that I should mention.

## Fuel and Speed Gauge

First of all, the speedometer and the fuel gauge are all dynamically controlled and change-based on vel and the amount of fuel you have remaining:

```
// Set the speed needle to indicate my speed
_root.stat.speedneedle._rotation = (Math.abs(vel) * 14) - 20;

// Set the fuel guage needle to show my fuel
_root.stat.fuelneedle._rotation = (Math.abs(_root.fuel) / 10);
```

The fuel needle and the speed needle are both instances of the same movie clip called speedneedle, which looks like this:

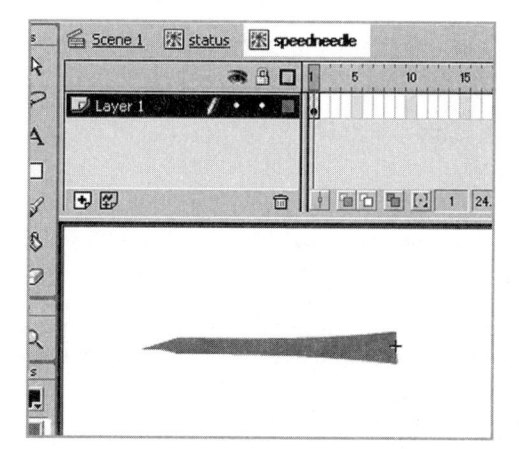

Notice that its right edge is the center of the object. This means that when the _rotation of a speedneedle instance is set to 0, it will be resting on the left. When the _rotation is 180, it will be pointing to the right.

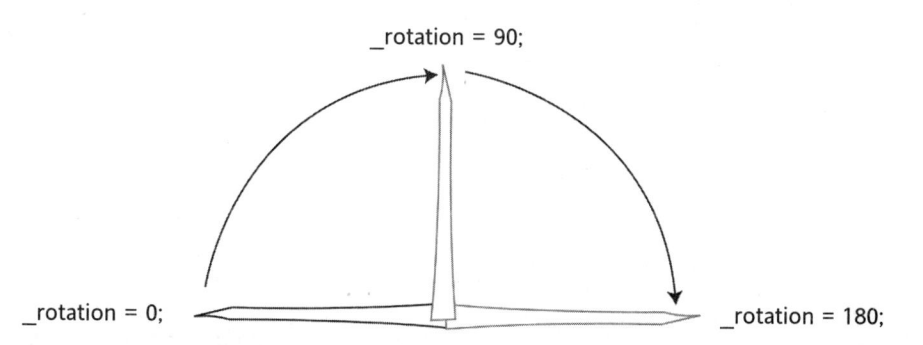

_rotation = 90;

_rotation = 0;            _rotation = 180;

Since the fuel level is a number from 0 to 1800, we can make the fuel gauge work by setting the _rotation of its needle to fuel/10-(0 to 180) to create an angle between 0 and 180 degrees. Setting the speedometer needle is a little more of a subjective calculation, for which

# Flash Games Studio

Since the fuel level is a number from 0 to 1800, we can make the fuel gauge work by setting the `_rotation` of its needle to `fuel/10-(0 to 180)` to create an angle between 0 and 180 degrees. Setting the speedometer needle is a little more of a subjective calculation, for which `(Math.abs(vel) * 14) - 20` seems to work best.

We also want to decrease the player's fuel based on how fast they're going and thus how much gas they're applying. This is accurate to real life where going at a higher speed makes your car use up more gas. We diminish the fuel with the following code:

```
_root.fuel -= (Math.abs(vel) + 1) / 10;
```

Here we're simply decreasing by the absolute value of `(vel + 1)/10`. This means that even if the car is completely stationary, and the `vel` is 0, you will still be losing 1/10 or 0.1 fuel every frame.

On the main stage, there's a movie clip known as the fuel pad. This has the instance name `fuelpad`, and when you are over the top of it, your fuel level slowly increases. This is how you refuel:

```
if (_root.fuelpad.hittest(_x, _y, false))
{
    maxspeed = 12;
    if (_root.fuel < 1800){
        _root.fuel += 4;
    }
}
```

We're simply checking to see whether the player's `_x` and `_y` (the nose of the car) is over yhe top of the `fuelpad`. If it is, we increase the fuel by 4 each frame until it is at 1800.

**KeyChange**
The remaining items have all been covered, until we reach this code:

```
if (id == _root.myid && keychange)
{
    st = "p," add Math.floor(_x) add "," add Math.floor(_y) add
➥"," add vel add "," add ang add "," add key_Up add "," add
➥key_Down add "," add key_Left add "," add key_Right add "," add
➥maxspeed add "," add remaininglaps add ",";

    if (_root.comm.connectstat)
    {
        _root.comm.sock.send(st);
    }
}
```

This is where our movement packets are constructed and sent to the server. At several stages throughout the frame, `keychange` could have been set to `true`. When this happens, it means that we have changed something important which must be sent through to the server so that the other players can see the change. We're also making sure that this is indeed the player's car (`id == _root.myid`).

# Multiplayer Applications

That's it. We've covered all the core functionality in the game, and what is required to make this multiplayer game happen. I hope you've gained an understanding of how Flash uses sockets and how we use packets to convey information about our game, and receive information about the other players' games.

## Synchronization

There's an unfortunate fact about the Internet – sometimes data gets lost. Have you ever seen a web site that just won't load unless you press reset and try again? Or an image that comes up as a broken link yet, upon refreshing, the image is there and intact. This is often due to lost data.

In the case of our multiplayer game, we must contend with the fact that sometimes packets will get lost and simply disappear. In these cases, cars will appear to run into walls, or keep turning in circles because, for example, the `key_Up` packet has been lost.

So, we try to compensate for this by ensuring that the cars act on their own accord, unless told otherwise. That's how this game works. If we don't get a packet from a player, at least the car won't stop dead on everyone else's screen; it will keep moving along its previous trajectory. This is often enough to carry us through until the next packet does arrive, and things are brought back into synch.

Unfortunately you will see the occasional car jump mysteriously to a new location, as the packet containing its correct location is finally received. This is simply a limitation of the technology, and very hard to overcome. Even the best commercial games get anomalies like this from time to time.

The best way to overcome synchronization issues is to ensure that your server is running on a fast, stable connection, and that your players have systems that are capable of handling Flash in general. Graphically speaking, this game isn't very intensive so if a computer can run most other Flash games, then they should be able to run this one just fine.

## The Server

So what is this server anyway? Well, basically the server is an application that I have made in Visual Basic 6.0. It uses the WinSock control to send and receive socket communications to and from clients.

Building a server requires the secondary knowledge of knowing a programming language other than ActionScript, and understanding how to architect such systems, and build full executable (EXE) applications. It also requires the hardware upon which to install, run and operate the server.

# 15  Flash Games Studio

The server program supplied in the source files is an EXE file that runs under a Windows environment (Windows 9x, ME, NT, 2000) and listens on a specific port for connecting players. The main application window looks like this:

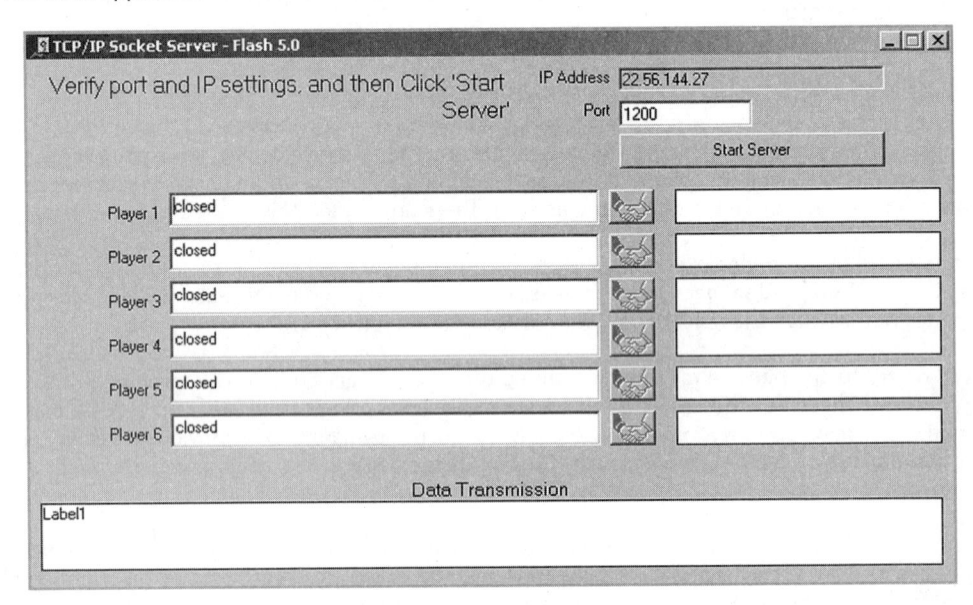

When you first run the program, you will see the IP address of the local machine in the IP address box at the top of the window. This cannot be changed – it's fixed to each machine. However, beneath it, you will see the port box. In here you can choose any port upon which to listen for incoming connection requests. Once you've chosen a port, click on Start Server, and the server will start running. It will look like this:

# Multiplayer Applications    15

Whatever value you select for the IP and port, the client must also set these in their login screen.

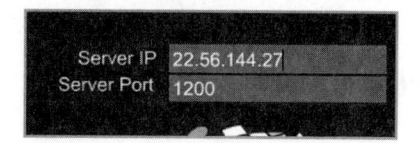

From the server window you'll see when players connect because a slot in the window will become occupied, and the player's coordinates and `remaininglaps` will appear in the box at right. For example, this is how the server could look if two players were connected to the game:

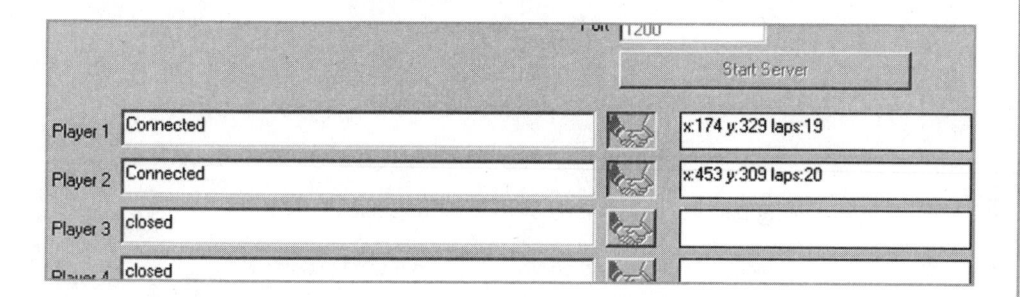

This allows the person running the server — the server administrator — to check the status of the game and see how many people are playing, and how the game is going. I would like to go further into detail on the functionality of the server, but this book isn't for Visual Basic programming.

You can run this server on your local machine, and then tell your friends that the server is running. If you give them copies of the SWF file (or make it into a projector file) they can connect to your server. However, some Internet service providers (ISPs) do not allow their customers to run servers or, more specifically, have people connect to an IP on their network. In some cases it represents a violation of the *terms of service* agreement you will have with your ISP. For this reason, be careful.

One other thing you could do is run this game/server on a local area network (LAN). This has the added advantage of being much faster. I recommend that you don't run the server and a client on the same machine. Let the server have its own machine because it's going to be commanding a lot of the processor.

# 15  Flash Games Studio

## Conclusion

So, now you know how to make a fast, socket-based multiplayer application in Flash. Yes, it can be done! Flash can handle it as long as you have a server that is capable of intelligently managing the game and informing the client when things happen in the game.

We've covered all this:

- Planning your systems requirements.
- IP addresses, port numbers and handling firewalls.
- Ways of connecting different computers to a Flash game – HTTP and Sockets.
- Introducing packets as methods of transmitting data.
- Types of packets – client and server – and how they are used.
- How to keep each players screen synchronized with the server.

Implementing a multiplayer application is simply a matter of running everything like a skilled conductor runs an orchestra. We must always know what's going on at every stage of the game, and we have to be on top of our information flow. We must think in terms of what our game is doing, what the server is doing, and how they're interacting.

Flash is the next great multiplayer platform because it already exists on the Web, so now it's our responsibility, as game designers, to make these worlds come to life.

However many players there are, with Flash you're on to a winner!

# Multiplayer Applications 15

**Introduction**
chapter 1
chapter 2
chapter 3
chapter 4
chapter 5
chapter 6
**Case Study 1**
chapter 7
chapter 8
chapter 9
chapter 10
chapter 11
chapter 12
chapter 13
**Case Study 2**
chapter 14
chapter 15
**Director Afterword**

# Director Afterword

# Flash Games Studio

## Director for Flash Users

I know, I know, what's a section on Director doing in a Flash games book? Well, Flash is perfect for low bandwidth games over the Internet, but what happens when you want to get a bit more... well... professional? When you want to add full quality video and polish to your games, but still keep your web-deliverability options open? Director is an obvious option to take, so rather than leaving you to hit it cold, we thought we'd give you an introduction to what you can expect to find and how easy it'll be for you to make the change.

This afterword has been written for all the Flash users out there who are in the process of adding Director to their list of multimedia tools. As with most people moving from one software application to another in the same related field, I looked at Director not in terms of 'what is Director 8.5?' but rather 'I want to learn this program as quickly as possible and the only way I can do that is by realizing the differences and similarities between Director and Flash'. By realizing the similarities, I could simply modify my old Flash workflow to Director, and hopefully transfer my existing skill-sets over. By realizing the differences, the theory was that I could home in on the parts of the Director documentation I needed to learn from scratch, and quickly build up the new skill-sets I needed.

This afterword looks at Director from the perspective of Flash converters. It's here to quick-start Flashers over to Director, pointing out the journey for people who started from the same initial point as I did.

This is a personal view on learning Director; there are no tutorials and no specific tips, it's more of a travelogue, taking a few snapshots along the way. I guess the friends Of ED Flash Foundation books helped a few people get into Flash, and now we, as the authors of those books are in exactly the same position with Director. This is how we found it, straight from the horse's mouth.

For those of you who just want the headlines, here they are:

- Perhaps the most daunting task to getting into Director is **the interface** itself – all those windows! Once you've realized that most of them can be safely closed during most of the development cycle though, the interface starts to look much less cluttered.

- Surprisingly (for me if no-one else), Director has a much better **animation system** than Flash. You can set tween paths with associated acceleration without ever having to touch a keyframe. As well as the surprisingly advanced low-level animation facilities, the **transition** and **effects** available are much more varied than those in Flash because they work on the bit plane level rather than the vector level.

- Director is a much easier environment to get into if you don't want to get your hands dirty with scripting. Director has **drag and drop** sewn up in a way that leaves Flash standing.

# Director Afterword

- For the Flash coder who does want to get into scripting, the disadvantage is that Director's resident **Lingo language is not based upon a 'standard' language** in the same way that ActionScript is a JavaScript derivative. Although this does mean that Lingo is something that must be learned from scratch, the good news is that it now supports a dot notation format, making it much more familiar.

- As well as web applications, Director is of course capable of **creating standalone applications**. The importance of this in building downloadable screensavers and desktop toys (possibly including Flash components) could be a critical consideration for the expert Flash designer looking to add a few additions to his skill-set.

- Finally, Director is a multimedia palette with a much larger number of colors. As the web world moves towards a broadband canvas that supports more and more content, Director is perhaps the only plug-in that contains **video**, **hardware driven 3D**, **fast bitmap scaling**, and **per pixel effects**, and all within a recognized industry standard plug-in.

## Culture Shock

The Software that people use as the basis of their careers is usually seen as 'just another application' by people on the outside, but for people who actually use things like PhotoShop, 3D Studio Max, Flash, or Director for a living will know better. There is always a community of professionals built up around the programs.

In his introduction to *New Masters of Flash: 2002 Annual*, Jonathan Gay, the creator of Flash, talks about this thing called 'community', that's part of Flash's success and personality. I've been a part of the Flash community that spans across countless boards and newsgroups – as well as the regular Flash conventions such as Flash Forward – for some time, and I have developed a feel for the community identity. Here's what I've found...

Flash is seen as the new kid on the block. Flash designers tend to be younger than, say, Director designers, and are more likely to have no graphic art background. Motion graphics was too new to have a standard route, and that wasn't a bad thing. The early gold rush of Flash design was all about bringing these motion graphics to the web – clever interfaces and mad, unfettered designs. There was commercial Flash of course, but much of the output was from designers like James Paterson, Yugo Nakamura, Joshua Davis, and Joe Cartoon – just doing it for its own sake; an underground of Flash designers and developers in direct opposition to the shackles of traditional HTML.

Director has been around since a time when multimedia was something new, and computers really did have 16 color palettes. It's traditionally been used by companies in the creation of CD-ROM and kiosk applications for the music and retail/promotional industries, and this is reflected in the community which, to a convert from Flash, will look a lot more polished and corporate. Even the Macromedia pricing of the two applications reflects this difference.

The effects of this on Director are subtle, but I guess the professional Flashers who do it all for a living will understand what I am talking about when I say that applications are not just programs to people who use them every day; the community and general output direction give them a personality.

# Flash Games Studio

As I was saying, the Director personality currently has a much more corporate feel and smell to it than Flash. This isn't something that I would class as necessarily good or bad, but just different. The fact that broadband will be more than just 'more of the same stuff' and will require rather more than a 'couple of Flash designers, an HTML guy and a server side guy' means that broadband will be more grown up in the same way Director already is. The amount of video, sound and all the other media required to put together a true broadband production tends to suggest a more planned route than the 'wow, here's a new interface concept, lets design a website around it'.

The relative maturity of Director also has its effect. Although we are constantly told about web-safe palettes and bit depths, no Flash designer I know takes a blind bit of notice of them. Anyone out there with a graphics card that doesn't display at least a 16-bit desk top more than likely doesn't know about Flash or the web either. No one uses VGA and CGA displays any more because even the old Matrox graphics cards of 5 years ago could display enough unique colors for us to ignore palette issues. The only remaining issue is possibly the relative brightness of PC and Mac displays, but apart from the few Photoshop graphic people who actually take the time to calibrate their monitors, no one actually cares. Yeah, I know some other folks write whole chapters on web safe colors, but we're a little more pragmatic when it comes to the realities of web design!

Director has a heritage from the time when a Hercules 256 color card was the best money could buy, and the interface is littered with references to file formats that allow us to set bit depths and all the other low level bitmap stuff.

Most Flash designers are by now used to just using JPEG/PNGs, or converting to vectors if there's lots of solid color. If that's the case with you, my advice is to do the same in Director too, unless there are compelling reasons otherwise (and I haven't found any practical ones so far).

## Why Director?

Of course, anyone who already has the big Director 8.5 box on their desk has already answered this question for himself or herself. Flash 5 is designed for low bandwidth applications, and suffers in other areas because of this. Its particular Achilles heels are performance and lack of multimedia options; at the heart of Flash is a real time vector rendering engine. Every frame in a Flash site is rendered from basic vector point and fill data on the fly, and this takes lots of processing power even when it feels like nothing much is happening. Although this factor is often given as an advantage to creative and novel thought (lots of designers have worked against this limitation to come up with killer Flash sites and applications), some things just can't be attempted in Flash. Because Flash is aimed at low bandwidth applications it doesn't have anywhere near the same sort of multimedia support that Director has.

Another issue that's apparent with Flash is its increasing instability as the file size increases. Flash is designed with small applications in mind, and as soon as you start to load it up with masses of high bandwidth assets the resulting large SWF file can become a little erratic and crash happy. Director on the other hand is tailor-made for handling this sort of content gracefully.

Also, the Flash executable (the SWF file) is an interpreted language system rather than a compiled one (an SWF is an FLA stripped of all authoring aids and compressed down to something called byte-code, which is then converted back to Flash plug-in readable code during runtime). A compiled language is read and converted to machine-readable data all in one go, making it more stable and quicker for standalone applications.

# Director Afterword

The look and feel of Director is of a compiled language (at least in the standalone non-Shockwaved version), which is a definite asset as we move to more complex and mixed media presentations, with their increasing need for good synchronization and stability.

So Director is a generic multimedia engine. Its output can be either streamed across the web, or compiled into true standalone and stable applications. Its native engine is bitmap based, which is much easier for computers to draw quickly because the images are effectively 'pre-drawn', and all that has to happen is that the image file is blitted around the video memory. Because it isn't primarily designed for quick download, the Director plug-in can handle a greater number of different media elements, and do them in the most efficient way; 3D support via hardware, video support and all the other cool stuff just isn't there in the 350k Flash plug-in.

Of course, the emerging new digital frontier has moved from simple Internet connectivity to The Broadband Web, and Director's old CD-ROM heritage coupled with its recent streaming abilities make it more ideal for this than Flash.

There are already some broadband Flash sites, and I had a look at some of them in researching this section. Broadband Flash takes as long (and on occasion longer!) than similar broadband Director sites simply because most broadband elements (bitmap, video, 3D) are not part of the Flash plug-in's design focus, and don't stream as well as vector based content. The upshot is that Flash loses much of its streaming capability in migrating to broadband.

There is a subtler problem as well: performance. Broadband Flash requires a very fast computer to work well. Flash based streaming video + sound solutions are particularly slow, and full screen update on a (pretty standard) 1024x 768 screen is something Flash struggles with even on non-broadband sites.

Director already equals Flash on the broadband streaming front, and is edging past it in the raw multimedia performance stakes. This is a contest well worth watching in the future as Macromedia develops the two programs.

Rather than replace it, Director looks like it will complement Flash in many web and other applications, supporting it where Flash cannot handle the heavy multimedia streams such as video and hardware assisted 3D. For this reason, knowing both applications is a valid strategy for future-proofing your skill-set.

## The Interface

The good news is that Director and Flash have got a lot closer to each other since Director version 8 (so my Director contacts tell me). The impression of the basic Director interface is reminiscent of Flash 4. Director hasn't had the 'tabbed palettes makeover' that occurred between Flash 4 and 5, and the main components (apart from the Director scripting windows) have a distinct Flash 4 feel. Despite this, the Director interface is much easier to use for the non-programming Flash user because of its true drag and drop scripting. Additionally, the Director help system now looks much like the Flash one, and given that you will use it a lot early on (I know I did!) this is another bonus to fast learning.

More on all this later, but first, let's tackle the basic graphic interface stuff.

### The Timeline/Score

The big joy of using Flash is its 'do it any way you want to' philosophy when it comes to using timelines. You can attach scripts, sounds or graphic elements pretty much on any keyframe of any layer. The freeform nature of Flash in this respect has perhaps more than anything helped its ability to draw in converts from non-multimedia backgrounds; it's just so easy to chop and change timeline animations so that they reflect your own personal preferences.

One of the biggest differences with Director is that it doesn't let you get away with this same freeform design, as it has a much more structured timeline:

***The Flash equivalent terminology to Director basic names is listed below:***

*Flash layer = Director channel*
*Flash timeline = Director score*
*Flash graphic, button or movieclip element on the stage = Director sprite*
*Flash ActionScript attached to a keyframe = Director behavior attached to the behavior channel*

Director only allows you to add certain elements in specific channels. Sound, for example, can only be attached to dedicated channels. The same goes for scripts. Note the first six channels in the Director score:

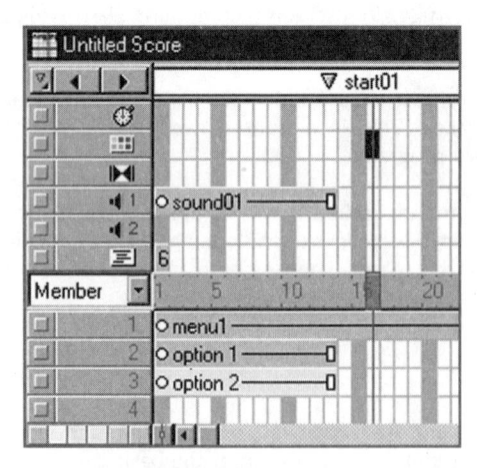

They are default channels called the tempo, palette, transition, sound (left channel), sound (right channel) and behavior channels. Although this in itself is not really a problem given that some of the channels in this group (called the effects channels) have no Flash equivalent, it does mean that you're more limited when it comes to sound. You can only have one sound stream for each of the 2 sound channels, whereas in Flash you can have up to 8 stereo sounds!

# Director Afterword

Most Flash users create a specific layer for the purpose of attaching scripts to the timeline (it's the actions layer in my Flash timelines), so the fact that Director forces you to do the same via the behavior channel is only forcing a good habit.

Being able to do things like changing the frame rate (via tempo changes in the tempo channel) is the sort of thing us poor Flash cousins wish we could do, so it's all swings and roundabouts... Also, the Director ink effects (the transition channel) are much more useful than the equivalent Flash instance effects (because Director works at the bitmap level rather than Flash's vector shapes, which can only address vector tint, brightness, and alpha transitions).

The real practical differences start when you begin adding things in the Director sprite channels (the channels that appear below the effects channels, and are also sometimes called member channels). You can hold several graphic elements at the same time per layer in Flash, but in Director it's strictly 'one channel, one sprite'. This means that you will tend to have a much larger number of channels in a Director score than you will in a Flash timeline. This can be annoying if like me, you like to place related graphics on the same layer in Flash. The Director alternative isn't just different, it requires a lot more forward planning if you want to manage your timeline in such a way that you don't start to lose sight of where stuff is.

Director is light years ahead when it comes to fine-tuning and editing the score, and controlling tween animation as befits a true multimedia-authoring tool.

For example, this spiral tween motion below took me 20 seconds to set up in Director:

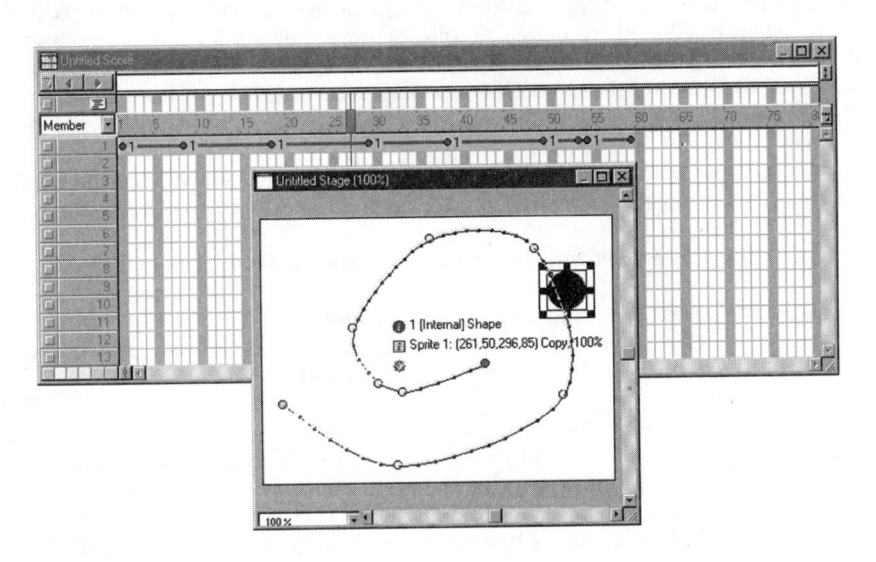

# Flash Games Studio

By moving points directly on the tween path, I can shape the sprite's direction and acceleration without having to touch a timeline. With Flash, I have to keep messing about with the timeline because there is no easy way to set up a path with acceleration in such an intuitive and graphical way. This is something that seems to be overlooked a lot; we hear that 'Flash is for the web and Director is for kiosks', but no-one really has a look under the hood and says things like 'wow, I never knew Director was better for hand-drawn animation, particularly because it supports vectors as well; I just thought Director was something to do with bitmaps and video...'.

The fact that Flash doesn't have this sort of low level animation usability is possibly one reason why the Flash community go straight for scripting solutions, but with Director animation is all so intuitive that scripting isn't needed as much – and when it is, there's usually a pre-built behavior you can use instead of reaching for the Lingo manual.

I've already started looking back at some of my old animation-heavy Flash movies and trying to get them working in Director. Some of this stuff is already looking really neat, particularly when you start adding ink effects into the mix. Another big bonus is of course the additional performance – Director is definitely faster.

It's not all good news though, because the Director implementation of movie clips is perhaps one of the things that takes the longest to get used to for the Flash designer.

For Flash, movie clips are the most important graphical element. They may seem like a minor point to Director users, but Flash designers base everything around them. Flash media is built around a flurry of movie clips triggered from buttons or events, and even advanced scripted presentations are heavily based around movie clips because they are the only true object based graphical element with properties and methods. Movie clips are so easy to create and modify in Flash because of the total reliance upon them; simply double click them from either the stage area or the library.

In Director the sprite or 'static graphic' seems to be the most basic element, and the concept of movie clips feels less complete. To create a movie clip in Director is a two-stage process;

- Create the movie clip content in the main Director timeline.

- Select the parts of the timeline you want to make into a movie clip and drag it into the Library. Once the movie clip is created you can't edit it again (although you can copy its contents back onto the main timeline for re-editing)

This means that you have to create all your movie clips before you create the main Director timeline, so the organic way you can easily chop and change movie clips in Flash is lost as soon as you cross over to Director. This is a major change to the typical Flash user, and is a major change to the normal free form Flash workflow. Of all the things that I had to learn in crossing over to Director from Flash, this was the hardest to get a handle on. Lingo and Havok were easy in comparison...

# Director Afterword

## The Cast

The Cast window is broadly equivalent to the Flash Library window. The main differences are that the Director environment allows you to have multiple casts, and to define special DIR files that essentially constitute an external cast. The differences are less apparent than the similarities however, and the Director Cast window feels much like the Flash Library window (for those who can remember, it feels a lot like the Flash 3 Library window).

## The Inspectors

About 60% of all your use of the Director interface will center on the Property Inspector. This is a context-sensitive tabbed window similar to the sort of thing seen in Flash 4:

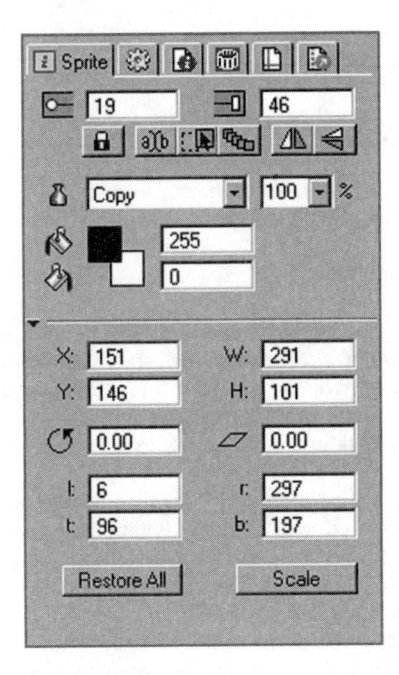

Only the tabs and requesters available for the currently selected element are shown (and if nothing is selected, the Inspector defaults to the tabs for the stage itself), making it totally intuitive as long as you understand the attributes of the thing you have just selected. It works in the same general way as the Flash 5 tabbed panels, so it's not even something new to learn. There are a few other inspectors for each of the more specialized functions – text, behaviors (scripting) and memory. Of particular note is the Behavior window, which is one of the greatest instances of parallel evolution I have come across. It is just like the Flash Actions window, and even has something very similar to the Normal/Expert script editing modes:

# Flash Games Studio

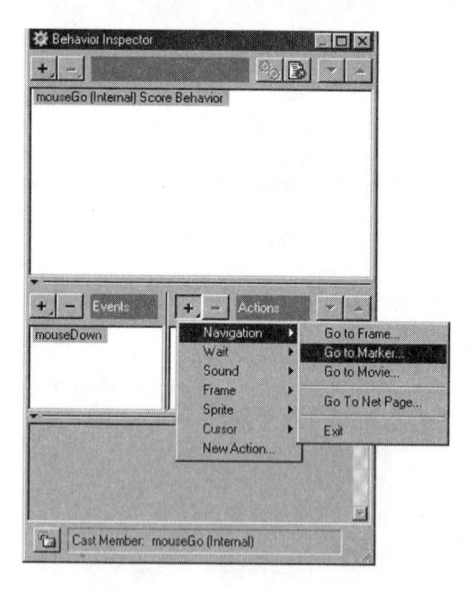

If you start a new script as a beginner, the Behavior Inspector window allows you to define your commands as event-action pairs selected from a set of pop-down menus, such as:

on mouseDown, go to frame 20

The great thing about scripting in this way is that it doesn't require knowledge of Lingo, but rather an understanding of simple events and handlers (which is something the typical Flash user knows all about already). I found myself writing scripts for a few trial Director sites within a few hours of opening the Director box (and some hours before opening any of the manuals!). This is exactly the way actions were entered way back in Flash 3 and 4, so it's not even something new to a lot of us.

Using the basic functionality is a bit limiting in that it only allows you to build basic navigation and the most elementary media control commands (about the level of scripting of the Flash 3 dialect of ActionScript), but I found using the basic scripting methods discussed here a good way of writing my own simple Lingo scripts. I then went into them via the true text entry window Expert Mode and started dissecting the raw Lingo and modifying the basic scripts I had created. That's how I learned Flash in the first place, and it's the best way to get into Lingo that I've found so far: create some simple 'drag and drop' Lingo and then go in and start playing with it close up:

# Director Afterword

## The Sprite Editing Windows

The Paint and Vector Shape windows allow you to create bitmap and vector based graphics within Director. I would recommend that you don't use them though. Any web design person worth their salt will already know Photoshop and Freehand (or whatever their chosen bitmap and vector programs are), and to be brutally honest, they are miles beyond the sort of thing you can do in the Director 'content creation' windows. Most of the Director people I spoke to tend to do the same thing, working in external programs and then importing all of the finished assets into Director for building into the final presentation. The Director editing windows only have one level of undo in any case, so the word is if you are more familiar with something else, use it instead - it will be better for work flow.

The only basic content creation window worth learning (apart from the new Shockwave 3D window of course!) is the text window:

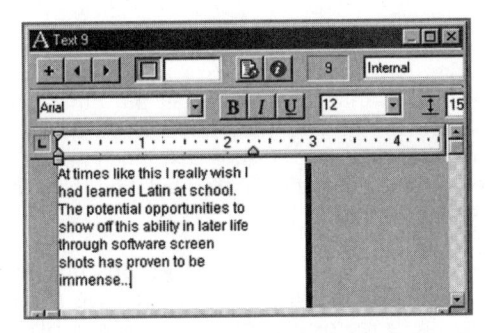

Given that this window is just a basic text editor, there's not much to learn in any case: I didn't have to consult the manual and I don't suppose anyone else will either.

Although there are a few other windows lurking about, these are all the elements that I had to address before I was well on my way in Director. As mentioned before, the only real problem I found is the lack of a movie clip object with the same ease of editing as we have in Flash. The next big challenge was learning Lingo...

## Scripting in Director

One of the big advantages of Flash is the accessible scripting language. In a total masterstroke, Macromedia changed Flash's scripting language (ActionScript) into a syntax very similar to the only other computer scripting language that web designers might actually know – JavaScript. This immediately made the creation of scripting heavy Flash sites accessible to a large number of the existing web design community.

Lingo is very different to ActionScript in that it's not a new language and therefore can't be changed in such a drastic manner. Lingo has a large user following and it's been maturing for a long time. One of the few recent major changes though has a large effect: most commands can now be expressed in dot notation, as well as the curiously wordy Lingo syntax. This will make Lingo particularly accessible to Flash designers crossing over. It's not quite a total implementation of dot notation however, and there are particular technical and historic inconsistencies;

# Flash Games Studio

- Lingo commands are not grouped into 'objects' such as occurs with Flash's Math or movieClip objects. This structure, along with dot notation means (in Flash) that if you think there should be a command to do something, you are probably half way to knowing what its syntax is, because dot notation used in conjunction with an object-based syntax makes for totally logically defined command structures.

- For example, there are a large number of Lingo commands that handle vector shapes, such as addVertex, antiAlias, backgroundColor, broadcastProps, and so on. In Flash dot notation, we would expect a 'vector object' and would call actions such as vector.addVertex, vector.antiAlias, vector.backgroundColor and so on. The Flash object-based action groupings are great for learning the language, because it is easy to find and pick off a command from a requester or drop down menu because the groupings are intuitive.

    Also, once you've used a command in a particular object (such as, say, the Date object's getSeconds method), you know all the other commands more or less by default because you only have to understand the particular object to understand all of that object's methods. Learning Lingo is that much harder than ActionScript because it doesn't follow a full dot notation implementation through to the actual structure of the language syntax itself.

- Lingo serves many more applications than ActionScript. For example there are large subsets of Lingo for 3D and video that don't have any comparable commands in ActionScript, so the Lingo dictionary of keywords is HUGE! My boxed Director 8.5 release has two 500-page books (the 'Lingo Dictionary' and the 'What's New in Director Shockwave Studio' book) that just contain lists of Lingo commands... scary! Because there is no true dot notation hierarchy applied to command syntax, there's a lot of syntax to learn out there in Lingo world.

- Many Lingo aficionados don't like dot notation, so there are two dialects. Some Lingo tutorials I have downloaded from the web switch from one to the other within the same DIR file. It's confusing to the beginner to say the least – rather like having to learn German and Spanish at the same time!

    Once I got into scripting in Lingo though, I found it to be much like any other language. There are a few commands that you use often, and lots of obscure ones that you'll hardly ever use. If you're well up on scripting in Flash, scripting in Lingo will be more of the same (albeit with a larger body of commands to get your head around). There's all sorts of Lingo specific terminology such as 'parent-child' scripting, but once you get down to it, it's not altogether different from the Flash movie clip-based animation hierarchies that the ActionScript divas use all the time.

    There are all sorts of cool additions in Lingo that make it worth the journey though: the greater number of events your scripts can trigger on, movies in windows, 3D, and, most of all, the raw increase in performance that Lingo gives you over and ActionScript. It's like test driving a fast car – exhilarating and fun!

# Director Afterword

## Conclusion

At the time of writing, I've been working with Director for about a month. I can't say that the first couple of weeks were not hard going – they were. But looking back that was all due to unfamiliarity and not a lack of understanding of basic principles; if you know one multimedia timeline-based tool you probably know them all.

I've already started to look at working with Director on some personal multimedia projects that just didn't get off the ground in Flash due to technical issues. One of my most ambitious is a multimedia version of a graphic novel I did years ago (it was cited as the first ever totally digitally created comic strip in Computer Arts Magazine way back when), and I'm using real time 3D (Character Studio and the others) along with bitmapped images:

My first love in digital art was always 3D, and Director has finally brought this back home in a form that brings together all of my favorite applications. 3D Studio Max for the 3D object creation, Flash for the cool interface elements, and Director to bind the real time 3D together with pre-rendered 3D video, sound and any other media streams I might want to add.

It's not really about choosing between Director or Flash or whatever. It's about saying 'here's a project I've wanted to do, what are the tools I can use to visualize this?' For me its getting really cool, because the stuff I had to pre-render three years ago can now be done in real time with some OpenGL hardware and a few alpha bitmaps to hide all the jaggies. All the programs I worked with separately only a few years ago are becoming integrated in one big workflow - and that's the truly exciting thing because as applications get more integrated, the possibilities for using them together grow exponentially. And the program that has finally come out from the shadows to integrate all this media into one big broadband delivery system looks set to be Director.

# Index

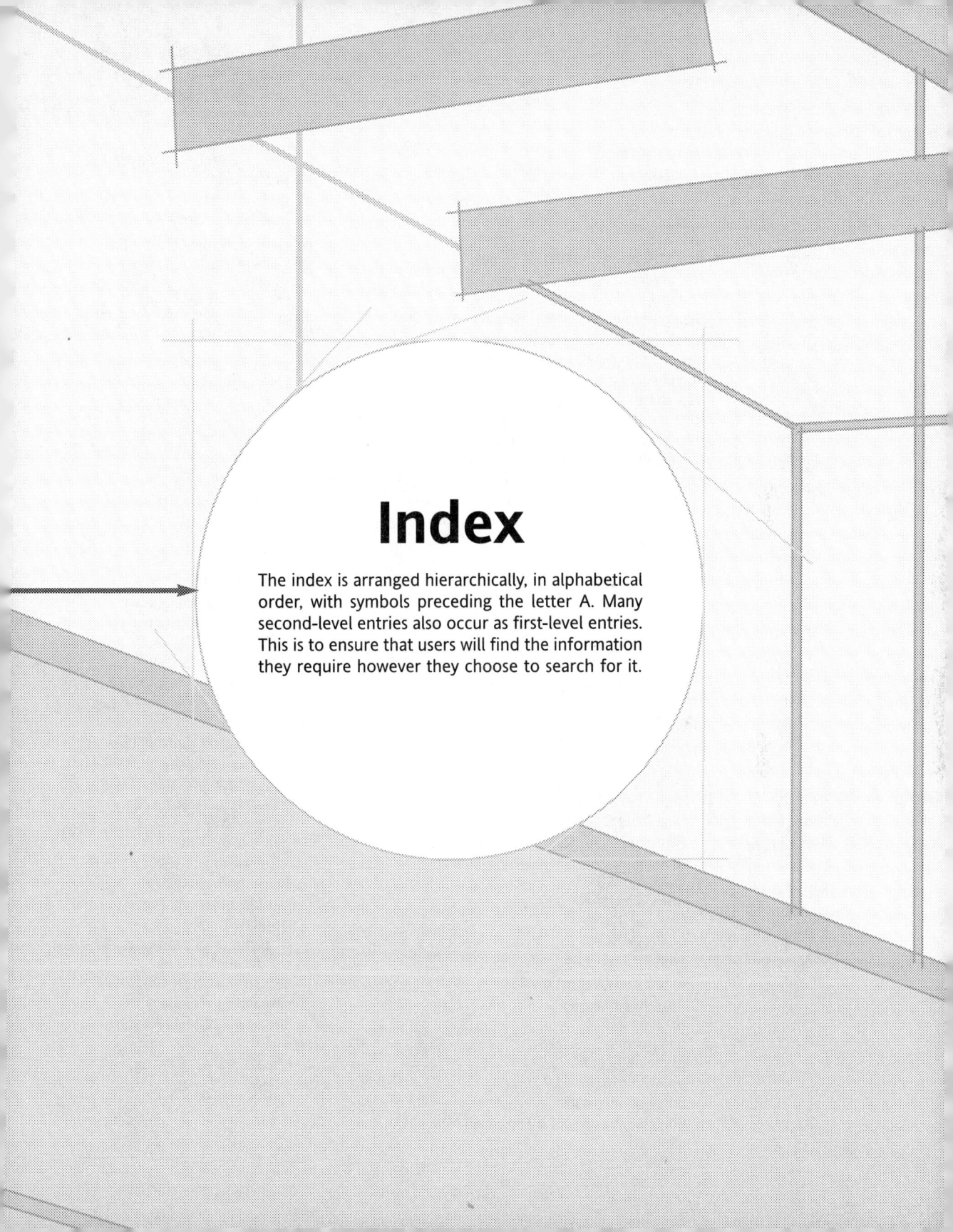

The index is arranged hierarchically, in alphabetical order, with symbols preceding the letter A. Many second-level entries also occur as first-level entries. This is to ensure that users will find the information they require however they choose to search for it.

# Flash Games Studio

## Symbols

! symbol 266
+= operator 518
3D. See also 3D Pong (tutorial) .See also line engine #1(tutorial). See also line engine #2 (tutorial). See also Manic Bounce (tutorial). .See also Mech Attack (case study). See also renderer (tutorial). See also polygon engine (tutorial). See also shine and flaring effects (tutorial). See also Star Cruiser (tutorial). .See also tiles (tutorial). See also trees (tutorial). See also wireframe3d function (tutorial).
   3D collision detection 130
   3D engines 6
   3D movement 22
   3D movies 228
   3D object definition 88
   3D polygons 22
   3D rendering programs 235
   3D sprites 22
   backface culling 59, 450
   bitmap images 234
   cameras 125
   constructor functions 89
   coordinate origins 87
   cube vertices 88
   defining shapes 87
   depth of field 227
   faux 3D 2, 226, 278
   Flash 233, 654, 657
   focus 227
   graphics 456
   isometric 3D 87, 227, 270
   layering 228
   line objects 90
   line3d function 90
   mathematical motion 654
   ordering 103
   parallax 228
   perspective 226, 228
   point objects 89
   point3d function 89
   polygons 89, 434
   polygons per second rendered 435
   pre-rendered 3D images 232
   projection 106
   quad objects 91
   real 3D 86, 226
   rendering shapes 99
   rotation 102
   scaling 101
   speed considerations for games 452
   stereoscopic vision 227
   textured surface bitmaps 435
   translation 100
   triangles and quads 434
   wireframe images 88, 434
   wireframe3d function 92
   z axis 87, 258
3D Pong (tutorial)
   3D collision detection 130
   ang variable 127
   ball object 127
   balldx and balldz variables 130
   camera buttons 128
   camera positioning 131
   camera3d constructor function 125
   collision events 130
   controller movie clip 128
   controlling rotation of paddle 129
   decelerating motion 132
   defining ground object 127
   destination variables 126
   dynamic text box 128
   enterFrame clipEvent 128, 129
   game loop 128
   ground object 127
   load clipEvent 125
   paddle object 127
   points variable 128
   possible improvements 132
   rendering ball 129
   setcam function 126
   setcamera routine 132
   speed variable 127
3D scaling 654
3D Studio Max 235, 242, 677, 687
8-bit games 536

# Index

## A

abs method 520
Acid (application) 415
ActionScript 540, 648
    code decentralization 2
    functions 2
    random number generation 6
    relative hierarchies 143
    sound implementation 612
    speed problems 649
    timeline animation versus ActionScript 208, 481
adaptive degradation 142
ADPCM (Adaptive Differential Pulse Code Modulation) 417
    bit depth 418
    sample rates 417
air combat simulators 657
Alpha effects 137, 470, 474
    frame rates 489
    processing requirements 514
alpha method 516
alpha property 514
ambient music 411
Amorphium Pro 235
animated sequences 668
animation. See also beach ball (tutorial)
    secondary animations 515
    timeline animation versus ActionScript 208, 481, 515
anti-aliasing 473
arbitrary polygons 439
Array object 503
    methods of Array object 509
arrays 286
    referencing values in arrays 63
artificial intelligence 532, 534. See also Sugar Monster (tutorial)
    crisp and fuzzy logic 205, 206
    emulating intelligent behavior 539, 560, 571
    non-linear behavior 207
Asheron's Call (game) 653
ASP 525, 542
Assembly Language 648
Asteroids (game) 536
Atari 516, 535, 536
audio filter programs 417
audio software
    Gigapiano 415
    loop-based composition programs 415
    multitrack recorders 414
    Reason 415
    Rebirth 415
    sequencers 414
    software synthesizers 415
    wave editors 415

## B

backface culling 59, 450
bandwidth 322, 493
beach ball (tutorial)
    += operator 518
    abs method 520
    ball movement (code) 518
    ball movie clip 517
    bouncing effect 520
    calculating ball rotation 518
    changing opacity of shadow 522
    onClipEvent (enterFrame) 517, 521
    onClipEvent (load) 519
    scaling shadow 522
    setting circumference variable 519
    shadow effect 521
    shadow movie clip 521
    sin method 520
Bemani games 658
Berkley Systems 413
bezier splines 465
bingo 318, 652
The Birds (film) 412
bit depth 418, 678
Bit Rate 614
bit-shift operator 115
bitmaps 463, 468
    bitmap scaling 677
    bitmaps versus vectors 470, 489
    Trace Bitmap tool 234
Black and White (game) 534, 539
blank game engines 547

Blizzard Entertainment 413
'bloatware' 620
bouncing effect 520
bowtie quads 92
broadband 678
buttons
    button event handlers 371
    hit areas 371

## C

C (programming language) 282, 436, 648
C++ 542
The Cable Guy (film) 310
cache 305
Cakewalk (application) 414
cameras 125
Candle in the Wind (song) 431
card games 651
Carmageddon (game) 655
Carrey, Jim (comedian) 310
casino games 652
challenge 667
chaotic systems 6
Character Studio 687
chess 310, 318, 536, 540, 571
chords
    chord progression 423
    types of chords 410
Chuckie Egg (game) 652
Civilization (game) 534
client-server architecture 312, 318. See also Radio Racer (tutorial)
    client connection speed 323
    firewalls 314
    server connection speed 323
clip events. See onClipEvent function
    clip events versus smart clips 527
clocks 458, 498
Close Encounters of the Third Kind (film) 408
code
    decentralization 2
    gathering code in top layer of frames 215
    object-oriented code 5

code optimization 136. See also Pong (tutorial)
    adaptive degradation 142
    enterFrame event scripts 140
    event-driven code versus frame-based code 140
    event execution periods 182
    logic loops 139
    look-up tables 141
    mutually exclusive conditionals 139
    optimizing conditional logic 138
    relative hierarchies 143
    staggered update 141
    varying redraw periods 141
collision detection 22, 245, 376, 525, 606
    hitTest method 576
collision systems 656
Color object 194, 503, 506
compiled languages 678
Computer Arts Magazine 687
computers
    minimum specifications 614
configuration 150
conflicting goals 537
constructor functions 89
    lines 90
    points 89
    quad3d function 91
    quads 91
controls 664, 667. See also customizing keys (tutorial)
    control keys 664
    custom controls 378
    intuitive controls 370
Cool Edit Pro 415
coordinate systems 87, 525
curly brackets 137
currentFrame property 511
custom controls 378. See also tank (tutorial). See also customizing keys (tutorial)
custom event handlers 376
customizable graphics 547
customizing keys (tutorial)
    converting key codes 384
    default key settings 387, 388
    display dynamic text field 382
    firing key control 388

# Index

key configurator movie clip 383, 387
key editor movie clip 383, 384
keys array 385
onClipEvent(mouseDown) 386
onClipEvent(keyDown) 383, 385
onClipEvent(load) 385
_parent movie clip 384
play button symbol 390
setKey function 384
String.fromCharCode character code convertor 384
tempKey variable 384

## D

Dante (tutorial)
acceleration 179
actions layer 180
Alien object 176, 188
alien timeline 192
AlienSpawner object 176, 196
ArcadeClassic font 173, 174
backdrop layer 183
blip movie clip 194
burstDuration timer 196
collision detection 174, 189
Cursor object 176, 185, 187
cursorX and cursorY variables 185, 188
danteOBD01.fla 177
database 177, 189, 193
database array points 191
database object 179
database.score 189
direction variable 185, 189
dummy movie clips 195
enterFrame Script 190, 196
game components and workflow 175
game controls 170
game engine 174
game graphics 172
game object definitions (list) 175
gameSprites 170, 182
gameWorld 174, 179, 199
gameWorld object 175
gameWorld object block diagram 178
guide layer 195
inertia 179
killGoal gameSprites 177
killLine status variable 189, 196
laser beam animation 196
LaserBeam object 176, 194
maxSpeed variable 179, 189
mouse properties 186
object block diagrams 175, 177, 179, 199
object of game 172
object relationships 177
physical constants 179
plasmaController movie clip 195
PlasmaController object 176
player's ship and alien BomberCraft graphics 173
PlayerShip object 176, 184
protectGoal gameSprites 177
Radar object 176
radar object block diagram and code 192
radar updateRate 193
score status 190
scoreKeeper object 176, 198
score[index] 179
screen extents 179
scrollerDemo.fla 174
scrolling 170
ship layer 184
ship movie clip 186
shipDead[index] status 179
shipGun bullet 191
shipX and shipY variables 179
Star object 175, 181, 199
star updateRate 182
stars layer 180
system level 186
SYSTEM object 176
system.flash variable 186
Terrain object 175, 183
viewPort 180
viewSpeed status variable 180, 182, 189
viewSpeed value 188
_visible property 190

world object 179
zero index 179
darkness 490. See also hovercraft (tutorial)
databases 170, 533
    database array points 191
    database connection information 296
    PHP-supported databases (list) 282
dataName variable 151
Dave's 3D Studio 255
Davis, Joshua (web designer) 677
debugging 160, 549
    limitations of Debugger 180
Defender (game) 536
defining shapes 87
delete key 598
demo2-1.swf 477
demo2-2.swf 480
demo2-3.swf 481
demo2-4.swf 482
demo3-6.swf 496
demo3-7.swf 496
demo3-8.swf 490
demo10-1.swf 408
demo10-2.swf 409
demo10-6 424
demo10-7 424
demo10-8m.fla/swf 419
demo10-9.fla 421
demo13-1.fla 440
demo13-1.swf 446
demo13-2.fla 98
demo13-2.swf 450
demo13-3.fla 99
demo13-4.swf 109, 120
demo13-5.swf 120
demo13-6.swf 124
demo15-1.xml 320
demo16-1.swf 228
demo16-3.fla 252
demo16-3.swf 252
demo16-4.fla 241
demo16-4.swf 241
demo16-5.fla 236
demo16-6.fla 272
demoCs2-1 71
depth 379
    depth conflicts 395
    modulo operator 395
    swapDepths function 393
depth of field 227
depth sorting 124
Director 186
    3D applications 687
    addVertex command 686
    animation system 676, 682
    antiAlias command 686
    backgroundColor command 686
    Behavior window 683
    bitmap scaling 677
    bitmap-based graphics 679, 685
    broadcastProps command 686
    Cast window 683
    CD-ROM 677, 679
    content creation windows 685
    default channels 680
    DIR files 683
    Director community 677
    dot notation inconsistencies 686
    downloadable screensavers 677
    drag-and-drop 676, 679
    editing score 681
    Flash equivalent terminology to Director basic names 680
    generic multimedia engine 679
    hardware-driven 3D 677
    Havok 682
    help system 679
    importing images into Director 685
    ink effects 681
    interface 676, 679
    kiosk applications 677
    Lingo 677, 682, 686
    member channels 681
    movie clips 682
    multiple casts 683
    Paint window 685
    per pixel effects 677
    performance 682
    Property Inspector 683
    scripting methods 684, 686
    Shockwave 3D window 685
    sound limitations 680

# Index

sprite channels 681
standalone applications 677, 679
tempo channel 681
text window 685
timelines 680
transition channel 681
transitions and effects 676
tween animation 681
using with Flash 676
vector-based graphics 685
video 677
DirectX 186, 436
Disney-Pixar 435
Donkey Kong (game) 652
Doom (game) 310, 654
dot notation 319, 677
download times 492, 659. See also external SWF files (tutorial). See also meter preloader (tutorial)
   ideal download times (table) 661
   loader bars 663
downloadable screensavers 677
do... while loops 558
drawobject function 453
Dreamworks SKG 435
dropTarget property 510, 526
   slash notation 511
Duke Nukem Forever (game) 654
duplicateMovieClip method 524
dynamic line renderers 96

## E

EA (games company) 534
electronic music 411
emulating intelligent behavior 539, 560, 571
   coding complex logic as functions 560
Encore (application) 414
end of game conditions 534
enterFrame event scripts 140
ethnic music 411
event execution periods 182
event handling 368. See also onClipEvent function. See also tank (tutorial)
   button event handlers 371
   custom event handlers 376
   keyPress event Handler 372
   on handler 405
Everquest (game) 653
EXE files 362
experimental music 411
Expert mode scripting 137
external SWF files (tutorial)
   box animation 496
   "Click here to load" movie clip 496
   container movie clip 497
   host movie clip 496
   parked movie clip 498
eye-candy 668

## F

F29 Retaliator (game) 310
faux 3D 2, 226, 278
fighting games 656
file compression 661
file size 476, 661
film soundtracks 408
Final Fantasy (game) 435, 653, 666
finite elements 5
Firestarter (song) 431
firewalls 314, 316
first person shooters 654, 670
Flash. See also frame rate counter (tutorial). See also meter preloader (tutorial). See also external SWF files (tutorial). See also polygon engine (tutorial). See also sockets (tutorial)
   3D in Flash 86, 88, 654, 657
   Actions window 683
   Alpha effects 137, 470, 474
   animation 7
   anti-aliasing 473
   bandwidth profiler 493
   basic Flash polygon engine 437
   bezier splines 465
   bitmaps in Flash 546
   broadband Flash sites 679
   cache problems 305
   color object 194

combining Flash with PHP 298, 649
command structures 686
comparative frame rates (tables) 487
complete soundtracks 419
curly brackets 137
debugger window 549
Director and Flash 676
dot notation 686
download times 492, 659, 663
drawing 3D images in Flash 233
drawing solid shapes at runtime 437
dynamic line renderers 96
dynamic text 475
effect of adding sound on game performance 613
Expert mode scripting 137
external SWF files 496
Flash 4 Edit Envelope window 617
Flash bottlenecks (list) 137
Flash community 677
Flash equivalent terminology to Director basic names 680
font-rendering engine 475
frame rate 456, 461, 614, 619
frame rate counters 483
frame rate on Macs 486
full-screen motion 652
globalToLocal function 594
goal-based strategy 536
gradients 475, 233
graphic potential of Flash 649
image quality 471
importing vector versions of 3D images 235
input devices 369
interpreted language 136
interpreting code from top to bottom layer 215
Key UP event 649
keyboard handling routines 649
lighting and shadow effects 236
limitations of Flash 649, 678
line engines 96
long scripts 542

look-up tables 137
math functions 137
Math object 686
maximum number of sound samples 431
modifing vertices of shapes at runtime 96
movie clips 5, 476, 502, 547, 682
movieClip object 686
music in Flash 415
nested timelines 210
object-oriented code 5
online data 282
Optimize command 465, 467, 475
optimizing images in Flash 467, 489
outlines 474
performance limitations 81
platform games 652
pre-rendered 3D images 232
preloaders 493
projectors 662
radians 97
rendering curves 465
running two Flash movies simultaneously 490
scaling and rotating 462, 468
scrolling 492
shine and flaring effects 236
simulations 657
slash notation 136
Socket communications 316
sound channels 614
sound file export options 415
sound file import options 613
sound object 615
start and stop sound object methods 616
streaming 136, 614, 679
string concatenation 137
targeting sounds 628
Trace Bitmap tool 234, 470
tweening 7, 13, 96, 475
updating text fields 137
vector engines 132, 463, 678
vector graphics 463, 649
write and read operations 470
XMLSocket object 317

# Index

Flash 5 ActionScript Studio (book) 118, 320, 640
Flash 5 Studio (book) 172
Flash Forward (conference) 171, 677
flight simulators 657
flowcharts 179
flying ball (tutorial)
    ball movie clip symbol 477
    blinking eye 481
    drawing green circle 476
    dx and dy variables 478
    onClipEvent() 477
    random momentum 480
    resolution and frame rate 476
    reversing horizontal momentum 479
    reversing vertical momentum 480
font-rendering engine 475
fonts
    ArcadeClassic font 173
for loops 392
frame rate 456, 459, 483, 516, 614
    comparative frame rates (tables) 487
frame rate counter (tutorial)
    dynamic text field 484
    frameratecounter movie clip 483, 485
    getTimer variable 485
    Math.ceil function 485
    onClipEvent () 485
    reset button 484
    text box 484
framesLoaded property 511
Freehand 685
friction 665
Fruity Loops (web site) 415
FTP (File Transfer Protocol) servers 313
full-screen motion 652
functions 2, 286
    coding complex logic as functions 560
    initializing functions 368
fuzzy logic 205, 214, 539. See also Sugar Monster (tutorial)
    crisp logic 206
    games theory 215, 217
    young and old analogy 205

## G

Galaxians (game) 535
game design
    animated sequences 668
    challenge 666
    controls 664, 667
    delivery options 662
    design on paper 660
    friction 665
    game physics 664
    gender differences 668
    gravity 664
    hidden secrets 669
    online games 662
    performance 662
    playability 659
    projectors 662
    random elements 669
    repeat playability 669
    resistance 665
    rewards 668
    stages of design process 658
    story 666
    systems requirements 663
    target audiences 661, 668
    testing 669
    unsuitable content 668
games
    1980s games 456
    3D games 513
    3D perspective 226
    8-bit games 536
    adding sound to games 619
    animated sprites 576
    archived high scores 5
    artificial intelligence 532, 534
    blank game engines 547
    card games 651
    casino games 652
    conflicting goals 537
    databases 533
    effect of adding sound on game performance 613
    end of game conditions 534
    fighting games 656
    first person shooters 654, 670
    game engines 144, 619
    game environments 533

game rules 533
games theory 215
gameWorlds and gameSprites 144
intelligent soundtracks 431
large maps 492
multiplayer games 310, 651, 655, 669
music 408, 414
non-linear games 669
non-player characters (NPCs) 534
objects for games 504
online games 5
platform games 576, 652
playability 659, 662
puzzle games 650
real-time game coding 136
real-time games 612
role-playing games 653
secondary animations 515
selling games 547
simulations 657
sound in games 612
sports games 655
turn-based games 532
wireframe games 437
games consoles 652
gameWorlds 200. See also Pong (tutorial). See also Dante (tutorial)
    communication between gameSprites 150
    configuration 150
    dataName variable 151
    gameSprites 145
    gameWorlds as software objects 148
    global variables 152
    graphical programming tool 199
    initial stages of gameSprite code 161
    large-scale applications 199
    relative hierarchies 146
    scrolling 146
    status versus configuration 152
    _visible property 146
Gay, Jonathan (programmer) 677
gender differences 668
GET and POST methods 315
getBounds method 525
getRGB method 505
getTransform method 505
getURL method 525
Gigasampler 415
global variables 152
globalToLocal function 525, 595
goal-based behavior 535
gradients 475, 173, 233
    frame rates 489
Grand Theft Auto (game) 411
graphics. See also flying ball (tutorial). See also frame rate counter (tutorial). See also hovercraft (tutorial). See also meter preloader (tutorial)
    adaptive degradation 142
    anti-aliasing 473
    comparative frame rates (tables) 487
    darkness 490
    gradients 475
    graphic complexity 173
    line thickness 469
    pixels 457
    resolution 458
    simple solutions 490
    slowing down games 457
    stages in pixel rendering (list) 459
    stand-in graphics 173
    varying complexity of stationary versus moving graphics 491
gravity effect 248, 655, 664
Gruber, Diana 671
GTInteractive 413

## H

Half-Life (game) 434, 654
Half-Life: Counter-Strike (game) 654, 670
hardware-driven 3D 677
height property 513
hidden secrets 669
hierarchy
    nesting 523
    relative versus absolute paths 523

# Index

high-score tables 282. See also mind reading (tutorial)
Hitchcock, Alfred 412
hitTest method 48, 245, 398, 525, 576
    movie clip to point collision 401
hovercraft (tutorial)
    cosine wave ActionScript 491
    motion blur 491
    removing outlines 491
    sky 491
    streetlamp images 490
HTTP (HyperText Transfer Protocol) 313, 315
    GET and POST methods 315, 318
    HTTP versus sockets 318
    loadVariables function 315
    speed and connection limitations 316

## I

Id Software 310
if statement 375
image quality 471
initialization 392
input devices 369
    intuitive controls 370
    keyboards 370
input properties and methods 375
Intel 540, 408
interactivity 648
interface design 182
Internet
    interactivity 648
    IP (Internet Protocol) addresses 313
    multiplayer games 310, 651, 669
    packet synchronization 361
    pinging 323
    role-playing games 653
    streaming rates 417
interpreted languages 678
inverse-square law 226, 259
invisible buttons 547
IP (Internet Protocol) addresses 313

isDown method 377
isometric 3D 227, 270. See also tiles (tutorial)
    character movement 271
    tiles 270
isometric perspective 2, 6, 87
ISPs
    server-running restrictions 363
iterative loops 392

## J

James Bond films 408
Java 282, 542
JavaScript 540, 542, 685
Jaws (film) 408
Jerusalem (song) 431
Joe Cartoon 677
junkmedia 668

## K

key codes 373, 375
Key object 508
Key UP event 649
keyboards 370. See also customizing keys (tutorial)
    keyboard types 370
    on(keyPress "key") command 372
keyDown events 375
keyPress event Handler 372. See also tank (tutorial)
    key codes 373, 375
Keystone Capers 516
keyUp events 375
Korg Electribe analog synthesizer 157

## L

layers 228. See also trees (tutorial)
    script layer 215
learned behavior 541
    advantages and drawbacks 541

neural nets 541
Lee, Bruce 656
level editor (tutorial)
- butterfly movie clip 590
- centerMovie(mc) function 595
- control layer 594
- coordinate systems 595
- creating map data 598
- creating toolbar 594, 597
- defining array 594
- deleteButton 597
- deleteSelected function 596, 598
- depthCounter variable 594
- editor layer 591
- editor movie clip 591, 595, 599
- editor window 590
- enemy movie clip 590
- extending the level editor 605
- fire movie clip 590
- generateMap function 599, 605
- globalToLocal function 594, 595
- largePlatform movie clip 597
- lastSelectedClip variable 596
- map button layer 600
- map layer 599
- mapData dynamic text field 598
- mapDisplay movie clip 598
- newGameElement function 595
- pickUp movie clip 591
- platform movie clip 591
- player movie clip 590
- properties window 605
- scroll buttons layer 593
- scrolling the editor 592
- scrollLeft button 593
- scrollRight button 593
- scrollSpeed variable 593
- setSelected function 592, 596
- sky movie clip 595
- snail movie clip 590
- tempPoint custom object 594
- toolbar functions 594
- toolbar layer 597, 598

level editors 589

level maps 578, 588. See also level editor (tutorial)
lighting and shadow effects 236. See also shine and flaring effects (tutorial)
Lightwave (application) 235
line engine #1(tutorial)
- calculating line angle 97
- calculating line length 97
- line1 movie clip 96
- _rotation property 97

line engine #2 (tutorial)
- line thickness 99
- _xscale and _yscale properties 98

line thickness 469
linkage sound objects 615, 643
- combining linkage sounds and targeted sounds 633
- setVolume, setPan, and setTransform methods 629
- sound control mixer stage 634

Linux 322
loader bars 663
loadMovieClip method 525
loadMovieClipNum method 525
loadVariables function 315, 525
loadVariablesNum method 525
local area networks (LAN) 310, 363
localToGlobal method 525
logic loops 139
look-ahead strategy 540
look-up tables 137, 141, 508
loop (tutorial)
- controller movie clip 422
- importing loop 422
- initializing sound object 422
- linking sound loop 422
- loop sound object 422

loop-based composition programs 415
loops 415, 421
- while... loops 558

lowpass filters 417
Lunar Lander (game) 21

# Index

## M

Macs
    COMMAND and OPTION keys 370
    Flash frame rate 484
mahjong 651
Manic Bounce (tutorial) 241
    3dbox movie clip 243, 244
    additional blocks 250
    ball movement 248
    ball movie clip 243
    block rendering 242
    clicking and dragging blocks 244
    collision detection 245, 249
    collisionbox movie clip 245, 249
    computing score 249
    depth levels 250
    dx and dy variables 248
    gradient-filled sphere 242
    gravity effect 248
    high-score 251
    hitTest method 246
    indicator arrow movie clip 250
    lighting effects 242
    lives and score dynamic text fields 243
    object of game 242
    pre-rendered 3D blocks 242
    setting current frame of box 243
Manic Miner (game) 652
manipulateobject function 453
master clocks 458
Math object 503. See also beach ball (tutorial)
    abs method 520
    look-up tables 508
    mathematic constants 508
    methods of Math object 508
    sin method 520
    trigonometry 508
Math.floor command 254
Math.random command 230, 258
matrix multiplication 118
Matrox 678
Maya (application) 235

Mech Attack (case study)
    3D sprite 552
    aa variable 562, 565
    alive variable 564, 566, 574
    ang variable 546, 578, 587
    animation playing assessment (code) 588
    avez variable 581, 582
    backface culling 572, 574, 579, 581, 587
    background 546
    break command 576
    capturerate variable 565
    captures variable 547
    ceiling limitation 587
    cityscape movie clip 545
    collision detection 532, 560, 589
    Color object 574
    compute button 533, 535
    controller movie clip 534, 570, 571
    controller object 561, 562
    converting world coordinates into screen coordinates 579
    cosang and sinang variables 578
    creating buildings in gamegrid 569
    creating gamegrid array and point arrays 572
    crosshair movie clip 549, 551
    currentframe property 535, 556, 576
    dang variable 585, 587
    dead variable 554, 568
    degrees to radians conversion 538, 577
    demoCs2-1.fla 541
    description of game 530
    drawline function 590
    dvel variable 568, 585
    dx, dy and dz variables 538, 558, 575, 587, 590
    editor.fla 532
    enterFrame ClipEvent of controller movie clip 577
    explosion animation 556, 560
    explosion layer 557
    frame rate 591

fuel, ammo and life variables 548, 568
ga variable 562, 565
game grid collision detection (code) 589
game improvements 592
game levels 533
game quality 572
gamegrid array 589
gamegrid value 570
gameover movie clip 545, 547
graphical altitude indicator 531, 547
gravitational pull-down effect 555, 587
gridxsize and gridzsize variables 569
GUI (Graphical User Interface) 546
GUI meters 547
gui movie clip 546, 548
healing polygons 562
helibomb movie clip 556, 559
helibomb player tracking 560
helibomb speed limit 560
hitTest method 558, 564
hittingsomething variable 552, 558, 566
hmoving variable 588
key game objects (list) 541
ku, kd, kl and kr variables 584
laser firing control 591
laser movie clip 550, 566, 590
level editor 532, 535, 587
level.txt 535, 540, 561
line-drawing engine 550
lives variable 547
loader movie clip 566, 567, 570
loadVariables action 567
master polygon 561, 572, 574
Math.round function 587
minime movie clip 547
mysin and mycos arrays 577, 587
nam string 564
object movie clip 552
object creation routines 533
objnum counter 568, 575
onClipEvent(data) handler 566
output text box 535

output variable 533, 540
performance limitations 591
perspective projection 579, 583
play command 560
player death code 544
player movement 540, 584
player movie clip 533, 559
player rocket pack 585
player state assessment 587
point counter 570
pointx, pointyt, pointyb and pointz arrays 570, 572
poly1 movie clip 561, 580
poly2 movie clip 582
polygon capturing 565
polygon rendering 579
polymast 574, 575
polynum counter 568, 574
power-up type selection 556
power-ups 531
powerup movie clip 553, 568
quad movie clip 533, 534
rendering sprite objects 582
renderpolygon function 571, 575, 582
RGB values 570
robot animation frames 542
robot controls 531
robot jump animation 544
robot movie clip 542, 562, 589
robot walk loop 544
_root.buildings global variable 571
_root.controller.gamegrid array 567
_root.controller.shooting variable 564
_root.loader.bldg variable 566
_root.points global variable 571
_root.robot.swapDepths command 584
rotation variable 538
setting robot depth level 584
setTransform command 574
setupObj function 568, 571, 574
setupPoly function 571, 573, 575

# Index

setupPoly function parameters 570
shooting global variable 558
shooting variable 591
sparks movie clip 552
spawnpowerup function 561, 571, 576
sprite objects 538
sprite scaling 583
streetlamp object 552, 570
stx and sty variables 539
swapDepths command 549, 582, 583
third-person perspective 579
tpointz variable 581
tr color transform object 565
tr object caller 562
transform object 574
tsx, tsyt and tsyb temporary variables 573, 578, 579
user interaction checking 584
vdying variable 588, 590
vel variable 538, 540
vfalling variable 588
visible property 551, 582, 583
vrising variable 588
whoiam variable 574
wx1, wy1t, wy1b and wz1 variables 578
x1, y1 and z1 variables 553, 555, 558
yloc variable 586, 587, 590
Meier, Sid (programmer) 534
melody 409
meter preloader (tutorial)
    needle rotation 495
    preloader movie clip symbol 494
methods. See also beach ball (tutorial)
    abs method 520
    alpha method 516
    duplicateMovieClip method 524
    getBounds method 525
    getRGB method 505
    getTransform method 505
    getURL method 525
    globalToLocal method 525
    gotoAnd method 524
    hide method 503, 507
    hitTest method 525
    loadMovieClip method 525
    loadMovieClipNum method 525
    loadVariables method 525
    loadVariablesNum method 525
    localToGlobal method 525
    nextFrame method 524
    prevFrame method 524
    prototype command 503
    removeMovieClip method 524
    scale method 516
    setPan method 506
    setRGB method 505
    setting methods 503
    setTransform method 503, 506
    setVolume method 506
    .show method 503, 507
    sin method 520
    startDrag method 510, 526
    stopDrag method 526
    swapDepths method 525
Microprose 534
MIDI (Musical Instrument Digital Interface) 414
mind reading (tutorial)
    adding functionality 285
    arrays 286
    check score movie clip 300, 303
    check_score movie 302
    Code layer 284, 287
    converting symbol graphics into buttons 288
    cpuChoice variable 286, 287
    Crystal Ball layer 284
    Crystal Content layer 284
    crystalball.swf 285
    database connection information 296
    db_include.php file 296, 305
    displaying message and score information 291
    doCorrect function 287, 288
    doWrong function 287, 290
    dynamic text fields 291, 300
    enter button 303
    enter your name graphic 303
    game over mechanism 293
    high score if statement 302

high-score table 294, 296, 298
highscore movie clip 304
highscore variable 298, 300
include command 296
input text field 303
loadVariables command 302, 304
lowplayer variable 298
lowscore variable 298
masterSymbol variable 287, 289
messages text box 291
movie timeline 284
mymessage variable 289, 292
myscore variable 289, 292
mySQL database 294, 305
newplayer variable property 303
num variable 297
on (release) code 304
onClipEvent (data) event 302
pAbility (score) dynamic textbox 303
pAbility variable 292
PHP 295, 304
player selection 287
playerChoice parameter 288
playerSelection function 287
psychic table 295
randomCorrectQuote variable 289
resetting masterSymbol value 290
score information query 297
Score layer 284, 300
scoreid variable 298
scores information (table) 295
selectSymbol function 286, 288, 292, 294
setting up psychic table structure 294
show_scores.php script 295, 297, 302
symbolArray variable 286
symbolNum variable 286, 292, 293
symbolsShown function 293
update_scores.php script 304, 305
while loop 297

mixing (tutorial) 423
    balanced mixing 431
    brass movie clip 425
    computing relative volumes 428, 430
    conductor movie clip 425
    controller movie clip 426
    creating loops for mixing 424
    creating sound object 426
    flute movie clip 425
    importing loops into Flash 425
    loop movie clips 425
    setting volumes as percentage of highest volume 429
    strings movie clip 425
    synch variable 426, 429
    synchronizing loops 427, 428
    vol variable 427, 429
modular software definition 154
modulo operator 395
monitors
    refresh rate 461
    screen resolution 462
Mortal Kombat (game) 656
Motorola 540
mouse 370
    features 370
    _xmouse and _ymouse properties 375
Mouse object 503
    methods of Mouse object 507
Mouse.hide method 503, 507
Mouse.show method 503, 507
mouseDown events 375
mouseMove events 375
mouseUp events 374
movie clips 5, 476, 481. See also flying ball (tutorial). See also frame rate counter (tutorial)
    clip events 510
    coordinate systems 525
    frame movie clips 157
    gameSprites 144
    methods of movie clips 510, 524
    nested movie clips 523
    properties of movie clips 510
    scripting libraries 526
    timelines 510
MP3 files 417, 613

# Index

       Bit Rate 418
       Quality setting 419
       streaming audio 418
multiplayer games 310, 651, 655, 669. See also Radio Racer (tutorial)
       firewalls 314
       limitations of multiplayer client/server games 322
       real-time and turn-based 310
       systems architecture 310
music. See also musical styles
       chords 410, 423
       complete soundtracks 419
       emotional impact 408, 431
       film soundtracks 408
       importance in games 408
       irritating jingles 410
       keys 423
       melody 409
       music in Flash 415
       tempo 409, 423
       types of audio software 414
       use in games 414
musical styles
       ambient music 411
       electronic music 411
       ethnic music 411
       experimental music 411
       orchestral music 411, 413
       rock music 411
mySQL. See also mind reading (tutorial)
       phpMyAdmin 283
       relational databases 282

## N

Nakamura, Yugo (web designer) 677
naming conventions 8, 46, 156
nesting 523
neural networks 206, 215, 541
New Masters of Flash: 2002 Annual (book) 677
nextFrame method 524
Nintendo 409, 412, 652, 662
non-linear behavior 207, 669
non-player characters (NPCs) 534
       control strategies (list) 534
       goal-based behavior 535
       learned behavior 541
       look ahead strategy 540
       weighted outcomes strategy 537

## O

object block diagrams 148, 152, 200
       object block diagrams versus flowcharts 179
Object object 504
object-oriented code 5
objects 502. See also beach ball (tutorial)
       Array object 503
       categories of objects (list) 502
       Color object 503, 504
       constructor functions 502
       defined objects 502
       Math object 503
       methods 503
       Mouse object 503
       Object object 504
       objects for games 504
       predefined objects 502
       Sound object 503
       spawned objects 379
on(keyPress "key") command 372. See also tank (tutorial)
onClipEvent function 368, 370, 376. See also tank (tutorial)
       keyDown events 375
       keyUp events 375
       mouseDown events 374
       mouseMove events 375
       mouseUp events 374
       onClipEvents for user input 374
       types of event handlers (list) 368
       user input related events 369
online data 282
online games 662
OpenGL 186, 687
Optimize command 465, 467, 475
optimizing conditional logic 138
optimizing images in Flash 467
       list of golden rules 489
orchestral music 411, 413

ordering 103
outlines 474
    frame rates 489

## P

Pac-Man (game) 652
packets 320
    packet synchronization 361
    packet-triggering events (list) 321
    syntax 321
page flipping 492
parallax scrolling 226, 228, 579, 587. See also trees (tutorial). See also Star Cruiser (tutorial)
    aligning layers 231
parallel projection 107
Parrapa the Rapper (game) 658
particle systems 6
Paterson, James (web designer) 677
PCs
    ALT and CTRL keys 370
peer-to-peer architecture 311, 318
per pixel effects 677
Perl 5, 282
perspective 108, 226, 228, 513
Photoshop 546, 677, 685
PHP (PHP Hypertext Preprocessor) 525, 649. See also mind reading (tutorial)
    calling PHP scripts from within Flash 298
    database connection information 296
    PHP-supported databases (list) 282
    PHP-supported protocols 283
    phpMyAdmin 283
    server-side HTML-embedded scripting language 282
pinging 323
pixels 457, 469, 498, 649
    line thickness 469
    stages in pixel rendering (list) 459
    write and read operations 470
PizzaDude (web site) 173
platform games 270, 576, 652. See also Rescue Run (tutorial). See also level editor (tutorial)
    game levels 588
    level editors 589
    player and platform collision detection 585
    side scrolling 579
playability 659, 663, 669, 535
polygon engine (tutorial)
    2D representations of 3D objects 446
    arbitrary polygons 439
    avez variable 446
    backface culling 450, 452
    center point of poly0 444
    checking visibility of back of polygon 449
    controller movie clip 447
    culling flag 450
    data representation 439
    defining edge 1 and edge 2 448, 451
    determining visibility of polygons 449
    limitations of engine 437
    local coordinate system 444
    obj variable 443, 446
    offscreen variable 450
    perspective-projecting 3D polygon on screen 448
    polygon movie clip 441, 443
    polygon rendering routine 445
    polygons defined in order around object 451
    squashing and stretching triangles 441
    top, mid, and bottom movie clips 441, 442
    _xscale and _yscale properties 440
    y1t and y1b variables 439
    z1 and z2 variables 447
polygon engines 659
polygons 89, 434. See also polygon engine (tutorial)
    basic Flash polygon engine 437
    polygon-rendering engine 51, 71
    per second rendered 435

# Index

shape manipulation options 436
speed considerations 452
textured polygons 52
textured surface bitmaps 435
Pong (game) 535
Pong (tutorial)
    actions layer 155, 158
    ball bounce effect 165
    ball script 163
    ballDir variable 168
    ballPos variable 168
    bat graphics 157
    batHeight variable 166
    bounce off walls beep 165
    boundaries 157
    collision detection 153, 164
    configuration and status of gameSprites 153
    configuration from main gameWorld timeline 161
    constants and physical properties 149
    court layer 155
    defining game elements 147
    defining rules 147
    detecting key ball positions 165
    entire game script 168
    frame layer 155
    frame movie clip 157
    gameSprites 150, 153, 159, 160
    gameWorld 148, 149, 150, 157
    handling many gameSprites 170
    if statements 163, 164
    inertia equation 163
    initialization 156, 160
    load event script 164
    myPos object 164
    myPos variable 161
    mySpeed object 164, 166
    myTarget variable 161
    NPC bat script 162
    npcPos variable 163
    npcScore movie clip 167
    onLoad event 160
    pieces layer 155
    player bat enterFrame script 162
    player bat gameSprite 159
    playerScore movie clip 167
    power up beep 158
    skillFactor variable 163
    sound objects 157
    splash screen 158
    startButton layer 155
    status data of gameSprites 152
    tennisFinal.fla 146, 155
    world object 156
ports 313
    choice of port 314
    port 80 (HTTP) 316
    reserved port numbers (list) 313
pre-rendered 3D images 232. See also Manic Bounce (tutorial). See also Star Cruiser (tutorial)
pre-rendering 654
predefined objects 502
preloaders 493, 526. See also meter preloader (tutorial)
prevFrame method 524
Pro Tools (application) 414
processor speed 458
projection 106
    parallel projection 107
    perspective projection 108
    view distance variable 108
projectors 662
properties
    alpha property 514
    animation with properties 515
    currentFrame property 511
    dropTarget property 510
    framesLoaded property 511
    height property 513
    quality property 514
    read only properties 510
    read/write properties 512
    rotation property 513
    totalFrames property 511
    visible property 514
    width property 513
    x and y properties 512
    _xmouse and _ymouse properties 512
    xscale and yscale properties 513
prototype command 503, 526

proximity-based behavior 5
Psycho (film) 408
Pulp Fiction (film) 408
puzzle games 650
Pythagoras' Theorem 400

## Q

quads
 bowtie quads 92
Quake (game) 654, 434
Quake III (game) 654
quality property 514

## R

radians 97, 239
Radio Racer (tutorial)
 ang variable 327
 captain dialog box 326, 344
 car controls 352
 car movement 327
 car movie clip 331
 chat box 326
 chat packets 340, 348
 chatclear variable 348
 client position server packet 340
 client-server communication events (list) 338
 collide movie clip 332
 collision map 332
 comm movie clip 342
 connect button 351
 connect function 351
 connection ID server packet 340
 connectStat variable 343, 347
 description of game 324
 disconnect server packet 341, 348
 doc string 346
 dx and dy variables 327, 333
 fuel gauge 325, 359
 fuel pad movie clip 360
 fuel variable 343
 game controls 326
 game screen 325
 general position client packet 339
 getTimer variable 334, 350
 hitTest method 331, 332, 336
 hitTimer variable 334
 ID packet 346
 id variable 337
 ipaddress text field variable 352
 j array 346
 key control code 330
 keyboard control keys checking 328
 keychange variable 330, 333, 360
 lap counter 325, 335
 laps variable 343
 login client packet 339
 login packet 347
 maxspeed variable 328
 msg text box 348
 msg variable 348
 msgmc movie clip 348
 msgmc.msg variable 348
 multiple cars control 337
 mynode variable 335, 343
 myOnConnect function 342, 352
 myOnXML function 342, 344
 nodes 334
 nodes layer 335
 numnodes variable 343
 obstacles layer 331, 332
 on_Road flag 331
 Play Local button 352
 player position packet 347
 refuelling 360
 remaininglaps variable 349
 restart client packet 340, 349
 restart global flag variables 349
 restart server packet 341
 roadsurface movie clip 330
 _root.countdown text box 350
 _root.myid gobal variable 337, 343, 346, 352
 _root.waitstart variable 350
 server-client communication events (list) 339

# Index

serverport text field variable 352
shadows effect 333
sidebar 325
sock object 342, 360
speedneedle movie clip 359
speedometer 325, 359
splash screen 350
st string 346
String.split function 346
success variable 343
vel variable 327
xd and yd variables 334
XMLSocket object 342, 351
random behavior 535
random elements 669
random number generation 6
RAW files 417, 613
real-time games 4, 136, 612
real-time mixing/layering 415, 423. See also mixing (tutorial)
refresh rate 461
relative hierarchies 143
removeMovieClip method 524
renderer (tutorial)
    addline function 110, 113, 116
    addpoint function 116
    bit-shift operator 115
    controller movie clip 110
    cube ActionScript 112
    d variable 111
    depth sorting 124
    drawing object on screen 113
    drawline function 116
    drawobject function 123
    drawsprite3d function 122
    duplicating line graphics 111
    iteration loop 114
    line movie clip 110, 113, 116
    line3d object 111
    linename object array 111, 116
    lnum global variable 111
    main timeline 110
    manipulateobject function 116, 123
    modulus operator 117
    mycos and mysin arrays 112, 117
    object definition 110
    object renderer 113
    onClipEvent(load) function 110
    p1ind and p2ind temporary variables 114
    perspective projection 115, 123
    rendering cube 119
    rendering sprite3d object 121
    _root.ballimage movie clip 121
    rotating points 118
    scale variable 121
    scaling points 118
    screencenterX and screencenterY variables 111
    source parameter 121
    sprite3d object constructor function 121
    swapDepths command 116
    tpointlist array 114, 119
    translating points 118
    xoff, yoff and zoff values 118
    yaw, roll and pitch temporary variables 117
rendering shapes 99. See also renderer (tutorial)
    object manipulations 99
    ordering 103
    projection 106
    rotation 102
    scaling 101
    translation 100
Rescue Run (tutorial) 577. See also level editor (tutorial)
    adapting the game engine 606
    additional graphics 607
    attack function 581
    deceleration variable 582
    decreaseHealth function 583
    defining map array 602
    displayNewLevel function 603
    dissolve function 608
    duplicateMovieClip method 605
    endLife function 583
    enemies 580
    enemy movie clip 578, 580, 582
    game structure 578
    gameEnd pick-up 578
    gameObject function 601, 603
    gameOver function 584

717

gameWorld movie clip 579, 587, 604
gameWorld reset function 584
goldCoin movie clip 607
health variable 582
hitTest method 579, 582, 586
identifying pick-ups and enemies 607
increaseScore function 583
initialize function 604
initializing player variables 583
jump function 584
jumpHeight variable 582
largePlatform movie clip 582
level maps 578, 587, 588
levels data structure 601
lives variable 582
loadlevel function 602
mainBackground movie clip 579, 587
mainGame movie clip 579
map movie clip 578, 602, 603
mapData string 603
mapName variable 602
mapSize variable 603
mapToDataStructure function 602, 603
maxSpeed variable 582
moveLeft function 584
object-based approach 578
parallax scrolling effect 587
pick-up movie clip 578, 580
pickUp function 580, 607
platform collision detection 579
platform types 582
platforms movie clip 579, 582, 604
player and platform collision detection 585
player movie clip 579, 587
player movie clip variables (list) 582
player reset function 584
removeMovieClip function 581, 605
reset function 584, 587
score variable 582
scrollLeft function 580, 587
scrollStart variable 586

smallPlatform movie clip 582
speedHoriz variable 583
speedVert variable 583, 587
springboards 607
storing level data 588
subType variable 580, 587, 588
superJump function 607
unloadLevel function 605
rescuerun_editor02.fla 593
rescue_run.fla 577
resistance 665
resolution 458
    screen resolution 462
rewards 668
Risk (game) 310
Robotron (game) 171
rock music 411
Rocky (film) 408
role-playing games (RPGs) 370, 653
rotation
    yaw, pitch and roll 102
rotation property 513

### S

sample rates 417, 614
save FS command 606
Savior (game) 172
scaling 101, 462, 516
    ordering 104
scaling and rotating 468
screen buffers 460
screen death 208
screen resolution 462
scripting libraries 526
scrolling 492, 146. See also Dante (tutorial)
    parallax scrolling 579, 587, 226
    scrolling shoot 'em up games 170
    scrolling worlds 608
Sega Master System 652
selling games 547
sequencers 414
servers 322. See also sockets (tutorial)
    EXE files 362
    FTP (File Transfer Protocol) servers 313

# Index

HTTP servers 313
ISPs 363
local area networks (LAN) 363
server application window 362
server building 361
server connection speed 322
socket servers 316
types of servers 313
setPan method 506, 629, 636, 643
    varying controls whilst sound is playing 640
setRGB method 505
setTransform method 503, 629, 643
    advanced features of setTransform 640
    crossover signals 642
    default settings for ll and rr values 641
    initializing setTransform definition code 640
    true mono sound 642
setVolume method 506, 629, 643
    varying controls whilst sound is playing 640
    volume values over 100% 630
shadow effect 521
shape tweening 96, 475
shine and flaring effects (tutorial) 236
    calculating relative position of sun 238
    description of effects 237
    lens flare circle 237
    object movie clip 240
    rotation property 239
    shadow coloring 240
    tree shadow 239
    yscale of shadow 240
Shockwave 679
Shrek (film) 435
Sim City (game) 667
Simon (game) 508
simulations 657
sin method 520
sine waves 520
slash notation 511, 136
smart clips
    clip events versus smart clips 527

sockets 316. See also sockets (tutorial). See also XML code (tutorial). See also Radio Racer (tutorial)
    bandwidth 322
    HTTP versus sockets 318
    packets 320
    real-time event response 316
    socket servers 316
    XMLSocket object 317
sockets (tutorial)
    doc variable 317
    ipaddress variable 318
    myOnConnect function 317, 318
    myOnXML function 317
    onConnect callback function 317
    onXML callback function 317
    opening a socket 317
    serverport variable 318
    success variable 317
    trace command 317
    XMLSocket object 317
software objects 148
    modular software definition 154
software synthesizers 415
sound. See also tennis with sound (tutorial). See also mixing (tutorial)
    adding sound to games 619
    attaching sounds from Library 507
    Bit Rate 614
    comparison to audio circuits 633
    controlling linkage sounds 616
    effect of adding sound on game performance 613
    Flash 4 Edit Envelope window 617
    hierarchical sound 643
    linkage 615
    linkage identifier 616
    methods of Sound object 506
    MP3 files 613
    offsets and looping 617
    RAW files 613
    sample rates 417, 614
    setPan method 506

setTransform method 506
setVolume method 506
sound file export options 417
sound file import options 613
sound in games 612
sound mixing 641
sound object definition 616
start and stop sound object methods 616
stereo sound 637
stopping individual sounds 616
streaming sound 614
targeting sounds 615, 628
true mono sound 642
using root timeline 618
volume control software model 633
Sound Forge (application) 415, 617
soundtrack (tutorial)
    Load button 420
    play button 420
    soundtrack movie clip 420
soundtracks 419
    intelligent soundtracks 431
spawning 379, 392
Speedball (game) 655
sports games 655
Sprint (game) 324
sprites 232, 576, 649
    center point positioning 42
    pre-drawn images 120
    sprite scaling 73
Square Pictures 435
staggered update 141
standalone players. See projectors
Star Cruiser (tutorial) 251
    adding orbs 260
    ang and sy variables 266
    checking health level 268
    collision detection 262
    controller movie clip 253, 260
    craft movie clip 255, 263
    depth variable 254
    dx and dy variables 267, 268
    explosion layer 256
    hit variable 262
    hitTest method 262
    initializing craft variables 266
    inverse square law 259
    kd and ku variables 267

    key-press variables 267
    kl and kr variables 267
    lasthit variable 262
    life depletion 262
    life, level and score dynamic text boxes 258
    lightning layer 257
    lightning movie clip 257
    limiting movement off screen edges 269
    Math.floor command 254, 258
    Math.random command 258
    object of game 251
    orb layer 257
    orb movie clip 256, 261
    orb speed 262
    parallax effect 254
    reaching right edge of screen check 268
    reset_orbs function 260
    _root.currentlevel variable 268
    setting current frame of craft 267
    shipframes layer 256
    shipframes movie clip 255
    spaceship movie clip 254
    star cruiser animation frames 255
    star field 252
    star movement 254
    star movie clip 253, 258
    stat movie clip 258, 267
    suggested modifications 270
    swapDepths function 255, 266
    z variable 258
Stargate (game) 171. See also Dante (tutorial)
startDrag method 510, 526
    bug 526
stereo sound 637
stereoscopic vision 227
stopDrag method 526
story 666
Strata 3D 235
streaming audio 418
Street Fighter (game) 656
string concatenation 137, 144
String object
    index methods 509
    methods of String object 508

# Index

parsing data 509
substring methods 509
String.fromCharCode character code convertor 384
Sugar Monster (tutorial) 207
    adjustSpring function 210, 216, 220, 222
    adjustTherm function 216, 221
    animation of pet 208
    choosing skill level 211, 221
    controls applied during animation cycle 209
    description of game 207
    diamond movie clip 213
    dynamic text box 213
    end-of-game screen 211
    energyCoeff variable 218
    food variable 214, 218
    frame rate 210
    function definitions 213
    fuzzy logic 214
    fuzzyTrust variable 214, 216, 220
    game controls 213
    game screen 211
    game structure 208
    gameLevel variable 217
    gotoAndStop command 212
    height of jumps 209
    hitGround function 210, 221, 222
    introductory screen 211
    loyalHeight value 220
    main timeline 210, 211
    Math.min method 220
    Math.random method 217
    Math.round method 219
    merc movie Clip 214, 221
    merc._height variable 214
    mode buttons 213
    mode switch 213
    mode variable 213
    mrGreen movie clip 209, 216, 218, 222
    myRand variable 219
    raise mode 213, 219, 221
    rndFood value 214, 215, 219
    rules screen 211
    springHeight variable 216, 218
    sugarmonster.fla 214
    sugarmonster.swf 207
    temp variable 214
    trust display 213
    trust variable 214, 215
    walk mode 213, 219
Super Mario Brothers (game) 412, 662, 664
Supercalifragilisticexpialidocious (song) 431
swapDepths method 525
Swift3D (application) 235, 255, 547
system levels 186
systems architecture 310
    client-server architecture 312
    peer-to-peer architecture 311
systems requirements 663

## T

tank (tutorial). See also customizing keys (tutorial)
    calculating cannon angle 396
    collision detection 398
    cursor key positions check 377
    deltaX and deltaY variables 400
    depth property 379
    explosion animation 404
    firing button 381
    firing timer 381, 394, 402
    for loop 401
    hitTest method 398, 400
    if statement 377
    initializing bullet speed 397
    initializing mines 394
    isDown method 377
    Key.LEFT and Key.RIGHT 377
    level variable 401
    Math object 379, 401
    Math.random method 394
    Math.sqrt method 400
    mine movie clip 392, 404
    modulo operator 395
    move function 380
    movement controls 379
    on(keyPress "key") command 373
    onClipEvent (enterFrame) 377, 400

## Flash Games Studio

    positioning mines 394
    Pythagoras' Theorem 400
    rotation property 374, 377, 380
    setting a level variable 392
    shot death by collision 404
    shot death by timeout 403
    shot movie clip 394, 404
    shot to mine detection 401
    shotCount variable 395
    tank movie clip 373
    timing out shots 402
    tread marks 380
    turret controls 377
    turret movie clip 373
    while loop 399
tankBlank.fla 373, 376
tankButton.fla 376
tankCustomKey.fla 378
tankFull.fla 378
target audiences 661, 667
targeted sound 643
    combining linkage sounds and targeted sounds 634
    distinguishing between linkages and target paths 628
    global volume and pan 629
    setPan method 629
    setTransform method 629
    setVolume method 629
    sound control mixer stage 634
    start and stop methods 628
    targeted sound object definition 628
    targeting hierarchies 635
    timelines 628
Tekken (game) 656
tempo 409, 423
tennis with sound (tutorial)
    actions layer 622
    batBounce sound 625
    enterFrame script of ball 623
    game over sound 627
    getVolume method 631
    globalSound sound object 631
    importing blips into Library 621
    initialization script 622
    initializing sound objects 622
    initializing vol value 631
    invisible button 622
    keyDown event script 632
    Linkage names 621
    main timeline 621
    mc.dummy movie clip 631
    mc.score movie clip 627
    miss sound 625
    miss2 sound 625
    setPan action 637
    setVolume action 632
    sound control script 631
    sound object definitions 622
    sound start actions 626
    sound-generating events in ball script 623
    soundControl layer 630
    sounds folder 621
    sounds needed (list) 620
    stereo sound 637
    tennisFinal.fla 628
    tennisMute.fla 619
    tennisMute2.fla 621, 630
    tennisSound01.fla 632
    tennisSound02.fla 638
    vol variable 632
    wallBounce sound 625
testing 669
Tetris (game) 650, 409
text 474
    updating text fields 137, 176
textured surface bitmaps 435
tic-tac-toe 537, 541. (tutorial)
    actions layer 543, 549, 552
    ActionScript-only layers 543
    advanced NPC routine 564
    bu.invisible button 547
    building the database 549
    checking rows, columns and diagonals for winning condition 568
    coding weighted intelligence NPC 568
    computer keyframe 557
    computer opponent 557
    creating graphics 545
    diagnostic information 555
    diagnostics layer 544, 548, 555
    do... while loop 558
    dynamic text fields 549, 552
    emulating intelligence 560
    endGame frame 559

# Index

events layer 544, 554
final player script 556
functions layer 566
game creation strategy 544, 553
game rules 544
gameSymbols.fla 545
goTaken variable 554, 556
graphics layers 543
if... else commands 563
implementing sub-rules 561
initialization loop 552
limitations of intelligence engine 570
Math.abs command 554
mc.dummy movie clip 547
mc.x and mc.o movie clips 546
mouse position detection 553, 554
onClipEvent (mouseDown) 554
player input 553
player move script 554, 562
random NPC moves 565
startGame keyframe 557, 559
state property 551
sy.tile symbol 545
textured background 546
tictactoe0.fla 548, 557
tictactoe1.fla 557
tictactoeFinal.fla 543, 560, 566
tile array elements 551
tile properties 550
update function 561, 564, 567
weight function 561, 566, 568
weighted outcomes engine 549
xWin, oWin, and noWin variables 567

tiles 270
    12 x 12 tiled map 272
    collision detection 275
    controller object 272
    depth computation 277
    duplicateMovieclip command 274
    dx and dz variables 274, 277
    independent collision testing of each axis 276
    invisible button 277
    object movie clip 272
    offx and offy variables 274, 277
    on-screen tile positioning 274
    player position and movement 274
    quad0 movie clip 272
    quadN array 273
    x and z co-ordinates 274

tiles (tutorial)
timers 392
Tomb Raider (game) 666
totalFrames property 511
Toy Story (film) 435
Trace Bitmap tool 234, 470
trace command 317
translation 99
    translate and then rotate 104
trees (tutorial)
    aligning layers 231
    controller movie clip 230
    cx and cy variables 231
    eye movie clip 231
    layers of depth 229
    layer_1 to layer_4 layers 229
    Math.random command 230
    navbox 229, 230
    rendering quality 230
    scaling of trees 231
    tree movie clip 230
    treeframe movie clip 230

Tribes (game) 434
Tribes II (game) 654
Turn (case study)
    addToCounter function 279
    aesthetic effect 265
    archived high scores 266
    arms movie clip 274, 275
    building game grid 271
    chaotic behavior 268
    checkNeighbors function 276
    cnt variable 272
    count global variable 279
    counter movie clip 269
    currentAngleNum global variable 274, 276
    description of game 264
    digit movie clips 277
    dynamic text field 277
    endAngleNum variable 274, 275
    FLA structure 265
    game score counter 266

    graphic design 268
    initializing game environment 270
    invisible button 274
    isFirstPos flag 274, 275
    isometric perspective 264, 268, 272
    linkage identifier 270
    main timeline 270
    myNum value 276, 277
    myRow value 277
    nested loop structures 271
    num variable 279
    numDiff variable 274, 275
    object movie clip 269, 271, 272
    object movie clip script 272, 275, 276
    origin of game 267
    player input 274
    proximity-based behavior 267
    real-time interaction 266
    resetCounter function 279
    rotation tweens 269, 274, 275
    score counter 277
    score display options 277
    setting global variables 271
    starting patterns 266
    turnMe function 274
    updateCounter function 279
    xCnt and yCnt variables 271, 276
turn-based games 532. See also tic-tac-toe (tutorial)
    end of game conditions 533
    game environments 533
    game rules 533
tweening 7, 13

## U

Ultima Online (game) 653
UNIX 322
Unreal Tournament (game) 413, 654
unsuitable content 668
user input handling routines 657

## V

values 375
Vecta3D (application) 235
vectors 463, 649
    vectors versus bitmaps 470, 489
Vegas Audio (application) 414
VGA and CGA displays 678
Video RAM (VRAM) 461
view distance variable 108
virtual reality goggles 228
_visible property 146, 514
Visual Basic 361

## W

Warcraft (game) 413
wave editors 415
Wavelab (application) 415
web-safe palettes 678
weighted outcomes strategy 537
    Black and White (game) 539
    emulating intelligent behavior 539
    fuzzy logic 539
    real-time applications 540
width property 513
Williams (games company) 536, 171, 630
Williams, John (composer) 408
Windows 2000 322
Windows NT Server 322
WinSock control 361
wireframe objects 6
wireframe images 88, 434
wireframe3d function (tutorial)
    addline function 94, 95
    addpoint function 94
    creating cube object 95
    defining cube vertices 95
    line3d objects 93
    linename array 94
    parameters of function 93
    point3d objects 93
    pointlist variable 93, 95
    scripting wireframe3d function 93

# Index

tpointlist array 93
write and read operations 470
write-access 649
www.mysql.com 283
www.php.net 283
www.phpwizard.net 283
www.pizzadude.dk 173

## X

x and y properties 512
Xara 3D (application) 235
XML (Extensible Markup Language) 318. See also XML code (tutorial)
    efficiency problems 320
XML code (tutorial)
    dot notation 319
    Funky variable 319
    onLoad function 320
    showresults function 320
XML object
    methods of XML object 509
XMLSocket object 317
xmouse and ymouse properties 375, 512
xscale and yscale properties 513

## Y

yaw, pitch and roll 102
You Don't Know Jack (game) 413

## Z

z axis 87, 258
Zadeh, Lotfi 205

Books | D2D | Code | News | Contact | Home | Search

**friendsof**
DESIGNER TO DESIGNER™

- Books
- D2D
- Code
- News
- Authors
- Interviews
- Web
- Events
- Contact
- Home

You've read the book, now enter the community.

friendsofed.com is the online heart of the designer to designer neighbourhood.

As you'd expect the site offers the latest news and support for all our current and forthcoming titles – but it doesn't stop there.

For fresh exclusive interviews and videos every month with our authors – the new and future masters like Josh Davis, Yugo Nakamura, James Paterson and many other friends of ED – enter the world of D2D.

Stuck with a design problem? Need technical assistance? Our support doesn't end on the last page of the book. Just post your query on our message board and one of our moderators or authors will make sure you get the answers you need – fast.

New to the site is our EVENTS section where you can find out about schemes brewing in the ED laboratory. Forget everything you know about conferences and get ready for a new generation of designer happenings with a difference.

Welcome to friendsofed.com. This place is the place of friends of ED – designer to designer. Practical deep fast content delivered by working web designers.

Straight to your head.

**www.friendsofed.com**

# freshfroot
## motion web mindfood

### seven day itch

freshfroot is where friends of ED fertilise the designer mind. It's a visual search engine, a daily creative resource and a hard-to-kick addiction. Everyday the froot pickers, along with a select band of celebrity guest editors, search through the web's good, bad and ugly to bring you the diamonds – categorised, critiqued and instantly searchable. freshfroot rejects the usual search engine criteria in favour of daily themes that pull together stylistically similar works and images to provide the rock solid creative resource to complement the technical resource on offer in our books.

freshfroot is the place where Mike Cina, James Paterson, Golan Levin, Mumbleboy, Brendan Dawes and many other new and future masters go to share their inspirations and be inspired. It's the place everyone goes when they need fresh ideas fast. Submit your own found or created masterpieces, spout your opinions and share ideas in the discussion forum. Get involved, be inspired and escape the mediocre.

stripes

warhol

seams & f

### my froot

shoe

### archive

a-z
date
keyword

search for: inspiration

james pate

hybrid

revolution

forward

playground

urban

brendan dawes

http://www.freshfroot.com

# friendsof ED

**DESIGNER TO DESIGNER™**

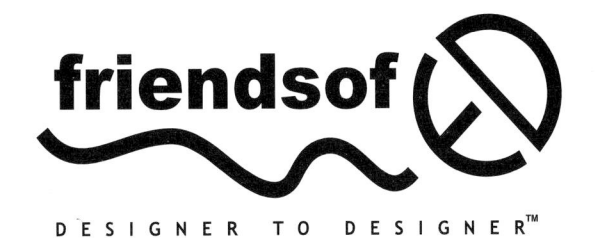

friends of ED write books for you. Any suggestions, or ideas about how you want information given in your ideal book will be studied by our team.

Your comments are valued by friends of ED.

Freephone in USA 800.873.9769
Fax 312.893.8001

UK contact: Tel. 0121.258.8858
Fax. 0121.258.8868

feedback@friendsofed.com

## Flash Games Studio - Registration Card

Name _____
Address _____
_____
_____
City _____ State/Region _____
Country _____ Postcode/Zip _____
E-mail _____
Occupation _____

How did you hear about this book?
☐ Book review (publication) _____
☐ Advertisement (name) _____
☐ Recommendation _____
☐ Catalog _____
☐ Other _____

Where did you buy this book?
☐ Bookstore (name) _____
☐ Computer Store (name) _____
☐ Mail Order _____
☐ Other _____

What influenced you in the purchase of this book?
☐ Cover Design          ☐ Contents
☐ Other (please specify) _____

How did you rate the overall contents of this book?
☐ Excellent              ☐ Good
☐ Average               ☐ Poor

What did you find useful about this book?

What did you find least useful about this book?

Please add any additional comments

What other design areas will you buy a book on soon?

What is the best design related book you have used this year?

*Note: This information will only be used to keep you updated about new friends of ED titles and will not be used for any other purposes or passed to any third party.*

# friendsof ED

**DESIGNER TO DESIGNER**™

NB. If you post the bounce back card below in the UK, please send it to:

friends of ED Ltd.,
30 Lincoln Road,
Olton,
Birmingham.
B27 6PA

---

NO POSTAGE
NECESSARY
IF MAILED
IN THE
UNITED STATES

**BUSINESS REPLY MAIL**
FIRST CLASS    PERMIT #64    CHICAGO, IL

POSTAGE WILL BE PAID BY ADDRESSEE

**friends of ED,
29 S. La Salle St.
Suite 520
Chicago Il 60603-USA**